T3-BOC-902

Thematic Threads in the Book of the Twelve

Beihefte zur Zeitschrift für die alttestamentliche Wissenschaft

Herausgegeben von
Otto Kaiser

Band 325

Walter de Gruyter · Berlin · New York
2003

Thematic Threads in the Book of the Twelve

Edited by
Paul L. Redditt and Aaron Schart

Walter de Gruyter · Berlin · New York
2003

BS
1560
.T44
2003

∞ Printed on acid-free paper which falls within the guidelines of the ANSI
to ensure permanence and durability.

ISBN 3-11-017594-0

Bibliographic information published by Die Deutsche Bibliothek

Die Deutsche Bibliothek lists this publication in the Deutsche Nationalbibliografie; detailed
bibliographic data is available in the Internet at <http://dnb.ddb.de>.

© Copyright 2003 by Walter de Gruyter GmbH & Co. KG, D-10785 Berlin

All rights reserved, including those of translation into foreign languages. No part of this book
may be reproduced or transmitted in any form or by any means, electronic or mechanical,
including photocopy, recording or any information storage and retrieval system, without permission in writing from the publisher..
Printed in Germany
Cover design: Christopher Schneider, Berlin

Foreword

At the end of the last century it became acceptable in scholarly biblical exegesis to view the Book of the Twelve Prophets as a literary unit. Several book length studies and numerous essays have demonstrated that any interpretation that takes the canonical text seriously has to understand the intention of the final composition of the twelve writings. There is no doubt that the individuality of each prophet is important. In contrast to Isaiah, Jeremiah, and Ezekiel, the Book of the Twelve lacks a superscription. Instead, some of the writings have their own. Nevertheless, the different prophetic writings are presented as diverse and sometimes controversial contributions to an ongoing process in which YHWH communicates to Israel what endangers its status as God's people and how YHWH will reestablish a blissful relationship with his sinful partner. Each prophet's individuality is construed by the final redactors in such a way that the message of each builds on his predecessors, picking up concepts, words, and text types from them. In this way each single prophet is portrayed as being capable of conceiving God's word clearly and formulating his own prophecy for his own contemporary audience. At the same time, the redactors who combined the writings into one book wanted the reader to look for, discover, and appreciate how the different thematic threads generate a colorful tapestry that reflects God's self disclosure in history.

This volume combines papers presented over the years 1999-2002 in the "Formation of the Book of the Twelve Seminar" of the Society of Biblical Literature. Since its foundation in 1994 this seminar has been a meeting point for those interested in the area of the Book of the Twelve. The international exchange, especially between North American and European scholars, turned out to be fruitful and inspiring. It is hoped that this volume will inspire even more scholars from all over the world to engage in the ongoing process to understand the formation of the Book of the Twelve Prophets.

We, editors and contributors, would like to thank Prof. Dr. Otto Kaiser and the publisher de Gruyter for accepting this anthology in its series BZAW.

Essen, Georgetown
Aaron Schart, Paul Redditt

Table of Contents

Thematic Threads

Introduction

In the heyday of form criticism, scholars analyzed biblical texts for their earliest oral forms and concerned themselves with the original, typical Sitz im Leben as the proper context for studying the passages. Later additions were dubbed "inauthentic," and often were treated with less interest. With the advent of redaction criticism, these additions became the subject of fruitful study, as exegetes sought to uncover the thematic and even theological and sociological interests of redactors. With regard to the Book of the Twelve, however, the unit of study remained the individual book, as it did even in Brevard Child's canonical critical study *Introduction to the Old Testament as Scripture.*[1] More recently, however, scholars have begun to focus more on the larger context of those prophetic collections, asking whether one should not also study the individual books in their larger *literary* context: the Book of the Twelve. Working off the insights of a few earlier scholars, Paul R. House, James D. Nogalski, Barry A. Jones, Aaron Schart, and Burkhard M. Zapff wrote their dissertation or *Habilitationsschrift* on topics that impinged on reading the Twelve as a unity.[2] In 1994,

---

[1]   Brevard S. Childs, *Introduction to the Old Testament as Scripture* (Philadelphia: Fortress, 1979), 373-498.

[2]   These studies found publication as the following: Paul R. House, *The Unity of the Twelve* (JSOTSup; Sheffield: Sheffield Academic Press, 1990); James D. Nogalski, *Literary Precursors to the Book of the Twelve* (BZAW 217. Berlin, New York: de Gruyter, 1993) and *Redactional Processes in the Book of the Twelve* (BZAW 218. Berlin, New York: de Gruyter, 1993); Barry A. Jones, *The Formation of the Book of the Twelve: A Study in Text and Canon* (SBLDS 149; Atlanta: Scholars press, 1995); Aaron Schart, *Entstehung des Zwölfprophetenbuchs* (BZAW 260; Berlin, New York: de Gruyter, 1998); Burkhard M. Zapff, *Redaktionsgeschichtliche Studien zum Michabuch im Kontext des Dodekapropheton* (BZAW 256; Berlin, New York: de Gruyter, 1997). All have participated in the Formation of the Book of the Twelve Consultation and then Seminar of the Society of Biblical Literature. Earlier scholars included, among others, Rolland E. Wolfe, "The Editing of the Book of the Twelve," (Ph. D. diss., Harvard University, 1933) and "The Editing of the Book of the Twelve," *ZAW* 53 (1935) 90-129; Alfred Jepsen, "Kleine Beiträge zum Zwölfprophetenbuch," *ZAW* 56 (1938) 85-100; 242-51; Dale Schneider, "The Unity of the Book of the Twelve" (Ph. D. diss., Yale University, 1979); Andrew Y. Lee, "The Canonical Unity of the Scroll of the Minor Prophets," (Ph. D. diss., Baylor University, 1985); David N. Freedman, "Headings in the Books of the Eighth Century Prophets," *AUSS* 25,1 (1987) 9-26.

under the hand of John D. W. Watts, a number of scholars formed the Formation of the Book of the Twelve Consultation of the Society of Biblical
Literature, which was followed by a Seminar that lasted eight years. With
this publication, all the papers presented in the annual meetings have been
published.[3] The first article in this volume, by Paul L. Redditt, reviews the
research conducted by the members of the Seminar.[4]

Four papers follow that deal with method. The first "The Ties That
Bind: The Identification of Verbal Parallels, Intertextuality, and Reading
Strategies in the Book of the Twelve," by Richard L. Schultz, examines the
issue of what constitutes intertextual citation. Schultz argues that scholars
should be more cautious in speaking of intertextuality between books than
within a given book. He finds convincing examples of intertextuality within
the Twelve, e. g., between Zech 2:14 (Eng. 2:10]) and Zech 9:9 (which he
treats as intertextuality between books) and in the use of Exod 34:6-7 in
several of the Twelve.

Aaron Schart offers a redaction-critical study of Amos 9, "The Fifth Vision of Amos in Context," which shows its growth through the various
stages of the Twelve and beyond. The original vision in 9:1-4* portrays
YHWH commanding Amos to strike the top of a column, thereby ruining
the temple and nullifying the boundary between holy space and profane
world. Tradition bearers added Amos 8:14 and 9:4b, applying the blow to all
sanctuaries involved in the sin of Samaria. Amos 9:7-10 derives from the
hand of the redactor responsible for an edition of the four books Hosea,
Amos, Micah, and Zephaniah. In this revision sinful Israelites will be eliminated, but righteous ones will survive. The hymn fragment inserted between
Amos 9:4 and 9:7 enjoins reciting YHWH's name to help usher in the action
of God. Next, Amos 9:11-15* applies the vision to the Babylonian destruction of the temple. Amos 9:12a, 13, written with Joel and Obadiah in view,
portrays Zion as the dwelling place of YHWH, where foreigners are not allowed. The Septuagint version sees in the vision a prediction of the destruction of the temple in Jerusalem, as do Christian redactors.

---

[3]   Papers from 1994 and 1995 appeared as pp. 85-302 in *Forming Prophetic Literature:*
      Essays on Isaiah and the Twelve in Honor of John D. W. Watts (ed. James W. Watts
      and Paul R. House; JSOTSup 235; Sheffield: Sheffield Academic Press, 1996); papers
      from 1996-98 appeared as *Reading and Hearing the Book of the Twelve* (ed. James D.
      Nogalski and Marvin A. Sweeney; SBLSymS 15: Atlanta: Society of Biblical Litera-
      ture, 2000).
[4]   For a review of a broader range of scholars, see Paul L. Redditt, "Recent Research on
      the Book of the Twelve as One Book," *CurBS* 9 (2001) 47-80.

Erhard S. Gerstenberger's study "Psalms in the Book of the Twelve: How Misplaced Are They?" asks how Psalms found a home in the Twelve. He suggests that scholars start, not with the presumed early prophet and ascribe everything we can to him, and then move on to the next level, ascribing what seems to fit there, and then to the next, etc. Instead, he suggests they start with the "final product" and work backwards, removing layer after layer. He thinks they would wind up ascribing much less to the original prophets, and have a much finer appreciation for the post-exilic scribes who sat in their circles and thought about the past and what the prophets of old must surely have thought and said about it.

The final article in this section is Edgar W. Conrad's study "Forming the Twelve and Forming Canon," in which he advocates the use of a form of reader criticism instead of redaction criticism. One job of a reader is to pay attention to the intention of the work (as opposed to the author or redactor. That intention, however, is communicated through codes in the text, codes that set limits on possible interpretations or readings. Conrad sets himself the task of reading the Twelve in light of its own codes, noticing groupings within the Twelve that employ such terms as "vision" (חזון), "the words of" (דברי), and the phrase "and it happened" (ויהי).

The next section of this volume contains four articles dealing in one way or another with the order of the books within the Twelve. Laurie J. Braaten, "God Sows the Land: Hosea's Land Theme in the Book of the Twelve," finds the land motif appearing at crucial intervals in the Twelve. It appears prominently in Hosea and Malachi and could be said to form a framing device for the Twelve. It also appears in Joel 1:2, 14, in contexts dealing both with judgment and blessing upon the people of the land.

The article "The Place and Function of Joel in the Twelve," by Marvin A. Sweeney argues on various grounds that the order in the LXX was original. (1) The LXX order treats the northern kingdom first (in Hosea and Amos, without interruption), then moves to the south, whereas the MT interjects Joel between Hosea and Amos, disrupting both historical and logical sense. (2) The MT breaks up the use of Obadiah in Joel, whereas the LXX preserves it so that references to Obadiah in Joel are immediately clear to the reader. Sweeney then employs these insights to determine which is earlier, arguing that the order in the LXX appears to reflect concerns within Judah during the late-monarchic, exilic, and early post-exilic periods, whereas the MT version appears to reflect the concerns of the later Persian period, particularly in the time of Ezra and Nehemiah.

In her study "The Repentance of Nineveh in the Story of Jonah and Nahum's Prophecy of the City's Destruction – A Coherent Reading of the Book of the Twelve as Reflected in the Aggada," Beate Ego assembles several ancient rabbinic texts that address the repentance of Nineveh, and thus implicitly the sequence of Jonah-Nahum in the MT, concerning the fate of Nineveh. While those texts address other issues (e. g., whether Jonah should be considered a false prophet for predicting something that did not occur – namely the destruction of Nineveh), they seem to offer an example of a consecutive reading of the Twelve.

A. Joseph Everson, "The Canonical Location of Habakkuk," argues that the Twelve is arranged in such a way that one can discern particular times of "days" when God's presence seemed evident. Hosea, Joel, Amos, Obadiah, Micah, Nahum, and Zephaniah all attempted to provide a framework for understanding history theologically by affirming Yahweh's sovereignty over the nations. By contrast, Jonah warns against the dangers of being overwhelmed by enmity, and Habakkuk focuses on the dangers of despair and disillusionment and encourages the faithful to remember the promises of Torah. By placing Habakkuk after Nahum, and before Zephaniah, the editors recall an era when chaos seemed to rule, but did not, and encouraged readers in similar times not to despair.

The more thematic oriented articles start with James Crenshaw's wide-ranging study "Theodicy in the Book of the Twelve." Especially after the Shoa, the issue has gained new urgency. Crenshaw differentiates between three basic ways YHWHs justice is addressed: The first way, found in Zeph 3:1-5 and Hos 14:10, denies that a problem exists and affirms in an apologetic way that YHWH's justice is beyond any doubt. The second approach questions the conviction that the virtuous prosper. It appears most prominently in the mouth of the opponents of Malachi (e.g. Mal 2:13-15). The third type tries to redefine YHWH's character in such a way that it does not match the believer's model of justice entirely. The Book of the Twelve contains all three options, thus giving the reader different possibilities. It even includes the statement that YHWH brings about evil (Am 3:8). The overall composition of the Book of the Twelve may provide a way for the reader to walk on the "edge between doubt and trust" in order to deepen the understanding of God's unconditioned grace.

There can be no doubt that the Day of YHWH is an important, recurring theme in many of the writings of the Book of the Twelve. Thirteen out of the fifteen occurrences of the phrase YOM YHWH in the Hebrew Bible appear in the Book of the Twelve. In "The Day(s) of YHWH in the Book of the Twelve" James Nogalski adds references to a day of a final intervention of YHWH in history with other expressions. In addition, certain imagery is typically associated with the actions on that day. Nogalski collects all the passages where the topic appears. Considering diachronic and synchronic issues as to how the passages are linked to one another, he finally explores how a reader can make sense of the order of the passages involved.

In "Die prophetische Ehemetaphorik und die Bewertung der Prophetie im Zwölfprophetenbuch," Gerlinde Baumann develops two independent topics. Since the Book of the Twelve opens with a text employing the marriage metaphor to refer to the relationship between YHWH and Israel (Hos 1-3), it is important to note how the book as a whole construes this image. It appears that the Book of the Twelve contains the most diverse and fully developed use of the imagery. Only the Book of the Twelve tells the full story of the love of YHWH to his unfaithful wife. This is probably due to a complex literary history behind the texts. Baumann differentiates between the thematic development within the tradition history, the redaction history, and the final canonical text. As it turns out, the completely unrelated topics of marriage and of prophecy display similar patterns of development throughout the Twelve.

In "Exile as Purification. Reconstructing the Book of the Four," Rainer Albertz reevaluates and refines the thesis of a four-prophets book comprising Hosea, Amos, Micah, and Zephaniah. Undoubtedly the four prophets book is the soundest and most widely-accepted precursor of the Twelve. However, the question of the exact shape of the book is not yet settled. Albertz compiles arguments concerning why Mic 5:9-13 should be seen as the original conclusion of Micah and Zeph 3:11-13 as the final conclusion of that book. These books see the Babylonian exile purification; every writing of the Book of the Four closes with a purification passage (Hos 14:2-4; Amos 9:7-10; Mic 5:9-13; Zeph 3:11-13). The judgment of YHWH is aimed at the final destruction of Judah's military forces and its idol cults, not at all the people. In close connection to passages from the version of Hosea, e.g. Hos 3,1-5*, the redactor developed his or her own understanding of the Babylonian exile. It is remarkable that the Book of the Four contained not a single hint that a Davidic ruler will play a role in Israel's future.

In "Futurism in the Preexilic Minor Prophets Compared with That of the Postexilic Minor Prophets," Simon J. De Vries explores phrases that mark temporal transitions, e.g. אז (then), עתה (now), והוה) ביום ההוא ([and it shall be] on that day), בימים ההם (in those days), בעת ההיא (at that time), הנה ימים באים (behold, days are coming). De Vries shows that redactors used specific formulas to expand or even reverse the original message of the prophets. Most notably, redactors used the phrases והוה) ביום ההוא ([and it shall be] on that day), בימים ההם (in those days), בעת ההיא (at that time), הנה ימים באים (behold, days are coming) in order to expand the salvific parts in postexilic times. Although there is no clear-cut shift in distribution from preexilic to postexilic times, some phrases were used more frequently in preexilic times than in postexilic ones. More and more the future of Israel and the world became the dominant topic of redactors, thus shifting from prophecy to apocalyptic visions. The high number of the phrase ההוא ביום (והוה) ([and it shall be] on that day) in Zech 12-14 shows, that those phrases finally became technical markers to refer to the end time.

In "Haggai-Zechariah: Prophecy after the Manner of Ezekiel," Steven S. Tuell investigates "four possible points of connection: the centrality of temple and cult in Haggai-Zechariah; the dating formulae, precise to the day, which structure this composite work; Zechariah's vision reports; and the use of the first person in Zechariah." Clearly, the concern for the temple is found in Haggai and Zechariah 1-8; however, only rarely is a clear literary dependence demonstrable (Zech 2,1-5 cites Ezek 40:3). In many respects it seems as if Haggai-Zechariah deliberately uses forms known form Ezekiel with different content. The redactors who added Haggai-Zechariah 1-8 to the precursor of the Book the Twelve apparently wanted to separate their temple and community concept from that of Ezekiel.

In "The Perspective of the Nations in the Book of Micah as a 'Systematization' of the Nations' Role in Joel, Jonah and Nahum?" Burkhard M. Zapff is concerned with the position of Micah between Joel and Jonah. He finds that the structure the last redactor of Micah gave this writing corresponds nicely with the position Micah has within the sequence Joel-Micah-Jonah. The different prophets would describe different stages of an eschatological drama similar to that envisioned in Zechariah 14. The many catchwords that Micah 7 especially has with Joel, Jonah, and Nahum 1 lead one to speculate whether the redactor of Micah 7 wanted to provide an overview over the fate of the nations as presented by the Book of the Twelve.

In "Endings as New Beginnings: Returning to the Lord, the Day of the Lord, and Renewal in the Book of the Twelve," Paul R. House examines a dominant motif in the Twelve. Many of the prophetic writings contain passages that urge the hearers to change their attitude, behavior or relationship to God. The relevant passages are read according to the setting the writings, especially their superscriptions, suggest. In many cases the prophets must state that the chance to "return" or to "seek the Lord" was already gone, but the hope that this would change in the future did not vanish. Every prophet envisioned a new beginning after the condemnation of sin, a future in which God and Israel together with the nations and nature will come together in new harmony.

The essays in this volume explore the formation of the Book of the Twelve with different approaches and they focus on different aspects. They all are concerned, however, to enrich the study of the Twelve as a unity. The reader will find many new observations and perspectives that try to make sense of connections of all kinds. Here and there the different essays confirm each other, so that it becomes clearer what theories are more stable;

sometimes the speculation goes in different directions. In any case, it is hoped that the volume presents many appealing ways of reading the Twelve as a multi-voiced whole. Not the least merit of this way of reading should be that the reader will be trained to read independent writings together. Within the process of reading from Hosea to Malachi the reader will identify with different prophets and observe the same theological issues from different angels and within different situations. This will open the reader to a deeper understanding of God and a better sense for plurality within a community of faith.

January 2003
Aaron Schart and Paul Redditt

List of Contributors

Rainer Albertz is Professor of Old Testament at Westfälische Wilhelms-Universität, Münster, Germany. He wrote *A History of Israelite Religion* (2 vols.; OTL; Louisville: Westminster, 1994). In his book *Die Exilszeit. 6. Jahrhundert v. Chr* (Kohlhammer, 2001) he dealt with the Book of the Four, Jeremiah, Ezekiel and Deutero-Isaiah. It will be translated into English in 2003.

Gerlinde Baumann is Wissenschaftliche Assistentin at the Philipps-Universität Marburg. She has written numerous publications on the subject of the Wisdom Figure in Proverbs 1-9, the prophetic marriage metaphor (YHWH-Israel/Jerusalem), and the body of God in the Old Testament.

Laurie J. Braaten, Ph.D. is Professor of Old Testament at Judson College in Elgin, IL. He has published articles and read papers on Hosea and the Book of the Twelve and on Creation Theology. He has five articles in the new *Eerdmans Dictionary of the Bible* (Adoption, Ancestors, Love, Pine, Poplar).

Edgar W. Conrad is Reader in and Head of Studies in Religion in the University of Queensland, Brisbane, Australia. He is the author of *Fear Not Warrior (Scholars) Reading Isaiah* (Fortress), *Zechariah* (Sheffield), and a forthcoming book *Reading Prophetic Books* (Sheffield). Recent articles focus on Isaiah and the Twelve.

James L. Crenshaw is the Robert L. Flowers Professor of Old Testament at the Duke University Divinity School. He is a leading interpreter of wisdom literature and also has published widely on biblical prophecy, including the recent commentary on Joel in the Anchor Bible. Among his numerous publications are *Old Testament Wisdom* (Westminster John Knox), *Ecclesiastes* (Westminster), and a collection of his essays, *Urgent Advice and Probing Questions and Education in Ancient Israel* (Mercer).

Simon J. De Vries is Professor Emeritus of Old Testament at the Methodist Theological School in Delaware, Ohio. He is the author of numerous works in OT exegesis and theology, the latest of which is *From Old Revelation to*

New, A Tradition-historical and Redaction-Critical Study of Temporal Transitions in Prophetic Prediction (Eerdmans, 1995). An exhaustive bibliography of his writings will appear in the forthcoming Festschrift in his honor, *God's World for our World.* Currently, he is preparing two additional books, one entitled *Isaiah in the Hands of John Calvin* and the other *Shining White Knight, A Spiritual Memoir.*

Beate Ego is professor of Old Testament Studies and Judaism in Antiquity (in German: Altes Testament und Antikes Judentum) at the University of Osnabrueck, Germany. She has written numerous publications in the field of Biblical and Rabbinic cosmology, the Book of Tobit, and Targum Sheni on Megillat Ester, as well as on other subjects of Biblical theology and the interpretation of the Hebrew Bible in early Jewish literature.

A. Joseph Everson is Professor of Biblical Studies at California Lutheran University in Thousand Oaks, California. He is the author of a number of essays relating to prophetic eschatology, in particular, the "day of Yahweh" motif in prophetic thought. His most recent publication is the entry on "The Book of Isaiah" in the *Eerdmans Dictionary of the Bible.*

Erhard S. Gerstenberger, native of the industrial Ruhr area in Germany, completed his Th. D. at Bonn University under M. Noth, studied and taught at Yale Divinity school and at the Brazilian Lutheran School of Theology at Sao Leopoldo. He also was a parish minister at Essen city and professor of Old Testament at Giessen and Marburg universities. His latest book is a form critical commentary on the Psalms, 2 vols., published by Eerdmans in 2001.

Paul R. House is Professor of Old Testament at Wheaton College, Wheaton, Illinois. He is the author of *The Unity of the Twelve* (1990), *1-2 Kings* (1995), and *Old Testament Theology* (1998), among other volumes.

James D. Nogalski is Associate Professor of Old Testament Interpretation at the M. Christopher White School of Divinity at Gardner-Webb University in Boiling Springs, North Carolina. He has written extensively on the Book of the Twelve, including two volumes in this series (BZAW 217 and 218).

Paul L. Redditt is Professor of Old Testament at Georgetown College, Georgetown, Kentucky. He contributed two volumes to the New Century Bible (*Haggai, Zechariah, Malachi* and *Daniel*) and has written articles on the Twelve and the book of Daniel.

Aaron Schart, born 1957, is Professor for Old and New Testament at the University of Essen, Germany. His research focuses on biblical theology and redaction critical questions of the Pentateuch and the prophets. He has published a book (*Die Entstehung des Zwölfprophetenbuchs*, in this series) and several articles on different aspects of the redaction history of the Book of the Twelve.

Richard Schultz is the Armerding Chair of Biblical Studies and Professor of Old Testament at Wheaton College (IL). He has written a monograph and several articles on the Hebrew Prophets.

Marvin A. Sweeney is Professor of Hebrew Bible at the Claremont School of Theology and Professor of Religion at the Claremont Graduate University. He is the author of *Zephaniah* (Hermeneia; Fortress, forthcoming 2003); *King Josiah of Judah: The Lost Messiah of Israel* (Oxford University Press, 2001); *The Twelve Prophets* (Berit Olam; Liturgical Press, 2000); *Isaiah 1-39, with an Introduction to Prophetic Literature* (Eerdmans, 1996) and many other books and studies in biblical literature and Jewish studies.

Steven S. Tuell is associate professor of Religious Studies at Randolph-Macon College in Ashland, Virginia. He has written *The Law of the Temple in Ezekiel 40--48* in the Harvard Semitic Monographs series, and a commentary on 1 and 2 Chronicles in the Westminster John Knox Interpretation series, as well as numerous articles on Ezekiel and on the Persian period. He has been a frequent contributor to the United Methodist Publishing House Adult Bible Studies curriculum, most recently a teacher's book on Daniel. Tuell is now at work on a new commentary on Ezekiel for the Hendrickson New International Bible Commentary series.

Burkard M. Zapff, born 1960, is Professor of Old Testament at the Catholic University Eichstätt-Ingolstadt, Germany. He is the author of two monographs on the redaction history of Isaiah and Micah, including *Redaktionsgeschichtliche Studien zum Michabuch im Kontext des Dodekapropheton* (de Gruyter). In 2001 he published a commentary on Isaiah 40-55 in the Series Neue Echter Bibel.

The Formation of the Book of the Twelve:
A Review of Research

Paul L. Redditt

The so-called "Minor Prophets" are called "The Twelve" and are reckoned as one book in the Hebrew Bible. The collection predates Sirach's prayer "May the bones of the Twelve Prophets send forth new life from where they lie" (49:10), even if that reference is to the prophets themselves, as David L. Petersen maintains.[1] The manuscript evidence from Qumran shows that the order of the Twelve in the MT itself goes back to at least 150 B.C.E., though 4QXII[a] might constitute an exception in which Jonah stood last.[2] Josephus also seems to have counted the Twelve as one book among the twenty-two he cited as the records of past times: five from Moses, thirteen recording events that transpired between Moses and Artaxerxes,[3] and four containing hymns and precepts (*Ag. Ap.* 1.8). Likewise, the Twelve seem to have counted as one among the twenty-four books Ezra is said to have dictated and made public (*2 Esd.* 14:44-45). The Babylonian Talmud provides instructions for copying the Twelve that stipulate leaving four lines between canonical books, but only three between the prophets in the Twelve.

To be sure, neither Jews nor Christians typically interpreted the Twelve in canonical fashion in the following centuries, using instead what modern

---

[1] David. L. Petersen, "A Book of the Twelve?" *Reading and Hearing the Book of the Twelve* (SBLSymS 15; eds. James D. Nogalski and Marvin A. Sweeney; Atlanta: Society of Biblical Literature, 2000) 4.

[2] Russell Fuller, "The Form and Formation of the Book of the Twelve: The Evidence from the Judean Desert," in *Forming Prophetic Literature; Essays on Isaiah and the Twelve in Honor of John D. W. Watts* (JSOTSup 235; eds. James W. Watts and Paul R. House; Sheffield: Sheffield Academic Press, 1996) 96. Fuller edited fragments of the Twelve from Qumran, discovering one fragment of the end of the corpus, which did not end with Malachi. Another fragment began Jonah, and Fuller concluded that it would fit the scroll after Malachi.

[3] His thirteen "historical" books almost surely would have included Joshua, Judges, Samuel, Kings, Isaiah, Jeremiah, and the Twelve, may have included Ezekiel, Chronicles, Ezra and Nehemiah, and perhaps even Daniel and all or part of the Five Megilloth. In any case, the Twelve would not have been omitted and could not have been counted individually.

exegetes might call a "proof-text" reading strategy.[4] Beate Ego, however, assembles several ancient rabbinic texts that address the repentance of Nineveh, and thus implicitly the sequence of Jonah-Nahum in the MT concerning the fate of Nineveh: Tob 14:4,8; Josephus *Ant.* 9.242, *b. Taan.* 16a, *Tg. Ps.-J. Nah* 1:1, *Pirqe R. El.* 43, *y. Taan.* 2.1, 65b, and *Pesiq. Rab Kah.* 24.11.[5] While those texts address other issues (e. g., whether Jonah should be considered a false prophet for predicting something – namely, the destruction of Nineveh – that did not occur), they seem to offer an example of a consecutive reading of the Twelve.

In the modern period, scholars have developed historical-critical methods, which typically study the Twelve in a reconstructed chronological order. Even so, members of the academy are all too aware of arguments over the dates of Joel, Obadiah, Jonah, Nahum, Habakkuk, Zechariah 9-14, and Malachi. Indeed, some scholars even challenge the dates supplied in the headings of one or more of the other six collections. Only a few have treated the Twelve canonically, but their work deserves notice at this point. As least as early as 1868, Heinrich Ewald proposed a redaction of the Twelve in three stages based on the superscriptions.[6] Carl Steuernagel found seven and Rolland E. Wolfe four.[7] More recently, Dale Schneider proposed a process in four stages: (1) Hosea, Amos, and Micah; (2) Nahum, Habakkuk, and Zephaniah; (3) Joel, Obadiah, and Jonah; and (4) Haggai, Zechariah, and Malachi.[8] Andrew Y. Lee posited a post-exilic redaction and enhancement during the time of Nehemiah of mostly authentic collections of saying by the prophets.[9] Terrence Collins also thought in terms of four steps: (1) an exilic stage combining Hosea, Amos (including chapter 9), Micah (including chapters 4 and 5), Nahum, Zephaniah, and Obadiah; (2) a post-exilic stage

---

[4]   See Paul L. Redditt, "The Production and Reading of the Book of the Twelve," in *Reading and Hearing the Book of the Twelve* (SBLSymS 15; eds. James D. Nogalski and Marvin A. Sweeney; Atlanta: Society of Biblical Literature, 2000) 26-31.

[5]   Beate Ego, "The Repentance of Nineveh in the Story of Jonah and Nahum's Prophecy of the City's Destruction: Aggadic Solutions for an Exegetical Problem in the Book of the Twelve," *SBLSP 2000*, 249-250.

[6]   Heinrich Ewald, *Die Propheten des Alten Bundes erklärt* (2nd ed.; Göttingen: Vandenhoeck & Ruprecht, 1868) 74-82. The first edition is not available to this author.

[7]   Carl Steuernagel, *Lehrbuch der Einleitung in das Alten Testament* (Tübingen: Mohr, 1912) 669-72; Rolland E. Wolfe, "The Editing of the Book of the Twelve," (Ph. D. diss., Harvard University, 1933) and "The Editing of the Book of the Twelve," *ZAW* 53 (1935) 90-129.

[8]   Dale Schneider, "The Unity of the Book of the Twelve," (Ph. D. diss., Yale University, 1979.

[9]   Andrew Y. Lee, "The Canonical Unity of the Scroll of the Minor Prophets," (Ph. D. diss., Baylor University, 1985.

spurred by the rebuilding of the temple, that added Haggai, Zechariah 1-8, expansions to Zephaniah, esp. Zeph 3:9-20, Jonah, and possibly Joel; (3) a stage from the mid-fifth century reflecting introspection that added Joel (if it was not already present), Habakkuk, Malachi, and some eschatological additions, notably to Zephaniah; and (4) later additions, especially Zechariah 9-14 and Mal. 3:22-24 [Eng. 4:4-6].[10] Finally, R. J. Coggins pointed to similarities in the shape of the Twelve when compared with the other prophetic books. They begin in the first six books with words of doom to the recalcitrant Israelite community, then move in the next three to a section dealing with the foreign nations, and conclude with hope for the restitution of the committee.[11]

The question for scholars participating in the Formation of the Book of the Twelve Seminar of the Society of Biblical Literature was not simply whether the Twelve had been preserved, collected, and edited, which they obviously had, but whether that editing linked the corpora in some unified or coherent way that one may uncover. Typically, they asked about editorial intention, but even if one discounts ever recovering the intention of redactors, the question of coherence remains valid. With the rise in interest in canonical order and structure permeating studies of the First Testament, they have begun recommending a canonical reading of the Twelve. Their overall thesis is that the Twelve underwent a process of growth that resulted in a coherent collection every bit as deserving to be called a book as Isaiah, Jeremiah, or Ezekiel. They argue that the Twelve exhibits an overall theme, plot, and/or direction greater than that of the sum of its twelve parts.

I. The Challenge to Demonstrate Coherence

The idea that the Twelve constitutes a coherent corpus capable of being read consecutively (and perhaps intended to be read that way) has not gone unchallenged. Ehud Ben Zvi objects to the enterprise for a number of reasons, including the following. (1) Collection does not prove coherence; ancient scribes collected anthologies with no coherent plan, one example from ancient Israel being the book of Proverbs. (2) Later communities, from Qumran to the rabbis, read the twelve as an anthology.[12] (3) The lack of a fixed

---

[10] Terrence Collins, *The Mantle of Elijah: The Redaction Criticism of the Prophetical Books* (Sheffield: Sheffield Academic Press, 1993) 62-64.

[11] R. J. Coggins, "The Minor Prophets -- One Book or Twelve?" in *Crossing the Boundaries* (eds. S. E. Porter, P. Joyce, and D. E. Orton; Leiden: Brill, 1994) 64.

[12] One may grant the point that the Rabbis rarely ever recorded a consecutive reading of the Twelve, but it proves little: they did not read other books in the Bible that way either.

order among the first six book militates against any argument that any given sequence is "correct."[13] (4) The superscription and the incipits set the prophets apart.[14] David. L. Petersen opts for a similar position. The mere fact of the collection could as easily support the view that the Twelve is an anthology as that it is a coherent book. In addition, he thinks the differences in order imply that the collection is an anthology. He does, however, find a consistent theme throughout the Twelve: "the day of the Lord." He argues, then, that the Twelve constitutes a "thematized anthology."[15]

Kenneth H. Cuffey suggests that there are four basic types of coherence: internal (or literary), structural, perspectival, and thematic. He finds examples of all four in Micah, and cites examples of all four adduced by Paul R. House and James D. Nogalski in their work on the Twelve (to be discussed later in this paper), but questions whether the Twelve as a whole exhibits coherence, for two reasons. First is the difference in scope between the Twelve and a given collection within it. The problem, as Cuffey sees it, is that the coherence claimed for the Twelve falls outside of units clearly marked by superscriptions.

Second, Cuffey says, it is harder to determine the intentions of a secondary redactor than it is a primary author.[16] In response, one might answer that the differences between Micah and the Twelve are only differences in degree, not of kind. If later voices have added to Micah anything like what critical scholars have attributed to them, a significant percentage, perhaps even a majority, of the book came from redactors. Moreover, the presence of the superscriptions -- if accepted as more or less historically accurate -- may assist understanding redaction in the Twelve. In the case of Isaiah, by contrast, there is no superscription naming a prophet after Isaiah 13:1, which

---

[13]   Stephen B. Chapman (*The Law and the Prophets* [FAT 27; Tübingen: Mohr Siebeck, 2000] 137) thinks that this argument is decisive, but it might not be. As will be shown later, Marvin A. Sweeney has proposed ways of reading both the MT and the LXX that also allow him to say which order came first.

[14]   Ehud Ben Zvi, "Twelve Prophetic Books or 'The Twelve': A Few Preliminary Considerations," *Forming Prophetic Literature: Essays on Isaiah and the Twelve in Honor of John D. W. Watts* (JSOTSup 235; eds. James W. Watts and Paul R. House; Sheffield: Sheffield Academic Press, 1996) 131-138. Recently, Michael H. Floyd ("The אֵשַׂמ [Maśśa] as a Type of prophetic Book," *JBL* 121 [2002] 401-422, esp. 409) joins Ben Zvi in his criticism.

[15]   Petersen, "A Book of the Twelve?" 3-10.

[16]   Kenneth H. Cuffey, "Remnant, Redactor, and Biblical Theologian: A Comparative Study of Coherence in Micah and the Twelve," *Reading and Hearing the Book of the Twelve* (SBLSymS 15; eds. James D. Nogalski and Marvin A. Sweeney; Atlanta: Society of Biblical Literature, 2000) 186-202.

certainly does not make the task of studying the growth of that back any easier.

Further, Collins has remarked that "there is no reason to suppose that the names of Hosea, Amos, and Micah were any less important than that of Isaiah. The quantity of material attached to their names was certainly as great, although the Isaianic collection was later to be expanded in ... a spectacular fashion."[17] In other words, for all one knows the redactional contributions to Isaiah were greater than those to the Twelve, and the redactors left no names behind other than Isaiah's. If Collins is right, the problems would be even greater for Isaiah than for the Twelve. Still, Richard L. Schultz has argued that scholars should be more cautious in speaking of intertextuality between books than within a given book. He finds convincing examples within the Twelve, e. g., between Zech 2:14 (Eng. 2:10])and Zech 9:9 (which he treats as intertextuality between books) and in the use of Exod 34:6-7 in several of the Twelve (see below).[18]

What types of coherence in the Twelve, then, have scholars adduced? With regard to literary coherence, Paul R. House thinks that the Twelve develops a "comic" plot, beginning on a negative note in Hosea through Micah with the sins of the nations, continuing with the punishment of sin in Nahum through Zephaniah, and concluding with the promise of a better day in Haggai, Zechariah, and Malachi.[19] In addition, the characters remain consistent: God serves as the hero, and Israel and the Gentiles are comic foils.[20] The prophets fulfill specific roles: as special servants they act out, transmit, and interpret and explicate the will, purpose, and word of God.[21] The implied author is God, and the point of view is third person omniscient, matching God's![22]

Clearly, the Twelve begin on a primarily negative note, and Haggai and Zechariah 1-8 look toward a new day when the temple was rebuilt. The comic plot, however, is more characteristic of individual books than the Twelve, since most follow the pattern of doom followed by hope (cf. Joel

---

[17] Collins, *The Mantle of Elijah*, 61.

[18] Richard L. Schultz, "The Ties That Bind: Intertextuality, the Identification of Verbal Parallels, and Reading Strategies in the Book of the Twelve," *SBL Seminar Papers, 2001* (SBLSP 41; Atlanta: Society of Biblical Literature, 2001), 46-51.

[19] Paul R. House, *The Unity of the Twelve* (JSOTSup 97; Sheffield: Almond, 1990). Cf. his article "Dramatic Coherence in Nahum, Habakkuk, and Zephaniah," *Forming Prophetic Literature: Essays on Isaiah and the Twelve in Honor of John D. W. Watts* (JSOTSup 235; eds. James W. Watts and Paul R. House; Sheffield: Sheffield Academic Press, 1996) 195-208.

[20] Ibid., 172-85, 203-219.

[21] Ibid., 185-203.

[22] Ibid., 226-41.

1:2-2:17 [doom] followed by 2:18-4:21 [hope] and Amos 1:2-9:10 [doom] followed by 9:11-15 [hope]), a pattern employed four times in Micah.[23] It might be more accurate, then, to speak of a double plot in the Twelve, developing the dual themes of progress (comedy) and regress (tragedy) or with Donald K. Berry to say it is open-ended.[24] He calls it an "epic," paralleling the historical epic of the Former Prophets and the epic narrative on the Torah, both of which have an open ending.

With regard to perspectival coherence, the shared implied author and point of view perhaps belong here also. Cuffey cites two postulated earlier corpora (Hosea, Amos, Micah, and Zephaniah on the one hand; Haggai and Zechariah 1-8 on the other) as possibly having perspectival coherence. The first may have come into being to explain the fall of Jerusalem, the second in relation to rebuilding the temple.[25] Another scholar, Margaret S. Odell, asked how the Twelve views the prophets. She uncovered a negative perspective toward the cult prophets of eighth-century Israel, and another toward the prophet Jonah.[26] "What Hosea and the Book of the Twelve suggest," she writes, "is that there is something greater than Jonah -- and all the prophets."[27] It is possible to push Odell's point further. This ambivalence toward prophets is not limited to Hosea and Jonah. It appears also in Amos 7:14-15 and in its echo in Zech 13:5. The resolution of the issue appears, perhaps, in Zech 1:5-6, which distinguishes God's servants the prophets from the word of God they delivered. The revealed word would live on, not the prophets. In the Twelve, it would live on in writing.

With regard to structural coherence, John D. W. Watts points to the significance of the superscriptions and incipits.[28] The fact that these elements create the appearance of twelve prophetic figures is the only basis one has

---

[23]   Cf. Cuffey's analysis of Micah in "Coherence," 190-6.

[24]   Donald K. Berry, "Malachi's Dual Design: The Close of the Canon and What Comes Afterward," *Forming Prophetic Literature: Essays on Isaiah and the Twelve in Honor of John D. W. Watts* (JSOTSup 235; eds. James W. Watts and Paul R. House; Sheffield: Sheffield Academic Press, 1996) 300.

[25]   Cuffey, "Coherence," 290.

[26]   Margaret S. Odell, "The Prophets and the End of Hosea," *Forming Prophetic Literature: Essays on Isaiah and the Twelve in Honor of John D. W. Watts* (JSOTSup 235; eds. James W. Watts and Paul R. House; Sheffield: Sheffield Academic Press, 1996) 159-68.

[27]   Ibid., 170.

[28]   John D. W. Watts, "Superscriptions and Incipits in the Book of the Twelve," *Reading and Hearing the Book of the Twelve* (SBLSymS 15; eds. James D. Nogalski and Marvin A Sweeney; Atlanta; Society of Biblical Literature, 2000) 110-124. Superscriptions are nominal headings over a book, a portion of a book, or a poem, introducing what follows, while incipits are the opening sentence of narratives, which serve the same purpose (p. 111).

for speaking of twelve prophets; critical scholars find evidence of many more hands at work in those books. Further, the superscriptions of Hosea, Amos, Micah, and Zephaniah are similar enough to posit one common hand (often called Deuteronomistic) as a redactor,[29] and Haggai-Zechariah 1-8 show so much similarity that critical scholars argue that they derived from the same redactional hand.[30] Thus, the superscriptions and incipits provide a structural (and often chronological) coherence to the Twelve and to two prior corpora.

Another issue related to structure is the order of the collections within the Twelve. The superscriptions in the early corpora outline the order from the eighth century (Hosea, Amos, Micah) to just before the exile (Zephaniah) and to the late sixth century at the time of the rebuilding of the temple (Haggai, Zechariah 1-8). These six collections do not vary in their placement relative to each other; nor does the sequence from Nahum to Malachi vary at all. The placement of the remaining three (Joel, Obadiah, and Jonah) varies between the MT and the LXX. A comparison of their respective order shows that the MT intersperses those three among the eighth century prophets Hosea, Amos, and Micah, while the LXX collects them after those three.

Order of the First Six of the Twelve: MT	Order of the First Six of the Twelve: LXX
Hosea	Hosea
Joel	Amos
Amos	Micah
Obadiah	Joel
Jonah	Obadiah
Micah	Jonah

This variation invites explanation, and as mentioned earlier some scholars consider it lethal to the view that the Twelve need to be read consecu-

---

[29]   See F. I. Anderson and David N. Freedman, *Hosea* (AB 24; Garden City, NY: Doubleday, 1980) 40-44, 143-9; David N. Freedman, "Headings in the Books of the Eighth-Century Prophets," *AUSS* 25,1 (1987) 9-26; Alfred Jepsen, "Kleine Beiträge zum Zwölfpropheten-buch," *ZAW* 56 (1938) 94-95; Gene M. Tucker, "Prophetic Superscriptions and the Growth of a Canon," *Canon and Authority: Essays in Old Testament Religion and Theology* (eds. George W. Coats and Burke O. Long; Philadelphia: Fortress, 1977) 69; P. Weimar, "Obadja. Eine Redaktionskritische Analyse," *BN* 27 (1985) 97; and Hans W. Wolff, *Hosea* (Hermeneia; Philadelphia: Fortress, 1974) 3-4.

[30]   See Carol L. Meyers and Eric M. Meyers, *Haggai, Zechariah 1-8* (AB 25B; Garden City, NY: Doubleday, 1987) xliv-xlviii. Cf. Paul L. Redditt, *Haggai, Zechariah, Malachi* (NCB; London: HarperCollins and Grand Rapids: Eerdmans, 1995) 11-12.

tively.[31] James D. Nogalski defends the order in the MT as original, citing catchwords between the end of one prophetic collection and the beginning of the next.[32] (See the next section of this paper.) For him, Joel was composed or extensively reworked for its place in the Twelve,[33] and serves as the anchor for a "Joel-related layer" (consisting of Joel, Obadiah, Nahum, Habakkuk, and Malachi) inserted into the two previously-existing corpora: the Deuteronomistic corpus and Haggai-Zechariah 1-8.[34] Obadiah, too, consists of the reworking of traditions with an eye towards other parts of the Twelve.[35] Jonah (and Zechariah 9-14, too for that matter) was a later addition to the Twelve, with Jonah disturbing the catchwords between Obadiah and Micah.[36]

By contrast, Marvin A. Sweeney argues on various grounds that the order in the LXX was original. (1) The LXX order treats the northern kingdom first (in Hosea and Amos, without interruption), then moves to the south, whereas the MT interjects Joel between Hosea and Amos, disrupting both historical and logical sense. The difference is significant for Sweeney. In the order in the MT, the positioning of Joel means that the Twelve emphasizes the role of Jerusalem and its relationship to Israel and to the nations throughout.[37] (2) The MT breaks up the use of Obadiah in Joel, whereas the LXX preserves it so that references to Obadiah in Joel are immediately clear to the reader.[38] With this same stroke Sweeney blunts the objection of Ben Zvi that the two books were too remote in the canon for a reader to note the similarities.[39] At the same time, it must be observed that the LXX order destroys the close connection between Joel 4:16 [Eng.. 3:16] and Amos 1:2, though the two passages could still stand as a case of quotation.

---

[31] Ben Zvi, "Twelve Prophetic Books or 'The Twelve,'" 137, Chapman, *The Law and the Prophets*, 137.

[32] James D. Nogalski, *Literary Precursors to the Book of the Twelve* (BZAW 217; Berlin, New York: de Gruyter, 1993) 20-57.

[33] James D. Nogalski, *Redactional Processes in the Book of the Twelve* (BZAW 218; Berlin: New York: de Gruyter, 1993) 13.

[34] Ibid., 275 and James D. Nogalski, "Joel as 'Literary Anchor' for the Book of the Twelve," *Reading and Hearing the Book of the Twelve* (SBLSymS 15; eds. James D. Nogalski and Marvin A. Sweeney; Atlanta: Society of Biblical Literature, 2000).

[35] Nogalski, *Redactional Processes*, 89-92.

[36] Ibid., 278-9.

[37] Marvin A. Sweeney, *The Twelve Prophets* (2 vols.; Berit Olam; Collegeville, Min.: Liturgical Press, 2000) 1.xxxii.

[38] Marvin A. Sweeney, "The Place and Function of Joel in the Book of the Twelve," *SBL Seminar Papers, 1999* (SBLSP 38; Atlanta: Society of Biblical Literature, 1999), 592.

[39] Ben Zvi, "Twelve Prophetic Books or 'The Twelve,'" 148.

Sweeney then employs these insights to determine which is earlier. The order in the LXX "appears to reflect concerns within Judah during the late-monarchic, exilic, and early post-exilic periods when Judean thinkers were attempting to come to terms with the Assyrian destruction of the northern kingdom of Israel and the threat to Jerusalem and Judah posed and later realized by the Babylonian Empire."[40] The MT version, which focuses on the role of Jerusalem, "appears to reflect the concerns of the later Persian period, particularly in the time of Ezra and Nehemiah, when concern shifted away from the north to focus almost entirely on Jerusalem as the holy center of Persian-period Yehud."[41] These implications point to one more difference between Sweeney and Nogalski: Sweeney thinks the Book of the Twelve was completed no later than the early Persian period, i. e. roughly the time of Ezra and Nehemiah, whereas Nogalski dates Joel in the late Persian period, Zechariah 9-14 in the Greek period at the end of the fourth and beginning of the third century, and Jonah early in the third century.[42]

As mentioned earlier, for the most part the Dead Sea Scrolls follow the order of the MT. One fragment, however, contains portions of Zechariah and Malachi and the beginning of another column. Another fragment contains parts of Jonah, which began two or three lines down from the top. Fuller edited these two fragments (4QXII[a]), concluding that they fit together and dating them 150 B.C.E., making them among the oldest fragments of the Twelve known from Qumran.[43] Barry A. Jones argues that 4QXII[a] preserves the original order, with both the MT and the LXX deriving from it.[44] He posits a stage in the growth of the Twelve when all but Joel, Obadiah, and Jonah were in place.[45] A new edition appeared with the addition of Joel and Obadiah, and yet another with the addition of Jonah.[46] Even if Fuller's textual reconstruction is correct, it might not carry the weight Jones attaches to it, because the people at Qumran are known to have changed the order of other biblical books to suit their own needs: specifically in the Psalms Scroll, the Habakkuk Pesher, the Temple Scroll, and the Great Isaiah Scroll.[47] In a later article, Jones argues that it is perhaps impossible to an-

---

[40] Sweeney, *The Twelve Prophets*, 1.xxxv.
[41] Ibid., 1.xxxvii.
[42] Nogalski, *Redactional Processes*, 57, 247, 272.
[43] Russell Fuller, "The Form and Formation of the Book of the Twelve," 96-98. See footnote 2.
[44] Barry A. Jones, *The Formation of the Book of the Twelve: A Study in Text and Canon* (SBLDS 149; Atlanta: Scholars Press, 1995) 130-132 and 167.
[45] Ibid., 53-58 and Table 6.2 on pp. 226-227.
[46] Ibid., 239-240, 139.
[47] Sweeney, *The Twelve Prophets*, 1.xxvii, n. 37.

swer the question of which text came first, and suggests instead that one think in terms of "an original *diversity* (italics Jones') of arrangements" of the Twelve, of which three have survived: MT, LXX, and 4QXII[a].[48]

With regard to thematic coherence, scholars have found several shared themes. Raymond C. Van Leeuwen points to the use of the confession of faith from Exod 34:6-7 in Joel 2:13, Jon 4:2, Mic 7:18, Nah 1:2-3, and possibly Hos 1:9.[49] Alan Cooper finds allusions to it in Hos 14:3, 5; Joel 2:13-14; Jon 3:8-4:2; Mic 7:18-20; and Nah 1:2-3a.[50] Petersen finds references to the "day of the Lord" to be so frequent in the Twelve that he identifies the phrase as its theme.[51] Similarly, Nogalski traces the use of the phrase in the first four prophets of the Twelve,[52] and Rolf Rendtorff finds it in Nahum, Habakkuk, Zephaniah, and Malachi as well,[53] and Everson argues that the Twelve is arranged in such a way that one can discern particular times of "days" when God's presence seemed evident. Hosea, Joel, Amos, Obadiah, Micah, Nahum, and Zephaniah all attempted to provide a framework for understanding history theologically by affirming Yahweh's sovereignty over the nations. By contrast, Jonah warns against the dangers of being overwhelmed by enmity, and Habakkuk focuses on the dangers of despair and disillusionment and encourages the faithful to remember the promises of Torah. By placing Habakkuk after Nahum, and before Zephaniah, the editors recall an era when chaos seemed to rule, but did not, and encouraged readers in similar times not to despair.[54]

---

[48]   Barry A. Jones, "The Book of the Twelve as a Witness to Ancient Biblical Interpretation," *Reading and Hearing the Book of the Twelve* (SBLSymS 15; eds. James D. Nogalski and Marvin A. Sweeney; Atlanta: Society of Biblical Literature, 2000) 69.

[49]   Raymond C. Van Leeuwen, "Scribal Wisdom and Theodicy in the Book of the Twelve," *In Search of Wisdom: Essays in Memory of John G. Gammie* (eds. Leo G. Perdue, Bernard Scott, and William Wiseman; Louisville: Westminster John Knox, 1993) 34-48.

[50]   Alan Cooper, "In Praise of Divine Caprice," *Among the Prophets; Language, Image and Structure in the Prophetic Writings* (JSOTSup 144; eds. Philip R. Davies and David J. A. Clines; Sheffield; Sheffield Academic Press, 1993) 160.

[51]   Petersen, "A Book of the Twelve?" 3-10. Cf. Theodor Lescow, *Das Buch Maleachi* (AzTh 75; Stuttgart: Calwer, 1993) 187.

[52]   James D. Nogalski, "The Day(s) of YHWH in the Book of the Twelve," *SBL Seminar Papers, 1999* (SBLSP 38; Atlanta: Society of Biblical Literature, 1999) 620; n. 10 offers a partial list of occurrences.

[53]   Rolf Rendtorff, "How to Read the Book of the Twelve as a Theological Unity," *Reading and Hearing the Book of the Twelve* (SBLSymS 15; eds. James D. Nogalski and Marvin A. Sweeney; Atlanta: Society of Biblical Literature, 2000) 78-86.

[54]   A. Joseph Everson, "The Canonical Location of Habakkuk," *SBL Seminar Papers, 2002* (SBLSP 41; Atlanta: Society of Biblical Literature, 2002) 248-57, esp. 256-57.

The Twelve also grapple with the issue of theodicy. James L. Crenshaw articulates three responses in the Twelve to the issue of theodicy in the Twelve: denying that a problem exists (Zeph 3:1-5; Hos 14:10, Eng. 14:9); questioning the validity of traditional affirmations about God (cf. Hab 1:2-4 and the opponents of the prophet in Mal 2:13-15, 17); and redefining Yahweh's character (Hab 1:13; 2:1-4).[55] Amos 4:6-12

> offers a theodicy in which misfortune is viewed instrumentally; suffering comes from God to stimulate repentance. Its lack of success leads to an even more alarming tactic, which has been described as doxology of judgment. Three hymnic fragments, scattered throughout the book, announce destruction while lauding Yahweh's justice in sending such calamity (Amos 4:13; 5:8-9; 9:5-6).... In this theodicy, Yahweh's attempt to educate a rebellious people does not find expression; indeed, the time has come for retribution. [56]

Crenshaw discusses one further in stance of theodicy. In Amos 3:3-8 Yahweh actually assumes responsibility for evil, as in Deut 32:39 and Isa 45:7. "The harshness of this type of theodicy," says Crenshaw, "is softened by a gloss in Amos 3:8 suggesting that Yahweh never acts destructively without alerting prophetic messengers, who will then, it is implied, make intercession for an endangered people."[57] Clearly, the Twelve do not speak with one voice on the subject, but that is not evidence of a lack of unity in the Twelve. Rather, the differences are at least partially explained by Crenshaw's observation that some events simply defy rationality.[58]

Finally, House argues, following Rendtorff, [59] that the theme of the day of the Lord is tightly bound to several others: returning to the Lord, considering one's ways, and fearing the Lord. Messages of condemnation were given to effect a returning to the Lord.[60] He also argues for a common theology in the Twelve, which offers a complex portrait of God as spouse, parent, judge, healer, creator, sovereign ruler, shepherd, deliverer, and refiner. These descriptions are not contradictory because they all point toward the

---

[55] James L. Crenshaw, "Theodicy in the Book of the Twelve," *SBL Seminar Papers, 2001* (SBLSP 41; Atlanta: Society of Biblical Literature, 2001), 9-16.

[56] Ibid., 17-18.

[57] Ibid., 18.

[58] Ibid., 1.

[59] Rendtorff, "How To read the Book of the Twelve," 86.

[60] Paul R. House, "Endings as new Beginnings: Returning to the Lord, the Day of the Lord, and Renewal in the Book of the Twelve," *SBL Seminar Papers, 2002* (SBLSP 41; Atlanta: Society of Biblical Literature, 2002), 258-84.

same God whose complexity cannot be reduced without distorting the portrait.[61]

In summary, scholars have attempted to answer the challenge to demonstrate coherence in the Twelve that validates the claim the book was edited to be read straight through, and that doing so yields valid results not obtainable otherwise. These scholars have demonstrated the presence of literary, perspectival, structural, and thematic evidence in support of their claim. In doing so, they have appealed often to the work of redactors. It is appropriate, therefore, to look more closely at the redactional techniques used in editing the Twelve.

II. Redactional Techniques in the Twelve

The study of the redaction of the Twelve inevitably involves intertextuality. Types of intertextuality include the quotation of or allusions to other texts and the use of catchwords, themes or motifs, and framing devices. Other redactional techniques include the use of designs (e. g., a chiasmus) and of rhetorical devices. All of these techniques appear in the Twelve. Mention has already been made of the redactional use of superscriptions and incipits to create the appearance of twelve collections; nothing more need be added here.

The next redactional technique is the use of catchwords, which Nogalski, in particular, has studied. He finds them at the beginnings and ends of the individual collections in the Twelve, in the seams between those collections in other words. The most obvious example is the repetition in Amos 1:2 of Joel 4:16 [Eng.. 3:16]: "YHWH roars from Zion, and from Jerusalem he utters his voice." Nogalski finds additional catchwords tying Joel 4:4-8, 14-21 [Eng. 3:4-8, 14-21] to Amos 1:1-2, 6-12, including the mention of Tyre, Philistia, and Edom.[62] He also finds catchwords between Hos 14:5-10 and Joel 1:1-12, Amos 9:1-15 and Obad 1-10, Obad 15-21 and Mic 1:1-7, Obad 11-14, 15b and Jon 1:1-8, Jon 2:2-10 and Mic 1:1-7, Mic 7:8-20, and Nah 1:1-18, Nah 3:1-19 and Hab 1:1-17, Hab 3:1-19 and Zeph 1:1-18, Zeph 3:18-20 and Hag 1:1-6, Hag 2:20-23 and Zech 1:1-11, and Zech 8:9-23 and Mal 1:1-14.[63] Zechariah 9-14, which itself draws upon other parts of the

---

[61] Paul R. House, "The Character of God in the Book of the Twelve," Reading and *Hearing the Book of the Twelve* (SBLSymS 15; eds. James D. Nogalski and Marvin A. Sweeney; Atlanta; Society of Biblical Literature, 2000) 144.

[62] Nogalski, *Literary Precursors*, 24-27.

[63] Ibid., 20-57. These pages reflect Nogalski's 1987 Th. M. thesis "The Use of Stichwörter as a redactional Unification Technique in the Book of the Twelve," written at the Baptist Theological Seminary, Ruschlikon, Switzerland.

Twelve, shares no catchwords with what comes before or after and thus appears to be a later addition.[64] Not all catchwords are said to derive from the hand of a final (or nearly final) redactor, and not all of the suggested catchwords are equally compelling, but enough are to conclude the Twelve was sewn together by this technique.

Technically speaking, the similarity between Joel 4:16 [Eng.. 3:16] and Amos 1:2 is a quotation. Other quotations and also allusions appear elsewhere in the Twelve. A few examples must suffice. Obadiah 17 announces that in contrast with the holocaust about to befall the inhabitants of Edom, "on Mount Zion there shall be those that escape," and Joel 3:5 (Eng.. 2:32) quotes the promise and applies it to a remnant in Jerusalem.[65] Also Joel 2:2 quotes, though not word for word, Zeph 1:14-15, and Joel 4:16a [Eng.. 3:16a] reverses Mic 4:3 (and Isa 2:4). Finally, Zech 13:5 places on the lips of future persons accused of being a prophet an altered version of the words of Amos in 7:14: "I am no prophet; I am a tiller of the soil."

The redactors of the Twelve also employed inclusion devices. Watts argues that Hosea 1-3 and Malachi constitute a frame for the Twelve, based on the love of God for Israel. This love did not preclude God's dealing harshly with the sins of the people, but the love remained constant.[66] Gerlinde Baumann also concludes that the love of God is a framing theme, though she denies that marriage constitutes a framing metaphor.[67] Sweeney, too, recognizes that Mal 2:10-16 forms a comment on the divorce of Gomer, but sees no indication that the text was written to perform that role.[68] Laurie J. Braaten finds the land motif running through the Twelve. It too appears in Hosea and Malachi and could be said to form another framing device.[69]

---

[64] For further discussion, see Nogalski's forthcoming study "Zechariah 13:7-9 as a Transitional text: An Appreciation and Reevaluation of the Work of Rex Mason," in *Bring Out the Treasure: Inner Biblical Allusion in Zechariah 9-14* (JSOTSup; Sheffield: Sheffield Academic Press, forthcoming; also the essay by Redditt, "Zechariah 9-14: The Capstone of the Book of the Twelve," in the same volume.

[65] Paul L. Redditt, "The Book of Joel and Peripheral Prophecy," *CBQ* 48 (1986) 235-7.

[66] John D. W. Watts, "A Frame for the Book of the Twelve," *Reading and Hearing the Book of the Twelve* (SBLSymS 15; eds. James D. Nogalski and Marvin A. Sweeney; Atlanta: Society of Biblical Literature, 2000) 210-217.

[67] Gerlinde Baumann, "Connected by Marriage, Adultery and Violence: The Prophetic Marriage Metaphor in the Book of Twelve and in the Major Prophets," *SBL Seminar Papers, 1999* (SBLSP 38; Atlanta: Society of Biblical Literature) 552-569.

[68] Sweeney, *The Twelve Prophets*, 2.713-4.

[69] Laurie J. Braaten, "God Sows the Land: Hosea's Place in the Book of the Twelve," *SBL Seminar Papers, 2000* (SBLSP 39; Atlanta: Society of Biblical Literature, 2000) 218-242.

Yet another redactional technique is the use of a chiasmus. Duane L. Christensen identifies one with significant implications for the formation of the Twelve in the structure of Nahum/Habakkuk.[70] The chiasmus is presented with slight modifications.

A Hymn of Theophany   Nahum 1
 B Taunt song against Nineveh   Nahum 2-3
  X The problem of Theodicy   Habakkuk 1:1-2:5
 B' Taunt song against the "wicked one" Habakkuk 2:6-20
A' Hymn of theophany   Habakkuk 3

Several points are in order here. (1) Nahum 1 (which begins with half of an acrostic) and Habakkuk 3 (which retains liturgical instructions) often are considered additions. Nah 1:2-3a quotes from God's theophany to Moses in Exodus 34, Nah 1:3b-4 speaks of his appearance in storms and Nah 1:6-8 of God's fury in God's protecting of the people, while Hab 3:3-15 reports a theophanic vision. (2) The nature of Nah 1:9-2:1 [Eng.. 1:9-15] is problematic, but seems somehow related to the theophanic half-acrostic, so calling the whole chapter a theophany is no misrepresentation of its last half. (3) Nothing in Nahum 2-3 identifies the materials as a taunt, but at least 3:8-9 and 14-19 (which address Nineveh in the second person) clearly are. (4) Hab 2:6 introduces the woe oracles that follow by saying they constitute a taunt. The implication of this structure is clear: the two were edited into one collection. Also, Nahum and Habakkuk employ the term *maśś'ā* (utterance, oracle) in the superscriptions. Whether the combined collection should be considered another precursor to the Twelve may remain open, but Nogalski leans toward the conclusion that the two underwent redaction as part of the "Joel-related layer."[71]

Kenneth M. Craig, Jr. points to the use of different types of questions in Haggai-Zechariah 1-8. He finds the following: rhetorical questions, sequential questions (or the "Pile Up" phenomenon), questions that function primarily to advance the plot, and questions that increase the number of characters in a scene. These questions function for Craig as a literary thread run-

---

[70] Duane A. Christensen, "The Book of Nahum: A History of Interpretation," *Forming Prophetic Literature: Essays on Isaiah and the Twelve in Honor of John D. W. Watts (JSOT*Sup 235; eds. James W. Watts and Paul R. House; Sheffield: Sheffield Academic Press, 1996) 193. Cf. James A. Watts, "Psalmody in Prophecy: Habakkuk 3 in Context," *Essays on Isaiah and the Twelve*, 214.

[71] Nogalski, *Redactional Processes*, 123-8; 180-1.

ning throughout Haggai and Zechariah 1-8, lending the two a kind of rhetorical or stylistic unity.[72]

Finally, Simon De Vries studies the use of several temporal transitions:
אָז (then), עַתָּה (now), וְהָיָה בַּיּוֹם הַהוּא ([and it shall be] on that day),
בַּיָּמִים הָהֵם (in those days), בָּעֵת הַהִיא (at that time), הִנֵּה יָמִים בָּאִים
(behold days are coming), אַחַר and אַחֲרֵי־כֵן (afterwards), and בְּאַחֲרִית
הַיָּמִים (at the end of the ages). He distinguishes between those that occurred
integrally (i. e., as part of the pericope either originally or redactionally) and
introductory transitions (i. e., as formulas for attaching materials redactionally). He discovers that

> the preexilic minor prophets Hosea, Amos, Micah, Habakkuk, Nahum and Zepha-
> niah exhibit the first two formulas, always in integral temporal transitions, whereas
> the postexilic minor prophets as a group lack them almost entirely and exhibit in-
> tegral temporal transitions only at Hag 2;23, Zech 8:11, and Zech 12:4.[73]

By contrast, בַּיּוֹם הַהוּא and וְהָיָה בַּיּוֹם הַהוּא appear in the preexilic
prophets exclusively as introductory or redactional formulas and in the post-
exilic prophets introductory formulas in all but three instances.[74]

In summary, the Twelve exhibits a series of redactional techniques that
shape it. The superscriptions and incipits delineate twelve prophetic individuals around whom the materials are shaped and according to whose dates
the traditions are arranged chronologically. Indeed, the superscriptions of
Hosea, Amos, Micah, and Zephaniah show a similar style that has caused
scholars to speak of them as a collection that served as the first precursor to
the Twelve. Catchwords appear in the seams between some or all of the
books and sew them together; quotations and allusions form thematic unity;
and inclusion devices frame the whole with the theme of the love of God.
The books of Nahum and Habakkuk form a chiasmus, and interrogatives tie
together Haggai and Zechariah 1-8, both techniques tying together two more
possible precursors to the Twelve. In view of the possible existence of such
precursors, it will be useful to turn next to views concerning the growth of
the Twelve.

---

[72] Kenneth M. Craig, Jr., "Interrogatives in Haggai and Zechariah: A Literary Thread?"
Forming Prophetic Literature: Essays in Honor of John D. W. Watts (JSOTSup 235;
eds. James W. Watts and Paul R. House; Sheffield: Sheffield Academic Press, 1996)
224-244.

[73] Simon J. De Vries, "Futurism in the Preexilic Minor Prophets Compared with That of
the Postexilic Minor Prophets," *SBL Seminar Papers, 2001* (SBLSP 41; Atlanta: Society of Biblical Literature, 2001), 20.

[74] Ibid.

III. Stages of Growth in the Twelve

As mentioned at the outset, scholars since Ewald have posited three or more stages in the growth of the Twelve. Nogalski's reconstruction (see above) involved four or five. He tentatively accepted the view that the Hosea, Amos, Micah, and Zephaniah constituted one and Haggai-Zechariah 1-8 another. The third was a "Joel-related layer," followed by the addition of Zechariah 9-14 and Jonah separately. In his study of Micah, Burkard M. Zapff accepts much of Nogalski's work, including his view about Deuteronomistic precursor.[75] He focuses on four Mican texts often considered redactional (2:12-13, 4:4-7, 5:6-7, and 7:1-20) in an attempt to relate Micah to the collections that stand on either side of it in the MT: Jonah and Nahum. He argues that the four additions constitute a new reading of the first collection of Micah by a redactor, who employed catchwords (as noted by Nogalski) to relate that collection to a new context in the emerging Book of the Twelve.[76] Sweeney objects that Zapff works with the MT. Hence, the connections that Zapff pursues obtain only for the MT.[77] Unless he can show that the order in the MT was original his argument fails. Hence, Zapff argues that the order for its originality on the grounds that it is more difficult to explain a shift of Micah from the third position behind Hosea and Amos (LXX) to the sixth position (MT) than to explain a reverse move.[78] In other words, those responsible for the order in the LXX simply moved Micah to a better position chronologically.

Aaron Schart acknowledges the importance of Nogalski's two volumes for this topic and builds upon them. He notes Nogalski's relative indifference to the rise of the "Deuteronomistic" corpus and starts there. He uncovers a two-volume first stage, comprised of early versions Amos and Hosea.[79] It was followed by the four-volume Deuteronomistic corpus, which consti-

---

[75] Burkard M. Zapff, *Redaktionsgeschichtliche Studien zum Michabuch im Kontext des Dodekapropheton* (BZAW 256; Berlin, New York: de Gruyter, 1997) 244-247.

[76] Ibid., 241-261.

[77] Marvin A. Sweeney, "Three Recent European Studies on the Composition of the Book of the Twelve," *RBL* 1 (1999) 32.

[78] Burkard M. Zapff ,"The Perspective of the Nations in the book of Micah as a 'Systematization' of the Nations' Role in Joel, Jonah, and Nahum? Reflections on a Context-Oriented Exegesis in the Book of the Twelve," *SBL Seminar Papers, 1999* (SBLSP 38; Atlanta: Society of Biblical Literature, 1999) 598-605.

[79] Aaron Schart, *Die Entstehung des Zwölfprophetenbuchs* (BZAW 260; Berlin, New York: de Gruyter, 1998) 128, 151-155; cf. Jörg Jeremias, "The Interrelationship Between Amos and Hosea," *Forming Prophetic Literature: Essays on Isaiah and the Twelve in Honor of John D. W. Watts* (JSOTSup 235; Sheffield: Sheffield Academic Press, 1995) 171-186.

tutes stage two.[80] (In connection with that corpus, Schart notes, for example, a repetitive "summons to hear" that appears among the first three [Hos 4:1, 5:1; Amos 3:1, 4:1, 5:1, 8:4; and Mic 3:1, 3:9, 6:2] and traces intertextual connections among them.)[81] Then, Schart addresses the rise of the remainder of the Twelve, disagreeing with Nogalski about the centrality of Joel. Stage three was the expansion of the Deuteronomistic corpus with the insertion of a Nahum-Habakkuk corpus.[82] A Haggai-Zechariah corpus was added in stage four, a Joel-Obadiah corpus in stage five, and then individually Jonah and Malachi.[83] These differences with Nogalski show how difficult it can be to reconstruct a lengthy redactional process. On the other hand, the superscriptions and incipits give some direction, as do references to identifiable, historical events. Joel, Jonah, and Zechariah 9-14 are hardest to pinpoint, at least partly because the dates for them are missing (for Joel and Zechariah 9-14) or because the collections themselves provide no pertinent information about the time of the real author (in the case of Jonah).

Rainer Albertz has joined Nogalski and Schart in arguing for a "Book of the Four." It consisted of Hosea 1-14 (minus 2;1-3, 20, 23-25; 3:5aβ); Amos 1:1-9:10; Mic 1:1, 3–3:12; 5:8-13; and Zeph 1;1-3:13. He identifies the hand of the redactor in Hos 3;1-5; Amos 9:7-10; Mic 5:9-13; Zeph 1:4-6 and 3:1-13, where he reformulated a previously existing text. These texts, along with Hos 14:2-5 which he took over, proclaim Yahweh's ongoing purifying judgments, by which Yahweh separates Israel and Judah from all the things and persons that led them to sin against him, including the cult, idols, the kingdom, weapons, fortresses, and even the upper class. These purifying acts reach their climax in the Exile and determine Israel's new start after the Exile.[84]

Byron G. Curtis has suggested a growth of four stages. He posits two collections of three books (one containing Hosea-Amos-Micah from the time of Hezekiah and another containing Nahum-Habakkuk-Zephaniah from the time of Josiah), with Obadiah inserted after Amos (with which it was programmatically and intertextually related) shortly after the destruction of

---

80 Schart, *Die Entstehung*, 156-223.

81 Ibid., 186-189.

82 Ibid., 234-251.

83 Ibid., 252-260, 261-282, 287-291, and 297-303. For this volume Schart prepared a study of Amos 9 ("The Fifth Vision of Amos in Context") that shows its growth through the various stages of the Twelve and beyond.

84 Rainer Albertz, "Exile as Purification: Reconstructing the Book of the Four (Hosea, Amos, Micah, Zephaniah)," *SBL Seminar Papers, 2002* (SBLSP 41; Atlanta: Society of Biblical Literature, 2002) 213-233, esp. 233. For a full discussion, see Rainer Albertz, *Die Exilszeit: Das 6. Jahrhundert.* (Biblische Enzyklopädie 7; Stuttgart: Kohlhammer, 2001) 163-85.

Jerusalem. Curtis also thinks that Haggai and Zechariah 1-8 circulated together and that Zechariah 9-14 and Malachi were added, forming yet another precursor before the whole corpus came into the Twelve.[85] He accounts for the "Deuteronomistic" superscription of Zephaniah simply as a
framing device that deliberately mimicked the superscriptions for Hosea,
Amos, and Micah added by the editor of the late pre-exilic corpus of six
books that ended with Zephaniah. He thinks the lengthy list of kings
(reaching back into the eighth century) in Zeph 1:1 is well explained by his
suggestion.[86] Then he turns to Zeph. 3:14-20, where he argues that 3:19-20
are actually prosaic and were added when Haggai was joined to Zephaniah.[87] Further, the "Zion-daughter oracle" has a literary connection with the
one in Zech 9:1-10, and the two oracles "were editorially and thematically
significant for the redactors responsible for appending Haggai-Zechariah-
Malachi to the trunk of the preceding books."[88]

Nogalski has written further on the connections between Zephaniah 3
and the rest of the emerging prophetic corpus. He thinks that Zeph 3:1-7 and
3:11-13, 18-19 interact with the Deuteronomistic corpus (e. g. Mic 4:6-7).
Further, he thinks Zeph 3:8, 14-17 picks up thematic themes developed in
Nahum, Habakkuk, and Zechariah, and he argues that Zeph 3:20 functions
as a deliberate transition to Haggai and exhibits verbal links with Joel 4. Finally, he thinks that Zeph 3:9-10 implants in Zephaniah the theme of the
remnant of the nations that is consistent with Zech 14:16-20.[89]

Edgar W. Conrad finds such studies speculative and unnecessary, though
not necessarily wrong. He suggests that a reader simply begin with the
Twelve as a whole, leaving the issue of its redaction aside. As a reader critic
he imagines

> that a model Author has coded a prophetic book to communicate something about
> the world of the prophets in ancient Israel. What is available to the reader is not an
> actual author's (redactor's) intention or an actual history of a prophetic book's de-
> velopment but a written text. As a real reader interested in a prophetic book com-

---

[85]   Byron G. Curtis, "The Zion-Daughter Oracles: Evidence on the Identity and Ideology
of the Late Redactors of the Book of the Twelve," *Reading and hearing the Book of the
Twelve* (SBLSymS 15; eds. James D. Nogalski and Marvin A. Sweeney; Atlanta: Society of Biblical Literature, 2000) 166-7, 171.

[86]   Ibid., 171.

[87]   Ibid., 181.

[88]   Ibid., 182.

[89]   James D. Nogalski, "Zephaniah 3: A Redactional Text for a developing Corpus,"
*Schriftauslegung in der Schrift; Festschrift für Odil Hannes Steck zu seinem 65. Ge-
burtstag* (eds. Reinhard G. Kratz, Thomas Krüger, Konrad Schmid; BZAW 300; Berlin, New York: de Gruyter, 2000) 218.

municating from the past, I can respect the *intentio operis* by paying heed to textual limits.[90]

He is concerned with reading the Twelve in light of its own codes, noticing
groupings within the Twelve that employ the terms "vision" (חזון), "the
words of" (דברי), and the phrase "and it happened" (ויהי), all of which en-
code various collections within the Twelve (and other prophetic texts as
well).[91] For purposes of this review, however, the significance of Conrad's
study is that he proposes to read the Twelve as a unified work.

Though scholars have not agreed on the number of stages in the growth
of the Twelve, four seems to be the minimum. They have also seen evidence
for four possible precursors: the Deuteronomistic corpus (with or without
Zephaniah), a seventh century corpus consisting of Nahum and Habakkuk
(with or without Zephaniah), a Joel-Obadiah corpus, and a post-exilic precursor consisting at least of Haggai-Zechariah 1-8 and possibly even the
whole of Haggai through Malachi. The growth of the Twelve consisted of a
series of additions of previously existing corpora and/or individual collections to an ever-growing corpus. The multiplication of "prophets" ended
when the number reached Twelve, though Zechariah 9-14 may well have
entered later. Following this direction of research, scholars also began to
look for connections between the Twelve and other emerging corpora
among the Latter Prophets, but in other parts of the First Testament too. The
next section will review briefly that issue.

IV. Relationship to Other Corpora

In his essay opposing scholars wanting to read the Twelve as a coherent
book, Ben Zvi criticizes a view that held to one or more "groups" standing
behind the collection of the different prophetic books. Instead of imagining
"Obadianic," "Zephanic," and "Jeremianic" (not to mention "Isaianic")
groups, he writes that it is "more reasonable to assume that in a wide sociological and historical sense the same groups developed the prophetic litera-

---

[90] Edgar W. Conrad, "Forming the Twelve and Forming Canon," *SBL Seminar Papers,*
2002 (SBLSP 41; Atlanta: Society of Biblical Literature, 2002) 240.

[91] Ibid., 240-42. He observes, for example, that Amos and Jeremiah, plus Ezekiel and to
a lesser extent Jonah, are "books" about extraordinary times. By contrast, Isaiah, Nahum, Obadiah, Habakkuk, Micah, and Joel all call themselves a vision (hazon). An ancient scribe responsible for such books "would have expected his Model Reader to understand" the meanings of those and other codes. Contemporary readers, by contrast,
do not have this information, but by comparative intertextual readings may acquaint
themselves with those codes.

ture."[92] Research into connections among the various corpora of the First Testament seems to point in just that direction. Among others, Wilhelm Rudolph called attention to the ending of Malachi in 3:22-24; (Eng. 4:4-6), arguing that it looks back over not just Malachi or the Twelve, but the Former Prophets and calls to mind Deuteronomy 34 as well.[93] Raymond F. Person has pursued the subject more extensively, and appears to have anticipated Ben Zvi in arguing that Second Zechariah derived from the same Deuteronomic School that was responsible for several editions of the Former Prophets and the book of Jeremiah.[94]

Steven S. Tuell argues that Haggai and Zechariah 1-8 are dependent on Ezekiel. He enumerates four possible points of influence: (1) the centrality of the temple, (2) the dating formulae, (3) vision reports, and (4) the use of the first person.[95] Obviously, contemporaries could influence each other, and clearly both Ezekiel and Haggai/Zechariah 1-8 exhibit the features Tuell notes. Those features are so general, however, that dependence one way or the other would be difficult to prove. Nevertheless, the so-called "Shepherd Allegory" in Zech 11:4-17 depends on Jer 23:1-4 and Ezekiel 34, and it reworks Ezek 37:15-28.

Also, Erhard S. Gerstenberger posits a post-exilic date for the final stages of all prophetic literature and points to psalmic passages interwoven in the Twelve as evidence that at the time and in the books of the Chronicler the prophet is merging into the Levitical singer. Hence, the single act of "singing hymns and prophesying is about the same demonstration of Yahweh's will (1 Chron 25:1-3). That means: Congregations at the time of the Chronicler (4th century B.C.E.?) did identify liturgical with prophetic activity."[96] In other words, the presence of hymns throughout the Twelve (and Isaiah, Jeremiah, and Ezekiel as well) suggests that it was the retroprojection of the late community set in worship rituals.

---

[92]   Ben Zvi, "Twelve Prophetic Books or 'The Twelve'"? 154.
[93]   Wilhelm Rudolph, *Haggai—Sacharja 1-8—Sacharja 9-14—Maleachi* (KAT 13/4; Gütersloh: Mohn, 1976) 291. Cf. Paul L. Redditt, "Zechariah 9-14, Malachi, and the Redaction of the Twelve," *Forming Prophetic Literature: Essays on Isaiah and the Twelve in Honor of John D. W. Watts* (JSOTSup 235; eds. James W. Watts and Paul R. House; Sheffield: Sheffield Academic Press, 1996) 254-6.
[94]   Raymond F. Person, *Second Zechariah and the Deuteronomistic School* (JSOTSup 167; Sheffield: JSOT Press, 1993), 13-14.
[95]   Steven S. Tuell, "Haggai-Zechariah: Prophecy After the Manner of Ezekiel," *SBL Seminar Papers, 2000* (SBLSP 39; Atlanta: Society of Biblical Literature, 2000) 265-280.
[96]   Erhard S. Gerstenberger, "Psalms in the Book of the Twelve: How Misplaced Are They?" *SBL Seminar Papers, 2000* (SBLSP 39; Atlanta: Society of Biblical Literature, 2000) 261-2.

Thus far most attention has focused on the relationship of the Twelve to Isaiah. Bosshard-Nepustil cites parallels between the Twelve and Isaiah primarily (though he cites parallels also to Jeremiah and Ezekiel), attempting to show not simply simultaneous development and parallel concerns, but a common origin as well. He thinks Hosea and Joel 1 parallel Isaiah 1-11, with Hosea berating the people of the northern kingdom, Joel the southern. The oracles against the foreign nations in Amos 1-2 and Obadiah parallel Isaiah 13-23. Isaiah 24-27 and can be seen as opposing Obadiah. Micah parallels Isa 28:1-4 in its concern with Judah; Nahum and Habakkuk focus on Assyria (and Babylon), paralleling Isaiah 33; and Zeph 3:14-18 parallels Isaiah 34 and 35. Nothing in the Twelve, however, derives from the exilic period to parallel Isaiah 40-55. In the post-exilic period the parallels resume. Haggai 2:6-9 parallels Isaiah 60; Zechariah 1-8 may parallel Isaiah 60-62 as a whole; and Zech. 14:16-19 parallels Isa 66:18-20.[97] He elaborated these views in his dissertation,[98] which Sweeney evaluated negatively on two basic counts. (1) Bosshard-Nepustil asserts the primacy of the MT without defending it. (2) His use of redaction criticism is based on tensions within the text and not, as Sweeney would prefer, on "secure historical foundations."[99]

Steck argues that late Isaiah and late Book of the Twelve materials arose in the same theological and temporal context. A chart will best represent this growth as he sees it.

A. Isaiah and the Twelve in the Persian Period

Isaiah	The Twelve
1-34, 36-39, 40-55+60-62	Much of the Twelve in place. Mal 1:2-5; 1:6-2:9 (vv. 13-16?) 3:6-12 added to Zechariah 1-8

B. Isaiah and the Twelve in the Time of Alexander the Great

(1) Twelve Preliminary Step I
Insertion of Zechariah 9:1-10:2
(between 332 and 323)

---

[97] Erich Bosshard, "Beobachtungen zum Zwölfprophetenbuch," *BN* 40 (1987) 30-36.
[98] Erich Bosshard-Nepustil, *Rezeptionen von Jesaia im Zwölfprophetenbuch. Untersuchungen zur literarischen Verbindung von Prophetenbüchern in Babylonischer und persischer Zeit* (OBO 154; Freiburg, Göttingen: Vandenhoeck & Ruprecht, 1997).
[99] Sweeney, "Three Recent European Studies," 23-25.

(2) Twelve Preliminary Step II
Insertion of Zech 10:3-11:3
(between 320 and 315)

(-) Twelve Expansion I
Addition of Joel, Obadiah, Zephaniah (slightly later)

(3) Isaiah Expansion I
First uniting of Isaiah 1-39 and 40-
55+60-62
Redactional additions: 10:20-23;
11:11-16; 13:5-16; chaps. 24-27;
30:18-26 (?); 34:2-4; chap. 35;
51:1-3, 4-5, 6-8, 10b-11; 54:2-3, 9-
10; 55:10-11 (/); 62:10-12

(4) Isaiah Expansion II
Redactional additions: 1:27-8; 4:2-
6; 29:17-24; 33:14-16; 48:22;
51:16; 56:9-59:21; 60:17-22; 61:2;
62:8-9; 63:1-6 (between 311 and
302/1)

(5) Twelve Expansion II
Redactional addition of Zech 11:4-
13:9 (slightly later)

(6) Isaiah Expansion III
1:29-31; 12:1-6; 14:1-3 (?); 54:11-
17; 56:1-8; 58:13-14; 60:12a; 61:3;
63:7-64:11 (all between 302/1 and
270); 65:1-66:24 (about 253, at
same time as 19:18-25)

(7) Twelve Expansion III
Redactional addition of Zechariah
14 (between 240 and 220)

C. Final Stage in the Formation of the Twelve

(8) Separation of Malachi from
Zechariah to form twelfth book. Addition of Zech 12:1a; Mal 1:1; 2:10-
12; 3:22-24 [Eng.. 4:4-6] (between
220 and 201 or 198 and 190)[100]

---

[100] Odil Hannes Steck, *Der Abschluss der Prophetie im Alten Testament: Ein Versuch zur
Frage des Vorgeschichte des Kanons* (Biblisch-Theologische Studien 17; Neukirchen;
Neukirchener Verlag, 1991) 196-8.

Steck's work is susceptible to criticism because of its assignment of small, at times isolated passages to a precise developmental sequence and because of the late dates of some of the material in the Twelve.

Paul L. Redditt has attempted to describe the implied circumstances of the production of the Twelve. It was produced for a readership who already agreed with the perspective of the final redactors or who could be persuaded to agree. Such readers would have been wealthy enough to have the leisure to read, but they would have been voluntary readers. No ecclesial or political power enforced reading or adhering to the Twelve. In terms of class, they would have been upper instead of lower. These editors reveal three theological influences: an emphasis on judgment, cultic confessions like Exod 34:6-7, and the book of Joel. They would have been male, as would their readers. Their inclusion of the late materials in Zechariah 9-14 suggests that they may have wanted to correct what they perceived as the shortcomings of Judah's leaders. As literati they appreciated the power of literature, and may have substituted it for political power, and they almost certainly worked in Jerusalem.[101] Redditt makes no attempt to name them or identify them with redactors working on other corpora, though some such identification might well be possible.

Attempts to relate the redaction of the Twelve to such corpora are in their infancy. These attempts are a logical extension from the attempt to see better the relationships among the collections in the Twelve, but they also involve the extra layer of uncertainty about intentionality that Cuffey mentioned.[102] Hence, issues of method and results of such studies will need further clarification. Even so, an increased interest in canon of late mandates attention to such connections.

V. Reading the Twelve

The final subject to be raised in this paper is how to read the Twelve as a redacted whole and the advantages for doing so. The principle issue has been whether to read the text diachronically or synchronically. Nogalski, Schart, and Bosshard-Nepustil advocate a diachronic reading, fully aware of redactional levels. Their work as redaction critics focused on the growth of the Twelve over centuries, and by its nature had to be diachronic. By contrast, House proposes a synchronic reading with a plot, repetitive themes, and a consistent, though dialectical, theology. Rendtorff and Sweeney suggest that both types of reading are necessary for a complete understanding of the

---

[101] Redditt, "The Production and Reading of the Twelve," 16-24.
[102] Cuffey, "Coherence," 201.

Twelve as a whole.[103] In his commentary on the Twelve, Sweeney states succinctly the case for using both:

> This commentary focuses on a synchronic literary analysis of the Book of the Twelve Prophets.... [I]t treats the individual books as discreet units within the Twelve and considers their relationships within the sequences of both the Masoretic and Septuagint forms of the book. The commentary necessarily includes diachronic considerations in order for the synchronic analyses to make sense. Such diachronic considerations include the historical, cultural, and linguistic contexts and circumstances in which the prophets and other authors of the twelve prophetic books spoke or wrote, and some indication of redaction-critical problems where necessary.[104]

Why, though, should the Twelve be read as a coherent whole? Other reading strategies having been pursued for centuries, and in recent time critical scholars have, for the most part, adopted a chronological strategy. They date the books from Amos to Jonah (or to whichever book they think came last) and read them in that order. There is much to commend such a reading, especially its facilitating an integral reading of the First Testament. It is nevertheless a fairly recent strategy beset by enough unresolved issues to cause some modern scholars to abandon it in favor of more literary (and synchronic) approaches. A chronological reading has other shortcomings as well. One needs mentioning here: it misses such obvious connections as that between Joel 3:16 [Eng. 4:16] and Amos 1:2. Modern scholars typically debate at most which influenced the other, but do not look to see what difference it makes that one follows the other by a scant seven verses (at least in the MT). To be sure, the Twelve itself is in part roughly chronological, containing three prophets from the eighth century, three from the seventh/sixth, and three from the post-exilic period, though its chronology appears to modern scholars to be wrong in some ways. For example, moderns date Hosea after Amos, but the Twelve switches the two. Apparently, something besides precise chronology drove that decision, and probably early on in the process of redaction. In addition, chronology is not the only factor at work, as is

---

103 Rendtorff, "How to Read the Book of the Twelve," 87; Sweeney, *The Twelve Prophets*, 1.xxxix.

104 Sweeney, *The Twelve Prophets*, 1.xxxix. Nowhere does Sweeney's approach opens new avenues of investigation in connection with Zechariah. Sweeney shows little interest in the connections between Haggai and Zechariah 1-8, but points to the so-called Shepherd Allegory in Zech 11:4-17 as a first person account that could have originated with the prophet Zechariah. He analyzes the collection as falling into three sections: 1:1-6 (introduction), 1:7—6:15 (visions), and 7:1—14:21 (oracles or pronouncements), each introduced by the putative date when the visions or oracles came to the prophet (2, 566).

shown by the placement of Obadiah, a piece reflecting the fall of Jerusalem, before Nahum, Habakkuk, and Zephaniah in every extant ms. It would seem appropriate, then, to seek other reasons for the sequence in the Twelve, and that is a question whose answer necessarily involves finding meaning in the placement of the various collections.

Two reasons for a holistic or canonical reading of the Twelve present themselves at once. Such a reading corrects some of the shortcomings of a chronological reading. Differently stated, it takes note of items in the biblical text that a chronological reading misses. Second, scholars working in this field have offered a remarkable amount of evidence in support of the contention that the Twelve is not simply a redacted piece, but a book intended to be read straight through. Obviously, one does not have to begin with Hosea in order to read Malachi with a great deal of sophistication and benefit, but if one never reads Malachi in the light of Hosea one misses framing devices, allusions, themes, and other devices used by the redactors of the Twelve in knitting the book together.

VI. Conclusions

Based on this research, one may draw at least five conclusions. First, there is sufficient evidence to warrant reading the Twelve canonically as a coherent unit, in addition to reading them individually. This coherence derives from superscriptions, framing devices and other redactional techniques, common themes and theology, and plot (which includes its own chronology). Besides, the Twelve has about as good a claim to being a unity as does Isaiah, which also contains traditions from eighth century to the post-exilic period, and perhaps a better claim than does the book of Jeremiah, whose structure baffles everyone.

Second, the Twelve grew in stages, still not completely delineated. There seem to have at least two precursors and maybe more. The post-exilic group may have enlarged to include Malachi (and perhaps Zechariah 9-14, though that seems less likely) even before entry into the emerging Twelve. The most difficult issue is accounting for the placement(s) of Joel, Obadiah, and Jonah.

Third, the original order of the Twelve remains unresolved. Of the three forms that survived in mss, 4QXII^a (with Jonah at the end) has not found wide support. It is difficult to choose between the order of the other two. The LXX collects Joel, Obadiah, and Jonah, placing Jonah last because of its obvious interest in God's punishing Nineveh, which it shares with Nahum. The MT scatters the three among the eighth century prophets, an order much more difficult to account for than that in the LXX, which Nogalski says simply moved the eighth century prophets Amos and Micah forward to a place behind Hosea. This suggestion also accounts for the order in the LXX with no other explanation needed.[105] Sweeney offered explanations for both orders, resulting in his judgment that the LXX order was primary. Time will tell which arguments will carry the day.

Fourth, the growth of the Twelve is probably related to the growth of other corpora. Its relationship to Isaiah has received the most attention, but its relationship to Jeremiah, Ezekiel, the Psalter, the Former Prophets, and even Deuteronomy (if not the whole Pentateuch) has been the subject of study. Insofar as the final stages of all of those corpora occurred in the tiny province of post-exilic Yehud, their completion most likely came at the hands of professional collectors and scribes, no matter how varied and oral their origins may have been. At some point they became the books of the literati, who no doubt shared much even though they may have disagreed on issues as varied as legitimacy of priests, roles for Levites, and cooperation with foreign rulers.

Finally, there are clear advantages to reading the Twelve this way beyond those gained from reading it chronologically or other ways. These advantages include the fact that such a reading attends to matters in the text missed by other reading strategies.

---

[105] James D. Nogalski, private correspondence. Cf. Zapff, "The Perspective of the Nations," 598-99.

The Ties that Bind: Intertextuality, the Identification of Verbal Parallels, and Reading Strategies in the Book of the Twelve

Richard L. Schultz

I. Intertextuality and the Book of the Twelve

Less than a decade ago, Terence Collins claimed that "the sound literary reasons for treating *The Twelve* as a single work have not received much attention."[1] However, much recent study of the Minor Prophets has focused on the evidence for coherence within the Book of the Twelve.[2] Rather than simply listing and discussing various types of indicators of unity, scholarly attention has been directed in particular towards their implications for how this canonical collection, despite being subdivided into twelve prophetic voices, is to be read as one book. In addition, numerous individual studies have offered suggestions regarding how the individual "books" are to be read in the light of their placement within and connection to the larger collection.[3]

In these studies several different kinds of indicators of coherence are cited, including similar thematic emphases, literary genres, or portrayals of the divine character. However, most frequently, scholars point to the hermeneutical significance of repeated words and phrases in linking texts. James Nogalski has subdivided the latter into subcategories, also offering

---

[1] Terence Collins, *The Mantle of Elijah: The Redaction Criticism of the Prophetical Books* (The Biblical Seminar 20; Sheffield: Sheffield Academic Press, 1993), 58.

[2] This newer emphasis is reflected in particular in two collections of essays, *Forming Prophetic Literature: Essays on Isaiah and the Twelve in Honor of John D. W. Watts* (ed. J. W. Watts and P. R. House; JSOTSup 235; Sheffield: Sheffield Academic Press, 1996); and *Reading and Hearing the Book of the Twelve* (ed. J. D. Nogalski and M. A. Sweeney; SBLSymS 15; Altanta: Society of Biblical Literature, 2000).

[3] Examples in the volume edited by Nogalski and Sweeney mentioned in the previous footnote include the essays by James D. Nogalski, "Joel as 'Literary Anchor' for the Book of the Twelve," 91-109, and Mark E. Biddle, "'Israel' and 'Jacob' in the Book of Micah: Micah in the Context of the Twelve," 146-165.

helpful definitions: quotations, allusions, catchwords, and motifs.[4] Most studies subsume these types of repetition under the term "intertextuality," which Nogalski defines simply as "the interrelationship between two or more texts." However, an examination of precisely how this term is employed in identifying and interpreting these claimed "interrelationships" reveals much diversity in perspective and considerable methodological imprecision. The purpose of this essay is to point out the difficulties caused by too broad a definition of intertextuality in the study of the Book of the Twelve (as well as the relationship of the Minor Prophets to the other prophetic books) and to suggest how focusing on verbal parallels that offer a more extensive textual basis for positing an *intentional* interrelationship is a more viable approach to the "ties that bind."[5]

Intertextuality has been the object of much recent scholarly attention.[6] Since, as Donald Polansky has noted, the term "intertextuality" already "has accumulated a bewildering variety of definitions and uses,"[7] it is useful at

---

[4] Nogalski, "Intertextuality and the Twelve," in *Forming Prophetic Literature*, 102-24. His fifth category, framing devices, admittedly broader and somewhat overlapping, includes superscriptions, genre similarities, structural parallels, juxtaposition of catchwords, and canonical allusions. Nogalski offers a fuller discussion and illustration of these devices in *Redactional Processes in the Book of the Twelve* (BZAW 218; Berlin: de Gruyter, 1993).

[5] The most extensive critique of the predominant approach to coherence in the Book of the Twelve has been offered by Ehud Ben Zvi, "Twelve Prophetic Books or 'The Twelve': A Few Preliminary Considerations," in *Forming Prophetic Literature*, 125-56. See also Richard L. Schultz, *The Search for Quotation: Verbal Parallels in the Prophets* (JSOTSup 180; Sheffield: Sheffield Academic Press, 1999) Ch. 2: "The Assessment of Prophetic Quotation."

[6] See especially *Intertextuality and the Bible* (ed. G. Aichele and G. A. Philips; Semeia 69-70; Atlanta: Society of Biblical Literature, 1995); also the *Congress Volume: Oslo 1998* (ed. A. Lemaire and M. Saebø; VTSup 80; Leiden: Brill, 2000), which includes essays on inter-textuality by Kirsten Nielsen, John Barton, Michael Fishbane, Antoon Schoors, Jean Louis Ska, and Patricia K. Tull. Other important discussions of intertextuality and biblical studies include *Intertextuality in Biblical Writings: Essays in Honor of Bas van Iersel* (ed. Sipke Draisma; Kampen: J. H. Kok, 1989); *Reading Between Texts: Intertextuality and the Hebrew Bible* (ed. Dana N. Fewell, Louisville: Westminster / John Knox, 1992); and Benjamin D. Sommer, "Exegesis, Allusion and Intertextuality in the Hebrew Bible: A Response to Lyle Eslinger," *VT* 46 (1996) 479-89.

[7] Donald C. Polanski, "Reflections on a Mosaic Covenant: The Eternal Covenant (Isaiah 24.5) and Intertextuality," *JSOT* 77 (1998), 58. According to Timothy K. Beal ("Ideology and Intertexuality: Surplus of Meaning and Controlling the Means of Production," in *Reading Between Texts*, 29) the term "intertextuality" was coined by Julia Kristeva in her 1969 volume, *Desire in Language: A Semiotic Approach to Literature and Art* (ed. L. S. Roudiez; trans. T. Gora, A. Jardine, and L. S. Roudiez; New York: Columbia University Press, 1980; French edition 1969).

the outset to distinguish three primary ways in which the term is employed. In its broadest application, intertextuality is to be understood, according to Peter Miscall, (1) as "a covering term for all the possible relations that can be established between texts. The relations can be based on anything from quotes and direct references to indirect allusions to common words and even letters to dependence on language itself."[8] Because of its current popularity, according to Ellen van Wolde, the term can also serve simply (2) as a trendy label for the traditional study of inner-biblical exegesis or inner-biblical allusion, i.e., "as a modern literary theoretical coat of veneer over the old comparative approach," such as that practiced by Michael Fishbane.[9] Between these two usages, there is another understanding of the term, which is shared by many contemporary literary critics. According to Benjamin Sommer, such intertextuality (3) "focuses on manifold linkages among texts or on connections between a text and commonplace phrases from the cultural systems in which the text exists ... [Thus] readers may notice links among many texts, whether the authors of the texts knew each other or not."[10] According to the third definition, intertextuality offers an alternative to the traditional approach to inner-biblical allusion that is *synchronic* rather than *diachronic* in emphasis, *reader*-focused rather than *author*-focused, and thus explores the *effect* rather than the *purpose* of such interconnections.

It is essential that one is aware of this ambiguity in the definition and usage of intertextuality (and related terms) when evaluating discussions of literary coherence in the Book of the Twelve. A comparison of two lists of intertextual relationship involving Malachi reflects this methodological difficulty. On the one hand, Andrew Hill's Anchor Bible commentary on Malachi contains an appendix listing examples of intertextuality, but he qualifies the examples as simply reflecting "interdependence" rather than

---

[8]   Peter D. Miscall, "Isaiah: New Heavens, New Earth, New Book," in *Reading Between Texts*, 44.

[9]   Ellen van Wolde, "Trendy Intertextuality?" in *Intertextuality in Biblical Writings*, 43. Gail O'Day, "Jeremiah 9:22-23 and 1 Corinthians 1:26-31. A Study in Intertextuality," *JBL* 109 (1990) 259-60, describes Michael A. Fishbane's work, *Biblical Interpretation in Ancient Israel* (Oxford: Clarendon Press, 1985), as the "single most important contribution to the study of intertextuality in scripture."

[10]   Sommer, "Exegesis, Allusion and Intertextuality in the Hebrew Bible," 486-87. See also van Wolde, 46. Miscall (*Isaiah* [Readings; Sheffield: JSOT Press, 1993] 20) in studying intertextual relationships within the book of Isaiah, admits that "one reader's parallels may not exist for another." The volume *Reading Between Texts: Intertextuality and the Hebrew Bible*, edited by Dana Fewell, illustrates this approach (see note 6 above).

claiming Malachi's "reliance" upon "the corresponding citation."[11] On the
other hand, Donald Berry offers several pages of "allusions or instances of
intertextuality" to canonical traditions in Malachi.[12] However, since Hill
focuses on verbal repetition while Berry emphasizes parallel motifs and
themes, there are only four textual parallels that appear on both lists: Mal
1:9 // Num 6:25; 2:10 // Deut 32:6; 3:1 // Exod 23:20; and 3:7 // Zech 1:3.
The nature and textual basis of Hill's examples vary greatly. Some are
introductory formulae (2:16 // Jer 11:3, etc.: "[thus] Yahweh, God of Israel,
has said – אמר יהוה אלהי ישראל;" 4:1 [Heb 3:19] // Zech 2:9,10 [Heb
2:13,14]: "for indeed" – כי־הנה), while others probably are idiomatic (2:2 //
Isa 42:25; 57:1,11; Jer 12:11: "lay it to heart" – שים על־לב). Some
represent extensive and unquestionably significant parallels, such as 4:5
[Heb 3:23] // Joel 2:31 [Heb 3:4] ("before the coming Day of Yahweh –
great and terrible" – לפני בוא יום יהוה הגדול והנורא), while others
employ similar words but in very different contexts or with divergent
referents (1:9 // Isa 50:11: "from your/my hand this [thing] has come" –
מידכם/י היתה זאת; 1:10 // Hag 2:3: "who [even one] among you?" – מי
בכם [גם־]). In still others the claim is based on a single Hebrew verb or
verb-preposition combination (1:13 // Hag 1:9: "to sniff, blow" - נפח; 2:3 //
Ezek 6:5: "and I will spread, scatter" – וזריתי).

This comparison of lists reveals a basic methodological problem. What
is true of Hill's and Berry's identification of examples of intertextuality is
true of many treatments of verbal repetition in the prophets -- the examples
cited range from extensive verbal parallels to individual words or motifs.
Even Nogalski, though carefully distinguishing between quotations and
allusions, when discussing catchwords, gives the impression that any word
that occurs at the beginning of one text and at the end of another is
significant. This leaves him open to the criticism that one could find similar
catchwords between nearly any two texts selected.[13] In discussing one
scholar's work, Aaron Schart complains that "one often has the feeling that

---

[11]   Andrew E. Hill, *Malachi* (AB 25D; New York: Doubleday, 1998), 401; "Appendix C:
       Intertextuality in the Book of Malachi," 401-12.
[12]   Donald K. Berry, "Malachi's Dual Design: The Close of the Canon and What Comes
       Afterward," in *Forming Prophetic Literature*, 270; Table 1, 270-72.
[13]   Kenneth H. Cuffey ("Remnant, Redactor, and Biblical Theologian: A Comparative
       Study of Coherence in Micah and the Twelve," in *Reading and Hearing the Book of
       the Twelve*, 203-4), does just that in the section of his paper entitled "A Random Case
       Study." See also Ben Zvi's extensive criticism of current methodologies, "Twelve
       Prophetic Books or 'The Twelve,'" 139-42.

the intertextual allusions cannot be controlled" and concludes that "the main difficulty for all the different models is establishing controls about what is considered deliberate redactional shaping and what is only accidentally connected."[14]

Kenneth Cuffey effectively summarizes the resultant methodological dilemma:

> How clearly does the canonical connection imply the books are to be linked? How are we to interpret the connections we find in the text? Do the links reflect an author's or editor's intentions? Or might we impose our own expectations and presuppositions on the text? Might the linkages merely be the result of chance associations noticed by the modern interpreter, but that were never anyone's intentional design?[15]

Despite all of these difficulties, Berry nevertheless claims, though rather vaguely: "Every point of correspondence means something."[16] The question, however, is precisely what that "something" is! Those who take a diachronic approach seek in intertextuality evidence of a conscious reuse or imitation of earlier traditions or authoritative prophetic utterances by later authors or editors in order to build upon, reinterpret, or link their prophetic oracles with the words of their predecessors, while some of those who take a synchronic approach seek in intertextuality an "adventure rich in interpretive possibilities…the encounter with tantalizing but tenuous connections among words and concepts in selected biblical texts."[17]

However, one wonders whether a false dichotomy has been suggested between methods. As a *text-based* phenomenon, intertextuality demands that the interpreter give attention both to author- and reader-related issues. On the one hand, even if intertextuality is associated with broader cultural influences, it is still appropriate to inquire regarding which texts formed part of a writer's intellectual world. On the other hand, regardless of whether verbal repetition is coincidental or intentional in origin, it is appropriate to inquire whether the competent reader also could (or must) note those intertextual links recently "identified" (or discovered) by various scholars in order to interpret a text properly, or whether this intertextuality

---

[14] Aaron Schart, "Reconstructing the Redaction History of the Twelve Prophets: Problems and Models," in *Reading and Hearing the Book of the Twelve*, 41, critiquing the work of Erich Bosshard-Nepustil (cf. note 44 below). See also Schart, 42-43.

[15] Cuffey, "Remnant, Redactor, and Biblical Theologian," 201.

[16] Berry, "Malachi's Dual Design," 272.

[17] Elaine A. Phillips, "Serpent Intertexts: Tantalizing Twists in the Tales," *BBR* 10 (2000) 233.

is simply the meaning created by a highly specialized (and motivated) kind of reader. Even if a text is composite, arising through a protracted and complex editorial process, its component parts are now read not in "chronological order" (i.e., in terms of their time of composition) but sequentially. Thus reading a later text or book (such as Joel) can affect how one reads an earlier one (such as Amos) if it is encountered subsequently in the reading process (for example, due to its later position in the Book of the Twelve).[18]

In a previous publication, this author suggested several criteria for identifying and an approach for analyzing verbal parallels, regardless of whether they can be labeled "quotations."[19] In seeking significant verbal parallels, one should look for *verbal and syntactical correspondence* that goes beyond one key or uncommon term or even a series of commonly occurring terms, also evaluating whether the expression is simply formulaic or idiomatic. Thus one also should look for indications of *contextual awareness*, including *interpretive re-use*, which indicates verbal *dependence* which is conscious and purposeful, even though one may not be able to determine the direction of borrowing with any certainty. If such dependence can be posited, one's knowledge of the *quoted* text will facilitate the proper interpretation of the *quoting* text. Neither an exclusively diachronic nor an exclusively synchronic analysis can do justice to the multi-functional nature of quotation -- or even of types of verbal correspondence that exhibit minimal intentionality. Though not questioning the validity of studying intertextual allusions, that is, those texts displaying

---

[18]   Thus Ben Zvi's ("Twelve Prophetic Books or 'The Twelve,'" 127, note 5) criticism of those who read individual minor prophets in the light of their present canonical sequence, that is "as an integral part of a unified Book of the Twelve" rather than "as a separate unit," is unwarranted. Although the implications that such interpreters deduce from (or impose on) intertextual links may be incorrect or excessive, suggesting what larger function a book may have within a larger canonical collection does not inherently subvert the effort to accurately assess the thematic thrust of the book itself.

For example, a reading of the book of Ruth which emphasizes the subtle interplay between divine providence and human action (highlighted by the juxtaposition of Ruth's chance and planned encounters with Boaz in chapters 2 and 3), covenantal kindness, and status changes is largely unaffected by the book's position within the Hebrew and Greek canonical collections. Following Proverbs, as in the MT, Ruth can be understood as the אֵשֶׁת־חַיִל (NRSV: "capable wife") of Prov 31:10, the worthy ancestress of King David. Following Judges, as in the LXX, the law-honoring Bethlehemites and resident-alien Ruth contrast with those throughout Israel who, during the period of the judges, instead did "what was right" in their own eyes.

[19]   Schultz, *Quotation*, 222-39. See also the helpful suggestions offered by Cuffey, "Remnant, Redactor, and Biblical Theologian," 204-08.

less extensive verbal and syntactical correspondence, such examples often entail greater methodological subjectivity and demand more reader competence than may be warranted.

II. Verbal Parallels and Coherence in the Book of the Twelve

In the following section, we will examine several examples of intertextuality based coherence involving the Book of the Twelve. It is our contention that *internal* links involving verbal parallels (such as those within the book of Zechariah) function differently from *external* verbal links (such as those between Isaiah and Micah), regardless of the compositional history of the individual books (e.g., the claim that the same prophetic group added a redactional layer to both the Major Prophets and the Book of the Twelve). Verbal repetition *within* one book functions as a type of self-quotation, a literary echo which takes its place alongside other forms of repetition, such as refrains, images, and themes, which have a unifying effect on the book.[20] The question at hand is whether the Book of the Twelve is sufficiently coherent so that intertextual relationships between the individual Minor Prophets, which might have functioned originally as *external* links, now function *internally*.   Indeed, it is Nogalski's contention[21] that most catchwords linking these books were redactionally inserted for the precise purpose of increasing coherence within the Book of the Twelve.

A. Zechariah 1-8 and 9-14

The dominant scholarly view today is that Zechariah 9-14 was composed and edited (and possibly also circulated) independently from Zechariah 1-8 but, manifests "a surprising compatibility" with "Proto-Zechariah."[22] Carol

---

[20]   This distinction was noted already in the late eighteenth century by Henry Owen (*Critica Sacra; or, a Short Introduction to Hebrew Criticism* [London: W. Bowyer and J. Nichols, 1774] 8 and lists on 22-23), who spoke of prophets "borrowing from themselves" or using the "same language on different occasions." See also Karl Elliger, *Deuterojesaja in seinem Verhältnis zu Tritojesaja* (BWANT 63; Stuttgart: Kohlhammer, 1933) 46. Nogalski ("Intertextuality and the Twelve," 110-11) makes a similar distinction. For a discussion of self-quotation within contemporary literary theory, see Schultz, *Quotation*, 197-98 and note 47.

[21]   Nogalski, *Literary Precursors to the Book of the Twelve* (BZAW 217; Berlin: Walter de Gruyter, 1993), especially 228-29, 262-67; *Redactional Processes*, especially 115-17, 176-79.

[22]   Brevard S. Childs, *Introduction to the Old Testament as Scripture* (Philadelphia: Fortress Press, 1979), 482; see also Paul L. Redditt, "Zechariah 9-14, Malachi, and the Redaction of the Book of the Twelve," in *Forming Prophetic Literature*, 258-61.

and Eric Meyers, drawing on the work of Rex Mason, argue for an even closer affinity between these two sections but wonder "whether the First-Second Zechariah interplay is…simply one of many instances of Second Zechariah's referential treatment of his scriptural forebears, notably prophets…"[23]

Two striking verbal parallels between the second and first sections of Zechariah occur together in chapter 9: 9:8 // 7:14 and 9:9 // 2:10 [Heb 2:14].[24] Zech 9:8 and 7:14 share the phrase מעבר ומשׁב ("[to go] to and fro") which occurs nowhere else in the Hebrew Bible and thus cannot easily be dismissed as idiomatic or characteristic prophetic speech. Zech 9:9 and 2:10 [Heb 2:14] share four elements which appear in the same order: (1) an imperatival call to rejoice, though with different verbs (גילי מאד הריעי // רני ושׂמחי), occurs only here in Zechariah; (2) the vocative address to daughter Zion (בת־ציון), also occurring only here in Zechariah, although the expression appears fifteen additional times in the prophetic literature; (3) the particle "behold" (הנה), which occurs a dozen times in Zechariah; and (4) the verb "come" (בוא), which occurs sixteen times in the Qal stem in Zechariah, the closest syntactical parallel to 2:14 being found in Zech 3:8 which uses the Hiphil stem.

The first parallel is striking and unique in its formulation, and the second, cumulatively, warrants attention as sufficiently extensive to be not merely coincidental. However, to pose Berry's previously cited question, what does this correspondence mean? First, it should be noted that 9:8 and 9:9 belong to distinct, though related, sub-units (vv 1-8; 9-10; 11-17). Further, 9:1-8 portrays the Divine Warrior as he disposes of Israel's enemies to the north and west, defeating, dispossessing, destroying, and, in the case of Philistia (vv 6-7, introducing first-person speech) purifying, and turning them into a "remnant for our God….like a clan in Judah." This unit closes with the assurance of divine protection for the Temple, so that no invader will go "to and fro." The portrayal of the Divine Warrior, employing theophanic language (v 14), resumes in vv 11-17, as he leads Judah and Ephraim in victory against Javan (i.e., Greece).

---

[23] Carol L. Meyers and Eric M. Meyers, *Zechariah 9-14: A New Translation with Introduction and Commentary*, (AB 25C; New York: Doubleday, 1993), 27-28, 38, referring primarily to Rex A. Mason's essay, "The Relation of Zech 9-14 to Proto-Zechariah," *ZAW* 88 (1976), 227-39.

[24] These parallels are cited by Joyce G. Baldwin as especially striking, *Haggai, Zechariah, Malachi: An Introduction and Commentary* (TOTC; Downers Grove, IVP, 1972), 68. All Scripture citations are from the NRSV unless otherwise noted.

The expression "to and fro" in 9:8 is repeated from 7:14, which concludes a unit (7:1-14) that recalls the message of the former prophets (vv 7, 12) and Israel's refusal to heed their instruction, thus incurring divine wrath (vv 11-12) and leading to exile and the destruction of their pleasant homeland (vv 13-14). No one from Israel "went to and fro" because the land had been desolated.[25] In contrast, 9:8 speaks of a future time when God's favor will be restored to his people rather than his wrath being provoked by them. Here those going "to and fro" refers to Israel's foes who no longer will threaten Jerusalem. According to Meyers and Meyers, "in evoking the past by way of a quotation of 7:14, the author/redactor may be attempting to emphasize the contrast between the past…and the present…"[26] This may be correct and would suggest that the phrase in 9:8 should not be deleted as an explanatory gloss as the editors of *BHS* and Paul Hanson recommend.[27] However, given the fact that the expression has a very different referent and context in 7:14 and that the expression in 9:8 is followed by "no oppressor shall again overrun (utilizing the same verb, עבד) them," the phrase in the latter verse is neither necessary nor does it explain anything.

Thus Meyers' and Meyers' additional comment, "Second Zechariah draws on an earlier passage and gives it a new meaning,"[28] is misleading. The phrase מעבר ומשב hardly constitutes an "earlier passage," and its larger context is not being reinterpreted by the author/editor of Zechariah 9. On the one hand, the reuse of the expression may be intended to recall its very different context and referent in 7:14 in order to highlight the change in Israel's present relationship to God and resultant circumstances. This would explain why the phrase is unnecessary in 9:8 and, syntactically, sits somewhat awkwardly in its context. (Consequently, the preposition מן probably should be taken privatively in both occurrences.) On the other hand, one need not recognize the verbal parallel in order to understand 9:8 (or 7:14); recognizing the parallel simply may help to explain its presence. As

---

[25] According to Meyers and Meyers, *Zechariah 9-14*, 119, this was because it was *unsafe* to move about. According to David L. Peterson (*Haggai and Zechariah 1-8: A Commentary* [OTL; Philadelphia: Westminster, 1984], 295), however, this was because the land had become too *unproductive* to attract even the "itinerant sheepherder."

[26] Meyers and Meyers, *Zechariah 9-14*, 119.

[27] Paul D. Hanson, *The Dawn of Apocalyptic* (Philadelphia: Fortress Press, 1979), 298. In the literature assessing verbal parallels, especially during the nineteenth century, one of the occurrences was frequently labeled a "secondary gloss."

[28] Meyers and Meyer, *Zechariah 9-14*, 119.

such, however, it does serve to underscore through its exact verbal repetition the more general thematic connections and contrast between Zechariah 1-8 and 9-14.[29]

The second parallel, Zech 9:9 and 2:10 [Heb 2:14], functions quite differently from the first. Zech 9:9 appears to draw on a number of prophetic traditions, primarily those concerning the coming king (Isa 9:6-7, 11:1-5, 32:1-8; Hos 3:4-5; Mic 5:2-4) and possibly also Gen 49:10-11. This verse begins with a shift to a second person address to the community personified as "daughter Zion" which is called upon to rejoice at the king's coming.   In v 10 the removal of implements of war is announced, reminiscent of Isa 2:4 // Mic 4:3.   As in several other prophetic texts, the divine speaker who establishes peace is distinguished from the king who reigns and administers justice (cf. especially Isa 9:1-7).   The extent of his realm is described in words identical to those found in Psa 72:8 ("from sea to sea, and from the River to the ends of the earth," מִיָּם עַד־יָם וּמִנָּהָר עַד־אַפְסֵי אָרֶץ) found only in these two texts. In sum, Zech 9:9-10 ex-hibits several significant intertextual links to texts other than Zechariah 1-8, thus offering support for the claim that "Zechariah 9-14 surpasses any other biblical work in the way it draws upon existing tradition."[30]

Unlike the previously discussed parallel, the contexts of Zech 2:10 [Heb 2:14] and 9:9 are quite similar. As in 9:9-10, the unit 2:6-13 [Heb 2:10-17] begins with a second person address to the community personified as daughter Zion. It is linked to the preceding account of the third vision (2:1-5) by the mention of glory (כָּבוֹד) and of God's dwelling in the midst of the people (2:5 [Heb 2:9 – אֶהְיֶה בְתוֹכָהּ] and 2:10,11 [Heb 2:14,15 – וְשָׁכַנְתִּי בְתוֹכֵךְ]), a phrase similar to the latter occurring elsewhere in the book only in Zech 8:3 (cf. also 8:8; i.e., not once in chapters 9-14). In addition to the four previously-noted similarities in formulation in 2:10 [Heb 2:14] and 9:9, the larger contexts of these two verses are linked by similar descriptions of the nations' benefiting from this future coming (2:11 [Heb 2:15]; 9:10).[31]

---

[29]   Zech 9:8 concludes with a reference to what God's "eyes" have seen, i.e., is watching over, forming an *inclusio* with 9:1 which states that the "eye" of all humanity, including all the tribes of Israel, is directed toward the LORD. Magne Saebø (*Sacharja 9-14: Untersuchungen von Text und Form* [WMANT 34; Neukirchen-Vluyn: Neu-kirchener Verlag, 1969], 161) notes the important role that the "eye" motif plays in Zechariah 1-8 (2:8 [Heb 2:12]; 3:9; 4:10; 5:6; 8:6), thus serving as an additional link between Zechariah 9 and 1-8.

[30]   Meyers and Meyers, *Zechariah 9-14*, 35.

[31]   This unit is also linked to Zech 9:1-8 by the motif of the divine "eye" (2:8 [Heb 2:12]; 9:8).

The verbal and conceptual parallels between the two texts are sufficient to evoke the former when one reads the latter, and they suggest dependence. In 9:9, the wording differs from 2:10 [Heb 2:14] (i.e., potentially has been modified) in several ways. The divergence in the imperatival call to rejoice may be insignificant, but the addition of "greatly" (מאד) makes the latter more emphatic. The divergence in the form of the verb "come" can be accounted for by the shift from first person ("I will come" in 2:10 [Heb 2:14]) to third person ("your king comes" in 9:9). Most significant, however, is the shift in agency. If one reads 9:9 in the light of 2:10 [Heb 2:14], one would understand that the divine re-election of Jerusalem to be blessed again by the divine presence and deliverance (2:12 [Heb 2:16]; ובחר עוד בירושלם) is signaled by the coming of the future (Davidic?) king to Jerusalem. At the same time, the first explicit promise of salvation addressed to (the inhabitants of) Jerusalem in Zechariah 1-8 is also linked to the first such promise in 9-14.[32] Although the two verbal parallels that we have just discussed function quite differently, both serve to link the two sections of the book of Zechariah.

B. The Book of the Twelve and the Pentateuch

Analyses of coherence within the Book of the Twelve usually emphasize the significance of catchword and thematic connections, such as common fertility, "day of the LORD," or theophany language, between (primarily adjoining) books within the collection. Another approach is to note how the individual books employ a common text from outside the Book of the Twelve. The use of Exod 34:6-7 within the Minor Prophets has received extensive treatment, focusing on the context and modifications of the individual occurrences.[33]

---

[32]   Ralph L. Smith (*Micah-Malachi* [WBC 32; Waco: Word, 1984], 255) and Meyers and Meyers (*Zechariah 9-14*, 121) both note the formal parallels between Zech 2:10 [Heb 2:14] and Zech 9:9, also citing Zeph 3:14 which shares only the first two parallel elements, but their recognition of these parallels does not enrich their interpretation of Zech 9:9.

[33]   See the essays by Josef Scharbert, "Formgeschichte und Exegese von Ex 34,6f und seine Parallelen," *Bib* 34 (1957), 130-50; Robert C. Dentan, "The Literary Affinities of Exodus XXXIV6f," *VT* 13 (1963), 34-51; Thomas B. Dozeman, "Inner-Biblical Interpretation of Yahweh's Gracious and Compassionate Character," *JBL* 108 (1989), 207-23; Alan Cooper, "In Praise of Divine Caprice: The Significance of the Book of Jonah," in *Among the Prophets: Language, Image and Structure in the Prophetic Writings* (ed. P. R. Davies and D. J. A. Clines; JSOTSup 144; Sheffield: JSOT Press, 1993), 159-63; Raymond C. Van Leeuwen, "Scribal Wisdom and Theodicy in the Book of the Twelve," in *In Search of Wisdom: Essays in Memory of John C. Gammie* (ed. L.

Before briefly examining this example, it is useful to summarize and assess the contributions of others in interpreting these texts. Given the extensive verbal parallels between Exod 34:6-7 and Joel 2:13, Jon 4:2, Mic 7:18, and Nah 1:2-3, Raymond Van Leeuwen's attempt to find evidence of Hosea's dependence on this same pentateuchal text is less convincing.[34] It is not clear that the use of רחם ("be gracious") and אהיה ("I will be") in Hos 1:6-9 recalls Exodus 32-34 unless one wants to make the same claim wherever these roots or forms occur in the prophets, such as the use of the former in Zech 1:12 and 10:6 and of the latter in Zech 2:5 [Heb 2:9] and 8:8, neither of which is noted by Van Leeuwen. Nor is it clear that Hos 14:9 [Heb 14:10] ("Those who are wise...know them. For the ways of the LORD are right") as a "redactor's creation" is "inexplicable apart from the use of Exodus 32-34...in Joel and Jonah,"[35] given the pervasive use of the verb "know" (ידע) in the Hebrew Bible and the repeated reference to the LORD's "ways" in the prophets (see, for example, Isa 2:3; 55:8-9; 58:2; 63:17; 64:5; also Zech 3:7). It is possible (and even likely) that the traditions underlying Exodus 32-34 may have influenced the formulation of some of the passages within the book of Hosea, but one must be cautious in drawing interpretive conclusions from too narrow a textual basis.

The fact that Joel, Jonah, Micah, and Nahum all draw upon Exodus 34 does more than simply highlight the foundational nature of this account of the revelation of the divine character. Not only does the intertextual connection of these books with the Exodus passage serve to create a sub-group out of the latter three prophets within the larger collection but also their modifications and recontextualizations of this text indicate the various historical implications that the divine character can have. If Nogalski is correct in arguing for Joel's role as the "literary anchor" for the Book of the Twelve, despite presumably being composed later than the books that adjoin it,[36] establishing the framework for the rest of the Book, then it is appropriate for Joel to be the first of the Twelve to use Exod 34:6 explicitly. Though the call to repent in Joel 2:12-13 is directed primarily to those in Zion (2:15), the cosmic and universal scope of the approaching "day of the LORD" (2:10-11; 3:9-17 [Heb 4:9-17]) suggests that a broader appropriation is possible, as illustrated in Jonah. In Van Leeuwen's words, "Joel serves as a paradigm for the day of the Lord that shows by way of anticipation that Israel could have averted the Assyrian 'Day' through

---

G. Perdue, B. B. Scott, and W. J. Wiseman; Philadelphia: Westminster/John Knox, 1993), 31-49.

[34] Van Leeuwen, "Scribal Wisdom," 34-39.

[35] Ibid, 36.

[36] Nogalski, "Joel as 'Literary Anchor' for the Book of the Twelve."

repentance and appeal to the compassionate name of YHWH."[37] Joel closely follows the formulation in Exodus: "he is gracious and merciful, slow to anger, and abounding in steadfast love," though adding "and relents from punishing" (ונחם על־הרעה), which Dozeman probably correctly explains as deriving from Exod 32:12,14.[38]

The quotation of Exod 34:6 in Jon 4:2 is virtually identical in formulation to that in Joel (other than its introductory words – כי אתה אל, cf. Joel 2:13 – אל־יהוה אלהיכם כי). The context of Jonah is explicitly linked to that of Joel through the Ninevites' carrying out the call to repentance in Joel 2:12-15, proclaiming a fast, mourning, turning from evil, and even using the same initial words in Jon 3:9 as appear in Joel 2:14 (מי יודע ישוב ונחם). Thus, according to Jon 3:10 (וינחם אלהים על־הרעה), the wicked Assyrians become the recipients of the divine compassion expressed in the expansion of the Exodus formulation in Jon 4:2 (ונחם על־הרעה), precisely what Jonah did not want to happen.

Thus, on the one hand, the linkage between Joel and Jonah is signaled through the parallel expanded Exodus formula and the parallel "who knows...?" question. Micah and Nahum, on the other hand, are linked by the fact that the former concludes with the verbal parallel from Exodus 34, applying it positively on behalf of Judah, while the latter begins with the verbal parallel, applying it negatively against Nineveh, thereby reversing the situation described in Jonah. Micah picks up the key words from Exod 34:6-7 which express divine forgiveness in 7:18-19:

[19] ישוב ירחמנו (corresponding to ארך אפים ורב־חסד)

[18]...נשא עון ...לא־החזיק לעד אפו כי־חפץ חסד הוא

In announcing judgment on Nineveh, Nah 1:3 begins with the same phrase which Mic 7:18 modifies ("The LORD is slow to anger..."), which could aptly describe the postponement of judgment in Jonah's day, and then makes its own modification to fit its context ("but great in power" וגדול־

---

[37] Van Leeuwen, "Scribal Wisdom," 45.

[38] Dozeman, "Inner-Biblical Interpretation of Yahweh's Gracious and Compassionate Character," 221, although his claim that Joel 2:1-17 as a whole constitutes an "inner-biblical interpretation" of Jon 3:1-4:11, 217, goes beyond the evidence. Joel also inverts the order of the word-pair "gracious and merciful," a common feature of verbal parallels (see Schultz, *Quotations*, 76, 125, 167, 293).

כה, instead of "and abounding in steadfast love" ורב־חסד). The verbal parallel concludes with the appropriate phrase from Exod 34:7 which the preceding three Minor Prophets understandably do not employ: "and the LORD will by no means clear the guilty" (ונקה לא ינקה יהוה).

To summarize, the repeated use of the verbal parallel from Exod 34:6-7 serves to link four of the Minor Prophets,[39] the author/editor in each case selectively quoting and modifying the formulation to facilitate the particular application of the text which is being made. Thereby, a larger message is conveyed concerning the implications of God's gracious character for the specific situation that each individual prophetic book addresses.

Though the reuse of Exod 34:6-7 is clearly the most striking verbal parallel between the Pentateuch and the Book of the Twelve, other intertextual links abound, especially between the formulations of the covenantal blessings and curses and the prophetic oracles of salvation and judgment. Douglas Stuart offers a helpful list of these elements, also noting where they occur in the first five Minor Prophets.[40] In many instances the parallels between the covenantal formulations and the prophetic threats and promises go beyond general motifs to the specific expressions. One threat which recurs in the Book of the Twelve is found in Deut 28:30b: "You shall build a house, but not live in it. You shall plant a vineyard, but not enjoy its fruit" (בית תבנה ולא־תשב בו כרם תטע ולא תחללנו). A related threat occurs in Deut 28:38-40:

> You shall carry much seed into the field but shall gather little in, for the locust shall consume it. / You shall plant vineyards and dress them, but you shall neither drink the wine nor gather the grapes, for the worm shall eat them. / You shall have olive trees throughout all your territory, but you shall not anoint yourself with the oil, for your olives shall drop off.

Amos 5:11-12 draws from both passages in pronouncing judgment against those in Israel who economically exploit the poor: "you have built houses of hewn stone, but you shall not live in them; you have planted pleasant vineyards, but you shall not drink their wine." The specific changes ("of hewn stone," "pleasant") serve to emphasize the perpetrators' affluence. A reversal of this curse is announced in 9:14. Mic 6:15 draws ex-

---

[39] Van Leeuwen, "Scribal Wisdom," by inference accounts for the lack of verbal parallel to Exodus 34 in Amos and Obadiah: the Israel of Amos' day and the Edomites of Obadiah's day could have repented and escaped punishment just as the Assyrians in Jonah's day did or experienced the divine forgiveness that Micah promised Judah.

[40] Douglas Stuart, *Hosea-Jonah* (WBC 31; Waco: Word, 1987) xxxi-xlii.

clusively from the latter text in announcing the future circumstances of those in Judah who, interestingly, also are wealthy while cheating others (6:10-12): "You shall sow, but not reap; you shall tread olives, but not anoint yourselves with oil, you shall tread grapes, but not drink wine." Here the formulation does not correspond as closely to Deuteronomy. However, the context of the parallels in Amos and Micah is quite similar and, thus, the curse is appropriate: the wealthy who exploit others economically will themselves be deprived of material pleasures. Zeph 1:13b uses a similar threat, here specifically pronounced against Jerusalem, which is closer to Amos 5 than Micah 6 in formulation: "Though they build houses, they shall not inhabit them; though they plant vineyards, they shall not drink wine from them." Rather than linking economic exploitation with this announced deprivation, Zeph 1:12 links the punishment with the sin by means of a vivid metaphor: "I will punish the people who thicken on their dregs." Adele Berlin comments regarding this expression:[41] "The people have become mired in their drinking and indulgent lifestyle. The image captures the decadence of Jerusalem's upper class." Just as the verbal parallels between Exodus 34 and the Minor Prophets emphasize that divine compassion has implications for every situation, so the verbal parallels between the covenant curses (and blessings) and the specific prophetic pronouncements in the Book of the Twelve emphasize the divine consistency in dealing with people (whether Israel or Judah; in the Assyrian or the Babylonian era): the oppressive and self-indulgent sins of the rich warrant the same punishment.[42]

C. Isaiah and the Book of the Twelve

Scholars have noted the similarity in scope between the prophecies contained in the book of Isaiah and the Book of the Twelve, spanning the Assyrian, Babylonian, and Persian eras, although only the latter explicitly distinguishes twelve prophetic voices.[43] Odil Hannes Steck and Erich

---

[41] Adele Berlin, *Zephaniah: A New Translation with Introduction and Commentary* (AB 25a; New York: Doubleday, 1994), 87-88. Jer 48:11 employs a similar image but with a different association.

[42] Additional examples of covenantal blessing and curse language in Zephaniah include, "they shall walk like the blind" (1:17 // Deut 28:28-29, cf. Isa 59:10) and "and no one shall make them afraid" (3:13 // Lev 26:6).

[43] See the literary approach of Edgar G. Conrad, "Reading Isaiah and the Twelve as Prophetic Books," in *Writing and Reading the Book of Isaiah: Studies of an Interpretive Tradition* (ed. C. C. Broyles and C. A. Evans; VTSup 70; 2 volumes; Leiden: Brill, 1997), I:3-17.

Bosshard(-Nepustil) along with Reinhard Kratz have developed this basic observation into complex redactional theories.[44] In essence, their view is that parallels in structure and content between Isaiah and the Book of the Twelve can be explained in part by the suggestion that both underwent the same redactional stages, most likely at the hands of the same redactors. Bosshard-Nepustil's primary evidence for an "Assyria-Babylon" redactional layer consists of parallels between various books from the Twelve and Isaiah 13, 21, 22, and 33.

Bosshard-Nepustil notes the following parallels between Joel 1:1-2:11 and Isaiah 13:[45]

1:5,11,13	13:6	Call for people of Judah to lament
1:15 (2:1-2,11)	13:6	Reason for lament
2:1	13:2	Call to sound alarm on a mountain/hill
2:2ff	13:3ff	Army's description on day of the LORD
2:6	13:7-8	Terrified response to army
2:9	13:16	Army plunders the houses

Although the parallel elements are not in the same order in both texts and their actual formulation is, for the most part, rather dissimilar, Bosshard-Nepustil's observation is grounded upon the extensive verbal correspondence between Joel 1:15 and Isa 13:6 (cf. also Ezek 30:2-3): "[Alas for the day / Wail,] for the day of the LORD is near; [and] it will come like destruction from the Almighty" (כִּי קָרוֹב יוֹם יהוה...כְּשֹׁד מִשַּׁדֵּי יָבוֹא).

On the basis of his comparison of Joel with Isa 13:2-8,14-16 (as well as Isa 5:26ff and Jer 4-6), Bosshard-Nepustil concludes (1) that Joel is dependent on the Isa 13 text, (2) that the day of the LORD in both texts refers to the attack of the Assyrian and/or Babylonian army, (3) that both passages were inserted for the same reason into the book of Isaiah (at the beginning of the oracles concerning the foreign nations) and the Book of the

---

[44] Odil Hannes Steck, *Der Abschluß der Prophetie im Alten Testament: Ein Versuch zur Frage der Vorgeschichte des Kanons* (BTS 17; Neukirchen-Vluyn: Neukirchener, 1991). Steck dates the decisive redactional work to the late fourth through the late third centuries BCE. Erich Bosshard, "Beobachtungen zum Zwölfprophetenbuch," *BN* 40 (1987), 30-62; Bosshard and Reinhard G. Kratz, "Maleachi im Zwölfprophetenbuch," *BN* 52 (1990), 27-46; Erich Bosshard-Nepustil, *Rezeptionen von Jesaja 1-39 im Zwölfprophetenbuch. Untersuchungen zur literarischen Verbindung von Prophetenbüchern in babylonischer und persischer Zeit* (OBO 154; Göttingen: Vandenhoeck & Ruprecht, 1997). For a critique of Bosshard and Kratz, see Paul Redditt, "Zechariah 9-14," 246-47.

[45] Bosshard-Nepustil, *Rezeptionen von Jesaja 1-39*, 292. He discusses the parallels on 292-97, 308.

Twelve (between Hosea and Amos), and (4) that the concluding question in Joel 2:11 ("who can endure [the day of the LORD]?") is not answered until Hab 1:1-2:16, the next insertion from this redactional layer. Somewhat similarly, Steck suggests that Joel corresponds to Isaiah 13, Obadiah to Isaiah 24-27, and Zephaniah to Isaiah 34-35, this editorial expansion taking place in 312/311 BCE.[46]

However, by limiting the unit to Isa 13:2-8,14-16, Bosshard-Nepustil can ignore 13:1 and 13:17-22 which indicate that it is the destruction of Babylon that is being described in the oracle, as well as vv 9-13, which contain proto-apocalyptic imagery. Both of these contextual factors make it unlikely that this verbal parallel offers conclusive evidence that Joel 1:1-2:11 is describing the Babylonian attack on Jerusalem, so that its future-oriented prophecy actually describes (from the perspective of its composition) past history. If that is the case, the book's central call to repentance (2:12ff) in the light of the approaching day of the LORD and God's readiness to forgive becomes meaningless. The rich prophetic imagery describing the day of the LORD resists any effort to narrow its referent to just one historical event. If this verbal parallel significantly links Joel and Isaiah 13, then it does so by emphasizing the certain and catastrophic nature of the day of the LORD, regardless of whether it is going to devastate Judah or Babylon. Furthermore, by focusing on just one verbal parallel between Isaiah and the Book of the Twelve, Bosshard-Nepustil downplays other striking verbal parallels between (other sections of) Isaiah and the book of Joel. James Crenshaw, for example, cites the following parallels:[47] 2:3b // Isa 51:3; 2:27 // Isa 45:5,6,18; 3:2 [Heb 4:2] // Isa 66:18; 3:10 [Heb 4:10] // Isa 2:4. If clear verbal parallels (such as that between Isaiah 13 and Joel) indicate parallel structures, why does neither Bosshard-Neupustil nor Steck give any attention to the striking parallel between Isa 52:7 and Nah 1:15 [Heb 2:1]?

A similar example is offered by Isa 2:2-4 // Mic 4:1-3. This parallel is the most extensive and most discussed of numerous verbal links between these two books. What is the structural effect of this vision being placed in a prominent position within both prophetic books? In light of the superscriptions, one may suggest either that Yahweh reveals essentially the same divine message to more than one prophet in a given generation or that a true prophet can quote a contemporary, since both are God's spokespersons.

---

[46]   Steck, *Der Abschluß der Prophetie*, 83. By analogy, one might have to claim also that Hosea corresponds to Isa 1-12 and Amos to Isa 14-23.

[47]   James L. Crenshaw, *Joel: A New Translation with Introduction and Commentary* (AB 24C; New York: Doubleday, 1995), 27-28.

Regardless of the origin of the oracle, these parallel texts were given equally prominent positions by those responsible for shaping the final form of these prophetic books. Early in Isaiah and at the midpoint of Micah, the reader is given a brief vision of Zion's glorious future, directly following a graphic portrayal of its current apostate condition. The remainder of each book sketches the long and twisted route to be traversed before the vision becomes a reality. However, in the final analysis, the divergent literary contexts and the distinctive emphases of each prophet (see Mic 4:4) reshape and redirect this close parallel. Thus even the virtually identical passages Isa 2:2-4 // Mic 4:1-3 evoke different applications (Isa 2:5, cf. Mic 4:5).[48]

Scholars have noted numerous less extensive verbal parallels between Isaiah and Micah, although many of these involve passages which some consider to be non-genuine in Isaiah, Micah, or both:[49]

Micah	Isaiah	Micah	Isaiah
1:11	47:2-3	5:5	9:6
2:13	52:12	5:13	2:8
3:5	56:10-11	6:7	1:11
3:8	58:1	6:8	1:17
3:11	48:2	7:1	24:13
4:7	24:24	7:2	57:1
4:9	13:8; 21:3	7:3	1:23
4:13	41:15-16; 23:18	7:17	49:23

In light of this list, it does not appear to be appropriate to interpret Isaiah 2 // Micah 4 primarily on the basis of the vision's relative location within the book of Isaiah and the book of Micah's place or function within the Book of the Twelve, as Steck's or Bosshard-Kratz's theories would suggest. These verbal parallels indicate more than chronological and theological proximity. As a result of the hermeneutical dynamics of verbal parallels such as these that are virtually impossible to date exactly, an intertextuality is established between the two books.

Childs has described the result:

> This common moulding has the effect that Isaiah serves as a commentary on Micah and *vice versa*. The use of a verbatim passage in such a central position consciously directs the reader to the other collection of prophecy. The two messages are not to

---

[48] For a fuller discussion of the parallel Isaiah 2 // Micah 4 see Schultz, *Quotation*, 290-307. See also Marvin A. Sweeney's recent comparison of these texts, "Micah's Debate with Isaiah," *JSOT* 93 (2001), 111-24.

[49] John H. Raven, *Old Testament Introduction: General and Special* (New York: Fleming H. Revell Co., 1906), 193, 230.

be fused since each has been preserved with a distinct shape as a discrete entity. Yet the two are to be heard together for mutual enrichment within the larger corpus of prophecy. The canonical shaping thus emphasizes an affinity which is far closer than that established by belonging to the prophetic division of the Hebrew canon.[50]

What is especially true of Isa 2:1-4 and Mic 4:1-3, and also has implications for how one reads the books of Isaiah and Micah as a whole, can apply to the proper identification and analysis of verbal parallels throughout the prophetic corpus or within the Hebrew Bible as a whole. With assessing some verbal parallels, methodological considerations such as those offered by John Sailhamer can be helpful:

> If...there is an authorially [or redactionally] intended inter-textuality, then it stands to reason that some loss of meaning occurs when one fails to view the text in terms of it. On the other hand, if there has been no intentional inter-textuality, then an attempt to read the text in terms of a supposed linkage with another text will likely distort the meaning of that text. Clear criteria of inter-textuality must therefore be established in biblical exegesis.[51]

However, even if no such "intent" can be detected or demonstrated, the identification of striking verbal parallels creates an intertextual dynamic that must be taken into account in developing a reading strategy for the prophets. It has been the goal of this essay to offer several criteria for identifying, as well as several examples of interpreting, the "ties that bind" together the prophetic corpus. We have thereby sought to illustrate why, in analyzing the almost countless words and motifs that are repeated *within* and *between* individual books and the larger collection of the Book of the Twelve, giving attention to fewer but clearer verbal parallels can be exegetically both more responsible and more illuminating.

---

[50] Childs, *Old Testament as Scripture,* 438. Robert P. Carroll, "Night without Vision: Micah and the Prophets," in *The Scriptures and the Scrolls: Studies in Honour of A.S. van der Woude's 65th Birthday* (ed. G. Martínez, A. Hilhurst, and C. J. Labuschagne; Leiden: Brill, 1992), 83-84, speaks similarly of the "intertextuality" of Micah and Isaiah.

[51] John H. Sailhamer, *Introduction to Old Testament Theology: A Canonical Approach* (Grand Rapids: Zondervan, 1995), 213.

The Fifth Vision of Amos in Context[1]

Aaron Schart

The five visions of Amos undoubtedly belong to the seminal texts of Israelite prophecy. At the end of the writing of Amos they form a well-designed composition, which reflects the private encounter of the prophet with YHWH in a visionary realm.[2] Two pairs of visions (Amos 7:1-3 // 7:4-6 and 7:7-8 // 8:1-2) lead the reader to the final "showdown." In the fifth vision (9:1-4), the prophet finally sees God directly at the center of the land, the temple.[3] God commands him to strike the temple building in order to destroy it. Apparently not every prophet or prophetess had so overwhelming an encounter with the God of Israel. After the downfall of Northern Israel and the temple of Bethel, Amos' vision cycle was acknowledged to have foreseen this downfall. Many generations of readers have found inspiration in these texts. It turned out that the texts were not only relevant for Northern Israel, but for Judah as well. Because visions, especially when they lead to a direct encounter with God, are emotionally overwhelming, but at the same time ambiguous and vague, words cannot grasp their meaning completely.[4]

---

[1] Earlier versions of this paper were given as lectures at the Universities of Tübingen (12.12.1998) and Bonn (12.07.2000). I am appreciative for the stimulating discussions there.

[2] A convenient, up-to-date overview of the mainstream interpretation of the vision cycle is provided by Siegfried Bergler, "'Auf der Mauer - auf dem Altar': noch einmal die Visionen des Amos," *VT* 50 (2000) 445-471, esp. 447-450. More sensitive to the theological issues involved is Jörg Jeremias, "Rezeptionsprozesse in der prophetischen Überlieferung - am Beispiel der Visionsberichte des Amos, in *Rezeption und Auslegung im Alten Testament und in seinem Umfeld* (ed. Reinhard Gregor Kratz and Thomas Krüger; OBO 153; Freiburg [Schweiz] Göttingen: Universitätsverlag / Vandenhoeck & Ruprecht, 1997), 29-44.

[3] The fifth vision picks up terminology from the third vision. To understand the relation of both it is important to notice that אֲדֹנָי in the third vision (Amos 7:7) was inserted very late; it is not yet attested in the Septuagint! Therefore in the original text the person that held the אֲנָךְ remained unidentified as in the first two visions. This explains why Amos' answer to the question "What do you see?" does not mention God (Amos 7:8); see Jörg Jeremias, *Der Prophet Amos* (ATD 24/2; Göttingen: Vandenhoeck & Ruprecht, 1995) 95; against Bergler, "Auf der Mauer – auf dem Altar," 455.

[4] Dalene Heyns, "Theology in Pictures: the Visions of Amos," in *Feet on Level Ground"* (ed. Koot van Wyk; Berrien Springs, Mich.: Hester, 1996) 132-172, esp. 164: "The prophetic proclamation may never get bogged down in verbal structures,

That is one reason why Amos entrusted his private experience to his followers. In the end it turned out that many generations could use the texts for reflecting on their own endangered situation before the God of Israel.

In this paper I want to investigate how the understanding of the fifth vision changed over time. It occurred mainly by modifying the context in which the vision was imbedded and understood. Since Brevard Childs has underlined the importance of context, redaction criticism now acknowledges that many of the redactors created complete and more or less coherent books.[5] As a consequence, it is imperative to read every text in its literary context. It is not sufficient, for example, merely to interpret the hymnic fragment in Amos 9:5-6 as a hymnic affirmation of God's superior name. One must ask what consequences the insertion of the hymn has for the sense of the fifth vision and the writing of Amos, and even the Twelve (or its precursors) as a whole. Through the course of redaction history the text of the vision proper remained remarkably stable; however, through the modification of the context the sense of the fifth vision was profoundly modified. I will follow the different stages from the oldest to the youngest.[6]

I. The Vision in the Hebrew Text

A. The Oldest Layer, Amos 9:1-4a*

The oldest literary layer of the fifth vision that can be reconstructed with any confidence comprises Amos 9:1-4a*.[7] There are three points to con-

---

may never only speak in stereotypes as the fixed forms of traditional images suggest. By means of symbols they open up wider possibilities for many-leveled interpretations of the divine word. In this way the visionary message remains new in each new situation." Yvonne Sherwood ("Of Fruit and Corpses and Wordplay Visions: Picturing Amos 8.1-3," *JSOT* 92 [2001] 5-27) offers a recreation of Amos' vision.

[5] Brevard Springs Childs, *Introduction to the Old Testament as Scr*ipture (Philadelphia: Fortress Press, 1979); idem, "The Canonical Shape of the Prophetic Literature," *Int* 32 (1978) 46-55. idem, "Retrospective Reading of the Old Testament Prophets," *ZAW* 108 (1996) 362-377. For an important sketch of this approach to treating the visions of Amos, see Jörg Jeremias, "Rezeptionsprozesse in der prophetischen Überlieferung."

[6] See Appendix 1. I presuppose the source-critical model of my book Aaron Schart, *Die Entstehung des Zwölfprophetenbuchs: Neubearbeitungen von Amos im Rahmen schriftenübergreifender Redaktionsprozesse* (BZAW 260; Berlin and New York: de Gruyter, 1998).

[7] Whether this layer of the vision belongs to the oldest layer in the writing of Amos or whether it even goes back to the historical prophet Amos is controversial, but need not be decided for the purpose of this paper. I, for one, do not see sufficient evidence to deny the authorship of the content to historical prophet , although the specific wording and structure may have been altered in order to fit better within the composition of five visions. For an overly skeptical and therefore implausible position, see Uwe

sider. First, the phrase עיני מנגד is clearly secondary in Amos 9:3. This
phrase was inserted together with Amos 9:4b in order to prepare a contrast
between the two verses. Second, the meaning of ובצעם בראש (and cut
them off on the head) in Amos 9:1 is unintelligible, probably due to an early
scribal error. It is clear that the action described should follow quite naturally out of the first imperative: "Strike …!" This could be done with a second imperative or a w=qatal. The subject of the verb could be Amos, but it
is at least equally possible that YHWH is the subject, as in the second colon
of this line. The object בראש may be correct, implying an appealing word
play on Amos 2:7; 6:7. In addition, there is an allusion to the verb רעש
(Amos 9:1) that arouses the reader's attention, because it was mentioned in
the superscription (Amos 1:1). The initial verb, however, cannot be recov-
ered. Third, it is questionable whether the passage is a literal unity. Some
scholars believe that vv. 2-4a are secondary.[8] Admittedly, some observations may point in this direction, but I doubt the hints are significant enough
to justify this hypothesis.

Turning to the content of this oldest layer, the first line depicts the vision proper. The rest of the account quotes the speech God has delivered to
Amos. The vision proper starts with an extraordinary statement: Amos
claims to have seen God.[9] No preparations for this direct visual encounter
are mentioned. Very probably the previous four visions are seen as such a
preparation leading to the final encounter. It is clear from the outset that
such a close contact with God must have an extraordinary message as its
outcome. Also the reader expects a temple as the location for such an encounter. The circumstances are mentioned very briefly, making every detail
of greatest importance. The prophet only mentions that YHWH has positioned himself on the altar. The verb נצב implies that some action by
YHWH will follow. Together with the following preposition על, the phrase

---

Becker, "Der Prophet als Fürbitter: Zum literarhistorischen Ort der Amos-Visionen,"
    VT 51 (2001) 141-165.

[8] Again Bergler ("Auf der Mauer – auf dem Altar," 452-454) has summarized the argu-
    ments. There are verbal and motive parallels with other texts, partly late ones. In most
    cases one can argue that the priority lies with Amos. Other authors studied his vision
    cycle, and it inspired them; for example Isaiah (6:1-4). Likewise, Dietmar Mathias has
    reviewed the arguments and concluded that the direction of dependence is at least pos-
    sible in both ways. Cf. his "Beobachtungen zur fünften Vision des Amos (9,1-4)," in
    Gedenkt an das Wort (ed. Christoph Kähler and Werner Vogler; Leipzig: Evangelische
    Verlagsanstalt, 1999), 150-174, esp. 164; contra Bergler, "Auf der Mauer – auf dem
    Altar," 469).

[9] We leave aside the question whether אדני in Amos 9:1 belongs to the oldest layer or,
    in my eyes more probable, was substituted for an original יהוה.

was probably chosen to allude to the *hieros logos* of Bethel, which stands behind the narrative of Jacob's dream in Bethel (Gen 28:10-22; the phrase נצב על appears in v.12).[10] מזבח is construed with the article. This can best be explained if it refers to the main altar of the temple, probably located in the center of the yard, and not in the temple building itself. That God stands at this place is unusual and frightening. It may be that in Bethel YHWH was imagined standing, instead of seated on a throne as in Jerusalem, but it was certainly not normal for YHWH to stand on the altar. On the contrary, when YHWH left his place inside the temple building, presumably over the cultic image of a golden bull, the harmonic order must have been disturbed.[11] God had left the normal place of God's presence. Why would God do this? In addition, God's standing on the altar made a cultic use of the altar impossible. This frightening scene becomes the setting for a shocking instruction in the following bicolon.

As in Isaiah 6, which is in many respects similar, in Amos 9 one finds the commissioning of the person having the vision following its depiction.[12] The imperative הך (Strike!) is meant as a command to Amos.[13] The text mentions neither another human nor heavenly beings accompanying God who could be the addressee.[14] Amos has to strike the כפתור, an act which will launch a seismic activity that finally reaches even the ספים (thresholds). Both Hebrew words have the article prefixed, although they have not been mentioned before. This can best be explained by assuming that the words refer to objects eternal to the text: while speaking, God points to the things God talks about. As a consequence, both terms must denote essential parts of the temple, which could be seen from the central altar.[15] The reader

---

[10]   See for example Friedhelm Hartenstein, "Wolkendunkel und Himmelsfeste: Zur Genese und Kosmologie der Vorstellung des himmlischen Heiligtums JHWHs," in *Das biblische Weltbild und seine altorientalischen Kontexte* (ed. Bernd Janowski and Beate Ego; FAT 32; Tübingen: Mohr Siebeck, 2001), 125-179; his illuminating comparison of Gen 28:12-13,17 with Amos 9:1-4 (and Amos 9:5-6) is on pp. 158-160.

[11]   In Isa 6:1 God is seen inside the temple building (היכל), sitting on a throne.

[12]   Compare Jörg Jeremias, "Das unzugängliche Heiligtum. Zur letzten Vision des Amos (Amos 9,1-4)," in *Hosea und Amos: Studien zu den Anfängen des Dodekapropheton* (FAT 13; Tübingen: Mohr Siebeck, 1996), 244-256, esp. 246: "Wo Jahwe andernorts in Visionen direkt geschaut wird, geht es um eine Beauftragung des Propheten (bzw. des 'Geistes') durch den himmlischen Hofstaat, der um den thronenden Himmelskönig Jahwe steht (1 Kön 22,19ff; Jes 6)."

[13]   A modification of the text is not necessary; cf. Bergler, "'Auf Der Mauer - Auf Dem Altar,'" 449.

[14]   One must not infer the seraphim from Isaiah 6.

[15]   As a consequence, all items are excluded that are located within the temple building; for example the cult image.

needs to imagine the situation concretely, in order to understand fully the significance of the situation (see picture in appendix 2).[16] The altar is probably located in the midst of the yard and is so large that a person can stand upon it. More difficult is the issue of where the סִפִּים (the thresholds) are located. Most of the commentators locate them at the entrance of the central temple building proper.[17] However, this suggestion does not fit with the plural of the noun, because that building had only one door. It is much more probable that סִפִּים refers to the thresholds in the outer wall of the yard, which marked the entrance to the whole temple precinct (*temenos*).[18] One may assume that at least three gateways existed. It is even more difficult to say what כַּפְתּוֹר means and where it was located. The term must have a technical meaning denoting some prominent part of the temple. Following the usual interpretation that כַּפְתּוֹר refers to the top of a column, one has to choose whether the text presupposes a column in front of the door of the temple building or a free-standing column somewhere in the yard.[19] Either way, it is clear that Amos is to deliver a blow or toward the center of the sanctuary. This single blow will initiate a shockwave that shakes the whole precinct as far as the outer wall. The temple in its entirety, from the center to the outer border, from the top to the foundations in the earth, will tremble.

Special emphasis, however, is placed on the shaking of the thresholds. They mark the border between inside and outside, between the holy place and the profane world. A holy place needs to be cut off from profane space, because the profane has the potential to contaminate the sacred. That is why

---

[16]   In order to help the reader imagine the situation, I have drawn a picture (cf. Appendix 2). This picture is not meant as an archaeological reconstruction of the site at Bethel, but as a visualization of the image that the text creates in the mind of the reader. In order to visualize it, one has to add many features not noted within the text; e.g., the relative measurements, the forms, and other things.

[17]   The main argument is that the כַּפְתּוֹר and the סִפִּים need to have an architectural connection, so that a strike on the one part can have an effect on the other; Hans-Walter Wolff, *Dodekapropheton 2: Joel und Amos* (BKAT 14/2; Neukirchen-Vluyn: Neukirchener Verlag, 3rd ed. 1985), 390: "Es muß sich hier um einen der Köpfe von Säulen handeln, die die Torschwellen flankieren. Sonst könnten darüber nicht die Säulenbasen und damit die Schwellen erbeben." See also Jörg Jeremias, "Das unzugängliche Heiligtum," 250; Bergler, "'Auf Der Mauer - Auf Dem Altar,'" 451. However in a visionary context it is normal that some rules of the ordinary reality are broken.

[18]   This is also true for Isa 6:4.

[19]   Archaeological evidence for a sole column in a temple precinct is lacking. The text does not exclude the possibility that two or more columns are present, but God's command singles out one Amos is to strike.

custodians for the thresholds and temple entrance liturgies are necessary.[20] If the thresholds do רעש (shake) – like an earthquake – they give up their function and can no longer block out the profane.[21] As a result, the holy place as such, which is the obligatory foundation on which a temple can be erected, ceases to exist. The temple is completely out of order.

Since the temple is the center that gives refuge, stability, and prosperity to life to the land, its elimination sets off disorder and death that will reach to its borders. Amos 9:2-4a* spells out this scenario in detail.[22] Shockingly, the temple is no longer a place of harmony with God and a source of protection. Instead, the deity residing at the sanctuary hunts down and kills the people, sparing no one.

At this point the decisive question arises: who are the people who will be killed? The vision report only speaks of כלם (all of them). The pronominal suffix must refer to the last mentioned group in the immediate context. Assuming that the main stream scholars are correct that the five visions originally formed a literary composition into which later redactors inserted the passages Amos 7:9-17; 8:3-14; 9:4b-15, the suffix refers to the fourth vision, where the end of "my people Israel" is announced. The reader must identify "all of them" with "my people Israel" (8:2). The expression "my people Israel" is no longer employed within the fifth vision, thereby signaling that the personal relationship between God and Israel has come to an end.

In sum, the oldest layer portrays YHWH as having left the place inside the temple building. Standing on the altar he commands his prophet to strike the top of a column (or something similar) in the center. This blow will initiate a shockwave, which will ruin the whole temple precinct. The shaking of the thresholds implies the nullification of the border between holy space and profane world, thereby expressing the total elimination of the sanctuary.

---

[20] Friedhelm Hartenstein (*Die Unzugänglichkeit Gottes im Heiligtum. Jesaja 6 und der Wohnort JHWHs in der Jerusalemer Kulttradition* [WMANT 75. Neukirchen-Vluyn: Neukirchener Verlag, 1997], Exkurs 4, pp. 116-122) has collected material from the Ancient Near East that illustrates the function of the thresholds.

[21] Here is an important difference from the vision in Isaiah 6. There the lexem נוע is used, which does not imply that the thresholds give up their function entirely.

[22] Cf. Jörg Jeremias, "Das unzugängliche Heiligtum," 255: "Es ist nun freilich keineswegs zufällig, daß diese Durchführung bis in kosmische Dimensionen ausgreift, weil der künftig unzugängliche Tempel eben kosmische Dimensionen besitzt." Also cf. Friedhelm Hartenstein, "Wolkendunkel und Himmelsfeste: Zur Genese und Kosmologie der Vorstellung des himmlischen Heiligtums JHWHs," in *Das biblische Weltbild und seine altorientalischen Kontexte* (ed. Bernd Janowski and Beate Ego; FAT 32; Tübingen: Mohr Siebeck, 2001), 125-179, esp. 154.

All people of Northern Israel will share its fate.[23] The name of the temple is
not mentioned, but in the context of the oldest layer it can only be Bethel.
No reason is given why YHWH would give up his temple, and nothing
gives the impression that Bethel is not an authorized sanctuary of YHWH.
Most likely the oldest layer depicted YHWH discarding Bethel because the
sanctuary and its cult "covered up" the oppression in the land, instead of
empowering the people to stop it.

B. The Tradition Bearers (*Tradenten*) of Amos, Amos 8:14 and 9:4b

The next stage of redaction activity was the insertion of Amos 8:14 between
the fourth and the fifth visions. The same redactor probably added Amos
9:4b and, less likely, the phrase עֵינַי נֶגֶד in Amos 9:3. This frame around
the fifth vision is heavily influenced by concepts from Hosea.[24]

The first of these concepts is that the wickedness of the capital Samaria
(Hos 7:1) is the foundation of all the sins of Northern Israel, among which
the monarch and the cult image are outstanding examples. Therefore, in Hos
10:7 the king is characterized as "*Samaria*'s king" and the cult image of
Bethel is designated as "*Samaria*'s calf" (Hos 8:5-6). Reading the fifth vision after Amos 8:14 makes it obvious that the temple at Bethel had to be
eliminated most of all because of the sin of Samaria. At the same time, the
redactor insists on mentioning the sanctuaries at Dan and Beersheba, which
also are involved in the sin of Samaria. The temple that is eliminated in the
fifth vision attains the role of an example to all of the godless בָּמוֹת (high
places, Amos 7:9). They too will be punished by YHWH.

The second point is that Amos 8:14 proposes, albeit in short statements,
reasons why the temple will be eliminated. The mention of swearing alludes
probably to juridic activities of an essential kind, including important economic transactions. Behind the MT must stand oath formulas directed towards a deity. If the accused people do not swear by other gods, they at
least invoke local manifestations or variants of YHWH at other sanctuaries.
This view, that the basic sin is seen in turning to other gods, is inspired by
Hosea. His critique that the accused persons have turned to Baal (Hos 2:10;
13:1) or to the Baalim (Hos 11:2) is relevant here.

Third, the ones who will be targets of YHWH's sword are defined
anew. Because of the insertion of Amos 8:14, the Hebrew כֻּלָּם (all of
them) in Amos 9:1 no longer refers to "my people Israel" mentioned in

---

[23] See Wolff, *Dodekapropheton 2: Joel und Amos*, 391: "Jeder Restgedanke ist so auf das
entschlossenste zurückgewiesen."

[24] See Schart, *Entstehung*, 126-128.

Amos 8:2, as in the previous layer, but to הנשבעים (those who swear) instead.[25] Only the people who rely on the false Northern cult in their juridic activities will "fall and never stand up."[26] Finally, the "eyes of God" in Amos 9:4b allude to Hos 13:14, where they also observe without mercy the destruction of the sinners through a hypostasized sword (Amos 9:4a; Hos 14:1).

All of these observations can best be explained by the thesis that early versions of Hosea and Amos together formed a "Two-Prophets-Book."[27] Followers of the prophets must have redacted the records, which they had available, in such a way that the message of one prophet could serve to nuance the understanding of the other.[28] Both prophecies now serve as independent but mutually confirming witnesses that YHWH warned his people before his patience came to a definite end (compare the significant phrase לא אוסיף עוד [I can no longer] in Hos 1:6 // Amos 7:8; 8:2). They also explain why he abandoned Northern Israel, especially its capital Samaria and its sanctuary Bethel. Within the writing of Amos alone, it does not become really obvious why the cult center Bethel and the people who relied on the Northern sanctuaries had to face such a harsh punishment, because Amos attacks the people who worship, not the cult or the sanctuary as such (cf. Amos 5:21: "*your* festivals, *your* solemn assemblies").[29] Perceived as the closing section to a Two-Prophets-Scroll, comprising early versions of Hosea and Amos, the fifth vision becomes fully understandable.

In sum, the tradition bearers understood the fifth vision in such a way that the blow that Amos had to deliver was aimed at all sanctuaries that were involved in the sin of Samaria. The unnamed temple was perceived as an example that illustrated the fate of all the others. However, the tradition bearers no longer think of a complete destruction of the whole people of Israel. Targets of God's punitive actions are only those who rely on the high places and sanctuaries in their juridic activities. This theological concept

---

[25] Mathias ("Beobachtungen zur fünften Vision des Amos [9,1-4]," 170) rightly asks for the referent of the plural suffix, but wrongly finds it in the persons accused in Amos 8:4.

[26] The allusion to the famous phrase from Amos 5:2 makes likewise clear who, according to the redactor of Amos 8:14, is meant by the metaphor "maiden Israel."

[27] For the full elaboration of this hypothesis, see Schart, *Entstehung*, 101-155.

[28] This is a practice, which is well attested in the Ancient Near East. For Mari, see Aaron Schart, "Combining Prophetic Oracles in Mari Letters and Jeremiah 36," JANESCU 23 (1995) 75-93. For the Neo-Assyrian prophecy, see Karel van der Toorn, "Mesopotamian prophecy between immanence and transcendence: a comparison of Old Babylonian and Neo-Assyrian prophecy," in *Prophecy in its Ancient Near Eastern Context* (ed. Martti Nissinen; SBLSymS 13; Atlanta, GA: SBL, 2000) 71-87, esp. 73-77.

[29] See Mathias, "Beobachtungen zur fünften Vision des Amos (9,1-4)," 172.

stems from the tradition bearers' version of Hosea, which formed the first part of their Two-Prophets-Scroll. In light of the background of Hosea it is most probable that they viewed the holy places of Northern Israel as sinful on the grounds that they had not been founded by YHWH. In addition, the plurality of sanctuaries stood in contrast to the exclusiveness of God's relation to Israel and Israel's devotion to God. And finally, the worship celebrated there was aimed towards other gods or strange local manifestations of YHWH.

C. The D-Layer, Amos 9:7-10

The next layer that interests us here is what may be called the D-Layer.[30] This layer added four new verses (Amos 9:7-10), thereby creating a new ending to Amos. Now YHWH no longer speaks to the prophet, but to all the Israelites. The passage takes up keywords from the vision (כפתור in Amos 9:1 // 9:7; "sword" in Amos 9:4a // 9:10; "evil" in Amos 9:4b // 9:10; "eyes of YHWH" in Amos 9:4b // 9:8). In this redactional layer the identity of Israel is deeply rooted within its history. It is within history that God has elected Israel, within history that Israel received its land, and within history that Israel will be punished. To be sure, the specific aim of Amos 9:8 is to deny a unique relationship on the part of Israel to YHWH, who has comparable relationships to other nations as well. Neither the temple nor the exodus guarantees that Israel will not suffer the destruction the fifth vision announces.[31]

The D-Layer has developed a distinctive idea of how the punishment of Israel will be executed, so that the sinful part will be eliminated but the other part will survive. The D-Redactor makes a fundamental distinction between the "sinful kingdom" (הממלכה החטאה) and the "house of Jacob," which will surely not be destroyed.[32] The concept of the "sinful kingdom" expands the idea of the tradition bearers that the political regime is responsible for the downfall of Israel. Whereas in Amos 7:9 a specific

---

[30] In order to avoid an imprecise use of the term "Deuteronomistic," I want to stress that this layer shows affinities to the Deuteronomistic History and its style, but does not use the characteristic phrases that would allow identification (see Norbert Lohfink, "Gab es eine deuteronomistische Bewegung?" in *Studien zum Deuteronomium und zur deuteronomistischen Literatur III* (Stuttgarter Biblische Aufsatzbände 20; Stuttgart: Katholisches Bibelwerk, 1995) 65-142.

[31] The wordplay on כפתור in Amos 9:1 and 9:7 must have had a special significance for a parallel between the temple as cosmic center and the historical roots of the Philistines, a parallel that is now lost because of our insufficient semantic knowledge.

[32] The formation לא + inf. abs. + yiqtol in Amos 9:8 seems to have this sense.

dynasty, the "house of Jeroboam," was seen as guilty, in Amos 9:8 it is the Northern kingdom as a whole, and very probably from its origin on, that needs eliminating.[33] At least this is the most plausible explanation for why the redactor cites the phrase "I will destroy it from the face of the earth" from 1 Kgs 13:34. There it is said that an unnamed prophet pronounced the downfall of the temple at Bethel. The D-Layer wants to demonstrate that Amos reaffirmed this message. According to Amos 9:9-10 the sinful kingdom also includes all those who have not believed the prophetic message, especially not the fifth vision (see the allusion to Amos 9:4b with רעה "evil"; cf. Amos 3:6). By contrast, this statement implies that those who do believe the prophet will belong to the house of Jacob.

The process of separating the house of Jacob from the sinful kingdom is described as the shaking of the house of Israel and compared to the shaking of a sieve (Amos 9:9). This concept certainly alludes to and reinterprets the shaking of the temple in Amos 9:1.[34] According to this layer, this shaking is only the first step in the process of shaking Northern Israel as a whole.

This layer must be viewed within the context of the D-Corpus as a whole. The four writings of Hosea, Amos, Micah, and Zephaniah present one coherent flow of prophetic critique. This unity is clearly marked, because all four writings not only have the same type of superscription, but also include similar information about their date and their audiences.[35] In the case of the Northern sanctuaries it is evident that the D-Redactors perceived them as illegitimate from their foundation by Jeroboam I onwards, and condemned them with the pejorative term "high places" (במות).[36] Applying this perspective to the interpretation of the fifth vision, it follows that YHWH never resided in the temple at Bethel. He came from Jerusalem (cf. Amos 1:2), conquered the city walls of Israel (Amos 7:7), and entered the temple yard to eliminate the high places, beginning with the temple in Bethel.

---

[33]   The D-Layer probably was inspired by Amos 7:9, because they understood the "house of Jeroboam" to mean the Northern kingdom. Christoph Levin has described how the D-Redaction has perceived the phrase, but not how the Tradents' version originally meant it ("Amos und Jerobeam I," *VT* 45 [1995] 307-317, esp. 309: "Es ist kein Zweifel, daß auch in Am. vii 9 Jerobeam I. gemeint ist").

[34]   The phrase בכל הגוים "among all the nations" in Amos 9:9 was added later. The Hebrew word הרבב must have an otherwise unattested meaning, probably a specific type of sieve. It may have been chosen in this context to allude to כבר, the channel where Ezekiel lived in Exile (Ezek 1:1).

[35]   See Schart, *Entstehung*, 39-46.

[36]   Whereas the tradition bearers presumably differentiated between "high places" and sanctuaries, the D-Redactors subsumed the latter under the former.

D. The Layer of the Hymnic Fragment, Amos 9:5-6

The next layer inserts a hymnic fragment between Amos 9:4 and 9:7.[37] As usual, some keywords and allusions are employed in order to make it obvious to the reader that a new understanding of the fifth vision is intended. Stefen Paas has summed up the allusions between Amos 9:1-4 and v. 5-6: [38]

- The earthen and heavenly temple stand in opposition.
- The striking of the כפתור paralleling the touching of the earth.
- The power of YHWH extends in all dimensions of the cosmos.
- The shaking of the threshold corresponds to מוג (staggering) of the earth.
- God controls the water, sea (Amos 9:3,6).
- Both use the tripartite model of the cosmos: heaven, earth, sea.

In addition, Paas shows that at least some elements fit well in a chiastic structure comprising all of the verses Amos 9:1-6.[39]

The insertion of the hymnic fragment expresses a new understanding of the fifth vision. As in the earlier layers, here also there is an allusion to the shaking of the thresholds. God touches the earth, with the consequence that the earth staggers (מוג). But now the shaking of the temple is seen as part of a cosmic action of YHWH himself. The action is no longer aimed specifically at Israel, but at "all inhabitants of the earth." In addition, the action of YHWH is compared to the rising and falling of the Nile. This leads one to ask whether YHWH's action is seen as a recurring phenomenon. At least one can be sure that after this particular period of ruin a period of restitution will follow.

Most importantly, the hymnic fragment contrasts what happens in the heavenly temple with what happens on earth. Whatever the exact concept of this heavenly dwelling place is, it is safe to say that YHWH is perceived as residing at a place in a different dimension of the cosmic building.[40] When-

---

[37] So also Wolff, *Dodekapropheton 2: Joel und Amos*, 393.

[38] Stefan Paas, "Seeing and Singing: Visions and Hymns in the Book of Amos," *VT* 52 (2002) 253-274, esp. 260.

[39] The allusions to the following passage are not so significant. Egypt, however, is mentioned in Amos 9:5 and 7, and על פני הארץ in Amos 9:6 alludes to על פני האדמה in 9:8. The destruction of the sinful kingdom is paralleled with the pouring out of the waters on the earth.

[40] The meaning of the building parts mentioned in Amos 9:6 is difficult to determine. A scribal error may even have been involved. The most intriguing interpretation is that given by Hartenstein ("Wolkendunkel und Himmelsfeste," 152-166). Following him, one can assume that the D-Redactors used concepts rooted in the self understanding of the sanctuary at Bethel to correct the concept of the temple in Jerusalem.

ever YHWH touches the earth, it staggers. The heavenly waters are poured out, but heaven itself is not affected by those destructive actions. God does not need a special location on earth in order to communicate with human beings. The downfall of mediating institutions between God's own sphere and the earth, of whatever kind, calls into question neither God's universal power nor God's accessibility. The hymnic recitation of God's name expresses astonishment and distance, but at the same time dependability and devotion. God's awe-inspiring transcendence is inconceivable from an earthly perspective. Belief in God's identity expressed in God's name and titles enables the reader to accept even destructive actions of cosmic proportions.

This portrayal of strict opposition between God and an earthly temple that can be eliminated by God without serious consequences for the communication between humans and God can best be understood as an answer to the question: How can YHWH possibly eliminate his *own* sanctuary? This opposition stands in sharp contrast with the D-Layer. To the redactors that added the hymn fragment, the temple of the fifth vision was not a dwelling place of YHWH, but one of the Northern high places where the people served other gods. If the hymn fragment recognized in the temple of the fifth vision YHWH's own sanctuary, that temple had to be the temple in Jerusalem. From there one may proceed to ask, then, whether for this layer there was a clear distinction between Northern Israel and Judah anymore.

Continuing further, this redaction must be seen in the wider context of Amos and the Nahum-Habakkuk-Corpus. Within Amos the hymnic fragment belongs to the same layer as the other fragments (Amos 4:13, 5:8, and 8:8). Together they implement a new cosmic framework that surfaces not only in Amos, but also in Hos 4:3, Hos 12:6, Mic 1:3-4, Zeph 1:2-3, and in a very elaborated way in the hymns in Nah 1:2-8 and Habakkuk 3. The prophetic message is no longer confined to the relation of YHWH and Israel. Instead YHWH is seen as the creator, ruler and sustainer of the whole cosmos. As such he is concerned with all forms of disturbances of the cosmic order. Among these disturbances one has to reckon the transgressions of Israel, but also the cruel imperialism of Nineveh (cf. Nahum) and Babylon (cf. Habakkuk). Similar accusations could be launched against Israel and

---

They picked up the concept of a heavenly dwelling place, but in contrast to Bethel, where it was believed that the heavenly place of God needed a firm connection to a specific holy place on earth (compare the "ladder" in Gen 28:12), the D-Redactors could imagine God without a fixed communication channel with an earthly basis. A praying person could get in contact with YHWH by invoking his name. In fact the process of reading the writing of Amos after the insertion of the hymnic fragments will eventually lead to places where YHWH's name and titles are invoked (Amos 3:13; 4:13; 5:8; 5:14,15,16; 5:27; 6:14; 9:5-6).

against foreign nations. Impressive is that the woe oracles, which Amos
(5:18; 6:1) and Micah (2:1) direct against Israel, are picked up by Nahum
(3:1) and Habakkuk (2:6,9,12,15,19) but they address foreign nations that
suppress Israel. Sometimes there are even verbal parallels (יום צרה) in Nah
1:7, Hab 3:16, and Zeph 1:15; "to build a city with blood" in Mic 3:10 and
Nah 2:12; "Woe to the city" Nah 3:1 and Zeph 3:1).

In sum, according to this layer the fifth vision occurs in Jerusalem. It
depicts YHWH, who had left his place in the holiest part of the temple
building, where he sat on his throne over the Ark of the Covenant, now
standing upon the central altar in the yard. From there YHWH, with the
help of the prophet, sets off a shockwave of destruction, before he retreats
to his heavenly temple. As a result, the whole earth staggers. However, reciting YHWH's name will help to end this period of frightening distance
from God. Then a new period will begin with the judgment of the nations
that so forcefully conquered Israel and Judah: the Assyrians (as spelled out
in Nahum) and the Babylonians (as elaborated in Habakkuk).

E. The Restitution Layer, Amos 9:11-15*

The next revision of the writing of Amos is no longer interested in the elimination of the temple, but elaborates on what will happen afterwards. In
contrast to the vision of downfall, the redactors added Amos 9:11-15* as
new ending.[41] With the well-known phrase "on that day" the passage portrays a future, in which the "fallen booth of David" will be rebuilt.[42] The
phrase "booth of David" introduces a metaphor not known elsewhere in the
OT. It is difficult to determine precisely what the redactor had in mind. It
was certainly his intention to introduce a new entity, which was to be identified neither with the "sinful kingdom" nor with the "house of Jacob" (both
in Amos 9:8) nor even with the temple of Amos 9:1. It would fit well within
the context if the "booth of David" were taken to refer to a small version of
the Davidic dynasty ("house of David"). Then the future would not bring a
restoration of the old glorious kingdom, but a modest version of political
independence.[43] However, assuming that the metaphor of rebuilding is con-

---

[41] The text in Amos 9:12a and 9:13 (without the introductory formula) was added later;
see James Nogalski, *Literary Precursors to the Book of the Twelve* (BZAW 217; Berlin, New York: de Gruyter, 1993) 108-110.

[42] The different suffixes in this passage are very difficult, because their referent is not
clear. The Septuagint has only 3. pers. sg. fem. pronouns, which refer to the "booth of
David." That is what one would expect. The MT is either due to scribal error or the
changing of referents. See James D. Nogalski, "The Problematic Suffixes of Amos IX
11," *VT* 93 (1993) 411-418.

[43] This is the interpretation of Jeremias, *Amos*, 134.

nected to the immediate context, one may see an allusion to the temple in Amos 9:1. The redactor would have understood the blow against the building to cause its destruction; however some ruins would remain. Whereas the downfall of the old temple initiated a shockwave of death, the erection of the "booth of David" is accompanied with prospering life and secure existence in the land. Whereas in Amos 8:2 the "end for my people Israel" was announced, in the new era YHWH will restore the covenant relation (Amos 9:14 "my people Israel"; Amos 9:15 "your God").

This concept fits well with Haggai and Zechariah, who proclaimed that the punishment of Israel was finished, that the temple lying in ruins (Hag 1:4, 9) will be rebuilt, albeit not in its former glory (Hag 2:3), and that YHWH will bring a new period of covenant relationship (e.g. Hag 2:5) and well being (e.g. Hag 2:18-19). Writings under their names were added to the Nahum-Habbakuk-Corpus, yielding what I call the Haggai-Zechariah-Corpus.[44] Within this corpus the vision cycle in Zech 1-6 forms a counterpart to the vision cycle of Amos. In five visions Amos saw the destruction of Israel coming, but in eight visions Zechariah sees the restitution of Israel and its glorious future. Certainly there are many differences between the two cycles, since they derive from different times and authors. However, as vision cycles they stand out from the rest of the prophetic words in the HZ-Corpus. In addition, there are some allusions from the later cycle to the former. Allusions to the fifth vision of Amos are found, for example, in the first vision of Zechariah (רָאִיתִי [I have seen] in Zech 1:8 // Amos 9:1; לְרָעָה [for evil] Zech 1:15 // Amos 9:4b[45]). Admittedly, the allusions are not very significant, but the over-arching composition of the book as a whole demonstrates that YHWH destroyed the first temple, and in the Persian Period reestablished it in Jerusalem. The prophecies of doom do not apply any longer to Israel. Instead, Zechariah expresses the distinct feeling that the period of the "former prophets" (Zech 1:4; 7:7) has come to an end and a new era of prophecy has begun. Now it is the primary goal of the prophet to offer comfort (Zech 1:17).

In sum, this layer perceived the fifth vision as the announcement of the Babylonian destruction of the temple in Jerusalem. However, the shaking of the thresholds did not result in a total elimination of the sanctuary, but only in a period during which the building stood in ruins. Amos 9:11-15* and the visions of Zechariah demonstrate that now a new era had begun, in which the temple would be rebuilt as well as the community around it.

---

44   Schart, *Entstehung*, 252-260.
45   Holger Delkurt, *Sacharjas Nachtgesichte. Zur Aufnahme und Abwandlung prophetischer Traditionen* (BZAW 302; Berlin / New York: de Gruyter, 2000) 81.

F. The Eschatological Layer, Amos 9:12a,13

Once again a redactor added a new ending to Amos (9:12-13*), alluding to the shaking of the thresholds by employing another image in which the hills loose their stability so that they "flow" (מוג, cf. Amos 9:13).[46] The staggering of the earth, which in Amos 9:1,5 is perceived as a frightening loss of stability, is now envisioned as sign for overwhelming fertility. A restitution of Israel in its land must be part of a fundamental transformation of nature. Otherwise it would not address the deepest sources of Israel's sin. In addition, Amos 9:12a expresses the idea that all the nations "over whom YHWHs name is called" must be come under the control of Israel. This is especially so for Edom, who is viewed as the ultimate enemy of God's people. The scale of this transformation is of such a character that it supersedes everything that could be realized within the course of history. Instead it envisions only the end of history to bring the solution to the deepest problems of Israel within its world. Therefore it may be labeled an eschatological understanding of the restitution of Israel.

This redaction is very closely related to Joel and Obadiah. Amos 9:13b is an almost verbatim citation of Joel 4:18. Both passages now form a kind of frame around the writing of Amos. Further, as Nogalski has noticed, "Amos 9,12a contains the essential elements of the message of Obadiah."[47] Joel and Obadiah are very closely connected in verbal and thematic aspects. Most of the verbal agreements are clustered around the concept of the "Day of the Lord" ("near is the day of the Lord," Joel 4:14 and Obad 1:15).[48] The redactors want the reader to perceive Amos within this hermeneutical frame. Reading the fifth vision from this point of view, the temple in Amos 9:1 cannot be identified with the one on Zion, because the Zion temple is unconquerable. In contrast, Joel 3:5 and Obad 1:17 clearly state that Zion will be the only place where one can safely escape destruction. This redaction must therefore interpret Amos 9:1-4 as the destruction of Bethel, which probably is understood as an example for all places where the name of YHWH is not called (compare Joel 3:5). Whereas the former layer of Amos 9:1-4 saw the vision of Amos fulfilled when the Babylonians conquered Jerusalem, the Joel-Layer views it as something what will happen when the day of the Lord comes. As Joel 4 spells out, the "day of the Lord" will bring

---

[46] To be sure, the redactor's allusion works by way of Amos 9:5, where the word מוג is used. A nice, almost humorous allusion contains the phrase דרך ענוים, which is found also in Amos 2:7 with only one consonant difference.

[47] Nogalski, *Literary Precursors,* 113; cf. the close thematic parallel to Obad 17-19 with "house of Jacob" in Obad 17-18 and Amos 9:8.

[48] See Schart, *Entstehung,* 272-274.

about a final battle, in which the evil forces of the world will invade and devour the land. Only at the last moment, when they gather in the valley Jehoshaphat in order to conquer Zion, will God defeat them forever. As the command in Joel 4:13 suggests, the people of God will be involved in this final battle, although the commands are highly metaphorical. This last battle is also depicted as a gigantic earthquake, which shakes "heaven and earth" (Joel 4:16 uses the same verb רעש as Amos 9:1).

In sum, from the standpoint of the Joel-Obadiah-Corpus, which is essentially informed by the dramatic events of Joel 4, Amos sees in his fifth vision YHWH, who has come on his day from Zion to fight the final battle against the evil forces of the nations. Since only Zion is the dwelling place of YHWH, all other sanctuaries and the people who seek refuge there will not escape destruction. Although it is God's irresistible voice that will cause the final shattering of heaven and earth (Joel 4:16), the people of God are called to take part in the last battle (Joel 4:13). The command to Amos to strike the top of the column then has to be seen as an example of how humans can be involved in God's final punishment. After this battle, however, those who have found refuge on Zion, together with the rest of nations (Amos 9:12) that have not taken part in the campaign against Zion, will live in peace within a nature that opens up abundant resources to human labor (Amos 9:13).

II. The Septuagint Version of Amos 9

The oldest Greek translation, the Septuagint, brought a new understanding of the fifth vision. Inevitably, every translation looses some semantic and structural elements that cannot be represented in the new language system. In addition, the translator of the Septuagint apparently had a poorly transmitted Hebrew Vorlage before him. Most significant for this paper, however, are *deliberate* changes in meaning made during translation. Those modifications can be classified as redactional activities. To be sure, in most cases it is impossible to decide whether a different sense of a Greek passage goes back to a Hebrew Vorlage different from MT, was incorporated within the process of translating, or was inserted within the transmission history of the Greek text. For the purpose of this paper I will concentrate on the verses Amos 9:1 and 9:11-12.

As is typical for the Septuagint of Amos, we find in Amos 9:1 a very literal translation, following closely the word order of the Vorlage, which almost certainly was identical with the MT.[49]

---

[49]   There is only one difficult case: בצעם. There is a good chance that the Vorlage did not contain the 3rd m. pl. suffix, since it is not represented in the Greek translation,

ראיתי את־אדני

נצב על־המזבח

ויאמר הך הכפתור

וירעשו הספים

ובצעם בראש כלם

ואחריתם בחרב אהרג

לא־ינוס להם נס

ולא־ימלט להם פליט

Ειδον τον κυριον
Εφεστωτα επι του θυσιαστηριου
και ειπεν Παταξον επι το
ιλαστηριον
και σεισθησονται τα προπυλα
και διακοψον εις κεφαλας παντων
και τους καταλοιπους αυτων
εν ρομφαια αποκτενω
ου μη διαφυγη εξ αυτων φευγων
και ου μη διασωθη εξ αυτων
ανασωζομενος.

In two cases, however, equivalents for Hebrew words are chosen, which imply a deliberate new meaning. First, כפתור (top of column) is translated as ἱλαστήριον (mercy seat). The translator probably intended to correct a scribal error. Since the Hebrew, probably written defectively as כפתר, was known to the translator as a geographical name (see Amos 9:7 where the word כפתור is translated as Cappadocia), he switched the last two letters of the word, which yielded the word כפרת (mercy seat).[50] Second, ספים (thresholds) was translated as προπυλον (porch). The translator probably had difficulty imagining the scene: how could it be that the pieces of the thresholds, which were located on the floor, hit people on the head? Therefore the translator inferred that here סף must have a technical meaning, denoting an architectural part of the temple building above their heads. Both cases indicate that the translator identified the temple of the fifth vision with that of Jerusalem. It was there where the mercy seat, which was built at Sinai, was brought, and it was there where the mercy seat in post-exilic time was of most importance for the ritual on Yom Kippur. In addition, a προ–πυλον was located in front of the temple building in Jerusalem. In Zeph 1:9 the translator used the lexem again, only this time it clearly referred to the

---

which otherwise represents every morpheme. It is sad, however, that at this point the LXX does not help to recover the original text, which must have meant something like "(And) I will smash the heads."

50   As many examples show, the Vorlage of the Septuagint was written much more defectively than the MT; e. g., כפתור was written כפתר. Cf. Emanuel Tov, *The Text-critical Use of the Septuagint in Biblical Research* (2d rev. and enlarged ed.; Jerusalem Biblical Studies 8; Jerusalem: Simor, 1997) 144-146.

temple in Jerusalem.[51] The destruction of this temple was, according to the Septuagint, specifically aimed at ending cultic propitiation, for which the ἱλαστήριον was used.[52]

In Amos 9:11-12 also there are two intentional modifications. In the first colon of Amos 9:12 the Septuagint changed יִירְשׁוּ (they will possess) to יִדְרְשׁוּ (they will seek) and vocalized אָדָם (human being, humankind) instead of אֱדוֹם (Edom).[53] Due to the first change, the subject of the sentence had to be modified, yielding a totally new understanding of Amos 9:12: "the 'rest of human beings' will seek…." The object of the seeking process is not explicitly mentioned because the literal style of translating did not allow inserting a word for clarification. The translator had in mind as the object either the "tent of David" or "YHWH," based on passages like Hos 3:5; Joel 2:32 (MT 3:5), and Zech 8:22.[54]

Unfortunately, it is very difficult to determine how the Septuagint understood the phrase "booth of David." The first point to be made is that σκηνή (tent, booth) has a wider meaning than the Hebrew סֻכָּה (booth). It also is used as the equivalent for the Hebrew אֹהֶל (tent) and sometimes מִשְׁכָּן (dwelling place). It is especially relevant that the first sanctuary for YHWH, which Israel built at Sinai, is a σκηνή (Exod 25:9; 26:1). In Chronicles (1 Chron 15:1; 16:1; 2 Chron 1:4) this tent was seen as a precursor to the Jerusalem temple. It was David's task to erect this tent within Jerusalem before Solomon built the temple. In some psalms the building itself is metaphorically described as a tent (σκηνή; Ps 26:6 = MT 27:6; 28:1 = MT 29:1; 30:21 = MT 31:21; 41:5 = MT 42:5). The exact phrase "booth (σκηνή) of David," however, occurs again only once more, in Isa 16:5 where it translates אֹהֶל דָּוִד. The passage there envisions an eschatological

---

[51] Although it was sometimes doubted, the hypothesis is nowadays generally accepted that the Book of the Twelve was translated by only one translator. The consistent use of προπύλον, which is not attested elsewhere in the Septuagint, may serve as an additional support.

[52] For the translation of כַּפֹּרֶת and the meaning of ἱλαστήριον, see Klaus Koch, "Some Considerations on the Translation of kapporet in the Septuagint," in *Pomegranates and Golden Bells* (ed. David P. Wright, David Noel Freedman, and Avi Hurvitz; Winona Lake, IN: Eisenbrauns, 1995) 65-75.

[53] In the first case, the very common interchange between Resch and Dalet established a difference between the Septuagint and MT. In the case of Edom, the Septuagint-Vorlage may have been written defectively so that there would be only a difference of vocalization between LXX and MT.

[54] Only later, presumably by early Christian scribes, "TON KYRION" was added as an object. This object was probably inferred by comparing passages with a similar theme, e.g. Hos 3:5; Joel 3:3; Zech 8:22.

ruler sitting on a throne within the "booth of David" striving intensely for truth and righteousness. As in Amos 9:11-12, this is the time when harmony between God's people and a foreign nation is established. So, on the one hand it is very probable, that the "booth (σκηνη) of David" in the Septuagint was viewed as a sanctuary in continuity with the temple of Jerusalem. On the other hand, the "booth of David" is the place where an unspecified future judge will enforce truth and justice, even between nations. If one is allowed to combine these two aspects, it would follow that the Septuagint perceived the "tent of David" as an eschatological equivalent to the Sinai tabernacle and the Jerusalem temple, providing a place where an unspecified eschatological figure will enforce God's justice.

In sum, from the point of view of the Septuagint the fifth vision foresees the destruction of the temple in Jerusalem, which is especially perceived as the place where the propitiation of YHWH takes place. In the end time, the ruins will be rebuilt to form a new religious center where an eschatological figure will judge (Isa 16:5). As a consequence, the "rest of human beings" will seek the "booth of David," especially the judge residing in it. Whether cultic activities or propitiation rites will be performed again is not mentioned.[55] This will have consequences not only for Israel but for all nations.

III. The Christian Redaction of Amos 9

A Christian redaction critic is not finished with the task of reconstructing the literary growth of the text until the context of the Christian Bible is reached. Christian redactors inaugurated a new understanding of the Greek canon of Jewish Scriptures by renaming it the "Old Testament" and attaching to it a collection of writings they called the New Testament. Even if the redactors had not changed a single letter of the Jewish Septuagint, they would have created a new sense of it through this redactional activity.[56] However, the Christian redactors made additional modifications in order to guide the reader towards a new understanding of Israel's scriptures.[57] Again I will focus on the opposition between Amos 9:1 and Amos 9:11-12, because in this case we have an explicit quotation in Acts 15, which allows us

---

[55] A reader of the whole Septuagint collection may speculate whether propitiation outside the temple cult through the death of the martyrs still remained a possibility (4 Macc 17:22).

[56] As we have seen so far, adding new closing sections to an existing text corpus was an established redactional method already within the growth of the writing of Amos.

[57] See David Trobisch, Die Endredaktion des Neuen Testaments: Eine Untersuchung zur Entstehung der christlichen Bibel (NTOA 31; Freiburg (Schweiz) / Göttingen: Universitätsverlag / Vandenhoeck & Ruprecht, 1996).

to elaborate the understanding of the Amos passage within the Christian Bible. I will confine myself to a few main points.

First of all, Christian scribes employed a special scribal technique to write the so-called *nomina sacra*. Throughout the Christian Bible a set of words the referents of which are closely related with the Trinitarian God (e.g. Kyrios, Jesus, Christ, the Spirit, David) are written in contracted form together with a horizontal line above.[58] This is probably meant as a signal to the reader that the three persons of the Trinitarian God are identical with YHWH, the God of Israel, his messiah and his spirit. It is the task of the reader to establish how precisely this identity can be conceived in every passage. One can safely assume that in cases where the New Testament quotes the Old Testament the reader has to use the NT understanding as starting point.

Amos 9:11-12	Acts 15:16-18
(11) Εν τη ημερα εκεινη Αναστησω	(16) Μετα ταυτα αναστρεψω και ανοικοδμησω
Την σκηνην ΔΑΔ την πεπτωκυιαν Και ανοικοδομησω Τα πεπτωκοτα αυτης Και τα κατεσκαμμενα αυτης αναστησω Και ανοικοδομησω αυτην Καθως αι ημεραι του αιωνος	Την σκηνην ΔΑΔ πεπτωκυια και τα κατεσκαμμενα αυτης ανοικοδομησω και ανορθωσω αυτην
(12) οπως αν εκζητησωσιν οι καταλοιποι των ανθρωπων Τον ΚΝ Αλεχανδρινυσ Και παντα τα εθνη εφ ους επικεκληται το ονομα μου επ αυτους Λεγει ΚΣ ο ποιων ταυτα	(17) οπως αν εκζητησωσιν οι καταλοιποι των ανθρωπων τον ΚΝ και παντα τα εθνη Εφ ους επικεκληται το ονομα μου Επ αυτους λεγει ΚΣ ποιων ταυτα (18) γνωστα απ αιωνος

---

[58]   See Colin Henderson Roberts, "Nomina Sacra: Origins and Significance," in *Manuscript, Society and Belief in Early Christian Egypt* (London: Oxford University Press, 1979) 26-48; Larry W. Hurtado, "The Origin of the Nomina Sacra: A Proposal," *JBL* 117 (1998) 655-673. In this paper it is not important to differentiate between the different stages of the development of the set of nomina sacra. By the time of the great Bible codices Alexandrinus, Vaticanus, and Sinaiticus the third level of development was universally in use.

Second, when one compares Acts 15:16-18 with Amos 9:11-12, it becomes obvious that the NT quotation differs significantly from the Septuagint text.[59] Some variants are probably due to the fact that the author of Acts
used for Amos 9:11 some other text tradition, presumably from a testimonia
collection, in which Amos 5:25-27 also was included.[60] The redactors of the
Christian Bible, although they included the Septuagint version of Amos in
their Old Testament, did not harmonize the passage in Amos with its quotation in Acts, therefore admitting a tension between Amos' original vision
and James' presentation of it at the summit meeting in Jerusalem.[61]

Let us consider the deliberate modifications.[62] First, Acts changed the
opening formula. Instead of "on that day," Acts 15:16 states that the predicted things will happen "when God returns after these things." Unfortunately, it is not clear to what "these things" refers. The natural explanation
would be that it is assumed the hearer of the quotation is familiar with the
original context of the quotation and therefore knows that what Amos had
predicted will happen before the booth of David will be rebuilt, namely the
destruction of the Jerusalem temple and the survival of "the rest" called the
"house of Jacob." Indeed, the author of Acts seems to have used many aspects of Amos, especially of chapter 9, to describe the *heilsgeschichtliche*
situation of the new Christian community. Stephan is accused of preaching
that Jesus would destroy the temple (Acts 6:14). By implication, the fifth
vision is reapplied and now directed against the Herodian temple in Jerusalem!

Two reasons are given as to why this will happen. First, according to
Stephan other gods are worshiped in the official cult of Israel from the

---

[59] For careful comparisons see Sabine Nägele, *Laubhütte Davids und Wolkensohn: Eine
auslegungsgeschichtliche Studie zu Amos 9:11 in der jüdischen und christlichen Exegese* (AGJU 24; Leiden, et al.: Brill, 1995). Significant differences in comparison to
the LXX and mixed quotations ("Mischziatate") are typical for the early Christian use
of scriptures (see Ernst Dassmann, "Umfang, Kriterien und Methoden frühchristlicher
Prophetenexegese," *Jahrbuch für biblische Theologie* 14 (1999) 117-143, esp. 123-
124). On the one hand the Christian communities had neither the money nor the social
standing to have access to the official manuscripts. On the other hand they were not
interested in accurate wording, but in the sense of the scriptures.

[60] See Martin Stowasser, "Am 5,25-27; 9,11f. in der Qumranüberlieferung und in der
Apostelgeschichte: Text- und traditionsgeschichtliche Überlegungen zu 4Q174 (Florilegium) III 12/CD VII 16/Apg 7,42b-43; 15,16-18," *ZNW* 92 (2001) 47-63. He has
shown that Amos 5:25-27 belonged to the same testimonia collection that contained
Amos 9:11.

[61] The Codex Alexandrinus, however, has adopted the variant τον κυριον from Acts and
inserted it into Amos 9:12. See Wilhelm Rudolph, *Joel, Amos, Obadja, Jona* (KAT
13,2; Gütersloh: Mohn, 1971), esp. 279.

[62] For the purpose of this paper we do not need to differentiate between variants made in
the testimonia collection and those made by the author of Acts.

time in the desert on (Acts 7:40-43). In this case the cult critique of Amos is adopted with the quotation of Amos 5:25-27. Second, the temple in Jerusalem *never* was a legitimate place for worship, since God does not inhabit a building made by human hands (Acts 7:48). Although there is no clear allusion to it, the hymnic passage in Amos 9:6 probably was read as referring to a heavenly sanctuary of God not made by human hands.

Another deliberate change seems to be the elimination of the phrase "according to the former times" from Amos 9:11. This may be explained with the assumption that the author of Acts did not want to stress the continuity between the New and the Old. The tent of David will have a new quality, although this newness is "known from old."

A further deliberate change is that the seeking process of the "human beings who remain" is perceived as being aimed towards "the Lord." The "Lord" may be YHWH. In this case, the author of Acts may have inferred from passages like Hos 3:5, Joel 2:32 (MT 3:5), and especially Zech 8:22 that the object of the seeking must be God. However, from the point of view of the redactors of the Christian Bible the "Lord" may also be Jesus Christ! This is obvious, for example, in Rom 10:13, where the citation of Joel 2:32 (MT 3:5) is understood in this way. It is clear from Rom 10:9 that "the Lord" is identified with Jesus. It is noteworthy that Paul states in this passage from Romans that there is no difference between Jews and Greeks "because they have the same Lord" (Rom 10:12). This is also what the James of Acts wanted to show (Acts 15:19) according to the redactors of the Christian Bible.

Turning now to the implicit adaptations of Amos 9:11-12, one may ask first how the redactors of the Christian Bible perceived the term "booth of David." In this case it is unambiguously clear that they identified David with Jesus Christ, because "David" is written as a nomen sacrum.[63] The background for this identification is that Jesus was seen as the true "son of David" (Lk 1:27; Rom 1:3). In addition, the body of the risen Christ could be metaphorically described as a new temple, which will replace the old destroyed one after three days.[64] The rebuilding of the "booth of David" was therefore viewed as the resurrection of Christ.

The last implicit modification of meaning I want to mention is the new understanding of the phrase "over whom my name is called" in Amos 9:12.

---

[63] To be sure, "David" belongs to the nomina, which were applied only late in the transmission process of the Bible. Within the great codices Alexandrinus, Vaticanus, and Sinaiticus, which attest the phenomenon of the Christian Bible in extant manuscripts, "David" is already among the nomina sacra.

[64] Act 6:14 alludes to this concept; see also Mk 14:58; 15:29; Mt 26:61; 27:40; Joh 2:19-22.

According to the redactors of the Christian Bible this must refer to the Christian mission, including specifically the act of baptism (see Acts 2:38; 19:5; Jas 2:7).[65] Through the Christian mission the gentiles receive the status as God's people (λαός, Acts 15:14) without being obliged to observe the Mosaic Law in full. It is sufficient to practice a very limited set of stipulations, which were laid down in the letter to Antioch.

In sum, according to the Christian redactors Amos foresaw in his fifth vision the destruction of the Jerusalem temple by the Romans. This destruction was seen as punishment for worshipping other gods. In addition, it was seen as the necessary precondition to erecting the sanctuary that will truly be a dwelling place for God, namely the "booth of David." This is what David had prayed for, but did not receive (Acts 7:46). This eschatological "booth" will not be made by human hands like the old temple, and, although this is not stated explicitly but may be inferred, does not need a "mercy seat" anymore. The metaphor "booth of David" refers to the body of the risen Jesus Christ, the true son of David.[66] Whoever responds in belief to the Christian mission will be included in the eschatological community out of Jews and gentiles. In the time when the author of Acts wrote, the process of realization of this end time prediction was impressively and irresistibly on the way.[67]

IV. Conclusion

In this article I have tried to show that the original sense of the oldest literary layer of the fifth vision only existed for a couple of years. The claim to go back to a direct visible encounter with YHWH's real presence, something that even prophets did not experience in every generation, the challenging images, together with the paucity of details, albeit important ones, served as a source for new inspiration in comparable situations. Since the claim of a direct encounter with God was proven valid in the course of history, many generations tried to find their own situation in the sparse wording and meager imagery of this vision report. As a result, generations of redactors elaborated their own experience with God in close connection to the

---

[65] Jostein Ådna, "James' position at the summit meeting of the apostles and the elders in Jerusalem (Acts 15)," in *The Mission of the Early Church to Jews and Gentiles* (ed. Jostein Ådna and Hans Kvalbein; WUNT 127; Tübingen: Mohr-Siebeck, 2000) 125-161, p.148. A good example how "calling God's name upon someone" can work is given in Acts 3:6-7 (cf. Acts 19:18).

[66] According to Paul every believer is part of the body of the risen Christ (1 Cor 12:27).

[67] The Hebrew text of the fifth vision was extraordinary faithfully transmitted by the Masoretes. Nevertheless some changes were made by the way of vocalization. The Masoretes, therefore, may not be classified as redactors.

famous predecessor. From early on this vision was perceived under the impression of other prophetic texts. Some of them were included within a growing Multi-Prophets-Book, thereby providing a new context out of which the sense of the fifth vision must be construed anew by the reader. Every stage of this redaction history and its version of the Multi-Prophets-Book deserves full attention. However, the redaction critic must not stop reconstructing this process at the end of the writing of Amos, or the Book of the Twelve, or the corpus propheticum, but has to reach the final canonical shape. This final stage is different for Jews and Christians. For both, however, the fifth vision helped readers imagine that God can destroy God's own temple. For the Christians any holy place and any cult became obsolete after the risen Christ had shown an alternative way to God the father. The new community out of Jews and gentiles, for whom the temple is employed as metaphor, will replace the temple, and their spiritual worship (Rom 12:1) will substitute for the temple cult. For Jews and Christians the fifth vision could serve as a reminder that God is greater than any manifestation God established in history. Both should be jointly on the way to the eschatological encounter with God face to face (1 Cor 13:12).

Appendix 1: The Growing Context for the Fifth Vision of Amos

1. Oldest literary layer: Amos 9:1-4a*
Book context, writing of Amos: Amos 1:1*; Amos 1:3-9:4a*

2. Tradition bearers layer: Amos 8:14 and 9:4b
Book context, Two-Prophets-Book: Hos 1:2-14:1*; Amos 1:1*; 1:3-9:4*

3. The D-Layer: Amos 9:7-10
Book context, D-Corpus: Hos*; Amos 1:1-9:10*; Mic*; Zeph*

4. The layer of the hymnic fragment, Amos 9:5-6
Book context, Nahum-Habakkuk-Corpus: Hos*; Amos 1:1-9:10*; Mic*; Nah*; Hab*; Zeph*

5. The restitution layer, Amos 9:11-15*
Book context, Haggai-Zechariah-Corpus: Hos*; Amos 1:1-9:15*; Mic*; Nah*; Hab*; Zeph*; Hag*; Zech*

6. The eschatological layer, Amos 9:12a,13
Book context, Joel-Obadiah-Corpus: Hos; Joel; Amos 1:1-9:15; Obad; Mic; Nah; Hab; Zeph*; Hag; Zech

7. The Septuagint version of Amos 9
Book context, Jewish collection of authoritative Greek books

8. The Christian redaction of Amos 9
Book context, Christian Bible comprising Old and New Testament.

Appendix 2: A Rough Sketch of the Temple Presupposed in Amos' Fifth Vision

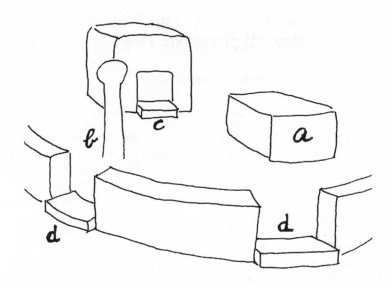

a: central altar, located in the yard, on which a person can stand
b: column in the yard; the word כפתור may refer to the top of it
c: threshold at the door of the temple building
d: thresholds in the outer wall of the temple precinct

Psalms in the Book of the Twelve:
How Misplaced Are They?

Erhard S. Gerstenberger

I. Paradigm Switches within the Study of the Hebrew Scriptures

Like other layers of the Old Testament tradition, the prophetic writings in the Hebrew Scriptures are undergoing new investigations because the modern exegete's style of living, thinking, and questioning has dramatically changed over the past decades.[1] Alterations in the reader's perspective and living conditions, according to any self-critical hermeneutical theory, necessarily result in fresh reconstructions of our own concepts of past history and theology. The Hebrew canon of three "large" and twelve "minor" prophets, being an important part of the *TaNaK* (Torah; Nebiim; Ketubim) consequently needs to be scrutinized almost from scratch in regard to composition, form- and tradition history, the profile of possible authors and transmitters, possible life-situations, and many other points of view. The results of such endeavors are amazing. They confront us with unfamiliar visions of the growth and use of prophetic literature within the social texture of exilic/post-exilic communities in Judah and perhaps other regions. They also reveal a characteristic remolding of prophetic images by later tradition, a result that calls into question our traditional concepts of "classical prophecy."

II. Liturgical Genres within the Prophetic Corpus

As a case in point we focus on the abundance of liturgical genres within the prophetic writings. It seems strange, indeed, that most of the fifteen prophetic books in the Hebrew Bible contain examples of what we may call psalmic genres, be they more on the side of purely "liturgical" and "hymnic" or else of "homiletical"[2] categories of text. Setting aside the latter for

---

[1] To cite but one effort of a fundamental reevaluation of the prophets and prophecy: Ferdinand E. Deist, "The Prophets: Are We Heading for a Paradigm Switch?" BZAW 185 (1989) 1- 18.

[2] Note this truly Protestant distinction between altar and pulpit, so to speak, or between fixed agendaric and more spontaneous parts of worship. Some scholars have already investigated prophetic texts under liturgical and homiletical perspectives; cf. Eberhard

the time being, we notice a wealth of passages which seem to belong to worship agendas, both in the form of unilateral prayers (i. e. prayers oriented from people to God) and of hymns sung in praise of Yahweh, both polyphonic and antiphonic (in a strictly "liturgical" shape), as a proclamation to and response of the community at hand. Thus we find almost full-scale communal complaints in Jer 14:2-14; Isa 63,7 – 64:10; Joel 1 – 2, while e.g. Hos 6:1-3; 14:3-4 apparently are fragments of more extensive collective prayers. The so-called "individual complaints" are at least mirrored in the "Confessions of Jeremiah" (Jer 11:18-22; 12:1-6: 15:10-21; 17:12-18; 18:18-23; 20:7-18). A full individual thanksgiving song is placed into narrative contexts (Isa 38; Jon 2), while a communal variety comes up in the "Isaiah Apocalypse" (Isa 26:1-6). Regular hymns or passages reminiscent of praise show up here and there, sometimes marking the end of collected sayings (cf. Isa 42:10-12; Hab 3; Zeph 3:14-20).[3] All in all, this phenomenon calls for fresh attention and explanation: Have these psalmic elements been placed in the context of prophetic utterances and discourses by mistake? Or imagining the opposite extreme: do the liturgical components constitute the original matrix of communal interaction out of which have grown prophetic sayings and speeches?

III. History of the Research on
Liturgical Components in Prophetic Corpora

The question just posed runs counter, of course, to everything we had been led to believe about prophets and prophetic utterances in biblical contexts. In contrast with anonymous, liturgical beginnings, we traditionally prefer a different anchoring of prophetic speech. One of the firmly entrenched and most influential views of prophetic activity through the 19th and 20th centuries has been that of personal identity and authorship of each individual messenger of God. Bernhard Duhm, for example, based his interpretation of

---

von Waldow, "Anlaß und Hintergrund der Verkündigung des Deuterojesja," (Ph. D. diss., Bonn 1953); Ernest W. Nicholson, *Preaching to the Exiles* (Oxford: Blackwells, 1970); Henning Graf Reventlow, *Liturgie und prophetisches Ich bei Jeremia* (Gütersloh: Gerd Mohn, 1963); William H. Bellinger, *Psalmody and Prophecy* (JSOTSup 27; Sheffield: JSOT Press, 1984). Also, Erhard S. Gerstenberger, "Höre, mein Volk, laß mich reden! (Ps 50,7)," *BK* 56 (2001) 21–25.

[3]   Hermann Gunkel and Joachim Begrich (*Einleitung in die Psalmen* [Göttingen: Vandenhoeck, 1933], 32-33) list a whole sequence of mostly brief prophetical passages classified as "hymns": Isa 6:3; 12:1-2, 3-6; 25:1, 5, 9; 30:18d; 40:12-17, 22-24, 26, 28-29; 41:13; 42:5, 10-12; 43:1, 14, 15, 16-17; 44:2, 6, 23, 24-28; 45:6-7, 11, 15, 18; 46:10-11; 47:4; 48:12, 17, 20; 49:5, 7, 13; 51:15, 22; 52:9-10; 57:15; 61:10-11; 63:7; Jer 2:6; 5:22, 24; 10:6-7, 10, 12-16; 31:7, 35; 33:2; 51:10, 15-16; Joel 2:21, 23; Amos 4:13; 5:8; 9:5-6; Nah 1; Hab 1:12-13; 3:18-19; Zeph 3:14-15; Sach 2:14; 9:9; 12:1.

prophetic writings exclusively on the authenticity of prophetic personality.[4] His lead has been followed by many Old Testament scholars. The historical figures named in superscriptions of prophetic books (and sometimes nowhere else!) were widely considered the authors of at least a nucleus of the respective writings. Disciples may have functioned as secretaries to these "men of God," but all later additions to their authentic "minutes" of divinely inspired kerygma were regarded as inferior or worthless, because they could not possibly match the genius of the prophetic mind and spirit, surpassing, as it were, by far the normal frame of contemporary conscience, experience and ethical standards.

This traditional, personalistic view by and large has been replaced by subsequent research with its changing hermeneutical parameters. One important moment in the shift certainly was the discovery of form criticism by Hermann Gunkel and Sigmund Mowinckel. The authors of biblical texts, especially of individual psalms, recede into the background. Instead, communicative situations are credited with the production of texts serving collective, i.e. communal, ends. Mowinckel in particular emphasized the thoroughly cultic character of the psalms. To his mind, temple servants and cultic singers composed the larger part of the psalms in the service of the temple community, and for collective use in worship.[5]

A second impetus for changing the traditional paradigm came from tradition-historical studies which reevaluated the formative forces shaping and inventing the inherited texts, be they orally transmitted or handed down in written form. Many exegetes today agree that considerably large parts of prophetic books have been molded (composed and_formulated) by transmitters and scribes in a long process of scriptural development. By the same token scholars today recognize that the *image* of prophets and prophecy has been at least partially if not completely formed by later interpretation.[6] Set-

---

[4]   Cf. Bernhard Duhm, *Die Theologie der Propheten als Grundlage für die innere Entwicklungsgeschichte der israelitischen Religion* (Bonn: Marcus 1875); idem, *Israels Propheten* (2nd ed.; Tübingen: J.C.B. Mohr, 1922).

[5]   Cf. Sigmund Mowinckel, *Psalmenstudien III: Kultprophetie und prophetische Psalmen* (Oslo: Kristiania, 1923; repr., Amsterdam: Schippers, 1961). He believed that the Prophets were cultic functionaries, yet theoretically free to communicate the word of God to the congregation using the first person of the deity.

[6]   To give but a few examples: Joseph Blenkinsopp freely admits the creative role of tradition in forming the biblical concepts of prophecy, e.g.: "It will now be apparent that those who edited and transmitted the book of Jeremiah over a period of several centuries, have been at pains to present him as fulfilling the paradigm of the prophetic role in Israel." Idem, *A History of Prophecy in Israel* (2nd ed.; Louisville: Westminster John Knox, 1996), 135; cf. my own epilogue ["Ausblick"] to the German translation entitled *Geschichte der Prophetie in Israel* (Stuttgart: Kohlhammer, 1998), 266–289. The research done by scholars like A. Graeme Auld, Robert P. Carroll, David L. Petersen,

ting aside, therefore, the idea of personal authorship of prophetic sayings, discourses, narratives – which certainly has had and further has its merits at some point – more and more interpreters are discovering the real depth dimensions of the prophetic traditions and the changes which went on through the centuries of Israelite and Judean history. Other parameters are also necessary in tracing this development. The growth of prophetic books and the understanding of their remote, "classical" eponyms cannot be pictured in terms of biographical, personalistic, historical factors, but has to be grasped within the whole context of group processes affecting the community of believers and worshippers that treasured and modulated that sacred heritage.[7]

Taking into account, furthermore, anthropological and sociological research on prophetic phenomena around the world, considering in this light more intensively and less dogmatically biblical evidence itself, we may conclude, that the agents of later communal organization were indeed paramount in forming the prophetic messages as well as the concepts of prophecy in general, as they now are extant in the Scriptures. This means that it has been principally the needs, aspirations, sufferings of the early Jewish community that have brought forth the prophetic books, using, as it were, rather faint memories of "classical" prophecy in Israel. Further, very few, if any, "authentic" words coming from the 8th and 7th centuries B.C.E. have been preserved.

IV. Psalms in the Twelve

Applying these new visions of prophecy to the Book of the Twelve and seeking psalm-like materials within the relevant writings, we will venture a rough purview and evaluation of the 82 printed pages in the Hebrew Bible according to Rudolf Kittel's edition, as well as the 96 pages of the Biblia Hebraica Stuttgartensia, provided by Karl Elliger. There is no claim, however, of being exhaustive at this time.

A. Psalms with an Opening Formula

From the outset it is clear that psalmic passages in the Book of the Twelve do belong to different genres, and they have been placed – if that is what happened to them – into their context in various ways. Some of them are

---

Ernest W. Nicholson, Robert R. Wilson, Ehud Ben Zvi, Bernhard Lang, Karl Friedrich Pohlmann and many others has paved the way for this kind of reassessment.

[7] The literature in regard to biblical prophecy is too extensive to be recited at this point, cf. instead John H. Hayes, "Prophecy and Prophets, Hebrew Bible," *DBI* 2:310–317; Klaus Koch, "Propheten / Prophetie II. In Israel und seiner Umwelt," *TRE* 27, 477 – 499.

highlighted by some kind of opening formula. Jonah 2:2 (RSV v. 1), on account of its context, is a narrative introduction: "Then Jonah prayed to Yahweh, his God, from the belly of the fish." It is followed by the formulaic expression "he said" (cf. Isa 38:9 ["I said"]; 1 Sam 2:1; Exod 15:1; Judg 5:1 etc.). Clearly, this is a case of inserting a narrative (oral or written, literary) psalm,[8] a thanksgiving song, to serve the plot of the story. Regardless of whether there are any liturgical implications in the position of such psalms, each inset text is entirely dependent on the use of the surrounding narrative. There are, in any case, no hints of the participation of worshippers intoning a song like this. The book of Jonah is the only true narrative text among the Twelve. Hence, it may be worthwhile to investigate more fully the rationale of its being there in the midst of so much prophetic proclaiming and preaching.

A second, and quite different, example of formal citation of a psalm is offered by Hab 3:1: "A prayer (תפלה) of the prophet Habakkuk according to *šigyonot* (שגינות)." This phrase is strongly reminiscent of redactional superscriptions, attributing a poem to some traditional singer, like Asaph, Korah, or David. In this case Habakkuk the *nabi'* is named the author or performer of the psalm, two details unknown in the Psalter.[9] The term שגינות, on the other hand, appears in a similar form in the headline of Psalm 7 (שגיון לדוד), while the designation "prayer" is part of five psalmic superscriptions (Pss 17; 86; 90; 102; 142). Furthermore, psalmic annotations do conclude the Habakuk text. The last two words are למנצח בנגינותי ("To the leader, with my stringed instruments"; cf. Pss 4:1; 6:1; 54:1; 55:1; 61:1; 67:1; 76,1). Thus, the psalm in Habakkuk is framed by elements which we know from superscriptions to Psalms. But how do we interpret this fact? Apart from the basic issue of how the superscriptions in the psalms may have worked, we ask: have parts of prophetic books been used in worship contexts, have they acquired a liturgical frame and then been inserted again into the original collection of prophetic sayings? Or has the psalm Habakkuk 3, a kind of theophanic victory song, attracted the discourses of Habakkuk 1 – 2?

From the beginning the liturgical frame featured an author's name, even specifying that the poet was a "prophet." So the psalm may have provided the prophetic identity for the whole book. Be it as it may, modern interpre-

---

[8]   Cf. James W. Watts, *Psalm and Story* (JSOTSup 139; Sheffield: Academic Press, 1992).

[9]   The only occurrences of the name Habakkuk are in Hab 1:1; 3:1. The designation *nabi'* appears three times in the Psalter, but never as an author: Ps 51:2 refers to the prophet Nathan, and Pss 74:9; 105:15 mention prophets of Yahweh in general.

tations vary greatly. Some experts follow the track that later readers of the prophetic writings may have extracted opportune texts, i.e. psalm-like prophetic sayings, from that tradition and remodeled them for use in worship service.[10] The Qumran Psalm tradition may be cited in support of this theory, but any relocation of the amended (liturgized!) version into the prophetic book remains enigmatic. Another hypothesis fully recognizes the liturgical provenance of Habakkuk 3 and makes the author a cultic prophet firmly anchored in the temple institution.[11] If the prophet really had been a liturgical leader of a temple community, then his message as a whole would have featured cultic traits and contents. For some scholars, consequently, the book of Habakkuk reveals a perfectly liturgical structure of prophetic complaint being answered by God. The text of Habakkuk itself this way becomes proof of the much-conjured institution of cult prophecy.[12]

The crux of this theory, however, is that it has to leave behind the conception of the prophets as free-lance divine messengers, so dear to the main stream of relevant research. If prophets are held responsible for cult liturgies in the prophetic writings as well as the Psalter, they hardly can remain spontaneous critics of social, political and religious conditions in Israel. They in fact become cult officials and functionaries. More serious, to my mind, and instrumental to that erroneous interpretation is the fact that this representation of prophecy (although recognizing correctly the liturgical character of some texts) still clings to outmoded views of an objective, author-to-audience relationship with textual creativity belonging to the author-speaker alone. The creative stimulus of communal action, in this case of corporate worship, does not enter into consideration at all. If, on the contrary, scholars would admit diverse forms of free mediation between people and God and perhaps some institutionalized ways of communication with the divine, and if scholars learned to consider all systematizing concepts of prophecy to belong to later periods of Israel's spiritual history, then the diverse phenomena might fall into place.

---

[10] Thus, e.g. Wilhelm Rudolph, Micha, Nahum, Habakuk, Zephanja (KAT XIII,3; Gütersloh: Gerd Mohn, 1975) 239-43.

[11] Cf. e.g. Friedrich Horst and Theodor H. Robinson, *Die Zwölf kleinen Propheten* (HAT I,14: Tübingen: J.C.B. Mohr 1954), 183–186; Jörg Jeremias, *Kultprophetie und Gerichtsverkündigung* (WMANT 35, Neukirchen-Vluyn: Neukirchener Verlag 1970), 85-100.

[12] Besides Jeremias, *Kultprophetie und Gerichtsverkündigung,* 99–100 n. 11, cf. Aubrey R. Johnson, *The Cultic Prophet and Israel's Psalmody* (Cardiff: University of Wales Press, 1979). Erhard S. Gerstenberger, "Psalm 12: Gott hilft den Unterdrückten. Zum Thema Kultprophetie und soziale Gerechtigkeit in Israel," in B. Jendorff und G. Schmalenberg, *Anwalt des Menschen* (Giessen: Fachbereich 07 der Justus Liebig Universität, 1983), 83–104.

The smallest of all prophetic writings within the Twelve is Obadiah, comprising only 21 verses, which partly coincide with Jer 49:9, 14-16. Biblical tradition does qualify these divine "threats against Edom" as typically prophetic utterances, namely, as a "vision" (חֲזוֹן) of the spokesman of Yahweh.[13] Seemingly, therefore, the genre "oracle against foreign nations" does not belong into the liturgical fold. Nevertheless, we may still surmise that such oracles have been used in worship situations as a means of Israel's self defense against foreign domination.[14] Furthermore, communal complaints in the Psalter do incorporate threats and curses against enemy nations and the oppressive rule of foreign powers (cf. Pss 60; 83; 137). Interestingly enough, all three psalms just referred to mention the neighboring rival Edom, besides other nationalities. We have good reason, therefore, to include oracles against foreign nations into the repertoire of liturgical texts. The little book of Obadiah, consequently, constitutes a prime example of agendaric material being placed between (or cut out from) Amos and Jonah, emphasizing salvation for Israel through destruction of Edom. Obadiah gained book status by a special headline, extremely short as it may be (v. 1, the first six Hebrew words). Nevertheless, it seems that the booklet acquired an important liturgical function in the context of the Twelve.

B. Psalms with no Opening Formula

There are, by contrast, psalm-like passages in the Book of the Twelve that stand out without being formally separated from their contexts by formulaic introductions or subscriptions. One example is Joel 1:2 – 2:27.[15] Some

---

[13]　"Vision" as a typical communication to messengers of Yahweh is used widely, especially in exilic/post-exilic prophetic texts; cf. Isa 1:1; Jer 14:14; 23:16; Ezek 7:26; 12:22-27; Hos 12:11; Mic 3:6; Nah 1:1; Hab 2:2-3, and heavily concentrated in Dan 8.

[14]　The genre and Sitz im Leben of these particular "oracles" have not been sufficiently studied so far. Cf. Peter Höffken, "Untersuchungen zu den Begründungselementen der Völkerorakel des Alten Testaments," (diss., Bonn, 1977); Bernhard Gosse, *Isaie 13,1 – 14,23 dans la tradition littéraire du livre d'Isaie et dans la tradition des oracles contre les nations* (OBO 78; Fribourg and Göttingen: University Press and Vandenhoeck, 1988); Joseph Blenkinsopp, *Prophecy in Israel,* 131–132; 175–176 et passim. Scholars in general agree on the exilic/post-exilic dates for the inclusion of these passages into the *corpus propheticum.*

[15]　Other divisions of the book are under discussion, e.g. between Joel 1:2 – 2:17 and 2:18 – 4:21 (Engl. 3:21). Cf. Erich Zenger, *Einleitung in das Alte Testament* (Stuttgart: Kohlhammer, 1995), 381–85. More important is Zenger's evaluation of the booklet as mere "literary prophecy and prophetic interpretation of prophetic writings... probably written to be placed into its present position in the Book of the Twelve" (383). Cf. James D. Nogalski, *Redactional Processes in the Book of the Twelve* (BZAW 218; Berlin: de Gruyter, 1993), 3-57. Determining the literary origin, however, does not solve the question of the Sitz, because literary texts may have been used in worship.

scholars consider this part of the book its authentic nucleus, declaring the subsequent passages as later accretions. The first two chapters of Joel contain elements of communal complaint[16] and responses by Yahweh. Many exegetes regard Joel 1 – 2 a full-fledged worship liturgy motivated by a locust plague or some other public calamity.[17] In fact, most interpreters think of some liturgical provenance for the text. The question remains, however, how such a special genre could possibly enter the prophetic canon to begin with. According to traditional presuppositions the prophet must enter the temple sphere and become a cultic functionary in order to make plausible the existence of a whole cluster of liturgical-agendaric genres in the prophetic collections, presumably consisting of freely communicated messages of Yahweh. The opposite view may be closer to ancient Israel's reality, but still misses the point by a wide margin. It claims that the prophet did not need to enter the cultic realm. Rather, the ideal figure of a communicator of Yahweh's word and will to the early Jewish congregation emerged from cultic practice, because that word had been synthesized right in the midst of the community's anxieties and hopes.

In Joel 1 – 2 we have an agendaric block of material to which, in the course of worship, other liturgical passages (Joel 3 – 4) have been added. (A similar relationship seems to prevail regarding Micah 7 and the preceding chapters of the book). At first glance it appears as if a liturgical block has been placed at the end of a collection of prophetic sayings.[18] For what purpose? Why would the composers of the book choose liturgical forms to conclude a written composition? And why, for that matter, did they occasionally use prayer language when shaping the body of the text (cf. Mic 1:8-16; 4:5; 5:4-5; 5:8; 6:6-8)? Would it not be more reasonable to image the reverse of this procedure, namely that prophetic sayings, in oral or written

---

"The liturgical character of these texts indicates that the prophetic books of which they are a part were read as part of the temple liturgy." Cf. Marvin A. Sweeney, *Isaiah 1–39* (FOTL XVI; Grand Rapids: Eerdmans, 1996) 17.

[16] As to the terms used here for genres – especially "complaint," "lament," "divine response." etc., cf. Erhard S. Gerstenberger, *Psalms, Part I* (FOTL XIV; Grand Rapids: Eerdmans, 1988) esp. 10–14; and *Psalms, Part II* (FOTL XV; Grand Rapids: Eerdmans, 2001) 506–543 (Glossary of genre terms).

[17] Cf. Gösta W. Ahlström, *Joel and the Temple Cult of Jerusalem* (VTSup 21; Leiden: Brill, 1971); Oskar Loretz, *Regenritual und Jahwetag im Joelbuch* (Altenberge: Ugarit Verlag, 1986).

[18] Ever since Hermann Gunkel ("Der Micha – Schluss", *ZK* 2 [1924] 145-178) exposed the liturgical character of this final chapter of Micah, scholars have speculated about the genre and function of these verses (Mic 7:8-20). There is a certain agreement on the basic forms being "agendaric," but many colleagues shun away from calling them "real liturgical texts." They think rather of literary imitations (cf. Rainer Kessler, *Micha* [HTKAT, Freiburg: Herder 1999], 296-312).

transmission, had been drawn into and molded by community services of exiled congregations.[19] Had these Yahwists fashioned prophetic sayings, just as early Christians incorporated and developed the words of Jesus in their texts?

Another example of sorts, again slightly different from the preceding two, is Nah 1:1-11. Clearly, there once was an alphabetical acrostic somewhere within or without the book of Nahum, parts of which have been preserved in Nah 1:2-8. Its lines successively begin, with some errors and omissions, with the letters Aleph to Kaph of the Hebrew alphabet. Equally clear is the fact that the text of an acrostic poem has been severely remodeled, perhaps to fit into the congregational philosophy and the liturgical practice of the ancient assembly. The enemies directly addressed (Nah 2 – 3) will suffer defeat from Yahweh's retaliating onslaught, and implicitly Israel will be liberated from her foes. This in all likelihood is the subject of liturgical celebrations, and the vividness of language and metaphors contributes to create this very impression.[20]

C. Psalms Reacting to Prophetic Speeches

A larger number of psalmic passages have been tightly interwoven with the regular "prophetic" contexts.[21] Apparently, they react to messenger speeches or prophetic denunciations of Judah or Israel. A good example is Hos 6:1-6. The preceding lines (Hos 5:8-14) are a terrible invective against the cities and tribes of northern Israel, conjuring – in military and accusa-

---

[19] Ehud Ben Zvi in his commentary *Micah* (FOTL XXIB; Grand Rapids: Eerdmans, 2000 [3-11; 171-72; 181-82])) emphasizes individual and communitarian reading of the written text. The "bearers" of this communicative office was a "circle of literati ... of high literacy in their society, and who took the role of brokers of the knowledge imparted by the book of Micah..." (181 and often). I do not see a reading culture in ancient Judah as early as the late Persian period. Rather, the texts in their dramatic orientation, preserved in the written sources, testify to authentic liturgical proceedings.

[20] Michael H. Floyd (*Minor Prophets* [FOTL XXII; Grand Rapids: Eerdmans, 2000], 10-20) decidedly rejects the idea of Nahum's being "an extended eschatological hymn" or "a prophetic liturgy," but he faces serious difficulties in explaining the vivid direct address discourse throughout the book as "resembling those [i.e. rhetorical conventions] that are home in some kind of ritual or ceremonial context ..." (12, cf. 15-18). "Although the conventions of direct address used in Nahum are somewhat similar to ones that might also be used in a ritual setting, they neither entail ritual acts nor reflect a cultic tableau" (17). His solution, then, is to locate the literary prophet in groups of scribes and wise men who "wrote books like Nahum to be studied among themselves, and to be used for the instruction of public officials and others ..." (19). For the book of Habakkuk, however, he partially admits cultic use (85, 87; etc.).

[21] Cf. Aaron Schart, *Die Entstehung des Zwölfprophetenbuches* (BZAW 260; Berlin: de Gruyter, 1998).

tory terminology – an enemy invasion. The diatribe culminates in a divine pronouncement of destruction and deportation (Hos 5:14b-15):[22]

> I myself will tear and go away;
> I will carry off, and no one shall rescue.
> I will return again to my place
> until they acknowledge their guilt and seek my face.
> In their distress they will beg my favor.

Thus the severe announcement of divine castigation ends up in giving the catchword for the following communal confession of guilt and declaration of confidence,[23] forms well known from collective complaints (to Hos 6:1-6 compare e.g. Pss 95:6-7; 100; 106:6; Neh 9:16-31; Ezra 9:9-15; Dan 9:5-16 etc.). The communal complaint of Hos 6:1-6, therefore, is an integral part of the prophetic text, and it makes the unit Hos 5:8 – 6:6 a true reflection of communal worship.

The same holds true or else may be reasonably claimed, e.g. for Zeph 3:14-15;[24] Hab 1:2-4, 12-14; Mic 4:1-5 (parallel to Isa 2:1-5); 6:6-8; and other passages. Even dirge-like poems, e.g. in Mic 1:8-16;[25] Amos 5:1-3, may have to be reevaluated under the hypothetical perspective of being an authentic witness of some sort of communal or perhaps individual (i.e. small group[26]) worship. This kind of intimate relationship between psalm-like passages and "prophetic" pronouncements can hardly be explained by any theories about cultic prophecy. Hans Walter Wolff may have come pretty close to the truth when summing up his observations as to the liturgical qualities of Mic 7:8-20:

---

[22] Analytical details can be found in Hans Walter Wolff, *Hosea* (2nd ed.; BKAT XIV/1; Neukirchen-Vluyn: Neukirchener Verlag, 1965) 131-167; Jörg Jeremias, *Der Prophet Hosea* (ATD 24/1; Göttingen: Vandenhoeck, 1983), 78-83.

[23] Wolff (*Hosea*, 1.48-49) calls it a "song of penitence" (Busslied).

[24] Cf. Erhard S. Gerstenberger, "Der Hymnus der Befreiung im Zefanjabuch," in Walter Dietrich et. al. (eds.), *Der Tag wird kommen* (SBS 170; Stuttgart: Katholisches Bibelwerk, 1996), 102-12.

[25] Cf. Kessler, *Micha*, 90-111.

[26] We should resolutely move away from the unilateral idea that worship in exilic/post-exilic times had consisted only in temple ceremonies, animal sacrifice and occasional pilgrimages to Jerusalem. There were manifold rites and rituals even under the influence of exclusivistic thinking in terms of monotheism. Cf. Erhard S. Gerstenberger, *Der bittende Mensch* (WMANT 51; Neukirchen-Vluyn: Neukirchener Verlag, 1980); *Yahweh the Patriarch* (Minneapolis: Augsburg Fortress, 1996), 55-66; and *Theologien im Alten Testament* (Stuttgart: Kohlhammer, 2001). The English translation is *Theologies in the Old Testament* (Minneapolis: Fortress; and Edinburgh: T&T Clark, 2002).

Relevant worship services comprised in the first place readings of old prophetic sayings announcing the evil ..., secondly contemporary prophetic utterances high-lighting the actual situation by biting critiques or comforting words ..., and finally the psalm-like response of the congregation, referring to the preceding kerygma.[27]

D. Psalms with no Apparent Connection with Their Context

Only a very few relevant psalm-like texts seem to have been included in prophetic books, like erratic pieces of non-prophetic origin, or meteor-like material witnesses of another world. Closer investigation still may yield contextual ligatures, though. The items most frequently discussed over an extended period of time are those fragmented parts (?) of Yahweh hymns found in the book of Amos (4:13; 5:8-9; 9:5-6; [Amos 8:8?]), the so-called doxological intrusions. They indeed have long puzzled exegetes, precisely for being so disconnected with their context.[28] Be that as it may, the inclusion of seemingly disconnected hymnic elements may constitute more evidence for the possible cultic origin and use of "prophetic" books. In an orderly written theological treatise, sudden hymnic exclamations hardly seem to fit.

V. Conclusions

A. The Role and Setting of Psalmic Texts in the Prophets

Psalmic texts are integrated into the Book of the Twelve in a variety of ways. We have to describe the modalities and functions these passages or literary units are performing in their respective contexts. A frame of introductory and/or concluding formulas in the fashion of Psalm superscriptions suggests the availability of the text for liturgical ends. Such redactional superscriptions are no mere literary dressing without meaning for the reader.

---

[27] Hans Walter Wolff, *Micha* (BKAT XIV/4; Neukirchen-Vluyn: Neukirchener Verlag, 1982), 194.

[28] Perhaps Karl Budde ("Zur Geschichte des Buches Amos," BZAW 27 [1914] 63-77) was the first to focus on this phenomenon. Friedrich Horst ("Die Doxologien im Amosbuch," ZAW 47 [1929] 45-54) gave the first comprehensive treatment of the form. To him doxologies are customary responses of those accused of crimes. They have to admit their guilt, so that they may be sentenced. Cf. also Werner H. Schmidt, "Die deuteronomistische Redaktion des Amosbuches," ZAW 77 (1965) 168-73; Werner Berg, *Die sogenannten Hymnenfragmente im Amosbuch* (Frankfurt: Bernhard Lang, 1974); Klaus Koch, "Die Rolle der hymnischen Abschnitte in der Komposition des AmosBuches," ZAW 86 (1974) 504-37. Koch rejects Horst's interpretation, arguing instead for each hymnic fragment's being a marker of a book division, which actually points back to some liturgical use of the texts (536). James L. Crenshaw (*Hymnic Affirmation of Divine Justice* [SBLDS 24; Missoula: Scholars Press, 1985] develops further Horst's position.

Instead, they contain real information about the use of the text in communal ceremonies, about which we may understand little from our historical distance. Unframed, semi-autonomous psalmic texts may be equally convenient pieces for worship services of the community. For a psalm-like text marked as in Habakkuk 3 and for most poems of the Psalter, one is hard pressed to imagine another than a liturgical purpose. Superscriptions consisting of personal ascriptions and technical terms hardly serve the interests of individual readers.[29]

Communicative and interactive uses of psalmic texts in "prophetic" writings may hint at the possibility that it was not the prophetic texts that attracted liturgical elements. Instead, cultic situations may have produced prophetic pronouncements and literature. At least, it seems to me, all the traditional theories of (a) the authentic, historical men of God in the name of Yahweh creating collections of oracles and proclamations, and (b) such collections migrating into the cultic memory are much less plausible. How and why would the voices of autonomous communicators of Yahweh's will, addressing themselves to very concrete and transient contemporary problems, be preserved over the centuries? It is much easier to imagine communities which – experiencing the pressures of the exilic/post-exilic age – looked backwards to find some explanation and orientation for their daily lives under the rule of Yahweh. They wanted to understand their destiny at the hands of Babylonians and Persians. They knew or invented prophetic figures in the past that should have known beforehand the plans of God for his people, the fate of the monarchy, and the spiritual uncertainties in a very pluralistic and hostile world. So whatever little information still was available of Isaiah, Jeremiah, Ezekiel and the Twelve would be brought into the assemblies, discussed and actualized there. The processes of collecting traditions of the past, of joining their bits of the "prophetic" heritage together, of actualizing the older sayings and exhortations by creating new "prophetic" proclamation were all interwoven as part and parcel of the same gradual compilation of the prophetic canon.

Only the erratic variety of willfully interspersed psalms or fragments of psalms in an apparently psalm resistant context could cause problems for our present tentative of interpretation. Why should later redactors place such texts into an alien context like "prophetic" discourse? The best explanation, it seems to me, is the real worship situation in exilic and post-exilic Judah (or Diaspora, for that matter). Perhaps congregations would respond

---

[29] To regard the Psalter (and the Prophets?) as private reading material has come into vogue in the past years. It seems to me, however, that the underlying concepts of writing and reading presuppose a modern literary society, which does not even exist in all countries of our world today. Investigations, e.g. in Latin America, show that less than 10% of the population read regularly.

to brutal announcements of doom by intoning hymns or staging complaint services. Hymn singing, in fact, can be a weapon against destruction and misery. Eulogizing the supreme power of God, the mighty benevolence of the Creator and Protector, all by itself may defeat the hateful powers or evil potencies. Thus, the Chronicler tells of military victory on account of hymn singing (2 Chron 20:21-22). And the legendary witnesses of Yahweh in Daniel 3, according to the Greek apocryphal tradition sing hymns in the midst of the "fire oven." Furthermore, hymnic passages may constitute part of complaint songs.[30] For these reasons the fragmented hymn of Amos should not seem too strange to us. On the contrary, it could be another piece of evidence for the origin and transmission of prophetic preaching, which solicits from the beginning communal response and participation.

B. Reading Texts in Post-exilic Judah

Textual analysis alone will not solve the enigmas in regard to prophetic tradition and prophetic office. Readers of ancient texts will always bring with them culturally acquired paradigms of ancient reality, which serve as background and matrix for the interpretation of individual texts. Thus our general ideas of what prophecy and prophetic tradition was like will determine to a large extent the results of our exegetical endeavors. As indicated at the beginning of this paper there are numerous basic issues to be critically evaluated before we come to grips with the psalmic passages in the Book of the Twelve. Here are some of the underlying questions. What has been the significance of putting prophetic proclamation into writing? Millions of words of different mediators between God and humans certainly have not been preserved in any kind of document. Why and to which end were some of them frozen into letters? How have the emerging written collections been used? Has there been already in Persian times a culture of reading books for private edification? If so, which parts of society were able to indulge in the luxury of buying and reading written documents? On the other hand, how can we visualize communities cultivating their own traditions in written form? The era of public libraries evidently began only in the Hellenistic period.[31] What kind of experts did they need to handle the written records? Quite naturally, learned scribes were highly important, but also theologians and spiritual leaders of sorts who determined the quality and authenticity of the written words.[32]

---

[30]   Cf. Gerstenberger, *Psalms, Part One,* 11-14.
[31]   Cf. Philip R. Davies, *Scribes and Schools* (Louisville: Westminster John Knox, 1998), 74-88; 107-25. 8
[32]   Cf. Joseph Blenkinsopp, *Sage, Priest, Prophet* (Louisville: Westminster John Knox, 1995).

Of these the most critical issue is this: what was the purpose of the written tradition, on the one hand for the *torah* of Moses, and on the other hand for the emerging prophetic canon? Can we claim the written word was destined principally for public recitation as in Neh 8:2-3 and – reduced to the royal court – Jer 36:4-26? If that has been the case, how much influence is to be attributed to the community of recipients of the words of God? In analogy to the "Gemeindebildung" (formulation of kerygma by the congregation) in New Testament times, the authorship of "prophetic" words to a large extent may be located in that living process of communal expectation and the shaping of contemporary (early Jewish) liturgical agendas promoted by the scribal and theological elite. Thus, considerable parts of the prophetic "books" prove to be retro-projected compositions of the late community, rather than the "classical" prophetic authors mentioned in the superscriptions.[33]

If this assumption is plausible, we have to investigate primarily the living conditions, theological outlooks and communitarian practices of the early Jewish community of the Persian epoch in order to understand correctly prophetic "books" and "writings." The life setting of prophetic words and psalms would not be "the book" as is sometimes erroneously claimed. Rather, written records of the congregations of believers in Yahweh in Persian times (beginning, as it were, under the dominance of the Babylonians) point to various worshipping rites in which written words were used, recited either from memory or by open and public reading. The people "told the scribe Ezra to bring the book of the law of Moses ... he read from it ... from

---

[33] The facts are quite obvious in case of the book of Isaiah. Cf. e.g. Otto Kaiser, *Das Buch des Propheten Jesaja Kapitel 1— 2* (ATD 17; Göttingen: Vandenhœck & Ruprecht, 1963); Uwe Becker, *Jesaja – von der Botschaft zum Buch* (FRLANT 178, Göttingen: Vandenhoeck, 1997). The facts are also clear for Jeremiah. Cf. e.g. Robert P. Carroll, *Jeremiah. A Commentary* (OTL, London: SCM Press, 1989); Winfried Thiel, *Die deuteronomistische Redaktion von Jer 1 – 25 / von Jer 26 – 45* (WMANT 41 and 51: Neukirchen: Neukirchener Verlag, 1973 / 1981); Karl-Friedrich Pohlmann, *Die Ferne Gottes* (BZAW 179; Berlin: de Gruyter, 1989). On Ezekiel, cf. e.g. Johan Lust (ed.), *Ezekiel and His Book* (BETL 74; Leuven: University Press, 1986); Bernhard Lang, *Ezechiel, Der Prophet und das Buch* (Darmstadt: Wissenschaftliche Buchgesellschaft, 1981). For Amos, cf. Werner H. Schmidt, "Die deuteronomistische Redaktion des Amosbuches," *ZAW* 77 (1965) 168 – 193; and Dirk U. Rottzoll, *Studien zur Redaktion und Komposition des Amosbuches* (BZAW 243; Berlin: de Gruyter, 1996). On Hosea, cf. Hans-Walter Wolff, *Hosea* (2nd ed.; BKAT XIV/1; Neukirchen: Neukirchen-Vluyn, 1965); Jörg Jeremias, *Der Prophet Hosea* (ATD 24/1; Göttingen: Vandenhoeck, 1983). On Micah, cf. e.g. Ehud Ben Zvi, *Micah* (FOTL XXIIB; Grand Rapids: Eerdmans, 2000); Kessler, *Micha*. It is strange, indeed, that many exegetes still ignore the facts and start their investigations from the alleged fountainhead, the historical prophet himself, instead of working backwards from the most productive, later communities towards earlier layers of tradition.

early morning until midday ..." (Neh 8:1, 3). "Baruch wrote on a scroll at Jeremiah's dictation ...", "you shall read the words of the Lord from the scroll that you have written at my dictation." (Jer 36:4, 6). "When Hilkiah gave the book to Shaphan he read it. ...Shaphan then read it aloud to the King." (2 Kings 22:8, 10). Moses "took the book of the covenant, and read it in the hearing of the people." (Exod 24:7). He "commanded them: Every seventh year ... you shall read this *torah* before Israel in their hearing." (Deut 31:10-11). Joshua "read all the words of the *torah*, blessings and curses, according to all that is written in the book of the *torah*." (Josh 8:34). There are a good number of Deuteronomistic passages hinting at the written precepts of Yahweh put down by Moses and communicated by him. All of these references may be understood as reflections of exilic/post-exilic habits of reading aloud the words of Yahweh to the assembled congregation. This also implies that where we hear of "reading the Word" in Hebrew Scriptures it is public recitation, not private musing (except in Deut 17:18; Ps 1:2?)[34] The recitation of Scripture by itself becomes a liturgical act, a scenario with the essential ingredients of authorized reader, scroll of *torah*, listening and responding community (which, by the way orders the scroll to be brought into the assembly; cf. Neh 8:1).

C. Post-exilic Worship as the Sitz im Leben of Prophetic Literature

Returning to the issue of psalms in the Twelve we may say that most scholars probably agree that the bulk of "psalmic" passages in the prophetic canon (and particularly in the Book of the Twelve) does have some affinity to liturgical texts and outlooks. Few, however, will accept the idea that these cultic elements may be the "Leitfossil" of the whole prophetic literature and especially the Book of the Twelve. I should like to argue that way. The psalm-like parts may betray the formative matrix at least for the compilation of the Book of the Twelve, and beyond this general frame they may hint at the enormously creative "Sitz im Leben" that brought forth a considerable part of retrospective "prophetic" proclamation and other divinely inspired discourse. Unfortunately, we do not have much direct, authentic information about the early Jewish communities and their leadership as being active in writing prophecies under the disguise of Isaiah, Jeremiah, Ezekiel and the Twelve. But all the Hebrew prophetic writings in their formative phases have been, as pointed out above, quite susceptible of becoming car-

---

[34] Cf. F. L. Hossfeld and H. Lamberty-Zielinski, *"qr'," ThWAT* 7,133–36: "The meaning "to read" for *qr'* is attested only from the exilic period onward ...." (134). "[P]ublic reading as part of covenant making acquired a cultic character..." (135); F. L. Hossfeld and E. Reuter, *"seper," ThWAT* 5,932 – 944.

riers of contemporary theology and preaching. It is only from this perspective that prophetic books as a whole become really understandable.

Prophetic speech in this regard becomes solidly grounded in community worship without the "classical" prophets becoming cultic functionaries. An additional, thorough investigation of speech forms (i.e. taking seriously congregational involvement in the production of prophetic books) in the Twelve and the bigger Three – I am thinking in particular of the frequent genres of "admonition" or "exhortation," "call for repentance," "ethical reflection," etc. – would without doubt greatly enhance the quest for a primarily cultic origin of "prophetic" compositions and discourses. There are some indications in the Hebrew canon itself that such a model of "prophecy" comes close to ancient reality.

We should e.g. reconsider the famous relationship of Jeremiah to his personal scribe Baruch under this angle. Ancient "prophetic" words and figures in fact need to be transmitted to posterity by mediation of "scribes." Classical prophets did not write down their messages. Nor were they called *nabi'* for that matter (cf. 1 Sam 9:9). Baruch wrote down the words of God communicated to Jeremiah and read them to the congregation, like court officials read the "prophetic" work to the king (cf. Jer 36). This beautiful and theologically most meaningful story, made up in Deuteronomistic circles, clearly depicts the mediation of the Word through written documentation. The "words of Jeremiah" are put down faithfully to be recited to the people, so that it can "amend its ways and its doings" (cf. Jer 7:3). Mediation through letters and literature is important. Therefore, the prophet is seen barred from the temple, in order that his (later) representative may communicate with the congregation. The destruction of the written Word is the imminent danger, not the possible demise of the prophet himself. Even the mediators of the Word of Jeremiah step into the background. The victorious writings prevail; they are victorious. The king may burn the first scroll, a new, enlarged edition will appear immediately at Jeremiah's dictation, containing all the speeches destroyed before, "and many similar words were added to them" (Jer 36:32). Of course, there is no explicit admission, that the mediators themselves enlarged some original collection of prophetic sayings. But everyone understanding the human genesis of sacred writings, and everyone who thoughtfully and attentatively reads our "prophetic" books in the Hebrew Bible should be able to recognize the growth of prophetic traditions. And the psalmic components indeed may lead us to the sources of prophecy and *nabi'*-hood: the proper community of faith struggling with its own past and for its identity and survival in turbulent times.

D. Hymns as Indicators of the Communal Authorship of the Prophets

With good evidence at hand of (a) the growth and shaping of "prophetic" traditions to have taken place in exilic/post-exilic times and (b) the unifying concept of Yahweh having sent in vain a whole series of prophets for the sake of his people to be a late systematization, we may finally compare the two approaches to prophetic literature, bearing in mind the lead of the psalmic passages in the Book of the Twelve.

The interpretation of prophetic texts in the past tried to start out from the historical person who communicated the will and verdict of Yahweh to his people in concrete historical moments of the life of Israel. Mentally starting from this point zero, the point of origin of individual texts, normally short sayings, modern exegetes tried to identify authentic messages and later, consecutive additions or modifications of these more or less divine words. Eventually, the main interpretative effort having cleared the very fountainhead of prophetic activity, the various layers of subsequent interpretations and comments had to be analyzed and explained, down to the Masoretic fixation of the Hebrew writings and the ancient versions as well as on through posterior theological debates in Jewish and Christian history of interpretation. A complete exegesis of a given text would include, therefore, a painstaking scrutiny of its first utterance as well as of its subsequent reworkings, alterations in diction and meaning. If later additions, corrections, etc. had overgrown the original "prophetic" word, the modern interpreter would have to muster his or her sharp tools of historical-critical and form- and social-critical research and cut back through the jungle of later interpretations in order to get to the fountainhead of that overarchingly significant first saying and its author.

The presence of psalm-like texts in the prophetic canon, which may point to the late, community-bound matrix of all "prophetic" texts, alerts us to the possibility of a very different approach. What we do have in the Hebrew prophetic books, especially in the Twelve, are pieces of literature probably going back to the fifth and fourth centuries B.C.E. We would have to take seriously the final shape and the late origin of these "prophetic" writings. First, the final literary product would have to be analyzed, including a probe into the social, cultural, theological conditions under which the book or writing came about. The creative interests prevalent in the group which used a given prophetic book or compilation have to be investigated. No human being and no group of people can avoid, while designing for him- or itself relevant pictures of the past, to impose his/its own, contemporary experiences on the older witnesses or interweave the bygone testimony with actual patterns of thinking and acting. This insight of everyone constructing the world in his or her own likeness is valid for biblical writers as well as for modern exegetes. In the case of the biblical tradition, the images of prophets and their messages as preserved in the Book of the Twelve to a very large extent are condensations of prophetic types and roles, known and/or invented exactly in the period under discussion. Having established the profiles of the youngest layer of tradition in the final written "prophetic" document, we would go upstream in order to recognize more clearly the historical depths of "prophetic" transmissions. Who knows whether one day we may come to discover or reconstruct one or two authentic words of some historical prophetic figure? In the case of the Twelve it seems obvious that we hardly encounter any trustworthy information about the eponyms of those booklets which carry their names.

Are the psalmic passages, then, misplaced in the Book of the Twelve? I trust that this is not the case. On the contrary, the psalm-like parts are not inserts at all in the fourth collection of "prophetic" words. They are treasures of prayers and hymns all testifying to a vivid Israelite community life in Persian times; and they open our eyes as to the wondrous world of preaching, teaching, debating theology, which must have gone on in many congregations of Yahwists within the small province of Judah as well as in Diaspora situations abroad.

Forming the Twelve and Forming Canon[1]

Edgar W. Conrad.

I. Introduction

In this essay I want to advance a reader-oriented position from which the formation of prophetic books is viewed from the perspective of text reception. My disagreements with a redactional-critical approach for understanding the formation of prophetic books, including the formation of the Twelve, have been published elsewhere,[2] and I do not intend to pursue these issues in this paper. I have argued earlier that redaction criticism downplays the active role of the reader in interpretation, that the external data necessary to outline the development of a book in terms of its inception is lacking, and that the recognition of "the unity" of a prophetic book undermines the recognition of the underlying sources that gives rise to the enterprise of redaction in the first place.[3]

A reader-oriented approach is sometimes dismissed because of the assumption that it is subjective, dismissing both the text and the historical context underlying a text's production. To be sure, some reader response critics have advocated a radical reader-oriented approach in which textual meaning is understood to rest solely with the reader. Such a position may be said to be represented by Stanley Fish.[4] A reader-oriented approach, however, does not necessarily imply such a radical position. While in past

---

[1]   I want to express my thanks to the Institute for Advanced Studies in the Humanities at the University of Edinburgh. My time as an elected Research Fellow at the Institute (January to July 2001) enabled me to reflect on these matters. I am particularly grateful to Prof. John Frow, Director of the Centre and to Prof. Graeme Auld of the Divinity School whose conversations with me on these matters were particularly helpful.

[2]   See, for example, my *Reading Isaiah* (OBT; Minneapolis: Fortress, 1991) 12-20; "Prophet, Redactor and Audience: Reforming the Notion of Isaiah's Formation," in *New Visions of the Book of Isaiah* (ed. R. Melugin and M. Sweeney; JSOTSup 214; Sheffield: Sheffield Academic Press, 1996) 306-25; and *Zechariah* (Readings: A New Biblical Commentary; Sheffield: Sheffield Academic Press, 1999) 16-18.

[3]   This is what John Barton (*Reading the Old Testament: Method in Biblical Study* [London: Darton, Longman and Todd, 1984] 57) calls "the trick of the disappearing redactor." See my *Reading Isaiah*, 18-20.

[4]   Stanley Fish, *Is There a Text in This Class? The Authority of Interpretive Communities* (Cambridge: Harvard University Press, 1980).

studies I have appealed to Stanley Fish as providing theoretical insight into the role of community in interpretation,[5] I have always advocated the central role of the text as an object of interpretation.[6] In this paper I want to further develop more clearly my understanding of the role of the text in interpretation by appealing to Umberto Eco's theory of semiotics. In particular, I want to build on the ideas outlined in his book *The Limits of Interpretation*,[7] especially his discussion of "the intention of the work" (*intentio operis*).[8] Eco's ideas have enabled me to develop notions of the formation of prophetic books, including the formation of the Twelve, from the perspective of the reader. I want to make it clear from the outset, however, that I am not pretending to be a semiotician. Nor am I appealing to Eco as a "canonical authority" on textual meaning. Rather, his work has become important as a dialogue partner in my own theoretical reflections on reading prophetic books.

In my paper I will also appeal to Philip Davies' work on canon, *Scribes and Schools: The Canonization of the Hebrew Scriptures*,[9] as providing insight into the formation of the Twelve as canon. However, while utilizing Davies' important ideas, I will depart from his diachronic discussion of canon to focus on the more synchronic activity of reading prophetic books as canonical formations.

II. Gunkel, Readers and Prophetic Books

There has been a long tradition in the critical study of prophetic books to regard them as unreadable. This position is outlined succinctly by Hermann Gunkel in his well-known essay, "The Prophets as Writers and Poets."[10] He offers the following advice to contemporary readers (italics mine):

> The prophets were not originally writers but speakers. Anyone who thinks of ink and paper while *reading* their writings is in error from the outset. "Hear!" is the

---

[5]   See *Reading Isaiah*, especially pp. 3-33.

[6]   Ibid., 27-33, especially p. 33.

[7]   Umberto Eco, *The Limits of Interpretation* (Bloomington: Indiana University Press, 1990). In this book he argues that his reader response approach [which he developed in his *The Role of the Reader: Explorations in the Semiotics of Texts* (London: Hutchinson, 1981)] was not meant to exclude the notion that there are textual limits in interpretation.

[8]   Ibid., 50.

[9]   Philip Davies, *Scribes and Schools: The Canonization of the Hebrew Scriptures* (Louisville: Westminster/John Knox, 1998).

[10] The article has appeared in English in *Prophecy in Israel: Search for Identity* (trans. J. L. Schaaf; ed. D. L. Petersen; IRT 10. Philadelphia: Fortress and London: SPCK, 1987) 22-73.

way they begin their works, not "Read!" Above all, however, if *contemporary readers* wish to understand the prophets, they must entirely forget that the writings were collected in a sacred book centuries after the prophets' wrote. *The contemporary reader must not read their words as portions of the Bible but must attempt to place them in the context of the life of the people of Israel in which they were first spoken.*[11]

He goes on to argue that literary context is of secondary importance and that the reader should question whether there is any such thing as the structure of a prophetic book. He observes that

> . . . in interpreting as well as in criticizing the prophetic books one must use the criterion of "context" only with great caution; and also that in attempting to indicate the structure of prophetic books such as Amos or Deutero-Isaiah one must first investigate whether such a thing exists at all.[12]

While Gunkel's contribution to the study of the Hebrew Bible has been immense, especially his challenge to appreciate it as literature, his observation that one should treat "the criterion of 'context'" with great caution and his questioning of whether prophetic books have a structure is, in the present climate of biblical studies, open to challenge. The significant redaction-critical work on prophetic books during the past decade, especially on Isaiah and the Twelve, has again brought literary "context" and structure to center stage. Prophetic books are now being seen not simply as random collections of the once oral words of the prophets. In a growing number of studies, it is argued that prophetic books evince structural design providing a *literary* context for the collected material. At the end of the century it has become easier for scholars to speak about the "intentionality" of a prophetic book than it was for Gunkel in the first half of the century.

The issue I now want to address concerns how one understands "intentionality" when speaking about what redaction critics refer to as "the final form" of the text. How are we to understand this final form? I want to offer an alternative explanation to the notion that this intention can be explained by tracing the formation of a prophetic book by attempting to reconstruct its diachronic development. Such an approach, as I have argued elsewhere, perpetuates the central role of the "author."[13] In the last fifteen years or so in biblical studies the redactor has emerged from the former role as a simple collector to that of an "author" fully engaged in shaping prophetic books into intentionally structured wholes.

---

[11]   Ibid., 24.
[12]   Ibid., 31.
[13]   Conrad, *Reading Isaiah,* 17-20.

Recent redaction critical work on prophetic books has been open to criticism because there has not been unanimity on how the intentionality of a particular prophetic book is to be understood in its final form. The question posed is, "Why is there so much disagreement among redaction critics about what constitutes the 'unity' of Isaiah or the Twelve?" This is Jeoshua Gitay's criticism of the scholars of the Isaiah seminar.[14]

Both Gitay and the redaction critics he is critiquing are working on notions of the "intentionality" of prophetic books that differ from the understanding of intentionality that I am proposing in this essay. Contemporary literary theory has helped us see that no literature can provide us with a direct avenue to author intention. The author of a prophetic book, like the author of any piece of written literature, is absent; and meaning emerges in the interaction of text and reader. Because the reader is involved in interpretation, it should be no surprise that redaction critical readers disagree. However, the indeterminacy in reading that this disagreement exemplifies should not lead one to conclude that prophetic books lack intentionality.

III. Umberto Eco, Intention and Textual Formation

I am arguing for a way of talking about intention and textual formation that moves the discussion away from the author (or redactor) to the work itself. In making this move I am following leads of Umberto Eco's semiotic approach examining how communication takes place in writing. According to Eco, for communication to take place an author will compose a text for a Model Reader who, the author expects, will employ codes and subcodes to decipher the text's intention. Eco says,

> To organize a text, its author has to rely upon a series of codes that assign given contents to the expressions he uses. To make this text communicative, the author has to assume that the ensemble of codes he relies upon is the same as that shared by his possible reader. The author has thus to foresee a model of the possible reader (hereafter Model Reader) supposedly able to deal interpretatively with the expressions in the same way as the author deals generatively with them.[15]

For Eco, the Model Reader is not a real reader but exists in the mind of the author. In turn what is accessible for the real reader is not the real author but an encoded text, which is limited by codes employed by the sender (author) for the envisaged Model Reader. Just as a real author can envisage

---

14   Jeoshua Gitay, "Prophetic Criticism – 'What are they Doing?': The Case of Isaiah – Methodological Assessment," *JSOT* 96 (2001) 101-27.
15   Eco *Role of Reader*, 7

a Model Reader, so a real reader can envisage a Model Author who has encoded a text for reading.

Therein lies a problem. "In the process of communication, a text is frequently interpreted against the background of codes different from those
intended by the author."[16] This situation is precisely the case with prophetic
texts whose envisaged Model Reader is imagined against a different social
context than that of a contemporary reader of a prophetic text. Such texts
according to Eco "obsessively aim at arousing a precise response on the part
of more or less precise empirical readers . . . and are in fact open to a possible 'aberrant' decoding. A text so immoderately 'open' to every possible
interpretation will be called a *closed* one."[17]

My concern in reading prophetic books can be defined in terms of Eco's
semiotics of reading. While I understand prophetic books to be closed texts
and open to all sorts of aberrant decoding, I am arguing that it is legitimate
for contemporary readers to focus on the intentionality of the book. This
intentionality is related to the coded information a Model Author provides
for the reader. In this essay I am particularly interested in how the beginnings of prophetic books offer coded information that the Model Author has
provided for a reader of prophetic books.

Before discussing how the superscriptions can be understood as providing codes employed by a Model Author, I want to speak a bit more about
how I imagine the Model Author of prophetic books. I understand that prophetic books have a compilational unity although they do not have the compositional integrity expected of authored works. In this sense they are more
like a collage than a composition. Prophetic books are the result of the
scribal activity of ordering, arranging and archiving material as well as
composition not unlike that described in Philip Davies' *Scribes and
Schools*.[18] However, unlike Davies, I assume that this ordered arrangement
arose at a point in time rather than resulting from a diachronic development
through time. I am not interested in how the particular text I am reading
came to be, but how the codes, for example those employed at the beginnings of prophetic books, provide information for the reader. To put this in
Eco's terms, I am interested in how a scribe, as a Model Author, compiled a
prophetic book for a reader. I am also interested in the way these prophetic
books as collections have been ordered and arranged by scribes for the
Model Reader.

---

[16]   Ibid., 8. It is for this reason that Eco would say meaning is indeterminate since what
an absent author intended is no longer available to a reader. What is accessible is only
the encoded text.

[17]   Ibid.

[18]   Davies, *Scribes and Schools*, 8-14, 57-59.

By creating a text for a Model Reader, according to Eco, the sender (author) has created a textual world.[19] In that textual world, codes are contextually based. This production of the text for the Model Reader is what Eco refers to as "the intention of the work" (*intentio operis*).[20] The "intention of the work" is not to be confused with "the intention of the author" (*intentio auctoris*), which is not available to the reader. What is available is a text encoded for the Model Reader, and it is the way the text works as a text that Eco identifies with "the intention of the work." As readers of these old texts we cannot get inside the head of the absent sender (author) to discover what the author might have had "in mind." As readers, however, we can get inside the text, which we bring to life as a message when we begin to read.

Because Eco wants to argue that the *intentio operis* limits interpretation, he makes a distinction between the *use* of a text and the *interpretation* of a text. Eco opposes radical reader response critics (such as Richard Rorty and one could include Stanley Fish mentioned above)[21] who take a pragmatic approach in understanding a text's meaning. For such critics a text's meaning is dependent entirely on the intention of the reader (*intentio lectoris*).[22]

According to Eco a pragmatic reading such as that of Rorty or Fish is designed "to use a text . . .in order to get something else . . ."[23] He understands that radical reader response critics use the text in this way because they maintain that there are no limits to interpretation. When they "use" a text, they beat it into a shape to serve their own purposes.[24] One could also argue that a form critic such as Gunkel was using the text "to get something else." He was using the text to reconstruct oral settings outside the text (*Sitze im Leben* or institutional background). Indeed, one could argue that the historical critical enterprise from source analysis to redaction criticism "uses" the text in this sense. The text has been beaten into a variety of shapes for a variety of uses. Historical critics use the biblical text "to get something else": underlying sources, *Sitze im Leben*, the intention of redactors, or a history of tradition. The text is used and left behind in search of something other than the *intentio operis*. Seen from this perspective, historical critics ironically can be seen as radical reader-response critics.

---

[19] Eco, *Limits of Interpretation*, 23.
[20] Ibid., 50.
[21] For a taste of this debate see Umberto Eco, *Interpretation and Overinterpretation* (ed. S. Collini; Cambridge: Cambridge University Press, 1992). The exchange in this volume with Richard Rorty, whose essay, "The Pragmatist's Progress," appears on pp. 89-108. Eco's response is on pp. 139-51.
[22] Eco, *Limits of Interpretation*, 50.
[23] Ibid., 57
[24] Ibid., 56.

In summary, then, as a real reader of a prophetic book I imagine that a
Model Author has coded a prophetic book to communicate something about
the world of the prophets in ancient Israel. What is available to the reader is
not an actual author's (redactor's) intention or an actual history of a prophetic book's development, but a written text. As a real reader interested in
a prophetic book communicating from the past, I can respect the *intentio
operis* by paying heed to textual limits.

IV. Openings of Prophetic Books and the Model Author

I want to turn now to the openings of prophetic books in order to look at
how they might be read as providing coded information from a Model
Author. The so-called superscriptions of prophetic books (that is, the Latter
Prophets—Isaiah, Jeremiah, Ezekiel and the Twelve) provide an interesting
array of information. The beginning of Isaiah informs the reader that this is
the "חֲזוֹן (vision) of Isaiah, the son of Amoz." This חֲזוֹן is something
which he saw (חָזָה) concerning Judah and Jerusalem. The חֲזוֹן is dated generally in the days of Uzziah, Jothan, Ahaz and Hezekiah, kings of Judah.

The beginning of Jeremiah provides the reader with similar but considerably different information. Here the reader is informed that what follows are "the דִּבְרֵי (words) of Jeremiah" — not a חֲזוֹן as in Isaiah. While
Jeremiah is identified as "the son of Hilkiah" just as Isaiah is identified as
"the son of Amoz," additional information is given, which has no correspondence in Isaiah. Jeremiah is among the priests (מִן־הַכֹּהֲנִים) who were
in Anathoth in the land of Benjamin. While both the "words" of Jeremiah
and the "vision" of Isaiah are dated, the words in Jeremiah are identified as
"the דְּבַר (word/thing) of Yahweh," and the dates are given with more precision than they are in Isaiah:

> "The word of Yahweh came to him in the days of Josiah, the son of Amon of Ju-
> dah, in the thirteenth year of his reign. It was also in the days of Jehoiakim, the
> son of Josiah, the king of Judah until the completion of the eleventh year of Zede-
> kiah, son of Josiah, the king of Judah until Jerusalem went into exile in the fifth
> month."

The opening of Ezekiel provides the reader again with rather different
information. The superscription opens by informing the reader about what
happened: "and it happened" (וַיְהִי). What happened is dated with even
more precision than in Jeremiah to "the thirteenth year, in the fourth month,
on the fifth day of the month." This date apparently refers to the period of
time he was in exile. There is no mention of Judean kings at this point and
no mention of his ancestry. The beginning of this book also is distinctive in

that Ezekiel speaks in the first person and his name is not immediately mentioned as in Isaiah and Jeremiah. What happened, he says, is that "when I was among the exiles by the river Chebar, the sky was opened and I had מראות (visions) of god." It is interesting to contrast this with Isaiah. The חזון of Isaiah is singular, but is dated over a long stretch of time: in the days of Uzziah, Jotham, Ahaz and Hezekiah kings of Judah. In contrast, what happened to Ezekiel is not identified as the חזון of Ezekiel, but in the plural as מראות of god that came to him in a very specific period of time, the thirteenth year, the fourth month and the fifth day of the month. In 1:2-3 Ezekiel is referred to in the third person, and the fifth day of the month is further clarified as the "fifth year of the exile of Jehoiachin." Interestingly, Jehoichin is not identified as the king of Judah. Just as the "words" (דברי) of Jeremiah are referred to as "the דבר (word/thing) of Yahweh," so the "visions" (מראות) that came to Ezekiel are referred to as "the דבר (word/thing) of Yahweh." Ezekiel is now identified as the son of Buzi and, like Jeremiah, he is associated with priests. Ezekiel is not *among* the priests as was Jeremiah, but he *is* "the priest (הכהן)." While Jeremiah was among the priests in "the land of Benjamin," Ezekiel is "the priest in the land of the Chaldeans." The opening information in Ezekiel concludes by saying, "the hand of Yahweh was upon him there."

How is a reader to understand this information at the beginning of prophetic books? What did an ancient author (scribe, compiler) expect his Model Reader to understand by this information coded at the beginning of prophetic books? As contemporary readers of what Eco would call "closed texts," we can only attempt to construct an answer to these questions by reading these texts intertextually with other prophetic books. Interestingly, the opening of the "books" of the Twelve contain superscriptions that parallel the openings of the Major Prophets.

"The דברי of Jeremiah" is matched in the Twelve only by the ספר of Amos, which begins in exactly the same way as Jeremiah, "the דברי of Amos." The superscription to Amos, like the superscription to Jeremiah, also identifies Amos as belonging to some group other than the prophets. Just as Jeremiah was "among the priests" of Anathoth so Amos was "among the shepherds (נקדים) from Tekoa." The significance of the coded information of "the words of" associated with a figure who comes from a non-prophetic group will become apparent below. For now it is important to note that both Amos and Jeremiah are books about the "words" of these two characters and also that they are associated with groups other than prophets. Amos is dated in the days of Uzziah, the king of Judah, and unlike Jeremiah he is also associated with a king of Israel, Jereboam. Like

Jeremiah, Amos' words are also dated with precision. However, rather than linking the precise date with the reign of kings, his words are dated as happening two years before the הרעש. This word is normally translated "the earthquake," but for reasons I will detail later, I think it is better translated as the "rumble" associated with war.

The significance of "the words of" is more clearly seen by focusing on what follows in Amos and Jeremiah. While the superscription informs the reader that Amos "saw" (חזה) "words" concerning Israel, Amos' words, like Jeremiah's words, are never identified as a חזון, as in Isaiah, nor as מראות of god, as in Ezekiel. Seeing in Amos and Jeremiah is of a different kind. When Jeremiah and Amos see "words," they see them in the visual world around them. Jeremiah sees such things as "a branch of an almond tree" (1:11), "a boiling pot facing away from the north" (1:13), a potter's house (18:2), a potter's earthenware jug (19:1), two baskets of figs (24:2) among other things. Amos sees two people walking together (3:3), a lion roaring (3:4), birds falling into snares (3:5), trumpets blowing in the city (3:6), locusts (7:1), fire burning the land (7:4), a plumb line (7:7), and a basket of summer fruit (8:1). Furthermore when seeing things, these two prophets take their words to the temple where they are confronted by priests since their words are a threat to kings. Amos goes to Bethel where Amaziah the priest says to Jeroboam, "Amos has conspired against you in the very center of the house of Israel; the land is not able to bear all his *words*" (7:10). Jeremiah is instructed by Yahweh (36:2-3).

> Take a scroll and write on it all the *words* that that I have spoken to you against Israel and Judah and all the nations, from the day I spoke to you, from the days of Josiah until today. It may be that when the house of Judah hears of all the disasters that I intend to do to them, all of them may turn from their evil ways, so that I may forgive their inquity and their sin.

Baruch is instructed to take this scroll and read it in the temple (36:5, see Jeremiah 7 and 26).

"The words of Amos" and "the words of Jeremiah" introducing prophetic "books" illumine one another when read intertextually. Both "books" speak of Yahweh roaring (שאג) and uttering his voice (נתן קולו) (Amos 1:2 and Jer 25:30) with the consequence that this will bring devastation to all the nations of the land. These unconventional prophets (one from among the priests and the other from among the shepherds) have the extraordinary role of prophesying the end of kingdoms and temples where Yahweh had been present. Amos announces the end of the northern kingdom of Israel including the sanctuary at Bethel, and Jeremiah announces the end of Judah and its temple in Jerusalem.

The announcement of the end of kingdoms is characteristic of unconventional prophets and highlights an important feature of my thesis on reading prophetic books coded for the Model Reader. (I do not have time to develop the notion fully.) Amos and Jeremiah are unconventional prophets who prophesy in extraordinary times concerning Yahweh who has made the decision to abandon his people, his land and his house (temple). Conventional prophets (like Isaiah, whom I will look at below) receive vision (חזון) from Yahweh, who is present in the temple. Conventional prophets go out from the temple with words of comfort and consolation. Unconventional prophets come to the temple deserted by Yahweh to announce the end.

Amos and Jeremiah are joined by Ezekiel, the other unconventional prophet, who is identified in the superscription as "the priest in the land of the Chaldeans" (1:3). Ezekiel will return to his role as a priest writing the torah of the temple at the end of the book (43:10-12; cf. Ezek 7:26-28; Jer 2:8; 18:18). This role as an unconventional prophet is suggested by the encoded information at the beginning of Ezekiel, "and it happened" (ויהי). What happened was that Ezekiel had "visions (מראות) of god" in the land of the enemy, the land of the Chaldeans. Unlike Isaiah he did not have a "vision" (חזון) in the temple.

The only other book to begin with the phrase, "and it happened" (ויהי) is Jonah. Although Jonah does not have "visions (מראות) of god," he is similar to Ezekiel in that Yahweh appeared to him in the land of the enemy.

What I am suggesting, then, is that Amos, Jeremiah, Ezekiel and, to a lesser extent Jonah, are prophetic "books" about extraordinary times. Amos, Jeremiah and Ezekiel, who are from groups other than prophets (נביאים), are themselves presented as extraordinary prophets. The language of the books backs up this observation. The verbal form of the root נבא "prophesying," which occurs only in Niph'al and Hithpa'el, is not evenly spread throughout the so-called Latter Prophets. It occurs once in Joel (3:1) and twice in Zechariah (13:3-4). In both cases it has to do with prophesying in the future and does not relate to the activity of either Joel or Zechariah. All the other references are found in the three books of the unconventional prophets: Jeremiah (over forty times), Ezekiel (over thirty times) and Amos (six times). In each of these "books"—and only in these three prophetic books—is the verb used to emphasize that Jeremiah, Ezekiel and Amos are engaged in prophesying. In the other prophetic "books," prophesying appears to be taken as a given.

This concentration of the verb "prophesying" is significant for understanding the information encoded in the "books" of Jeremiah, Ezekiel and Amos for reading. In each "book" the superscription emphasises the non-conventional origin of the figure, and each "book" makes repeated emphasis that each of these individuals (Amos, Jeremiah or Ezekiel) is prophesying by repeatedly drawing attention to the activity of prophesying.

Isaiah, as a prophet of חזון is a more conventional prophet. Other prophetic books, which have similar information in the superscription, are Obadiah ("The חזון of Obadiah") and Nahum ("An oracle concerning Nineveh. The book of the חזון of Nahum of Elkosh"). But I would also understand that "the oracle that the prophet Habakkuk saw" is a חזון. In Hab 2:2-3 Habakkuk is told,

> Write down the חזון;
> > make it plain on tablets,
> > so that a reader may run with it.
> For there is still a חזון for the appointed time;
> > It speaks of the end, it does not tarry.

These words in Habakkuk outline the main characteristics of a חזון. It is written down to be read out by a messenger who reads it. A vision is also something for which one waits. I understand that the vision of Isaiah shares these characteristics. See, for example, Isa 8:16 where Isaiah gives instructions to record his vision and to wait for it.

The notion that a חזון is written down so that a reader may run with it helps explain words immediately following the superscription in Isaiah. The announcement that this is the חזון of Isaiah in 1:1 is followed in 1:2 by imperative verbs summoning the sky and the land to "hear" and to "give ear."

> Hear, O sky and listen O land;
> > for Yahweh has spoken:
> I reared up children and brought them up,
> > but they have rebelled against me.

While I do not have time to develop the arguments fully here, I would also suggest that the books of both Micah and Joel should, like the book of Isaiah, be understood as a vision (חזון). While neither of these books uses the word חזון in the superscription, the verses following the superscriptions in both books, as in Isaiah, are a call to hear.

Hear this, O elders,
> Give ear, all inhabitants of the land. (Joel 1:2)

Hear, you peoples, all of you;
> listen, O land, and all that is in it
and let the lord Yahweh be a witness against you,
> the lord from his holy temple. (Mic 1:2)

In summary, then, I have argued that the openings of prophetic books supply the reader with information that the Model Author has intended for the reader that expresses the intentionality of the material that follows. The openings are not to be understood as arbitrary information about an equally arbitrary compilation of material that follows. To read Jeremiah and Amos as "the words of" involves the reader in a different exercise than in reading Isaiah, Nahum, Obadiah, Habakkuk, Micah and Joel as "vision" (חֲזוֹן). Furthermore, to read Jonah and Ezekiel as narrative introduced with "and it happened" distinguishes the reading of these from the reading of other prophetic texts.

V. Forming the Twelve and Forming Canon

While an ancient scribe would have expected his Model Reader to understand how to read prophetic books beginning with the "the words of," "the vision of" and "and it happened," contemporary readers of these books do not have this information at their immediate disposal. I have suggested in this essay that the codes can become available by reading intertextually books that have similar beginnings. To understand the intentionality of a prophetic book is not to discover the particular process of text production, but to learn how to read a prophetic book. Intentionality for a contemporary reader has to do with the reception of the text rather than its inception. Again I want to add that the prophetic book is not to be understood as a composition by a single author. Reading a prophetic book in its final form is reading it as a collection of materials arranged as a compilational whole – as a collage.

It is interesting that we have in the Twelve a collection of סְפָרִים identified as "vision," "words of" and "and it happened." Collecting and ordering prophetic material are not only important for understanding the individual books with openings such as "vision," "the words of" and "and it happened"; they also are important for understanding the collection of books in canonical order. This observation is consistent with the notion of canon outlined by Philip Davies, who understands the canonical process as a scribal process of collecting, arranging and ordering not only material in a scroll such as the Twelve but also collections of scrolls themselves into a canonical order.[25]

While I do not have space to outline my arguments in full detail here, I want to point out that the prophets of Isaiah, Jeremiah and Ezekiel are parallelled by The Twelve as a canonical collection of books brought together on one scroll. The Twelve is parallel to Isaiah, Jeremiah and Ezekiel in two ways. First, the books are introduced with similar superscriptions – the "vision of Isaiah" is parallelled by the "visions" of Joel, Micah, Obadiah, Nahum, Habakkuk and Zephaniah. "The words of Jeremiah" are parallelled by the "words of Amos;" the statement "and it happened to Ezekiel" is parallelled by "and it happened to Jonah." Second, just as Isaiah, Jeremiah and Ezekiel provide prophetic background to the fall of Judah, including the temple in Jerusalem and the restoration of the community in Zion/Jerusalem with the construction of the temple, so also The Twelve provides a prophetic background to the fall of Israel (the northern kingdom) and the restoration of the community in Zion/Jerusalem. Let me be more specific. The Twelve begins with Hosea. Hosea does not sit easily with any of the major genres of prophetic books and acts as an introduction to the Twelve and, as "the beginning of Yahweh spoke," also serves as the time frame for understanding the prophetic corpus as a whole. Yahweh first spoke to Hosea about his intention to empty the land. A major theme in Hosea is the call to return.

Following Hosea are books that emulate genres in the collection of the Major prophets: Isaiah ("vision"), Jeremiah ("the words of") and Ezekiel ("it happened"). Vision is represented in the books of Joel, Micah, Obadiah, Nahum, Habakkuk and Zephaniah, although the genre is not as clearly identified in the opening superscriptions of all of these books as in Isaiah. "The words of Amos" like "the words of Jeremiah," announce the end of Israel. "It happened to" Jonah narrates the appearance of Yahweh in Nineveh, the land of the enemy, mirroring the foreign element in Ezekiel. Whereas Isaiah, Jeremiah, and Ezekiel refer to Judah, the whole of the Twelve has a northern focus. Even the last book in the collection (Malachi) is an oracle to Israel. However, in these books restoration has to do with Yahweh's return not to Israel but to Judah and Jerusalem.

The Twelve ends with extraordinary prophets, Haggai, Zechariah and My Messenger. These prophets have to do with the extraordinary situation of temple restoration. This is the period of return, when Jerusalem will be the center of the whole land. Here Yahweh will dwell and all the nations of the land will pay allegiance to Jerusalem because of Yahweh's presence.

---

[25]   Davies, *Scribes and Schools*, 115-17.

VI. Summary and Conclusion

I understand the openings of prophetic books, then, as indications of intentionality in relation to the compilation of individual scrolls and also to the collection arrangement and ordering of prophetic scrolls in their totality. All this poses an important observation concerning canon. Reading the books intertextually, with attention to similarities and differences, enables us to recognize codes that give us clues to the literary integrity of a disparate collection of scrolls.

God Sows: Hosea's Land Theme
in the Book of the Twelve

Laurie J. Braaten

The Minor Prophets have been passed down as a single collection titled "The Book of the Twelve." Recent studies have explored ways of reading the Twelve as a unity. One approach looks for unifying elements in framing devices such as *inclusios*, key words, motifs, and themes.[1] In the Society of Biblical Literature's Formation of the Book of the Twelve Seminar, recent suggestions for such devices include love[2] (Watts, 1997), marriage imagery (Baumann, 1999), and the Day of Yahweh (Rendtorff, 1997, Nogalski, 1999). Others note such themes as Yahweh's relation with Israel and Judah, return and/or repentance, the changing roles of the nations, and vegetational motifs.[3]

The current study is a thematic approach based primarily on a synchronic reading of the MT form of the Book of the Twelve.[4] It begins by looking for literary clues concerning the text's meaning. What is the reader

---

[1] For this method see James D. Nogalski, "Intertextuality and the Twelve," in *Forming Prophetic Literature: Essays on Isaiah and the Twelve in Honor of John D. W. Watts* (JSOTSup 235; ed. James W. Watts and Paul R. House; Sheffield: Sheffield Academic Press, 1996) 102-24.

[2] John D. W. Watts, "A Frame for the Book of the Twelve: Hosea 1-3 and Malachi," in *Reading and Hearing the Book of the Twelve* (James D. Nogalski and Marvin A. Sweeney, eds.; SBLSymS 15; Atlanta: SBL, 2000), 209-17.

[3] A full literature survey regarding issues of reading the Twelve as a unity will not be attempted; see the treatments in the revised Seminar Papers in *Reading and Hearing the Book of the* Twelve), and in this volume, especially the surveys by Marvin A. Sweeney, Aaron Schart, and Paul L. Redditt.

[4] Examples of fruitful thematic approaches include Paul R. House, *The Unity of the Twelve* (JSOTSup 97; Sheffield: Almond Press, 1990); Terence Collins, *The Mantle of Elijah: The Redaction Criticism of the Prophetical Books* (BibSem 20; Sheffield: JSOT Press, 1993) 59-87; and Raymond C. Van Leeuwen "Scribal Wisdom and Theodicy in the Book of the Twelve," *In Search of Wisdom: Essays in Memory of John G. Gammie* (ed. L. Perdue, B.B. Scott, and W. J. Wiseman; Louisville: Westminster/John Knox, 1993) 31-49. The current study will not pursue questions of the variant textual order attested in the LXX. For such a study see Barry Alan Jones, *The Formation of the Book of the Twelve: A Study in Text and Canon* (SBLDS 149; Atlanta: Scholars Press, 1995).

expected to find *in* the text and what is the reader expected to bring *to* the text? It will also seek answers concerning the *utility* or functionality of the text. What is the text supposed to do *to* or *for* the reader? and who *is* the reader?[5] Answers to these questions will not only help us determine the Book's *meaning*, but will guide us in proposing the text's *setting* and *purpose*.

I. Thematic Elements in Hosea 1-3

The opening and closing oracles in the Book of the Twelve provide hints concerning key thematic elements of the whole.[6] The first is an *inclusio* formed by the word "land" (אֶרֶץ). Hosea 1:2 reads "Go, take a woman of whoredom and children of whoredom, for the *land* commits whoredom away from Yahweh." The final oracle in Malachi (MT) warns that God is going to send Elijah to restore father-son unity, "lest I come and strike the *land* with a ban of destruction" (Mal 3:24 [Engl. 4:6]).[7] Interpreters typically treat these two occurrences of land as references to the inhabitants, or people of the land, and not to the land *per se*.[8] Given the importance of the land in the Hebrew Bible and the frequent use of vegetational imagery[9] in the Twelve, however, it is possible that the collector(s) wished to designate *land* as an important theme throughout the work. How did Hosea, as the introduction to the Twelve, employ this theme? We will begin with an examination of the oracles in Hosea 1.

---

[5]   "Hearer" is a more appropriate designation for the original audience since the work probably was written to be proclaimed aloud, as we will propose below. Likewise "Scroll" more accurately describes the early form of The Twelve than "Book," which technically designates a bound or codex form originating in post-biblical times. Nevertheless, the current study will sometimes employ these anachronisms due to their current widespread usage.

[6]   These texts may also serve as *inclusios* for the individual prophetic work or earlier collections. Some texts serve multiple duty, the presence of specific terms being responsible for the placement of material in its current location. See James Nogalski, *Literary Precursors to the Book of the Twelve* (BZAW 217; Berlin: de Gruyter, 1993) 14-15.

[7]   Translations are the author's unless otherwise stated. Also when the numeration of verses differs between the MT and the English translation, the numeration of MT will be given first.

[8]   This is especially the case for Hos 1:2, e.g., Hans Walter Wolff, *Hosea* (Hermeneia; Philadelphia: Fortress, 1974) 15. Beth Glazier-McDonald (*Malachi: Divine Messenger* [SBLDS 98; Atlanta: Scholars Press, 1987] 258-59) understands the reference in Malachi to connote the territory circumscribed by the families mentioned in the oracle, and comments on the intimate connection between land and people in the Hebrew Bible. David L. Petersen (*Zechariah 9-14 and Malachi* [OTL; Louisville: Westminster John Knox, 1995] 227, 232) sees Malachi's reference as cosmic in scope; the threat is against "the earth."

[9]   See Collins, *The Mantle of Elijah*, 67-68, 77, 80, *passim*.

Hosea 1:2-9 contains four commands to the prophet involving symbolic acts or namings. The first (quoted above) commands a marriage and the engendering of children who are a sign of an accusation: "the land commits whoredom away from Yahweh." The second oracle is a command to name the firstborn son "Jezreel." The symbolic significance of the name is explained by another accusation: the house of Jehu is accountable for the "bloodshed (דמים) of Jezreel." The name is mentioned again in the pronouncements of judgment: the house of Jehu will experience a divine visitation, and God will put an end to the dominion of the House of Israel by breaking its military power (bow) in the valley of Jezreel (1:3-5). The next two oracles are sentences of judgment symbolized by the names of the last two children. Israel is declared "Not-Found-Compassion" and "Not-My-People" (1:6-9), whereby Yahweh rejects Israel as a parent would disown an unwanted child.[10]

These two oracles raise questions that are only answered elsewhere in Hosea, the Book of the Twelve, and the Hebrew canon. The first oracle usually gets the most attention. Questions about the meaning of "a woman of whoredom" have resulted in much speculation about the character of Gomer and the nature of Hosea's marriage. A more fundamental issue, however, is what it means to accuse the *land* of whoredom? If land is really meant here, in what sense can the land be guilty of offense? A related issue is the meaning of "children of whoredom" and their connection with the land.

The second oracle also raises questions. "Jezreel" is unlike the other names in both form and function. First, it lacks the negative particle prefixed to the other names, and is therefore directly amenable to a positive interpretation.[11]   Second, although this name comprises a short self-contained sentence — "God sows" — its significance is not immediately borne out in a sentence containing one of its elements as occurs in the other names, and as is usual in symbolic namings in the Hebrew Bible. The reader expects the name to carry more significance than simply as the name of the location where sin and judgment occur; and so the reader is left to ponder, "What does (will) God sow?"

The reader has at hand two means to answer these questions. One is to draw upon the traditions Hosea presupposes in the Elijah cycle; the other is to look for further information in Hosea and the Twelve. Both options bear

---

[10]   The disownment language in Hos 1-2 is discussed in Laurie J. Braaten, "Parent-Child Imagery in Hosea," (Ph.D. diss., Boston University, 1987) 220-72.

[11]   "Jezreel" may portend either judgment or salvation, unlike the other names, which only symbolize salvation by dropping the prefixed "not." See 1:7; 2:1-3[1:10-2:1], 24-25[22-23].

much fruit. First, the references to Jezreel and Jehu immediately bring to mind the Elijah and Elisha traditions concerning the House of Ahab, Naboth, and Jehu. This approach is verified by another thematic clue that the Twelve provides: the (MT) Book of the Twelve concludes with an explicit reference to Elijah in Mal 3:23 [4:5]. These two invocations of the Elijah tradition function as another frame around the Twelve. A quick glance at the Elijah tradition in Kings reveals that the house of Ahab is charged with "bloodshed" (דמים) and "whoredom" (זנונים) for crimes of murder, land seizure and Baalism. Joram is charged corporately with the sins of his parents, and specifically with the "whoredom" of his mother Jezebel.[12] In a similar manner Hosea charges Ephraim with bloodshed and false worship, the latter often characterized as "whoredom."[13] Moreover, as in the Book of Kings, Hosea charges the children with the whoredom of their mother (see below).

The reader returns to Hosea for more clues concerning the meaning of the first symbolic act. The "woman of whoredom" whom Hosea marries bears "children of whoredom." These children receive names indicating they symbolize God's people, Israel. If the children represent Israel, then who or what does the woman symbolize? Does she also signify Israel as is usually suggested? A survey of the family imagery in Hosea outside of Hosea 1-3 discloses that Israel/Ephraim is always represented by masculine imagery: he is the offspring or son of Yahweh, but never God's bride.[14] Some interpreters have suggested the woman, as portrayed in Hosea 2, symbolizes a city in a manner similar to the way Isaiah depicts Jerusalem as a whore in Isaiah 1.[15] The solution is closer at hand. When one views the

---

12   According to 2 Kgs 9, crimes of "bloodshed" (דמים, vv. 7, 26) orchestrated by Ahab and Jezebel are laid at Joram's door – the murder of the prophets, God's servants, and Naboth and his children. Furthermore, Jehu charges Joram with his mother Jezebel's "whoredom" (זנונים, v. 22), which no doubt includes the Baal worship by Jezebel and the Ahab dynasty mentioned throughout the Elijah-Elisha cycle.

13   For "whoredom" (זנונים and תזנות), see Hos 2:4[2], 6[4]; 4:11, 12; 5:4; 6:10. For "bloodshed," see Hos 4:2; 6:8; 12:15[14]. Both appear throughout the Twelve, and the two are attested in the accusations against Nineveh in Nah 3:1-4.

14   It is generally supposed that the prophet's accusations of "whoredom" are grounded in the image of Israel as an unfaithful wife. Schmitt observes, however, that the older material in Hosea (Hos 4-14) always employs the masculine forms of the verb זנה when accusing Israel of whoredom, unless specific women are in view (4:14). The same usage is attested throughout the Pentateuch. Generally speaking, the references to God's people in the Hebrew Bible are masculine, with Israel (a patronymic!) depicted as the "son/sons of God." See John J. Schmitt, "The Gender of Ancient Israel," JSOT 26 (1983) 115-25.

15   Schmitt, "The Gender of Ancient Israel," 120. In several articles and papers Schmitt has proposed Samaria as the bride in Hos 2; see "The Wife of God in Hos 2," BR 39

land and agricultural imagery applied to the bride in chapter 2 in light of the statement in Hos 1:2 – that the "woman of whoredom" represents the whoredom of the *land* – then it is clear that Yahweh's bride in Hosea 1-2 is the land *per se*. It is only in Hosea 3 that the bride unequivocally represents Israel.[16]

This puzzling accusation of "whoredom" against the land leads the reader to ask an important question: how can Yahweh hold the land accountable for such sin? Since elsewhere in Hosea (and the Hebrew Bible), land or earth are only judged as a result of human sin, one suspects that the same holds true here. The issue is clarified in Hosea 2. According to 2:4[2], Yahweh summons his children (the Israelites) to join him in a lawsuit against their mother (the land). This call to participate in a legal action can be compared to Isaiah's appeal to the people to render judgment against "the vineyard" (Isa 5:1-7; cf. 5:3). Like Isaiah, Hosea soon turns the charges against the people (children) who are guilty of their own share of whoredom and misdeeds (Hos 2:6[8], 8[10]b). In other words, Hosea's charges of whoredom against the land serve a rhetorical function. The charge of whoredom and the summons to join Yahweh in a legal action involve the readers (i.e., the children) in making judgments by which they ultimately condemn themselves.[17] The children are the responsible party; their bloodshed and whoredom — sins that violate the sanctity of the land

---

(1989) 5-18. Gale A. Yee (*Composition and Tradition in the Book of Hosea: A Redaction Critical Investigation* [SBLDS 102; Atlanta: Scholars Press, 1987] 124-25) points to the references to Jacob's (unnamed) wife in Hos 12:13 and Rachel in Jer 31:15, and suggests the woman is Rachel. The major weakness of these interpretations is that no such female figures are mentioned in Hos 1-3.

[16] The land as bride imagery is consistently applied only to the land through Hos 2:15[13]. Beginning with the salvation oracles in 2:16[14] the bride *includes* Israel, whom Yahweh will take *into* the wilderness. This differs from 2:5[3] where the bride (land) will be made *like* a wilderness. The major Greek codices resolved this tension by translating v. 15 as "I will designate her as (τάξω . . . εἰς) a wilderness" (cf. LXX 2:5, see *BHK*). Formerly I argued that this change in imagery was a result of a Judean redaction and reinterpretation of Hosea's oracles that culminates in the late exilic reformulation reinterpretation of Hos 3 (Braaten, "Parent-Child Imagery in Hosea," 46-72 and n. 27 below). I am now convinced that whatever its literary history, the present form of chapter 2 functions to indicate land/people solidarity. From one perspective the land is Israel's mother; from another, land and people are united in their fate and experience of both judgment and salvation. It is also noteworthy that the references to symbolic marriage in Hos 1 and 3 form a frame around Hos 2 and the content of these chapters function to focus culpability clearly on the people, unlike chapter 2 with its accusations against the land. See my "Earth Community in Hosea 2," in *The Earth Bible: Earth Story in the Prophets* (vol. 4.; ed. Norman C. Habel; Sheffield: Sheffield Academic Press, 2001) 190-95.

[17] See Braaten, "Earth Community in Hosea 2," 190.

— result in the land's "whoredom."[18] The fate of Land and people are united in corporate solidarity.

Keeping in view the above qualifications concerning the accusations against the land, the following image emerges. The people commit whoredom by worshipping Baal as their provider god instead of Yahweh, thereby "wedding" the land to Baal (Hos 2:10b[8b]). The bride land "commits" whoredom due to the people's action, resulting in the land's being allied to "lovers." The bride – like her children – attributes her gifts to these lovers rather than to her real husband Yahweh (2:7-10a[5-8a]). Intimately tied to the land as her offspring, the people are polluted by land's "whoredom" in much the same way that Joram shared the whoredom of his mother Jezebel (2 Kgs 9:22).[19] In response to her unfaithfulness Yahweh divorces his wife and strips her as an act of shame and punishment (2:4-5[2-3], 12[10]) by denuding her of the agricultural products that God has provided as her clothes (2:11[9]).[20]

The significance of "God sows" is becoming more apparent. The agricultural bounty of the land is a gift of God; it has been sown by God so to speak. As such, God can take it back as an act of judgment. Likewise, the people, who are the offspring of their father Yahweh and the land,[21] had been sown on the land, and are expected to take root there and bear fruit for God. What God has sown God can disown and remove (or "harvest"), however, as an act of judgment. "God sows" can also recover its positive significance if God decides to bless Israel in the future. This positive significance of Jezreel is found in two sets of salvation oracles which bracket

---

[18] For the effect of "bloodshed" on the land see Num 35:33. Making one's daughter a prostitute (Lev 19:29) or the remarriage of a divorced woman (Jer 3:1) results in the *land* committing prostitution or being defiled. Ps 106:34-39 lists the sins of the settlement as mingling with the Canaanites, worshiping their idols, sacrificing children, polluting the land with blood, and prostituting themselves. Hosea may have been the first to set forth such ideas. See Tivka Frymer-Kensky, "Pollution, Purification, and Purgation in Biblical Israel," in *The Word of the Lord Shall Go Forth; Essays in honor of David Noel Freedman in Celebration of His Sixtieth Birthday* (ed. Carol L. Meyers and M. O'Connor; Eisenbrauns, Winona Lake, IN: 1983) 406-412.

[19] The major difference being, of course, that Jezebel is held accountable for her "whoredom," while the land in Hosea is implicated in whoredom due to her children's deeds.

[20] For vegetation and herds as the land's clothing provided by God see Ps 65:10-14[9-13]. The marriage and divorce laws and customs reflected in the imagery of Hos 2 are discussed in Braaten, "Parent-Child Imagery in Hosea," 261-78.

[21] Sexual imagery is not in view here; rather the notion that God is the father/creator of individuals, expressed both in terms of creation in the womb of the human mother and creation in the womb of mother Earth (2 Esd 5:43-55; 10:7, 14; cf. Ps 139:13-16; Qoh 5:14[15]; Sir 40:1; cf. Job 1:21). See Braaten, "Parent-Child Imagery in Hosea," 280-92; also see Don C. Benjamin, "Israel's God: Mother and Midwife," *BTB* 19 (1989) 117.

Hosea 2.[22] In the first oracle God promises that the judgment on the children will be reversed "in the place where" (במקום אשר) they were disowned, viz. the land (Hos 2:1[1:10]). The children's names will be reversed and then they will "grow up out of the land (ועלו מן־הארץ), for great is the day of Jezreel" (Hos 2:2[1:11]).[23] God's sowing on the "day of Jezreel" will reverse the judgment "on that day" connoted by the name Jezreel in the first oracle of judgment in Hos 1:5.

The second salvation oracle playing upon the name Jezreel is found in Hos 2:23-25[21-23]; it begins with another reference to "on that day" (cf. 2:18[16], 20[18]). The reader must begin with the immediately preceding oracle, which announces that Yahweh will enable his wife to confess that Yahweh is "my husband" by removing the title "my Baal" from her mouth (2:18-19[16-17]). A creation wide salvation event will ensue, in which God will make a covenant with the animals, protect the land by removing warfare from her, and betroth his wife by rendering bridewealth consisting of "righteousness and justice, loving commitment and compassion ... [and] faithfulness."[24] This all-encompassing salvation event sets off a chain of cosmic responses with fertility implications: Yahweh "will answer the Heavens, and they will answer Earth, and Earth will answer the grain, the wine and the oil; and they shall answer 'Jezreel!'" (2:23-24[21-22]). Here the name Jezreel functions as a proper confession and acclamation by the grain, wine and oil: "God sows!" The confession completes the promise of vv. 18-19[16-17]; it acknowledges the God of Israel as the one who provides salvation and agricultural bounty, rather than the Baals as the unfaithful bride once reckoned (2:19[17]; cf. 2:7[5], 9[7], 10[8], 12[10], 13-15[12-13]). This divine sowing is restated in the continuation of the oracle in

---

[22]   Yee, *Composition and Tradition*, 71-76.

[23]   For עלה used for the growth of plants see Hos 10:8; for sprouting see Amos 7:1; with מארץ see Isa 53:2; for other references BDB s.v. qal 4. (The interpretation of עלו מן as "sprout" in 2:3[1:11] with reference to 2:25[23] was first suggested by Th. C. Vriezen, *Hosea, profeet en cultuur* [Groningen, 1941], 13, 22; cited by Wolff, *Hosea*, 28.) If the events of Hos 2:2[1:11] are understood to be prior to the salvation in the land mentioned in 2:1[1:10], then it is tempting to interpret the phrase "go up from the land" as also containing a promise of a new exodus (see Exod 1:10 cf. Gen 50:24). So Yee (*Composition and Tradition*, 75), who proposes that ועלו מן־הארץ "is open to both levels of interpretation," — i.e. as the people going up from the land of exile and as the people growing up like plants when they are sown on the land of homecoming. Wolff's (*Hosea*, 24, 28) proposal to interpret the phrase as "take possession of the land" is based on another interpretation of the phrase in Exod 1:10.

[24]   For this interpretation of Hos 2:18-22[16-20] see Braaten, "Earth Community in Hosea 2," 195-99.

2:25[23]; "I will sow it (וזרעתיה[25]) for myself in the land." In other words, through the cosmic chain of answering, God will sow "in the land"[26] the salvation promised in vv. 20-22[18-20].

The first two chapters of Hosea serve to introduce the hearers of the Scroll of the Twelve to the "God sows" theme.[27] We are now in a position to answer more fully the question, what does God sow? On the one hand, God will sow judgment on a people who violate their neighbor and God's land through bloodshed and whoredom. On the other hand, God promises to act for the sake of the created order and reverse this judgment and sow salvation for God's people, land, and even the animals. In the days of the post-exilic hearers of the Twelve, the intergenerational people of God have experienced, to some extent, both types of God's sowing. The hearers of the Twelve themselves, however, stand once again between these two poles of God's sowing; they have experienced God's judgment and await anew the promises of salvation. The Book of the Twelve thus serves both as a justification of the past judgment of God, and as warning and promise: a warning concerning the possibility of further judgment for a rebellious community, the promise of salvation for a repentant community. As the Book of the Twelve unfolds, the hearers find God's actions, as well as their own, described in the imagery of sowing, planting and harvesting. The fate of God's people and land stands in the balance. To this we will now turn.[28]

---

[25] For the various proposals for interpreting the feminine suffix (ה-) see the commentaries. For the 3rd pers fem sing suffix referring to a previous sentence or plurals see GKC § 135 p; cf. § 122q. This collective interpretation was first proposed by Bernhard F. Batto, "The Covenant of Peace: A Neglected Ancient Near Eastern Motif," *CBQ* 49 (1987) 202. For the interpretation employed here see Braaten, "Earth Community in Hosea 2," 199-200. For a similar idea see Zech 8:12, which forms an inclusio with Hos 2:25[23].

[26] Because of the cosmic salvation depicted in this context it is possible to understand ארץ in its more comprehensive meaning as "Earth."

[27] As indicated earlier (n. 16), Hos 3 is an alternative interpretation of Hos 1-2. It does not deal directly with the "God sows" theme or mention the land; rather, Hos 3 presents Israel's punishment and restoration as the loss of monarchy and cult, and eventual return to David and Yahweh's "good." (For this return to David cf. the reference to the people's appointing for themselves "one head" after their return to the land in Hos 2:2[1:11]). Hos 3 thereby functions as a second introduction to the Twelve by adding a messianic element, as Ps 2 does for the Book of Psalms. This chapter also has verbal and thematic links with Hag — Zech 8 with which it functions as an inner frame for the Twelve (proposed in Braaten, "That God May Heal the Land: A Liturgical Setting for the Book of the Twelve" [paper presented at the New England Society of Biblical Literature, April 27, 2001] 5-6).

[28] The current study will trace this imagery through Hosea and Joel with some concluding observations on Malachi. A brief survey of the land motif throughout the Twelve is undertaken in my unpublished paper "That God May Heal the Land."

II. Thematic Elements In Hosea 4-14

The lawsuit in Hos 4:1-3 introduces chapter 4 and the second major division of Hosea (chaps. 4-14). As in the opening judgment oracle in chapter 1, Hos 4:2 summarizes Israel's sins as bloodshed. In both cases the land and its people are adversely affected. In Hosea 4, however, the land is clearly presented as a victim, suffering unjustly for the sins of her human inhabitants. The land responds to this suffering as sufferers often react in the Hebrew Bible—she "mourns" (4:3).[29] In her recent dissertation Katherine M. Hayes has isolated nine examples of the "earth mourning" metaphor in the prophetic literature, three of which occur in the Book of the Twelve. Hayes observes that in these texts the mourning earth is usually depicted as responding to human distress or transgression.[30]

The land is presented as a victim whose fate is corporately linked to the actions of her sinful human inhabitants. If the people persist in their sin and refuse to change, then the land will continue to suffer. It might be possible, therefore, to see the mourning of the land as encompassing a repentance ritual, a response occasioned both by the land's miserable "dying" condition and the corporate sin afflicting her. The beginnings of this ritual may be hinted at in Hosea 2. Here God warns his bride that if she does not voluntarily give up her "whoredom" she would be stripped as an act of judgment. Hayes suggests this is the initiation of an imposed mourning.[31] After the

---

29 אבל can connote both "mourning" and "drying up." Some conjecture two roots for the word (KBL s.v.), but it is more likely that the two meanings are interrelated. See the discussion in Katherine M. Hayes, "'The Earth Mourns': Earth as Actor in a Prophetic Metaphor," (Ph.D. diss., Catholic University of America, 1997) 14-23. This dissertation has now been and published as "The Earth Mourns." Prophetic Metaphor and Oral Aesthetic (Academia Biblica; Boston, Leiden: Brill, 2002), but it appeared too late to be incorporated into this paper.

30 Hayes ("The Earth Mourns," 2-3) isolates the metaphor (chronologically) in Amos 1:2; Hos 4:1-3; Jer 4:23-28; 12:1-4; 12:7-13; 23:9-12; Isa 24:1-20; 33:7-9; and Joel 1:5-20. She observes (pp. 19-20) how earth's condition and appearance during a drought can be likened to human mourning rituals.

31 Stripping as a mourning ritual is one of six motifs Hayes identifies in the metaphor. She suggests the threatened stripping in Hos 2:4-15[2-13] (cf. 13:15 and 10:1-2) is an "imposed mourning" (see 2:13[11]) on the bride whom she identifies as Israel connoting both community and land. She sees a similar sequence of whoredom, pollution, and stripping (of Jerusalem) in Ezek 16:30-52 and 23:26-30 ("The Earth Mourns," 69-73). Perhaps there are allusions to the stripping of ornaments as a sign of mourning and contrition in Hos 2:4[2], 15[13], cf. the stripping of ornaments in Exod 33:4-6 as imposed mourning and contrition. Likewise, in Isa 32:9-20 Yahweh commands women to strip, don mourning attire (v. 11), then lament because of God's impending judgment—which includes the agricultural demise of the land. In her discussion of Amos 1:2, Hayes speculates that the mourning Earth metaphor may include multiple

judgment of Hosea 2, Yahweh promises he will restore her to the marital relationship and return the previously stripped agricultural products. The mourning of the land in Hosea 4, then, would signal that she has submitted to this judgment, so she now anticipates the promised renewal. Yet for the transformation to be complete, the sinful inhabitants of the land — who continue to pollute her with their unfaithfulness, violence and whoredom — must also acknowledge their sin and follow the example of the mourning and repenting land.[32] Since the land's fate is corporately bound up with that of her inhabitants', she will continue to suffer under (their) judgment until the people repent (שוב) or are removed from her.[33]

The languishing of the land and removal of her creatures points ultimately to the downfall of her inhabitants. Here we may have an allusion to the Jezreel, or "God sows" motif. Hayes suggests that in Hos 4:3 the verb נאסף, "being destroyed," could also be rendered "being gathered" or "harvested." God's judgment is manifested here as a reversal of creation, or a taking back or harvesting of what God has sown on the earth: "... what God has originally sown, or planted on the earth, he is now gathering up."[34] This

---

nuances (41-43), including implications of repentance rituals. She makes no mention of a connection with repentance rituals when she deals with Hos 2, however.

[32] Humans joining in with the mourning land (or similar personified mourners) is a typical response in such texts. See Delbert R. Hillers, "'The Roads to Zion Mourn' (Lam 1:4)," *Per* 12 (1971) 126-30. In Israel's broader cultural context mourning behavior, as is well known, is the usual response to such catastrophes as drought. In the Ugaritic Aqhat epic crops languish in a drought resulting from Aqhat's murder. Aqhat's father Danel and sister Pughat respond to the drought with mourning behavior—even *before* they learn of his death; see *ANET* 152-54; cf. Simon B. Parker, *The Pre-Biblical Narrative Tradition. Essays on the Ugaritic Poems* Keret *and* Aqhat (SBLSBS 24; Atlanta: Scholars Press, 1989) 122-24. An allusion to repentance is found in Hos 3:5 in the future "return" (ישבו)" of the sons of Israel to Jerusalem (i.e., David, Yahweh, and "his goodness," discussed in Braaten, "That God May Heal the Land," 5-6). Repentance is constantly called for throughout Hos 4-14 (see below).

[33] For the fate of land and people linked under the judgment of God see Hayes, "The Earth Mourns," 62 (especially n. 35). A similar linking is found in the priestly material which warns Israel that if they defile (טמא) themselves and the land with prohibited sexual practices, the land will protect itself from human incurred judgment and "vomit out" the offenders, as it did the previous inhabitants, Lev 18:24-30 (cf. Ezra 9:10-15 and Ezek 36:16-21). For the effect of bloodshed and whoredom on the land see the references in n. 18 above. The defilement of the land ultimately results in Israel's demise. "It is the land that is finally abused. Such action fouls the nest of Israel. And there is no alternative but to be rejected, because the land must be cared for." See Walter Brueggemann, *The Land: Place as Gift, Promise and Challenge in Biblical Faith* (OBT; Philadelphia: Fortress, 1977) 119.

[34] Hayes, "The Earth Mourns," 80, n. 83. For the allusions of Hos 4:3 to the tradition attested in the P creation narrative see Michael De Roche, "The Reversal of Creation in Hosea," *VT* 31 (1981) 400-409.

not only applies to the languishing plant life, but extends to all creatures or "seed," beasts of the field, birds of the air, and fish of the sea — and ultimately, to God's unrepentant people. From this point on in Hosea and the Twelve much attention is given to the motif of the people's failure to repent properly and their resulting tenuous relationship with the land.

After the introduction in Hos 4:1-3, the second section continues from Hos 4:4-5:7, which exhibits a high degree of thematic unity.[35] The prophet continues to announce threats of God's judgment against a straying people whose efforts to approach God are misguided. They lack knowledge and reject God's torah (Hos 4:6); they dedicate themselves to literal and spiritual whoredom (4:10, 12, 13-15, 18). Not only do they not know God, but also their deeds of whoredom have become a spiritual power rendering them incapable of returning to God (5:3-4, cf. 4:19). Their inadequate attempts to seek Yahweh reveal their unfaithfulness: new offspring are not the children of Yahweh, they are "sons of strangers" (5:6-7a). Therefore the fertility festivals will be turned against the people, and the new moon will devour them (יֹאכְלֵם 5:7b; cf. 4:10) and their land allotments (נַחֲלוֹת).

The third section, Hos 5:8-7:16,[36] takes up the theme of Israel's misguided efforts at repentance more directly, as evidenced by the frequent use of the keyword שׁוּב. Many interpreters see a shift here from a cultic to a historical focus, but they also recognize some continuity with the previous section.[37] The opening commands to blow the shophar and to "cry out" (5:8) are generally regarded as military terms: viz., the prophet is issuing

---

[35] Most commentators divide the passage in multiple units based on consideration of form, style, or content; e.g., Wolff (Hosea, 73-74 and 95) finds separate "transmission units" in 4:4-19 and 5:1-7. If one reads the material straight through, however, thematic unity is found in the addressees as "priests" (4:4, 6, 9; 5:1), the attack on the cult (throughout), the accusation of "whoredom" (4:10, 11, 12, 13, 14, 15; 5:3, 4, note "spirit of whoredom" in 4:12 and 5:4), which is connected with the desire for children (4:10; 5:7). The accusation that the people do not know Yahweh practically frames the unit including the introduction (4:1, 6; 5:4), as does the mention of the demise of the land (4:3) and of the fields' being devoured (5:7).

[36] Wolff (Hosea, 108) finds syntactic, stylistic, and thematic unity in the material.

[37] Wilhelm Rudolph (Hosea [KAT XIII/1; Gütersloh: Gerd Mohn, 1966], 125), claiming to follow a consensus, asserts that 5:8 is a new beginning, marked by a shift from the cultic to the political. A. A. Macintosh (Hosea [ICC; Edinburgh: T & T Clark, 1997], 194), following Jerome, sees the immediate connection between the sections as follows: "what God had threatened through his prophet is now fulfilled in the events of history." Francis Landy (Hosea [Readings; Sheffield, Sheffield Academic Press, 1995] 73) proposes that this section and the previous one are linked by a cultic occasion during which the priestly portions (5:7) would be consumed. See below the discussion on the shophar.

the war alarm.[38] While the military background is certainly connoted, the most one could say here is that such an alarm warns the people to seek refuge from the enemy in a city.[39] The alarm serves a more important function: it announces the "day of punishment" (5:9) and the need for a corporate acknowledgement of guilt — presumably in a public assembly.[40] Previously the prophet had warned that because of the people's unfaithfulness Israel's festivals would consume their land allotments (5:7). Now the prophet announces that Yahweh will strike the people with maladies that affect land, crops, and people ("maggots," "rottenness," "sickness," and "wounds" 5:10-12, NRSV). Instead of repenting, the people seek healing from Assyria (5:11-13). So God threatens to become like a lion that will "tear" and "carry off (from the land[?])" his people (5:14). Then God will "return" (אשובה) and await their acknowledgment of guilt (5:15). Instead, the people's "return" (נשובה) results in a superficial confession of God's willingness to heal and restore fertility (6:1-3). They expect clouds bearing life-restoring showers, but they will not come because the people's "loving commitment" lacks its restorative effect. Rather, it is like a fleeting morning cloud or a quickly dissipating dew (6:4-6), disappointing the farmer and leaving the land parched and the vegetation wilting. Both city and priests commit bloodshed (6:8-9), and Ephraim's whoredom continues to defile (טמא) Israel (6:10-11). Since they are land grabbers, God will also remove Judah as a "harvest" (קציר, 6:11; cf. 5:10).

God's efforts to restore (שוב שבות) and heal only bring the people's sin into sharper relief (6:11b-7:16). They do not ponder ("say to their hearts") that Yahweh remembers all their wickedness (7:2). Although fallen, they refuse to call upon God (7:7). Israel's guilt is self-evident, yet they refuse to return to (שוב) or seek Yahweh their God (7:10). Instead they vacillate between Egypt and Assyria for help (7:11). The prophet takes up a lamentation (woe oracle) against them because they continue to stray, rebel, and actually plot evil against God (7:13-16). God no doubt expects rites of contrition and confession, but their mourning rituals are not from the

---

[38] For the blowing of the *shophar* as connoting a war alarm or signal, see Judg 6:34; 1 Sam 13:3; 2 Sam 2:28; 18:6; KBL s.v. 3. For רוע (hiph) as a war alarm, as cry or trumpet blast, see Num 10:9; Josh 6:10, KBL s.v. 3.

[39] So Macintosh, *Hosea*, 194; see Amos 3:6. In view of the rest of the book, Hosea would hardly be calling the people to war.

[40] The *shophar* was often used to announce theophanies and/or cultic gatherings, including days of fasting and repentance (see Pss 47:6[5]; 81:4[3]; Joel 2:1, 15; KBL s.v. A.1, 2. The verb רוע was also employed in cultic rejoicing (Pss 47:2; 65:13) or laments (Mic 4:9); see Stuart A. Irvine, "Enmity in the House of God," *JBL* 117 (1998) 647-48; KBL s.v. 5, 6.

heart. Instead of repenting they attempt to move their God to reward them by gashing themselves in the manner of the Canaanites (7:14).[41] Again the prophet mentions that when the people turn (שׁוּב), it is not to God (Hos 7:16a).[42] The people whom God had once trained for warfare have become like a deceitful bow, they will fall by the sword and be brought into mockery in the land of Egypt (7:15-16).

In the two units comprising Hosea 8-13, the prophet continues to accuse the people of straying and failing to return to God, only now the punishment consists of land degradation and decreed loss is heightened and seems more certain. Section four consists of Hos 8:1 – 9:9.[43] It is linked with the previous section: both begin with a command to blow the *shophar* (Hos 8:1; cf. Hos 5:8). Here, however, Yahweh commands the prophet[44] to sound the alarm. War is again the immediate danger, the enemy is depicted as a vulture about to swoop down upon "the house of Yahweh," the land as *Yahweh's* dwelling place.[45] But the *shophar* reference could again connote a call to cultic assembly, as the appropriate place for prophetic speech and Israel's response.[46] Israel is called once more to follow the land's lead in mourning and repenting for sins.

---

[41] See Wolff, *Hosea*, 128. Self-mutilation was practiced by the Canaanite prophets, whom Elijah confronted on Mt. Carmel (1 Kgs 18:28). Prohibitions against this custom are found in Deut 14:1, and in Lev 19:28 immediately before the command not to profane the land by making one's daughter a prostitute. On the other hand, it is possible to understand from texts such as Jer 16:6 that such gashing was standard practice in mourning rituals when observed outside the Canaanite cults.

[42] ישׁובו לא על is difficult to translate, although it is clear that the people are not returning to God. The textual traditions suggest correcting the text to read "They turned, [but] not to a yoke," or "they turned to [what does] not profit." It is also possible to emend the text to read "they turned, but not to me"; see Wolff, *Hosea,* 108.

[43] This division is also adopted by C. F. Keil, *Biblical Commentary on the Twelve Minor Prophets* (2 vols; Edinburgh: T & T Clark, 1869), 1:111.

[44] With Macintosh (*Hosea,* 292) contra Wolff (*Hosea,* 133), who objects that this would be the only place in Hos 4 — 14 where Yahweh addresses the prophet directly. Rudolph (*Hosea,* 161) observes "wenn Jahwe seinen Propheten in Kap. 1 u. 3 anredet, warum soll er es nicht auch in Kap. 8 tun können?"

[45] Rudolph (*Hosea,* 162) interprets it as "'der Raum, das Gebiet Jahwes', d.h. das heilige Land wie in 9,15." Given the family imagery of Hosea, it is also possible to view this as Yahweh's family allotment. Francis I. Andersen and David Noel Freedman (*Hosea* [AB 24; Garden City: Doubleday, 1980] 486) interpret the phrase as "the promised land as Yahweh's realm or estate." Although most recent commentators reject a reference to the Temple here, given the cultic allusions in the chapter it is conceivable that both land and temple are in view.

[46] Collins (*Mantle of Elijah,* 62-63) suggests cultic settings for the production of the Twelve. The first edition reflects the "preaching and liturgical prayers" of the exilic assemblies, where the mood "varied from resigned acceptance and regret in the early years to hope and determination, even optimism as time went by." The second edition

Calling as the voice of Yahweh, Hosea announces that Israel has broken the covenant, transgressed torah, and is guilty of idolatry and other cultic irregularities (8:1, 4, 6, 12, 13). Israel shows that they still do not accept the charges, and desperately attempt to reassert their status as the covenant people. "They cry in lament (יזעקו) to me, 'My God, we know you — (it's) Israel!'" (8:2). Nevertheless, their political and cultic sins affect their relationship with Yahweh and the land. Hosea expresses this change in proverbial speech with a twofold application. "Because they sow wind (רוח יזרעו) the whirlwind they will harvest" (8:7a). First, their sins literally affect their harvest; the grain will not yield as expected (8:7b).[47] If there should be some growth, then "strangers will swallow it" (זרים יבלעהו, 8:7c). Second, the prophet speaks of the people's displacement from the land, using the catchword "swallow;" Israel will be "swallowed up" by the nations (8:8).

This application of the proverbial "to reap what one sows" is augmented by the broader context of Hosea. The רוח Israel has sown and reaped is the רוח זנונים, the "spirit/wind of whoredom" (Hos 4:12; 5:4; cf. 4:19), which robs Ephraim of the ability to return to God. They hoped through their whoredom to multiply and have abundant fertility, instead they bore "children of strangers." Here the prophet adds the charge that their political alliances are misguided because they bargain for lovers in Assyria (Hos 8:9-10). The result has been that Ephraim "has flourished by himself," but it is short-lived.[48] The people have sinned against Yahweh, the land, and one another, so Yahweh is about to "gather them up" for his harvest.[49] Ephraim will reap the consequences; "strangers" (with whom they bargained!) will "swallow" what is left of their crops, and then Israel itself. They have strayed so far from Yahweh that now no matter how much God should write his "torahs" (תורתי) the people would consider it "as (something) strange" (זר, 8:12). Israel would rather offer sacrifices than return, so "to Egypt they shall return" (ישובו, 8:13). God's sowing has apparently failed; he will "harvest" the inhabitants from his land. Both God and Israel will reap what they have sown.

---

was set in the "prayers and reflections associated with religious gatherings" at the post-exilic Jerusalem temple.

[47] Macintosh (*Hosea,* 313-14) notes the connection here between the natural world and moral sphere, as seen in Hos 4:1-3.

[48] Reading with the LXX. See Stuart A. Irvine, "Politics and Prophetic Commentary in Hosea 8:8-10," *JBL* 114 (1995) 292-93. I find it unnecessary, however, to transpose this phrase to v. 8 with Irvine.

[49] For קבץ pi. used in a harvest context in the Twelve see Mic 4:12.

The prophet reiterates the charge of "whoredom" (9:1).   Although the cult is directed to Yahweh, Israel is really just imitating other "peoples" (9:1-5).   The rituals have the same consequence as elsewhere in Hosea: the desired fertility will not result (9:2).   Yahweh will not be pleased with the sacrifices, which, like mourner's bread, will defile Israel, and will not be permitted in the house of Yahweh (9:4).[50] Israel will no longer be allowed to "dwell in the land of Yahweh" (9:3) — an allusion to the charge against "those who dwell in the land" (Hos 4:1-3). Israel will be gathered and buried by Egypt; their goods and pilgrim tents[51] will be dispossessed[52] by nettles and thorns (9:6b), as the land returns to its unpeopled condition. Furthermore, the prophet indicates that the "day of the festival of Yahweh" has initiated Israel's destruction, the "days of punishment" and "retribution" have come (9:5-7). Israel refuses to believe God has treated them fairly and "cries out" in lamentation (9:7).   Irvine argues that the setting of this passage is "a communal lament service at a national sanctuary," the "house of God" (9:8).[53] In this service a cultic prophet complains that Yahweh has failed to protect the nation during an enemy invasion. Hosea rebukes this prophet as foolish and mad and as perpetrating enmity in the house of God (9:7-8).[54] The lamenting of the people is still misdirected. Hosea closes by reiterating God's determination to "remember their iniquity" and "punish their sin" (9:9, cf. 8:13).

Section five (Hos 9:10 – 10:15) is bound together by its increased use of plant imagery to connote Ephraim's relation with the land, Yahweh, and one another. There is also a heightened tendency to direct oracles against

---

[50] Here "house of Yahweh" is a place of worship, and so lends support to the suggestion that the "House of Yahweh" in 8:1 indicates a cultic setting, possibly Bethel or Samaria. If this phrase is a redactional gloss, as Wolff (*Hosea,* 155) maintains, then it may indicate a post-exilic Jerusalem setting for the reading of the Book of the Twelve. Both meanings may apply, however, as Hosea receives a new application in its new setting in the Twelve.

[51] See Wolff, *Hosea,* 156.

[52] For the rendering of ירשׁ in contexts of inheriting or disinheriting see KBL, s.v. 1-3. Note again that the land is designated as belonging to Yahweh, who will protect his estate by removing its destroyers.

[53] For the emendation of ידעו to ירעו see *BHS*. For its translation see the discussion of Hos 5:8 above. Irvine ("Enmity in the House of God," 652) identifies in this passage several allusions to lamentation rituals and a number of terms characteristic of lament psalms.

[54] Recent studies have argued convincingly that Hos 9:7b-8 are the words of Hosea against a prophet, and not Hosea citing words spoken against him. See Irvine, "Enmity in the House of God," 645-48; and Margaret S. Odell, "Who were the Prophets in Hosea?" *HBT* 18 (1996) 83-87. The widespread view that 9:7b are the people's words goes back at least to Julius Wellhausen (*Die kleinen Propheten* [3rd ed.; Berlin: Georg Reimer, 1898] 123), who interprets 9:7b as a dispute ("Rede und Gegenrede").

Ephraim's children, rather than crops, as judgment for participation in the fertility cult. The text alternates with remarkable consistency between plant imagery, the fertility cult, and judgment on offspring. Threats of punishment are even more certain and serious than in the previous section, and include more references to the king and his officials, and Israel's political and military intrigues. The passage seems to be an explanation of the oracle pronounced against king and kingdom by the symbolic name of the first child, Jezreel, or "God sows." The escalating references to children bring to bear the disownment implied in the names of the second and third children, "Not-Found-Compassion" and "Not-My-People."[55]

The passage is a speech of Yahweh with brief interjections by the prophet, sometimes emerging as dialogue.[56]   Yahweh once regarded (רָאִיתִי) Israel as grapes in the wilderness, the first fruits of the fig (Hos 9:10a), a palm-shoot[57] planted in a meadow (9:13a), a fruitful vine (10:1). But from the beginning they committed themselves in love to Baal (9:10b). Yahweh will take away childbirth, but if they should bear children he will bereave them[58] and pronounce his woe over them when he departs from them (9:11-12). Indeed, Ephraim is about to produce children for the executioner (9:13b).[59] The prophet responds by praying they will neither give birth to nor nurse children (9:14). Yahweh replies that he has hated them since the days when they camped at Gilgal. God no longer loves them so he will disown[60] them, casting them out of his "house" (9:15), i.e., God's land and family, and to the exilic and postexilic reader his temple. At this point

---

55 Likewise Macintosh, *Hosea*, 369, 377.

56 Wolff (*Hosea*, 162-63) considers 9:10-17 "a sketch of an audition account" of Hosea to the inner circle that transmitted his sayings. Congruent themes continue, however, through Hos 10, for which Wolff recognizes a similar setting, seeing the material as delivered to the same inner circle (172).

57 See Macintosh, *Hosea*, 370-71, Rudolph, *Hosea*, 180, 182, and NRSV.

58 Cf. the sequence in Hos 8:7b, where there will be no production of grain, but if some should grow it will be consumed by others.

59 וְאֶפְרַיִם לְהוֹצִיא אֶל־הֹרֵג בָּנָיו; for the translation "about to (lead)" see GKC §114h, k. הוֹצִיא can mean "lead, bring out (to, אֶל)," or "generate," usually of plants; cf. BDB s.v. hiph, 1g, j. It is also used of God's agency in birth in Job 10:18, perhaps related to the image of Yahweh as the divine midwife. See Benjamin, "Israel's God: Mother and Midwife," 115, 118-19. In Hos 9 the plant imagery suggests both of these meanings. Perhaps a third meaning would be apparent to the post-exilic reader, "put away, disown" as in Ezra 10:3, 19.

60 "Hate, love, and cast out" (גָרַשׁ) are often interpreted as divorce language here, but the terms also connote disownment. Since the dominant family image of Israel in Hosea is the father/son relationship and disownment (Hos 1), disownment is probably in view here as well. See Braaten, "Parent-Child Imagery in Hosea," 308-15; cf. 40-41 and 88-134.

the plant metaphors take on negative connotations. Ephraim will no longer take root, God will kill their children in the womb as the prophet requested (9:16). The prophet summarizes the outcome of Ephraim's lack of response since the initial call to hear, "My God will reject them since they have not heard him, they will be wanderers in the nations."[61] Since Israel has failed to hear and respond to the accusations concerning their crimes against the land, God will reject them, disowning them from his land, rendering them landless wanderers.

In the remainder of the section the prophet continues to use plant imagery in indictments against Israel and its leaders. As the bounty of Yahweh's land (אֶרֶץ) increased, so did their altars and pillars. When Israel worships, "their heart is divided."[62] Israel will be held guilty, and Yahweh will destroy these cult objects (10:1-2). Yet Hosea still hopes that Israel will admit that their political demise is due to their not fearing Yahweh (10:4a).[63] Perhaps a small starting point will be their mourning over the calf of Beth-aven, which will soon be deported to Assyria (10:5-6). Until they repent sincerely, though, the prophet will continue to accuse them of bearing bad fruit; judgment sprouts like poisonous plants because of their empty covenants (10:4). When the king and cult are removed, briers and thistles (cf. Gen 3:18 and Isa 7:23-25) will grow up over their altars, reclaiming their domain (10:7-8).

Hosea now tells Israel how to receive the restoration they earlier claimed Yahweh had unfairly withheld (8:2). They need to sow according to righteousness, and they will reap according to the loving commitment (חֶסֶד) they have lacked (see Hos 4:1; 6:6). This will be nothing less than Judah's and Ephraim's breaking fallow ground (10:11). It is now time for Israel to act, to seek Yahweh, and await his rain of righteousness upon them (10:12). Formerly they have sown (plowed) wickedness and reaped injustice. Thus they are bearing the consequences of eating the fruit of lies (10:13a), concerning which they have been warned (Hos 4:2).

Section six (Hos 11—14) contains two major subdivisions. The first, chapters 11:1-14:1[13:16], is thematically connected by references and allusions to the Exodus tradition. Although the imagery differs from Hosea 1-2, it is linked with these chapters by oracles of judgment against God's rebellious son, and God's determination to redeem him. This subdivision also contains increased direct appeals to repent through the use of שׁוּב, some-

---

61 This is the first time the verb "hear"(שׁמע) has been used since the introduction and opening section (Hos 4:1 and 5:1).
62 For the vocalization of חָלַק in 10:2, see *BHS*.
63 For the interpretation of these verses see Wolff, *Hosea,* 174; Macintosh, *Hosea,* 392-94.

times offering a renewed sense of hope to the reader. Yet prophetic accusations and threats of punishment continue to foster an urgency for repentance, which is anticipated in the second subdivision Hos 14:2-10[1-9].
Again, although the imagery is slightly different, this passage is linked to
the salvation and fertility oracles of Hosea 1—3.

The section begins with Hos 11:1-7 portraying the Exodus as an act of
adopting Israel as God's son. Israel later violated this relationship by offering service to the Baals instead of Yahweh, his loving and nurturing parent.[64] Having refused to return (שוב) to Yahweh, Israel will return (ישוב) to
the land of Egypt (and Assyria, 11:5). Israel will be destroyed and consumed, and because Yahweh's people are "bent on turning away from me"
(תלואים למשובתי), they will find no nurture from Baal[65] (11:6-7). Still,
judgment and destruction will not mean the complete end of God's son.
Yahweh's compassion moves him to promise that he will not again (שוב)
destroy Ephraim (11:8-9). This resolve is a major turning point in the book;
Yahweh is now ready to "return them (הושבתים) to their houses" (11:11),
thereby reversing their disownment from Yahweh's house in 9:15.

To move toward that goal, Yahweh announces his lawsuit against
(Judah and) Jacob to "repay (ישיב) him according to his deeds." Since the
suit is patterned after God's relationship with the patriarch Jacob there is
hope, for despite his undesirable past, when Jacob wept and sought God's
favor the divinity met with him at Bethel (12:3-7[2-6]).[66] The prophet
promises God's aid: "And you, with the help of[67] your God shall return
(תשוב); maintain loving commitment and justice, and hope for your God
continually" (12:7[6]). Although Ephraim is still unwilling to confess his
guilt in cheating others for his wealth (12:8-9[7-8]), Yahweh stands ready to
restore him to the lost festival tents (12:10[9]).[68] Again Ephraim is compared to Jacob, and warned that the prophets have been sent as bearers of

---

[64] The adoption from Egypt imagery differs from the land as mother image elsewhere in
Hosea; see Braaten, "Parent-Child Imagery in Hosea," 292-308.

[65] Emending על to בעל; cf. 11:2; see *BHS*.

[66] For this interpretation see Wolff, *Hosea*, 211-14. He says "Israel . . . should take the
course of its ancestor: weeping and supplication, submission and repentance. In
Bethel Yahweh's word will once again come to those willing to return" (213).

[67] *Beth instrumenti*, for the translation see Macintosh, *Hosea*, 491.

[68] On relating this verse to 9:5, see the commentaries. Rudolph (*Hosea*, 223, 234) suggests the tents are symptomatic of the poverty of exile in contrast to the comfortable
life of the monarchy. He thus interprets the oracle as a threat of exile and understands
the reference to a festival as ironic.

God's revelation, either for Ephraim's destruction or protection.[69]   Since
Ephraim has given offence, however, God will return (יָשִׁיב) his reproach to
them (12:11-15[10-14]).

Ephraim once spoke with authority, but he quickly fell into the fertility
cult. When the people experienced satiation in their pasture and "lifted their
heart" they forgot Yahweh (13:1-7). Again God threatens to devour his
people as a lion, leopard, bear, or beast of the field (13:7-8), perhaps repre-
senting some of the "inhabitants of the land" that are suffering due to Israel's sins (Hos 4:3). Yahweh would be Israel's helper,[70] but Israel would
rather rely on ineffective political leaders (13:9).

Before a final word of judgment (13:15-14:1[13:16]), and the final appeal to repent (14:2-9[1-8]), there is an interesting notice regarding
Ephraim's condition as son. A record of his sin has been placed in storage,[71] the record declaring that he is an "unwise" son because he fails to
come to the birth canal when "the pangs of the woman giving birth (יוֹלֵדָה)
are upon him" (13:12-13). Hosea only presents one figure as the birth
mother of Israel — the land (Hos 1:2; 2:4[2], 6[4]; possibly 4:5). The land
is once more a victim, for Ephraim's refusal to come to term not only portends certain death for himself, but also for his mother. The wise son would
surrender to the birth process, i.e., return to Yahweh from the heart, obeying
in matters of worship, loving commitments, and politics. As the concluding
epilogue summarizes, the "wise . . . walk in the ways" of Yahweh (Hos
14:10[9]). Although Ephraim's destruction is deserved, Yahweh decides to
ransom the people from sheol, and redeem them from death—he will not
change his mind (נָחַם, 13:14).[72] This redemption is not only for the sake of
the child—it will also save mother land. The connection between Hos
13:13 and 14 is through the allusion to Ephraim dying in the womb of the
(mother) land, for אֶרֶץ can also connote the "underworld"[73] or sheol. Instead of letting the womb become sheol for his son, however, Yahweh will
redeem him.

---

69   For the translation of נשׁמר בּ in Hos 12:14[13] as "be guarded by" or "be attentive
to" see KBL s.v. niph, 1, 2; against Odell, "Who were the Prophets in Hosea?" 88.

70   Hos 13:9a is obscure; either Yahweh or Israel could be understood as the cause of
Israel's destruction. See the commentaries, esp. Macintosh, *Hosea*, 533-34, and T. K.
Cheyne, *Hosea, with Notes and Introduction* (CB; Cambridge: Cambridge University
Press, 1884) 122.

71   Macintosh, *Hosea*, 542.

72   For this understanding of vv. 13-14 cf. KJV. The translation of these lines as a question (see NRSV) is gratuitous (see Cheyne, *Hosea*, 124; Keil, *Minor Prophets*, 159,
and Artur Weiser, *Das Buch der zwölf kleinen Propheten* [ATD 24/I; 2d ed.; Göttingen: Vandenhoeck & Ruprecht, 1956] 98).

73   KBL, s.v. 5.

Before the way of repentance is presented, the subdivision ends with a warning concerning agricultural disasters due to the wind of Yahweh[74] and war (13:15-14:1[13:16]). The gruesome concluding oracle (14:1[13:16]) threatens Samaria with the death of her inhabitants, including dashing children on the rocks and ripping open pregnant women. The references to births not coming to term are another example of the bereavement motif in Hosea. In addition, this oracle forms a bracket with 13:13-14 with which it is in tension. In the first passage Yahweh promises to redeem the unborn child for the sake of the land and people; in the second there is a threat of certain punishment due to the guilt of Samaria.[75]

The tension just observed between God's resolve to redeem people and land and God's threats of judgment are resolved in the second subdivision of the section (14:2-10 [1-9]), which is also the conclusion of the book. The prelude to redemption has been envisaged as a return of the people to their God. Yet every effort to initiate such a return through appeals for corporate repentance and acknowledgment of guilt has failed. The confessions have been superficial, the people have refused to admit their sin; instead they blame Yahweh for not responding according to their desires. Unless one party changes, Ephraim and the land are headed for certain destruction.

Such a change is forthcoming; indeed it was hinted at in God's commitment to redeem his wayward and unwise son. Hosea 14 begins with two more appeals to return (שׁוּב, 14:2[1] and 3[2]), but with some new elements. First, the prophet provides Ephraim with a prayer of confession. The people are to request that God take away their iniquity, then promise to offer sacrifices of thanksgiving.[76] They must admit they cannot find help in political alliances or handcrafted gods. They are to conclude by confessing "in you the orphan will find compassion (יְרֻחָם)" (4[3]). The reversal of the name "Not-Found-Compassion" (Hos 1:6; cf. 2:3[1], 23[25]) is transparent.

---

[74] The terms used of the drying wind (רוּחַ, קָדִים, יֵבֹשׁ, חֶרֶב) are also employed in Exod 14:21-22 to connote Yahweh's drying of the sea. Thus allusions to the Exodus are placed at the beginning and the end of the subdivision (Hos 11:1-14:1[13:16]). This subdivision also has an inner frame with references to God's uncooperative son in Hos 11:1-6 and 13:12-13.

[75] This personification of the city might lend some support to Schmitt's thesis that the bride of Yahweh and mother of Israel in Hos 2 is Samaria (see n. 15 above). If Samaria were personified as bride and mother throughout, however, we would expect the city's inhabitants (see 10:5) to be referred to here as "her children." In the only other Hosean passage that might be viewed as a personification (7:1), Samaria appears to be synonymous with Ephraim, connoting the collective sinful behavior of the people.

[76] Lit. "bulls of our lips," 14:3[2]; see Odell, "The Prophets and the End of Hosea," in *Forming Prophetic Literature*, 166.

The second new element is this significant change in Ephraim's status from unfavorable son to orphan. A "son of whoredom" or a rebellious son might be disowned or publicly executed,[77] but an orphan is always granted protective status by the gods.[78]

The third new element is Yahweh's promise to enable his people to return. "I will heal their faithlessness ("turning away" מְשׁוּבָה), ... for my anger has turned (שָׁב) from me" (14:5[4]). In other words the "turning" will occur in God before it takes place in the people. If he relies no more on idols, then Ephraim will have his fruit from Yahweh (6-9[5-8]). God's restorative power will be like the dew to Ephraim, who will thrive and flourish like a healthy plant in the land. Yahweh will be like a protective tree for Israel. Instead of seeking their fertility under the shade of trees at questionable cult sites (Hos 4:13a), the Israelites will "return (יָשֻׁב) and dwell beneath his shade, they will grow grain and flourish like a vine" (14:8[7]).[79] Through God Ephraim will blossom and strike root; his shoots will spread out, and he will flourish. This divine planting of Israel and God (!) on the land will reverse the judgment of earlier chapters, recalling the positive connotations of Jezreel, or "God sows."

Before continuing we will summarize our results in outline form.

Table 1: Thematic and Structural Elements of Hosea

I. HOSEA 1-3 (A)
  A. Literary Frames: Hosea 1-2 with Mal 3[4]
    1. Land Inclusio: Hos 1:2 ↔ Mal 3:24[4:6]
    2. Elijah (/Elisha) Tradition(s) Frame: Jezreel – Jehu in Hos 1:4 ↔ Mal 3:23[4:5]
    3. Parent– Child: Yahweh [& Land!] – Israel in Hosea 1-2 (etc.) ↔ Mal 1:6; 3:17
  B. Themes & Inner Frames: Introduction to Hosea *and* Book of the Twelve (Hos 1-2)
    1. Whoredom & Bloodshed (Hos 1:2, 4; 2:6-7[4-5]); false worship & violence → land pollution
    2. Jezreel, "God Sows" -/+ significance (Hos 1:4-5; 2:2 [1:11]; 24-25 [22-23])

---

[77] As mentioned above, the compassion shown the repentant is a reversal of the name לֹא־רֻחָמָה, the disownment oracle of Hos 1:6. For the execution of a rebellious son see Deut 21:18-21. Cf. Elizabeth Bellefontaine, "Reviewing the Case of the Rebellious Son," *JSOT* 13 (1979) 13-31.

[78] Ps 82:3-4; Exod 22:22-24; Deut 10:18; 24:17; 27:19. See F. Charles Fensham, "Widow, Orphan, and the Poor in Ancient Near Eastern Legal and Wisdom Literature," *JNES* 21 (1962) 129-39.

[79] The connection between the shade of outdoor cult sites and the shade provided by Yahweh is made by Phyllis Bird, "'To Play the Harlot': An Inquiry into an Old Testament Metaphor," in *Gender and Difference in Ancient Israel* (ed. Peggy L. Day; Minneapolis: Fortress, 1989) 93 n. 39. The agricultural terms link this verse with Hos 2; see Nogalski, *Literary Precursors*, 70-71, esp. n. 44.

3. Judgment threatened, appeal, restoration of bride/mother *land* (Hos 1:2b; 2:4-25[2-23])

4. Disownment & restoration of child(ren) (Hos 1:6-7, 1:9-2:1[1:10]; 2:3 [1], 6[4], 25[23])

  C. Judgment and return, Davidic hope: Hos 3 ↔ Hag – Zech 8

II. HOSEA 4:1-5:7 (B)

  A. Hos 4:1-3. Second Introduction: Lawsuit against people, Land Mourns: *Land / Earth as example for unrepentant people

  B. Hos 4:1-5:7. Indictments for bloodshed, lack knowledge of God, whoredom, Israel bears sons of strangers

III. HOSEA 5:8-7:16 (C)

  A. *Assembly*: Shophar & cry (5:8) coming *"day* of punishment" (5:9), God awaits confession (5:15) [Anticipates Day and Repentance of Joel 1-2]

  B. Presumptuous and false efforts at repentance (6:1-6; 7:10, 13-16); bloodshed & whoredom (6:7-11)

IV. HOSEA 8:1-9:9 (C′)

  A. *Assembly*: Shophar & (false) cries (8:1, 2; 9:7), festival *day* of visitation // recompense inescapable (9:5-7) [Anticipates Day and Repentance of Joel 1-2]

  B. Israel continues in idolatry (8:3-14): whoredom & defilement; *threats:* lose land & crops (9:1-4)

V. HOSEA 9:10-10:15 (B′)

  A. Increased *threats*: plant imagery applied to Ephraim, bereavement, woe oracles, disownment (9:10-17)

  B. Harvest imagery: Yahweh's punishment is Ephraim reaping what sown; *appeal* to seek Yahweh (10:1-15)

VI. HOSEA 11:1-14:10[9] (A′)

  A. *Threat:* Israel to be punished as rebellious adopted son; Yahweh decides to *spare!* (11:1-11), threats & appeals (12:1-13:11)

  B. Land in travail with Ephraim, unwise son, Yahweh's decides to *redeem*; *Threat*: warfare, bereavement for Samaria (13:12-14:1[13:16])

  C. Conclusion: *Appeal* for Israel to repent, provision for confession and offer to heal and grant *mercy* to *orphan*; fertility images (14:2-10[1-9]) [Anticipates Joel 1-2]

Explanation. The six-part structure of Hosea generally follows a chiastic ABC // C′B′A′ pattern. The turning point is found in sections III and IV (C and C′) with a call for an assembly of lamentation and confession anticipating the *day* of Yahweh's punishment / visitation.

III. Thematic Elements in Joel

Joel further develops Hosea's themes by employing language reminiscent of that book's themes. Joel begins with a summons for a group of leaders to "hear" (שִׁמְעוּ) and the mention of "(all) those who dwell in the land" (יוֹשְׁבֵי־הָאָרֶץ; see Joel 1:2, 14, cf. Hos 4:1-3 and 5:1). The prophet then queries (v. 2): "Has *this* occurred in your days, or in the days of your fathers?" Nogalski has convincingly argued that *this* (זֹאת) refers to the repentance and promises of Hosea 14, which have not yet occurred. Hosea ends with the *promise* that if the people respond, God will enable them to repent and then will heal them. There is no indication, however, that the people have responded to this offer.[80] After the prophet's question, Yahweh speaks of the devastation of "my land" (אַרְצִי, v. 6) and its produce, then issues a summons to lament (1:4-13). Specific affected groups are *commanded* to participate in mourning rites: drunkards (v. 6), a female subject (1:8), priests[81] (1:9, 13), and farmers and vinedressers (1:11). There is only one who immediately *responds* to the command: "the ground (אֲדָמָה) mourns" (1:10) – apparently the unnamed female subject called upon to wail in 1:8.[82] This is a variation on the "land mourns" imagery of Hos 4:1-3.[83] As in Hosea, the land (or ground) is the first to respond in mourning over the effects of sin and judgment, while her inhabitants' response is still pending. Once again the land's mourning becomes an example for human subjects to imitate.

In Joel 1:14 there is another call for a fast and assembly at the house of God, during which "all those who dwell in the land" (cf. Hos 4:1-3) are to "cry in lamentation" (אֹזְעַק) to Yahweh. The response of the land's non-human inhabitants is depicted in language suggestive of laments: animals sigh (אָנַק), cattle are confused (בּוּך), sheep bear guilt (נֶאְשָׁם), beasts of the fields long for (עָרַג) Yahweh.

---

[80] Nogalski observes that Hosea 14 presumes Israel will suffer future punishment, then offers promises of restoration after repentance. Joel anticipates the punishment and calls for *this* repentance. He also suggests that the "missing" accusation of sin in Joel is supplied by its position after Hosea in the Twelve. See *Redactional Processes in the Book of the Twelve* (BZAW 218; Berlin: de Gruyter, 1993) 15-17, 22; and "Joel as 'Literary Anchor' for the Book of the Twelve," *Reading and Hearing the Book of the Twelve*, 101.

[81] With LXX, reading אֵבְלוּ in 1:9 as an imperative. Cf. 1:13; see *BHK*.

[82] Nogalski notes the connections of the agricultural imagery in the Joel passage with Hos 2 (and elsewhere), and argues that the bride of Hosea and Joel are the same, which he regards as Zion (but he also uses "Israel"). He comments on the merit of Bergler's suggestion that the reference could be to land; see *Redactional Processes*, 7-8 (cf. n. 25), 18-22; "Joel as Literary Anchor," 101-103, n. 23; and *Literary Precursors*, 21-24, 58-73. Since there is a mourning female subject ("ground") in the immediate context and in Hosea, it is unnecessary to construct a hypothetical example (as do many commentators) or to bring in an outsider such as the Virgin Anath lamenting over Baal (as does Hillers, "The Roads to Zion Mourn, 127-30.

[83] For a discussion of this passage see Hayes, "The Earth Mourns," 260-302.

The appeal is continued with a command to blow the *shophar* in Zion and to cry out (Joel 2:1). This command is reminiscent of Hos 5:8 and 8:1. In Joel, however, the *shophar* and the cry clearly announce the dawning judgment as the Day of Yahweh (2:2-11).[84] The call to assembly continues with a double call to repentance (שוב), accompanied by fasting, weeping and mourning from the heart (2:12-13a), something Israel's rites lack in Hosea.[85] The call is grounded in the gracious and merciful character of Yahweh (2:13b-14).[86]

The last command for this fast – again announced by the *shophar* in Zion – concerns the gathering of the people and the intercession of the priests (Joel 2:15-17). The heightening of the gravity of the situation is portrayed by the universal summons: in contrast to the selective summons of Joel 1, the assembly is now to be attended by all, from the elderly to the nursing infant (2:16; cf. 2 Chr 20:3-4, 13). A turning point is announced by an oracle of salvation, which is conditioned upon a future repentance of the *people*:[87] "Yahweh will be zealous for his *land*, and will have compassion (חמל) for his people" (2:18). Significantly, it is the land that first receives God's attention (cf. 2 Chr 7:13-14). In regard to the people, the agricultural bounty lost and promised again in Hosea[88] will be restored and the enemy expelled (2:19-27). But the oracle of assurance ("do not fear") comes first to those who first repented and mourned — the ground (אדמה) and the

---

[84] It is possible that Hosea's frequent references to "days of divine intervention," as days of impending judgment—often in association with the *shophar* and cry or call for repentance (Hos 5:8-9; 8:1-2; 9:5-7; cf. 7:5)—influenced Joel's depiction of the Day(s) of Yahweh. As noted above, these days are sometimes associated with Yahweh's house (8:1; 9:4, 8, 15) and have prepared the way for this first reference to "the Day of Yahweh" in the Twelve. Observe also the frequent references to (a) "day(s)" of judgment or salvation in Hos 1-3. Particularly noteworthy is the anticipation of Israelite repentance and the restoration of the Jerusalem cult and monarchy "in the latter days" in Hos 3:4-5 (cf. n. 32 above). A more thorough treatment of the connection of Day of Yahweh with the land theme in the Twelve is a subject for another study. For a survey of the days of divine intervention in Hosea through Obadiah see Nogalski, "The Day(s) of YHWH in the Book of the Twelve," in *Society of Biblical Literature 1999 Seminar Papers* (SBLSP 38; Atlanta: Scholars Press, 1999) 617-42.

[85] Hos 7:13-14; cf. Nogalski, "Joel as Literary Anchor," 101.

[86] Van Leeuwen ("Scribal Wisdom and Theodicy," 39-40), who traces the theme of God's mercy (per Exod 34:6-7) in the Twelve, notes that Hos 2:13b-14 is the first explicit formulation of this theme in connection with the Day of Yahweh in the Twelve.

[87] Likewise Nogalski (*Redactional Processes*, 4), who states that 2:18 "constitutes the assurance of YHWH's positive response to the people presuming the people do indeed *repent*" (emphasis his). My only qualification is the observation that, like Hos 4:3, a partial repentance has begun with the mourning of the ground (Joel 1:10) and its non-human inhabitants (2:17-20).

[88] Hos 2:10-14[8-12], 24[22]); likewise Nogalski, "Joel as Literary Anchor," 97-98.

beasts of the field (2:21-22)! In another act of restoration (associated with another Day of Yahweh), Yahweh promises to pour out "my spirit" (רוחי) upon all flesh (Joel 3:1-4[2:28-31]). This aid will enable all people to prophesy by Yahweh, and thereby reverse the negative imagery connected with wind/spirit in Hosea.[89]

Although much more could be said about the land imagery in Joel, we will close this section with a final brief note. Joel ends with a reference to the bloodshed and wilderness imagery first initiated in Hosea 1-2. Only now it is (the lands of) Egypt and Edom that will become a desolate wilderness because they have poured out "innocent blood" (דם־נקיא) "in their [Judah's] land" (בארצם, Joel 4[3]:19-20).

IV. Thematic Elements in Malachi

Malachi has much in common with Hosea; a short list follows. The book employs father-son imagery for the relationship between God and his people.[90] Malachi says that God will not bless the priests and will punish their offspring because they have not been committed from the heart (2:2), and they have mishandled torah (2:4-9). God does not honor the men's weeping and sighing (בכי ואנקה) at the altar due to their broken covenant with their wives and consequent failure to produce "seed of God" (2:13-16). The people complain that God seems inconsistent and unjust (2:17).

The repentance sought in Hosea and Joel (and throughout the Twelve) is still required. Although God has not changed his mind concerning his standard, the people have not changed "since the days of their fathers" but have turned aside from God's statutes.[91] Therefore God calls them to "return (שובו) to me and I will return to you" (3:6-7). If the people renew their commitment by paying their tithes (3:8-10a), God will rebuke the devouring locust that destroys their land's crops and grant the agricultural abundance

---

[89] Cf. the "spirit of whoredom" (Hos 4:12, cf. 19; 5:4); the people "sow" and "herd" wind (8:7; 12:2[1]); the cultic prophets are "persons of the spirit" (9:7); and Yahweh's רוח is a wind of judgment (13:15).

[90] Mal 1:6; 2:10; 3:17; perhaps 4:5 LXX.

[91] A previous "return" involving a spatial return to Jerusalem and also repentance took place in Zech 1:3-6. Zech 8 ends on a hopeful note for Jerusalem, Israel, the nations, the land and all creation. See Edgar W. Conrad, *Zechariah* (Readings, Sheffield: Sheffield Press, 1999) 47-54; and Braaten, "That God May Heal the Land," 13-14. Collins (*The Mantle of Elijah*, 79) calls Zech 1:6b a "model response" of repentance which functions to "influence our reading of *The Twelve*." The change in the people was apparently short-lived, so Malachi once again attests to the need for repentance.

they lack (3:10b-11). Then even the nations will notice as they (!) become a
land of delight (3:12).[92]

The last word the people speak in Malachi (and the Twelve) shows that
many still resist change. Some complain that repentance rituals are point-
less (3:13-15). "[They] say, 'It is vain to serve God, and what is the use of
us observing his obligations, or that[93] we should go about in mourning
clothes (הלכנו קדרנית)[94] before Yahweh of hosts'" (3:14). Thus the
mourning or repentance rituals called for by earlier voices is resisted. What
would be the point of repenting, since evildoers prosper and get away with
testing God (3:15)?

After these complaints the "fearers of Yahweh" spoke with one another.
In response, "Yahweh paid attention and heard" and a "Scroll of Remembrance" (ספר זכרון) was "written before him for[95] those who fear Yahweh
and esteem his name" (3:16). Then Yahweh will make them his own, his
special treasure, and he will spare them like a father spares his son (3:17).
The result is to be repentance: Yahweh tells the community "you will return
(ושבתם) and discern between the righteous and the wicked, between the
one serving God and the one not serving him" (3:18).

This momentous series of changes begins with the writing of the "Scroll
of Remembrance." What is the significance of this document?[96] First, it is
possible to link it with the last command in (the MT of) Malachi through
the catchword "remember": "*Remember* (זכרו) the torah of Moses, my servant, which I commanded him on Horeb, concerning all Israel — the statutes and the ordinances" (3:22 [4:4]). Taken together, these references to
writing, remembering and torah in Malachi may be another example of
linking between Malachi and Hosea. Both books charge that the priests fail
in their obligations to teach torah. In Hos 8:12-14 God says it would do no
good for him to *"write"* more *"torahs"* since the people consider them

---

92 Here ארץ is a comprehensive term for the land as gift and place of blessing, which
  includes the people who inhabit it and benefit by it; see our discussion of the land-
  people solidarity in the final form of Hos 2 above. Cf. Rudolph, *Haggai — Sacharja
  1-8 — Sacharja 9-14 — Maleachi* (KAT XIII/4; Gütersloh: Gerd Mohn, 1976) 285.
93 For this use of כי in a consecutive clause depending on an interrogative clause see
  GKC §107u.
94 The hapax legomena קדרנית is probably connected with mourning customs. Cf. the
  similar phrase הלך* קדר in lament contexts (Pss 38:7[6]; 42:10[9]; 43:2; Job 30:28;
  cf. Pss 36:14); refer to the lexicons and commentaries for conjectures concerning
  translation.
95 For נכתב־ל as "to be written for" see BDB s.v. niph 1; cf. qal 1 c, see Hos 8:12.
96 See the commentaries for the various proposals concerning a divine ledger based on
  Exod 32:32-33; Pss 69:28; 87:6; Dan 12:1.

"strange." The people continue to offer sacrifices not pleasing to God, with the result that God will *remember* their iniquity and visit their sins upon them, and the people will *return* to Egypt. Israel's problem is that "he has forgotten his maker."[97] Malachi appears to be presenting this Scroll of Remembrance as a means of beginning the reversal of the situation in Hosea; the people are being offered a way they can *remember torah* and *return*.

Second, the Scroll of Remembrance may function as both torah and words of the prophets. There was a growing perception in the postexilic community that *the prophets* taught the "fathers" the law and statutes of Moses.[98] These prophetic words were cited, proclaimed or read aloud during fasting or repentance rituals, which were often concerned with the fate of the land.[99] If the Scroll of Remembrance is such a prophetic scroll, then it is plausible to identify this scroll as the Scroll of the Twelve as Nogalski has proposed.[100] Such a description of the Scroll of the Twelve as words of torah and words of the "former prophets" read during days of fasting,

---

[97] For other cases of God's "remembering" Israel's sin in Hosea see Hos 7:2; 9:9. Hos 8:12 is the first reference to "writing" in the Book of the Twelve. Others include the reference to the "scroll of the vision of Nahum" (Nah 1:1), God's command for Habakkuk to write his vision on tablets (Hab 2:2), and this Malachi passage.

[98] Second Kgs 17:13-18; Zech, 1:4-6. According to Collins (*The Mantle of Elijah*, 84), the command to remember the law in Mal 3:22 "brings us back to Zech 1:2-6 and ultimately to . . . Moses." See the discussion of the connection of the Law of Moses with the prophets in Glazier-McDonald, *Malachi*, 265-67 and Paul L. Redditt, "Zechariah 9-14, Malachi, and the Redaction of the Book of the Twelve," in *Forming Prophetic Literature*, 254-55.

[99] The proclamation of written prophecy at fast days is first attributed to Jeremiah. In an effort to move the Judean pilgrims to pray for mercy, he had Baruch *write* his words on a scroll to be *read* at the temple on a fast day (Jer 36:4-8). Zech 7:1-14 (cf. 8:19) speaks of fasting and mourning rituals in conjunction with the fulfilled words of the former prophets. Conrad suggests that the former prophets mentioned in Zech 1:2-6 and 8:9 are the written and read-aloud words of Hosea through Zephaniah. See "Reading Isaiah and the Twelve as Prophetic Books," in *Writing and Reading the Scroll of Isaiah: Studies of an Interpretive Tradition* (VTSup 70/1; ed. Craig C. Broyles and Craig A. Evans; New York: Brill, 1997) 8-14; and idem, *Zechariah*, 28-29, 42. These prophets proclaimed God's torah and word through the spirit, and when the people refused to listen they were scattered and the *land* became desolate (Zech 7:12-14). In another context an assembly gathered as Ezra fasted in mourning attire and prayed about the potential for the Judeans to defile the *land*, like the Canaanites before them, because they failed to keep the commandments of "your servants the prophets" concerning intermarriages (Ezra 9:5-10:1; cf. Neh 9:1-37). Daniel, fasting in sackcloth and ashes, confesses that God's people did not listen to the law of Moses spoken through the prophets, which brought wrath to Jerusalem and God's people (Dan 9:3-19). According to Solomon's vision in Chronicles, when Yahweh causes fertility to cease due to sin, if the people humble themselves and repent God will forgive them and heal the *land* (2 Chr 7:12-14).

[100] Nogalski, *Redactional Processes*, 206-12.

mourning and repentance is consistent with the proposals of this study. This scroll preserves for the postexilic community the remembrance of the torah of Moses taught to the "fathers" by the earlier prophets, and now employed for the comfort and warning of subsequent generations.

The conviction that obedience to Mosaic torah is a condition for maintaining a relationship with the land also links the end of the book of the Twelve with Joshua, the opening book of the prophetic canon. As one would expect, there are frequent references to the land in Joshua 1 (vv. 2-3, 4, 6, 11, 13, 14, 15 [2x]). Here Israelite success in taking possession of the land is made conditional upon Joshua's obeying "the torah which Moses my servant commanded you" (Josh 1:7).[101] Similarly, the hearers of the Twelve are enjoined to "remember the torah of my servant Moses which I commanded him" (Mal 3:22[4:4]) so as not to endanger their relationship with the land (Mal 3:24[4:6]).

The hearing of the Scroll of the Twelve also may have had a setting in familial torah instruction. The book of Deuteronomy, which influences Malachi, emphasizes the connection between the public reading of Mosaic torah and the parental responsibility for teaching it.[102] For such teaching to be effective there must be mutual respect between the generations. Children must honor their parents (Deut 5:16a, cf. Mal 1:6) and fathers are told to "set to your heart" the words recited in the cult and to command your sons "to observe all the words of this torah" (Deut 32:44-47; cf. Mal 1:1b LXX). Without this intergenerational respect, family members will risk disobedi-

---

[101]   As Michael Fishbane (*Biblical Interpretation in Ancient Israel* [corr. ed.; Oxford: Clarendon Press, 1986] 384-85) has observed, God's speech to Joshua in Josh 1:6-9 reformulates Moses' speech to Joshua in Deut 31:7-8 by making the possession of the land conditional upon obedience to Mosaic torah. Likewise, the book concludes with an association between obedience to torah and completing the conquest (of the אדמה) in Joshua's final speech (Josh 23:12-13). We would add that the Book of the Twelve is similarly framed. For a discussion of the linking of the last chapter of the Pentateuch with the first and last chapters of the Prophets by references to "my servant Moses" (Dt 34:5; Josh 1:2, 7 and Mal 3:22) see Rudolph, *Haggai...Malachi*, 291, and Nogalski, *Redactional Processes*, 185, 244-45.

[102]   For the presence of children at the reading of the Deuteronomic law see Deut 29:10-11; 31:12-13; cf. Christopher J. H. Wright, *God's People in God's Land: Family, Land, and Property in the Old Testament* (Grand Rapids: Eerdmans, 1990) 81-84. For teaching the commandments in the home associated with long life and fertility see Deut 6:1-8, esp. vv. 2-3, 7; for children's participation in festivals see Deut 16: 11, 14. Particularly noteworthy is that the context for teaching torah is the anticipation of "the great and terrible Day of Yahweh" (Mal 3:23[4:5]). We have already observed the intergenerational (familial) participation in important fast days (2:16; cf. 2 Chr 20:3-4, 13; see the discussion on Joel above). Joel associates such a gathering with a Day of Yahweh. If the conjecture is correct that the Twelve was read at fast days, the implication of the above is that these days were associated with a Day of Yahweh.

ence to Yahweh's commands and the "long life" of blessing on the *land* will be forfeited (Deut 5:16b; 32:47). This would explain the significance of (the MT form of) the Book of Malachi's closing words. Elijah will return to "restore (השיב) the heart of the fathers to the sons and the heart of the sons to the fathers, lest I come and strike the land with a ban of destruction (חרם)" (3:24[4:6]). Familial disobedience will result in community disobedience, and as we learn from Hosea, community disobedience will result in the land suffering the consequences.   But a remedy is anticipated, Malachi looks forward to a new work of an old prophet.   Elijah will restore the conditions necessary for hearing anew the torah of Moses and the words of the prophets, now written in the Scroll of the Twelve.   These words offer the hope that God's land might not be harmed by its human inhabitants, and that those sown in her may be deeply rooted and flourish.

The Place and Function of Joel
in the Book of the Twelve

Marvin A. Sweeney

I. Introduction

Recent scholarly discussion of the so-called "Minor Prophets" has begun to recognize that these twelve prophetic compositions can no longer be treated exclusively as twelve discrete prophetic works. Their consistent appearance as a single book in all canonical forms of the Jewish and Christian Bibles, where they are known respectively as עשׂר תרי or "Dodekapropheton," as well as in three distinct manuscripts from the Judean wilderness (MurXII; 4QXII[a]; 8HevXIIgr), and finally their collective citation in several apocryphal and pseudepigraphical sources (Sir 49:10; 4 Ezra 1:39-40; Martyrdom and Ascension of Isaiah 4:22; Lives of the Prophets), demonstrate that ancient readers from as early as the second century B.C.E. understood them as a single unit or collection. Although the bulk of modern critical treatment of the Twelve Prophets focuses on their interpretation as individual compositions, scholars increasingly address both the literary form and compositional history of the Book of the Twelve as a whole.[1]

---

[1]   For discussion of the issue, see Karl Budde, "Eine folgenschwere Redaktion des Zwölfprohetenbuchs," *ZAW* 39 (1921) 218-229; Roland Emerson Wolfe, "The Editing of the Book of the Twelve," *ZAW* 53 (1935) 90-129; Peter Weimer, "Obadja. Eine redaktions-kritische Analyse," *BN* 27 (1985) 35-99; Erich Bosshard, "Beobachtungen zum Zwölfprohetenbuch," *BN* 40 (1987) 30-62; Paul R. House, *The Unity of the Twelve* (JSOTSup 97; BLS 27; Sheffield: Almond, 1990); Erich Bosshard and Reinhold Gregor Kratz, "Maleachi im Zwölfprohetenbuch," *BN* 52 (1990) 27-46; Odil Hannes Steck, *Der Abschluss der Prophetie im alten Testament. Ein Versuch zur Frage der Vorgeschichte des Kanons* (BibThSt 17; Neukirchen-Vluyn: Neukirchener, 1991); Terence Collins, *The Mantle of Elijah: The Redaction Criticism of the Prophetical Books* (BibSem 20; Sheffield: JSOT Press, 1993) 59-87; James D. Nogalski, *Literary Precursors to the Book of the Twelve* (BZAW 217; Berlin and New York: Walter de Gruyter, 1993); idem, *Redactional Processes in the Book of the Twelve* (BZAW 218; Berlin and New York: Walter de Gruyter, 1993); Barry Alan Jones, *The Formation of the Book of the Twelve: A Study in Text and Canon* (SBLDS 149; Atlanta: Scholars Press, 1995); R. J. Coggins, "The Minor Prophets--One Book or Twelve?" *Crossing the Boundaries* (BibInt 8; Fest. M. D. Goulder; eds. J. Barton and

Especially noteworthy are the attempts to employ intertextual references as well as generic and thematic similarities within the Twelve and with Isaiah to reconstruct a multi-staged redactional history of the book. Steck and Bosshard-Nepustil, for example, argue that the Book of the Twelve appears to have been deliberately composed in stages in relation to the basic theological outlook, chronological progression, and compositional history of the book of Isaiah.[2] Nogalski and Schart note the similarities in form and outlook of several sub-collections within the Book of the Twelve, i.e., Hosea, Amos, Micah, and Zephaniah; Nahum and Habakkuk; and Haggai, Zechariah, and Malachi, as well as other features of materials within the Twelve, such as the lack of historical specificity in Joel, Obadiah, and Jonah and the numerous intertextual citations in Joel, particularly of the other books of the Twelve. On this basis, they attempt to reconstruct the redactional development of the Twelve through several stages as collections are formed and redactionally expanded into the present form of the book. Although the details of their respective models differ, both posit early collections in Hosea/Amos/Micah/Zephaniah; Nahum/Habakkuk; and Haggai/Zechariah that are brought together and organized by a late redaction based upon a collection that includes Joel and Obadiah and other writings, such as Jonah; Zechariah 9-14; and Malachi.[3]

For the most part, these studies presuppose the priority of the Masoretic text, which presents the books of the Twelve according to the order Hosea; Joel; Amos; Obadiah; Jonah; Micah; Nahum; Habakkuk; Zephaniah; Haggai; Zechariah; and Malachi. Other orders are extant, however, such as the LXX (Hosea; Amos; Micah; Joel; Obadiah; Jonah; Nahum; Habakkuk; Zephaniah; Haggai; Zechariah; and Malachi) and 4QXII[a] (Hosea; Joel; Amos; Obadiah; Micah; Nahum; Habakkuk; Zephaniah; Haggai; Zechariah; Malachi; and Jonah). Jones notes that the differing orders of these versions

---

D. J. Reimer; Macon, GA: Mercer University Press, 1996); James W. Watts and Paul R. House, editors, *Forming Prophetic Literature: Essays on Isaiah and the Twelve in Honor of John D. W. Watts* (JSOTSup 235; Sheffield: Sheffield Academic Press, 1996); Erich Bosshard-Nepustil, *Rezeptionen von Jesaia 1-39 im Zwölfprophetenbuch* (OBO 154; Freiburg: Universitätsverlag; Göttingen: Vandenhoeck & Ruprecht, 1997); Burkhard M. Zapff, *Redaktionsgeschichtliche Studien zum Michabuch im Kontext des Dodekapropheton* (BZAW 256; Berlin and New York: Walter de Gruyter, 1997) Aaron Schart, *Die Entstehung des Zwölfprophetenbuchs* (BZAW 260; Berlin and New York: Walter de Gruyter, 1998); James D. Nogalski and Marvin A. Sweeney, editors, *Reading and Hearing the Book of the Twelve* (SBLSymS 15; Atlanta: Society of Biblical Literature, 2000); Marvin A. Sweeney, *The Twelve Prophets* (Berit Olam; 2 volumes; Collegeville: Liturgical, 2000).

2 Steck, *Abschluss*; Bosshard-Nepustil, *Rezeptionen von Jesaia 1-39*.
3 Nogalski, *Literary Precursors*; idem, *Redactional Processes*; Schart, *Entstehung*.

of the individual prophets contained within the Twelve may have some bearing on the compositional history of the book as a whole.[4] Based upon his assessment of the differing orders of books in the MT; LXX; and 4QXII[a], he likewise argues that Joel and Obadiah entered the book of the Twelve at a relatively late stage (but prior to Jonah), and play a constitutive role in shaping the final form of the book in all three of these textual versions. He further contends that the original order of books within the Twelve is that of 4QXII[a], which is in turn a variation of the LXX. Jones' position is based especially on the observations that Joel, Obadiah, and Jonah appear in different positions within the respective orders of these three versions of the book of the Twelve, that Joel and Obadiah provide little indication of their historical settings, and that Joel contains a large number of intertextual references to other books among the Twelve.

Jones' work in particular points to the need for an assessment of the overall form or arrangement of books in each version of the Book of the Twelve, both as a means to understand the hermeneutical perspective of each and as a basis for reconstructing the compositional history of the book. Indeed, he makes some pertinent observations concerning the overall form of the various versions of the Twelve, particularly when he notes that Joel introduces a concern with foreign nations that is carried through in Obadiah, Jonah, and Nahum in the LXX version of the Twelve, but he does not provide a full analysis of the rational underlying the sequence of books in any version of the Twelve. The present writer has made a preliminary attempt for the MT and LXX versions of the book in a recently published paper.[5] It argues that the LXX version of the Twelve is based in a concern to demonstrate that the experience of the northern kingdom of Israel in the Assyrian period provides the paradigm for the experience of Jerusalem and Judah in the Babylonian period and beyond. This is evident in the first three books, Hosea, Amos, and Micah, all three of which provide the rationale for the punishment of northern Israel prior to addressing the future of Jerusalem, Judah, and the nations in Micah. Joel then focuses on the fate of Jerusalem in relation to the nations that occupies the attention of the balance of the book. In contrast, the MT introduces Joel immediately after Hosea and places Micah after Jonah so that concern with Jerusalem, Judah, and the nations appears throughout the Twelve. Nevertheless, the paper provides only an overview, and a more detailed analysis is needed.

---

[4] Jones, *Formation.*

[5] Marvin A. Sweeney, "Sequence and Interpretation in the Book of the Twelve," *Reading and Hearing the Book of the Twelve,* 49-64; see also idem, *The Twelve Prophets,* xxvii-xxxv.

This paper attempts to meet the need for such a detailed analysis in relation to Joel. Clearly, the book of Joel plays a key role in the overall form and compositional history of the Book of the Twelve,[6] but a full assessment of Joel in relation to the overall form of both the LXX and MT versions of the Twelve is necessary. Several aspects require treatment. First is an assessment of the overall form of the book of Joel, including its literary structure and generic characteristics in order to determine its intention as a discrete unit within the Twelve. Second is an assessment of its intertextual relationships, particularly with other books from the Twelve, in order to define its interrelationships with the other individual units that form the Twelve and to determine further its intention. Third, is an assessment of the place and function of Joel within the sequence of books in each version of the Twelve in order to determine the distinctive outlook of each. Fourth is a reconstruction of the setting in which each version of the Twelve must have developed and functioned.

II. The Form of the Book of Joel

Scholarly assessment of the overall form and function of the book of Joel has been unduly influenced by concern with establishing the compositional history of the text and the socio-historical setting or settings in which the book or its major components were composed.[7] It has also been heavily influenced by the theological presupposition that authentic prophets must somehow speak a message of judgment against the people of Israel and that messages of restoration or divine favor for Israel must be the work of later priestly or apocalyptic writers, who sought to transform the prophetic message of judgment into one of salvation. As a result, scholars have generally followed the early works of Rothstein and Duhm, who argue that the key to the structure of the book lies in the distinction between the authentic words of prophetic judgment in Joel 1-2 and later "apocalyptic" additions in Joel 3-4.[8] Indeed, Duhm argues that the shift actually takes place in Joel 2:18, which turns to YHWH's jealousy on behalf of Israel and marks the beginning of the second half of the book. Although many later scholars have

---

[6]   See James D. Nogalski, "Joel as 'Literary Anchor' for the Book of the Twelve," *Reading and Hearing*, 91-109.

[7]   See the overviews of research on Joel in Theodore Hiebert, "Joel, Book of," *ABD*, 3:873-880; Rex Mason, *Zephaniah, Habakkuk, Joel* (OT Guides; Sheffield: JSOT Press, 1994) esp. 103-112.

[8]   For discussion of Rothstein's position in his 1896 annotated German translation of S. R. Driver's *Introduction to the Literature of the Old Testament*, see Mason, *Joel* 105; B. Duhm, "Anmerkungen zu den Zwölf Propheten," *ZAW* 31 (1911) 1-43, 81-110, 161-204, esp. 184-188.

argued for the unity of the book on various grounds, particularly in relation to its cultic or liturgical character, the shift from judgment to salvation in Joel 2:18 continues to serve as the basis for claims that Joel comprises two basic structural components, i.e., prophetic or liturgical calls to lamentation and repentance in Joel 1:2-2:17 and apocalyptic oracles predicting salvation in Joel 2:18-4:21.[9] The contention that the book of Joel is, at least in part, an apocalyptically-oriented composition that looks beyond the concerns of the historical present to posit eschatological salvation has frequently resulted in dismissal of the book's significance.[10] Such an evaluation of the book is no doubt fueled in part by the difficulties in establishing its historical setting.

Nevertheless, there are grounds to question this assessment of the book of Joel as scholars increasingly point to the need for a systematic synchronic analysis of texts as communicative entities, which in turn provides the necessary prerequisite for diachronic literary analysis.[11] The standard two-part division of Joel is not based on a full assessment of its synchronic textual linguistic form, including its syntactic and semantic forms of expression; rather, it is based largely upon the book's most basic thematic motifs, i.e., judgment and restoration, which are conveyed by its linguistic form. Indeed, such motifs likely play a role in the so-called "deep" or "conceptual" structure of the book, but they do not define the formal literary structure of the text as presented to the reader. The proposed transition between Joel 2:17 and Joel 2:18, for example, is marked by a *waw*-consecutive formation, וַיְקַנֵּא ה' לְאַרְצוֹ, "and YHWH is jealous for his land," which indi-

---

9   E.g., Arvid S. Kapelrud, *Joel Studies* (UUÅ 4; Uppsala: A.-B. Lundequist; Leipzig: Otto Harrassowitz, 1948); Hans Walter Wolff, Joel and Amos (Hermeneia; trans. W. Janzen et al; Philadelphia: Fortress, 1977) 6-12.

10   See, e.g., the assessment of Joel by Wilhelm Rudolph, *Joel--Amos--Obadja--Jona* (KAT XIII/2; Gütersloh: Gerd Mohn, 1971) 24-29.

11   Rolf Knierim, "Criticism of Literary Features, Form, Tradition, and Redaction," *The Hebrew Bible and its Modern Interpreters* (ed. D. Knight and G. M. Tucker; Chico: Scholars Press, 1985) 123-165 (reprinted in *Reading the Hebrew Bible for a New Millennium: Form, Concept, and Theological Perspective. Volume 2: Exegetical and Theological Studies* [SAC; eds., W. Kim, D. Ellens, M. Floyd, and M. A. Sweeney; Harrisburg, PA: Trinity Press International, 2000] 1-41); idem, "Old Testament Form Criticism Reconsidered," *Int* 27 (1973) 435-448 (Reprinted in *Reading the Hebrew Bible for a New Millennium*, 42-71; Marvin A. Sweeney, "Formation and Form in Prophetic Literature," *Old Testament Interpretation: Past, Present and Future* (eds., J. L. Mays, D. L. Petersen, and K. H. Richards; Nashville: Abingdon, 1995) 113-126; idem, "Form Criticism," *To Each Its Own Meaning: Biblical Criticisms and their Application* (eds., S. L. McKenzie and S. R. Haynes; Revised and expanded edition; Louisville: Westminster John Knox, 1999) 58-89.

cates a syntactical relationship with the preceding material that must be taken into account. Other linguistic features, such as the commands to "hear this, O elders" (שמעו־זאת הזקנים) in Joel 1:2 or to "blow the *shofar* in Zion" (תקעו שופר בציון) in Joel 2:1 and 2:15, indicate an effort to address a listening or reading audience from the outset of the book that must also be considered. Such features point to a need to consider the rhetorical function of this text, i.e., is it designed merely to convey an expectation of salvation in some distant, undefined future that can be safely ignored by its contemporary audience, or is it designed to have an impact on the perspectives of its audience that will prompt it to some sort of decision or action?[12]

In considering the formal literary structure of the text,[13] the first observation concerns demarcation. The book of Joel is clearly identified within the Book of the Twelve by its initial superscription in Joel 1:1, "The word of YHWH which was unto Joel ben Pethuel," which introduces and identifies the following material.[14] No other superscription appears until the following book, Amos 1:1 in the sequence of the MT and Obadiah 1a in the sequence of the LXX. The superscription marks the book of Joel as a discrete unit within the Book of the Twelve.

The second observation concerns the generic character and function of the superscription in relation to the rest of the book. The objective third person form of the superscription clearly indicates that the narrator of the book is the speaker, and its reference to the word of YHWH that was unto Joel ben Pethuel clearly indicates that the following material must be identified as that word. At no point in the rest of the book is there a clear indication that the narrator of the book appears once again. Consequently, the superscription is generically distinct from the following material. It stands apart from Joel 1:2-4:21 in that it introduces and identifies that material as the word of YHWH that was unto Joel ben Pethuel. The superscription in Joel 1:1 therefore constitutes the first major structural component of the book, and the word of YHWH that was unto Joel ben Pethuel in Joel 1:2-4:21 then constitutes the second major component.

---

[12] See the recent analysis of Joel by Stephen L. Cook (*Prophecy and Apocalypticism: The Post-Exilic Social Setting* [Minneapolis: Fortress, 1995] 167-209), who argues that Joel is designed to mobilize the Judean community to support the programs of the Zadokite priesthood.

[13] For full discussion of the formal literary structure of Joel, see my commentary, *The Twelve Prophets*, 1:145-187.

[14] For discussion of the formal character and role of superscriptions, see Gene M. Tucker, "Prophetic Superscriptions and the Growth of the Canon," *Canon and Authority* (ed. G. W. Coats and B. O. Long; Philadelphia: Fortress, 1977) 56-70.

In assessing the literary structure of Joel 1:2-4:21, it must be observed at the outset that this text is formulated as an imperative address to its audience. This is clear from the initial commands in Joel 1:2, "Hear this, O elders, and give ear, all inhabitants of the land." This command then introduces statements throughout Joel 1:3-20 that are concerned with a plague of locusts that threatens the land and that identify that threat as a manifestation of the "Day of YHWH" (v. 15). Indeed, a series of imperatives in vv. 2, 5, 8, 11, and 13 appear to define the basic literary structure of this text. Joel 1:2-4 introduces the basic premise of the entire passage, i.e., that a plague of locusts threatens the land that the audience must tell their children and future generations about it. Joel 1:5-7 addresses the audience as drunkards who must weep because an enemy nation has invaded the land and laid waste to the vines, fig trees, etc., of the land. Inherent in this section is the metaphorical portrayal of the enemy as locusts who would strip the land bare of its agricultural growth. Joel 1:8-10 calls upon the audience to lament like a young woman who has lost her husband, because this disaster threatens the grain and drink offerings of the Temple and indeed the entire crop of grain, wine, and oil, that support life in the land. Joel 1:11-12 then calls upon the farmers and vintners to wail over the loss of the grain and fruit crops. Finally, Joel 1:13-20 culminates in a call to the priests to declare a fast and solemn assembly in the Temple to mourn and to petition YHWH concerning the disaster that the land has suffered. It is clear that the text presupposes that the disaster comes from YHWH as vv. 15-18 identify it as the "Day of YHWH," which brings destruction and famine as food is cut off from the land. Verses 19-20 specify that the fast is designed to appeal to YHWH to put a stop to such suffering. In short, Joel 1:2-20 constitutes a distinct literary sub-unit that must be identified as "a call to communal complaint concerning the threat of the locust plague on the Day of YHWH."

Imperative formulations appear to play key roles in the balance of the book as well. Joel 2:1, "Blow the *shofar* in Zion, and raise a shout on my holy mountain," introduces a second address that also warns of the coming "Day of YHWH" (v. 1b), but it employs theophanic language to characterize the threat to the land as a military invasion that is led by YHWH. Joel 2:1-14 calls upon the people to return to YHWH (v. 12) so that the threat might cease. It therefore builds upon Joel 1:5-7, which metaphorically compares the locust plague to the invasion of an enemy nation, but it drops the metaphor entirely. The passage therefore presents military invasion as the human counterpart to the locust plague described in Joel 1:2-20. The structure of the passage appears to be defined by the presence of quotations by YHWH in v. 1a, "blow the *shofar* in Zion, raise a shout on my holy mountain," and v. 12-13aα, "'And also now,' utterance of YHWH, 'return to me with all your heart and with fasting and with weeping and with mourning, and tear your heart and not your garments,'" which then serve as the basis for the prophet's own statements that build upon YHWH's words. Thus, Joel 2:1-11 constitutes the prophet's theophanic portrayal of the threat against the land posed by YHWH's invading army on the "Day of YHWH." Joel 2:12-14 then comprises the prophet's call to the people to appeal to YHWH for relief, particularly as he reiterates YHWH's own appeal for return in v. 13aβ-b, "and return to YHWH, your G-d, because he is gracious and merciful, slow to anger and full of loyalty, and he relents concerning evil." To a certain extent, Joel 2:1-14 is parallel to Joel 1:2-20 in that it calls upon the audience to appeal to YHWH for deliverance from the threat of military invasion on the Day of YHWH. Joel 2:1-14 must therefore be identified as "a call to communal complaint concerning the threat of invasion of the Day of YHWH."

A third major imperative appears in Joel 2:15 that is initially parallel to that in Joel 2:1, "Blow the *shofar* in Zion, sanctify a fast, call a solemn assembly." Verses 15-17 then build upon this command by calling upon the entire people to gather for cultic assembly in which the priests will appeal to YHWH to spare the people from YHWH's threat. This call culminates in a rhetorical question, "Why should they say among the nations, 'Where is their G-d?'" that is obviously designed to provoke YHWH's response. The report of that response begins in Joel 2:18 and continues throughout the balance of the book.

Most interpreters view the structure of this sub-unit quite differently.[15] Joel 2:15-17 is frequently viewed as the conclusion to the previous material because it calls upon the people to gather at the Temple to appeal to YHWH for deliverance, much like Joel 1:19-20 and 2:15-17 that also call for the people to cry out to YHWH. Joel 2:18-4:21, however, focuses specifically on YHWH's response and promises to deliver the people. Several factors call for a reconsideration of this view. First, the initial imperatives in Joel 2:15-17, "blow the *shofar* in Zion," "sanctify a fast," "gather the people," etc., take up not only the initial call of Joel 2:1, "blow the *shofar* in Zion," but language in Joel 1:2-20 as well, i.e., "hear this, O elders, give ear, all inhabitants of the land" (1:2) and "sanctify a fast, call a solemn assembly. Gather the elders and all the inhabitants of the land" (1:14). Joel 2:15-17 does not simply provide a rhetorical inclusio for Joel 2:1-14, but it does recapitulate the major concerns of Joel 1:2-20. Second, in recalling elements from the previous units of the book, Joel 2:15-17 does not simply sum up the preceding text, but it also looks forward so that it constitutes an

---

15   For an overview of the discussion, see most recently, James L. Crenshaw, *Joel* (AB 24C; New York: Doubleday, 1995) 29-39.

introduction to the following material. It does not call the people together for the purpose of lamentation; that has already been accomplished in Joel 1:2-20 and 2:1-14. Rather, it calls the people together so that they may hear YHWH's answer to their complaint in Joel 2:18-4:21. Whereas Joel 2:1-14 announced the "Day of YHWH" as a day of coming threat to the people, the question posed YHWH in Joel 2:15-17 points to YHWH's anticipated action to deliver the people from that threat, viz., "spare your people, O YHWH, and do not make your heritage a mockery, a byword among the nations. Why should they say among the nations, 'Where is their G-d?'" Furthermore, the beginning of the announcement of YHWH's response in Joel 2:18 is linked syntactically to Joel 2:15-17 by a *waw*-consecutive formulation, "then YHWH became jealous for his land and had pity on his people. . ." The material beginning in Joel 2:18 is meant to be read together with Joel 2:15-17, whereas the disjunctive imperatives in Joel 2:15-17 indicate that it is the beginning of a new unit. Finally, Joel 2:1-14 concludes with the call to "return" to YHWH and the speculation that YHWH will show mercy for such a request. Joel 2:15-4:21 constitutes precisely such an attempt to appeal to YHWH for mercy together with YHWH's answer.

The structure of Joel 2:15-4:21 is defined by a succession of syntactically disjunctive introductory imperatives in Joel 2:15-16, "Blow a *shofar* in Zion. . . "; 2:21-22, "Do not fear, O land, celebrate and rejoice because YHWH has prepared to act. Do not fear, O beasts of the field, for the pastures of the wilderness are green; for the tree bears its fruit, the fig tree and vine give their yield"; 4:9-11, "Proclaim this among the nations, sanctify/prepare for war, rouse the warriors, . . ." Joel 2:15-20 therefore begins the sub-unit with the prophet's presentation of YHWH's response to the people's appeal for mercy in which YHWH promises to send grain, wine, and oil, and to remove the northern threat against the people, i.e., the army that had threatened them.[16] Joel 2:21-4:8 conveys YHWH's reassurance to restore the natural world of creation and to deliver the nation from its oppressors. Indeed, this passage is tied together by syntactical conjunctives in 3:1 (וְהָיָה אַחֲרֵי־כֵן), "and it shall come to pass afterwards") and 4:1 (כִּי הִנֵּה בַּיָּמִים הָהֵמָּה וּבָעֵת הַהִיא אֲשֶׁר), "for behold, in those days and at that time when. . ."), and specifies that YHWH will restore the fortunes of Judah and Jerusalem (4:1). Finally, Joel 4:9-21 presents the prophet's call to the nations to assemble themselves at the Valley of Jehoshaphat for YHWH's judgment, which in turn will lead to the restoration of fertility in the natural world together with Judah's and Jerusalem's eternal security.

---

[16] For discussion of the significance of YHWH's response to national lament in Joel, see Graham S. Ogden, "Joel 4 and Prophetic Responses to National Laments," *JSOT* 26 (1983) 97-106.

Altogether, Joel 2:15-4:21 constitutes "the prophet's announcement of YHWH's response to protect the people from threats."

The structure of the passage may be outlined as follows:

The Book of Joel: YHWH's Response to Judah's Appeals for Relief from Threat	1:1-4:21
I. Superscription	1:1
II. Body of Book: YHWH's Response to Judah's Appeals for Relief from Threat	1:2-4:21
A. Prophet's Call to Communal Complaint concerning the Threat of the Locust Plague	1:2-20
1. The basic premise: threat posed by locusts	1:2-4
2. The threat to the grape harvest and wine	1:5-7
3. The threat to the people of the land and the offerings at the Temple	1:8-10
4. The threat to the grain crop	1:11-12
5. Appeal for fasting and mourning on the day of YHWH	1:13-20
B. Prophet's Call to Communal Complaint concerning the Threat of Invasion	2:1-14
1. Theophanic portrayal of the threat posed to the land by YHWH's army	2:1-11
2. The call to appeal to YHWH for mercy	2:12-14
C. Prophet's Announcement of YHWH's Response to Protect People from Threats	2:15-4:21
1. Presentation of YHWH's response to the people: deliverance from threat	2:15-20
2. Presentation of YHWH's reassurance to restore creation and to deliver the nation from oppressors	2:21-4:8
3. Announcement concerning YHWH's response to protect the people from threats	4:9-21

Several conclusions may be drawn from this analysis of the literary structure and generic characteristics of Joel. First, the book is identified by the superscription as "the word of YHWH that was to Joel ben Pethuel," which lends it a certain truth claim to its status as divine revelation, even if Joel ben Petheul is otherwise unknown. Second, the body of the book is identified as the prophet's presentation of YHWH's response to Judah's appeals from threat. Insofar as that response promises deliverance for Judah and Jerusalem and punishment of the nations that threaten Jerusalem/Judah, it must be taken as YHWH's pledge to undertake such action. Third, insofar as the response is delivered in relation to the prophet's calls to communal complaint to YHWH concerning the threat, YHWH is also viewed as responsible for bringing or allowing the threats in the first place. In this sense, YHWH is portrayed as exercising absolute control over the fate of Jerusalem, Judah, and the nations. Furthermore, the threat posed against Jerusalem/Judah and its agricultural produce is portrayed simultaneously as the armies of enemy nations and as locusts or sheaves of grain that are cut down. This suggests a certain mythological dimension in the conceptualization of the entire scenario in which the events of the human world are also conceived as events in the natural world of creation and in the heavenly realm. The entire scenario is presented in relation to the Day of YHWH, as both a day of threat against Jerusalem/Judah and as a day of deliverance for Jerusalem/Judah. Insofar as the Day of YHWH is portrayed elsewhere as a cultic event that portends both threat and deliverance for the people, Joel must be considered as an expression of the patterns of thought inherent in the ancient Jerusalemite/Judean cult and liturgy, i.e., threat and deliverance appear successively as a cyclical pattern much like the seasons of the year, and both stem from YHWH. In short, YHWH will take action to remove a threat to Jerusalem in response to the appeals of the people. Such a contention plays a major role in defining Jerusalem's/Judah's expectations of YHWH in time of crisis, i.e., YHWH may bring the crisis, but YHWH has the capacity to end it based upon the repentance and appeal of the people. Finally, Joel presents its scenario of threat and deliverance in anonymous terms; it therefore constitutes a basic pattern of threat and divine response to threat that can be read in relation to any particular historical situation in which the same patterns apply.

III. The Intertextual Relationships in Joel

The second major facet of Joel to be treated is its intertextual relationships, particularly in relation to the other constituent books of the Book of the Twelve. Several intertextual relationships require examination.[17] Apart from those pertaining to the Book of the Twelve, they include first of all the use of the Exodus tradition, particularly the plagues of locusts in Exod 10:1-20 and darkness in Exod 10:21-29. The use of the Exodus tradition includes the Sharav or Hamsin, the dry desert wind that brings locusts and perhaps the darkness to depict YHWH's defeat of threats against the people (Exod 10:13, 19; cf. Exodus 14-15; Isa 11:11-16). Other traditions employed include the "Day of YHWH" tradition that depicts punishment against Israel's enemies as well as against Israel itself (Isa 2; 13; see also Amos 5:18-20; Obadiah; Zephaniah; Zechariah) and 2 Chronicles 20, which portrays King Jehoshaphat's defeat of the nations, Ammon, Moab, and Edom, that threatened Jerusalem. Intertextual references to the book the Book of the Twelve include the citation of Amos 1:2 and 9:13 in Joel 4:16,

---

[17] For a full study of the intertextual relationships in Joel, see Siegfried Bergler, *Joel als Schriftinterpret* (BEATAJ 16; Frankfurt/Main: Peter Lang, 1988).

18; the use of Mic 4:1-5 (cf. Isa 2:2-4) in Joel 4:10; and citations from the book of Obadiah that appear throughout Joel 3-4.

The use in Joel of the locust plague from Exod 10:1-20 has already been noted by scholars. Bergler's recent dissertation studies the extensive intertextual relationships between Joel and the Exodus narrative, including parallels in Joel 1:3; 2:26-27 and Exod 10:1, 2 concerning YHWH's self-identification and the instruction to the people to tell their children about YHWH's actions; Joel 2:19, 25 and Exod 10:4 concerning the motif of "sending"; Joel 1:4; 2:25 and Exod 10:5, 12, 15 concerning the devouring of the remnant or what is left over; Joel 1:2; 2:2 and Exod 10:6, 14 concerning the threat posed by the locusts to houses that has not been seen since the days of the people's ancestors; Joel 2:20 and Exod 10:17, 19 concerning YHWH's capacity to remove the threat from the land; and Joel 3:3-4 and the general pattern of signs and wonders in the Exodus.[18] Bergler's examination of these intertextual relationships stresses that Joel creates an Exodus typology in which the specific setting of the locust plague against Egypt in the Exodus account is removed so that the pattern of the locust plague may be applied to the situation of threat that is articulated in Joel. It should be noted, however, that Joel does not present a particular situation of threat, i.e., no specific enemy is identified, rendering it impossible to tie Joel's depiction of threat to any specific historical situation or event. The presentation of threat against Jerusalem and Judah in Joel is almost entirely anonymous. Apparently, this is deliberate in that the creation of such an Exodus typology enables the book of Joel to be read in relation to any threat, whether real or potential, that might be posed against Jerusalem and Judah. In this respect, Joel draws upon past tradition to assert that YHWH has the capacity to bring a threat against Jerusalem and Judah and to deliver Jerusalem and Judah from that threat, just as YHWH did at the time of the Exodus from Egyptian slavery.

It is noteworthy, therefore, that Joel 3:1-5 employs the motif of YHWH's "wind" or "spirit" that will be poured out over all flesh so that all the people, including slaves and maidservants, will prophesy and Jerusalem and Judah will be saved. It is not insignificant that this passage follows immediately the reference in Joel 2:27 in which YHWH states, "and you shall know that I am in the midst of Israel; and I am YHWH your G-d and there is no other, and my people shall not be ashamed forever." As noted above, the motif of YHWH's self-identification and the instruction to tell the children constitutes one of the key intertextual connections between Joel and the Exodus narrative of the locust plague. Although many interpreters correctly read the reference to YHWH's pouring out of the divine "spirit" or

---

[18]   Ibid., 247-294.

"wind" (Hebrew, רוח) on the people in relation to the following statements concerning their ability to prophesy (cf. Num 11:16-20; 1 Sam 10:6; 19:20-24), the statement also relates to the Exodus locust narrative in that the locusts are brought upon Egypt by an "east wind" (Exod 10:13) and later removed by a "west wind" that was changed by YHWH (Exod 10:19). The east wind in particular is a frequent motif in the Hebrew Bible that is to be identified with the Sharav (Hebrew) or Ḥamsin (Arabic), a strong dry desert wind, much like the Santa Ana winds of Southern California, that blows in from the desert at times of seasonal transition in Israel, either from the dry summer to the wet winter in October of from the wet winter to the dry summer in April. These winds can be very destructive as they reach high velocities, and they frequently blow in a great deal of dust and debris that blocks out the sun, thus darkening the land and causing the moon to appear as a deep red or blood-like color as described in Joel 3:3-5. In this respect, the imagery of Joel 3 also relates to that of the plague of darkness as described in Exod 10:21-29, which is variously understood in relation to a solar eclipse or the Sharav/Ḥamsin that is common to the region.[19]

The use of the image of the Sharav/Ḥamsin once again speaks to a concern to portray YHWH's actions of threat and deliverance in relation to the cosmic patterns of nature, i.e., YHWH brings destruction as well as deliverance, and the cyclical nature of such events, i.e., just as YHWH brought about such actions at the time of the Exodus, so YHWH is capable of bringing them about once again. Indeed, the use of the Sharav/Hamsin as a symbol for YHWH's deliverance is known in Exodus 14-15 and Isaiah 11:11-16 in which the wind divides the water of the Red Sea or the River of Egypt, and enables Israel to return from exile in Assyrian as well as in Egypt. Joel's images of the portents in heaven and earth, blood, fire, and columns of smoke are also noteworthy in that they combine the images of the natural phenomenon of creation in the Sharav/Ḥamsin with those of sacrifice at the Temple altar. Indeed, the cyclical pattern of threat and deliverance that is conveyed by the Sharav/Ḥamsin also appears in Temple sacrifice in which the images of blood, fire, and columns of smoke speak to the act of destruction in the killing and consumption of the sacrificial animal as well as the deliverance or the restoration of cosmic order that such an action embodies. The imagery of the Sharav/Hamsin and the Temple sacrifice are both transformative in that both mark the transition from threat to order or security that underlies the basic pattern of Joel.

Such a concern also underlies the use of the "Day of YHWH" motif in Joel. The "Day of YHWH" is mentioned explicitly in Joel 1:15; 2:1; and

---

[19] For discussion of the Sharav or Ḥamsin, see "Israel, Land of (Geographical Survey)," *EncJud*, 9:189-193.

4:14, and it appears to underlie the entire scenario of threat and deliverance in the book. Although the "Day of YHWH"is not well understood in that it is variously identified in relation to the holy war, cultic/Sukkot, royal, or eschatological/apocalyptic traditions,[20] it is clear that the "Day of YHWH" elsewhere signifies both a day of threat against Israel and a day of deliverance for Israel from its enemies. Thus, Amos 5:18-20 indicates that the people of Israel might desire the Day of YHWH as a day of light or deliverance; in fact, it is to be a day of darkness and threat. Isaiah 2:6-21 portrays it as a day of threat against all the arrogant of the earth or land; Isaiah 13 portrays it as a day in which YHWH's warriors will bring down Babylon; and Isaiah 34 presents it as a day of YHWH's vengeance against the nations, especially Edom. Ezekiel 30 presents it as a day of judgment against Egypt; Obadiah presents it as a day of judgment against Edom; and Zechariah 14 presents it as the day that YHWH will defeat the nations and bring them to Zion to worship YHWH at the festival of Sukkot. Like Amos, Zephaniah portrays it as a day of judgment against those in Jerusalem/Judah and the nations who resist YHWH's sovereignty. As the various images of the day demonstrate, it is present as a day of cultic sacrifice at the Temple (Zeph 1:7-9; Zech 14:20-21; cf. Isa 34:5-7) in which theophanic images of warfare, darkness, gloom, thick clouds, and *shofar* blast predominate (Ezek 30:3; Amos 5:18-20; Zeph 1:14-16; cf. Isa 13:10; 34:8-10). Insofar as the "Day of YHWH" motif permeates the entire book of Joel, it appears to define the entire scenario of threat against Jerusalem/Judah by the nations and deliverance from that threat throughout the book of Joel as a whole. Again, the general scenario is anonymous in that can be applied to various nations.

The motif of the Day of YHWH especially appears to define the use in Joel 4:9-21 of the tradition concerning King Jehoshaphat's defeat of the Moabites, Ammonites, Meunites, and Edomites from 2 Chronicles 20. Scholars have already noted Joel's dependence upon some form of this tradition in that Jehoshaphat's defeat in the Valley of Berachah of the nations that threatened Jerusalem underlies Joel's call to prepare for war against the nations in the "Valley of Jehoshaphat" or the "Valley of Decision."[21] The reason for the use of this particular tradition in Joel is unclear, but it does seem to play on the name of the valley where Jehoshaphat won his victory in that the Valley of Berachah (Hebrew, עמק ברכה) means "valley of blessing," which of course calls to mind the motif of YHWH's deliverance in a time of threat. More importantly for the present purposes, the text in Joel initially renders the nations anonymous so that the scenario may be applied once again to any situation of threat against Jerusalem. Further-

---

20   See the discussion by K. J. Cathcart, "Day of YHWH," *ABD*, 2:84-85.
21   E.g., Nogalski, *Redactional Processes*, 30-37.

more, Joel introduces both the motifs of the Day of YHWH and the cosmic transformation of the son and the moon that darken, in keeping with the previously discussed use of the Sharav/Hamsin from the Exodus plague narratives. Again, the agricultural motifs from the first part of the book of Joel appear as YHWH's deliverance ensures the harvest of grain and wine that were previously threatened by the locusts. By the end of the passage, however, the general threat against the nations that threatened Jerusalem and Judah is directed specifically against Egypt and Edom. The basis for the mention of Egypt is clear since Joel makes such extensive use of the Exodus tradition. The mention of Edom likewise becomes clear when one considers the use of Obadiah, which is formulated as an oracle of judgment against Edom, throughout Joel 3-4.

Indeed, scholars have long noted the extensive allusion to texts from Obadiah in Joel 3-4.[22] The allusions include Joel 3:5 and Obadiah 17-18 concerning the remnant for Jerusalem/Judah in Zion and the lack of one for Esau; Joel 4:17 and Obadiah 17, 11 concerning the foreigners who threaten YHWH's mountain in Zion; Joel 4:3 and Obadiah 11 concerning the lot cast against Jerusalem; Joel 4:3 and Obadiah 16 concerning the nations who drink at Zion; Joel 4:4, 7 and Obadiah 15 concerning recompense for deeds against YHWH/Zion; Joel 4:6 and Obadiah 18 concerning YHWH's spea-king; Joel 4:19 and Obadiah 10 concerning Edom's slaughter of Judah or Jacob; Joel 4:9, 11 and Obadiah 1 (cf. Jer 49:14) concerning the call to war; Joel 4:11 and Obadiah 9 concerning warriors; Joel 4:14 and Obadiah 19-20 concerning the sale or exile of Jerusalem/Judah to Greece or Sepharad; and Joel 4:12, 17 and Obadiah 21 concerning YHWH's judgment against Esau and the nations. Based upon his analysis of the allusions to Obadiah in Joel 3-4, Bergler argues that Joel typologizes Edom so that it becomes a repre-sentative of the nations at large. This is in contrast to Obadiah, which con-demns Edom specifically for wrongs done against Jacob and Jerusalem. He maintains that the typologization of Edom thereby provides the link in Joel between the initial locust plague of the book and its later judgment against the nations. This is apparent especially from Joel 4:19 where Egypt and Edom are placed together and condemned for the violence that they have done against Judah in shedding innocent blood. Clearly, Joel is dependent upon Obadiah, and employs Obadian texts to build its typological portrayal of YHWH's bringing nations against Jerusalem for judgment and then de-livering Jerusalem from the threat when the people repent. The use of Oba-diah is apparently linked to the use of 2 Chronicles 20 with its portrayal of Jehoshaphat's defeat of the nations, including Edom/Esau, that threatened Jerusalem. Whereas 2 Chronicles 20 depicts the defeat of Edom and the

---

[22]   See Bergler, *Joel als Schriftinterpret*, 295-333.

other nations, Obadiah provides a prophet's condemnation of Edom for its crimes against Jerusalem.

The concern with the threat against Jerusalem and YHWH's deliverance of the city from that threat also appears to motivate the use of Amos 1:2 and 9:13 in Joel 4:16 and 18 respectively.[23] In portraying YHWH's actions against the nations, Joel 4:16 states, "and YHWH will roar from Zion, and from Jerusalem he will give his voice, and heaven and earth will tremble (וְרָעֲשׁוּ)," which draws directly from Amos 1:2, "YHWH will roar from Zion, and from Jerusalem he will give his voice," which appears immediately following the reference to the earthquake (הָרַעַשׁ) in Amos 1:1. Likewise, in portraying the coming day of YHWH's deliverance, Joel 4:18 states, "and it shall come to pass in that day that the mountains will drip fresh wine, and the hills shall flow with milk," which draws upon the portrayal of Israel's fecundity in Amos 9:13, "and the mountains shall drip fresh wine, and all the hills shall flow (literally, 'melt, dissolve') with it." The use of these verses clearly supports Joel's attempt to portray Jerusalem's deliverance from threat by YHWH as well as the overall portrayal of the threat against Jerusalem and its deliverance in cosmic imagery or natural terms. It must also be noted that these verses respectively introduce and conclude the words of Amos as presented in his book so that they encapsulate Amos' message of judgment against various nations and northern Israel and the restoration of Israel under Davidic kingship or Jerusalemite rule as the goal of that punishment. In short, Joel apparently reads Amos as an expression of its own scenario in which Jerusalem is under threat, this time from northern Israel, and YHWH takes action to remove that threat and to restore Jerusalem to its rightful state of existence.

Finally, scholars have also long noted the use of Micah 4:1-5 or Isaiah 2:2-4 in Joel 4:10.[24] As part of the general call to battle against the nations, Joel 4:10 states, "beat your plowshares into swords and your pruning hooks into spears (רְמָחִים)," whereas Micah 4:3/Isaiah 2:4 state, "and they shall beat their swords into plowshares and their spears (חֲנִיתוֹתֵיהֶם/חֲנִיתֹתֵיהֶם) into pruning hooks," as part of the overall scenario of world peace that will ensue when the nations recognize YHWH's sovereignty at Zion. Although the reference to spears differs slightly as חֲנִית may refer to a lighter javelin whereas רֹמַח may refer to the heavier lance, the passage clearly draws upon some version of the text that appears in Micah or Isaiah. It is impossible to determine upon which text it is dependent, or even if it is dependent upon a third text. Nevertheless, it draws its power of expression from the

---

23   Cf. Nogalski, *Redactional Processes*, 42-48.
24   E.g., Wolff, *Joel and Amos*, 80.

reversal of the motif of world peace depicted in these texts, and thereby serves Joel's agenda of declaring YHWH's judgment against the nations that threaten the security of Jerusalem, the city of peace that stands at the center of the cosmos. Again, no specific nations are singled out, but they are treated as a whole to serve Joel's interests in depicting typologically the resolution of a threat to the cosmos.

IV. Joel's Place Within the Book of the Twelve

Clearly, Joel depends heavily upon other biblical texts, including texts from the Book of the Twelve as well as other biblical writings. Although Joel's use of other biblical texts has implications for establishing the date of Joel, Joel's use of other texts from the Book of the Twelve also has implications for understanding Joel's place or setting within the major versions of the Twelve. Insofar as the Twelve appears within different sequences of books in its MT and LXX versions, the sequence of Joel's appearance in relation to the other books that it cites appears to have some bearing in understanding the arrangement of the Twelve in both versions.

The use of Mic 4:3/Isa 2:4 in Joel 4:10 is particularly noteworthy. This citation appears at the outset of the last discrete sub-unit of the book in Joel 4:9-21 in which the prophet calls for the gathering of warriors who will enforce YHWH's judgment against the nations that threaten Jerusalem in the Valley of Jehoshaphat. The reversal of this statement makes for a particularly powerful rhetorical impact upon the audience because the Mican/Isaian text was apparently very well known (see Zech 8:20-23; Isa 37:32/2 Kgs 19:31; Isa 51:4), which presuppose the Mican/Isaian oracle) and because it conveyed a very compelling image of peace among the nations that is shattered in Joel. One can account for its function in Joel even if Joel appears prior to Micah in the sequence of the Twelve as is the case in the MT. If Joel is read first, then the reversal of the image actually occurs in Mic 4:1-5 as Joel's image of judgment among the nations is resolved when the nations voluntarily stream to Zion for YHWH's judgment and rework their weapons in the Mican text.

This sequence does create problems in that Micah defines an ideal situation in the middle of the Twelve that is not resolved until nearly the end of the sequence. Zech 8:20-23 portrays the nations grasping onto the garments of Jews in Zech 8:20-23 so that they might come to Jerusalem and suffer YHWH's punishment before finally celebrating Sukkot in Zechariah 14. In such a sequence, it is not clear why the judgment should be mentioned near to the outset of the Twelve, only to point to an ideal in the middle of the sequence, and then to return once again to judgment and its resolution near the end of the sequence. The MT order highlights the experience of Jerusalem throughout, but it does not present a smoothly flowing sequence for the definition and realization of Jerusalem's ideal state of being in relation to the nations. The LXX order, which places Micah prior to Joel, appears to make much better sense. Insofar as the LXX sequence of the Twelve treats the experience of northern Israel as a paradigm for that of Jerusalem and Judah,[25] Micah points to the ideal future of Jerusalem as the sequence makes the transition from Israel to Jerusalem. Joel then imitates the scenario of judgment against the nations with typological portrayal that is specified with successive treatment of Edom (Obadiah), Assyria (Jonah; Nahum), Babylon (Habakkuk), and Jerusalem (Zephaniah) prior to the images of Jerusalem's restoration in the midst of the nations (Haggai; Zechariah) and a concluding book that calls for the realization of this scenario (Malachi). In short, the ideal is defined, and then the process by which that ideal is to be achieved follows in a logical progression.

Similar considerations apply to the citation of Amos 1:2 and 9:13. Once again, the citation of these texts appears in the concluding sub-unit of the book of Joel, which portrays the prophet's summons of the warriors to the Valley of Jehoshaphat for YHWH's judgment against the nations. As noted above, these verses appear at the beginning and end of the book of Amos. Amos in turn presents its own scenario of YHWH's judgment against the nations and the northern kingdom of Israel that culminates in the call for the destruction of the Beth El altar and the restoration of Davidic kingship, and thus Jerusalem's central role, over all Israel. In this respect, Amos 1:2 and 9:13 encapsulate the message of the book of Amos as a whole, and thus provide Joel with an abbreviated reference to that message that points to YHWH's capacity for judgment from Zion and the resolution of that judgment in a restored state of fecundity and order in creation. Naturally, this reference can be lost if Joel appears prior to Amos as it does in the MT. Although this problem might be resolved by the recognition that biblical books are intended to be read and reread,[26] the MT sequence nevertheless creates tension in that the book of Amos addresses a fundamental judgment and transformation of the northern kingdom of Israel which has an impact on Jerusalem, whereas Joel is concerned with Jerusalem and Judah throughout. If Amos is read first, as is the case in the LXX sequence of the Book of the Twelve, then the situation of the northern kingdom of Israel is addressed first, with its implications for Jerusalem, and Joel subsequently treats the

---

[25] See Sweeney, "Sequence and Interpretation."

[26] For discussion of the reading and rereading of prophetic books, see the commentary on Micah by Ehud Ben Zvi, *Micah* (FOTL 21; Grand Rapids and Cambridge: William Eerdmans, 2000) 9-11; idem, *A Historical-Critical Study of the Book of Obadiah* (BZAW 242; Berlin and New York: Walter de Gruyter, 1996) 3-6.

issue of Jerusalem as a next stage in the sequence. In this case, the citation of Amos 1:2 and 9:13 in Joel provides a cryptic reference to the scenario of judgment that recalls the experience of northern Israel just as Jerusalem and Judah undergo their own experience of judgment and transformation. Once again, the LXX sequence appears to make a great deal of sense whereas the MT sequence appears to create tension.

Finally, the use of the Obadian passages in Joel also appears to make greater sense when read in the LXX sequence of the Twelve. As noted above, Obadiah apparently portrays the judgment against Edom as an actual historical situation whereas Joel employs Edom together with Egypt as a typological portrayal of the nations at large. In both the MT and LXX sequences of the Twelve, Joel appears before Obadiah so that in both cases, Joel presents the typology and Obadiah presents the realization of that typology. But Amos appears between Joel and Obadiah in the MT sequence, and this break the connection between the two books to a certain extent, i.e., the interrelationship between the two books is somewhat lost due to the appearance of the intervening book of Amos. This is addressed, in part, by the often noted reference to David's or Judah's possession of the remnant of Edom and all the nations in Amos 9:11-12. There are questions as to whether this reading is the result of redactional emendation, because the LXX reads Hebrew אֱדוֹם, "Edom," as אָדָם or Greek των ἀνθρώπων, "humanity," so that the passage reads as a reference to David's/Judah's possession of the remnant of humanity and all the nations.[27] It is not entirely certain, however, that the LXX reading is original as the recovery of Edom would have been a major issue in Israel and Judah throughout the late-ninth and eighth centuries B.C.E.[28] Apart from this issue, the LXX sequence, which places Joel immediately prior to Obadiah, makes a great deal of sense because the references to Obadiah in Joel are immediately clear to the reader, who encounters Obadiah after having just completed Joel. Edom then becomes the first of the nations mentioned in Joel's typological portrayal, and the other nations then follow as indicated earlier.

---

[27]   See the discussion in Nogalski, *Literary Precursors*, 113-116.

[28]   See 2 Kgs 8:20-22, which notes Edom's revolt against Judah during the reign of Jehoram/Joram. Cf. 2 Kgs 10:32-33, which notes the loss of the Trans-Jordan to Israel during the reign of Jehu. 2 Kgs 14:25 refers to Jeroboam ben Joash's restoration of Israel and 2 Kgs 14:7 refers to Amaziah's defeat of the Edomites, but it is not clear that Edom was ever brought entirely under Israelite/Judean control during this period.

V. Setting and Function Within the Versions of the Twelve

The preceding observations clearly indicate that Joel's place in the LXX sequence of the Book of the Twelve provides for a far more logically consistent progression among the individual books that holds out the experience of northern Israel in Hosea, Amos, and Micah as a model or paradigm for that of Jerusalem. In addition, it places books concerned with the nations together as a block in Obadiah (Edom), Jonah (mercy for Assyria), Nahum (fall of Assyria), and Habakkuk (Babylon), prior to returning to concern with Jerusalem's judgment in Zephaniah, its restoration at the center of the nations in Haggai and Zechariah, and the projection that the entire process is about to begin (Malachi). Thus, Joel, with its typological concern for the threat posed to Jerusalem by the nations and YHWH's pledge to deliver Jerusalem from that threat, provides an ideal transition between Hosea--Micah and Obadiah--Malachi. In the MT sequence, which focuses on Jerusalem throughout, tension appears among the various books as Joel provides a typological portrayal of Jerusalem's experience in relation to the nations, but the following sequence only highlights Jerusalem's idealization in the middle (Micah) prior to taking up the issue as to how that ideal will be realized in Zephaniah--Malachi.

This has some bearing on the historical setting in which the two forms of the Book of the Twelve were assembled insofar as they point to two very different concerns. The interest in comparing the experience of northern Israel, with its destruction and exile at the hands of the Assyrian empire in the late eighth century B.C.E., would have been of paramount concern in the late-monarchic period as well as during the exile and the early years of the Persian period. During these periods, Judean thinkers were attempting to come to terms with the destruction of the northern kingdom and its implications for Judah and Jerusalem. Such concern was inherent in the attempts by the southern kingdom of Judah to reestablish Davidic rule over the north, perhaps as early as the reigns of Ahaz or Hezekiah and as late as the reigns of Josiah and his successors. With the emergence of Babylon in the late seventh and early sixth centuries, concern would shift to understanding the implications of Israel's downfall in relation to the threat posed to Jerusalem and ultimately realized in the Babylonian exile. Certainly, the composition of the so-called Deuteronomistic History, with its posited Hezekian and Josian editions and its final exilic or early post-exilic edition,[29] demonstrates considerable interest in the fate of the northern kingdom of Israel and

---

[29]   See my *King Josiah of Judah: The Lost Messiah of Israel* (New York and Oxford: Oxford University Press, 2001) for full discussion of the redaction of the Deuteronomistic History.

the implications this had for Judah. In the case of the earlier editions, the presentation of ideal Davidic monarchs would support a program of reunification of all Israel under Davidic rule. In the case of the final edition, it would look toward the restoration of Israel.

Such concerns are also inherent in the early edition of Jeremiah, which apparently is to be identified with the Hebrew *Vorlage* of the present form of LXXJeremiah.[30] The book begins in chapters 2-3 by articulating the prophet's concern for judgment against Israel and then it shifts to treatment of Judah and Jerusalem in chapters 3-25. Like the LXX form of the Book of the Twelve, LXXJeremiah places the oracles concerning the nations in the middle of the book (LXXJeremiah 25-32) prior to returning to its portrayal of Jerusalem's fall in LXXJeremiah 33-52. Similar patterns that point to a concern with understanding the fall of Israel in relation to Jerusalem's and Judah's experience appear in the book of Isaiah, in both its posited seventh and sixth century editions.[31] In the former instance, Isaiah 5-12 points to the fall of Israel as the impetus for a restored Davidic state prior to turning to the issue of judgment against the nations in Isaiah 13-23 and the judgment and restoration of Jerusalem in Isaiah 28-33. In the latter instance, the patterns of Isaiah 1-39 remain intact, and Isaiah 40-55 first treats the exile of Jacob in chapters 40-48 prior to the restoration of Zion in chapters 49-55. Indeed, the earliest edition of the Book of the Twelve posited by Nogalski and Schart, which includes early forms of Hosea, Amos, Micah, and Zephaniah, demonstrate a similar concern for the fate of Israel as a model for that of Jerusalem and Judah.[32] Although there are no early manuscripts of the Book of the Twelve that order the books according to their sequence in the LXX, concern with the judgment of Israel as a model for the experience of Jerusalem and Judah would not have been a major issue in the late-Persian, Hellenistic, Hasmonean or Roman periods when Judean attention focused especially on Jerusalem.

The MT sequence of the Book of the Twelve, which focuses especially on Jerusalem throughout, appears to be the product of the later Persian period when concern shifted away from the north to focus especially on Jerusalem. This concern is particularly noticeable in the period of Ezra and Nehemiah when Jerusalem was truly restored as the center of Persian-period Yehud, and various conflicts arose between the Jerusalem-based exiles who returned with these figures and the Persian-appointed authorities in Sa-

---

[30] See Jack R. Lundbom, "Jeremiah, Book of," *ABD*, 3:706-721, esp. 707-708, for an overview of the issue.

[31] See my *Isaiah 1-39, with an Introduction to Prophetic Literature* (FOTL 16; Grand Rapids and Cambridge: William Eerdmans, 1996).

[32] Nogalski, *Redactional Processes*, 274-280; Schart, *Entstehung*, 156-233.

maria. The specific concern with Jerusalem is evident in both the books of Ezra-Nehemiah and in the books of Chronicles, which apparently excises materials from the DtrH that are concerned with the north to focus almost entirely on Jerusalem and Judah. A similar agenda may be observed in the MT form of the book of Jeremiah, postulated by many to be an expanded and later edition of the book. Jeremiah 2:2, for example, expands this verse to indicate that Jeremiah's initial oracles concerning Israel are addressed to the people of Jerusalem (cf. LXXJer 2:2, which lacks reference to Jerusalem). Likewise, the oracles concerning the nations are placed at the end of the book in chapters 46-51 so that chapters 1-45 are ultimately concerned with Jerusalem and Judah throughout. Even the posited fifth century edition of the book of Isaiah begins and ends in chapters 1 and 56-66 with oracles that take up the fate of Jerusalem.[33] Indeed, the earliest manuscripts of the Book of the Twelve, i.e., the MurXII and 8HevXIIgr, reflect the MT order of the books, but these manuscripts are apparently the products of the Hasmonean period when concern with the restoration of Jerusalem from foreign/Seleucid rule was paramount.

In conclusion, it appears that the book of Joel does indeed play a key role in the Book of the Twelve. Although the book was likely composed in a relatively late period,[34] its typological character, its place, and its function in both the MT and LXX versions of the book apparently defines the overall outlook of each. Joel's typological character and the difficulties in establishing its historical setting make it an eminently mobile text within the sequence of the Twelve, and that mobility enables it to shape the sequence of the Twelve so that the Book of the Twelve as a whole might address two very different hermeneutical agendas that originated ultimately in different historical settings.

---

[33] Sweeney, *Isaiah 1-39*.

[34] Wolff, for example, places the composition of the book in the early fourth century B.C.E. (*Joel and Amos*, 5); cf. Mason, *Joel*, 113-116, who points to the difficulties in dating the book. See also Sweeney, *Twelve Prophets*, 1:149-150.

The Repentance of Nineveh in the Story of Jonah and Nahum's Prophecy of the City's Destruction – A Coherent Reading of the Book of the Twelve as Reflected in the Aggada

Beate Ego

A coherent reading of the story of Jonah within the literary unit of the Book of the Twelve poses the problem of its relationship to the prophecy of Nahum. Under the assumption that the single works of this literary unit appear in a chronological order, the question arises: why did Nahum[1] have to prophecy to the destruction of Nineveh after its people had already repented in the time of Jonah?[2] However, within the Book of the Twelve, the reader finds no explicit answer to this question; nor are there unambiguous clues that the question was even taken seriously. The modern interpreter of the Book of the Twelve may infer a solution from implicit hints in the text;

---

[1] The dating of Nahum appears to be difficult, since there is neither a date in the superscription nor are there unambiguous other hints. Josephus dates him in the time of King Jotham (756-741 B.C.; cf. *Ant. 9.239*). His date is puzzling, since a reader of the Book of the Twelve would expect that Nahum spoke some time after Micah. Josephus seems to presuppose that the undated prophet Nahum is to be located in the same time as his dated antecedent. This rule could be deduced from the fact that Jonah belonged to the same time as Amos, although neither Obadiah nor Jonah dates itself. Others prefer to place Nahum in the time of King Manasseh (696-642 B.C.); cf. *Seder Olam Rabba 20*; see also Louis Ginzberg, *The Legends of the Jews*, (7 vols.; Philadelphia: The Jewish Society of America, 1946-1955) 6.314 n. 56; 373 n. 200; Anna Maria Schwemer, *Die Viten der kleinen Propheten und der Propheten aus den Geschichtsbüchern. Übersetzung und Kommentar* (vol. 2 of *Studien zu den frühjüdischen Prophetenlegenden Vitae Prophetarum*; TSAJ 50; Tübingen: J.C.B. Mohr [Paul Siebeck], 1996) 88. Although both dates conform with Nahum's position in the sequence of the Twelve, the latter is closer to the modern dating.

[2] According to traditional Jewish exegesis, the prophet Jonah is identical with the prophet of the same name mentioned in 2 Kgs 14:25, and therefore is placed in the time of Jeroboam II (787-747 B.C.). On this issue see Hartmut Gese, "Jona ben Amittai und das Jonabuch," in *Alttestamentliche Studien* (Tübingen: J.C.B. Mohr [Paul Siebeck], 1991) 122-138, esp. 126-127; Hans Walter Wolff, *Dodekapropheton 3: Obadja und Jona* (2d ed.; BKAT 14/3; Neukirchen-Vluyn: Neukirchener Verlag, 1991) 53.

however, such a hypotheses would be strengthened if it could be demonstrated that ancient readers already were aware of the problem and felt the need to offer an explanation.[3] In this article, traditional Jewish exegesis will be reviewed. It turns out that there are interpretations of Jonah that allow the reader to construe a coherent relationship between Jonah and Nahum, although it must be admitted that this relationship may not in all cases be the only or even preeminent aim of the ancient interpreters.

I. The Relationship Between Jonah and Nahum

The earliest reference to the question is to be found in the book of Tobit, which was probably written in the eastern Jewish Diaspora around 200 BC.[4] In his imposing farewell address, the aged Tobit advises his children to flee Assyria, since its capital, the city of Nineveh, will be destroyed in the near future. Whereas the long version of the book of Tobit G^{II}, which, in all probability, is to be seen closer to the original text,[5] refers in this context to "those things which Nahum spoke to Nineveh" (Tob 14:4), in the shorter and younger version G^{I} we read: "Go into Media, my son, for I surely believe those things which Jonah the Prophet spoke to Nineveh, that it shall be overthrown" (KJV).

It seems to be very unlikely that the name "Nahum" here was erroneously changed to "Jonah," especially since in Tob 14:8 G^{I} there exists — without a parallel in the text of the version G^{II} — a further reference to the prophecy of Jonah concerning the destruction of Nineveh: "And now, my son, depart out of Nineveh, because that those things which the prophet Jonah spake shall surely come to pass" (KJV). The references to Jonah seem to imply that the reception of the book of Jonah was focused, in this context, on his prediction against Nineveh (cf. Jon 1:2; 3:4), while the fact that the Ninevites carried out repentance from their evil deeds, as told in Jon 3:5-10, is simply ignored. From this perspective the prophecy of Jonah could be identified with the prophecy of Nahum, since both prophets are

---

[3] For this problem in general, cf. Aaron Schart, *Die Entstehung des Zwölf-prophetenbuches. Neubearbeitungen von Amos im Rahmen schriftübergreifender Redaktionsprozesse* (BZAW 260; Berlin/New York: de Gruyter, 1998) 26-27, 291; Brevard Springs Childs, *Introduction to the Old Testament as Scripture* (Philadelphia: Fortress Press, 1997) 425; James D. Nogalski, *Redactional Processes in the Book of the Twelve* (BZAW 218; Berlin/New York: de Gruyter, 1993) 270-271.

[4] Beate Ego, *Buch Tobit* (Jüdische Schriften aus hellenistisch-römischer Zeit, vol. II: Unterweisung in erzählender Form; Gütersloh: Gütersloher Verlagshaus, 1999) 899-900, with references to further literature.

[5] Concerning the question of the relationship of the two versions of Tobit, cf. Ego, *Buch Tobit*, 875-6, with references to further literature.

considered harbingers of the destruction of Nineveh. Jonah's prophecy seems to be the same as Nahum's message concerning the destruction of the Assyrian capital, and in this way the contradiction between Jonah and Nahum appears to be solved.

An analogous tendency of interpretation is apparent in Josephus' retelling of the story of Jonah in *Ant. 9,214*:

> Then, having prayed to God to grant him pardon for his sins, he went to the city of Ninos and, standing where all could hear him, proclaimed that in a very short time they would lose their dominion over Asia; after giving them this message, he departed. And I have recounted his story as I found it written down.[6]

Because Josephus ignores the thematic motif of the repentance of the Ninevites and replaces the precise biblical statement that Nineveh "will be overthrown in forty days" (Jon 3:4) with the vague "in a very short time," and also because in this passage, the message of judgment is emphasized, one gets the impression once again that Jonah's prediction is quite similar to the prophecy of Nahum.[7]

However, these passages should also be viewed in the context of another factor that played an important role in early exegesis about Jonah. As Elias Bickerman has demonstrated, these literary units are also to be considered in the light of the question of whether Jonah is to be accused of being a false prophet. "Jonah went to Nineveh, announcing in the name of God that in forty days the city would be overthrown. Yet, the *fata denunciativa* did not materialize. Was he a false prophet, who only pretended to speak in the name of God?"[8] This issue is clearly addressed in the book of

---

[6]   *Josephus*, Ant 9, 214 (Ralph Marcus).

[7]   See also *Ant. 9.242* concerning Nahum's prophecy. Cf. Schart, *Entstehung des Zwölfprophetenbuches*, 28: "Jona wird dargestellt, als habe er für eine unbestimmte Zukunft den Untergang Ninives angekündigt. Nahum hätte diese Botschaft des Jona dann später aufgegriffen und ausgebaut. Beide Propheten hätten mit ihrer Untergangsankündigung schließlich Recht behalten und sich als wahre Propheten erwiesen. Die Leserschaft soll darüber staunen, daß die biblischen Propheten ein Ereignis bereits so lange vorher angekündigt haben. Josephus hat einen Zusammenhang geschaffen, der das Problem des Verhältnisses von Jona und Nahum löst, mußte aber dazu wesentliche Teile der Jonaschrift verschweigen."

[8]   Elias Bickerman, *Four Strange Books of the Bible. Jonah / Daniel / Kohelet / Esther* (Schocken Books: New York, 1967) 33-38. This aspect was recently stressed and embellished by Schwemer (*Prophetenlegenden Vitae*, 69-72). Cf. the "Vita of Jonah" in *Vitae Prophetarum*: "Jonah was from the district of Kariathmos near the Greek city of Azotus by the sea. And when he had been cast forth by the sea monster and had gone away to Nineveh and had returned, he did not remain in his district, but taking his mother along he sojourned in Sour, a territory (inhabited by) foreign nations; for he

Tobit and in the writings of Josephus. "It will all come true; everything will happen to Assyria and Nineveh that was spoken by the prophets of Israel whom God sent," says the author of Tobit (14:4; G^{II}). "Not a word of it will fall short; everything will be fulfilled if the time comes"(NEB). Also Josephus, in the context of his discussion of Nahum, stresses in the same way the fact that all the predictions of the prophets were fulfilled:

> And many more things beside did this prophet prophesy about Nineveh, which I have not thought it necessary to mention, but have omitted in order not to seem tiresome to my readers. But all the things that had been foretold concerning Nineveh came to pass after a hundred and fifteen years (*Ant. 9.242*).[9]

II. The Repentance of the Ninevites

Before turning to the question of how the sages dealt with the contradiction between the narration of Jonah and the prophecy of Nahum, it should be underlined that the thematic motif of the repentance of the Ninevites plays a very important and significant role in rabbinic tradition. The earliest rabbinical reference concerning the reception of Jonah's message in 3:8-10 is to be found in the *Mishnah*. Here, the repentance of the Ninevites appears as "the type" for repentance in general, and the gentile Ninevites are portrayed as shining examples for the doing of penance.

---

said: 'So shall I remove my reproach, for I spoke falsely in prophesying against the great city of Nineveh.'" Translation by D. R. A. Hare, "The Lives of the Prophets," in *The Old Testament Pseudepigrapha* (vol. II; ed. J.H. Charlesworth; Garden City, New York: Doubleday & Company, Inc., 1985) 383-99, here: 392. Concerning Nahum it is stated: "Nahum was from Elkesi on the other side of Isbegabrin of the tribe of Simeon. After Jonah this man gave to Nineveh a portent, that it would be destroyed by fresh water and an underground fire, which also happened." Cf. the solution of this problem in *Pseudo-Philo, De Jona c. 46 §186* based on the exegesis of Jon 3:4: "Forty more days and Nineveh shall be overturned (נֶהְפָּכֶת)" by using the double meaning of the Hebrew הָפַךְ – "to turn, to change, to destroy, to overturn": The city was not destroyed, but the hearts of the Ninevites were changed. On this issue cf. Folker Siegert, *Drei hellenistisch-jüdische Predigten. Ps.-Philon, "Über Jona", "Über Simson" und "Über die Gottesbezeichnung 'wohltätig verzehrendes Feuer'"*, vol. I *Übersetzung aus dem Armenischen und sprachliche Erläuterungen* (WUNT 20; Tübingen: J.C.B. Mohr [Paul Siebeck], 1980) 43f.; vol. II: *Kommentar nebst Beobachtungen zur hellenistischen Vorgeschichte der Bibelhermeneutik* (WUNT 61; Tübingen: J.C.B. Siebeck [Paul Mohr], 1992) 211-212 with references to further literature.

9   Josephus, *Ant.* 9.242 (Ralph Marcus). On this issue in the work of Josephus, see Schwemer, *Prophetenlegenden*, 70.

M.Taan. 2.1, a tradition which very likely originated in the liturgy of the sanctuary and which was later used in the context of service for fast days outside the temple,[10] describes this service in the following manner:

> What is the order [of service] for fast days? The ark is taken out to the open space of the city, wood ashes are placed on the ark, on the head of the Nasi and on the head of Ab-beth. Everyone else puts ashes on his head; the elder among them addresses them with words of admonition [to repentance] thus, "Our brethren, scripture does not say of the people of Nineveh, 'and God saw their sackcloth and their fasting,' but, 'and God saw their works, that they turned from their evil way' (Jonah 3:10); and in the prophets it is said, 'and rend your heart and not your garments'" (Joel 2:13).[11]

The final quotations from Jon 3:10 und Joel 2:13 show clearly that in relation to the repentance of the Ninevites it was not the rites of penance that were important, but a conversion of outer actions accompanied by an inner conversion of the heart.[12]

In the Gemara of the *Babylonian Talmud*, i.e. in *b. Taan. 16a*, in reference to the passage quoted above, the explanation affirming the sincere and deep repentance of the people of Nineveh is confirmed and embellished. Starting with a concrete example, the Gemara makes clear the radical manner in which the Ninevites understood Jonah's prophecy to repent. The penance of the Ninevites did not stop at fasting and praying. Their deeds showed that they were determined to lead a better life: if a man had usurped another's property, he sought to make amends for his iniquity; some went so far as to destroy their palaces in order to be able to give back a single brick to the rightful owner. The determination of the Ninevites to lead a better life is made evident in the above mentioned passage by a tradition attributed to R. Samuel, who interpreted the phrase in Jon 3:8 "from the violence that is in their hands" (מן החמס אשר בכפיהם) in the following manner: "Even if one had stolen a beam and built it into his castle he should raze the entire castle to the ground and return the beam to its owner."[13]

---

[10] On this issue see Joseph Heinemann, *Prayer in the Talmud. Forms and Patterns* (SJ 9; Berlin/New York: Walter de Gruyter, 1977) 108-9.

[11] Quotation from *The Babylonian Talmud. Translated into English with notes, glossary and indices* (35 vols.; ed. Isidore Epstein; London: Soncino Press, 1935-1952) ad loc.

[12] For a more detailed analysis of this text, see Beate Ego, "Denn die Heiden sind der Umkehr nahe. Rabbinische Interpretationen zur Buße der Leute von Ninive," in *Die Heiden. Juden, Christen und das Problem des Fremden* (ed. R. Feldmeier, U. Heckel; WUNT 70; Tübingen: J.C. B. Mohr [Paul Siebeck], 1994) 158-76, esp. 159-60.

[13] Quotation from *The Babylonian Talmud*, ad loc. An embellished version of this midrash is to be found in the medieval *Midrash Jonah (Bet haMidr. I, pp. 96-105)*. Cf.

Thus, it can be seen, that on the one side, in rabbinic literature, great importance has been attached to the repentance of the people of Nineveh. In this field of Jewish tradition, however, new light has also been shed on the interpretation of Jon 3:8-10, which implies a further solution for the contradiction between Jonah and Nahum. For example, *Ps.-J. Nah 1:1* makes a direct reference to Jonah:

> Previously Jonah the son of Amittai, the prophet from Gath-hepher, prophesied against her and she repented of her sins; and when they sinned again, there prophesied once more against her Nahum of Beth Koshi, as is recorded in this book.[14]

This means that the Ninevites' new attitude toward life did not last very long and that they returned very soon to their evil deeds, thereby requiring the appearance of another prophet foretelling the destruction of the city. In support of this interpretation, one has also to understand a passage contained within the *Midrash Pirqe de Rabbi Eliezer*. This midrash, which represents the genre of "rewritten bible,"[15] dates from early mediaeval times. After an impressive description of the deeds of repentance based on the tradition described in *b. Taan. 16a*, which serves to show the power of repentance in general, *Pirqe R. El. 43* continues with the very brief, but nevertheless harsh statement: "After forty years they returned to their many evil deeds, more so than their former ones, and they were swallowed up like the

---

also *Tg. Esth. II Est 4:1*, where Mordecai says: "People of the house of Israel, beloved and respected ones, let us proceed to look at the people of Nineveh, when the prophet Jonah son of Ammitai was sent to it, to overturn the city of Nineveh. So when the word reached the king of Nineveh, he rose from his precious throne and removed the crown from himself, covered himself in sackcloth, rolled himself in ashes, and issued a proclamation in Nineveh which said: It is the decree of the king and his princes as follows: No man or beast, herd or flock should go out to pasture or drink any water. They should repent from their evil ways and from the violence that is in their hands; then He retracted through his memra the evil thing He planned to do unto them and did not do (it). Let us also do like they (did), and let us decree fast days and proclaim fasts because we were exiled from Jerusalem." Quotation from B. Grossfeld, *The Two Targums of Esther, translated with Apparatus and Notes* (The Aramaic Bible 18; Edinburgh: T&T Clark Ltd, 1991), 152-53.

14 Quotation from K.J. Cathcart and R.P. Gordon, *The Targum of the Minor prophets* (The Aramaic Bible 14; Edinburgh: T&T Clark Ltd, 1989), 131. Cf. also *Rashi ad Nah 1:1*: "It was already written about them, and this is the prophecy of Jonah ben Ammitai; and hence, now Nahum is predicting against them ..." Then follows the quotation from *Tg. Ps.J. Nah* 1:1.

15 For this literary genre cf. Günter Stemberger, *Einleitung in Talmud und Midrasch* (8th ed.; Munich: C.H. Beck, 1992) 321-23; Josef Heinemann, *Aggadot we-toledotehen* (Sifriyat Keter, Jerusalem: Keter Publishing House, 1974), 181.

dead, in the lowest Sheol, as it is said, "Out of the city of the dead they groan" (Job 26:12).[16]

It is worth noting that in modern research reference is usually made in particular to this midrash in order to underline the midrashic tendency towards harmonizing Jonah and Nahum in rabbinic exegesis.[17] This effect, however, is only achieved when it is assumed that Nahum prophesied quite soon after Jonah against Nineveh — perhaps as stated in *Seder Olam 20*, during the reign of King Manasseh,[18] and that the narrator of *Pirqe de Rabbi Eliezer* was not aware of the exact historical background and chronological framework of the real destruction of Nineveh by Nebuchadnezzar, King of Babylon in 612 B.C. David Luria (1798-1855), the Lithuanian rabbi, scholar, and commentator on *Pirqe de Rabbi Eliezer*, apparently was aware of this problem, and stated that after its destruction Nineveh was built again and that Nahum appeared preaching against the city subsequent to this rebuilding.[19] Perhaps also here one has to take into account the issue of defending Jonah from the accusation of being a false prophet. As explicitly stated in this context, the "forty years" which this midrash posits between Jonah's prophecy and the city's destruction correspond to the biblical "forty days" in the prophecy of Jonah (Jon 3:4).

Finally, there is another aggadic tradition that harmonizes the narration of Jonah and the prophecy of Nahum. It is to be found in the Gemara of the Jerusalem Talmud based on *m. Taan. 2.1.* Here the thematic motif of Nineveh is considered in a quite different way, and the biblical story itself is changed. In *y. Taan. 2.1, 65b* we have a tradition that is attributed to R. Simeon ben Laqish and R. Yohanan:

> Said R. Simeon ben Laqish, The repentance that the men of Nineveh carried out was deceitful ... Said R. Yohanan, What they had in their hands they gave back, but what they had hidden in chests, boxes and cupboards, they did no give back.[20]

Although the Gemara of the *Babylonian Talmud* stresses the severeness of the repentance of the Ninevites, the *Jerusalem Talmud* maintains that this

---

[16] See also the parallel *Yal. Sh. Jonah § 550 (430c)*.

[17] For example Schart, *Entstehung*, 28.

[18] See above the notes concerning the dating of Nahum.

[19] Cf. Y. Horowitz, "Luria, David Ben Judah," *EncJud,* 11.571.

[20] Quotation from Jacob Neusner, *The Talmud of the Land of Israel. A Preliminary Translation and Explanation* (vol 18; *Besah and Taanit*; Chicago Studies in the History of Judaism [Chicago: The University of Chicago, 1987]), 180-181. The same tradition is quoted in *Midrash Jonah* in the context of a very positive description of Nineveh's repentance.

repentance was hypocritical und superficial. The biblical phrase החמס
אשר בכפיהם — literally: "the violence which was in their hands" (Jon
3:8), which was interpreted in *b. Taan. 16a* as an admonition to give back
all property acquired in iniquity, is understood by R. Johanan in a strongly
literal manner. Only the stolen property that was actually in the hands of the
Ninevites at the time of Jonah's homily was given back; everything else that
was stolen before this time, the Ninevites kept for themselves. Thus, the
penance of the Ninevites was no more than a deception, a "trick" to outwit
God.

It should be stressed, however, that in this connection no one has found
an explicit reference to Nahum's prophecy. As I have shown in a previous
study,[21] the motif of the hypocritical and superficial repentance of the Ninevites' functions in particular in order to comfort Israel. This becomes clear
in the midrashic context of *Pesiq. Rab Kah. 24.11*. In this passage, the thematic motif of hypocritical repentance is integrated with a homily, which
seeks to comfort and console Israel in its distress and humiliation. The tradition here is part of a homily for Hos 14:2, — the beginning of the Hafta-
rah for the Parashah האזינה. Its Sitz im Leben is Shabbat Shuva between
Rosh-ha-shanah and Yom Kippur. After several calls for repentance it is
stated: "Master of the Universe, if we will carry out repentance will you be
prepared to accept us?" The homily answers by explaining that the ten days
between Rosh-ha-shanah and Yom Kippur are destined in a special manner
for the repentance of man. In other words, within this time God is willing to
accept even imperfect forms of penance. The Ninevites' repentance appears
— as also in the case of Ahab, David or Manasseh — as a paradigm for an
imperfect repentance that nevertheless is accepted by God.

Great importance is attached here to the following consoling, paracletical issue: God did not refuse the imperfect repentance of the gentiles, so
why should he refuse his own people? The acceptance of the superficial,
indeed hypocritical penance of the Ninevites serves as a kind of guarantee
for God's everlasting mercy with his own people.[22]

Moreover, as Ephraim Urbach has already shown,[23] some of the above-
mentioned texts were even employed in the context of anti-Christian polemics. The rabbinic teachers may have changed their interpretation of the nar-

---

[21] Ego, *Heiden*, 165-166.

[22] Cf. also Apostolic Constitutions 8,9,9 (SC 336, Metzger 163).

[23] Ephraim Urbach, "Tᵉshuvat anshe ninive wehaviquaḥ hayehudy noṣry," *Tarbiz* 20
(1949/50) 118-122. Cf. also Elias Bickerman, "Les deux erreurs du prophète Jonas,"
RHPR 45 (1965) 232-264, esp. 240; Bickerman, *Four Strange Books*, 17, without explicitly referring to Urbach's article.

ration of Jonah as a reaction to the anti-Jewish form of interpretation of the Church Fathers, who used this story of Nineveh for demonstrating the stubborn attitude of the people of Israel.

The paradigmatic character of this repentance, both as it appeared in rabbinical literature and as it was employed in order to criticize Israel,[24] led to its utilization in the exegesis of the Church Fathers. On the one hand, Christians are admonished to imitate the behavior of the Ninevites;[25]on the other hand, the Ninevites' willingness to do penance is seen as an admonition against Israel. This thematic motif, although originating in inner-Jewish self admonition, was now being turned against Israel from outside. E. Bickerman described this process as follows: "Les Pères de l'Eglise acceptèrent l'interprétation juive mais la retournèrent contre ses auteurs."[26] Situated against this background, the negative attitude towards Nineveh's repentance as found in the rabbinical literature seems to be very plausible.

III. Summary

In summing up the various results of the analysis of these passages, it becomes obvious that aggadic exegesis solves the tension between Jonah and Nahum in different ways:
— by ignoring the thematic motif of repentance of the people of Nineveh (Tob 14:4.8 and *Ant. 9.214*);
— by starting from the assumption that after their repentance the people of Nineveh started once again to commit sins (*Tg. Ps.-J. Nah 1:1; Pirqe R. El. 43*);

---

[24] Cf. for example *Mek. pisḥa* 1 *(Horowitz/Rabin 3-4.)*: "Jonah said: I will go outside of the land, where the divine presence does not reveal itself, for since the Gentiles are more inclined to repent, I might be causing Israel to be condemned." Cp. also *Lam Rab. Petiḥta* 31 (17b*)*: "Why couldn't it (scil. Jerusalem) learn from Jonah's city, Nineveh? One prophet I sent to it and they repented, but how many prophets I have sent to Jerusalem and they didn't repent?!"

[28] See also *1 Clem* 3:4-6:4; 7:7; for further references cf. Eugen Biser, "Zum frühchristlichen Verständnis des Buches Jonas," *BK* 17 (1962) 19-21, esp. 20; Yves-Marie Duval, *Le livre de Jonas dans la littérature chrétienne grecque et latine. Sources et influence du Commentaire sur Jonas de saint Jérôme* (2 vols.; Sources Augustiennes; Paris: Études Augustiennes, 1973), vol. II, Index *Metanoia; *Pénitence nécessaire des païens.

[26] Elias Bickerman, "Les deux erreurs," 240; Bickerman, *Four Strange Books*, 16. The earliest reference to this fact is to be found in Justin's work "Dialogue with the Jew Trypho," 108:1-3, which dates to the second half of the Second Century A.D. Here Israel is exhorted to act like the Ninevites and to carry out repentance. It seems, that in the fourth and in the beginning of the fifth century, utterances of this kind were increasing. For a collection of this material see Ego, *Heiden*, 169-173.

— by interpreting the repentance as being hypocritical and superficial (*y. Taan 2.1, 65d; Pesiq. Rab Kah. 24.11*).

It must be emphasized, however, that apart from *Tg. Ps.-J. Nah 1:1* and — in a special manner — the variants of Tob 14:4, no special reference to the prophecy of Nahum is made. For this reason, because of the complexity of the traditions it seems to be appropriate to differentiate between an explicit and an implicit aggadic solution in order to explain the contradiction between the narration of Jonah and Nahum's prophecy. In addition, one should take into account that there are further motifs of interpretation to be reflected on when dealing with these passages. One has to consider, for instance, the tendency towards the defending of Jonah against the accusation of being a false prophet. Special attention should also be given to the motif of the superficial and hypocritical repentance of the Ninevites. This includes, on the one hand, a paracletical tendency towards Israel, through which the people should be comforted and encouraged; God is also prepared to accept imperfect forms of repentance. On the other hand, this motif should be regarded within the context of anti-Christian polemics. In relation to the above, it can be seen, that the traditional forms of Jewish exegesis for the story of Jonah make up a complex process that includes several different factors and interpretative intentions.

The Canonical Location of Habakkuk

A. Joseph Everson

The book of Habakkuk provides only limited evidence for determining a historical setting against which to understand the message of this prophetic work. The superscriptions in 1:1 and 3:1 simply identify the author as "Habakkuk the prophet." Marvin Sweeney has summarized well the variety of historical settings that have been proposed for understanding Habakkuk. He points to the wide range of dates that have been suggested "from Sennacherib's invasion of Judah in the late 8th century (701 B.C.E.) (Betteridge 1903) to Alexander the Great's conquest of the Near East in the 4th century (Duhm 1906; Torrey 1935)."[1] He cites other proposals, including the work "Bel and the Dragon" (2nd century B.C.E.), which sees Habakkuk as a contemporary of Daniel during the Babylonian exile; the midrashic historical work "Seder Olam Rabbah" from the 2-3rd ntury C.E., which locates Habakkuk in the reign of Manasseh (687-642 B.C.E.); and Clement of Alexandria writing in the 2-3rd century C.E., who contended that Habakkuk was a contemporary of Jeremiah and Ezekiel.[2]

In recent years the work of the Formation of the Book of the Twelve Consultation/Seminar of the Society of Biblical Literature has brought a new mode of analysis to these so-called "minor prophets."[3] Instead of presupposing that each work should be analyzed separately, scholars have been examining evidence suggesting that the Book of the Twelve should more properly be understood as a larger literary work. The purpose of this paper is to explore the implications of the canonical location of the book of Habakkuk and to ask about the significance of its location and message for understanding the larger theological perspective seen by the editors of the Book of the Twelve. I suggest that both the location and the internal evidence in Habakkuk indicate that the book was remembered in

---

[1] Marvin A. Sweeney, "Habakkuk, Book of," *ABD* 3:1-6.
[2] Ibid., 2.
[3] See the collection of seminar essays collected in James D. Nogalski and Marvin A. Sweeney (eds.), *Reading and Hearing the Book of the Twelve* (SBLSymS 15:Atlanta: Society of Biblical Literature, 2000).

conjunction with the tragic death of Josiah in 609 B.C.E., but advocates patience and faithfulness instead of despair and disillusionment.

I. The Book of the Twelve as a "Theology of History"

The evidence from Qumran is somewhat problematic for understanding the history of the Habakkuk scroll. The Habakkuk Pesher from Qumran (The Ain Feshka Scroll), which appears to date from the first century B.C.E., includes the text and a midrashic interpretation of chapters 1 and 2 in light of the early history of the Qumran sect.[4] Some scholars have contended that the Ain Feshka scroll provides evidence that chapter 3 was not yet a part of the Habakkuk literary tradition. And further, they have wondered whether this Qumran text suggests that a larger Book of the Twelve was not yet a reality.[5] What we know is that a Scroll of the Twelve was extant in the 2nd century C.E. at Wadi Murrabbat, a scroll that included all three chapters of Habakkuk, at a time only a few decades after the probable determination of the MT Textus Receptus (Jamnia, about 90 C.E.). Similarly, we know that from earliest versions of the LXX (Aquila, Theodotian, Symmachus), as well as from the Scroll from Nahal Hever (8 Hev XIIgr), that Habakkuk was part of a book of the Twelve and in its present location by the early second century C.E. The three-chapter work became part of the standard accepted Greek translation tradition.[6] Our concern is to ask what the editors of the Twelve had in mind when they arranged the books in their present order. What specifically did they see as the function and theological message of Habakkuk (including the third chapter) in the succession of prophetic writings?

I suggest first of all that there is a fundamental "theology of history" preserved within the collected anthology or "book" of the Twelve. The first

---

[4] Millar Burrows, John Trever and W. H. Brownlee, *The Dead Sea Scrolls of St. Mark's Monastery* (vol.1; New Haven: Yale University press, 1950), cited by Sweeney, *ABD* 3:2.

[5] Considerable discussion has been devoted to the questions of whether the twelve works were combined primarily because they fit together on one reasonably long scroll. Were they intended to imitate in size the approximate length of the Isaiah, Jeremiah or Ezekiel scrolls? See David L. Peterson, "A Book of the Twelve?" in *Reading and Hearing the Book of the Twelve* (eds. James D. Nogalski and Marvin A. Sweeney; SBLSymS 15; Atlanta: Society of Biblical Literature, 2000) 5. Peterson writes: "As a scroll, probably a leather one, the Twelve would have been relatively long. For example, 1QIsa runs almost seven and one-half meters, whereas the Nahal Hever Minor Prophets scroll is more than ten meters long (Tov, *Textual Criticism of the Hebrew Bible*, 204). Relatively short books they might be, but when written together the Twelve filled a scroll of a length similar to the Major Prophets."

[6] Sweeney, *ABD* 3:2.

six works, which open the scroll (Hosea – Micah), are preserved as reflections on the dramatic events that occurred in northern Israel and southern Judah in the 8th century B.C.E. This is evident from the superscriptions that introduce Hosea, Amos, and Micah, all of which recall kings and events from the 8th century B.C.E.[7] Similarly, specific references to the post-exilic Persian emperor, Darius, in Haggai (1:1; 2:1) and Zechariah (1:1; 1:7; 7:1) indicate that these two books, along with Malachi, are part of an intentional chronological ordering of the books of the Twelve. Set together, the Twelve preserve theological reflections from the eras of Assyria, Babylon and Persia.[8]

II. Day of Yahweh Rhetoric in the Book of the Twelve

With Rolf Rendtorff and David Peterson, I am convinced that in the theology of history preserved in these works, "day of Yahweh" (יום יהוה) rhetoric and imagery provide a fundamental unifying theme.[9] Motifs or allusions related to this prophetic theme permeate all twelve of the works. Instead of understanding or interpreting references to the "day" as expectations of a distant future event, however, I suggest that it is helpful to stand with the editors and look backwards to see how ancient prophetic writers used this poetry to anticipate specific events. With the editors, we can dis-

---

[7] On the order of the writings, see Aaron Schart, "Reconstructing the Redaction History of the Twelve Prophets: Problems and Models" in *Reading and Hearing the Book of the Twelve* (eds. James D. Nogalski and Marvin A. Sweeney; SBLSymS 15; Atlanta: Society of Biblical Literature, 2000) 34-48. Schart suggests (p. 37) that "a meaningful superstructure points toward a deliberate ordering, for example, the historical ordering of the writings with Hosea first (because it mentions the "House of Jehu" in Hosea 4) and Malachi last (because it presupposes an operative second temple)." In the Septuagint, the first six writings are Hosea, Amos, Micah, Joel, Obadiah and Jonah. For the purposes of this paper, the different ordering is not significant since Habakkuk falls eighth in both orders.

[8] Helpful in this regard are the observations of Peterson, "A Book of the Twelve?", 9-10. He suggests that the Isaiah scroll encompassed a time frame of approximately 240 years (743-500 B.C.E.), Jeremiah about 40 years (627-580 B.C.E.), and Ezekiel, about 23 years (593-570 B.C.E.). By contrast, the era embraced by the Book of the Twelve involves roughly 400 years (750-350 B.C.E.)

[9] See Rolf Rendtorff, "How to Read the Book of the Twelve as a Theological Unity" in *Reading and Hearing the Book of the Twelve* (eds. James D. Nogalski and Marvin A. Sweeney; SBLSymS 15; Atlanta: Society of Biblical Literature, 2000) 75-87; Peterson "A Book of the Twelve?", 3-10; A. Joseph Everson, "The Days of Yahweh," *JBL* 93 (1974) 329-337 and "Serving Notice on Babylon: The Canonical Function of Isaiah 13-14" *Word and World* 19,2 (Spring, 1999) l33-140.

cern patterns of promise and fulfillment.[10] In retrospect, they saw specific
events in history that allowed later generations to discern God's presence,
either as punishment or as rescue.[11] They were events, usually of war, that
seemed to turn history in one direction or another, often with enormous
consequences for people or nations.   When prophetic writers employed the
rhetoric of Yahweh's "day," they could use various rhetorical tricks or
patterns of dramatic reversal, and assume that their audience would have a
preconceived understanding.   Such a "trick" is seen, for example, in the
bold reversal of expectations set forth in the well known announcement of a
"day of Yahweh" in Amos 5:18-20. The day was announced as "darkness,"
not "light."   The anticipated event would not be what the people expected!
Similarly, in Jer 46:2-12, an army of warriors was envisioned going forth to
battle with great confidence. "Proud Egypt" went up to fight at Carchemish,
certain that their forces would have a day of victory over Babylon in
support of the Assyrians.   Then the poet exclaims (46:5) "But what do I
see?" (מדוע ראתי), as he depicts a defeated army returning from Carchemish in devastation and disgrace.[12]   Instead of a "day of victory," Egypt
experienced a "day of judgment." The author declares (46:10): "That day is
the day of the Lord God of hosts, a day of vengeance, to avenge himself on
his foes" (והיום ההוא לאדני יהוה צבאות יום נקמה להנקם מצריו).

In retrospect, it seems clear that later generations and the editors of the
book of the Twelve remembered the fall of the northern kingdom of Israel
(721 B.C.E.) as a "day of Yahweh" for the northern kingdom.   The
destruction brought by Assyria confirmed the reliability of the warnings
spoken earlier by Hosea, Joel, Amos, Obadiah and Micah. The events about
which they warned had come to pass! While the warfare came at the hands
of the Assyrian forces, the prophets declared that those events were the
work of Yahweh, judging and punishing his own arrogant people.

---

[10]   I disagree with Schart ("Reconstructing the Redaction History of the Twelve
Prophets," 42) when he writes "the reader may also infer that every reference to a
decisive day, on which YHWH will punish sin and restore the true Israel – for
example, "on that day" (Amos 2:6;8:3) or "day of trouble" (Nah 1:7) – points toward
the one Day of YHWH." There is no "one" Day of YHWH. I am convinced that the
poetic references need to be understood as prophetic rhetoric, which the authors could
employ to refer to any number of important events – past, present, or future, events
that had the potential of turning history in one direction or another.

[11]   Peterson ("A Book of the Twelve?"3-10) sees specific references to "day of Yahweh"
(yom adonai) in Hos 9:5; Joel 3:4; Amos 5:18-20; Obad 15; Mic 2:4; Hab 3:16; Zeph
1:7-16; Hag 2:23; Zech 14:1 and Mal 4:1. He sees the theme explicitly in all but two
of the Twelve (Jonah and Nahum). I believe the theme is also present in those books.

[12]   On Jer. 46: 2-12, describing the battle in 605 B.C.E., see John Bright, *A History of
Israel* (Philadelphia: Westminster, 975) 324.

In a similar manner, Assyria is remembered as being first warned and then taunted by Nahum for her arrogance. Like other ancient (or modern) empires, Assyria suffered from the disease of "arrogance of power," convinced that her gods had blessed her. Assyria seems to have believed that the ultimate reality about political power in the world is "might makes right!"[13] In the eyes of Israel's prophets, that belief contributed directly to her downfall. Nahum declares (1:7-8, 14):

> The Lord is good,
> a stronghold in the day of trouble;
> He knows those who take refuge in him.
> But with an overflowing flood
> he will make a full end of his adversaries,
> and will pursue his enemies into darkness
>
> ....
>
> The Lord has given commandment about you (Assyria):
> "No more shall your name be perpetuated;
> from the house of your gods I will cut off
> the graven image and the molten image.
> I will make your grave, for you are vile."

Later generations clearly remembered the fall of Nineveh (in 612 B.C.E.) as another "day of Yahweh," one that had now come for Assyria. In the overall arrangement of the Book of the Twelve, it is interesting that Habakkuk is located just after Nahum. From beginning to end, Nahum presented a fierce and bitter partisan tirade against the horrors of Assyria. Thus it seems that the editors are suggesting that the message of Habakkuk should be remembered in light of events after the fall of Nineveh (612 B.C.E.), the event that confirmed the word of Nahum.

By contrast, the book of Zephaniah, which immediately follows Habakkuk, is remembered primarily in conjunction with the traumatic events that resulted in the destruction of Jerusalem and the southern kingdom of Judah (military conflicts in 604, 598 and 587 B.C.E.). The superscription (1:1) locates Zephaniah as a prophet from the era of King Josiah (640-609 B.C.E.). While the "day of Yahweh" poetry in Zephaniah includes images of universal destruction, the focus is clearly on imminent destruction for Judah. Thus it seems equally clear that the editors want Habakkuk to be understood within the world of Judah prior to the destruction and deportations brought by Babylonian (598 and 587 B.C.E), the events that confirmed the prophetic warnings of Zephaniah. By its canonical location, Habakkuk seems to be located after Nahum and before

---

13   See further, Hab. 1:5-11; Isa 10:5-19.

Zephaniah to recall a particularly difficult time in Judah's history between 612 and 598 B.C.E.

It is important to note that when prophetic writers used "day of Yahweh" rhetoric, they could still hold out hope for those who were faithful. From the earliest texts, it appears that "day" rhetoric had a dual meaning: events that proclaimed judgment for the arrogant could also mean rescue or salvation for those who were faithful. This perspective seemed to have been confirmed by the events that brought an end to Judah's "Babylonian captivity" era (539-520 B.C.E.). The fall of Nebuchadnezzar's dynasty was viewed as a new "day of Yahweh," now for Babylon (see Isa 13-14; Jer 50:41-46; Jer 51: 1-64). While those events meant judgment for Babylon, they also signaled the beginning of a new era of hope for captive Hebrew people (see esp. Isaiah 61 and 63).[14] In this sense, "day" rhetoric contributes to the larger perspectives of Israel's covenantal theology.

III. "Theodicy" and the Day of Yahweh in Habakkuk

When compared with Zephaniah, "day of Yahweh" rhetoric in Habakkuk is muted but still readily evident. Chapter 1 is dominated by images of war. In 1: 2-4, the world is portrayed as being filled with destruction (שֹׁד), violence (חמס), strife (רִיב) and contention (מדון). What is most striking, however, is that this prophetic work begins with a lament about divine governance rather than with a more traditional judgment speech.[15] The enemy is at the center of the theological reflection and the fundamental question of the book is posed in the opening lines (Hab 1:1-4):

> O Lord, how long shall I cry for help, and you will not listen?
> Or cry to you "Violence!" and you will not save?
> Why do you make me see wrongdoing and look at trouble?
> Destruction and violence are before me;
> Strife and contention arise.
> So the law becomes slack
> And justice never prevails.
> The wicked surround the righteous—
> Therefore judgment comes forth the perverted.

---

[14]   Even Zephaniah includes words of hope and consolation (Zeph 3:11-20); see further, the hopeful words in Hos 14:5-9; Joel 3:1-17; Amos 9:11-15; Obad 17-21. The full field of evidence for discerning the prophetic use of the motif of the 'day of Yahweh" should also include texts such as Isa 2:12-17; 13:1-22; 22:1-14; 34:1-17; Ezek 13:1-16.

[15]   See further, Theodore Hiebert, "The Book of Habakkuk" *The New Interpreter's Bible* (12 vols; Nashville: Abingdon, 1996) 7.632-3.

The portrait preserved in Habakkuk attempts to make sense of a tumultuous era in Judah's history that saw Assyria, Egypt and Babylon in conflict, with Judah and other small countries caught in the intrigue.[16]   In the opening poem (Hab 1:5-11), it is clear that the rise of Babylon is the major puzzle within the Habakkuk scroll. The author sets forth Yahweh's word (1:6): "Behold I am rousing the Chaldeans ..." (הנני מקים את הכשדים). He describes in great detail the brutality and ruthlessness of this foreign invader, who is understood to be executing Yahweh's judgment.Yet, the scenario in Habakkuk also declares that in time the Babylonian forces will also be punished. In 3:1-16, the writer envisions Yahweh coming in another event of war and declares (Hab 3:16): "I will quietly wait for the day of trouble" (אנוח ליום צרה). This latter time will bring vindication for the ruthless invader. This pattern of thought is seen also in Lamentations, where the author reflects on the fall of Jerusalem as a "day of Yahweh" (1:12) and then a few verses later makes the request (Lam 1:21): "Bring the day you have announced, and let them be as I am" (הבאת יום קראת ויהיו כמוני).[17]

What is remembered most in the book of Habakkuk is the anguish of oppression by a foreign power. The dominant theme is theodicy. How, amid the chaos of the world, was it possible to make sense of God's sovereignty in this era of history, especially when innocent people were caught in war and devastation?[18] I suggest that, in retrospect, the editors of the Book of the Twelve were recalling an event such as the death of Josiah when they located the book of Habakkuk within the Twelve. Josiah's untimely death at Megiddo was clearly remembered as a puzzling contradiction by later generations. In the entire Deuteronomistic tradition,

---

[16] For an analysis of the macrostructure of Habakkuk, see James Nogalski, *Redactional Processes in the Book of the Twelve* (BZAW 218; Berlin: Walter de Gruyter, 1993) 129-181.

[17] See further, the prophetic imagery in Isa 10:5-19. Note also the similar rhetoric in Isa 13:1-22. There a prophetic word announcing a "day of Yahweh" for Babylon (13:6) includes a word about the envisioned instrument of Yahweh's judgment with the declaration in v. 17: "Behold I am stirring up the Medes" (הנני מעיר עליהם את מדי).

[18] I see the memories preserved in the book of the Twelve as being more complex than is suggested by a simple scheme of "sin-punishment-restoration" (Paul. R. House, *Unity of the Twelve* [JSOTS 97; Sheffield: Sheffield Academic press, 1990] 63-109). As Schart ("Reconstructing the Redaction History of the Twelve Prophets," 38-39) has pointed out, those themes appear in Malachi as well as in Joel and other works remembered from pre-exilic settings.

Josiah is remembered as the best of the reformer kings, the one who, probably before and after finding an ancient law code during a temple restoration, carried out massive reforms throughout the country.[19] No other king of Judah can match the high marks given to Josiah (2 Kgs 23:25):

> Before him there was no king like him,
> who turned to the Lord with all his heart,
> with all his soul and with all his might,
> according to all the law of Moses; nor
> did any like him arise after him.

Josiah had been designated as king when he was only eight years old; in 609, he was still only 39 years old when he was killed in battle attempting to slow the advance of an Egyptian army under Pharaoh Necho on the plain near Megiddo. That Egyptian force was heading north to assist Assyria in her defense against the new insurgent forces of Babylon. Josiah was evidently in league with Babylon, yet Babylon would turn out to be the great oppressor of Judah. The memories connected with Josiah's death raised precisely the kind of questions that seem to be addressed by the Habakkuk scroll.[20]

When a king who "turns to Yahweh with all of his heart" still dies a tragic death at an early age, the words of the farmer's song at the end of Habakkuk take on a particularly appropriate focus. They are words of encouragement for the faithful (Hab 3:17-18):

> Even when there is no fruit on the vines;
> Even when the olive oil fails,
> And when the fields yield no food;
> When the flocks are cut off from the fold,
> And when there is no herd left in the stall,
> I will still rejoice in the Lord;
> I will exult in the God of my salvation!

The words are remembered as encouragement to people, urging patience and trust in the promises that God had given, even when the world does not make sense.

---

[19] On Josiah, see Marvin A. Sweeney, *King Josiah of Judah: The Lost Messiah of Israel* (New York: Oxford, 2001) and the treatment of the topic "Josiah: Man of Torah" in Walter Brueggemann, *1 and 2 Kings* (Macon, Ga.: Smyth & Helwys, 2000), 543-565.

[20] The Chronicler author attempts to address the issue of theodicy by suggesting that Josiah failed to listen to the word of God spoken to him through Necho (II Chr 35:7).

IV. Concluding Observations

I have suggested in this paper that the message preserved in the Habakkuk scroll comes into clearer perspective when viewed from the larger context of the Book of the Twelve and the rhetoric of the "day of Yahweh" tradition. There were decisive moments in Israel's history. There were times when the suzerain role or kingship of Yahweh was particulary apparent to later generations. The book of the Twelve is arranged in such a way that one can discern particular times or "days" when God's presence seemed evident. Hosea, Joel, Amos, Obadiah, Micah, Nahum and Zephaniah all attempted to provide a framework for understanding and affirming Yahweh's sovereignty over nations. Among the Twelve, two books provide a rather different focus: Jonah and Habakkuk. In a sense, they almost provide moments of respite from the relentless recitation of the horrors of war that came for northern Israel, for Assyria, for Egypt, for Judah, and then for Babylon and for other countries.

Jonah brings a word of caution about vindictiveness. That scroll includes a warning about the dangers of being consumed by feelings of hostility and revenge for an enemy nation. In Jonah, the author reminds the reader that all people are creatures of God, and that even their cattle are precious in the sight of God (Jon 4:11).

Habakkuk, by contrast, focuses on the dangers of despair and disillusionment, and he calls the reader to a posture of patience and faithfulness, even amid the memories of past horrors. Events of history are not always such that people can readily discern covenantal blessings or punishments. Sometimes events simply defy explanation. The author encourages the faithful to remember the promises of the Torah even when events seem meaningless (Hab 2:3-4):

> ...there is still a vision for the appointed time;
> it speaks of the end, and does not lie.
> If it seems to tarry, wait for it;
> It will surely come, it will not delay.
> Look at the proud!
> Their spirit is not right in them,
> But the righteous will live by their faithfulness!

In Habakkuk, life is not simply a matter of the wicked being punished and the righteous prospering. The innocent also die! But the life of faith has its own rewards. So people of faith are called to a vision of life that involves justice (מֹשְׁפֵּט, 1:4), righteous life (צַדִּיק, 2:4), faithfulness (אֱמוּנָה, 2:4) and mercy (רַחֵם, 3:2), all of which seem bound together with Habakkuk's vision of meaningful life and what it means "to know the glory of the Lord" (לדעת את כבוד יהוה, 2:14). In locating Habakkuk after Nahum and before Zephaniah, the editors recall an era when chaos seemed to rule. The reader is encouraged not to despair when situations seem similar, especially in those times when Yahweh's sovereignty or righteousness does not seem readily apparent in the world.

Theodicy in the Book of the Twelve

James L. Crenshaw

Because some historic events defy rationality, they append a huge question mark to fixed belief, transforming a society accustomed to affirmation into one plagued with interrogatives. The twentieth century alone witnessed several such transformative events beginning with World War I and concluding with the AIDS epidemic that continues to claim millions of lives in the new millennium. For many historians, the singular event of a century captivated by ethnic consciousness took the lives of over six million Jews and others targeted for elimination or condemned by association. Response to the Shoah has varied from a type of muscular Judaism aimed at defeating Hitler's ultimate goal (Emil Fackenheim) to an abandoning of theism altogether in favor of voluntarism determined to establish a safe haven for the Jewish people in the modern state of Israel (Arthur A. Cohen). Between these extremes, others have given up the long-standing conviction that God works within history, rewarding virtue and punishing sin, and blessing a chosen people (Irving Greenberg); they have opted for cyclical repetitiveness of nature (Richard Rubenstein); or they have stressed ultimate mystery and, ironically, the necessity of silence in the face of the unspeakable (Elie Wiesel). Victims have been viewed as martyrs, their suffering construed as vicarious, or they have been considered the ugly consequence of freedom bestowed on humankind by a deity who has hidden the divine face.[1] Consequently, the relationship between creator and sentient creature,

---

[1] Steven T. Katz, "Holocaust: Judaic Theology and the," *The Enclopedia of Judaism* (ed. Jacob Neusner, Alan Avery-Peck, and William Scott Green; Leiden: E. J. Brill, 1999) 406-20. Perhaps one should distinguish between theodicies and responses to the sheer magnitude of evil encountered in the Holocaust such as mystery and silence (William Scott Green, "Facing the One God Together," *PRSt* 26 [1999] 308). With few exceptions, Judaic responses have exonerated God or left the traditional conception of God intact, according to Green, who adds (p. 309) that "Post-Holocaust Jewish prayer is like pre-Holocaust prayer: same blessings, same petitions, same questions, same answers." One is reminded of a story by Eli Wiesel about a trial of God by three Talmudic scholars at Auschwitz. They listened to witnesses and weighed evidence for several evenings, finally issuing a unanimous judgment. "The Lord God Almighty, Creator of Heaven and Earth, was found *guilty* of crimes against creation and human-

once thought crystal clear, has become clouded with mystery. Two previously held convictions have become problematic: that God controls history and is compassionate, just, and powerful. Perhaps a third assurance has also fallen by the way: that God *is*.

Christian theology, unexplainably less touched by the Shoah, has nonetheless taken a direct hit, particularly liberalism's optimism, its belief in progress, and its exalted view of human nature. Here, too, extreme responses occurred, ranging from Neo-Orthodoxy's ringing reaffirmation of traditional beliefs to the announcement that God is dead. The phenomenon of fundamentalism flourishes as believers refuse to be overwhelmed by the *anomie* that characterizes modern existence.[2] Divine favoritism, once widely extolled, has become an embarrassment, except to those who consider themselves God's chosen, and the historical paradigm associated with the idea of an elect people has lost its appeal in a global society where competing religious claims must be taken into account.[3] In such a context, the question of God's character has assumed center stage for theists, and with it, the issue of theodicy in its purest sense, specifically a defense of divine

---

kind. And then, after what Wiesel calls an infinity of silence, the Talmudic scholars looked at the sky and said, 'It's time for evening prayers,' and the members of the Tribunal recited Maariv, the evening service" (Robert McAfee Brown, introduction to E. Wiesel's play, *The Trial of God* [New York: Schocken, 1995]) 7.

[2]   The single term, lawlessness, captures best the lack of rhyme or reason that has replaced an earlier view of an order governing the entire universe. The resurgence of religious intolerance represents the conservative response to a threatened collapse in theological orthodoxy. When individuals see cherished doctrine under attack, the natural inclination is to reaffirm it rather than explore the reasons others consider the belief no longer adequate. Aggressive reaffirmation thus undercuts any possible dialogue with persons who hold different religious views. For the term *anomie* and the social aspects of theodicy, see Peter L. Berger, *The Sacred Canopy: Elements of a Sociological Theory of Religion* (Garden City: Doubleday, 1969) 53-80. Walter Brueggemann ("Theodicy in a Social Dimension," *JSOT* 33 [1985] 3-24) faults Old Testament scholars for ignoring the social aspect of theodicy, but James L. Crenshaw ("The Sojourner Has Come to Play the Judge: Theodicy on Trial," in *God in the Fray: A Tribute to Walter Brueggemann*, [ed. Tod Linafelt and Timothy K. Beal; Minneapolis: Fortress, 1998], 83-92) demurs.

[3]   Clark M. Williamson (*Way of Blessing Way of Life: A Christian Theology* [St. Louis: Chalice, 1999], 67-72) deals helpfully with the question, "Is there one true religion, or are there many?" and discusses the possibility of inter-religious dialogue. He examines five options to this question: (1) the exclusivist claim that Christianity is the only true religion and that salvation is granted only to Christians; (2) the inclusivist position that Christianity is the one true religion but one's ultimate salvation is a separate issue; (3) the pluralist option, in which all religions are equally true and salvation is granted to all; (4) a view that salvation does not adhere to a single religion, for other religions may be true; and (5) Christian claims are true but stand under the judgment of revelatory events that make Christians forgiven sinners.

justice.[4] Eighteenth and nineteenth century understandings of theodicy as (1) attempts to show that belief in a deity can coincide with belief in a mechanistic universe and (2) to demonstrate the intellectual credibility of an infinite being or power differ markedly from theodicy as manifest in the Bible and in its ancient Near Eastern context. Such Post-Enlightenment efforts to buttress faith have come under attack recently, for valid reasons,[5] but earlier discussions of divine justice are not vulnerable to these criti-

---

[4]   In the introduction to the journal referred to in note 1 (Green, "Facing the One God Together"), David Nelson Duke conveniently specifies various types of theodicy at the turn of the twentieth century. He lists theodicies of: (1) fatalism, (2) accountability and calculation, (3) instrumental purpose, (4) expressivity, and (5) denial. Duke includes theodicies emphasizing God's impenetrable mystery in the first category, and he notes the magical dimensions of control underlying the second type, the human attempt to escape the consequence of evil through mental gymnastics such as prayer or positive thinking, akin to bootstrapism. In the third type he sees the danger of self-abuse encouraged by an abusive deity; in the fourth he recognizes a form of escapism from the real world; and in the fifth category he notices signs of trivializing evil through sloppy language and improper use of analogies. Other contributors to this volume of *Perspectives in Religious Studies* address the general problem of theodicy in the Hebrew Bible (Walter Brueggemann), the particular case of Job (Samuel E. Balentine), insights from Buddhism and the possibility of compassion as a practical theodicy (Wendy Farley), the problem of the white Christ from the perspective of Dietrich Bonhoeffer (Josiah Ulysses Young), and Dostoevsky on evil as a perversion of personhood (Ralph C. Wood). The editors, Duke and Balentine, conclude the issue with an impassioned plea that Jews and Christians rethink the concept of God. The ramifications of bold rethinking can be seen in my forthcoming article entitled "The Reification of Divine Evil" and in David Penchansky, *What Rough Beast? Images of God in the Hebrew Bible* (Louisville: Westminster John Knox, 1999), as well as the various articles in *Shall Not the Judge of all the Earth Do What Is Right: Studies on the Nature of God in Tribute to James L. Crenshaw* (ed. David Penchansky and Paul L. Redditt; Winona Lake: Eisenbrauns, 2000).

[5]   Terrence W. Tilley (*The Evils of Theodicy* [Eugene, Oregon: Wipf and Stock, 2000[1) argues that theodicy creates evil by silencing powerful voices of insight and healing. On the basis of a theory of speech act, he considers the silencing of Job and the distortion of subsequent texts; specifically Augustine's *Enchiridion*, Boethius' *The Consolation of Philosophy*, Hume's *Dialogues Concerning Natural Religion*, and George Eliot's *Adam Bede*. Tilley dislikes the theoretical nature of Post-Enlightenment theodicies and insists on the need for practical responses to evil, together with the use of spiritual texts such as Job, Boethius, Julian of Norwich, and Simone Weil. For Tilley, the most shocking feature of modern theodicies is the effacement of Job (p. 245), which may be true of theologians in general but does not apply to biblical scholars. *Theodicy in the Old Testament* (Philadelphia: Fortress, 1983) which I edited will soon give way to a comprehensive *Handbook of Theodicy* in the ancient Near East to be edited by Antti Laato and Johannes C. de Moor and published by E. J. Brill and by a volume that I have given the provisional title *Deities on Trial: Questioning Divine Justice in the Bible*, to be published by Oxford University Press. The present essay should be supplemented by my contribution to the *Handbook of Theodicy*, specifically "Theodicy and Prophetic Literature."

cisms. Like modern ones, however, biblical theodicy, although remote from purely intellectual exercises, arises from the anomalies of existence and endeavors to make sense of reality in the light of the prevailing worldview.[6]

I. Theodicy in the Bible and Parallel Literature

A. Wisdom and Apocalyptic Literature

Within the Bible, theodicy finds its purest expression in the book of Job, usually linked with the wisdom books of Proverbs, Ecclesiastes, Sirach, and Wisdom of Solomon.[7] The deutero-canonical Second Esdras, an apocalyptic masterpiece, rivals the biblical book of Job in posing the question of divine justice. Together these books raise the issue as it pertains to an individual and to humanity at large. Whereas the book of Job focuses on divine abuse of a faithful servant, Second Esdras nationalizes the issue, indeed comes close to universalizing it. An exquisite Psalm, the seventy-third, transforms a personal experience of wrestling with theodicy into a communal occasion for openly facing doubt without loss of trust in divine goodness.[8] Parallels to these texts dealing with Yahweh's justice have much in common with them: a brief section in the Egyptian "Admonition of Ipuwer," the Sumerian parallel to Job, the Babylonian "I Will Praise the Lord of Wisdom," and the Babylonian Theodicy. Less directly, but nonetheless related, are Ecclesiastes and its parallel, A Dialogue between a Master and his Slave, possibly also the Ugaritic Epics of Kirtu and Dan'el. The answers provided in this literature, less profound than the vetting of the issue,

---

[6] In a forthcoming article entitled "Theodicy, Theology, and Philosophy: Early Israel and Judaism," in *Religions of the Ancient World: A Guide* (Cambridge, Mass.: Harvard University), I describe the cultural assumptions in the ancient Near East that underlie discussions of evil.

[7] Classifying the book of Job as wisdom literature requires that one put more emphasis on content than style, as various critics have underscored. The prominence of lament does not override the dominant intellectual query about the adequacy of interpreting suffering on the basis of a rigid theory of act and consequence. The cognitive dimension almost equals the affective one in the powerful exploration of the right response to suffering and the possibility of disinterested virtue. Still, it must be conceded that the book of Job includes features otherwise absent from wisdom literature, most notably theophanic addresses.

[8] The interplay of realism and imagination turns this majestic psalm into what is arguably the theological center of the Psalter, despite unresolved questions about the exact scope of the union with the deity in the closing verses, or even the nature of the transforming experience in El's sacred place (v. 17). Both the literary artistry and theological profundity of this assessment of the belief that God is good to the pure in heart occupy pride of place in my discussion of this psalm in *The Psalms: an Introduction* (Grand Rapids: Eerdmans, 2001) 109-27.

range from blaming the gods for creating perverse humans to condemning people as guilty, from acknowledging ignorance in the face of ultimate mystery to assurance that obedient worship will bring divine favor once more, from despair to hope. Because the sages responsible for this remarkable literature belonged to the intellectual elites[9] of society, their reflections on life's deepest mysteries occasion no surprise.

B. Popular Sentiment

Neither does the hue and cry of the less cerebral among the populace, ordinary women and men who faced adversity and were unable to accommodate calamity with ancestral beliefs transmitted over the generations.[10] Their openness to doubt, forced on them by episodic and rampant evil, grew out of the inadequacy of a religion founded on calculatable morality once individualism surged to dominance. In addition, the conviction that Israel and Judah enjoyed the status of a favored nation plunged precipitously as successive empires from Assyria and Babylon wreaked havoc on the two kingdoms. Judging from complaints within the Psalter, the loss of honor that accompanied these defeats and the painful mockery heaped on Yahwists evoked a profound theological crisis. The question "Where is your God?" yielded no easy answer. Religious pragmatism, encouraged by the dogma of reward and retribution, more often than not led to abandonment of traditional belief, particularly in a culture with no really dominant belief system. With faith up for grabs, the prominence of theodicy in popular sentiment makes sense.

---

9   Few investigators into the level of literacy in ancient Israel consider it high, given the agrarian economy and managed control by the elite scribes who profited from its scarcity. Analogies with the sophisticated cultures in Mesopotamia and Egypt cut both ways. The tiny percentage of literate people, perhaps approximating one percent, and the greater demand for scribes than in Israel point one way, even as the simplicity of Hebrew when compared with cuneiform and hieroglyphics points another way. On this complex issue, see James L. Crenshaw, *Education in Ancient Israel: Across the Deadening Silence* (New York: Doubleday, 1998).

10   The investigation of popular belief, which captured my imagination over three decades ago (*Prophetic Conflict: Its effect Upon Israelite Religion* [BZAW, 124; Berlin and New York: de Gruyter, 1971] and "Popular Questioning of the Justice of God in Ancient Israel," *ZAW* 82 [1970]: 380-95) has begun to intrigue others who bring different questions to the table from those preoccupying me then. Without assuming that citations attributed to the people accurately reflect fact on one level, we may credibly imply verisimilitude; otherwise the literary fiction would have floundered. There is no evidence that readers rejected the attributions as unreliable descriptions of popular belief. Moshe Greenberg (*Biblical Prose Prayer as a Window to the Popular Religion of Ancient Israel* [Berkeley: University of California, 1983]) uses a similar argument to justify his treatment of fictional prayers as true to life.

C. Prophetic Literature

Where such questioning of divine justice seems out of place, however, is within biblical prophecy. By its very nature, prophecy conveys a divine message to society's leaders and ultimately to the populace in general, whom it also represents to the deity. This intermediary role implies a unique relationship between prophets and their divine commissioner, one based on a calling to service and implying affinity of intellect and affect. The titles associated with biblical prophets emphasize their unique relationship, a bond resulting from having been summoned, from the actual task of speaking on behalf of the deity (נביא), or from possession (האלהים איש, איש הרוח). Alternatively, they stress either the prophet's access to divine secrets through special insight, usually called clairvoyance, or divinatory technique (ראה, חזה). Given the bond linking prophet and deity, and the peculiar vocation of the former, one hardly expects theodicy to come into play. That seems the case in extra-biblical prophecy as preserved in ancient Mari and in Neo-Assyrian texts from the seventh century, where ecstatics (muhhum), diviners (sabru, sailu, apilum), and proclaimers (raggimu) communicate messages from various deities, especially Adad and Ishtar, to ruling authorities – Zimri-Lim at Mari, Esarhaddon and Ashurbanipal in Nineveh.[11]

Biblical prophets distance themselves from Yahweh long enough to ponder the anomalies of history and their impact on the divine character, particularly the aspect of justice. They do so from a sense of personal affront and from a perception that the forces of chaos have gained the upper hand. Yahweh's failure to honor his promises to a loyal prophet like Jeremiah and to Moses and King David in regard to Israel and Zion reflected negatively on the divine character, just as the argument about the natural order of things and the causal nexus of sin and its consequences grew increasingly more problematic. Above all, liturgical renderings of

---

[11] Recent interpreters of these prophetic texts have concentrated on their social context more than their theological content, with the exception of Simo Parpola, *Assyrian Prophecies* (SAA 9; Helsinki University, 1997), whose speculative description of a monotheistic religion involving Ishtar of Arbela argues for a continuity with later Graeco-Roman and Hellenistic philosophy. Martti Nissinen, *References to Prophecy in Neo-Assyrian Sources* (SAAS 7; Helsinki: The Neo-Assyrian Text Corpus Project, 1998) and "Spoken, Written, Quoted, and Invented: Orality and Writtenness in Ancient Near Eastern Prophecy," in *Writings and Speech in Israelite and Ancient Near Eastern Prophecy* (ed. Ehud Ben Zvi and Michael H. Floyd; Atlanta: Society of Biblical Literature, 2000) 235-71 and Karel van der Toorn, "From the Oral to the Written: The Case of Old Babylonian Prophecy," in *Writings and Speech in Israelite and Ancient Near Eastern Prophecy*, 219-34 examine the phenomenon of prophecy – its institutional setting, official titles, mode of proclamation, and preservation in writing.

events in terms of instrumental purpose, even when that goal meant catastrophe for those who saw themselves as the elect, introduced theodicy into the act of worship itself. The inexplicable fall of Jerusalem despite belief in its inviolability and razing of Yahweh's residence demanded a prophetic response that answered the charge of divine impotence or malice.[12]

In Ezekiel's case, a persistent attack on divine justice by the people exacerbated the issue and resulted in a virtual shouting match venting more fury than insight. When calm prevailed, he caught a glimpse of a deeper meaning in Yahweh's departure to Babylon, symbolized by the כבד, and perceived the utter nothingness of idols.[13] His closing shout, reaffirming divine presence in a restored Zion, now made idyllic, stands in stark contrast to the lonely descent into despair attributed to Jeremiah in the so-called confessions. The empty affirmation of Yahweh's justice (12:1a) slipped precipitously when Jeremiah dared to direct charges against the deity (20:7). Innocence, the forensic meaning of צדיק, quickly changed to its opposite, guilt.

II. Theodicy in the The Minor Prophets

The Minor Prophets differ little from Isaiah, Jeremiah, and Ezekiel in this regard. For some of them, Isaiah's near silence about theodicy becomes normative; for others, the examples of Ezekiel and Jeremiah prevail. The only investigation into the problem of theodicy within the entire Book of the Twelve of which I have any knowledge advances the argument that the issue never surfaced in genuine prophecy but was inserted into the text by scribal editors who wished to shape the reading of prophetic literature in a desired direction.[14] This interpretation of the facts avoids the difficulty dis-

---

[12] These five occasions for theodicy are developed in my "Theodicy and Prophetic Literature."

[13] John F. Kutsko, *Between Heaven and Earth: Divine Presence and Absence in the Book of Ezekiel* (Biblical and Judaic Studies 7; Winona Lake, Ind.: Eisenbrauns, 2000) clarifies the importance of theodicy to the prophet Ezekiel, particularly in regard to idolatry. Kutsko emphasizes the means by which Ezekiel comes to Yahweh's defense, above all the relegation of idols to non-entities and the departure of the divine presence but ultimately its return and the restoration of a chastened people. Kutsko's argument, thoroughly philological, makes good use of literary features to illuminate the theological context in which Ezekiel moved.

[14] Raymond C. Van Leeuwen, "Scribal Wisdom and Theodicy in the Book of the Twelve," in *In Search of Wisdom: Essays in Memory of John Gammie* (ed. Leo G. Perdue, Bernard Brandon Scott, and William Johnston Wiseman; Louisville: Westminster John Knox, 1993) 31-49. Van Leeuwen traces allusions to Exod 34:6-7 in the Book of the Twelve, arguing that forerunners of Ben Sira introduced theodicy as an

cussed above – the possibility that individuals commissioned by Yahweh could question the justice of the one in whose service they proclaimed a divine word – but misconstrues the actual religio-historical context of prophecy.[15]

A. Modalities of Thinking

In a given society some people continue to believe what they have been taught about the deity regardless of historical circumstances. Others abandon traditional teachings at the drop of a hat. However one explains these dispositions to question everything or to accept things without reservation, they introduce a distinct dynamic into a religious community. The resulting struggle for dominance frequently overlooks the positive contribution of such tension. Each view represents a partial truth. Many, if not most, traditional beliefs have stood the test of time and will probably survive the present crisis. Therefore, its detractors need a reminder that considerable time and energy have been invested in the teaching. Nevertheless, not all beliefs can pass muster when confronting major shifts in cultural assumptions.[16] The inadequacy of these features of the belief system are thus exposed to full view, opening its adherents to mockery. Occasionally, the imperative mood carries the day as a result of subjecting the declarative to the interrogative, and authority figures issue the great demands that, if obeyed, keep the tradition intact. We can see all three perspectives at work in the Book of the Twelve.

---

explanation for the catastrophic events in 722 and 587 BCE. He discusses Hos 14:10 (also 1:6, 9); Mic 2:7-8a; 7:18-20 via 4:5 and Ps 25:4-13; Joel 2:12-14; 4:21 [3:21]; Amos 4:13; 5:8-9; 9:5-6, Obad (the references to Yahweh's day); Jonah 3:5-10; 4:1-2, 3-11; Nah 1:2b-3a; and Habakkuk. Indeed, Van Leeuwen thinks Mic 6-7 comprises a miniature theodicy.

[15] By placing the controversy over Yahweh's justice in the circle of the wise, Van Leeuwen isolates biblical prophets from daily life in a way that flies in the face of their frequent readiness to wrestle with difficult theological questions. It is more probable that biblical prophets joined the fray and thus were not insulated from the challenges to traditional belief but experienced them both professionally and personally. Their concept of God and theology of election guaranteed the emergence of theodicy. Nevertheless, Van Leeuwen's initial insight, that some of these texts that rush to defend divine justice are editorial glosses, cannot be faulted. The issue, then, becomes one of origin, whether scribal or prophetic.

[16] The modern references to a shift in paradigm from history to literature indicate an awareness that the manner of interpreting texts for nearly two centuries has given way to a rival one that never really disappeared. Similarly, the furor over Post-Enlightenment views and the desire to replace them with older ways of viewing the world reveal the emotional involvement in cultural assumptions.

B. Denying That a Problem Exists

When this tension eases, a religious community tends to abandon the tradition altogether or to pretend that no problem exists. The latter approach occurs in Zeph 3:1-5, which denies the mere possibility of divine injustice.

> Ah, soiled, defiled, oppressing city!
> It has listened to no voice;
> > it has accepted no correction.
> It has not trusted in the Lord;
> > it has not drawn near to its God.
> The officials within it are roaring lions;
> its judges are evening wolves
> > that leave nothing until the morning.
> Its prophets are reckless, faithless persons;
> its priests have profaned what is sacred,
> > they have done violence to the law.
> The Lord within it is righteous (צַדִּיק);
> > he does no wrong (עַוְלָה).
> Every morning he renders his judgment,
> > each dawn without fail;
> but the unjust knows no shame.[17]

The exuberant confidence of the prophet Zephaniah matches that exemplified in Psalm 92, which envisions a just society with God unfailingly rewarding the righteous and finally crushing the wicked. The psalmist acknowledges the mystery of momentary success on the part of evildoers but attributes lack of understanding to human laziness and divine profundity (92:5-6). In this Lord who causes the righteous to flourish like a well-watered palm the psalmist can detect no sign of injustice. The prophet Zephaniah suffers no delusions as to the extent of corruption in the holy city, but this moral laxity contrasts with the deity's perfection. Human leaders, without exception, are judged to be guilty--officials, judges, prophets, and priests. For them, the usual deterrent to ravenous conduct, a wish to avoid the slightest hint of shame, has lost its power, leaving them bereft of honor. Over against this perfidy stands a divine incapacity to do wrong, at least as the prophet sees things. Others may berate Yahweh for failing to keep times of judgment, but Zephaniah detects no such dereliction of duty.[18]

---

[17] The translations in this article come from the NRSV.

[18] Ignoring the first half of verse 5, the assertion that the righteous Yahweh can do no wrong, Adele Berlin concentrates on the concluding half-verse and compares its single idea, in her view, to Psalm 19, which associates judgment and sunlight (*Zephaniah* [AB 25A; New York: Doubleday, 1994] 130. J. Schreiner, "ʿawel, ʿwla, ʿwl, ʿiwwal," *TDOT* X (1999) 529 contrasts the biblical insistence on Yahweh's freedom from

A similar passage in Ezek 22:23-31, an oracle attributed to the deity, lacks the assertion of divine justice but has the negative assessment of Judah's leaders. The behavior of its princes is likened to roaring lions; its priests have violated the teaching with respect to the sacred and the profane; its officials act like hungry wolves; its prophets invent visions and proclaim lies; and the people of the land commit extortion and robbery against the powerless. The expansionist nature of this text when compared with Zeph 3:1-5 makes it difficult to determine the precise relationship between the two, but the resemblances are too close to be accidental. Zephaniah's oracle about the defiled city and its leaders does not stop with this negative assessment but shifts to divine speech announcing a purging of the citizens, leaving a few humble people incapable of wrongdoing (3:6-13). Ezekiel mentions nothing beyond the outpouring of divine indignation, although the prophet will have more to say later about the restoration of Israel and Judah. An eschatological dimension seems to hover over Zephaniah's words, with the gathering of nations for judgment and invocation of the Lord recalling Joel's remarkable look into the future.[19]

The gloss that concludes the book of Hosea also denies that divine injustice exists.

> Those who are wise understand these things;
>   those who are discerning know them.
> For the ways of the Lord are right (יְשָׁרִים),
>   and the upright (צַדִּקִים) walk in them,
>   but transgressors stumble on them. (Hos 14:10).

The difference between this affirmation and Zephaniah's is noteworthy. Whereas Zephaniah characterizes Yahweh as צַדִּיק, indeed incapable of doing עַוְלָה, the gloss in Hosea refers to divine activity, rather than the de-

---

wrongdoing (e.g., in Ps 92:15 [16], Zeph 3:5; Deut 32:4) with the people's proclivity to engage in sinful acts.

[19] For Joel's anticipation of a day when Yahweh will sit in judgment over the nations, see James L. Crenshaw, *Joel* (AB 24C; New York: Doubleday, 1995) 186-96. Historical events made it increasingly necessary to explain the dominance of foreigners over a covenant people, and the resulting sense of helplessness fueled eschatological hope that Yahweh would eventually punish the nations for their harsh treatment of his devotees. (According to Zech 1:7-17 those nations who exceeded the divine mandate to punish [Israel and] Judah were particularly vulnerable to Yahweh's wrath). The fundamental basis for this optimism was the conviction that Yahweh's justice could not be compromised.

ity's nature, uses a word indicating straight dealings, and reserves the adjective צדקים for obedient people.[20]

C. Questioning the Traditional Affirmation that the Virtuous Prosper

The book of Malachi represents the opposite perspective from Zephaniah, for the issue of theodicy occupies a prominent place in the heated discussion between prophet and detractors.[21] Indeed, the divine character opens itself to a charge of favoritism at the very beginning (1:2-5), a preference for Jacob over Esau expressed in terms of love and hate. Like the gloss in Hos 14:10, Malachi's opponents concentrate on Yahweh's activity, or lack of it.

> You have wearied the Lord with your words. Yet you say, "How have we wearied him?" By saying, "All who do evil are good in the sight of the Lord, and he delights in them." Or by asking, "Where is the God of justice?" (Mal 2:17)

The prophet prefers silence to the relentless pursuit of answers, relegating into oblivion the problem of delayed recompense for evil and reward for virtue. His detractors possess too much integrity to remain silent; their disappointment in Yahweh takes extreme form--the idea that the deity actually delights in wickedness. Small wonder they inquire about the whereabouts of a God who values משפט. The deity smarts from the intensity of attack.

> "You have spoken harsh words against me," says the Lord.
> Yet you say, "How have we spoken against you?"
> You have said, "It is vain to serve God. What do we profit by keeping his command or by going about as mourners before the Lord of hosts? Now we count the arrogant happy; evildoers not only prosper, but when they put God to the test they escape." (Mal 2:13-15)

---

[20] The claim that the gloss in Hos 14:10 derives from sages rests on the dubious assumption that they held a monopoly on cognitive vocabulary. Were the prophets interested in being understood and in addressing discerning hearers? The answer to this question can only be a resounding "yes." It follows that the open expression of this wish to have astute hearers (and readers) does not necessarily indicate the interests of a different sociological group. The language consists of nothing that belongs exclusively in wisdom literature, for everything in the verse fits nicely within prophecy.

[21] Like the book of Jonah with its single oracle of five words, Malachi rests uneasily in the prophetic corpus. The prevailing tone is that of discussion, or even argument, with a wide range of issues from moral to ritual (Julia O'Brien, *Priest and Levite in Malachi* [SBLDS 121; Atlanta: Scholars Press, 1990]).

Here we encounter the age-old problem of a misfit between the comforting belief that a principle of reward and retribution governs the universe and life as it is actually experienced. Here, too, the author sacrifices present reality by gazing into the future when, he thinks, a heavenly book[22] will reveal the names of those who have trusted Yahweh in spite of everything and when justice will finally dawn on earth.

The vexing disparity between virtue and its reward lies at the heart of the circumstances that elicited disquieting remarks attributed to Habakkuk in 1:2-4. An endless cry for help has fallen on deaf ears, or so it appears, and injustice prevails as perverse judgments favor the wicked. The prophet's language suggests the extent of his exasperation; intercession on his part has met with stony silence rather than expected deliverance. Neither persistence, implied by עד־אנה, nor extreme duress, suggested by the combination of the verb אזעק and the noun חמס,[23] has moved Yahweh to ameliorate the situation. Furthermore, Habakkuk expresses resentment at being forced by Yahweh to observe such total overturning of society's values. On the surface, at least, the facts hardly support traditional belief that Yahweh cares deeply about justice.

The divine response in 1:5-11 uses a common prophetic motif, foreigners as instruments of Yahweh's punishment, to open Habakkuk's eyes to a deeper dimension of the problem. The idea is presented as if unprecedented, something the prophet would have difficulty believing. The observation that the Babylonians decide what constitutes justice (1:7) stands in perfect harmony with the final statement that might makes right (1:11).[24]

---

[22] Shalom M. Paul ("Heavenly Tablets and the Book of Life," *JANESCU* 5 [1973] 345-53) discusses the scope of ancient Near Eastern speculation about the deity's active role in determining an individual's ultimate destiny by means of a written record. This early version of "Santa Claus lore" ("He's making a list and checking it twice; gonna find out who's naughty or nice") blossomed in later apocalyptic, bringing comfort to an oppressed people. Underlying the idea is a calculating morality, according to which one's fate depends entirely on a final weighing of good deeds against evil ones reminiscent of the Egyptian belief that one's virtues would be weighed against the goddess of justice, Maat.

[23] The language of lament, by nature raw, includes subtle indictment, for the champion of the oppressed should hasten to the rescue on hearing about bloodshed and violence. In this instance, the prophet has cried out repeatedly, without receiving any answer. This rare cluster of words (עד־אנה, אזעק, and חמס) pertaining to theodicy refutes any suggestion that the issue was merely an intellectual enterprise.

[24] Justice is always conflicted, as Ralph Waldo Emerson observed: "One man's justice is another man's injustice." A better articulation of the idea would substitute the word "tyranny" for "injustice." The struggle for justice often becomes a striving for power, which engenders rival theodicies, one for the group in control and another for the disenfranchised.

D. Redefining Yahweh's Character

Obviously unsatisfied by this troublesome response that has redefined justice and deity, Habakkuk presses further by exploring the matter of the divine character. Having first settled the question of Yahweh's eternality in language so shocking to later scribes that they altered its sense ("You shall not die" becomes "we shall not die"), Habakkuk wonders about the inconsistency between divine purity and an evil eye that seems to wink at the grossest malice possible.

> Your eyes are too pure to behold evil,
>   and you cannot look on wrongdoings.
> Why do you look on the treacherous,
>   and are silent when the wicked swallow
>   those more righteous than they? (Hab 1:13).

This accusation of divine instability or hypocrisy illustrates the confusion resulting from continued belief in Yahweh's justice regardless of the evidence undercutting such conviction. The assertions, "You cannot" yet "you do" cancel each other out, although Habakkuk refuses to reach this obvious conclusion.

In another oracle Habakkuk receives a vision that instructs him to write the divine word as a testimony to its veracity and to proclaim it abroad, but also to trust it in the face of possible delay (2:1-4). This vision ends with the much-discussed word about the righteous living by their faith or faithfulness. The likely object of באמונתו, the prophetic vision, is described as truthful but directed toward a specific time.[25] Moreover, it possesses an internal contradiction; it may seem to tarry but will not delay. With this curious language the prophet endeavors to protect himself in the event that expectations generated by the vision are not met with immediate gratification. The closing hymn in chapter 3 acknowledges the uncertainty of grand promises, even when originating above, and conveys the prophet's determination to remain faithful in unpromising circumstances. These sentiments usher the reader into the company of others who cherish divine presence above presents, especially the unknown author of the majestic seventy-third psalm.

---

[25]   On the antecedent of the suffix attached to אמונה, with a prefixed preposition, see J. J. M. Roberts, *Nahum, Habakkuk, and Zephaniah* (OTL; Louisville: Westminster/John Knox, 1991) and Robert D. Haak, *Habakkuk* (VTSup 44; Leiden: Brill, 1991). Donald E. Gowan, *The Triumph of Faith in Habakkuk* (Atlanta: John Knox, 1976) 20-50 raises the theological issue of divine justice.

1. Jonah and the Compassion of God

Although a putative historical event figures prominently in the book of
Jonah, specifically the sparing of Nineveh, the issue of theodicy arises from
reflection on the deity's nature as proclaimed to Moses in Exod 34:6-7.[26]
Because Jonah understands Yahweh to be compassionate, he shrinks from
carrying out the mission entrusted to him by the Lord, and when compelled
by circumstances to finish the original task, Jonah explains his reluctance to
become a pawn in the divine game of chess.

> O Lord! Is not this what I said while I was still in my own country? That is why I
> fled to Tarshish at the beginning; for I knew that you are a gracious God and
> merciful, slow to anger and abounding in steadfast love, and ready to relent from
> punishing. (Jon 4:2)

Having experienced Yahweh's readiness to forgive even a wayward messenger, Jonah resents this same compassion being extended to a city guilty
of horrific malice directed at his own people. Rather than unleashing divine
wrath against a disobedient prophet, Yahweh demonstrates the patience
announced in the ancient confession and provides an object lesson intended
to persuade Jonah that truly repentant creatures deserve a second chance,
regardless of their ethnicity or pedigree.

Jonah has a point. Should guilty individuals escape responsibility for
the calamities they have brought to others? Should repentance, even if genuine, remove the punishment demanded by their atrocities?[27] Where is the
justice in letting guilty people escape the recompense due them? Who
wants to live in a world devoid of justice, one in which evildoers can sin
with impunity? The operative word here is evildoers, not foreigners, for
elsewhere the book describes foreign sailors in admirable terms. Readers of
the book would probably have known that Nineveh eventually fell to
Babylonian soldiers, making Jonah's objection a moot point. The over-

---

[26]   James L. Crenshaw, "Who Knows What Yahweh Will Do? The Character of God in
the Book of Joel," in *Fortunate the Eyes That See: Essays in Honor of David Noel
Freedman,* (ed. Astrid Beck et. al. [Grand Rapids: Eerdmans, 1995]) 185-96 and
Terence E. Fretheim, "Jonah and Theodicy," *ZAW* 90 (1978) 227-37.

[27]   In trying to justify curses against enemies in the Psalter, C. S. Lewis reflects on the
consequences of letting evildoers escape punishment. For him, anger over wickedness
demonstrates a conscience, whereas tolerating cruelty indicates indifference. He also
stresses the harm inflicted on the innocent by generating hatred within them
(*Reflections on the Psalms* [New York: Harcourt, Brace and Company, 1958], 20-33).

turning of the hated city, whether by repentance or by subsequent invasion,[28] served as a מָשָׁל of divine solicitude.

Jonah's legitimate objection therefore pales before the astonishing
illustration of Yahweh's concern for the wellbeing of all creatures. Dogma,
however revered, means less to the author of this book than divine
compassion. After all, the belief in justice stands in tension with mercy,
and when the two come into conflict mercy will prevail.[29] This message
stands out in a conflicted medium, one freely employing irony, humor, and
satire. Has the author faced theodicy and rendered it impotent? If so,
Jonah's petulance in the open-ended tale must be judged unseemly. His
protest becomes even more telling when we move from fiction to stark
reality long enough to ponder the fact that divine compassion was not
sufficiently strong to spare that great city and its inhabitants. In the end,
theoretical treatments of theodicy do not suffice, for concepts of God that
do not accord with reality, however inspiring, amount to little more than
proverbial whistling in the dark.

Jonah was not alone in trying to reconcile the characterization of
Yahweh as preserved in Exod 34:6-7 with everyday experience. The
prophets Joel, Nahum, and Micah join Jonah in this arduous endeavor.
Affinities between the texts of Joel and Jonah go beyond coincidence, but
lacking valid criteria for dating the two books we cannot detect the line of
dependence. The problem confronting Joel differs profoundly from that of
Jonah; no evidence of guilt on the part of an afflicted people surfaces in the
biblical text, although modern interpreters, like Job's friends, have labored
long and hard to indict the innocent.[30] To them it seems obvious that sin has
brought punishment in the form of a plague of locusts and drought. Joel
urges the community to turn to Yahweh in supplication, relying on the
deity's character as specified in Exod 34:6. His confidence is rewarded and
Yahweh has compassion on the people (Joel 2:12-27). Elsewhere Joel
insists on an exact measure for measure when Yahweh finally gets around

---

[28] Jack M. Sasson, *Jonah* (AB 24B; New York: Doubleday, 1990) 234-37 recognizes the
      ambiguity of the word נֶהְפָּכֶת, its potential for both a threatening and a hopeful sense.
      Nineveh faced a choice, whether to be overturned through external force or to be
      turned around in repentance.
[29] On this dynamic, see James L. Crenshaw, "The Concept of God in Old Testament
      Wisdom," in *In Search of Wisdom*, 1-18 (also in Crenshaw, *Urgent Advice and Prob-
      ing Questions: Collected Writings on Old Testament Wisdom* [Macon: Mercer
      University, 1995], 191-221; pages 141-221 of this book deal with theodicy).
[30] James L. Crenshaw, "Joel's Silence and Interpreter's Readiness to Indict the Inno-
      cent," in *"Lässet uns Brücken bauen..." Collected Communications to the XVth
      Congress of the International Organization for the Study of the Old Testament,
      Cambridge 1995* (BEATAJ 42; Frankfurt: Peter Lang, 1998) 255-59.

to punishing foreign kingdoms for implementing slave trade and other atrocities against Israel and Judah. Like Joel, the prophet Obadiah envisions an exact retribution against the Edomites (v 15). The doxological conclusion to Micah reaffirms Yahweh's compassionate nature and views this readiness to exalt mercy over justice as unique (Mic 7:18-20) – like Nahum's application of the negative aspects of Yahweh's character to Nineveh (Nah 1:2-3). Without exception, the other uses of the credal affirmation in Exod 34:6-7 stop short of mentioning Yahweh's exacting punishment, for they appeal to the compassionate side, hoping for pity. Nahum, however, has revenge in mind, and he does not hesitate to recall Yahweh's penchant for justice. Like Jonah, Nahum insists on exact retribution against a hated enemy, for in Nineveh's collapse, here graphically depicted, he recognizes an act of divine justice.

2. A Liturgy of Wasted Opportunity

The liturgical function of the confession about Yahweh's essential nature corresponds to specific texts in the book of Amos with destructive acts affecting an elect nation. The people's fondness for proclaiming Yahweh's salvific acts (צדקות) prompts Amos to mimic such liturgical moments. Looking back over the remembered past, he calls to mind devastating events – famine, drought, infestation of crops, pestilence, unspecified calamity like that at Sodom and Gomorrah – and explains them as Yahweh's discipline (Amos 4:6-12). In effect, the prophet constructs a liturgy of wasted opportunity,[31] concluding each segment with Yahweh's haunting words, "Yet you did not return to me." The prophet offers a theodicy in which misfortune is viewed instrumentally; suffering comes from God to stimulate repentance. Its lack of success leads to an even more alarming tactic, which has been described as doxology of judgment. Three hymnic fragments, scattered throughout the book, announce destruction while lauding Yahweh's justice in sending such calamity (Amos 4:13; 5:8-9; 9:5-6). The hymn celebrates Yahweh's creative accomplishments, his control over nature itself, and his use of torrential rain as judgment. The contexts of the fragments highlight human guilt, justifying a final act of destruction. In this theodicy, Yahweh's attempt to educate a rebellious people does not find expression; indeed, the time has come for retribution.[32]

---

[31] From a human perspective, the discipline amounts to a squandered opportunity, whereas from a divine viewpoint it represents a pedagogical failure (James L. Crenshaw, "A Liturgy of Wasted Opportunity: Am. 4:6-12; Isa. 9:7-10:4," *Semitics* 1 [1971]: 27-37).

[32] James L. Crenshaw, *Hymnic Affirmation of Divine Justice* (SBLDS 24; Missoula, Montana: Scholars Press, 1975).

3. Natural Calamities and the Attribution of Evil to Yahweh

The shift from history to the realm of nature figures prominently in Amos 3:3-8, where the prophet argues from cause to effect. A series of logical deductions relating to causal events culminates in the attribution of evil to Yahweh. Just as one can deduce from a lion's roar that it has captured prey and from the sound of alarm that fear has been generated in the populace, the incidence of misfortune indicates divine activity. In this theodicy Yahweh assumes full responsibility for evil, as in Deut 32:39 and Isa 45:7. The harshness of this type of theodicy is softened by a gloss in Amos 3:8 suggesting that Yahweh never acts destructively without alerting prophetic messengers, who will then, it is implied, make intercession for an endangered people.[33]

IV. Conclusion

The Minor Prophets, like Jeremiah and Ezekiel, experienced an intolerable discrepancy between the anomalies of life and theological belief. They felt this defect most acutely as a result of historical events that threatened what they held most dear, as a consequence of personal interaction with Yahweh that constituted an affront, and as a challenge to their understanding of the deity's essential character. While some prophets denied the problem altogether, others acknowledged its persistence and tried to grasp its fundamental nature and to construct a valid response. Caught in the tension between justice and compassion, they refused to relinquish either one. Hosea's terrible announcement that compassion is hidden from Yahweh's eyes (13:14) alternates with a proclamation of divine courtship (2:14-15 [2:16-17]), but the prophet comes short of saying that Yahweh's abandonment is momentary whereas compassion lasts forever (cf. Isa 54:7-8; Ps 30:5). Like faithful believers today, Israel's prophets learned the hard fact that life has a way of forcing them to walk the razor's edge between doubt and trust. Their integrity demanded that they pose the issue of theodicy to the very one into whose service they had been called.

---

[33] On this extraordinary instance of rational deduction within prophetic literature, see Jörg Jeremias, *The Book of Amos* (OTL; Louisville: Westminster John Knox, 1998) 51-5; Hans Walther Wolff, *Joel and Amos* (Hermeneia; Philadelphia: Fortress, 1977) 179-88; and Shalom Paul, *Amos* (Hermeneia; Minneapolis: Fortress, 1991) 104-14.

The Day(s) of YHWH in the Book of the Twelve

James D. Nogalski

In 1997 Rolf Rendtorff presented a paper in the SBL Formation of the Book of the Twelve Seminar in which he argued that the concept of the day of YHWH showed significant promise as a unifying theme of the Book of the Twelve.[1] He also suggested that it was unwise to limit the concept merely to those texts, which specifically use the construct chain יוֹם יהוה. Twenty five years earlier, Joseph Everson and others carried on a rather lively debate about the extent to which the background of יוֹם יהוה required that one study only those texts, which contained this term.[2] Dissenters exist, but the majority of scholars concurred with Everson that other terms could refer to this day, and that the day in question could lie in the past as well as the future. This paper will attempt to investigate these suggestions systematically by asking two questions. First, if other expressions potentially evoke the concept of יוֹם יהוה, how does one recognize which terms do and which do not? Second, how does one evaluate the possibility that this recurring concept provides an avenue into the unifying elements of the Twelve?

---

[1] Rolff Rendtorff, "How to Read the Book of the Twelve as a Theological Unity," *SBL Seminar Papers, 1997* (SBLSP 36; Atlanta: Scholars Press, 1997): 420-432. The article also appeared in *Reading and Hearing the Book of the Twelve* (ed. James D. Nogalski and Marvin A. Sweeney; SBLSymS; Atlanta: Society of Biblical Literature, 2000) 75-87.

[2] A. Joseph Everson, "The Days of Yahweh," *JBL* 93 (1974) 329-37. Other works preceded Everson's article and responded to it. A selection of these writings is mentioned here: Gerhard von Rad, "Origin of the concept of the Day of Yahweh," *JSS* 4 (1959) 97-108; Klaus Dietrich Schunck, "Strukturlinien in der Entwicklung der Vorstellung vom Tag Jahwes," *VT* 14 (1964) 319-30; Paul Emile Langevin, "Sur l'origine du 'Jour de Yahvé,'" *Sciences Ecclésiastiques* 18 (1966) 359-70; Patrick D. Miller, Jr., "Divine Council and the Prophetic Call to War," *VT* 18 (1968) 100-107; Klaus Dietrich Schunck, "Die Eschatologie der Propheten des Alten Testaments und ihre Wandlung in exilisch-nach-exilischer Zeit," in *Studies on Prophesy, VTSup 26* (Leiden: Brill, 1974) 116-132; C. van Leeuwen, "The Prophecy of the Yom YHWH in Amos v 18-20," in *Language and Meaning*, (OtSt 19; Leiden: Brill, 1974) 113-134; Douglas Stuart, "The Sovereign's Day of Conquest," *BASOR* 221 (1976) 159-64; Yair Hoffmann, "The Day of the Lord as a Concept and a Term in the Prophetic Literature," *ZAW* 93 (1981) 37-50; Hermann Spieckermann, "Dies irae: der alttestamentliche Befund und seine Vorgeschichte," *VT* 39 (1989) 194-208.

Once one opens the door to other terms, one must decide which terms to include. An attempt to investigate the literary cohesion must look at any text that could have been interpreted as a day of YHWH text by those compiling the Twelve. I have therefore assessed those texts which refer to a day of divine intervention in the Twelve for reasons discussed below. This decision greatly increased the number of texts to be evaluated, and it forced a limitation of the discussion in two ways. First, the study was limited to the first four writings of the Twelve. Advantageously, this limitation includes two writings with superscriptions claiming 8th century settings (Hosea and Amos) and two non-dated writings (Joel and Obadiah), which the discipline generally dates later than Jerusalem's destruction. Second, I chose to focus the discussion upon passages where multiple terms were present. The volume of texts and the intricacy of the interrelationships make it impossible to treat every text in the space available.

I. Identifying Day of YHWH Texts

Any study of the day of YHWH must include more than the phrase יום יהוה. This construct chain appears 15 times in the Hebrew Bible, but this statistic only begins to tell the story.[3] All 15 references appear in the Latter Prophets, and 13 of 15 appear in the Twelve. In addition, a closely related expression, "the day of the wrath of YHWH," occurs three times, and two of these references appear in the Twelve.[4] A third syntactical variant contains the *lamed* preposition before YHWH, the day (belonging) to YHWH (יום ליהוה). This form appears exclusively in the Latter Prophets *when referring to the day of YHWH*, but a close parallel (היום ליהוה) appears elsewhere and refers to a day of ritual celebration.[5] In short, "day of YHWH" appears in variant forms, and these forms demonstrate a remarkably consistent association with the Latter Prophets, and especially with the Twelve.

However, other formulas and idiomatic expressions can refer to the day of YHWH and its effects. Two formulas, "on that day" (ביום ההוא) and "in those days" (בימים ההם), manifest conceptual similarities. Prophetic

---

[3] Isa 13:6, 9; Ezek 13:5; Joel 1:15; 2:1, 11; 3:4; 4:14; Amos 5:18, 20; Obad 15; Zeph 1:7, 14 (twice); Mal 3:23.

[4] Zeph 2:2, 3; Lam 2:22.

[5] The phrase יום ליהוה, when referring to the day of YHWH, appears in Isa 2:12; Ezek 30:3; 46:13; Zech 14:1. This phrase appears five times (Exod 16:25; 32:29; Lev 23:34; Deut 26:3; 1 Chr 29:5) in narrative texts, always with the definite article (היום ליהוה). This latter form refers to a particular day of ritual celebration.

usages of these phrases differ from their use in other parts of the canon. These phrases can refer to a day when YHWH acts or days which manifest the effects of YHWH's activity, and thus relate to the day of YHWH. The expression "in those days" appears 39 times in the Hebrew Bible, and the 25 instances outside the Latter Prophets always refer to the past.[6] By contrast, the phrase appears 14 times in the Latter Prophets, and all but two refer to the future when the effects of YHWH's action will be operative.[7] These formulaic phrases should be evaluated with the same criteria as other יום sayings.

The second formula, "on that day" (ביום ההוא), also functions distinctively in the Latter Prophets. The phrase occurs 206 times in the Hebrew Bible with a significant number (170) in the *Former and Latter Prophets*. The phrase occurs in the Latter Prophets 107 times where it overwhelmingly anticipates a future event. By contrast, outside the Latter Prophets, the phrase typically refers to past events. This phrase is far more prominent in Isaiah (45 times, with all but one appearing in Isa 1-31) and the Twelve (40 times) than in Jeremiah (10 times) or Ezekiel (12 times). With only a few exceptions, ביום ההוא refers to a past event in narrative literature and a future event in the Latter Prophets. Only six times (out of 107) does the formula not refer to the future.[8] References outside the Latter Prophets are even more instructive. In the Torah, DtrH, and the *Ketubim*, only 10 of the 99 do not refer to past events.[9] Five of these 10 references occur in DtrH or Chronicles, and always in the mouth of a prophet. All five pentateuchal references occur in prophetic speeches by Moses. Conversely, several future references within the Latter Prophets occur in prophetic oracles within *narrative* contexts (e.g., Jer 39:16, 17; Hos 1:5). This phrase, when referring to future events, connotes prophetic activity. The two meanings of this phrase (past or future) do not vary because one predominates in narrative literature (versus poetic), but because the future references carry prophetic connotations.

---

[6]   Gen 6:4; Exod 2:11; Deut 17:9; 19:17; 26:3; Josh 20:6; Judg 17:6; 18:1 (twice); 19:1; 20:27, 28; 21:25; 1 Sam 3:1; 28:1; 2 Sam 16:23; 2 Kgs 10:32; 15:37; 20:1; Esth 1:2; 2:21; Dan 10:2; Neh 6:17; 13:15, 23; 2 Chr 32:24.

[7]   Isa 38:1; Jer 3:16, 18; 5:18; 31:29; 33:15, 16; 50:4, 20; Ezek 38:17; Joel 3:2; 4:1; Zech 8:6, 23. Isa 38:1 refers to the past, but it utilizes 2 Kgs 20:1 as its source. Zech 8:6 uses this expression to refer to the present. The remaining texts refer to future events.

[8]   Jer 39:10 uses the phrase in a narrative account about a past event. Ezek 20:6; 23:38, 39 use the phrase in a divine speech to refer to a past event. Zech 6:10 implies the present day or the very near future. Isa 22:12 refers to the past action of YHWH.

[9]   Exod 8:18; 13:8; 31:17 (2 times), 18; 1 Sam 3:12; 8:18 (2 times); 1 Kgs 22:25; 2 Chr 18:24.

In addition to the formulas, references to a day of YHWH's intervention using idiomatic expressions appear in over 100 texts.[10] These expressions include terms for YHWH's destructive activity (e.g. wrath, vengeance), the effect of that activity (your overthrow), or the name of the recipient (e.g. Egypt, Midian). The majority of these terms refer to contexts of judgment and punishment, but both the idiomatic expressions and the formulas also appear in contexts which speak of salvation or deliverance. To what extent are these phrases associated with the concept of the day of YHWH? In several cases, these phrases occur as parallel expressions for the day of YHWH, meaning that one cannot eliminate these terms without careful reasoning from a discussion of the day of YHWH.

How does one recognize references to the day of YHWH if one cannot isolate these references based solely on terminology? All prophetic day of YHWH texts presume a point of divine intervention into human events. This intervention may be anticipated, recounted, or interpreted. The divine intervention may be direct or it may involve YHWH's use of some entity to accomplish a given task. By collating multiple qualities referring to a day when YHWH intervenes, one can develop a composite picture of the expectations and explanations of what will happen or has happened. These qualities include the following: the type of action, the recipients of the intervention, the reason for the intervention, the time of the intervention, and potential literary connectors.

---

[10]   These idiomatic expressions include at least the following: the day (Mic 7:4, 12; Zech 14:1; Jer 30:7; 31:6; 47:4; Mal 3:19; Ezek 7:7, 12, 19; 12:23; 30:2, 18; 39:8; Zeph 2:2), your day (Ezek 22:4; Jer 50:31), one day (Isa 10:17; 47:9; Zech 3:9), the latter days (Isa 2:2; Jer 23:20; 49:39; Mic 4:1; Jer 30:24; 48:47). In addition, the following construct chains also refer to the "day of . . . x," where x = battle (Amos 1:14; Hos 10:14; Zech 14:3), bitterness (Amos 8:10), building your walls (Mic 7:11), calamity (Jer 12:3; 18:17; 46:21; Amos 6:3), clouds (Ezek 30:3; Joel 2:2; Zeph 1:15), darkness (Joel 2:2; Zeph 1:15), destruction (Obad 12; Zeph 1:15), disaster (Jer 17:17, 18; Obad 13), distress (Isa 37:3; Jer 16:19; Obad 14), Egypt (Ezek 30:9), his burning anger Isa 13:13; his coming (Mal 3:2), his disaster (Obad 13), his misfortune (Obad 12), his preparation (Nah 2:4), his rebellion (Ezek 33:12), his sin (Ezek 33:12), his turning from wickedness (Ezek 33:12), indignation (Ezek 22:24), its (Assyria) going to sheol (Ezek 31:15), Jezreel (Hos 2:2), light (Amos 8:9), Midian (Isa 9:3), my rising (Zeph 3:8), my visiting (Jer 27:22), panic (Isa 22:5), punishment (Isa 10:3), rebuke (Hos 5:9), salvation (Isa 49:8), sickliness (Isa 17:11), strangers carrying off his wealth (Obad 11), east wind (Isa 27:8), great slaughter (Isa 30:25), trouble (Nah 1:7; Zeph 1:15), trumpet and battle cry (Zeph 1:16), vengeance (Isa 34:8; 61:2; 63:4; Jer 46:10), woe (Jer 17:16), wrath (Zeph 1:15), YHWH's anger (Zeph 2; 2, 3), YHWH's sacrifice (Zeph 1:8), your fall (Ezek 26:18; 32:10), your brother (Obad 12), your overthrow (Ezek 27:27). Plural construct chains also appear that require examination, including phrases that are translated "the days of . . . " punishment (Hos 9:7), retribution (Hos 9:7), the Baals (Hos 2:15), your slaughter (Jer 25:34), and my dealing with you (Ezek 22:14).

Two basic types of action can be noted, positive and negative, but individual texts display a wide variation regarding how the desired action will be achieved. Negative actions essentially involve judgment, but the judgment can be framed as total annihilation, as a purification that will leave a remnant, or as punishment designed to last until specific behavior changes. Positive actions can be portrayed as salvation, deliverance, or restoration.

The recipients of the divine intervention also vary significantly. Not only can the day of YHWH be directed toward YHWH's people or toward foreign nations, but distinctions within these general categories carry different connotations. Intervention may be directed toward Israel or Judah for different reasons, at different points. Foreign nations may also be cited for specific reasons.

The time of the intervention can be past or future. Past references tend to be used as illustrations to coerce some type of change on the part of the current addressee. Future references may imply the distant future or the very near future.

Reasons for divine intervention usually relate to some transgression which YHWH will not tolerate. However, the accusations involve cultic, ethical, or military activities. Sorting through these rationale can provide insights into the theological and literary agendas associated with various texts.

Potential literary connectors also demand reflection. The passage's form and context affect how one interprets a reference. Other indicators may provide clues about the literary horizon of a given passage. Does one text quote or allude to another? Does a text refer to the day of intervention by using idiomatic or formulaic language? Do the anticipated events "recur" in another text?

Evaluating these characteristics can help to determine how the "day of YHWH" functions within the Twelve, where the proliferation of יוֹם texts, when compared with other writings, suggests common transmission, or at least a shared orientation on the part of the tradents of these twelve writings. However, without additional validation, repetition of יהוה יוֹם, the phrase or the concept, does not necessarily provide evidence of literary cohesion for the corpus. The remainder of this paper will investigate texts in Hosea through Obadiah that refer to a day of divine intervention as a step toward clarifying the role of the day of YHWH in the Twelve. Time and space dictate that several texts function as focal points of the investigation because they contain multiple references to a "day" of divine intervention.[11]

---

[11]   Hos 2; 9; Joel 1-4; Amos 5:18-20; 8-9; and Obadiah. If space permitted, other passages meeting these criteria could be treated: Mic 4-5; 7:8-20; Zeph 1:2-2:3; Zeph 3; Zech 8; 12; 13; 14; Mal 3. In addition to texts containing multiple references to a day of divine

II. Hosea 2

Hosea 2 contains the second of three extended units which utilize a marriage metaphor to convey a message that moves from judgment to restoration. However, Hosea 2 depicts YHWH, not the prophet, as the husband. It becomes increasingly clear that the wife is the land (of Israel) personified as mother and wife. This role parallels the role played by the personified Lady Zion in other prophetic texts, but Hosea 2 reflects its context.[12] Both the judgment sayings and the salvific promises of Hosea 2 draw upon the names of the children mentioned in Hos 1:1-9.

Hosea 2 illustrates how the aforementioned qualities can help to characterize days of divine intervention. "Day" appears eight times in the chapter (2:2, 5, 15, 17 [2 times], 18, 20, 23), but only four times (2:2, 18, 20, 23) does יוֹם refer explicitly to a period of divine intervention. All four instances refer to the future. Three of these four texts explicitly anticipate divine intervention, while the fourth implies intervention by using an easily recognized allusion to the literary context. Hos 2:2 refers to a future time when Israel and Judah will be reunited under one king, hence a time of political restoration. This verse contains no *explicit* reference to divine intervention, but its concluding statement calls the time the "day of Jezreel." This unique phrase alludes to the interpretation of the name of the first son in Hos 1:5: "And it will happen *on that day* that *I* will break the bow of Israel in the valley of *Jezreel*." Hos 1:5 thus interprets the name Jezreel as anticipating a day of divine judgment against Israel, while Hos 2:2 alludes to that action as the "day of Jezreel," but reinterprets the action as a promise of political restoration when Israel and Judah will be united under a single king.

---

intervention, isolated references to a day of divine intervention also occur (e.g., Mic 2:4, Hab 3:17; Zech 2:15, etc). A complete study would need to evaluate these texts as well.

12   Several prophetic texts express Jerusalem's relationship to YHWH by personifying Lady Zion (e.g., Isa 60; Jer 30:12-17; Ezek 22; Mic 7:8-13; Zeph 3:14-19). Increasingly, the role of Lady Zion as the consort of YHWH and the mother of the children of Jerusalem has come into focus. For the background of this concept, see the writings of Aloysius Fitzgerald, "The Mythological Background for the Presentation of Jerusalem as a Queen and False Worship as Adultery in the OT," *CBQ* 34 (1972) 403-416; Mark E. Biddle, "The Figure of Lady Jerusalem: Identification, Deification and Personification of Cities in the Ancient Near East," in *The Biblical Canon in Comparative Perspective* (eds. B. Batto and others; Scripture in Context 4; Lewiston, NY: Mellen Press, 1991), 173-194; Julie Galambush, *Jerusalem in the Book of Ezekiel: The City as Yahweh's Wife*, SBLDS 130 (Atlanta: Scholars Press, 1992); John J. Schmitt, "The Motherhood of God and Zion as Mother." *RB* 92 (1985) 557-569.

Hos 2:18, 20, and 23 all refer to future intervention using the formula "on that day." Hos 2:18-19 anticipate a restoration of the relationship between YHWH and Israel "on that day." The restoration results from YHWH's intervention: "For *I* will remove the names of the Baals from her mouth so that they will no longer be mentioned by their names." This reference reflects its context, essentially contrasting the future restoration "on that day" with the past "days of the Baals" in 2:15.

Hos 2:20 uses the ביום ההוא formula to introduce a short promise of a restored relationship. The verse draws upon creation language (cf. Gen 1:30) to reverse the judgment pronounced in Hos 2:14. In the larger context, this creation imagery appears again in Hos 4:3; 7:12; and Zeph 1:2-3, within pronouncements of judgment against Ephraim and Judah respectively. In 2:20, YHWH restores the relationship between mother Israel and the animal realm, but YHWH serves as the mediator of the covenant, not one of the covenant partners.

Hos 2:23 introduces a promise (2:23-25) that has intra-textual connections and provides an added thematic dimension. YHWH's response will restore the course of nature for Israel: "It will happen *on that day* that I will respond to the heavens and they will respond to the earth, and the earth will respond to the grain, the new wine, and the oil, and they will respond to Jezreel" (Hos 2:23-24). As with the other promises, "that day" reverses judgments pronounced in the extended context. This promise restores elements from nature which YHWH had removed earlier in the chapter (2:10-11). The concluding reference to Jezreel in 2:24b not only refers back to the name of the first son, it also introduces word plays in 2:25 which reverse the judgment symbolized in the names of all three children: "I will sow (זרע) her for myself in the land, and I will have compassion (רחם) on her who had not obtained compassion (לא־רחמה), and I will say to those who were not my people (לא־עמי), you are my people." This promise also serves as the source text for a promise in Joel 2:19, following predictions of the day of YHWH against Zion.

In summary, references to a day of divine intervention in this chapter are contextually bound to Hosea as seen by their awareness of the names of the children and their reversal of earlier pronouncements of judgment. Hos 2:23 is cited in Joel 2:19. These texts expand restoration promises to the political, religious, and natural realms.

III. Hosea 9

Hosea 9 contains five references to יום (9:5 [2 times], 9:7 [2 times], 9:9), but only three refer to days of divine intervention, albeit to different events.

Hos 9:7 refers to the immediate future as "the days of punishment" (יְמֵי הַפְּקֻדָּה) and "the days of retribution (יְמֵי הַשִּׁלֻּם) for Ephraim. Both terms appear in similar forms in other prophetic literature.[13] The third term (the days of Gibeah) alludes to intervention in the distant past as narrated in Judges 18-21.[14] Hos 9:9 announces judgment upon Ephraim (cf. 9:3) for its "iniquity" like the "days of Gibeah." Hos 10:9 uses this same phrase to mark the length of time that the people of Israel had sinned while anticipating a future battle when YHWH will cause the nations to attack. Hos 9:6-8 refers to Ephraim, Israel, Samaria, and Bethel (*Aven*), indicating that this passage concerns the Northern Kingdom. Both the related passage in 10:9 and the allusion to Judges imply that the punishment will come in the form of an enemy attack, with the presupposition that YHWH will instigate the enemy to attack (cf. especially 10:10).

Hos 9:7-9 thus anticipates a period in the near future when YHWH will intervene for judgment against Israel. Hos 9:9 draws upon knowledge of traditions from Judges 19-21 (cf. especially 20:18-28) to affirm both the extent of Israel's guilt and YHWH's ability to accomplish the judgment. Hos 9:7-9 is linked to another text (Hos 10:9-10) by the unusual phrase "days of Gibeah" as well as the reaffirmation of YHWH's decision to chastise Israel by sending other nations against Israel (the Northern Kingdom) to punish it for its failure to worship YHWH properly. The remaining phrases in 9:7, "days of punishment" and "days of retribution," do not find direct citations elsewhere in the Book of the Twelve, although very similar phrases occur in Isaiah and Jeremiah. The presence of the word pair punishment (פְּקֻדָּה) and retribution/recompense (שִׁלֻּם) appear in reverse order in Mic 7:3-4 in a judgment oracle against the people of Jerusalem.[15] Amos 3:14 uses a similar phrase "on the day I punish Israel" to refer to YHWH's

---

[13] Isa 10:3 uses the singular form "day of punishment" to refer to an attack commissioned by YHWH from which there is no escape. Jeremiah uses the phrases the "time of their punishment" (10:15; 48:44; 50:27; 51:18) and the "year of their punishment" (11:23; 23:12) to refer to YHWH's intervention against Judah and/or foreign nations. Isa 34:8 uses the term "year of retributions" in synonymous parallelism with "day of vengeance."

[14] The reference alludes to the account of the punishment of Gibeah and the sons of Benjamin in Judg 19-21 by the sons of Israel following the rape of the Levite's concubine. Note especially the successive consultations of YHWH over three *days* in Judg 20:18, 23, 26-28. See Hans Walter Wolff, *Hosea* (Hermeneia; Philadelphia: Fortress, 1965) 158; Jörg Jeremias, *Der Prophet Hosea* (ATD 24/1; Göttingen: Vandenhoeck & Ruprecht, 1983) 118; Wilhelm Rudolph, *Hosea* (*KAT* 13/1; Gütersloh: Gerd Mohn, 1975) 179-180.

[15] Mic 7:3-4 use the two terms in close proximity. Mic 7:3 uses the term שִׁלֻּם (meaning recompense in the sense of bribery) as an accusation and "your *punishment* (פְּקֻדָּתְךָ) will come on a day of your posting a watchman" (cf. Hab 2:1?).

impending judgment on Israel. Amos 3:14 may represent one of several examples of knowledge of the message of Hosea appearing in Amos.[16] Hos 9:7-9 can function meaningfully within a coherent reading of the Twelve, but does not provide direct evidence that it plays a role in shaping the corpus literarily. This finding differs from the more direct citation of Hos 2:22 by Joel 2:19.

IV. Joel

Joel contains eleven םוי texts that refer specifically to divine intervention and use a significant variety of phrases: the day (1:15), the day of YHWH (1:15; 2:1, 11; 3:4; 4:14), day of darkness and gloom (2:2), day of clouds and thick darkness (2:2), in those days (3:2, 4:1), and on that day (4:18). More significant than the terms themselves, the type of action anticipated in these contexts reflects the movement of Joel from presumed judgment to a call for repentance, to promised restoration, to judgment on the nations who oppressed Judah and Jerusalem. This observation suggests that the meaning of similar terminology changes based upon the literary intention of the immediate and extended context (for Joel and the Twelve). The intended recipients of the day of divine intervention also play a significant role in the changing terminology within Joel.

Joel 1 opens with an extended communal call to repentance. Various groups among the inhabitants are singled out and addressed directly (cf. 1:2, 5, 11, 13). These calls *presume* the guilt of these people and describe how the devastation of the land affects each group.[17] The first explicit mention of the day of YHWH comes in 1:15, which warns that a military attack on Jerusalem and Judah will follow the devastation of the land. Subsequent texts in Joel explicate the form of that judgment, especially 2:1-11, which describes the day of YHWH as the attack of an army of unprecedented strength. This army is depicted using the extended metaphorical imagery of a locust plague, but the recipients of the attack are people of the city, not the crops. The description also carries cosmic overtones (2:10-11).

This expectation that the devastation of nature will be followed by a divinely initiated military attack corresponds to the manifestation of divine intervention in the two םוי texts from Hosea. Hosea 2 anticipates YHWH's

---

[16]   The use of the writing of Hosea in Amos occurs in virtually every level of the transmission of Amos. See Jörg Jeremias, "Die Anfänge des Dodekapropheton: Hosea und Amos," *VTSup* 61 (Leiden: Brill, 1995) 87-106; also in *Hosea und Amos*, (FAT 13; Tübingen: Mohr, 1996), 34-54.

[17]   For a treatment of how Joel 1 presumes the accusations of guilt from Hosea, see my treatment of the context in James D. Nogalski, *Redactional Processes in the Book of the Twelve* (BZAW 218; Berlin: de Gruyter, 1993), 17-18.

removal of resources from Israel that can lead to a time of restoration while Hos 9:7-9 predicts a military attack against the Northern Kingdom by an army of nations whom YHWH assembles. Joel 1-2 mirrors the essential thematic movement of the day of divine intervention in Hosea with one exception. The recipients in Joel are the people of Judah and Jerusalem, not the Northern Kingdom. Could the compilation of Joel reflect its literary context? Joel's quotations of Hos 2:23 (Joel 2:19), Amos 1:2, and 9:14 (Joel 4:16, 18) point in that direction. Could the thematic similarity of the day of YHWH merely result from a limited number of ways that divine judgment was portrayed in these ancient texts? Perhaps, but the multiplicity of the links between Joel and its context in the Twelve must be taken into account. When one sees the extent of thematic development, the dovetailing of genres, the use of catchword connections, and direct citations in Joel, the probability of Joel's cognizance of its *literary* context between Hosea and Amos becomes more plausible than the presumption of coincidence piled upon coincidence.[18]

Joel uses several terms to announce days of divine intervention, a remarkable percentage of which appear elsewhere in the Twelve.[19] These parallels function as markers for Joel's paradigm of history that transcends, but does not replace, the chronological shape of the Twelve. This paradigm provides an eschatological perspective (reinforced by periodic notes to the reader of the Twelve) that Joel's predictions have occurred or are in the process of unfolding. The utilization of Joel imagery in the Twelve occurs with several motifs, not just the day of YHWH.[20]

The character of the days of divine intervention in Joel changes after 2:11, in keeping with this writing's literary movement. The remaining "day" texts promise intervention on Judah's behalf. These promises include

---

[18] The distance between the two ideas in the day of divine intervention texts of Hosea 2 and 9:7-9, when compared with the interweaving of the ideas in Joel argues that Joel is combining ideas already present in Hosea. See also James D. Nogalski, "Intertextuality and the Twelve," in *Forming Prophetic Literature: Essays on Isaiah and the Twelve in Honor of John D.W. Watts* (ed. James W. Watts and Paul R. House; JSOTSup 235; Sheffield: Sheffield Academic Press, 1996), 102-24.

[19] Ten of the eleven references appear in citations, close parallels, and verbal parallels elsewhere in the Twelve. Compare the following parallels: Joel 1:15 // Zeph 1:14; Joel 2:1 // Hos 9:7 (verbal combination); Joel 2:2 // Zeph 1:15; Joel 2:11 // Mal 3:23; Joel 3:4 // 2:10b and Mal 3:23; Joel 4:1 // Zeph 3:20; Joel 4:14 // Joel 1:15 and Zeph 1:14; Joel 4:18 // Amos 9:13. Only Joel 3:2 has no close parallel elsewhere in the Twelve. See the chart and my discussion of these parallels in "Joel as a Literary Anchor to the Book of the Twelve," in *Reading and Hearing the Book of the Twelve* (ed. James D. Nogalski and Marvin A. Sweeney; SBLSymS 15; Atlanta: Society of Biblical Literature, 2000), 106.

[20] See Nogalski, "Joel as Literary Anchor for the Book of the Twelve," 91-109.

the outpouring of YHWH's spirit, deliverance on the day of universal judgment, and judgment of the nations. All of these texts presume this positive intervention will come *if and when* the call to repentance in 1:2-2:17 is accepted (although Joel never states whether that repentance occurs). Joel 3:2 (with 3:1) promises the universal outpouring of YHWH's spirit at a point in the distant future. The outpouring of YHWH's spirit is chronologically more vague (cf. "afterward" in 3:1 and "in those days" in 3:2). The divine intervention is directed toward "all flesh," sons and daughters, the youth, the elderly, and even the slaves. No direct verbal connections tie this text to others within the Twelve, though thematic similarities to other texts exist. Zech 8:23 and Mal 1:11-14 offer similar positive orientations toward people beyond the borders, as does the book of Jonah, but one cannot establish these connections via the day of divine intervention.

The promissory nature of that time of divine intervention takes an ominous twist in Joel 3:3-5 which anticipates a "great and terrible day of YHWH." The reference to the "great and terrible day of YHWH" in 3:4 occurs in only one other place, at the conclusion of the Twelve, in Mal 3:23.[21] In addition, similar wording occurs in Zeph 1:14-15 which contains several terms from Joel concerning the imminent destruction of Judah and Jerusalem on the great day of YHWH.[22] Like Joel 2:1-11, the day of YHWH anticipated in 3:4 draws upon cosmic images, even quoting 2:10b. One may extrapolate the recipients of judgment as those *not* calling on YHWH's name, since 3:5 states that those who call on YHWH's name will be saved in a verse that appears to cite Obad 17.

Joel 4:1 again uses the phrase "in those days," formally linking it with 3:1-5. The divine intervention of 4:1-21 continues the dual focus of the restoration of Judah and Jerusalem and the punishment of the recalcitrant nations. The chronological formula and the promise in Joel 4:1 are cited in Zeph 3:19-20, the last verses which separate the "preexilic" portion of the Twelve from the postexilic section. Zeph 3:19-20 promises restoration to Judah and judgment upon the nations who took advantage of Judah by taking up the language of Mic 4:6-7 and Joel 4:1 respectively. Immediately thereafter, the Twelve presumes that YHWH's people are back in the land after the exile. In the larger context of the Twelve, Zeph 3:19-20 implies that Joel's promises of restoration and recompense were not immediately fulfilled. When one reads Joel as an eighth century prophetic voice, based on its context in the Twelve not the date of its composition, then the chrono-

---

21 The word pair "great and terrible" occurs in eight other contexts, but refers to the wilderness (Deut 1:19; 8:15), God (Deut 7:21; Dan 9:4; Neh 1:5; 4:8), God's name (Ps 99:3), or God's actions (Deut 10:21).

22 Zeph 1:2-2:3 demonstrates the same blending of images that combine a day of YHWH against Judah and Jerusalem on the one hand, and against all creation on the other.

logical markers of Joel 3:1, 2, 4; and 4:1 do not indicate the immediate repentance of the people following Joel 2:17. In other words, while an isolated reading of Joel often assumes that the people repent following 2:17,
the Twelve does not narrate the repentance of YHWH's people prior to the
generation of Haggai and Zechariah.[23]

Joel 4:14 mentions the day of YHWH as a day of judgment against the
nations. It functions within a larger unit (4:9-17) that promises divine intervention. Joel 4:14-16 present a series of quotations which adapt judgment
pronouncements against Judah into pronouncements against the nations.
Joel 4:14 repeats the threat of the imminent day of YHWH from Joel 1:15
except Joel 4:14 portrays the nearness of the day of YHWH against the nations, not Judah. Joel 4:15 cites 2:10 with a similar change, and Joel 4:16a
quotes Amos 1:2 thereby linking the upcoming oracles against the nations
in Amos with the eschatological emphasis of Joel.[24] These quotes culminate
in an explanation (4:17) that this divine intervention will demonstrate
YHWH's beneficence toward Zion and Jerusalem.

Joel 4:18 contains the final specific reference to a day of divine intervention in Joel. It links Joel with the end of Amos by the citation of Amos
9:13. This citation introduces the final literary unit of Joel, a unit which
reverses the devastation of Joel 1-2 by using catchwords to previously mentioned elements. The formula "on that day" places the expected time frame
in conjunction with the promised judgment of the nations in the remainder
of the chapter.

The images of days of divine intervention in Joel are diverse yet interwoven with the immediate and extended contexts. Joel's use of self-quotes
helps move the reader from judgment against Judah to potential restoration
and then to judgment against the nations. However, these references to days
of divine intervention also provide threads of cohesion within the Twelve.
By means of thematic combinations and direct citations, the days of divine
intervention present a complex picture that picks up where Hosea leaves off
and moves to Amos. References back to Joel's language associated with
divine intervention also play a significant role in the Twelve at key points
(cf. especially Zeph 1:14-15; 3:19-20; and Mal 3:23).

---

[23]   Not until Zech 1:2-6 does a prophetic text in the Twelve clearly indicate that the peo-
       ple repent. The superscription in Zech 1:1 precedes the date of the last messages in
       Haggai (see Hag 2:10, 20). Elsewhere only the Ninevites in Jonah repent.
[24]   See Aaron Schart, *Die Entstehung des Zwölfprophetenbuch* (BZAW 260; Berlin: de
       Gruyter, 1998), 262-265.

V. Amos

Amos 5:18-20, 8:4-14, and 9:11-15 anticipate days of divine intervention with more than a single reference to the day. Amos 5:18-20 is often cited as the earliest text in the Hebrew Bible specifically using יום יהוה. The three uses of this phrase polemically contrast two different perceptions of the day of YHWH. Through a series of rhetorical questions, the voice of the prophet tells those who anticipate a day of divine intervention on their behalf that they are mistaken. The day of YHWH will bring darkness (חשך) and gloom (אפל) rather than light (אור) and brightness (נגה). These verses thus make two affirmations about the day of YHWH: (1) it will come as a day of judgment against the Northern Kingdom and (2) when the day comes, escape will be impossible.

Amos 5:18-20 existed within Amos long before Joel's composition, but at least two indicators suggest they should be read with Joel by the reader of the Twelve. Joel 4 (with its expectation of a day of divine judgment against the nations) contains quotations that link that chapter to the beginning and end of Amos. To this extent, one can say that Joel anticipates and interprets Amos literarily, though Joel's composition is much later than the core of the Amos material. Moreover, Joel 2:2 links to Amos 5:18-20 via the explicit reference to the day of YHWH as a day of darkness (חשך) and gloom (פלה). In fact, Amos 5:18-20 appears as the second of three texts in the Twelve which use this phrase.[25]

For the reader of the Twelve, the link between Amos 5:18-20 and Joel 2:2 provides evidence of deliberate association, but for what purpose? Does anything in the Amos context account for Joel's citation apart from the reference to the day of YHWH? One should not miss three intriguing associations. First, in Amos 5:16-17, the unit immediately preceding Amos 5:18-20, one finds several thematic and verbal links with the mourning of the farmers (cf. Joel 1:10-11), and the wailing "in all the streets" and "in all the vineyards" (cf. Joel 1:12; 2:12). Second, in the context preceding Amos 5:18-20, the chapter begins with the pronouncement of a dirge following a divine report of Israel's repeated refusals to return to YHWH using the refrain "yet you did not return to me," also used in Joel 2:12 as an admonition, "yet even now, return to me." Third, the context of Amos relates the dirge (5:1) and the proclamation of the imminence of the day of YHWH (5:18-20) to the destruction of the House of Israel with particular reference to Bethel and Gilgal (5:5).

---

[25] See Zeph 1:15. See also the discussion in Schart, *Entstehung*, 220-222.

When reading Hosea, Joel, and Amos sequentially, an interesting phenomenon occurs. Hosea ends with an open call to repentance to the Northern Kingdom, and Joel begins with a call to repentance for Judah and Jerusalem before the arrival of the day of YHWH. The day of YHWH in Amos 5:18-20 is again directed toward the Northern Kingdom, but it presumes the day of judgment will result from *Israel's* refusal to return to YHWH. By contrast, Zion receives a temporary reprieve (cf. Mic 7:8-20) before the day of YHWH pronouncement in Zeph 1:14-15 shows that Jerusalem will suffer the same fate on the day of YHWH just as Joel 2:2 had warned.

Amos 8 uses יום six times in the context of a day of divine intervention (8:3, 9 [2 times], 10, 11, 13). Amos 8:3 contains the formula "on that day," but it refers to a day of judgment rather than a promise. The phrase in 8:3 refers to the day of judgment which will bring an end to Israel. It appears within the explanation of the fourth vision. The verse is thus closely tied to its immediate context.

Amos 8:9-10 contains three references to יום. Amos 8:9-10 stands out as a small subunit by the introductory formula and the change of speaker to divine first person speech. While this speaker continues in 8:11-14, those verses signal a new paragraph by another introductory formula in 8:11. Amos 8:9 uses ביום ההוא as an introductory formula to refer to a day of divine intervention for judgment upon Israel. Day also appears in reference to YHWH's divine intervention that will make the sun grow dark in the middle of the day. Amos 8:10 refers to this coming day of judgment as a "day of bitterness," a phrase which has its closest parallel in Zeph 1:14, a text which also played a role in the connection between Amos 5:18-20 and Joel.[26] Three things stand out about these verses. First, 8:9 uses ביום ההוא to introduce motifs already explicated within Amos 5:16-17, 18-20, 21-23. The darkening of the day sounds very much like 5:18, 20, and the festivals/songs turned to mourning in 8:10 recalls 5:21-23. Second, this association confirms a presumption noted at the beginning of this paper that the phrase "on that day" *can be* conceptually related to the concept of the day of YHWH. Third, the verbal links in this verse point to the larger context of Amos and to a lesser extent the (developing) Book of the Twelve. Amos 8:9-10 refers to the day of YHWH context of Amos five, but it also contains echoes of language from Hosea, Micah, and Zephaniah.[27] However, these images cannot be unambiguously labeled as direct citations.

---

[26] Zeph 1:14-18 contains several terms for the day of YHWH from elsewhere in the Twelve.

[27] In addition to the day of bitterness connection to Zeph 1:14, the "mourning for an only son" sounds much like YHWH's attitude toward Ephraim in Hos 11, although the term

Amos 8:11-12, 13-14 contains two additional formulas introducing a day of divine intervention. In 8:11, "Behold, the days are coming" offers a new introduction, but the images used in these verses do not explicitly link with the motifs of Amos 5 or to the broader context of the Twelve. Amos 8:11 refers to a famine in the *coming days*, but it is YHWH's word, not agricultural elements, that is lacking. Amos 8:13 contains another ביום ההוא formula which formally looks back to the time of the famine mentioned in 8:11. This verse does use images that appear in Amos 5. The verse refers to the *virgins* (בתולות) and the young men (הבחורים) who will faint from thirst. It leads to condemnation of those who swear by the guilt of Samaria . . . who will fall and not rise again." Similarly, Amos 5:2 refers to "the Virgin Israel (בתולת ישראל) who has fallen and will not rise."

In summary, the references to a day(s) of divine intervention in Amos 8 show a strong awareness of texts from Amos 5. This link is significant since it correlates day of YHWH statements with ביום ההוא formulas. The "day" references in Amos 8 also contain images from the larger context of the Twelve, with links to Joel 2 and Zeph 1:14-15 being the strongest. As with the references to the day of YHWH in Amos 5, these verses also anticipate judgment upon the Northern Kingdom.

Amos 9:11-15 uses יום twice to refer directly to divine intervention. Amos 9:11 contains two references to "day." One uses ביום ההוא to refer to YHWH's future restoration, and one compares this future day to the ideal "days of old." In its current form, this promise continues through 9:12 and vows to restore the kingdom under a single ruler. The promise in 9:11 links thematically with other royal restoration texts (e.g. Hos 2:2), although the link does not have strong verbal connections, making the question of deliberate association difficult. The image of restoration evoked by this promise functions on multiple levels. First, the promise presumes the destruction of Jerusalem, not just the split of the Northern and Southern Kingdoms, as can be seen from the language of rebuilding the city walls.[28] Since the setting of Amos is placed in the eighth century by the book's superscription, the promise of 9:11ff serves a metahistorical function.[29] Second, the anticipated restoration of the kingdom goes beyond the reunification of the two king-

---

"only son" does not appear there. The term "baldness" appears only in Amos 8:10 and Mic 1:16 within the Book of the Twelve.

[28] See discussion in James D. Nogalski, "The Problematic Suffixes of Amos 9:11," *VT* 43 (1993): 411-418; and *Literary Precursors to the Book of the Twelve*, (BZAW 217; Berlin: de Gruyter, 1993), 105-8.

[29] On the concept of metahistory, see Odil Hannes Steck, *Prophetenbücher und ihr theologisches Zeugnis* (Tübingen: Mohr, 1996) 50-54 (English translation: *The Prophetic Books and their Theological Witness* [St. Louis: Chalice Press, 2000], 49-52).

doms since 9:12a also anticipates the retaking of "the remnant of Edom and all the nations who are called by my name." Amos 9:12 summarizes the message of Obadiah by announcing Edom's destruction (Obad 1-15) and the restoration of the Davidic kingdom by the combined house of Jacob and house of Joseph (Obad 18) as it (re)possesses Edom and the surrounding territory (Obad 19-21).[30] Again, ביום ההוא and יום יהוה are linked.

Amos 9:13 contains a new introductory formula, "behold the days are coming," followed by a promise of astounding fertility (9:13) and restoration of the cities and crops (9:14-15). Several indicators point to editorial expansion of this short unit. The promise of continual agricultural abundance makes the promise of normalcy seem anti-climactic. Also, the explicit citation of Joel 4:18 in Amos 9:13b creates the suspicion that this reference has been added to establish the concluding link to Joel in Amos. By contrast, the promise of 9:14-15 presumes the devastation of the land and its cities will be restored with the return of "my people," the rebuilding of the cities, and a return to the land's ideal fertile state. The character of the divine intervention implied in these verses does not have the aggressive political overtones of 9:11-12. Apart from the direct link to Joel, the underlying promises in the two parts also have thematic links with the promises of Hos 2:1-25 where one finds the names of Hosea's children used to combine promises of political reunification (2:2), devastation (2:14), exile to the wilderness (2:16), and restoration of the relationship that leads to normal agricultural patterns for "my people" (2:23-25).

The promises of divine intervention in Amos 9:11-15 connect thematically to the promises of Hos 2:2-25, but they also contain verbal links backward to Joel and forward to Obadiah. This multiplicity of connections gives Amos 9:11-15 the feel of a pastiche, combining several images of what will happen once YHWH intervenes on the people's behalf. This passage suggests that the day of divine intervention functioned as a stack pole for creating meaning across the multi-volume corpus as it developed.

VI. Obadiah

The Hebrew word יום appears 12 times in Obadiah, and all twelve relate to a day of divine intervention. When one analyzes the events of those various days, one notes that the actual intervention combines more than one image. The terms begin with ביום ההוא (Obad 8) and end with a specific refer-

---

30   This association, when noted, was explained by the assumption that two completed works were placed side by side. Recent work suggests this association was created redactionally by inserting part of this verse. See Nogalski, *Literary Precursors*, 217, 115-116, and Schart, *Entstehung*, 271-272.

ence to the day of YHWH (Obad 15) on all the nations. The ביום ההוא
formula introduces a pronouncement of a divinely guided destruction of the
wise and the mighty (Obad 9) on the mountain of Edom.

In the remaining instances, ten idiomatic expressions refer to the day of
Jerusalem's destruction, accusations about Obadiah's role in that destruction, and the resulting punishment of Edom on the day of YHWH.[31] These
idiomatic expressions can be noted in Obad 10-15, which address Edom
directly:

> [10]For the violence (done to) your brother Jacob, you will be covered with shame.
>   And you will be cut off forever.
> [11]*On the day* you stood far off,
>   *On the day* when strangers captured his wealth,
>   And foreigners entered his gates and cast lots over Jerusalem,
>   Moreover, you were like one of them.
> [12]Do not look *on the day* of your brother, *on the day* of his calamity.
>   Do not rejoice about the sons of Judah *on the day* of their destruction.
>   And do not boast *on the day* of distress.
> [13]Do not enter into the gate of my people *on the day* of their disaster.
>   Do not look, especially you, on his wickedness *on the day* of his disaster.
>   Do not loot his wealth *on the day* of his disaster.
> [14]And do not stand in the crossroad to cut off his fugitives.
>   And do not deliver up his survivors *on the day* of distress,
> [15]because the *day of YHWH* is near on account of all the nations.
>   Just as you have done it will be done to you.
>   Your recompense will return upon your own head.

Unlike Obad 8, the יום sayings in 11-15 allude to the destruction of Jerusalem as the day of divine intervention while warning Edom not to participate
in Judah's punishment lest the same fate befall Edom on the day of YHWH
for all nations. These verses convey this message using linguistic forms that
display a bifurcated sense of time. On the one hand, the accusations against
Edom presume knowledge about Edom's role in Jerusalem's destruction.
On the other hand, most of the יום sayings use formulations which presume
those events have not yet taken place. Obad 12-14 uses the syntax of negative commands (אל + imperfect), whose chronological perspective assumes
they are issued prior to an event. However, Obad 11 and 15 demonstrate
knowledge that Edom *has already* done what vv. 12-14 say not to do. This
dichotomy is overcome when one understands the metahistorical perspective of Obadiah. Like Joel, Obadiah demonstrates awareness of its literary

---

[31]   For a discussion of יום יהוה in Obadiah, see S. D. Snyman, "Yom (YHWH) in the
        Book of Obadiah," in *Goldene Äpfel in silbernen Schalen* (BEATAJ 20; Frankfurt:
        Peter Lang, 1992) 81-91.

location when it was compiled. Obadiah's position among the eighth century prophets in the Twelve functions as a warning that justifies YHWH's punishment of Edom for indifference and/or its active participation in Jerusalem's destruction.[32] The Jacob/Esau language of Obadiah implies Edom should have known better because of its lengthy relationship with YHWH's people. From the perspective of the Twelve, Edom receives a warning which paralleled the warning given to the Northern Kingdom.[33]

The יום sayings in Obadiah contain verbal and thematic ties to other Edom texts in the Latter Prophets, although it can be difficult to classify every link as idiom, parallel, allusion, or citation. One example of these idiomatic expressions illustrates the difficulty. The phrase "day of distress" occurs in Obad 12 and 14. This phrase occurs some 15 times in the Hebrew Bible.[34] The phrase appears almost as often in the Writings (6 times) as in the Prophets (8 times), even though the phrase occurs more often in the Twelve (5 times) than any other book.[35] The phrase could thus be a common idiom that has no definable role when reading the Twelve. However, it is striking that the phrase appears in texts with ties to the broader context of the Twelve and to the punishment of foreign nations in retaliation for their role in threatening Jerusalem.

This contextual connection provides a certain cohesiveness to the recurring phrase as one reads the Twelve. However, despite the verbal similarity, one cannot say that the phrase was always originally used with the Twelve in mind. In Nah 1:7 the phrase already existed in the acrostic poem that was modified and incorporated into Nahum with an eye toward the context of the developing multi-volume corpus.[36] It was thus not written for the Twelve, but the phrase could have served a role in selecting the theophanic hymn to be placed at the start of Nahum. *In that context*, Nah 1:7 functions

---

[32] See Nogalski, *Redactional Processes*, 218, 89-92.

[33] See my discussion of the parallel structure of Obadiah and Amos 9 in Nogalski, *Redactional Processes*, 61-68; and "Jeremiah and the Twelve: Intertextual Observations and Postulations," a paper presented to the Society of Biblical Literature (1998).

[34] Gen 35:3; 2 Kgs 19:3 = Isa 37:3; Jer 16:19; Obad 12, 14; Nah 1:7; Hab 3:16; Zeph 1:15; Pss 20:2; 50:15; 77:3; 86:7; Prov 24:10; 25:19.

[35] In comparison, the phrase appears does not appear in Ezekiel and appears only once in Jeremiah (16:19). The only time it appears in Isaiah (37:3), it appears in the parallel to the Hezekiah story from 2 Kgs 19:3.

[36] Exactly when these hymns were incorporated into Nahum and Habakkuk is a matter of some debate. I have argued that they entered with the Joel-Related Layer (see *Redactional Processes*, 218) while Schart (*Entstehung*, 234-251), and Erich Bosshard-Nepustil (*Rezeptionen von Jesaia 1-39 im Zwölfprophetenbuch: Untersuchungen zur literarischen Verbindung von Prophetenbüchern in babylonischer und persischer Zeit* [Göttingen: Vandenhoeck & Ruprecht, 1997] 269-432) raise significant arguments that (portions of) Nahum and Habakkuk entered the developing corpus prior to Joel.

as the threat of a day of divinely delivered distress upon Assyria because they have threatened Judah. Similarly, the theophanic hymn in Hab 3:16 refers to the day of distress against Babylon *after* they attack Jerusalem.[37] However, in both instances, one would not *hear* these verses in the same way if these hymns appeared in Psalms (cf. Pss 20:2; 50:15; 77:3; 86:7) or Proverbs (24:10; 25:19). The odds are higher, however, that Obad 12, 14, and Zeph 1:15 were written specifically for a larger, developing corpus. In both contexts one finds the dual association of a threat to Jerusalem followed by a day of divine judgment against the nations. The fact that Zeph 1:14-18 contains links to Joel, Amos, and Obadiah makes it likely that these verses (along with other parts of Zeph 1:1-2:3) functioned as a collecting point for phrases related to the coming day of YHWH's intervention.

The greatest difference in these "day of distress" texts comes in the identity of the nation who threatens Jerusalem and who will subsequently be judged. Yet, even this difference makes sense when viewed within the metahistorical framework of the Twelve. The pronouncements against Edom, Assyria, and Babylon depend upon their location in the Twelve. Nahum and Habakkuk function within the chronological framework of the Twelve to anticipate YHWH's use of Assyria and Babylon to confront the people of Judah, while at the same time affirming that YHWH will remove these powers from the scene because they overstep the role which YHWH sent them to perform. Obadiah transcends the chronological framework by virtue of its location among the eighth-century prophets, but its composition deliberately creates structural and thematic parallels to Amos 9, thereby comparing the ultimate fate of Edom with Israel (the Northern Kingdom) while still anticipating Jerusalem's punishment. The complexity of the "day of distress" applies to other phrases as well.

The day of YHWH saying in Obad 15 functions similarly. This verse transitions to a day of divine intervention on the nations (especially those of the Davidic Kingdom) that will play out *after* Edom has been judged (Obad 18) and possessed (Obad 19) by the "house of Jacob" and the "house of Joseph." The careful reader of the Twelve recognizes that the expression "the day of YHWH is near" has occurred in Joel. It reappears again in Zeph 1:7, 14.[38] Two observations raise questions about the function of the day of YHWH sayings in the Twelve. First, the particular form of "near" (קָרוֹב)

---

[37]   The prophetic first person response in Hab 3:16-19 to the theophanic description of 3:3-15 does not presume that the threat of the day of distress has been removed, only that God will provide strength and salvation. The context of the hymn in Habakkuk virtually demands that the reader should associate Babylon with the attacking enemy.

[38]   The same formulation כִּי קָרוֹב יוֹם יהוה appears in 1:15; 4:14. See also the closely related formulation in 2:1.

appears only in conjunction with day of YHWH texts (Joel 1:15; 2:1; 4:14; Obad 15; Zeph 1:7, 14 [twice]).[39] Second, this phrase does not appear in any of the writings that function as "postexilic" writings in the Twelve. In other words, this phrase does not appear in Haggai, Zechariah, or Malachi.[40]

The identity of those whom YHWH will use to destroy Edom in Obad 18 should not be overlooked. The combination of the house of Jacob and the house of Joseph denotes a reunified kingdom. The phrase "house of Joseph" is particularly instructive. It appears 17 times in the Hebrew Bible, but only three times in the Latter Prophets, and never in the Writings.[41] The Former Prophets identify the term with the territory of Ephraim and Manasseh (see Josh 17:17, 2 Kgs 11:28). All three uses of the term in the Latter Prophets appear in the Twelve. Amos 5:6 uses the same metaphor of the consuming fire to pronounce judgment upon the house of Joseph that Obad 18 uses to depict judgment upon Edom. The house of Jacob appears 21 times, most frequently in the Isaiah corpus (9 times) and in the Twelve (6 times).[42] In Isaiah and Micah the phrase refers to Judah, which makes the most sense in Obad 17-18 because of the combination of the house of Jacob/Joseph. The term appears twice in Amos with 3:3 referring to the Northern Kingdom as the house of Jacob while 9:8 refers to the remnant of the kingdom as the house of Jacob. The combination of these two entities appears only in Obad 18, and connotes restoration that reflects the reunification of the Davidic kingdom.

Obadiah's role in the literary context of the Twelve and the prophetic corpus should be noted. First, Obadiah was compiled for its position in the Twelve. Its careful structural, thematic, and verbal imitation of Amos 9 make this perspective plausible (and in my mind probable).[43] Second, Obadiah's threefold movement of the day of divine intervention also plays a role in Malachi, the final writing in the Twelve. Obadiah anticipates a day of judgment on Jerusalem that will lead to a day of judgment on Edom as the first of the surrounding nations to be judged on the Day of YHWH against the nations. In the Twelve, Edom receives periodic mention in Joel

---

[39]   Compare the fact that this phrase appears elsewhere only three times in the Latter Prophets (Isa 13:6; Ezek 7:7; 30:3), while the adjective קָרוֹב appears some 72 times in the Hebrew Bible.

[40]   Those writings tend to portray a day of divine intervention differently, in a manner that suggests awareness of their postexilic function in the Twelve, but that is the subject of another paper.

[41]   Gen 39:22; 43:17; 43:18, 19, 24; 44:14; 50:8; Josh 17:17; 18:5; Judg 1:22, 23, 35; 2 Sam 19:21; 1 Kgs 11:28; Amos 5:6; Obad 18; Zech 10:6.

[42]   Gen 46:27; Exod 19:3; Isaiah 2:5, 6; 8:17; 10:20; 14:1; 29:22; 46:3; 48:1; 58:1; Jer 2:4, 20; Ezek 20:5; Amos 3:13; 9:8; Obad 17, 18; Mic 2:7; 3:9; Pss 114:1.

[43]   See Nogalski, *Redactional Processes*, 61-68; and "Jeremiah and the Twelve: Intertextual Observations and Postulations."

and Amos, and is the subject of extensive treatment in Obadiah, but it is not mentioned again until Malachi.[44] More interestingly, the threefold movement of the day of divine intervention in Obadiah is presumed to be in process in Malachi. Elsewhere I have demonstrated how Mal 1:2-5 displays knowledge of Obadiah, not just nebulous traditions about Edom, except both the judgment on Jerusalem and the desolation of Edom are now in the past.[45] Thus, two of the three "days of divine intervention" anticipated in Obadiah have come to pass, while the third movement is not mentioned in Mal 1:2-5. However, reference to the day of YHWH virtually concludes Malachi with the citation of Joel 3:4 in Mal 3:23: "Behold I am going to send you Elijah the prophet before the *coming of the great and terrible day of YHWH*." The coming day of YHWH in Mal 3:23 will be directed at the wicked, not just the nations, but this alteration reflects the situation presented by Malachi where YHWH's people as a whole have returned to false worship practices just as at the beginning of the Twelve, while some of "the nations" have begun turning toward YHWH (cf. Mal 1:11-14). Thus, Jerusalem has been punished, Edom has been destroyed, and on the coming day of YHWH, the righteous will defeat the wicked (Mal 3:21). One sees a similar dynamic in the Isaiah corpus (cf. Isa 34:5-6, 63:1-6) where verbal links unite two widely separated texts in the expectation of the divine warrior's victory on the day of recompense against the nations (cf. Isa 34:8) that begins with Edom's destruction.

In summary, the day of divine intervention in Obadiah appears as a sequence of days of judgment with three recipients: Edom, Judah, and the nations. Judah's punishment (destruction and exile) is presumed (Obad 10-15, 20), even though the event is set in the future, and the reason for the punishment is never addressed. Edom's punishment is portrayed as a future event that will occur *after* Jerusalem's destruction as a result of Edom's hostility toward Jerusalem.

VII. Conclusion

Significant verbal and thematic links show that the concept of a day of divine intervention provides literary cohesion to the writings of Hosea through Obadiah. These links suggest that the other writings of the Twelve

---

[44] The Twelve specifically mentions Edom in Joel 4:19; Amos 1:6, 9, 11; 2:1; 9:12; Obadiah; and Mal 1:4.

[45] Nogalski, *Redactional Processes*, 218, 190-1.

are also involved. These links include more than the phrase יום יהוה. All four writings demonstrate thematic links, while the later writings (Joel and Obadiah) show more explicit signs of deliberate verbal links which combine references to days of divine intervention across the writings of the Twelve.

Die prophetische Ehemetaphorik und die Bewertung der Prophetie im Zwölfprophetenbuch

Eine synchrone und diachrone Rekonstruktion zweier thematischer Fäden

Gerlinde Baumann

Es ist eine geläufige Metapher, dass Texte den Charakter von Geweben haben. Der besondere Charakter des „Gewebes" Zwölfprophetenbuch (im Folgenden: XII) ist in der jüngeren Forschung in unterschiedlicher Weise erkannt und erforscht worden. Das ganze Textstück XII erinnert an einen Quilt oder eine Patchwork-Arbeit, die aus einzelnen, bereits vorhandenen Stücken zu einem neuen Werk zusammengefügt werden. Dabei kommen bei der Betrachtung des gesamten Stückes nicht so sehr die einzelnen Ursprungsstoffe zur Geltung als vielmehr deren Auswahl und Zusammenstellung zu dem neuen Stück. Die Komposition fällt ins Auge: Muster, Farben und graphische Anordnungen.

Auf dem Hintergrund dieser Metaphorik gedeutet glich die historisch-kritische Forschung am XII über lange Zeit eher der Betrachtung der Einzelstoffe. Das historisch-kritische Instrumentarium wurde überwiegend dafür genutzt, kleine und kleinste Textstücke auf ihren Ursprung hin zu untersuchen. Der Ort der Einzeltexte in der Gesamtkomposition ist dabei häufig unberücksichtigt geblieben. Erst in jüngster Zeit wird, überwiegend aus der Perspektive der Endtextexegese, auch Aufmerksamkeit auf verbindende Elemente oder auf die Gesamtkomposition gelegt. Manches vorher Vernachlässigte ist dadurch stärker in den Blick gekommen: So etwa die Stichwortverknüpfungen zwischen einzelnen Schriften des Zwölf-prophetenbuchs[1] oder Beobachtungen zu einzelnen Büchern, die Rück-schlüsse auf redaktionelle Schichtungen erlauben.[2] Thematische oder

---

[1] So vor allem J.D. Nogalski, Literary Precursors to the Book of the Twelve, BZAW 217, 1993; Redactional Processes in the Book of the Twelve, BZAW 218, 1993, sowie Intertextuality and the Twelve, in: J.W. Watts/P.R. House (Hg.), Forming Prophetic Literature. FS J.D.W. Watts, JSOT.S 235, 1996, 102-124.

[2] So v.a.: A. Schart, Die Entstehung des Zwölfprophetenbuchs. Neubearbeitungen von Amos im Rahmen schriftenübergreifender Redaktionsprozesse, BZAW 260, 1998.

motivliche Linien durch das XII rücken an einzelnen Punkten in den Fokus der Forschenden: so etwa das Thema der „Liebe Gottes" mit seiner rahmenden Funktion,[3] verbindende Motive wie der Tag JHWHs[4] mit der Gottesnamen-Anrufung,[5] die Gnadenformel aus Ex 34,6f[6] oder die sich durch die Geschichte hindurch verändernde Erfahrung Israels mit JHWH.[7]

Linien dieser Art sollen in diesem Beitrag im Zentrum der Aufmerksamkeit stehen. Dabei gehe ich davon aus, dass sowohl der diachrone Blick als auch die synchrone Lektüre des Endtextes bei der Erforschung des XII ihre Berechtigung haben. Erst mit Hilfe beider Perspektiven kann sowohl die spezielle Aussage eines Einzeltextes als auch der Charakter der Gesamtkomposition gewürdigt werden. Die diachrone Perspektive kann dabei nicht nur auf kleine Texteinheiten angewendet werden, sondern auch auf das gesamte XII und seine prägenden thematischen Strukturen. Es ist davon auszugehen, dass im XII einerseits jede kleine Texteinheit für sich bedeutsam ist, dass sie andererseits aber in Linien und Muster eingefügt wurde, innerhalb derer gelesen sie einen neuen Sinn entfaltet. Die Untersuchung thematischer „Längsschnitte" möchte ich anhand zweier Beispiele durchführen, die bislang kaum erforscht wurden.

---

3   J.D.W. Watts, A Frame for the Book of the Twelve, in: J.D. Nogalski/M.A. Sweeney (Hg.), Reading and Hearing the Book of the Twelve, SBL Symposium Series 15, 2000, 209-217.

4   Der Tag JHWHs als das XII verbindende Motiv wird in mehreren neuen Publikationen genannt, so z.B. bei D.L. Petersen, A Book of the Twelve? in: Nogalski/Sweeney (Hg.), Reading and Hearing (s. Anm. 3), 3-10, hier: 10; A. Schart, Reconstructing the Redaction History of the Twelve Prophets: Problems and Models, in: Nogalski/Sweeney (Hg.), Reading and Hearing, 34-48, hier: 40; J.D. Nogalski, Joel as „Literary Anchor" for the Book of the Twelve, in: Nogalski/Sweeney (Hg.), Reading and Hearing, 91-109, hier: 104f, sowie J.D. Nogalski, The Day(s) of YHWH in the Book of the Twelve, im vorliegenden Band.

5   R. Rendtorff, Alas for the Day! The „Day of the LORD" in the Book of the Twelve, in: T. Linafelt/T.K. Beal (Hg.), God in the Fray. FS W. Brueggemann, 1998, 186-197, sowie ders., How to Read the Book of the Twelve as a Theological Unity, in: Nogalski/Sweeney (Hg.), Reading and Hearing (s. Anm. 3), 75-87; dargestellt bei R. Scoralick, Gottes Güte und Gottes Zorn. Die Gottesprädikationen in Ex 34,6f. und ihre intertextuellen Beziehungen zum Zwölfprophetenbuch, Herders Biblische Studien 33, 2002, 138-140.

6   So R.C. van Leeuwen, Scribal Wisdom and Theodicy in the Book of the Twelve, in: L.G. Perdue/B. Scott/W. Wiseman (Hg.), In Search of Wisdom. In Memory of J.G. Gammie, 1993, 31-49, sowie ausführlicher Scoralick, Gottes Güte (s.o. Anm. 5), 131-207.212f.

7   So P.R. House, The Unity of the Twelve, JSOT.S 77, 1990, sowie ders., The Character of God in the Book of the Twelve, in: Nogalski/Sweeney (Hg.), Reading and Hearing (s. Anm. 3), 125-145.

Inzwischen ist anerkannt, dass das XII über mehrere Stufen gewachsen ist. Um die jeweiligen Sinnverschiebungen im Rahmen der Ergänzung des jeweiligen Mehrprophetenbuchs beurteilen zu können, muss zunächst ein Modell dieser Ergänzungen oder Erweiterungen vorgestellt werden. Als hypothetisches Modell eines Wachstums des (masoretischen)[8] XII möchte ich eine sehr grob gehaltene Synthese aus den Entwürfen von Zenger[9] sowie von Schart[10] vorschlagen; Einzelheiten und Begründungen finden sich jeweils bei den Autoren. Die beiden Modelle divergieren an einigen Stellen. Zengers „Mehrprophetenbuch I"[11] enthält die Schriften Hosea, Amos, Micha und Zephanja und entspricht damit grob Scharts D-Korpus.[12] Dies ließe sich als ein erstes Stadium des Wachstums ansetzen. Chronologisch scheint mir nun Scharts „Nahum-Habakuk-Korpus" in einem zweiten Stadium dazugekommen zu sein. Es umfaßt, grob gesagt, neben Teilen von Hosea, Amos, Micha und Zephanja weitgehend die Schriften Nahum und Habakuk.[13] In einem dritten Schritt könnten Haggai und Sacharja 1-8 ergänzt worden sein.[14] Danach wurden vermutlich Joel, Obadja, Sach 9-14 sowie Maleachi angefügt.[15] Als Abschluß wird schließlich Jona als jüngste der zwölf Schriften hinzugefügt worden sein.

---

8   Die Reihenfolge der LXX (Hos – Am – Mi – Joel – Obd – Jona) unterscheidet sich im ersten Teil des XII vom masoretischen Kanon (Hos – Joel – Am – Obd – Jona – Mi). Den Konsequenzen der Unterschiede in der Anordnung von MT und LXX für thematische Schwerpunkte widmet sich z.B. die Untersuchung von M.A. Sweeney, Sequence and Interpretation in the Book of the Twelve, in: Nogalski/Sweeney (Hg.), Reading and Hearing (s. Anm. 3), 49-64.

9   E. Zenger, Das Zwölfprophetenbuch, in: ders. et al., Einleitung in das Alte Testament, ³1998, 467-533, v.a. 467-472.

10 Schart, Entstehung (s. Anm. 2), passim, v.a. 304-314.

11 Zenger, Zwölfprophetenbuch (s. Anm. 9), 470. ,

12 Schart, Entstehung (s. Anm. 2), v.a. 218-233. Die genannten Schriften sind allerdings jeweils nicht in den kanonischen Endfassungen enthalten, sondern nur in Vorformen. Schart entwirft für dieses Korpus zudem noch eine eigene Vorstufe, das „Zweiprophetenbuch der Tradenten von Hosea und Amos", v.a. 151-155.

13 Schart, Entstehung (s. Anm. 2), v.a. 246-251.

14 Zenger, Zwölfprophetenbuch (s. Anm. 9), 470 als „Mehrprophetenbuch II"; Schart, Entstehung (s. Anm. 2), 252-260.

15 Hier weiche ich allerdings von beiden Entwürfen ab. Zenger differenziert seinen dritten Redaktionsgang – m.E. zu Unrecht – nicht mehr; er spricht lediglich davon, dass es sich um eine „(sukzessive?) Einfügung von Joël, Obd, Jona, Nah, Hab, sowie Fortschreibung von Sach 1-8 durch Sach 9-11.12-14 (sukzessiv) und schließlich Abschluß durch Mal im 4. und 3.Jh." (470). Schart wiederum (Entstehung [s. Anm. 2], 291-299) weist Maleachi dem letzten Ergänzungsstadium zu, was m.E. mit der dort geschilderten sozialen Situation nicht in Einklang zu bringen ist.

Den ersten thematischen Längsschnitt werde ich bei der prophetischen Ehemetaphorik legen.[16] In dieser wird JHWH in metaphorischer Weise als „Ehemann" der „Ehefrau" Israel oder Jerusalem/Zion vorgestellt. Die Metaphorik besteht aus mehreren Motiven und zieht sich durch alle vier Prophetenbücher der Hebräischen Bibel sowie die Threni.[17] Jedes Prophetenbuch setzt dabei seinen eigenen Akzent. Welche Besonderheit läßt das XII gegenüber den anderen Prophetenbüchern erkennen, und welche Rückschlüsse lassen sich daraus für die Komposition des XII ziehen?

Die zweite Linie werde ich bei einem völlig anderen Thema ziehen, nämlich bei der Bewertung der Prophetie. Hier geht es weder um Metaphern noch um eine Erzählung, sondern um ein Phänomen, das in den Texten unterschiedlich dargestellt und beurteilt wird. In diesem Rahmen kann ich nur erste Ansätze einer solchen Linie andeuten. Es geht mir darum, den Blick für solche thematischen Linien zu öffnen. Lassen sich bei dem ganz anders gelagerten Thema der Bewertung der Prophetie ähnliche Ergebnisse wie bei der Ehemetaphorik erzielen? Was ist aus den Unterschieden und Gemeinsamkeiten beider Längsschnitte für die Absichten und Umsichten einer Redaktion des XII an Erkenntnissen zu gewinnen?

I. Die prophetische Ehemetaphorik im Zwölfprophetenbuch

Die Ehe als Metapher für das Verhältnis JHWH-Israel/Jerusalem zieht sich durch das gesamte alttestamentliche Prophetencorpus. Das Vokabular der prophetischen Ehemetaphorik kommt, entsprechend der kanonischen Reihenfolge, in folgenden alttestamentlichen Texten vor: Jes 1,21; 47,1-4; 49,15-26; 50,1; 51,17-52,2; 54; 57,6-13; 60; 62,1-9; 66,7-12; Jer 2*; 3,1-13; 13,20-27; 22,20-23; 30,12-17; 31*; Lam 1*; Ez 16; 23; Hos 1-3*; 9,1; Am 5,2; Mi 1,6f.13-16; 4,9-14; Nah 3,4-7 sowie Zeph 3,11f.14-19, und Mal

---

16   Zur Metapher der Ehe zwischen JHWH und Israel/Jerusalem habe ich mich andernorts eingehender geäußert (G. Baumann, Liebe und Gewalt. Die Ehe als Metapher für das Verhältnis JHWH – Israel in den Prophetenbüchern, SBS 185, 2000; die Publikation der amerikanischen Übersetzung unter dem Titel „Love and Violence: Marriage as Metaphor for the Relationship between YHWH and Israel in the Prophetic Books" ist für 2003 geplant.) sowie mit dem Schwerpunkt auf der Ehemetaphorik im Zwölfprophetenbuch: Connected by Marriage, Adultery and Violence: The Prophetic Marriage Metaphor in the Book of the Twelve and in the Major Prophets, SBL.SP 38, 1999, 552-569. Die Ausführungen zur Ehemetaphorik sind eine Weiterentwicklung des zuletzt genannten Beitrags.

17   Während bei Daniel die Ehemetaphorik nicht verwendet wird, ist dies in Thr 1 der Fall; dazu vgl. Baumann, Liebe und Gewalt (s. Anm. 16), 175-182.

2,10-16. In dieser Aufzählung sind auch eine Reihe von Texten enthalten, die das Vokabular nur ausschnittsweise verwenden oder darauf nur anspielen.

Nur in wenigen Texten allerdings wird ein relativ „normales" eheliches Verhältnis vorausgesetzt: Dieses beinhaltet, dass ein Mann eine Frau „heiratet" (בעל oder nur לקח) und ihr „Ehemann" (בעל) wird. Er kann die Beziehung dadurch beenden, dass er sie „wegschickt" (שלח) bzw. ihr einen „Scheidebrief" (ספר בדיתות) gibt. In der Mehrzahl der Fälle erscheint das vorausgesetzte Eheverhältnis gestört, am häufigsten erscheint dann das Wort זנה, „huren", und seine Ableitungen.[18] זנה kann deshalb als eine Art Leitwort der prophetischen Ehemetaphorik angesehen werden. Zusammen mit זנה wird häufig נאף als Terminus für Ehebruch verwendet. Die Bestrafung der „Ehefrau" wird häufig mit Worten zum Ausdruck gebracht, die – zumindest für heutige Leserinnen und Leser – Szenen sexueller Gewalt darstellen. Die Geschlechtsteile (ערוה, מעה, נבלת, שבל oder שול) der „Frau" etwa werden „aufgedeckt" oder „enthüllt" (גלה), so dass alle ihre „Scham" oder „Schande" (קלון oder חרפה) „sehen" (ראה) können.

Innerhalb der prophetischen Ehemetaphorik läßt sich ein ganzes Bündel an Motiven ausmachen. Neben der Ehe zwischen JHWH und seiner „Ehefrau" Israel oder Samaria gibt es eine ähnliche Geschichte JHWHs mit Jerusalem/Zion oder Juda. Beiden „Frauen" wird „Hurerei" zugeschrieben, d.h. Abkehr von JHWH. Dessen Reaktion besteht in strafendem Handeln oder in der Ehescheidung. Die Strafe wird meist in Szenen sexueller Gewalt geschildert. In manchen Texten vergibt JHWH nach einer bestimmten Zeit der Bestrafung oder des Leidens der „Frau" und setzt sie wieder in einen heilvollen Zustand ein.

Des weiteren gibt es Texte, die sprachlich eng mit der Ehemetaphorik verwandt sind, sich jedoch nicht auf eine „Ehefrau" JHWHs beziehen, sondern auf eine andere weibliche Personifikation. Auf der einen Seite sind hier fremde Nationen zu erwähnen, die als „Frauen" oder „Töchter" personifiziert werden. Deren Bestrafung wird ebenfalls im Vokabular sexueller Gewalt geschildert (Jes 47,1-4; Nah 3,4-7). Auf der anderen Seite gibt es die „Jungfrau Israel" (Am 5,2), die „Tochter Zion/Jerusalem" oder die „Tochter mein Volk" (häufig bei Jes, Jer oder z.B. in Sach 2,10-17*;

---

18 Zur Bedeutung von זנה vgl. u.a. D.T. Setel, Propheten und Pornographie: Weibliche sexuelle Metaphorik bei Hosea, in: L.M. Russell (Hg.), Befreien wir das Wort, 1989, 101-112, sowie Ph. Bird, „To Play the Harlot": An Inquiry into an Old Testament Metaphor, in: P.L. Day (Hg.), Gender and Difference in Ancient Israel, 1989, 75-94, sowie Baumann, Liebe und Gewalt (s. Anm. 16), 52-56.

9,9), die häufig nicht „Ehefrau" JHWHs sind, aber ebenfalls JHWH zu- und untergeordnet sind – wie eine Tochter ihrem Vater.[19]
Grundsätzlich dient die Ehemetaphorik der Beschreibung von JHWHs Festhalten an einer Beziehung mit Israel/Jerusalem trotz deren negativen Verhaltens. Bei genauerer Untersuchung läßt sich erkennen, welchen historischen Sachverhalt sie theologisch umsetzt. In den meisten Texten steht hinter dem „Ehebruch" Israels oder Jerusalems, dass die IsraelitInnen andere Gottheiten verehren oder aber mit den falschen Großmächten paktieren (Ez). Bei der Bestrafung durch JHWH steht der Fall Samarias (722 v.Chr.) oder das Babylonische Exil der BewohnerInnen des Südreichs (586-538 v.Chr.) im Hintergrund. Texte mit dem Thema der Umkehr JHWHs oder der Wiederherstellung der „Ehefrau" sind dagegen eher in exilischer oder nachexilischer Zeit verfaßt worden und verarbeiten die Erfahrung, dass die Beziehung JHWHs zu seinem Volk auch nach dem Exil eine Fortsetzung findet.

Ein kurzer Überblick über die Ehemetaphorik in den drei großen Propheten soll es ermöglichen, im Vergleich den besonderen Zuschnitt der Ehemetaphorik im XII beurteilen zu können.

Zu Beginn des Jesajabuchs spielt die Ehemetaphorik kaum eine Rolle.[20] Bei PrJes wird sie nur an einer Stelle erwähnt; zudem in einem Vers, der vermutlich redaktioneller Herkunft ist: Jes 1,21 tituliert Jerusalem als „Hure", ohne diese Zuschreibung einzuordnen oder zu erläutern – die Ehemetaphorik wird offensichtlich als bekannt vorausgesetzt. Dies ist auch im zweiten Buchteil der Fall. Ohne zu entfalten, was Jerusalem sich hat zu Schulden kommen lassen, wird bei DtJes häufig auf die Ehemetaphorik älterer Texte angespielt.[21] Vor allem in Heilsorakeln wird das Schicksal Jerusalems geschildert: JHWH leugnet die Scheidung von ihr (50,1) bzw. nimmt die Beziehung zu ihr wieder neu auf (49,14-18; 54). Bezeichnenderweise hat nicht sie gesündigt, sondern ihre „Kinder", die Israelitinnen und Israeliten; für diese mußte sie die Strafe erleiden (50,1). Ihre exilische „Kinderlosigkeit" wird in Kinderreichtum verkehrt (49,20f;

---

[19] Dazu vgl. E. Seifert, Tochter und Vater im Alten Testament. Eine ideologiegeschichtliche Untersuchung zur Verfügungsgewalt von Vätern über ihre Töchter, Neukirchener Theologische Dissertationen und Habilitationen, 9, 1997.

[20] Hierzu breiter: Baumann, Liebe und Gewalt (s. Anm. 16), 183-211.

[21] Zu diesem Aspekt der prophetischen Ehemetaphorik habe ich mich bereits an anderer Stelle breiter geäußert: Prophetic Objections to YHWH as the Violent Husband of Israel. Reinterpretations of the Prophetic Marriage Metaphor in Second Isaiah (Isaiah 40-55), in: A. Brenner (Hg.), Prophets and Daniel. A Feminist Companion to the Bible, Second Series 8, 2001, 88-120, v.a. 99-110. Dabei rekurriere ich an wichtigen Stellen auf P.T. Willey, Remember the Former Things. The Recollection of Previous Texts in Second Isaiah, SBL.DS 161, 1997.

54,1). Erst bei TrJes mischen sich wieder kritische Töne in die Ehemetaphorik; dtr Wendungen entwerfen erneut die Perspektive „ihres" Fehlverhaltens (57,6-13).

Im Jeremiabuch spielt die Ehemetaphorik von Beginn an eine Rolle.[22] Jerusalem wird in Jer 2,1-3,5 als JHWHs Braut bezeichnet.[23] Sie aber betrügt ihn und verehrt andere Gottheiten. Als Reaktion erwägt JHWH die Ehescheidung von ihr; bereits früher hat er sich aus ähnlichen Gründen von Israel scheiden lassen (3,6-10). Doch Jerusalem ändert ihr Verhalten nicht, so dass JHWHs Zorn in einer Szene sexueller Gewalt kulminiert (13,20-27). In 22,20-23 wird ihr und ihren Liebhabern Vernichtung angesagt. In den vermutlich später angefügten Kapiteln Jer 30f wird für Israel wie Jerusalem umfangreiche Wiederherstellung angesagt. Hier werden auch Termini der prophetischen Ehemetaphorik verwendet.[24] Im weiteren Verlauf des Buchs ist dies aber nicht mehr der Fall.

Im Ezechielbuch erscheint die Ehemetaphorik einerseits geschlossener und andererseits stärker ausgearbeitet als in den anderen Prophetenbüchern.[25] Die Ehemetaphorik ist Ezechiel vermutlich durch Jeremia bekannt.[26] Genaugenommen bietet Ezechiel zwei Varianten der Ehemetaphorik. In Ez 16 wird das ausgesetzte Kind Jerusalem von JHWH gefunden und adoptiert. Das Mädchen wächst bei ihm auf, und er heiratet es später. Sie aber wendet sich von ihm ab und anderen Liebhabern zu. Im Unterschied zu den anderen prophetischen Büchern repräsentieren die Liebhaber dabei Großmächte und nicht andere Gottheiten. JHWHs Strafe wird wiederum in Bildern sexueller Gewalt geschildert. In Ez 16,44-52 wird die Metaphorik um die Schwestern Samaria und Sodom erweitert; sie teilen Jerusalems Geschichte mit JHWH. Dagegen variiert Ez 23 die Ehemetaphorik auf andere Weise: Nun wird die Geschichte der zwei

---

[22] Hierzu ausführlicher in Baumann, Liebe und Gewalt (s. Anm. 16), 111-141.

[23] Die Metaphern der „Liebe in der Wüstenzeit" und der „Hurerei" gehen vermutlich auf hoseanische Ursprünge zurück. M. Schulz-Rauch hat dies näher untersucht (Hosea und Jeremia. Zur Wirkungsgeschichte des Hoseabuches, CThM 16, 1996, 194): „Man kann Jer 3,20 als direkte Parallele zu Hos 3,1 verstehen, während Jer 3,1 als eine kreative Weiterentwicklung des hoseanischen Vorbildes zu deuten ist ... Die jeremianische Verwendung der Eheanalogie knüpft mit großer Wahrscheinlichkeit an hoseanische Vorbilder, insbesondere an den Ehevergleich Hos 3,1 an und entwickelt deren Einsichten weiter." Schulz-Rauch nimmt zudem an, dass Jeremia kein schriftlich verfaßtes Hoseabuch vorliegt, sondern dass er eher mit der groben Richtung der hoseanischen Botschaft vertraut ist (237).

[24] Beispielsweise bezieht sich Jer 30,15 auf 13,22 zurück.

[25] Hierzu eingehender: Baumann, Liebe und Gewalt (s. Anm. 16), 142-174.

[26] Zu den Verbindungen zwischen beiden Büchern, allerdings ohne speziellen Fokus auf die Ehemetaphorik, vgl. D. Vieweger, Die literarischen Bezüge zwischen den Büchern Jeremia und Ezechiel, BEAT 26, 1993.

Schwestern Ohola/Samaria und Oholiba/Jerusalem erzählt. Sie „huren" bereits vor ihrer Ehe mit anderen Liebhabern und sind folgerichtig auch ihrem späteren „Ehemann" JHWH nicht treu. Die Strafe fällt hier drastischer aus als in den anderen Texten der prophetischen Ehemetaphorik: Nicht nur Szenen sexueller Gewalt, sondern der Tod der „Frauen" wird auf mehrfache Weise erzählt. Ezechiel verzichtet auf die Wiederherstellung der „Frauen"; das Buch entfaltet aber in den Kapiteln 40-42 die Neuschaffung Jerusalems als Bauwerk.

Im XII findet sich die Ehemetaphorik heterogener als bei den großen Propheten. Das Buch beginnt mit der Parallele zwischen Hoseas Ehe mit der „Hure" Gomer und JHWHs Ehe mit Israel. Israel „hurt" mit Baal, womit hier der kanaanäische Gott bezeichnet wird.[27] Eine Ehescheidung von JHWH und Israel wird in Hos 2,4 angekündigt. Israel wird bestraft, was auch in einer Szene sexueller Gewalt geschildert wird (2,12). Später jedoch versucht JHWH seine Frau zurückzugewinnen, was auch gelingt (2,21f). In 9,1 allerdings wird Israel wiederum als „Hure" bezeichnet. In Hos 11 wird JHWHs Liebe zu Israel erneut beschrieben; diesmal ist Israel aber eine männliche Figur, nämlich JHWHs Sohn. So endet die Metaphorik des Verhältnisses JHWH-Israel bei Hosea mit der Wiederherstellung des maskulin personifizierten Israel. Von JHWHs Vergebung gegenüber seiner „Frau" ist nicht auf explizite Weise die Rede.

Amos erwähnt die „Jungfrau Israel" nur einmal (5,2), aber nicht als JHWHs „Ehefrau". Sie ist gefallen und steht nicht wieder auf. Dies rekurriert auf den Fall Samarias 722 v.Chr. und kann als Anspielung auf Hosea 2,12 interpretiert werden.

Als nächste Schrift verwendet Micha die prophetische Ehemetaphorik. Nur in einem kurzen Rückblick wird Samaria als „Hure" bezeichnet, die andere Götter liebt (Mi 1,5-7). Sie wurde bereits von JHWH bestraft. In Mi 1,13 betritt die „Tochter Zion" die Bühne des XII. Sie wird noch nicht als JHWHs Ehefrau angesehen; das ist erst in Mi 4,9-15 der Fall, wo ihre Bestrafung zusammen mit ihrer Wiederherstellung angekündigt wird. In Mi 7,8-10 erzählt die „Frau" von ihren Racheplänen gegen ihre – weibliche! – Feindin.

In der Abfolge der Schriften im XII gelesen, folgt nun eine weitere Szene der Bestrafung einer weiblichen Personifikation: In Nah 3,4-7 wird die Bestrafung Ninives durch JHWH in Bildern sexueller Gewalt dargestellt. Auf diese Weise findet sich im XII auch dasjenige Vokabular, das sonst vor allem dazu verwendet wird, die Bestrafung von JHWHs „Ehefrau" zu schildern. Die Züchtigung oder Vernichtung eines als Frau

---

[27] In Jes 54,5; 62,4f bezeichnet בעל JHWH als Jerusalems Ehemann und nicht als Gott wie bei Hosea.

personifizierten Fremdvolkes wird mit Hilfe dieses Vokabulars nur – neben Jes 47,2f – in Nah 3,4-7 zum Ausdruck gebracht.

Im Blick auf das XII endet nun das Leiden und die Bestrafung der „Frauen". Zeph 3,14-17 erzählt von der Freude und Wiederherstellung der „Tochter Zion/Jerusalem". JHWH verliebt sich erneut in sie, was ein Hinweis auf ihre Rolle als „Ehefrau" ist.

Ähnlich wie bei Zephanja ist auch in Sach 2,14 und 9,9 von Freude und Wiederherstellung der „Tochter Zion" die Rede. In Sach 5,5-11 korrespondiert eine negative Personifikation diesem positiven Frauenbild: Die „Bosheit" (רשעה) wird als „Frau im Fass" personifiziert und nach Babylon abtransportiert. Nach ihrer Deportation ist sie in Israel nicht mehr zu finden.

Maleachi stellt schließlich die andauernde Liebe JHWHs zu seinem Volk fest. Am Beginn dieser letzten Schrift des XII wird JHWHs Liebe direkt ausgesprochen (Mal 1,2a). Aber auch die Schwierigkeiten der Israeliten und Israelitinnen, JHWH ihrerseits zu lieben, werden zum Ausdruck gebracht. Die Passage in Mal 2,10-16 über die „Mischehen" ist mehrdeutig und kann auch so gelesen werden, dass sie transparent für JHWHs Liebe und Ehe zu seiner (ersten) „Ehefrau" Israel/Jerusalem ist.

Dieser Text kann nicht nur als Mahnung an die nachexilische Gemeinschaft gelesen werden, sondern auch als Feststellung JHWHs, er habe die „Frau seiner Jugend" nie verlassen. Auf diese Weise wird durch das Motiv der JHWH-Liebe ein Rahmen um das XII gelegt.[28] Aber die „Liebesobjekte" unterscheiden sich: Zu Beginn des XII ist es Israel, das aber schließlich JHWHs Liebe verloren hat. Jerusalem hat sich zwar nicht besser verhalten, aber nach dessen Bestrafung erfolgt immerhin eine Wiederherstellung. Nach Höhen und Tiefen der göttlichen Liebe werden in Mal die einzelnen Israeliten und Israelitinnen als Gegenüber der JHWH-Liebe angesprochen. Zudem können die Anspielungen auf die Ehemetaphorik in Mal 2,11b auch als deren bewußte Destruktion verstanden werden: Juda wird als Ehemann bezeichnet, der die Tochter eines fremden Gottes zur Frau genommen hat – statt JHWHs, wie kundige Lesende ergänzen.[29]

Auf dem Hintergrund der bekannten Ehemetaphorik gelesen würden hier die Geschlechterrollen in einer Weise verkehrt, die jedes weitere Reden von JHWH als „Ehemann" der „Frau" Israel/Jerusalem unmöglich macht: Denn nun erscheint JHWH in der Rolle der Frau und nicht mehr des Mannes.

---

[28] Dies ist bereits von Watts, Frame (s. Anm. 3) herausgearbeitet worden.
[29] Dazu vgl. J.M. O'Brien, Judah as Wife and Husband. Deconstructing Gender in Malachi, JBL 115 (1996), 241-250.

Innerhalb des Kanonteils Nebiim der Hebräischen Bibel, so läßt sich dieser kurze Vergleich auswerten, kommt nur im XII das gesamte Spektrum der Motive der prophetischen Ehemetaphorik zur Anwendung: JHWHs Beziehung zu Israel/Samaria, ihre „Hurerei" weg von JHWH und seine deshalb erfolgende Bestrafung, die leidende „Tochter Zion/Jerusalem" und ihre spätere Wiedereinsetzung als geliebte „Ehefrau" JHWHs als Bild der wieder aufgebauten Stadt. Zusätzlich finden sich auch zwei Motive aus dem weiteren Bereich der prophetischen Ehemetaphorik, nämlich die Bestrafung einer ausländischen Nation und die „Tochter Zion/Jerusalem", die nur teilweise als JHWHs Ehefrau gesehen wird. Interessant ist zudem, dass der Gedanke der Rache an den Feinden Jerusalems nicht erst bei Nahum geäußert wird, sondern bereits bei Micha aufscheint.

Verglichen mit der Verwendung der prophetischen Ehemetaphorik in Jesaja, Jeremia und Ezechiel deckt das XII die größte thematische Breite ab. Dies ist angesichts der langen Entstehungsgeschichte und des „Patchwork-Charakters" des Buches erstaunlich. Während Jesaja den Schwerpunkt auf die Wiederherstellung Jerusalems und die Bestrafung ihrer Widersacherin setzt, Jeremia von Israel und Juda, von „Hurerei", Bestrafung und Wiederherstellung spricht und Ezechiel eine Biographie insgesamt dreier Schwestern – Israel/Samaria, Sodom und Jerusalem – erzählt, an deren Ende nach grobem Fehlverhalten keine Wiederherstellung folgt, erfahren die Lesenden nur im XII die komplette Geschichte der weiblichen Personifikation Israel/Jerusalem/Zion in ihrer Beziehung zu JHWH. In der Anordnung des XII läßt sich eine inhaltliche Linie nachzeichnen, die plausibel und folgerichtig ist.

Wie hat sich nun die Ehemetaphorik im Zuge des Wachstums des XII entwickelt? Die Geschichte Israels mit JHWH wird bereits im ersten Stadium eines Mehrprophetenbuches mit den wichtigsten Motiven erzählt. Die ehemetaphorischen Passagen in Hos 1-3* verstehe ich dabei nicht erst als nachexilische Redaktion eines größeren Buchcorpus, sondern bereits als Bestandteil von Hos/Am/Mi/Zeph.[30] Fortgesetzt wird die Ehemetaphorik in diesem Corpus mit dem Fall Israels/Samarias (Am 5,2; Mi 1,6f). Auch die Bestrafung der zwischen „Tochter" und „Ehefrau" schillernden Größe Jerusalem/Zion wird angekündigt (Mi 1,11.16), wobei auf die Ehemetaphorik aber nur angespielt wird. Das Strafmotiv wird etwas später aufgenommen, wenn das Motiv der Bestrafung einer als „Frau" personifizierten ausländischen Nation deutlich ausgearbeitet in Nah 3,4-7 dazutritt. Nahum wird zusammen mit Habakuk dem vorhandenen Mehrprophetenbuch angefügt.

---

30 Zur Problematik der Datierung habe ich bereits in Liebe und Gewalt (s. Anm. 16), 91, kurz Stellung genommen.

Vermutlich schon zu Beginn der Exilszeit wird die Bestrafung der „Tochter Zion" dann in Mi 4,9-13 breiter ausgemalt.[31] Ideen der Bewahrung und Wiederherstellung Zions werden erst später, in nachexilischer Zeit, geäußert (Zeph 3,14-17).[32] Was dann noch folgt, sind Wiederaufnahmen der bereits genannten Motive: Auf der nächsten Erweiterungsstufe klingt mit dem Abtransport der Bosheit in Sach 5,5-11 die Bestrafung einer fremden Nation als „Frau" an. Im dritten und vierten Ergänzungsstadium gibt es weitere Rückverweise auf bereits ausgeführte Motive: zunächst in Sach 3,14 und später auch in Sach 9,9. Wiederum geht es um die Freude der wiederhergestellten „Tochter Zion", und zwar vermutlich mit Bezug auf den ähnlich lautenden Text Zeph 3,14-17.[33] In den Maleachi-Anspielungen wird dann das Ende der Ehe JHWHs mit Israel/Juda angedeutet.

Die inhaltliche Linie der Ehemetaphorik stimmt demnach – grob gesagt – in etwa mit der vermutlichen historischen Entstehung des XII aus einzelnen Vorläufern überein: Die historisch frühen ehemetaphorischen Texte stehen zu Beginn, die späten Texte eher am Schluß des XII. Allerdings findet sich am Buchschluß die elaborierte Fassung der Ehemetaphorik nicht mehr, sondern nur noch Anspielungen. Auch sind im ersten Vorläufercorpus mehr und prägnantere ehemetaphorische Texte zu finden als in den späteren Ergänzungen. Zum Schluß des XII wird bei Maleachi eine Verschiebung der „Beziehungspartner" vorgenommen. Nun steht nicht mehr das Verhältnis des Volkes zu JHWH, sondern der Individuen zu JHWH im Mittelpunkt. Dies läßt sich als Bemühen darum verstehen, dass das XII als Abschluß des Propheten-Kanon-Teils auch mit der prophetischen Ehemetaphorik abschließen soll: Sie findet sich durchgängig in den Prophetenbüchern, wird aber nur im XII ausführlich und komplett dargestellt und zu einem Ende gebracht. Es ist spürbar, dass es bei der Endredaktion des XII auch darum gegangen ist, eine kohärente

---

31 R. Kessler, Micha, Herders Theologischer Kommentar zum Alten Testament, 1999, 196-216 setzt diese Passage in die frühbabylonische bzw. frühexilische Zeit und hebt hervor, dass sich in diesen Texten starke Rachegedanken finden.

32 Beide Texteinheiten Zeph 3,14f sowie 3,16f sind als „metahistorisch" geprägte vermutlich spät anzusetzen; zur Diskussion vgl. J.D. Nogalski, Zephanaiah 3: A Redactional Text for a Developing Corpus, in: R.G. Kratz/Th. Krüger/K. Schmid (Hg.), Schriftauslegung in der Schrift, FS für O.H. Steck, BZAW 300, 2000, 207-218, hier: 214f.

33 B.G. Curtis (The Zion-Daughter Oracles: Evidence on the Identity and Ideology of the Late Redactors of the Book of the Twelve, in: Nogalski/Sweeney [Hg.], Reading and Hearing [s. Anm. 3], 167-184) votiert dafür, dass Zeph 3,14-20 der Einstiegstext für die Zions-Wiederherstellungs-Texte des XII ist (181-183), zu denen an vorderster Stelle auch Sach 9,9 zählt.

Geschichte JHWHs mit seinem Volk zu erzählen – zumindest kann das für die prophetische Ehemetaphorik gesagt werden. Auch haben sich die Maleachi-Redaktoren um ein Ende bemüht, das die Metaphorik sowohl abschließt als auch einen der veränderten Situation angemessenen Ausblick auf das „neue" Gottesverhältnis zu den Einzelnen ermöglicht.[34]

Im Blick auf die Ehemetaphorik im gesamten Prophetencorpus kann beobachtet werden, dass es von Jesaja bis zum XII eine deutliche Steigerung gibt: Während Jesaja die Ehemetaphorik relativ spärlich verwendet, bietet das XII die gesamte Breite der Motive. „Ehemetaphorisch gesehen" wäre also eine Klimax zu beobachten. Nicht nur im XII, sondern auch innerhalb der Prophetenbücher insgesamt sorgt die Ehemetaphorik auf der inhaltlichen Ebene für eine größere Kohärenz der Texte. *Eine* Metaphorik zieht sich durch und wird zudem gegen Ende des Gesamtwerkes verstärkt eingesetzt. Ich halte es für durchaus möglich, dass solche Intentionen bei der Endredaktion des XII oder der Prophetenbücher eine Rolle gespielt haben.

Lassen sich diese am Beispiel der prophetischen Ehemetaphorik getroffenen Beobachtungen generalisieren, oder sind sie auf dieses eine Thema zu begrenzen? Dies soll die folgende „Gegenprobe" anhand des Themas Prophetie zeigen.

II. Die Bewertung des Phänomens der Prophetie im Zwölfprophetenbuch

Die Frage nach der Bewertung der Prophetie ermöglicht – wie die prophetische Ehemetaphorik – einen Blick auf die Geschichte der israelitischen Prophetie. Den Zugang zum Phänomen der Prophetie wähle ich vor allem über das Wortfeld נבא/נביא, חזה/חזון, משא. Ein erster Blick wird die Befunde wieder synchron, d.h. nach der Anordnung der Texte im kanonischen XII sichten. In einem zweiten Durchgang werde ich die Aussagen dann diachron, d.h. im Rahmen des hier zugrundegelegten Entstehungsmodells des XII darstellen.

Die Erzähllinie nimmt bei Hosea einen positiven Anfang. Wichtigste Aufgabe der Prophetie in der Nachfolge des Mose ist es, „Jahwe ein *neues*

---

34   Um dieses auszusagen, wird eine Veränderung der Metaphorik vorgenommen: Anknüpfend an die Eltern-Kind-Metaphorik, die für das Verhältnis JHWH-Israel bereits bei Hosea (11,1-4) verwendet wird, kann Maleachi von der Vaterrolle JHWHs für die einzelnen Israeliten und Israelitinnen sprechen. Diese Metaphorik findet sich nur in der ersten und letzten Schrift des XII.

Volk zu schaffen."[35] So gesehen steht Joels Ankündigung einer „Demokratisierung" der prophetischen Gaben in künftigen Zeiten (Joel 3,1f) nicht unbedingt im Widerspruch zu Hosea, sondern kann als Ausarbeitung der bei Hosea in der Fortführung von Num 11,29 angelegten Linie interpretiert werden. Zudem wird schon bei Joel die Hochschätzung „gelehrter Prophetie"[36] vorbereitet. Von Amos an verzweigt sich die Linie der Bewertung der Prophetie in zwei Richtungen: Immer dort, wo konkrete prophetisch redende Personen im Blick zu sein scheinen, wird heftige Kritik laut; wo es dagegen um die prophetische Aufgabe selbst geht, ist die Bewertung positiv.

Auch wenn dem verkündigenden Unheilspropheten ein schweres Schicksal auferlegt wird, besteht bei Amos die unbedingte Notwendigkeit, das prophetische Wort an Israel zu übermitteln (Am 2,11f; 3,1-8).[37] In den vermutlich redaktionellen Versen in Am 3,1-8 sind konkrete Träger und Trägerinnen des prophetischen Amtes im Blick. Noch werden sie positiv als Künderinnen des JHWH-Ratschlusses angesehen. Amos selbst dagegen distanziert sich vom Prophetentitel (Am 7,14).[38] Die sich hier andeutende kritische Haltung wird bei Jona verstärkt; die prophetische Aufgabe wird hier als eine fast unlösbare hingestellt: Wie gelähmt steckt Jona im Dilemma von prophetischem Auftrag und den Kriterien für wahre Prophetie aus Dtn 18,15-22. Von hier aus fällt es schwer, nachzuvollziehen, dass das XII überhaupt fortgesetzt und weiter prophetisch geredet wird. Liegt ein Grund darin, dass Jona nicht nur auf die Schwierigkeiten des prophetischen Amtes, sondern auch auf die Themen der gelungenen Umkehr und der Gnade Gottes fokussiert? Von hier fiele der Anschluß an die folgende Micha-Schrift leichter, für die die Umkehr des sündigen Jerusalem zentral

---

[35] So E. Zenger, „Durch Menschen zog ich sie ..." (Hos 11,4). Beobachtungen zum Verständnis des prophetischen Amtes im Hoseabuch," in L. Ruppert/P. Weimar/ders., (Hg.), Künder des Wortes. FS J. Schreiner, 1982, 183-201, hier:195, im Blick auf die Nordreichs-Prophetie in 1 Kön 19.

[36] Diesen Terminus hat H.W. Wolff geprägt (Amos. BK.AT 14/2, ³1985, 94).

[37] J. Jeremias (Die Rolle des Propheten nach dem Amosbuch, in: ders., Hosea und Amos. Studien zu den Anfängen des Dodekapropheton, FAT 13, 1996, 272-284) führt aus, dass das Phänomen Prophetie bzw. das „Wort JHWHs" in der Amosschrift in Texten verschiedener Redaktionsstufen (in etwa: zuerst 7,1-8; 5,1f; 9,1-4; 3,3-6.8; dann [noch vorexilisch; a.a.O, 277] 7,10-17 und schließlich nachexilisch 2,11f; 3,7; 8,11f sowie 9,9f.; a.a.O., 272 u.ö.) unterschiedlich gewertet wird, wobei sich trotzdem eine Linie nachzeichnen läßt. Insgesamt ist die prophetische Unheilsansage für die überlebensnotwendige Umkehr Israels unverzichtbar („Extra verbum prophetae nulla salus." a.a.O., 283).

[38] Dies ist vermutlich eher auf einen Konflikt zwischen Priester und Prophet zurückzuführen als auf eine pauschale Ablehnung von Prophetie; so J. Jeremias, Rolle (s. Anm. 37), 278.

ist. Daneben widmet sich Micha wieder konkreten Prophetengestalten. Ihnen gilt seine scharfe Kritik (Mi 3,5-11). Chriffriert unter der Gestalt Mirjams (Mi 6,4) sind Prophetinnen und Propheten als Gruppe allerdings wichtig für das Israel der Zukunft;[39] hier wird die Amos-Linie fortgeführt. Wiederum beim Namen genannt und ins Kreuzfeuer genommen werden die betrügerischen Propheten bei Zephanja (Zeph 3,4). Habakuk (Hab 1,1; 3,1) setzt mit der Selbstbezeichnung wieder einen positiven Gegenakzent; in gleicher Richtung ist PrSach (1,1.7) zu intepretieren. Nun aber wechselt die Perspektive: Von jetzt an wird Prophetie retrospektiv betrachtet und als ein Phänomen der Vergangenheit angesehen (Sach 1,6; 7,3.7.12; 8,9).[40] Daher gewinnt das sich abzeichnende Ende der Prophetie, wie es in Sach 13,2-6 angekündigt wird, an Plausibilität. Maleachi negiert diesen Gedanken zwar nicht explizit, unterwandert ihn aber, wenn die Botengestalten teilweise prophetische Aufgaben übernehmen sollen (3,1) und ausdrücklich mit der Gestalt des Elia als Rahmenfigur um das Prophetencorpus verknüpft werden (3,23).

Diese Nacherzählung zeigt zunächst, wie schwierig es ist, hier eine argumentative Linie auszumachen. Einige „Klippen", die Ausweichbewegungen im argumentativen Fluß notwendig machen, stellen vor allem Joel, Jona und Sach 13 dar. Die durch sie gesetzten Akzente lassen sich als – in später historischer Zeit offensichtlich notwendige – Vorverweise auf das Ende der Prophetie zusammenfassen, das je nach Ausgestaltung unterschiedlich ausfällt: Es besteht entweder in der Demokratisierung des Phänomens Prophetie (Joel 3,1), im Betonen der Spannung zwischen strikter prophetischer Unheilsverkündigung und dem gnädigen Gott (Jona), oder im Ende der mündlichen JHWH-Prophetie, die auf eine Weiterführung prophetischer Verkündigung allein in Schriftform schließen läßt.

Gegenüber dieser eher mühsam nachzuvollziehenden Argumentationslinie läßt sich die diachrone Entwicklung des Themas im Rahmen der Entstehung des XII leichter nachzeichnen.

Die vorexilischen Propheten, die zu einem ersten Vorläufer des XII zusammengebunden wurden, stehen dem Prophetentum und dessen Repräsentanten von vornehrein zwiespältig gegenüber. Ungebrochen positiv beurteilt das Phänomen der Prophetie und die konkreten Propheten

---

[39] Dazu R. Kessler, Mirjam und die Prophetie der Perserzeit, in: U. Bail/R. Jost (Hg.), Gott an den Rändern. Sozialgeschichtliche Perspektiven auf die Bibel. FS W. Schottroff, 1996, 64-72, sowie R. Kessler, Zwischen Tempel und Tora. Das Michabuch im Diskurs der Perserzeit, BN 44 (2000), 21-36.

[40] An diesem Punkt stimme ich Conrad zu: „Prophecy in the Twelve is valued as a past institution that is coming to an end." (E.W. Conrad, The End of Prophecy and the Appearance of Angels/Messengers in the Book of the Twelve, JSOT 73 [1997], 65-79, hier: 67) Für die Perspektive von Hosea bis Haggai gilt dies m.E. allerdings nicht.

in vorexilischer Zeit nur Hosea, wie an mehreren älteren und jüngeren Stellen zum Ausdruck kommt.[41] Deutlich ist vor allem, dass das prophetische Amt schon in der Mosezeit gestiftet wurde und sich auf ganz Israel bezieht.[42] Von Hosea aus ist vermutlich auch bei Amos eine positivere Einschätzung der prophetischen Rolle für Israel herausgestellt worden (3,1-8).[43] Dass Prophetie für Israel überlebensnotwendig ist, hält Amos fest, obwohl er selbst es von sich weist, in Bethel als Prophet bezeichnet zu werden (Am 7,14). Die Gruppe der Propheten bei Micha ist vermutlich Teil des höfischen Beamtenapparats; ihre Angehörigen werden als gut bezahlte Lügner und Opportunisten hingestellt (Mi 3,5-11).[44] Eine ähnliche Einordnung trifft Zephanja; auch hier werden die Propheten als Betrüger tituliert (Zeph 3,4).

Auf der nächsten Erweiterungsstufe, bei Nahum und Habakuk, finden sich keine expliziten Aussagen zum Thema. Habakuk bezeichnet sich allerdings selbst zweimal (1,1 und 3,1) als Propheten. Er ist damit das erste Individuum im XII, das sich diese Selbstbezeichnung in positiver Absicht zulegt[45] – auch ein Hinweis auf die Gebrochenheit, in der Prophetie im XII zuvor gesehen worden ist.

Die folgende Ergänzungsstufe ist in nachexilischer Zeit durch zwei Tendenzen im Umgang mit dem Phänomen der Prophetie charakterisiert: Zum einen stehen nun nicht mehr die konkreten Propheten als Berufsstand in der Kritik. Jetzt geht es um die Frage der Legitimität von JHWH-Prophetie. Proto-Sacharja kann noch ungebrochen positiv von sich als Prophet sprechen (Sach 1,1.7) und auf die Propheten der Vergangenheit als Künder wichtiger JHWH-Botschaften rekurrieren (Sach 1,6; 7,3.7.12; 8,9).[46] Eine Micha-Redaktion weist der Prophetie, erwähnt in der Person Mirjams, eine wichtige Rolle neben Priesterschaft und politischer Führung zu (Mi 6,4).

Auf der vorletzten Stufe dagegen bricht die Sacharja-Fortschreibung (Sach 9-14) mit der Wertschätzung der Prophetie. Nicht das Vorhandensein weiterer Prophetie wird geleugnet, sondern deren Legitimation durch JHWH (13,2-6). Eine zweite Bestreitung zukünftiger Prophetie kommt ohne solch direkte Ablehnung des Bisherigen aus. Maleachi arbeitet unter Ausweitung von Sacharjas Anfängen die Gestalt des „Boten" (מַלְאָךְ) aus,

---

41 Dazu vgl. J. Jeremias, TRE XV, 587.
42 So Jeremias ebd. sowie E. Zenger, Menschen (s. Anm. 35), 195.
43 Dazu vgl. J. Jeremias (Die Anfänge des Dodekapropheton: Hosea und Amos, in: ders., Hosea und Amos [s. Anm. 37], 34-54), v.a. 42-45.
44 Hierzu vgl. Kessler, Micha (s. Anm. 31), 159f.
45 So Conrad, End of Prophecy (s. Anm. 40) 72.
46 Dazu vgl. a.a.O., v.a. 73-78.

die teilweise prophetische Aufgaben zu übernehmen hat (Mal 3,1). Joel negiert durch seine „Demokratisierung" der Geistbegabung als Fähigkeit für alle Israelitinnen und Israeliten (Joel 3,1-5) die prophetische Individualexistenz, Einzelbegabung und -erwählung durch JHWH. Seine Perspektive ist durch die Ankündigung des Tages JHWHs mit Gericht und Heil verknüpft. Die häufigen Anknüpfungen an ältere Texte führen vor, dass mit Joel das Zeitalter „gelehrter Prophetie" in Schriftform beginnt.

Bei der Komplettierung des XII führt Jona schließlich das individuelle Prophetenschicksal angesichts von Gottes Gnade erzählerisch *ad absurdum*. Dem Ruthbuch vergleichbar wird hier nicht auf argumentative, sondern auf narrative Weise eine in nachexilischer Zeit ausgearbeitete Erkenntnis älteren Einsichten entgegengestellt. Die Gnade Gottes kontrastiert bei Jona mit der historisch älteren Unheilsprophetie – ohne dass den Lesenden eine eindeutige Lösung des Konflikts vorgeschlagen würde. Dies hält ihnen die Möglichkeit offen, trotz der prophetiekritischen Tendenz Jonas auch die folgenden Texte des XII positiv zu rezipieren. Ein solches Vorgehen macht es auch möglich, als Schlußwort des Prophetenkanons (Mal 3,23) das Wiederkommen des Elia, eines der ersten Propheten, anzukündigen.

Das historisch-chronologische Endstadium der Prophetie im XII fällt auch mit dem erzählten Ende zusammen. Auch wenn diese Linie der Bewertung von Prophetie nach der hier zugrunde gelegten historischen Abfolge weitaus weniger deutlich ist als die für die prophetische Ehemetaphorik konstatierte, besitzt sie doch deutlich weniger Klippen als die zuvor entworfene Linie des kanonischen Endtextes des XII. Ein zweiter Durchgang durch die Argumentation soll dies verdeutlichen:

Im ersten Stadium (Hos, Am, Mi, Zeph) wird bereits die Hochschätzung von Prophetie mit gleichzeitiger Kritik an den konkreten Amtsträgern verknüpft. Als Teil der zweiten Erweiterung fügt PrSach das Element des Rückblicks an; Prophetie erscheint nun zwar in positiver, aber bereits historischer Perspektive. Auch Maleachi mit der Einführung der den Propheten beerbenden Botengestalt und Joel mit der „Demokratisierung" der Prophetie und der Weiterführung als „schriftgelehrte Prophetie" setzen die positive und eher rückwärtsblickende Haltung fort. Sach 13,2-6 setzt einen Schlußpunkt unter das Auftreten leibhaftiger Prophetengestalten. Dies darf allerdings nicht abgekoppelt von der vorangegangenen Wertschätzung der schriftlich niedergelegten Prophetie betrachtet werden. Auf dieser fußt auch Jona; das erzählte Dilemma eines Einzelpropheten im Konflikt zwischen göttlicher Gnade und Auftragserfüllung setzt einen weiteren Endpunkt sozusagen von der Seite der Betroffenen aus: das Prophetenschicksal ist kein erstrebenswertes.

Die Linie der Bewertung von Prophetie im XII (MT) beginnt also bei Hosea und Joel positiv, teilt sich bei Amos in zwei Stränge – der positiven

Bewertung des Amtes und der negativen Beurteilung konkreter Träger –, um ab Sacharja zurückzublicken. Die Teilung ermöglicht es, dass Maleachi schließlich am Schluß des XII die Substanz des Amtes – die Vermittlung von JHWHs Willen an die Israelitinnen und Israeliten – unbeschadet der konkreten Verfehlungen einzelner Propheten in ein neues Amt überführt. Dieses Amt des „Boten" (מלאך) ermöglicht mehrere Anknüpfungen: Zum einen diejenige an andere alttestamentliche Traditionen mit ihren Mittlergestalten wie beispielsweise die Weisheitsgestalt aus Prov 1-9 und weitere spätere Engel- oder Zwischenwesen.[47] Zum anderen ermöglicht sie durch den Verzicht auf eine durchgängig negative Beurteilung von Prophetie auch den Blick für gelehrte Schriftauslegung älterer Prophetentexte; diese wird als „Tradentenprophetie"[48] eine neue Ausformung israelitischer Prophetie. Das Lesen der Schrift (Jes 34,16) tritt teilweise an die Stelle des Hörens auf das durch die Propheten vermittelte Wort JHWHs (Hos 4,1 u.ö.).[49]

III. Auswertung und Ausblick

Obwohl sich bei beiden betrachteten Themen relativ kohärente inhaltliche Linien entwerfen lassen, ist diejenige beim Thema Prophetie deutlich verschränkter, komplizierter und rekonstruktionsbedürftiger als bei der Ehemetaphorik. In beiden Fällen läßt sich nicht nur in der vermutlichen historischen Abfolge der Texte, sondern auch in der Anordnung im XII und von einer vermuteten Entstehung des XII aus Vorläufercorpora eine sinnvolle Aussage ermitteln. Dabei stimmt bei der Ehemetaphorik die diachrone Linie in etwa mit der Anordnung der Texte im vollendeten XII überein. Gleiches läßt sich für das Thema der Bewertung der Prophetie allerdings nicht sagen. Hierin liegt ein weiterer Grund, warum das zweite Thema im XII schwieriger nachzuzeichnen ist: Es trennen sich historische und textliche Linien, und es entstehen je nach Herangehensweise zwei

---

[47] Die Entwicklung von der Propheten- zur Botenfigur zeichnet Cohen nach (N.G. Cohen, From *Nabi* to *Mal'ak* to „Ancient Figure", JJS 36 [1985], 12-24); sie stellt auch heraus, dass in nachexilischer Prophetie die Aufgabe der klassischen Schriftpropheten von Boten übernommen wird (20; Mal 2,4-8) und die Grenze zwischen „irdischen" Propheten und „himmlischen" Boten verschwimmt (21).

[48] So der Terminus von O.H. Steck, z.B. in: Die Prophetenbücher und ihr theologisches Zeugnis: Wege der Nachfolge und Fährten zur Antwort, 1996, 167.

[49] Darüber hinaus weist Overholt (T.W. Overholt, The End of Prophecy. No Players without a Program, JSOT 42 [1988], 103-115, auch mit Besprechung von Literatur zum Thema) darauf hin, dass Prophetie in nachexilischer Zeit nach dem Wegfall des Königtums – mit dem König als Gegenspieler der Propheten – notwendig ihre Gestalt wandeln muß.

unterschiedliche Muster. Während die historische Linie – auch mit Hilfe von anderen alttestamentlichen Texten und weiterem historischen Wissen – relativ gut erschlossen werden kann, kann die textimmanente Linie des XII erst bei einem relativ groben Überblick gesehen werden. Um die textimmanente Linie erkennen zu können, ist das Wissen um die historische Entwicklung der Prophetie eine große Hilfe; stehen doch dadurch Kategorien und Deutungsmuster für sie bereit. Diese Beobachtung kann als Aufforderung gewertet werden, die diachrone und die Endtextperspektive bei der Untersuchung weiterer Motive und Themen des XII gemeinsam zur Anwendung zu bringen.

Werden die Untersuchungsergebnisse zu beiden Themen – trotz ihrer Unterschiedlichkeiten – zueinander in Beziehung gesetzt, so eröffnet sich eine weitere Dimension des XII. Konstrastierend zu einer zunehmend negativen Bewertung der Prophetie entwickelt sich des Schicksal Israels mit JHWH in der prophetischen Ehemetaphorik positiver. Obwohl die beiden thematischen Bögen so unterschiedlich begonnen wurden, zeigen ihre jeweiligen Enden gewisse Ähnlichkeiten, insofern die vorangehenden Gedanken nicht nur einfach abgeschlossen werden. Bei beiden Topoi deuten sich Weiterentwicklungen auf die größeren inhaltlich-theologischen Umwälzungen Israels hin an. Die Ehemetaphorik wird im Stichwort der „Liebe" transparent für das Verhältnis JHWHs zu den Einzelnen, und die Prophetie behält weiterhin Mittler in Gestalt von „Boten" bei. Beide Perspektiven werden in nachexilischer Zeit ausgeprägt. In dieser Epoche finden sich ähnliche Entwicklungen auch in anderen Büchern.

In diesem Beitrag konnte ich nur anhand zweier Beispiele andeuten, was ein Überblick über einzelne Themen im XII erbringen kann. Besonders das zweite Thema konnte hier nur angerissen werden. Zudem blieb bei der Prophetie auch die unterschiedliche Reihenfolge der Darstellungen in MT und LXX unberücksichtigt. Hier wären weitere Untersuchungen sehr lohnend.

Die Unterschiedlichkeit der Ergebnisse bei den zwei Themen möchte ich als Aufforderung verstehen, sich bei der Untersuchung weiterer Themen für ganz andere Linien und Systematisierungen offen zu halten. In der Zusammenstellung der Einzelstoffe im „Gesamtkunstwerk Zwölfprophetenbuch" sind noch viele Muster verborgen, die darauf warten, entdeckt zu werden.

Exile as Purification.
Reconstructing the "Book of the Four"

Rainer Albertz

I. Previous Studies

In doing his pioneer work on the redactional history of Book of the Twelve, James Nogalski discovered that the core of the four prophetic books, Hosea, Amos, Micah and Zephaniah, had probably formed an older redactional unit composed during the exilic period.[1] He named it the "Deuteronomistic corpus" after Dtr phrases and topics in its redactional layer. In this estimation he took up the observations of Werner H. Schmidt on a Dtr redaction of the book of Amos[2] and of Jörg Jeremias on an exilic edition of the book of Micah.[3] Additionally, Nogalski observed that the headings of those four books take a similar shape, set under the common title of יהוה דבר and dated during the reigns of Israelite and Judean kings. He noticed that two prophets from the North are followed by two from the South in an obvious systematical and chronological order. He pointed out, that these two phases of prophecy are deliberately linked in the beginning of the book of Micah (Mic 1:2-9). Finally he uncovered several catchwords that linked these four books together. So, in his view the "Deuteronomistic corpus" comprised Hosea 1-14, Amos 1:1-9:6, Mic 1-3+6, and Zeph 1:1-3:8a*. However, Nogalski was aware that his hypothesis was not yet fully developed, because he was not able to investigate all the text of the four books in detail.[4]

---

[1] James Nogalski, *Literary Precursors to the Book of the Twelve* (BZAW 217; Berlin, New York: de Gruyter, 1993) 278–80; idem, *Redactional Processes in the Book of the Twelve* (BZAW 218; Berlin, New York: de Gruyter, 1993) 274–75.

[2] Werner H. Schmidt, "Die deuteronomistische Redaktion des Amosbuches. Zu den theologischen Unterschieden zwischen dem Propheten und seinem Sammler," *ZAW* 77 (1965) 168-193.

[3] Jörg Jeremias, "Die Deutung der Gerichtsworte Michas in der Exilzeit," *ZAW* 83 (1971) 330-354.

[4] Nogalski, *Literary Precursors*, 278.

Fortunately, Nogalski's hypothesis was confirmed and further developed by Aaron Schart.[5] By calling the Book of the Four the "D-Korpus" (abbreviated "DK"), he indicated that the composition had its own specific language and topics, which cannot be identified with those of the typical Dtr literature (DtrH, JerD) completely.[6] Having investigated in detail the book of Amos literary-critically, Schart pointed out more redactional links than Nogalski had and was able to describe a particular set of theological intentions for this composition. In contrast to Nogalski, he supposed that the books of Hosea and Amos were already connected in the late pre-exilic period and presumed that the addition of the books of Micah and Zephaniah took place in two steps. In my view, however, these last two assumptions seem to complicate the thesis unnecessarily and are less convincing.[7] Regardless, the "D-Korpus" reconstructed by Schart agrees mainly with Nogalski's Book of the Four, apart from some smaller modifications and uncertainties (Hosea*; Amos 1:1-9,10*; Mic 1,1-3,12*; 6,1-16*; Zeph 1,1-3,8* [11-13?]).[8]

In spite of such impressive results, the redaction-historical work concerning the Book of the Twelve is still on shaky grounds. For example, Erich Bossard-Nepustil, one of the co-founders of this new approach, in spite of his general agreement with Nogalski, disputed the thesis that the book of Zephaniah belonged to Deuteronomistic corpus.[9] Moreover, Ehud ben Zvi has raised several material and methodological objections,[10] which

---

5   Aaron Schart, *Die Entstehung des Zwölfprophetenbuchs* (BZAW 260; Berlin, New York: de Gruyter, 1998).

6   Schart, *Entstehung*, 46.

7   The linguistic and structural correspondences between Hosea and Amos (e.g., calls for hearing in Hos 4:1; 5:1; Amos 3:1; 5:1 and the opening sections Hos 4:1-3; Amos 3:1-2), as already pointed out by Jörg Jeremias ("Die Anfänge des Dodekapropheten: Hosea und Amos," *Hosea und Amos: Studien zu den Anfängen des Dodekapropheton* [FAT 13; Tübingen: Mohr, 1996] 34-54), can be explained sufficiently by the assumption that the pupils of both prophets knew each other and do not call for a literary dependency.

8   According to Schart (*Entstehung*, 316-17) the DK-redaction can be identified in following verses: Hos 1:2b*; 2:6; 3:1*; 4:1*; 5:1-2*; 8:1b; 14:2-4; Amos 1:1-2, 9-12; 2:4-5, 10-12; 3:1b, 7; 4:6-11*; 5:11, 25-26*; 8:4-7, 11-12; 9:7-10; Mic 1:1, 2b, 5a, 6-7, 13b; 2:3*; 6,2-16; Zeph 1:1, 6, 13b, 17aβ.

9   Erich Bosshard-Nepustil, *Rezeptionen von Jesaja 1-39 im Zwölfprophetenbuch: Untersuchungen zur literarischen Verbindung von Prophetenbüchern in babylonischer und persischer Zeit* (OBO 145; Fribourg & Göttingen: Universitätsverlag Freiburg Schweiz and Vandenhoek & Ruprecht, 1997) 344–350. His argument that without the book of Zephaniah the supposed parallels with Isa 1-39 would fit better is too hypothetical to be convincing.

10 Ehud ben Zvi, "Twelve Prophetic Books or 'The Twelve.' A Few Preliminary Considerations," *Forming Prophetic Literature: Essays on Isaiah and the Twelve in Honor of*

should be taken seriously. I will only take up three of them, which seemed to me of the most interest for our subject. First, neither the Book of the Twelve, nor the supposed Book of the Four ever received a comprehensive heading.[11] Thus none of the Minor Prophets is necessarily a part of the composition, but can still be read and interpreted as a separate volume. Second, the argument that redactors used catchwords to form redactional links between different prophetic books seems to be doubtful,[12] since the mere fact that one more or less unspecific word occurs in two different literary units can be accidental in many cases. Interpreting such cases as deliberate links is arbitrary and unconvincing. Third, there is the danger that an interpretation on the wider redactional level can conceal the original meaning of a certain book and may lead to misunderstanding.[13] Thus, the question of how properly to interpret a big redactional unit, in which not only the redactor, but also the older voices edited by him say their own word at the same time should be answered.

II. Methodological Reflections

When I was confronted with the decision few years ago of whether I should deal with the new thesis of the Book of the Four in my new textbook about the exilic period,[14] I was skeptical and hesitated for a long time. The whole enterprise seemed to me too difficult and too complex, the objections too serious against it. I have to confess, though, that Nogalski and Schart convinced me as far as the Book of the Four is concerned that there are basic pieces of evidence that are not touched by Ben Zvi's objections. Moreover, I think it is possible to overcome most of the methodological and hermeneutical problems he raised and to arrive at more certainty.

First, I think we should restrict what we are entitled to call an "intentional link." The mere occurrence of the same word in two different literary units is not sufficient. There must be a specific expression consisting of several words, a reiterated word or several words, before we can speak of a catchword at all. Moreover, both literary units, or at least one of the units comprising the catchword, must be secondary in their or its context; only then we are allowed to speak of an intentional redactional link.

John D. W. Watts (eds. James W. Watts and Paul R. House; JSOTSup 235; Sheffield: Sheffield Academic Press, 1996) 125-156.

[11]   Ibid., 137, 151.

[12]   Ibid., 139–49.

[13]   Ibid., 126–27

[14]   Cf. Rainer Albertz, *Die Exilszeit: Das 6. Jahrhundert* (Biblische Enzyklopädie 7; Stuttgart: Kohlhammer, 2001) 164–85.

Second, each one of the four books under consideration should be investigated in detail. Only if the full range of tradition-historical and literary-critical levels of every book is clarified will there be a basis for correctly identifying all passages that probably belong to the redaction of the Book of the Four. This identification is crucial, since we may not start with the assumption that the redaction of the Book of the Four speaks a language that can clearly be specified as Dtr. Schart had already noticed some differences between the two. As far as I can see, the redactor's language, which undoubtedly shows many Dtr idioms of some kind, is also heavily influenced by Hosea, and less by Amos, Micah, and Zephaniah (or Jeremiah and Isaiah either). Thus, in reconstructing the Book of the Four we may not look for Dtr-stamped passages exclusively. Those passages may belong to the redaction, but need not. Also, there are passages that show no Dtr features, but may belong to it anyway. What is decisive is not the language and the style of the passage, but its redactional nature, its intention, and its dating relative to the redaction history of the book.[15]

Two examples will make this point clearer. On the one hand, Mic 6:1-13, mentioned by both Nogalski and Schart, clearly shows Dtr features, but it cannot belong to the Book of the Four because its position and its motives point clearly to the post-exilic period.[16] On the other hand, Mic 5:9-13 contains no typical Dtr language, but shows many connections to all four prophetic books. Specifically, it has clear features of a compositional text and is connected with other passages, which are already recognized as part of the redactional layer (Mic 1:6-7, 13b). Therefore, it probably belonged to the Book of the Four. What can be learned from redactional history in other parts of the Hebrew Bible (Pentateuch, DtrH, Isaiah, Deutero-Isaiah, Jeremiah) is also valid for the Book of the Four: redactors should not be restricted only to smaller additions, since often they were authors who could contribute larger parts to the books they were editing.

Third, I plead for the use of both the composition-critical and the redaction-historical method in order to gain more certainty in reconstructing a

---

[15] It may be dangerous, I am aware, to weaken the stylistic criterion, so I plead for supporting the 'Tendenzkritik' with redactional, compositional, and literary-historical arguments.

[16] Micah 6-7 clearly constitutes a later addition to the book. Mic 6:1 presupposes the framing of the earlier chapters by means of 1:2 and 5:14. This framing presents the book as YHWH's dispute with the foreign nations. This is a new perspective in contrast with Micah 1-3 as a whole, and it is exilic at the earliest. Consequently, the disputation in Mic 6:2-7 about Israel's proper offerings (which presupposes the existence of the temple cult) must be post-exilic. For this dating see Hans W. Wolff, Dodekatonpropheten: Micha (BKAT XIV/4; Neukirchen-Vluyn: Neukirchener Verlag, 1982), xxxii-xxxiii, 144–45; Rainer Kessler, Micha (HTKAT; Freiburg: Herder, 1999) 47, 255–56.

redactional unit. To demonstrate the existence of a Book of the Four, one has to show for it a sensible and structured composition, constituted by a programmatic beginning, a sequence of sub-units, and a meaningful conclusion. Of course, such a redactional composition like the Book of the Four, whose existence must be deduced from the larger Book of the Twelve, cannot be as clear in its structure as a literary unit that was independently formulated. Nevertheless, some kind of unity, some kind of progress, and some kind of a final solution should be discernible, if there was a rational editor at work that wanted to give any clear pieces of advice to his audience. Thus, such a prophetic composition, supposedly written in the later exilic period, cannot end in total destruction and hopelessness, particularly since it started with a much more hopeful perspective in the book of Hosea (2:16-17; 3:5; 11:8-11; 14:2-9). Thus, it is very unlikely that Zeph 3:8a formed the end of the Book of the Four, as Nogalski proposed.[17] It seems to me that Schart was on better grounds in asking whether the end should not be seen in the promise in Zeph 3:11-13.[18] On the basis of the composition-critical method the decision is clear: either Zeph 3:11-13 ended of the Book of the Four or that book never existed. Additionally, because this decision can be literary-critically confirmed by the insight that Zeph 3:1-8bα.10-13 constitutes a literary unit,[19] we have a clear result with a high degree of probability.

Fourth, I argue for a tradition-historical interpretation of such a complex redactional unit as the Book of the Four appears to be. In my view, the interpretation cannot be restricted to the redactional level, because the older levels of the prophetic traditions constitute the biggest part of the text and have to be recognized in some way. Still, the problem is to determine to what degree they should be recognized and how far they participate in shaping the theological profile of the whole composition. What shall we do with those passages which do not fit that profile properly or even oppose it in some way? I would like to propose that the interpreter should start with the redactional passages in order to determine the main theological intentions of the editor. Then one should study how far these intentions agree or differ with the messages offered by the older layers of the given prophetic books. Finally, one should describe in detail what the editor has learned from the

---

[17] Cf. Nogalski, *Literary Precursors*, 175–78. It seems that Nogalski meant Zeph 3:8bα. He noted some uncertainty concerning 3:9-11.

[18] Cf. Schart, *Entstehung*, 214; he noted several links to central parts of Hosea, Amos, and Micah.

[19] Cf. the same address of Jerusalem and several verbal correspondences: מ/בקרבך Zeph 3:3, 5, 11, 12; עליל ותך Zeph 3:7, 11, עשה עולה Zeph 3:13, cf. 3:5. God's judgement in Zeph 3:8 is directed against the officials of Jerusalem (3rd person plural!) accused in 3:3–4 and removed in 3:11. Zeph 3:8bβ.9-10 belongs to a later redaction with a universal horizon, cf. 1:3aβ.b.18b; 2:10-11.

traditions of one prophet or the other, what he has altered, what he has interpreted in a new fashion, and what he has put aside. Thus, the result can be the description of a vivid dialogue between the editor and the prophetic voices that he wanted to present in a new shape.

III. My Own Proposal

A. The Headings

As Nogalski and Schart have already shown, the best starting point for the hypothesis is constituted by the headings of the four books (Hos 1:1; Amos 1:1; Mic 1:1; Zeph 1:1). The four prophets are ordered in a chronological line, starting from the days of Uzziah and Jeroboam II (Hosea, Amos), continuing through the days of Jotham, Ahaz and Hezekiah (Hosea, Micah) and ending with the days of Josiah (Zephaniah). Hosea was set in the first position and given a long-lasting career that overlapped Amos, the oldest of the four prophets. (The reason for the inversion will be shown later.) Apart from the book of Amos, which preserved an older type of heading ("words of Amos"), the other three books are all titled as "word of YHWH" (דבר יהוה). The title shows that the Book of the Four claims to comprise the one word of God, which was revealed to the four prophets over the course of about 150 years concerning Israel and Judah. In the first stage of the book (Hosea, Amos) the divine word concerned Israel (Amos 1:1); in the second phase (Micah, Zephaniah) it shifted from Samaria to Jerusalem (Mic 1:1). Thus we can see the redactor's intention not only to parallel YHWH's judgments on Israel with those of Judah, but also to point out the common divine message of these four prophets that his exilic audience should hear.

B. Micah

As Nogalski pointed out, the transfer of the word of YHWH from Samaria to Jerusalem, hinted at already in Mic 1:1, is realized in Mic 1:2-9.[20] YHWH's theophany first resulted in a prophecy of doom over Samaria (1:6-7) and then continued as an "incurable stroke" against the gate of Jerusalem (1:8-9). Nogalski considered Mic 1:2-4 as a literary unit. That would lead to the consequence that the whole overture of the book of Micah must be considered redactional and could not be dated before the Persian period.[21] To

---

[20] Cf. Nogalski, *Literary Precursors*, 129-137; he is followed by Schart, *Entstehung*, 177–181; Kessler, *Micha*, 80–94.

[21] So consequently Kessler (*Micha*, 80-5) who argues that Mic 1:2-7 must be considered as *vaticinium ex eventu* that presupposes the chapter 6 (cf. the links between Mic 1:2 and 5:14; 6,1), which can clearly be dated in the Persian period; cf. note 16 above.

prove that the Four-Prophets-Redactor (FPR) actually connected a form of
the book of Micah with the other three prophetic books, it is of crucial importance to recognize the redactional traces in Mic 1:2-9. Wolff has pointed
out that Mic 1:2, including transitional first two words of 1:3 (הנה כי), belongs to a later edition of the book that stresses the universal dimension of
its message.[22] Already in 1938 Alfred Jepsen showed that the theophany
originally ran directly towards Jerusalem and thus Mic 1:5b-7 is to be considered secondary.

Micah 1,5a For the crime of Jacob is all this,
            for the sins of the house of Israel.
      5b   What is the crime of Jacob?
                      Is it not Samaria?
                      And what are the high places of Judah?
                      Are they not Jerusalem?
      6   I will make Samaria into a ruin in the field
                      a place to plant vineyards.
                      I will pour out her stones into the valley,
                      and uncover her foundations.
      7   All her images shall be smashed;
                      all her Ashera shall be burned by fire;
                      all her idols I will lay waste.
                      For she collected them as the fee of a harlot,
                      so to the fee of a harlot they shall revert.[23]

The secondary character of this passage becomes clear if one realizes
that the two terms "Jacob" and "Israel" in v. 5a (which elsewhere in the
book of Micah clearly denote the Southern kingdom; cf. Mic 3:1, 9; cf.
1:14-15; 2:7) are reinterpreted by the two questions of v. 5b. There, "Jacob"
– the redactor wanted the audience to acknowledge – meant "Samaria,"[24]
while "Israel" referred to "Judah." From this reading of 1:5a, the FPR concluded (in 1:5b) that Micah had also prophesied over the Northern Kingdom. Thus he found the warrant to add his view that YHWH had pronounced a verdict against Samaria (1:6) similar to that on Jerusalem (3:12).

---

[22] Wolff, *Micha*, xxviii-ix, 14-5, 23-4; cf. the doublet Mic 1:2b and 3a and the lack of
      any universal perspective in 1:3-9. Both divergent perspectives are artificially con-
      nected by the term עד. YHWH's judgment over his people is a warning for the nations
      that something similar could happen to them (5:14).
[23] The English translation is taken from James L. Mays, *Micah: A Commentary* (OTL;
      London: SCM, 1976) 41, 45–6.
[24] Actually, as it turns out, the word referred only to some part of the Northern Kingdom,
      not the whole people.

Moreover, he aligned the prophetical messages by introducing Hosea's accusation against idolatry (cf. Hos 1:2; 2:12, 14; 4:17; 11:2) into the prophecy of Micah. The redactor agreed with Hosea that the typical sin of the North had been idolatry, but he was of the opinion that likewise the people of the South, who trusted wrongly in the temple (Mic 3:11), turned the holy place into an illegitimate high place (cf. במה in 1:5b and 3:12).

In the view of the FPR, Zion's "chief sin" was her illusionary trust in weapons, especially horses and chariots, as he announced in Mic 1:13b, a passage long considered secondary.[25] But his general statement about the sins of Jerusalem and God's judgment on the city can be found in 5:9-13, a passage that constitutes an alien body in the context of the salvation oracles of Micah 4-5 and could have originally followed directly the concluding prophecy of doom in 3:9-12.[26] As already mentioned, the text is highly compositional. It has many connections to the other books[27], and the close links between Mic 5:9, 12-13 on the one hand and 1:13b, 6-7 on the other verify that it belongs to the same redactional layer.

Micah 5,9 It shall be in that day, oracle of YHWH,
           I will cut off your horses from your midst
           And I will wreck your chariots.
       10 I will cut off the cities of your land
           And I will overthrow all your fortresses.
       11 I will cut off sorceries from your hand,
           And you have no soothsayers.
       12 I will cut off your images
           And your pillars from the midst.
           You shall not bow down again
           to the work of your hands.

---

[25] Ibid., 52; cf. Wolff, *Micha*, 18; Kessler, *Micha*, 108.

[26] Cf. the same expression בקרב in Mic 3:11 and 5:9, 12; in the passage 5:9-13, with the addressee in the 2nd Pers., now punctuated as masc. gender according to 5:6-7, probably Jerusalem has been meant originally. The verse 5:14 concerned again with the nations, belongs to a later universal redaction (cf. 1:2; 6:1). Also the introduction 5:9aα modelled on 4:6, might be a later addition. Perhaps the verse 5:8, understood as lament of the people, could have served as a bridging link to 3:12. In my view all the salvation oracles in between must be seen as later additions; cf. Albertz, *Exilszeit*, 170.

[27] Concerning the horses and chariots in Mic 5:9b cf. 1:13; Hos 10:13; 14:4; concerning the cities and fortresses in 5:10, 13 cf. Hos 8:14: 10:14; 13:10; Amos 5:9; Zeph 1:16. The sorceries and soothsayers are forbidden in Deut 18:10, which reminds one of the Dtr list in Jer 27:9. Concerning the idols, pillars and Asherim in 5:12 cf. Hos 3:4; 10,1-2; Mic 1:7. The expression "work of your hands" in 5:12 reminds one of Hos 14:4b.

     13 I will root out your Asherim from your midst
        And I will destroy your cities.

The thesis that Mic 5:9-13 derived from the FPR, a possibility which has been overlooked so far by scholars like Nogalski and Schart, has two far-reaching consequences. First, it reveals how the exilic redactor understood the destruction of Jerusalem and Judah in 587 B.C. In his view, YHWH's judgment had to be understood as an act of purification. By his judgment YHWH wanted to separate Judah from all those things that had led the people to sin against him: weapons, fortresses, sorceries, idols and other cult symbols. Thus the loss of all these things, a loss Judah had lamented following the catastrophe, must have come about for her benefit.

Second, the passage Mic 5:9-13, which once constituted the end of the exilic book of Micah, does not stand in isolation. On the contrary, the concept of purifying judgment constitutes the redactional chain of the whole composition. Passages comprising the same concept can be also found at the end of the book of Amos (9:7-10) and at the end of the book of Zephaniah (3:11-13). Another passage occurs in the beginning of the book of Zephaniah (1:4-6) that shows close verbal and motive correspondences to Mic 5:9-13.[28] So all these passages were probably composed by the same redactor. If we have a look at the book of Hosea we can notice two similar passages: first Hos 3:1-5, where YHWH withdraws all the benefits from his adulterous wife for a long time; and second 14:2-4, where – after YHWH's judgment – a contrite Israel himself pledges that it will no longer trust in weapons and idols, but only in God. Both passages belong to the inherited Hosean tradition and therefore do not fit the redactional concept totally; nevertheless the FPR integrated them into his composition. If we include the two Hosean passages into our consideration, the Book of the Four shows a clear compositional structure. We have one purification passage at the end of each of the four books (Hos 14:2-4; Amos 9:7-10; Mic 5:9-13; Zeph 3:11-13), and one additional purification passage in the beginning of the first and of the last book each (Hos 3:1-5; Zeph 1:4-6). The unifying concept of an ongoing purification, combined with that clear symmetric structure are – apart from the headings that Nogalski has shown – another strong argument for the thesis that a redactional composition, which comprises these four prophetic books, really existed. The following investigations will confirm this.

---

28   Cf. the typical וְהִכְרַתִּי , four times in Mic 5:9-12 and one time in Zeph 1:4b; cf. also
    the long enumeration of objects that will be wiped out.

C. Zephaniah

As already mentioned, Mic 5:9-13 is closely linked with Zeph 1:4-6. This passage stands outside the "Day of the Lord" composition (1:7-2:4) and is redactional throughout.[29] In the view of the FPR, YHWH's purifying judgment in the days of Hezekiah was repeated in the days of Josiah. All the cults of foreigners that invaded Judah during the 7th century would be wiped out, including their priests, idols and worshippers. Schart has already pointed out that the strange expression "the rest of the Baal" (שְׁאָר הַבַּעַל) can only be understood in the wider horizon of the Book of the Four.[30] It includes all that remained after Hosea's damnation of Baalism (Hos 2:10, 15; 7:15; 11:2, 7; 13,1). As often noticed, there exist clear parallels between Zeph 1:4-6 and 2 Kings 23 (cf. esp. vv. 4-5, 12).[31] So the FPR wanted to interpret Josiah's cult reform in the sense of a purifying judgment, which had been announced by Zephaniah.[32]

However, the cleansing of the cult from idolatry did not remove all the sins of Judah. At the end of Zeph 1:4-6 some people are mentioned "who have not sought (בִּקֵּשׁ) YHWH or consulted (דָּרַשׁ) him." By that clause the FPR created the possibility of appending Zephaniah's prophecy about a horrible day of wrath (1:7-2,4*)[33] that would come over all the vain officials and the ill-gotten riches of Jerusalem. YHWH had to announce another judgment that would remove the corrupt upper class. In the view of the editor, only the pious poor who seek YHWH (בַּקְּשׁוּ) and do his law perhaps would have a chance (2:3a).

This divine judgment is demonstrated in the second part of the book, Zeph 2:5-3,13*.[34] According to my literary-critical analysis, this part is en-

---

[29] Schart (*Entstehung*, 107–109) attributed only Zeph 1:6 to the "D-Korpus." As Klaus Seybold (*Satirische Prophetie: Studien zum Buch Zephanja* [SBS 120; Stuttgart: Katholisches Bibelwerk, 1985] 85) has shown, the whole passage has Dtr. features and is redactional throughout.

[30] Cf. Schart, *Entstehung*, 209.

[31] Cf. Marco Striek, *Das vordeuteronomistische Zephanjabuch* (BBET 29; Frankfurt am Main: Lang, 1999) 95–106.

[32] Similarly, Seybold, *Satirische Prophetie*, 85.

[33] Zeph 1:13b (cf. Amos 5:11); 1:17aβ; 2:3a (cf. Amos 8:4) are insertions of the FPR into the older composition.

[34] The oracles in Zeph 3:14-20 do not presuppose a partial salvation any longer and are therefore later additions. Further, 3:14-15 shows influences of Deutero-Isaiah and can be dated in the late exilic time (539-520 B.C.). The rest of the oracles are even later. For the dating of the first edition of Deutero-Isaiah in the year 521 B.C., see Albertz, *Exilszeit*, 296-301.

tirely composed by the FPR,[35] using older materials like oracles against foreign nations (2:5-6, 8-9a, 12, 13-15) and a hymn verse (3:5). Combining prophecies of doom against foreign nations with those threatening doom against Jerusalem, he wanted to create a counterpart to Amos 1:3-2:16 and to give a similar message. YHWH's threatening word (דבר יהוה) had come over the nations (Zeph 2:5) and caused heavy destructions, especially of the Assyrian empire (2:13-15), but the elite of Jerusalem did not learn their lesson (3:2), as YHWH hoped they would (3:6-7). Instead, they continued with their cruel and corrupt activity (3:3-4), so God in his justice (3:5) decided to pour out his anger over this arrogant upper class (3:8abα) and remove it from Jerusalem (3:10). After this last purifying judgment, YHWH would start a new history with the "humble and poor people," who were left in Jerusalem (3:11). So, at the end of his composition the FPR draws an ideal picture of a totally purified society without any officials, palaces, fortified cities, arms, and idols, which would have learned to trust only in God and to avoid any deceit and injustice (3:12).

D. Amos

Having established the conclusion of the Book of the Four, it is possible to reconstruct its earlier form with near certainty. As far as the redactional portions in the book of Amos are concerned, scholars have reached more of a consensus. Schmidt, who discovered the Dtr. redaction in the book of Amos, ascribed to it the following verses: Amos 1:1*; 1:9-12; 2:4-5; 2:10-12; 3:1*, 7; 5:25-26.[36] Wolff considered adding Amos 8:11-12.[37] Examining these results in his detailed investigation, Schart arrived at a similar result. His major differences are the addition of Amos 4:6-11; 8:4-7; 9:7-10 to the texts named before.[38] If we examine these additional passages, we will get different results: As Wolff and Jeremias had already shown, Amos 4:6-13 constitutes a literary unit;[39] thus this passage belongs to an exilic redac-

---

[35] Striek (*Zephanjabuch*, 169-171, 187) has ascribed the verses Zeph 3:2, 7 to a Dtr redaction with sound reasons (cf. Jer 7:28, 35:13 both JerD), but it is impossible to remove them from their wider context. Consequently the whole composition belongs to that redaction. Only Zeph 2:7, 9, 10-11; 3:8bβ, 9-10 are later additions.

[36] Cf. Schmidt, "Die deuteronomistische Redaktion," 169–190.

[37] Cf. H. H. Wolff, *Dodekapropheton 2: Joel und Amos* (BKAT XIV/2: Neukirchen-Vluyn: Neukirchener Verlag, 1969) 136–37.

[38] Cf. the listing in Schart, *Entstehung*, 317; he also included Amos 5:11, but that is uncertain.

[39] Wolff, *Amos*, 253; Jörg Jeremias, *Der Prophet Amos* (ATD 24/2; Göttingen: Vandenhoeck & Ruprecht, 1995) 47–56. Bossard-Nepustil, *Rezeptionen*, 348, considered all the Amos doxologies as part of Book of the Four redaction, but that is even more improbable.

tion which prepared the book of Amos for its use in the cult. This redactional layer, to which the other doxologies 5:8-9 and 9:5-6 also belong in my view, precedes the Book of the Four.[40] In contrast to Schart's opinion, the passage Amos 8:4-7 should be dated pre-exilic,[41] because the Sabbath mentioned here still has the shape of a lunar festival (par. הַחֹדֶשׁ), celebrated every fortnight, rather than the shape of a weekly celebration separated from the moon cycle, which was introduced during the exilic period.[42]

However, Schart's insight that with Amos 9:7-10 the FPR created a new conclusion to the book of Amos is a very nice advance in our research. This is especially so since Nogalski's opinion that the book should end in 9:1-6 with the purpose "to pronounce the destruction of Israel"[43] would not fit the hopeful perspective that we have found at the end of the books of Micah and Zephaniah. My compositional argument confirms Schart's redaction-critical decision very nicely: the passage Amos 9:7-10 deals again with a purifying judgment of YHWH.

The main problem the FPR had to struggle with was the radical and total divine judgment that Amos and his early pupils had announced: Israel would come to its end (Amos 8:2); even experiencing the exile would not improve its chances of survival (9:4). That view seemed to exclude any hope. On the one hand, therefore, the redactor tried to explain this horrible judgment of God by stressing the sins that Israel had committed. It had not only promoted injustice and oppressed the poor, but it had also – as could be seen in the expulsion of Amos – repressed the word of God proclaimed by the prophets (2:11-12). Therefore, in the throes of the disaster, the word

---

[40]   Cf. Albertz, *Exilszeit*, 177-78. Schart's view is founded on the observation that Amos 8:8 constitutes a redactional link between 8:4-7 and the doxology in 9:5-6. Since he regards 8:4-7 as part of the redaction of the Book of the Four, he is forced to conclude that the doxologies presuppose these verses. But Amos 8:4-7 is older; see below. On the contrary, by inserting the verb וְדֹרֵךְ into Mic 1:3, the FPR probably establishes a link to the doxology in Amos 4:13.

[41]   In my view the passage is part of a late pre-exilic edition of the book, to which the passages Amos 1:2; 3:13-14; 5:26; 8:4-7, 9-10, 13-14; 9:1-4 belong. I also reckon with an earlier edition of the late 8th century B.C., which comprised Amos 1:1-8:3*. For more details see Albertz, *Exilszeit*, 177–78.

[42]   Cf. the pre-exilic parallels 2 Kgs 4:23; Isa 1:13; Hos 2:13; Lam 2:6 for differences from the exilic praxis shown in Deut 5:12-15. For the probable development cf. Rainer Albertz, A *History of Israelite Religion in the Old Testament Period* (2 vols; OTL; Louisville: Westminster, 1992) 2:408-410.

[43]   Nogalski, *Literary Precursors*, 121.

of YHWH (דבר יהוה) was no longer available, although Israel would need it now more than daily bread (8:11-12).[44]

On the other hand, the FPR tried to open the end of the book to the possibility of survival by appending a new ending.

Amos 9:7 Are you not like the Cushites to me, Israelites? – oracle
of YHWH –
Did I not bring Israel up from the land of Egypt,
the Philistines from Caphtor, and Aram from Kir?
8 Behold, the eyes of Adonay-YHWH are on that sinful kingdom,
I will wipe it off the face of the earth.
However, I will not wipe out the house of Jacob totally.
9 Behold, I will give my orders
and I will shake [...][45] the house of Israel
as a sieve is shaken to and fro
and not a pebble falls on the ground.
10 By the sword all sinners of my people shall die,
who say: "You will not let the disaster come near and meet us."

First, the FPR rejected any attempt to avoid the terrible prophecy of Amos by referring to the election of Israel. What could be learned already from Amos 3:1-2 was that Israel was no less guilty than its neighbors so far as sinfulness was concerned. Second, the editor restricted the application of the awful message that YHWH had fixed his eyes on evil (9:4) with regard to the "sinful kingdom," which would be wiped off the face of the earth (9:8a). Israel as a whole, as the redactor interpreted the older prophecy, was not that kingdom and would not be wiped out totally (9:8b). It would, to be sure, have to undergo a purifying judgment in which God would shake all Israel in a big sieve. All those who still denied the word of God prophesied by Amos would be kept in the sieve and killed by the sword. As for those who accepted the prophetic message and corrected themselves, we may infer they would have the chance to bypass the sieve and constitute God's new people.

We must now raise the question of how the abolition of the "sinful kingdom" is to be understood. Schart thinks that the kingdom of the Northern state is meant, not only here but in the Book of the Four throughout.[46]

---

[44] Notice the use of the singular in Amos 8:12 as in the headings. The plural in 8:11 is textually uncertain. Cf. the use of בקש as in Zeph 1:6; 2:3; the clause might be modelled on Hos 5:6.
[45] Delete בכל־הגוים as a later addition, which spoils the parable. It interpreted the diaspora existence rather than the foreign invasion as the purifying instrument.
[46] Cf. Schart, *Entstehung*, 227-229.

He refers to the fact that most of the criticism against kings and kingship occurs in the books of Hosea (1:4; 3:4; 5:1; 7:7; 8:4; 10:7, 15; 13:9-11) and Amos (7:11). Additionally, of course, the post-exilic editor who appended Amos 9:11-12, announcing the reestablishment of the Davidic kingdom, understood 9:8b in such a restricted sense. To me, however, Schart's understanding seems to be mistaken. We have to remember that some criticism is raised also against the Judean royal family in Zeph 1:8, and that in the vision of the ideal future society of Jerusalem at the end of the whole book (3:11-13) no Davidic king is mentioned. If we take into account that the FPR wanted to make parallel the messages of the Northern and Southern prophets in order to present them as the "one word of YHWH" to his exilic audience, it will be improbable to suggest that he wanted to underline a difference between them at just that crucial point of future kingship. I think the Judah passage (Amos 2:4-5) in the overture (1:3-2:16) inserted by the FPR, testifies that he wanted to apply the whole book of Amos to a Judean audience. To report a verdict against the Northern kingdom alone would simply make a theoretical statement, so Schart's interpretation seems unlikely.

We know from other texts that the question of whether the Davidic rule should be restored was hotly debated during the exilic and the early post-exilic period (2 Kgs 25:27-30; Jer 22:24-30; Hag 2:20-23; Isa 55:5).[47] Amos 9:8 can easily be understood as a voice in this discussion. Since all promises of a new Davidic kingdom in Hos 3:5, Amos 9:11-12, and Mic 5:1-2 are later additions, and never belonged to the Book of the Four, it is most probable that the FPR – as radical as the Dtr. pupils of Jeremiah – intended to proclaim a general rejection of Israelite and Judean kingship. For FPR the monarchy belonged to the institutions that caused the people to sin against God.[48] Therefore it had to be removed by YHWH like other state attributes such as arms and fortresses. Understood in this way, the book of Amos too fits in the series of purifying judgements investigated so far (Mic 5:9-13; Zeph 1:4-6; 3:11-13).

E. Hosea

Finally, at the beginning of his work the FPR positioned the book of Hosea. This choice was by no means natural. It distorted to some degree the chronological order of the composition. Since Amos was the oldest prophet it should have been placed first. Probably this decision has a theological

---

[47]   Cf. Rainer Albertz, "In Search of the Deuteronomists: A First Solution to a Historical Riddle,"in *The Future of the Deuteronomistic History* (ed T. Römer; BETL 147; Leuven: Leuven University Press and Peeters, 2000) 1-17; idem, *Exilszeit*, 249-50.
[48]   Cf. Amos' expulsion from Bethel, the monarchic sanctuary (Amos 7:13). It is pronounced by the priest Amaziah, but surely ordered by the king.

basis. As will be seen from many motives and ideas that shaped the whole composition, the book of Hosea achieved paradigmatic significance for the editor. Moreover, Hosea has the most developed perspective of salvation of all four books. So it was suitable for the entrance of a work that aimed at having a look beyond the catastrophe.

A serious problem in research into the Book of the Four is that so far nearly no traces of a Dtr. edition of Hosea have been found. Since the work of Lothar Perlitt, only Hos 8,1b had been accepted as a Dtr. addition.[49] Schart proposed adding more verses, taking Hos 1:1, 2b*; 2:6; 3:1*; 4:1*; 5:1-2*; 8:1b; 14:2-4 as part of the "D-Korpus." However, his proposals are not all equally convincing. In 3:1bβ we can find a Dtr. expression ("although they resort to other Gods"; cf. Deut 31:18, 20). The insertion of the phrase דבר יהוה into 4:1 may have been made by the FPR. Perhaps there might be a slight realignment in Hos 5:1-2*.[50] Hos 1:2b and 2:6 are admittedly redactional, but they belong to the older composition of Hosea 1-3*. Further, the passage Hos 14:2-4 does play an important role in the Book of the Four, but cannot be ascribed to the FPR in my view, because vv. 2aα and 5aα are already cited in Jer 3:22a and must be dated earlier.[51] Thus only Hos 1:1; 3:1bβ; 4:1*; 8,1b can be considered certain.

Be that as it may, some other verses considered secondary and ascribed to Judean redactions or not assigned at all,[52] are appropriate candidates for the FPR, provided we do not look for Dtr. features exclusively but also for topics that fit well with other redactional passages in the Book of the Four. In Hos 1:5, 7 the well-known theme of destroying weapons is taken up prominently (cf. Mic 5:9); and in Hos 8:14, a verse that can surely be dated late exilic, the building of palaces and fortified cities is said to be a special sin of Judah. This latter accusation is similar to Zeph 1:16 (cf. Mic 5:10).[53] The polemic against cult places outside Jerusalem in Hos 4:15 constitutes a

---

[49] Lothar Perlitt, *Bundestheologie im Alten Testament* (WMANT 36; Neukirchen-Vluyn: Neukirchener Verlag, 1969) 146-152.

[50] Schart, *Entstehung,* 186-87.

[51] Jörg Jeremias (*Der Prophet Hosea* [ATD 24/2; Göttingen: Vandenhoeck & Ruprecht, 1983] 171–72, ascribed Hos 14:2-9 to the pupils of Hosea, perhaps after they fled to Judah around 722 B.C. I regard Jer 3:19-4:2 as part of Jeremiah's early prophecy, which was still directed to Northern Israelites, spoken before the death of Josiah, 609 B.C., cf. Rainer Albertz, "Jer 2-6 und die Frühzeitverkündigung Jeremias," *ZAW* 94 (1982) 20-47.

[52] Cf. the listing presented by Jörg Jeremias, "Hosea/Hoseabuch," *TRE* 15:586-598, esp. 592.

[53] Cf. the allusions to Deutero-Isaiah (Isa 44:2; 51:13). The compositional character of the verse can be seen in the fact that the announcement of judgment refers to Amos 1:4 et al.

redactional link to Amos 8:14; also the secondary polemic against idols in Hos 8:6a fit the topic of idolatry (cf. Mic 1:6-7; 5:12-13). Finally, the clearly secondary remark about Israel's refusal to turn back in Hos 11:5b, which takes up Jer 5:3; 8:5 and reminds one of Zeph 3:2, may be ascribed to the FPR. Thus, in all probability, the hand of FPR can be seen in Hos 1:1, 5, 7; 3:1bβ; 4:1*, 15; 8:1b, 6a, 14; 11:5b. To be sure, these verses constitute only traces, but they show that the book of Hosea demonstrably belongs in the Book of the Four.

Otherwise I agree with Schart's statement that the small amount of re-dactional work in Hosea can be explained by simply saying that "Die D-Redaktion ihre theologische Konzeption in dieser Schrift auch ohne größere Eingriffe ausgesprochen fand."[54] Actually, in the book of Hosea the FPR could find all the topics that were important to him: the basic evil of idola-try (Hos 2:4-17; 4:14-14 et. al.; cf. Mic 1:6-7; 5:12-13; Zeph 1:4-6), a sinful trust in arms and allies (Hos 5:11-14; 7:8-9, 10-11; 8:9; 10:13-14; 14:4; cf. Mic 1,13b; 5:9-10, 13; Zeph 1:16), a criticism of kingship (Hos 1:4; 3:4; 5:1; 7:7; 10:7, 15; 13:10-11; cf. Amos 9:8) and of the officials (Hos 5:1-2; 7:3-7, 16; cf. Zeph 3:3-4). Even social criticism, otherwise untypical for Hosea, appears once (Hos 4:1-2). Multiplied by Amos and Micah, it founded the "social gospel" at the end of the Book of the Four (Zeph 2:3; 3:11-13). Finally the important topic of rejecting the prophets, with which the redactor dealt in Amos 2:10-11 (cf. 7:9-17; Zeph 3:2, 7), appeared in Hos 9:7-9, 17.

The FPR did not need to add substantially to the Hosean prophecy, but he did want to underscore some of its themes. He used Hosea's verdict against the Northern Kingdom announced in the overture of the book (Hos 1:4) to introduce his criticism of weapons (1:5). Not only would Israel's kingship come to an end, but also its bows would be broken. In contrast to Israel's condemnation symbolically pronounced by Hosea, the editor an-nounced a divine rescue of Judah that would happen not by arms and war, but by mysterious, God-like measures (1:7). This overture fits perfectly in a book that will go on to tell about the removal of the kingdom (Amos 9:8), of arms and fortresses (Mic 5:9-10; Zeph 1:16), and arrogant officials (Zeph 3:11) by divine, purifying judgments, leaving only a poor and humble peo-ple at the end.

The awful aberrations of the North denounced by Hosea led the FPR to teach his audience a lesson. With his warning to Judeans in Hos 4:15 not to visit the cult places in Gilgal, Bethel and Beersheba, he perhaps wanted to prevent the exilic people's abandoning the centralization of the cult achieved under Josiah because of the destruction of the temple in Jerusalem

---

[54]   Schart, *Entstehung*, 169.

by the Babylonians. By inserting the Dtn.-Dtr. term ברית in Hos 8:1b he wanted to show that all the misdeeds of Northern Israel that Hosea had condemned in this chapter were transgression of God's covenant and violations of his תורה written in the book of Deuteronomy. When the FPR repeated in Amos 2:4 a similar accusation against Judah (מאס תורת־יהוה), he wanted to equate the transgressions of the two nations on a fundamental theological level. Although the sins of Israel and Judah were different in some respect, they both had broken the covenant. The Judeans could not boast to their Northern brothers.

More than in the other three books, Hosea offers the possibility of a new beginning after destruction. Several promises of salvation occur here, either originally included in prophecies of doom (Hos 2:4-17; 11:1-11) or attached later (2:18, 21-22; 14:2-9). Most of the salvation oracles of the book[55] can be dated pre-exilic, thus preceding the FPR. So we can imagine that they were of crucial importance for him, since he wanted to open future prospects for the exilic generation. It can be shown that he developed all the theological concepts of his work on the basis of what is said about the relation between divine judgement and salvation in the Hosean prophecy.

In the book of Hosea one can find a repeated movement from judgment towards salvation (Hos 2:4-18, 21-22; 3:1-5; 4-11; 12-14). In accordance with this structure, the FPR arranged his work generally in that way, with passages comprising the hopeful purifying judgments being set at the ends of the books (Amos 9:7-10; Mic 5:9-13; Zeph 3:11-13). By that arrangement he surely wanted to give his exilic audience a piece of advice: any chance for survival could be found only by accepting YHWH's judgment, not by denying its results.

From the book of Hosea, the FPR could learn that judgment and salvation are both part of God's lawsuit (ריב) with his unfaithful people (Hos 2:4; 4:1, 4; 12:3). Both are founded in God's passionate love; both aimed to bring his beloved people back to him (2:4-17; 11:1-11). Thus, all judgment of YHWH aimed at Israel's repentance (2:9b; 5:15; 11:11; 14:2-4); all judgement of God had a pedagogical intention. It never ended his relationship to Israel, but aimed at making a new start possible. This insight drawn from Hosea permitted the FPR to alter the hopeless ending of the books of Amos and Micah.

Moreover, from Hosea the FPR learned that God's judgment itself consists of saving elements. By removing all his blessings (Hos 2:11, 14; 9:2) YHWH intended to lead Israel to the recognition it owed all its wealth to

---

[55] The salvation oracles Hos 2:1-3, 20, 23-25 are considered post-exilic additions, cf. Jeremias, *Hosea*, 48–9.

God. By removing all the things that led Israel astray, from the baalized cult to the bull icon of Bethel (2:13, 15, 19; 9:4-5; 10:5), Israel could be brought back to YHWH.

All these elements are bound together in the symbolic act in Hos 3:1-5* where the prophet is ordered to marry an adulterous woman in order both to keep her away from all her lovers and to withdraw from her all loving care. This symbol act comprises at the same time love and punishment, and it aimed at Israel's return to her divine husband. The second part of the passage runs as follows:

Hosea 3:3 Then I said to her:
"Many days you will sit in my house
and not play the harlot
and have no intercourse with a man, nor I with you."
4 For the Israelites will sit there without king or official
without sacrifice or pillar, without ephod or teraphim;[56]
5 but after that the Israelites will turn back
and will seek (בקשׁ) YHWH, their God, [...]
and will anxiously approach to YHWH and to his goods [...].[57]

The divine punishment consists of the withdrawal of all that Israel has loved instead of God and all that seduced it to apostasy: the kingdom, the officials, the sacrifices, cult places, and all oracle instruments.

I think that the FPR developed his concept of purifying judgment directly from this Hosean idea of divine punishment, founded on God's love and aiming at Israel's education. Moreover, it seems to me that Hos 3:1-5* especially constitutes the textual basis on which the FPR modelled his own purification passages. The stylistic feature of listing those things that YHWH would withdraw, reminds one of Mic 5:9-13; Zeph 1:4-6; 3:11. It is not by chance that four of the six elements named in Hos 3:4 are literally taken up in those passages and that the remaining two elements have their material equivalents.[58]

---

[56] Ephod and teraphim should be interpreted here as oracle instruments; see Judg 17:5; 18:14-20; 1 Sam 23:9-12; 30:7-8; Ezek 21:26; and Jeremias, *Hosea*, 56.

[57] Jeremias (*Hosea*, 57–8) ascribed Hos 3:5 to an early addition because it was presupposed in Jer 2:19 (Syr., Vetus Latina). In any case it preceded the FPR. However, postexilic additions to v. 5 were, according to Jeremias, the ill-fitting phrase "and David, their king" and the eschatological formula "at the end of the days."

[58] Concerning מלך cf. ממלכה in Amos 9:8; concerning שׂר cf. Zeph 3:3, 11; concerning זבח cf. Amos 5:25; concerning מצבה cf. Mic 5:12. Concerning the oracle instruments cf. the sorceries and soothsayers in Mic 5:12.

Of course there is a little difference between the two concepts: Hosea spoke of withdrawal, the editor of purification. The latter used harsh words in order to stress the total destruction and complete removal of all the seducers.[59] However, even this difference can be explained by the Hosean prophecy. Hosea underlines several times that Israel's return to God would be difficult (Hos 6:1-6; 7:10, 16) or even impossible (11:7). Since Israel became so enslaved by its seducers, YHWH was forced to use severe measures to heal its apostasy (14:5). The FPR developed this idea just a bit further. Since Israel was incapable of dissociating itself from all those seductive powers, God himself would destroy them with all his might. By his purifying judgement, the scene would be so completely cleansed that no relapse would be possible. Thus the book of Hosea can be considered the model that shaped the concept and the structure of the Book of the Four.

IV. Concluding Remarks

The drastic way in which Israel's salvation is realized according to the Book of the Four excludes the idea that the new beginning could be done by restoring the pre-exilic conditions simply. On the contrary, by pronouncing that state attributes like the kingship, the officials, the fortified cities, palaces, chariots, horses and other weapons are removed by God forever, the book pleads for a radical new start. Not the old upper class, but the poor and humble, who should be immune to arrogance and injustice, would characterize the future society.

Judged by this concept the FPR belonged to the most radical groups of the exilic period.[60] He stood in opposition to the group behind the DtrH, who pleaded for the full restoration of the pre-exilic state, though in the shape that it had found during the reforms of Josiah. Also the reform priests around Ezekiel wanted a radical new start, but they still reckoned with the old elites, the priest and the king, although the latter, according to this group, would be much more restricted in power. More radical were the authors of the Dtr books of Jeremiah, who rejected the restoration of the Davidic rule and pleaded for a religious and moral renewal of all the people. But they did not denounce the upper class at all.

As can be seen, the FPR was generally oriented towards the Dtn and Dtr theology, but this orientation was in no way exclusive. His theology and language were also strongly influenced by the four prophets whose books he edited. As shown, he was most closely related to Hosea. Amazingly

---

[59] Cf. הכרית Mic 5:9-12; Zeph 1:4; השמיד Amos 9:8; שבר Hos 1:5.

[60] For details concerning the different exilic literature and their tradents cf. Albertz, *Exilszeit*, 163-323.

enough, the FPR referred also to the prophet Isaiah, especially to his criticism of enthusiasm for military might (Isa 14:32; 30:1-5, 15-16; 31:1-3), which was only partly taken up by the pupils of Hosea (Hos 14:4).

Since the FPR seems to know the DtrH (cf. Zeph 1:4-6 and 2 Kgs 23:4-5, 12) and the first edition of JerD (cf. Zeph 3:2 and Jer 7:28), he can probably be dated in the later exilic period (after 550). Because of the relationship to Isa 47:8, 10 in Zeph 2:15, and to Ezek 22:25-31 in Zeph 3:3-4, 8 one could consider a location in Babylonia. But Hos 4:15 deals with a concrete Judean problem, so a location in Judah seems to me more likely. However, this hypothesis should be taken cautiously until a more precise historical and social classification will be possible.

V. Summary

Proposing some methodological clarifications, the hypothesis developed by Nogalski and Schart that there existed a Book of the Four is developed further. The book consists of the passages Hosea 1-14 (without 2:1-3, 20, 23-25; 3:5ab); Amos 1:1-9:10; Mic 1:1, 3-3:12; 5:8-13; Zeph 1:1-3:13*. It constitutes an intentional composition, structured by a chain of passages that proclaim YHWH's ongoing purifying judgments: Hos 3:1-5*; 14:2-5 (where judgment had already been announced in the tradition), and Amos 9:7-10; Mic 5:9-13; Zeph 1:4-6; 3:1-13* (where judgment is newly formulated). By his judgments YHWH separates Israel and Judah from all those things and persons that have led the people to sin against him: the cult, the idols, the kingdom, the weapons, the fortresses, and the upper class. Thus, in the view of the book, all those losses, which had been lamented between 732 and 587 B.C., actually happened for the benefit of Israel. Moreover, God's purifying acts radically determine Israel's new start after the exile.

The work of the Book of the Four redaction can especially be seen in Hos 1:5, 7; 3:1bb; 4:1*, 15; 8:1b, 6a, 14; 11:5b; Amos 1:1b, 9-10, 11f.; 2:4-5, 10-12; 3:1b*, 7; 5:25(?); 8:11f.; 9:7-10; Mic 1:1, 5b-7, 13bβ; 5:8(?), 9-13; Zeph 1:1, 3-6, 13b, 17aβ; 2:3a; 2:5-3:8bα*, 11-13 (without 2:7, 9, 10-11; 3:8bβ-10).

Futurism in the Preexilic Minor Prophets Compared with That of the Postexilic Minor Prophets

Simon J. De Vries

In my book, *From Old Revelation to New, A Tradition-Historical and Redation-Critical Study of Temporal Transitions in Prophetic Prediction*, published by Wm. B. Eerdmans in 1995, I examined in detail the temporal phrase אָז (then), עַתָּה (now), (וְהָיָה) בַּיּוֹם הַהוּא ([and it shall be] on that day), בַּיָּמִים הָהֵם (in those days), בָּעֵת הַהִיא (at that time), הִנֵּה יָמִים בָּאִים (behold, days are coming), אַחַר and אַחֲרֵי־כֵן (afterwards), and הַיָּמִים בְּאַחֲרִית (at the end of the ages). Certain important distinctions become apparent. Sometimes these expressions function as integral transitions (i.e., as an original and structural element within a given pericope, whether original or redactional from a compositional point of view), while most often they function as introductory transitions (i.e., as formulas for attaching redactional appendages). Some of them appear only integrally and others only as redactional introductions.

The first two formulas in the list, אָז and עַתָּה, are exclusively integral. Of special interest is the fact that the pre-exilic minor prophets Hosea, Amos, Micah, Habakkuk, Nahum and Zephaniah do exhibit these two formulas -- always as integral temporal transitions -- whereas the postexilic minor prophets as a group lack integral temporal transitions almost entirely, having them only at Hag 2:23, Zech 8:11, and Zech 12:4. The formula הִנֵּה יָמִים בָּאִים belongs almost exclusively to the Deuteronomistic and Jeremianic redactions, appearing either as an integral or as an introductory transition. The remaining expressions on this list are always redactional. בַּיּוֹם הַהוּא and וְהָיָה בַּיּוֹם הַהוּא appear in the pre-exilic group of minor prophets exclusively as introductory (which is the same as saying "redactional") formulas, but in the postexilic group of minor prophets mainly as introductory formulas, apart from the three exceptions mentioned. This strong preference is a mark as well in the redaction of the books of Isaiah and Ezekiel, while Jeremiah has his own rich and distinctive pattern of temporal formulas, both in integral and in introductory positions.[1] With this introduction, I shall proceed to summarize from more detailed treatments the most important redactional and ideological developments characterizing each of the pre-exilic and post-exilic Minor Prophets.

I. The Pre-exilic Minor Prophets

A. Hosea

There are integral temporal transitions in the following verses of Hosea:

> 2:12 Now (עַתָּה) I will uncover her lewdness in the sight of her lovers, and no
> one shall rescue her out of my hand.
> 3:5 Afterward (אַחַר) the Israelites shall return and seek Yahweh their god
> [and David their king] and shall come in fear to Yahweh and to his goodness
> [in the latter days][2]
> 5:7b Now (עַתָּה) the new moon shall devour them with their fields.
> 7:2b Now (עַתָּה) their deeds encompass them, they are before my face.
> 13:2 And now (וְעַתָּה) they sin more and more, and make for themselves
> molten images.

Hosea also has *introductory* temporal formulas for the following passages:

> 1:5 And it will happen on that day (וְהָיָה בַיּוֹם הַהוּא) that I will break the
> bow of Israel in the valley of Jezreel.
> 2:18 [Eng. 2:16] And it will happen on that day (וְהָיָה בַיּוֹם הַהוּא), oracle of
> Yahweh, that you will call me, "My husband" and no longer "My master."
> 2:23 [Eng. 2:21] And it will happen on that day (וְהָיָה בַיּוֹם הַהוּא), oracle of
> Yahweh, that I will answer the heavens and they shall answer the earth.

A brief scrutiny of the work of one of the very first writing prophets brings to light some important distinctions for the others that follow. We may observe that the man Hosea occasionally introduced temporal transitions for the purpose of connecting Israel's sinful act to its consequent judgment (2:12 [E 10], 5:7, 7:2, 13:2) or of predicting an act of divine grace following judgment (3:5). The work of three successive redactors employing introductory rather than integral temporal transitions may be seen in the "biographical" section comprising chapters 1-3.

---

[1]   On Isaiah, see Simon J. De Vries, *From Old Revelation to New: A Tradition-History
and Redaction-Critical Study of Temporal Transitions in Prophetic Prediction* (Grand
Rapids: Eerdmans, 1995) 110-29. On Jeremiah see pp. 130-60, and on Ezekiel see pp.
161-181.

[2]   This explicative gloss functions as a time-identifier rather than as a temporal transition.

There was first a disciple who composed the prose account of 1:2-9. He did not employ temporal transitions, but a redactor from late in the seventh century did interject his own special interpretation of the Jezreel naming at 1:5, employing a synchronizing והיה ביום ההוא. Chronologically in between these two additions, very probably in close temporal proximity with the first, is the work of the disciple-redactor who expanded the faithless wife poem of chap 2 in terms of Yahweh's eventual intention, again employing the transition, (והיה ביום ההוא (2:18, 23 [Engl. 2:16, 21]), to introduce scenes of bliss following upon Gomer's eventual restoration. It cannot be gainsaid that, in their respective reinterpretations of Yahweh's purpose, the expansion in 1:5 appears as trivial, while those of chap 2 seem theologically momentous. Nevertheless, they all assume that the Deity may change his attitude toward Israel. For the redactor of chap 2, this is posited on a prior repentance on the part of the guilty -- an authentic biblical theme. For the later redactor of 1:5, on the contrary, the shift is arbitrary and unmotivated.

B. Amos

Amos has the following *integral* temporal transitions:

> 4:2 Adonay Yahweh has sworn by his own holiness, "Behold the days are coming upon you (הנה ימים באים עליכם) when they shall take you away with hooks, even the last of you with fishhooks."
>
> 6:7 Therefore now (לכן עתה) they shall be the first of those who go into exile, and the revelry of those who stretch themselves shall pass away.
>
> 7:16 So then (ועתה) hear Yahweh's word: You say, "Do not prophesy against Israel and do not preach against the house of Isaac"; accordingly thus says Yahweh: "Your wife shall be a harlot in the city (etc.)."

Amos has also the following *introductory* temporal transitions:

> 8:9 And it will happen on that day (והיה ביום ההוא), oracle of Adonay Yahweh, that I will make the sun go down at noon, and darken the earth in full daylight.
>
> 8:11 Behold, days are coming (היה ימים באים), oracle of Adonay Yahweh, when I will send a famine on the land, not a famine of bread nor a thirst for water, but of hearing the words of Yahweh.
>
> 8:13 On that day (ביום ההוא) the fair virgins and young men shall faint for thirst -- those who swear by Ashima of Samaria (etc.).
>
> 9:11 On that day (ביום ההוא) I will raise up the booth of David that is fallen and repair its breaches, and raise up its ruins, and rebuild it as in the days of yore.
>
> 9:13 Behold days are coming (הנה ביום באים), oracle of Yahweh, when the plowman shall overtake the reaper, and the treader of grapes him who sows the seed.

Certain important features of the composition and redaction of Amos have been illuminated by my study of temporal transitions. Those found in the prophet's own oracles at Amos 4:2, 6:7 and 7:16 are integral to their context and are fresh and natural in their styling. Each passage predicts imminent calamities for the unrepentant. The addressees are certain wayward groups or individuals within Israel whose doom foreshadows that of the entire nation.

On the contrary, the employment of temporal formulas in the two redactional series at 8:9-14 and 9:11-15 approaches a stereotype of form paralleling a notable monotony in theme. Here it is the nation, without distinction, that is consigned to judgment or promised a paradisiacal bliss. Still, the three pericopes of Amos 8:9-10, 11-12 and 13-14 refurbish recognizable themes from the authentic preaching of the prophet. It is Amos 9:11-12 and 9:13-15 that introduce themes for which there is no direct parallel in the authentic sections of the book, the first being the rebuilding of Jerusalem and the conversion of foreign nations, the second being the motif of prolific nature. The appendages in Amos 8 served a disciple of Amos, possibly during the prophet's lifetime, to round off the preserved records of his preaching in the form of a permanent record. Those of Amos 9 bear witness to the fact that soon after the destruction of the "booth of David," there were others who gave the book a one hundred-eighty degree spin, reinterpreting Amos' grim prophecies in terms of Yahweh's more ultimate purpose to save, now in application to Jerusalem rather than to Samaria.

Both in the employment of הנה ימים באים and in that of הנה יהוה, I have discovered a close formulaic connection between the Deuteronomistic redaction, the redaction of Jeremiah, and the redaction of Amos. The affinity with the Deuteronomistic school should come as no surprise, but that with the Jeremian redaction is rather surprising. The fact that the occurrence of introductory temporal transitions in Amos stand in anacrusis to poetry and introduce poetry, whereas such transitions in Jeremiah introduce prose, may be a decisive clue that the direction of influence was from Amos toward the Deuteronomistic history and then to the redaction of Jeremiah.

C. Micah

Integral temporal transitions appearing in Micah are the following:

3:4 Then (אז) they will cry to Yahweh but he will not answer them, but he will hide his face from them [at that time] because they have made their deeds evil.

4:9 Now (עתה)[3] why do you cry out loud? Is there no king in you? Has your
counselor perished that pangs have seized you like a woman in travail?

4:10b For now (כי עתה) you shall go forth from the city and dwell in the open
country, you shall go to Babylon.

4:11 And now (ועתה) nations are assembled against you, saying, "let her be
profaned, and let our eyes gaze upon Zion."

4: 14 [Engl. 5:1] Now (עתה) you are walled about with a wall, siege is laid
against us, with a rod they strike the ruler of Israel on the cheek.

Micah also has *introductory* temporal transitions in the following verses:

2:4 On that day (ביום ההוא) they shall take up a taunt song against you, and
wail a bitter lamentation, and say (etc.).

4:1 And it shall happen in the sequel of days (והיה באחרית הימים) that the
mountain of Yahweh's house shall be established as the highest of the
mountains, and be raised up above the hills.

4:6 On that day (ביום ההוא), oracle of Yahweh, I will assemble the lame, and
gather those who have been driven away and those whom I have afflicted.

5:9 [Engl. 5:10] And it shall happen on that day (והיה ביום ההוא), oracle of
Yahweh, that I will cut off your horses from among you and destroy your
cities.

The book of Micah is unique as a relatively short composition showing
many levels of redaction. If it does anything, this testifies to the especially
high regard in which the man Micah was held over two centuries and more.
His own "eschatology" coming to expressing in the integral use of temporal
transitions in 3:4 and 4:9, 10, 11, 14 was limited to matters of imminent
concern, first Yahweh's refusal to be available to the oppressing class, and
second the emergence of a new ruler in a new "now," terminating the perils
of Assyrian siege. The futuristic ideology of his early redactors (2:4, 5:9)
was rooted in present deficiencies and involved judgment for wayward
groups or for Israel/Judah as a whole. That of his late and very late
redactors (seen in 4:1, 6), on the other hand, assumed a return from exile
already past and envisaged an ideal bliss for and through Jerusalem.

Micah himself used only the time expressions אז and ועתה as integral
transitions. Like the redactors of Isaiah, the redactors of Micah employed
(והיה) ביום ההוא or והיה באחרית הימים (cf. Isa 2:2), either in anacrusis
or in a formal rubric. In view of the fact that Isaiah's redactors used the
same two formulas, and the first rather frequently -- though almost always
in prose expansions -- it is noteworthy that Micah's redactors also stuck to
poetry, with the temporal formula in anacrusis, for introducing such

---

3   LXX reads ועתה.

expansions. This is further evidence of a remarkable linguistic and formulaic tenacity among Micah's redactors.

In light of the fact that the prophet did not use the oracle formula, its attachment to temporal formulas in the redactional verses, Mic 4:6 and 5:9 [Engl. 5:10], is especially important. The seventh-century redactor who added 5:9-14 [Engl. 5:10-15] was calling attention to Yahweh's anger toward the continuing idolatry of hypocritical Judahites gloating because the menacing Assyrian empire had fallen. On the contrary, the late post-exilic redactor who was responsible for inserting 4:6-7 was intent on counteracting the grand universalism of 4:1-4, identifying Jerusalem as a haven for returning Jewish exiles rather than as a goal of universal pilgrimage.

It seems ironic that these two impulses run directly counter to each other. Both aspirations are emphatically claimed, by the addition of the oracle formula יהוה נאם, to be God's more ultimate revelation. Nevertheless, they seem to reach out in opposite directions while expressing ideas that were of no special concern to the prophet Micah himself. The first expansion resists a chauvinism that misinterprets divine justice when brought to bear on the foreign nations, excusing oneself of blame for unrepentant sin, while the other qualifies the notion that God may intend the well-being of all mankind by reemphasizing his special purpose with regard to his much-injured people, Israel. Each claim is asserted as a more ultimate expression of the divine intention. Depending on one's vantage point, each is indeed true in certain conditions. This only points up the need for ongoing new revelation and the continuous reinterpretation and reapplication of that revelation.

D. Nahum and Habakkuk

There is no *introductory* temporal transition and but a single *integral* temporal transition in each of these short books:

Nah 1:13 And now (ועתה) I will break his yoke from off you, and will burst your
   bonds asunder.
Hab 1:11 Then (אז) they shall sweep by like the wind and go on, guilty men
   whose own might is their god.

Neither Nahum nor Habakkuk has been expanded literarily through the use of the kind of redactional transitions that I have studied. These two compositions may not have enjoyed sufficient stature within the exilic and post-exilic communities to have attracted significant redactional expansions of the sort that we find in the previously discussed books. To put it otherwise, these two prophets probably did not enjoy the support of personal schools of adherents surviving over decades and centuries, as adherents surviving over decades and centuries, as was the case with the three major prophets, Isaiah, Jeremiah and Ezekiel, along with the three minor prophets previously analyzed.

Both Nahum and Habakkuk contain a single integral temporal transition. Nahum did not foresee the looming menace of a new threat to the nation's independence and well being in the form of the Neo-Babylonian empire; he saw only the end of Judah's affliction under the Assyrians and rejoiced at a fleeting moment of liberation. It is understandable that this kind of "eschatology" did not invite redactional readjustment to a situation of new and far more severe affliction.

Habakkuk's complaint is of a general perversion of justice under Jehoiakim's misrule (1:2-4), to which Yahweh responds by calling his attention to the Chaldeans, who are to serve Yahweh in bringing punishment on Judah for these wrongs (1:5-11). This last verse (1:11) is climactic in this vision and points to what lies directly ahead within the proximate future. The Chaldeans are *just now* attacking Judah. It is the proximate future that looms. Nevertheless, Yahweh has a more ultimate purpose in the future that lies immediately beyond this crisis.

E. Zephaniah

A single *integral* temporal transition is the following:

> 3:11b For then (כִּי אָז) I will remove from your midst your proudly exultant ones, and you shall no longer be haughty in my holy mountain.

Zephaniah has also the following occurrences of *introductory* temporal formulas:

> 1:10 And it will happen on that day (וְהָיָה בַיּוֹם הַהוּא), oracle of Yahweh, that a cry will be heard from the Fish Gate, a wail from the Second Quarter, a loud crash from the hills.
>
> 1:12 And it will happen at that time (וְהָיָה בָּעֵת הַהִיא)[4] that I will search Jerusalem with lamps, and I will punish the men who are thickening upon their lees (etc.)
>
> 3:9 For then (כִּי אָז) I will change the speech of the peoples to a pure speech, that all of them may call upon the name of Yahweh and serve him with one accord.
>
> 3:11a On that day (בַיּוֹם הַהוּא) you shall not be put to shame because of the deeds by which you have rebelled against me (etc.).
>
> 3:16 On that day (בַיּוֹם הַהוּא) it shall be said to Jerusalem, "Do not fear, O

---

[4]   Read LXX הַהוּא בָּטֶעַם וְהָיָה; cf. De Vries, *From Old revelation to New*, 47.

Zion; let not your hands become weak!"
3:20 At that time (בעת ההיא) I will bring you home, even at the time when I
gather you (etc.).

The temporal transitions in Zephaniah 1 differ from those of chap 3 in two
respects: (1) they predict judgment rather than salvation for Israel/Judah
under the imagery of the awesome "day of Yahweh"; and (2) they pertain to
the proximate rather than the remote future. With regard to futuristic
ideology, Zephaniah himself stood with Jeremiah and Ezekiel. Like them,
he could see only the imminent and ineluctable end. He placed the foreign
peoples under a parallel judgment, yet his oracles against them did not
produce ideological expansions introduced by temporal formulas of the type
under study. Those in 1:10, 12 LXX, along with that in 1:8, authentically
communicate Zephaniah's own expectation; they were composed either by
him or by a close disciple. Any other disciples he may have had during his
own lifetime made no effort to amend his grim predictions. Nevertheless,
his postexilic redactors believed that they were entitled to expand – even
reverse – his grim prophecies. For them, the same Yahweh who had
brought the exile intended the restoration.

Finally, it may be noted that the oracle formula נאם יהוה is attached to
a temporal formula only in 1:10. As in the Yahweh speeches at 1:2, 1:3 and
2:9, it invokes a special level of revelational authority. Apparently because
they were not at all anxious about the question of authority, the redactors
who employed the temporal formulas in chap 3 made no use whatever of
the oracle formula.

F. Eschatology and Redaction Among the Preexilic Minor Prophets

The following quotation will summarize the foregoing analysis.[5]

> Among the preexilic minor prophets, we have noted the virtual absence of the kind
> of prose expansions that use an introductory temporal formula, seen regularly in
> Jeremiah and Ezekiel, but especially in Isaiah.
>
> 1) Original materials in the preexilic Minor Prophets have integral formulas and
> are always poetic; secondary materials having temporal formulas of transition are
> also in poetry, but have their temporal transitions either in anacrusis or in a
> liturgical rubric (Zeph 3:16).
> 2) Original and early redactional materials always announce judgment, while exilic
> and postexilic materials always announce salvation.

---

[5]   De Vries, *From Old Revelation to New*, 205-6. The author and editors gratefully thank
Eerdmans Publishing Company for permission to print this excerpt.

3) The expansions introduced in Hos 2:18, 23 [Engl. 2:16, 21] alter Israel's judgment as Israel's salvation; this is also the case in Micah's composition in 4:9-14, in exilic Amos 9:11, and in postexilic Mic 4:1 and Zeph 3:9.
4) Mic 5:9 [Engl. 5:10] has a remarkable reversal of Israel's victory into Israel's (and the nations') punishment.
5) The extension of Israel's salvation as further salvation is always postexilic (Amos 9:13, Mic 4:6, Zeph 3:11, 16, 20).

We are able to observe very little change in futuristic ideology from one preexilic minor prophet to another. They are steady in their prediction of looming calamity. Sometimes it is their early redactors, but mainly it is their late redactors, who have modified their grim prophecies in terms of the salvific events that will emerge from Israel's ordeal of purging.

In this respect the preexilic minor prophets take their stand with the three "great" prophets, Isaiah, Jeremiah, and Ezekiel. Micah and his redactors show especially strong affinities with the Isaiah school. The redactors of Amos show direct influence from -- or have exerted influence upon -- the Jeremianic redaction. Otherwise, each of the early minor prophets speaks with his own peculiar voice, giving witness out of his own special situation to Yahweh's sovereign work in history.

II. The Postexilic Minor Prophets

A. Jonah and Malachi

There are no integral or introductory temporal transitions in these books of the kinds that I have studied. Nevertheless, the authors and/or redactors of each had distinctive views of "eschatology." The futuristic affirmation of Jonah is a subtle rebuke of the prophet's caricature of divine justice and an affirmation of Yahweh's sovereign freedom in exercising clemency toward those who repent. The futurism of the book of Malachi, apart from redactional expansions in chapter 4, is distinctly imminentistic; i.e., this-worldly, first in condemning current misbehavior (Mal 1:1-2:17, 3:13-15), second in correcting misconceptions of the day of Yahweh (3:1-12), and third in reporting a quasi-ritual for Yahweh's acceptance of the repentant (Mal 3:16-18). Although both Jonah and Malachi are directed against erroneous beliefs or misguided practices within the postexilic Jewish community, they both show a peculiar awareness of the salvability of peoples outside this community. Their affinities with Nahum, proto-Zechariah, and proto-Joel, in strong contrast to second Joel and second Zechariah on this issue, clearly place them within the Persian era.

B. Joel

There are no *integral* temporal transitions in Joel, but it does have three *introductory* transitions of the kind we have been discussing:

> 3:1 [Engl. 2:28] And it shall happen afterwards (וְהָיָה אַחֲרֵי־כֵן) that I will pour out my spirit on all flesh; your sons and your daughters shall prophesy, your old men shall dream dreams and your young men shall see visions; even upon the menservants and maidservants in those days, I will pour out my spirit.
> 4:1 [Engl. 3:1] For behold, in those days and at that time (כִּי הִנֵּה בַּיָּמִים הָהֵמָּה וּבָעֵת הַהִיא), when I restore the fortunes of Judah and Jerusalem, I will gather all nations and bring them down to the valley of Jehoshaphat, and I will enter into judgment with them there (etc.).
> 4:18 [Engl. 3:18] And it will happen on that day (וְהָיָה בַיּוֹם הַהוּא) that the mountains shall drip sweet wine and the hills shall flow with milk; and all the streambeds of Judah shall flow with water; and a fountain shall come forth from the house of Yahweh and water the valley of Shittim.

The authentic material in Joel involves a "here and now" futurism that stands in stark relief over against the highly developed cosmic eschatology of the book's redactors. The temporal transitions created by these redactors point to conditions or situations of ultimate finality: the universal presence of the divine spirit, a calling of wrong-doers to retribution, and an idyllic transformation of nature, with Jerusalem at the center of all, as in Ezekiel 47 (cf. Revelation 22).

The original book (Joel 1-2) reflects an "eschatology" of imminent catastrophe, occasioning a public religious act to elicit Yahweh's beneficent response. Ideological as this part of the book may have been, its futurism remains within the realm of the historically possible and the traditionally appropriate.

Perhaps the most profound difference between chapters 1-2 and chapters 3-4 is that those concerned with Yahweh's irruptive act in the latter are neither a famine-ridden community of postexilic Jews nor the generation that first returned from Babylonian exile; rather, they are the ultimately faithful pious adherents of the one true religion, now separated decisively from the wicked. Their coming to Zion is cosmologically final rather than another "day" in the series of "days of Yahweh" that are equivalent to calamitous historical events in Israel's historical experience.

Although all the materials in Joel 3-4 were added incrementally and indicate significant nuances in ideology, they together show the clear marks of emerging apocalypticism. It is important to observe how drastically innovative 3:1-3 [Engl. 2:28-29] is in comparison with the context into which it has been inserted. It shifts the scene from "my people" and "Israel" in 2:26-27 to "all flesh"; in other words, from the context of the biblical covenant to that of religious anthropology. Even if the redactor's intent went no further than to universalize prophetic inspiration within Judaism alone, it had a striking and even elegant universalistic dimension in its radical laicizing of spiritual empowerment.

Finally, it is important to call attention to the innovative ideology of Joel 4:1-3 [Engl. 3:1-3], which interprets cosmic judgment as instrumental to the salvation and vindication of Yahweh's covenant people. As a motif that is seen elsewhere only in the early apocalyptic literature, it serves to reverse the incipient universalism of 3:1-3. This fact reminds us that we should not assume that all the apocalypticists held to identical visions of the future.

C. Haggai

Haggai has no *introductory* temporal transitions and one *integral* temporal transition:

> 2:23 On that day (ביום ההוא), oracle of Yahweh Sebaoth, I will take you,
> Zerubbabel my servant, the son of Shealtiel, oracle of Yahweh, and I make
> you like a signet ring; for I have chosen you, oracle of Yahweh Sebaoth.

There can be no mistaking the crucial significance of sequences and durations in this small and very early postexilic book of prophecy. What one would infer from the fact that all the oracles are dated is confirmed by the special emphasis that is placed on the immediate future in Hag 2:15, 18. Here is a twice-repeated command to take stock of the opportunities of the present moment: "Place your attention on what is to happen from this day forward (שׂימו־נא לבבכם מין היום הזה ומעלה)." This is a counter-weight to a similar, past-oriented command in 1:5, repeated redactionally in 1:7, "Place your attention on what have been your ways (שׂימו לבבכם על־דרכיכם)."

The immediate future of Yahweh's effectual action that will justify the people's faith and reward their obedience is forecast in Hag 2:6-7 and 2:19b. Following the messenger formula in 2:6a is a peculiar expression that defines a short duration in the immediate future, "It is yet for one short moment (עוד אחת מעט היא)." At the end of this brief moment, as it were, Yahweh will agitate the whole earth in order also to agitate the nations, in effect shaking loose their treasures to be used for the benefit of the temple in Jerusalem. This is the assurance that nullifies the past and present devastation of the temple. A corresponding assurance eases the persistent evidence of poverty, fulfilling Yahweh's promise in 2:19b that "from this day onward (מן־היום הזה)" he will surely bless them.

On the very day of receiving this second assurance, Haggai received his fourth and climactic oracle (Hag 2:20-23). The first two oracles had been addressed to Zerubbabel and Joshua together, while the third had been for the priests and the people. This final oracle is for Zerubbabel alone. This descendant of David is designated as פחה (governor), but he is here addressed as a soon-to-be king. Yahweh repeats the announcement of v. 6 that he is shaking the heavens and the earth (2:21), but the purpose is no longer to provide treasures for the temple, as in 2:7. Now it is for the specific purpose of undermining any and all political or military forces that might threaten to prevent Zerubbabel's investiture.

It is just here in the last verse of Haggai's book that we come across its only futuristic transition. It is integral rather than introductory in function -- appropriate to the fact that it is original and not redactional. Also it is climactic within the pericope and within the book. The formula ביום ההוא is an emphatic synchronizer between the imminently future events of vv 21-22 and the intended effect of those events, which is Zerubbabel's investiture (v 23). Yahweh's intention is revealed in the announcement of two actions in sequence, both of which are confirmed by further occurrences of the oracle formula. Yahweh announces that he will take (impf.) Zerubbabel, that is, separate him out from all potential candidates; this is guaranteed by the immediately following נאם יהוה. The purpose of this, expressed by a *wâw*-consecutive perfect, is to effectuate the second action; that is, make him "like a signet ring." The use of the comparative indicates that this is a symbolic action or typological function in distinction from an actual, public ceremony. The pericope is concluded by a grounding clause indicating Zerubbabel's special election and confirmed by a final oracle formula.[6]

Thus Haggai's expectation was sharply focused upon events of the immediate future. This focus included the removal of ritual uncleanness, the end of the famine, the arrival of supplies for beautifying the restored temple, and the symbolic placing of a royal ring upon the finger of Zerubbabel. The last expectation is far from messianic in the traditional sense. Furthermore, it is not predicted for a remote and ideal future, but for the situation of the very moment.

---

[6]   This book's variegated formulation of this traditional formula is remarkable and may seem excessive. Usually Haggai has נאם יהוה צבאות (1:9, 2:4(2), 8, 9(2), 23(1,3), but צבאות is dropped in 1:14, 2:4(1), 14, 17, 23:(2), while אמר יהוה צבאות is substituted in 2:7, 9(1). Also "Thus says Yahweh Sebaoth," occurs five times. Since this is Haggai's style, we should try to appreciate rather than censure the florid usage at the climax of his book.

Accordingly, this short book ends with a sharply focused private oracle, whose prediction is underscored by the thrice-occurring oracle formula. It should be noted that Haggai's futuristic ideology conceives of Yahweh's action in the world at large, which is to be instrumental in salvific events on behalf of Israel, here as in 2:7-8 (cf. Isa 45:1-8.). Haggai insinuates, but does not directly state, that the nations who are thus involved in Israel's restoration are at the same time receiving punishment. This is what especially distinguishes Haggai's "eschatology" from the proto-apocalyptism that was emerging at the same period. That ideology placed special emphasis on the judgment of the nations as a precondition for Israel's full enjoyment of Yahweh's favor (cf. Isa 24:21-23, Ezekiel 38-39, Joel 4, Zechariah 12-14).

D. Zechariah

There are two *integral* temporal transitions in this book:

> 8:11 But now (וְעַתָּה) I will not deal with the remnant of this people as in the former days, oracle of Yahweh Sebaoth.
>
> 12:4 On that day (בַּיּוֹם הַהוּא), oracle of Yahweh, I will strike every horse with panic, and its rider with madness (etc.).

In addition. there are 15 *introductory* temporal transitions:

> 3:10 On that day (בַּיּוֹם הַהוּא), oracle of Yahweh Sebaoth, every one of you will invite his neighbor under his vine and under his fig tree.
>
> 8:23 In those days (בַּיָּמִים הָהֵמָּה) ten men from the nations of every tongue shall take hold of the robe of a Jew, saying, "Let us go with you, for we have heard that God is with you."
>
> 12:3 And it will happen on that day (וְהָיָה בַיּוֹם הַהוּא) that I will make Jerusalem a heavy stone for all the peoples; all who lift it shall grievously hurt themselves, and all the nations will come together against it.
>
> 12:6 On that day (בַּיּוֹם הַהוּא) I will make the clans of Judah like a blazing pot in the midst of wood, like a flaming torch among sheaves (etc.).
>
> 12:8 On that day (בַּיּוֹם הַהוּא) Yahweh will put a shield about the inhabitants of Jerusalem so that the feeblest among them on that day (הַהוּא בַיּוֹם)[7] shall be like David (etc.).
>
> 12:9 And it will happen on that day (וְהָיָה בַיּוֹם הַהוּא) that I will seek to destroy all the nations that come against Jerusalem.
>
> 12:11 On that day (בַּיּוֹם הַהוּא) the mourning in Jerusalem will be as great as the mourning for Hadadrimmon on the plain of Megiddo.

---

[7]   A time indicator without transitional function

13:1 On that day (בַּיּוֹם הַהוּא) there shall be a fountain opened for the house of
David and the inhabitants of Jerusalem to cleanse them from sin and uncleanness.

13:2 And it will happen on that day (וְהָיָה בַיּוֹם הַהוּא), oracle of Yahweh Sebaoth, that I will cut off the names of the idols from the land, so that they shall be
remembered no more (etc.).

13:4 And it will happen on that day (וְהָיָה בַיּוֹם הַהוּא) that every prophet will be
ashamed of his vision when he prophesies: he will not put on a hairy mantle to
deceive.

14:6 And it will happen on that day (וְהָיָה בַיּוֹם הַהוּא) that there shall be neither
cold nor frost, and there shall be continuous day (etc.).

14:8 And it will happen on that day (וְהָיָה בַיּוֹם הַהוּא) that living waters shall
flow out from Jerusalem, half of them to the eastern sea and half of them to the
western sea; it shall continue in summer as in winter.

14:9b On that day (הַהוּא בַיּוֹם) Yahweh will be one, and his name one.

14:13 And it will happen on that day (וְהָיָה בַיּוֹם הַהוּא) that a great panic from
Yahweh shall fall on them, so that each will lay hold on the hand of his fellow,
and the hand of the one will be raised against the hand of the other.

14:20 On that day (בַּיּוֹם הַהוּא) there shall be inscribed on the bells of the horses,
"Holy to Yahweh" (etc.).

1. Zechariah 1-8

The question of redactional continuity is especially acute in the book of
Zechariah. It can scarcely be argued, as might be possible with respect to
Isaiah, that late expansions still significantly articulate the essential ideology
of the earlier part of the book. In matter of fact, the futuristic expectation of
Zechariah 1-8 and that of chapters 9-14 are worlds apart. It must have been
a purely editorial convention that attached these latter chapters to the
original collection.

Not only do the dating formulas in Zechariah 1-8 place the prophet
Zechariah's activity in the same historical situation as Haggai; but also their
frequency of occurrence indicates that here, too, sequences and durations
play a major role in defining the intention of individual pericopes and the
composition as a whole. Unfortunately, the insertion of epexegetical comments and some rearranging have created confusion. Most scholars agree
that Zech 6:9-14 has been reworked to eliminate an original reference to
Zerubbabel. If Galling is correct in transferring 1:7 to this passage,[8] it is
very tempting to interpret it in the light of Hag 2:21-23. The Haggai
passage, predicting an imminent investiture for Zerubbabel, is dated to the
twenty-fourth day of the ninth month in Darius' second year, so Zech 6:9-
14 would be dated to the twenty-fourth of the eleventh month, precisely two

---

8   Kurt Galling, "Die Exilswende in der Sicht des Propheten Sacharja," *Studien zur
Geschichte Israels im persischen Zeitalter* (Tübingen: Mohr, 1964) 109.

months later. The crowning with gold was for Zerubbabel rather than Joshua the high priest and may have been intended as an actualization of Hag 2:21-23, which as I have suggested above may have been purely symbolic. In any event, we may be certain that the original Zechariah's own "eschatology" was for the "here and now." His futuristic ideology included no more than the return from the exile, the rebuilding of the temple, and probably the special recognition of Zerubbabel as the secular leader of the community.

The only integral temporal transition in these chapters is in the middle of the probably original passage, Zech 8:9-13, an oracular exhortation closely similar to those of Haggai. Emphatic ועתה (a situational "so now") at the beginning of v. 11 provides the major turning point in this pericope. It is set in contrast to three expressions of time occurring in the preceding context, and to yet another in v. 11, each of which functions as a time identifier rather than as a temporal transition of the kind I have been studying.

"In these days" in 8:9 marks an ongoing present, beginning with the event ("since the foundation of the temple of Yahweh Sebaoth") that has led to the present situation. In order to give special prominence to this momentous present, another duration ("before those days" in v.10) is also mentioned, a time of wagelessness, insecurity and strife. In contrast to all of this, a new and decisive present and an imminent future are defined in vv. 12-13. Negatively stated, this new day is not to be like the earlier days (הראשנים כימים). Positively stated, this will bring peace, increase, honor, and salvation.

This striking interplay of temporal durations and sequences is precisely what characterizes the time ideology of Haggai. He and Zechariah, with certain unidentified others (8:9), believed that they stood at the very climax of Yahweh's work in the history of Israel: "Let your hands be strong, you who in these days have been hearing these words from the mouth of the prophets...that the temple might be built."

It is otherwise with the two introductory – i. e., redactional – temporal transitions in this section. Zech 3:10 is like Mic 4:4 in repeating an ancient saying (cf. 1 Kgs 4:25) about the amazing hospitality that goes with universal prosperity. It reinterprets a private oracle to Joshua concerning his and the community's *proximate* future to refer to his *remote* future. Zech 8:23 reinterprets the intra-Israelite universalism of 8:20-22 in terms of a multinational universalism in which the Jewish people, rather than the covenant community as such, are identified as the mediators of salvation to all mankind.

2. Zechariah 9-14

In my book *Yesterday, Today and Tomorrow*,[9] I was able to identify היום in Zech 9:12 as a time identifier within an identifying characterization, ההוא ביום in 9:16 as part of a futuristic epitome, and ביום ההוא in Zech 14:21 as part of another futuristic epitome. These conclusions are important for the exegesis of the passages in which they are found.

It will be seen that all the temporal transitions of Second Zechariah fall within the apocalyptic complex, Zech 12:1-13:6 plus Zechariah 14.[10] The most important difference between the "eschatology" of Zechariah 9-11 and that of these chapters is that the former still refers to events of the historical present and imminent future, such as the returning king of Zech 9:9-10 and the symbolic act of the annulled covenant king of 9:9-10 and the annulled covenant of 11:4-16, while the latter refer only to a *remote* – though not specifically final – future. Zechariah 9-10 resulted from a process of continuous accretion, and the two pericopes, Zech 11:4-16 and Zech 12:1b-13:6, arose independently until redactionally joined to chapters 9-10 by the employment of Zech 11:1-3, 17; 12:1a and 13:7-9 as linking elements. The last mentioned verses provide the definitive redactional perspective of the entire complex.

Zechariah 14 must be seen as a still later addition to the book. Utilizing the results of my work on the three major prophets in the light of the brilliant analysis of Magne Saebø,[11] I have been able to rationalize a place and function for each of the thirteen temporal transitions in Zechariah 12-14.

First is the pericope Zech 12:1b-13:6. There was an original day-of-Yahweh oracle in 12:2-4 in which ביום ההוא נאם יהוה functions as an integral temporal transition with following oracle formula, and to which vv 2b and 4b have been added as glosses. Redactional expansions to this core concerned the themes of (1) victory for Jerusalem/Judah, vv 3a, 5-8, (2) internal renewal, 12:9-13:1, and (3) religious purging, 13:2-6. Each of these units included a Yahweh-speech (12:3a, 9-10, 13:2, respectively) commencing with והיה ביום ההוא (the last adds נאם יהוה) and shows secondary third-personal development. Furthermore, each terminates with epexegetical additions, the first on Judah's fervor in 12:6, the second on

---

9   Simon J. DeVries, *Yesterday, Today and Tomorrow* (Grand Rapids: Eerdmans, 1975).
     245-6 and 321-2.
10   The liturgical poem of Zech 13:7-9 has been added redactionally as the original con-
     clusion to Zechariah 9-13.
11   Magne Saebø, *Sacharja 9-14, Untersuchungen von Text und Form* (Neukirchen-Vluyn: Neu-
     kirchener Verlag, 1969).

Jerusalem's shield in 12:8a, the third on ritual mourning in 12:11, the fourth on cleansing in 13:1, and the fifth on the termination of prophesy in 13:4-6. Evidently to make an emphatic synchronistic association with the preceding divine events, each of these epexegetical additions is introduced by a temporal formula.

There were strong tensions within the community of Zechariah's redactors, and their "eschatology" envisaged the resolution of these tensions rather than the usual postexilic problems of returning and rebuilding, which are the major themes of chaps 1-8. Yet the community itself would be called upon to participate in bringing Yahweh's action to its fullest potential. What needed to take place on their part would occur synchronously with Yahweh's primary deed of defeating Jerusalem's enemies.

In Zechariah 14 there is a somewhat similar pattern of redefining the nature of Yahweh's great day of self-revelation. Little of the emphasis on distinction and separation that comes to expression in 12:1-13:6 is to be found in chapter 14. On the contrary, it is distinction and separation that provides the *premise* for this new and final addition to the book. Verse 2 assumes a separation, but only one between the Jerusalemites who are to be lost in the nations' attack and those who survive it. The actual or potential animosity of the nations is thematic, but this is eventually resolved in favor of unity and universality. What is the most striking is that it develops even further the thematic tendencies of proto-apocalypticism, proliferating the use of the two variants of the ביום ההוא formula with as much apparent abandon as in the pericope to which it has been editorially attached.

There is another original day-of-Yahweh oracle in 14:1-3, 9a. An extraneous gloss commencing with ביום ההוא has been added in v. 9b. Again there are three complex literary expansions. (1) The first expansion elaborates a theophany motif (a divine appearance on the mount of Olives, vv 4-5a; a restoring river, introduced by והיה ביום ההוא, vv 8, 10a), including a gloss on Jerusalem's exaltation. (2) The second elaboration follows a holy-war motif (vv 6, 7b), with introductory והיה ביום ההוא postulating an endless day. Vv 13, 14b employs introductory והיה ביום ההוא to introduce the theme of panic and spoils of war. To this second elaboration epexegesis on the plague has been added in vv 12 and 15. (3) The third expansion has a comprehensive and cult-ideological orientation and features two special themes: an universal feast of booth, vv. 16-19, and comprehensive holiness, vv 20-21, with introductory ביום ההוא and the mighty epitome at the end of v 21, "And there shall no longer be a trader in the house of Yahweh Sebaoth on that day (ביום ההוא)." Nothing could be more apparent than that Zechariah 9-14 originated in an era quite separate and distinct from that of chaps 1-8. The lack of a redactional link between these two sections of the book apart from the word משׂא is in itself an indication of an extremely tenuous connection existing between the eschatological ideology of Second Zechariah and the this-worldly ideology of First Zechariah. These latter chapters of the canonical book have clearly been more strongly influenced by themes from the great prophets, Isaiah, Jeremiah and Ezekiel, than by themes from First Zechariah. The gap between the two sections of the book is wider, therefore, than that within the great book of Isaiah, where at least the main thematic source for Deutero-Isaiah has clearly been Proto-Isaiah itself.

Very little can be said with assurance about the historical background of Second Zechariah, and it is best to refrain from unwarranted speculation. It does however seem likely that Alexander's conquest lies behind Zechariah 9, and a permanent rupture between Judah and Israel (11:14) probably reflects the Samaritan schism -- whenever that occurred. But who the sheep and the shepherds were in this passage remains obscure, as well as the identity of the saved remnant.

The community for whom Zechariah 9-14 were written was confronted by three unwelcome realities: (1) the imperial powers that held them in subjugation were more of a threat than a source of assistance and relief; (2) the return from exile had not resulted in an ideal reunification of all Israel, and what unity did exist was constantly being threatened by strife and estrangement within the covenant community; and (3) the temple cult had neither cleansed the people of sin nor given them spiritual renewal. The effect of these tenacious problems was, for the proto-apocalypticists of Second Zechariah, despair about the possibilities of history along with encouragement to look beyond the events which they were experiencing to an ideal state of being in which (1) all external perils would be removed, (2) all that was truly Israel would be united together, and (3)Yahwistic religion would at last be fully purged.

The scenario of such a future is certainly more sharply focused in Zechariah 14 than in chapters 9-13. Saebø explains that the redactor of chapters 9-13 bound Zech 12:2-14 into these chapters under the motif of a severe coming judgment which was to lead in the end to Israel's purging and reconversion, at the same time restoring a new sense of distinctive peoplehood within the covenant with Yahweh (13:8-9). Thus the great battle of 12:2-14 is not, in fact, the last event of history, but a battle that leads to the restoration of covenant living within history.

This is the answer that the redactor of Zechariah 9-13 gives to the apocalypticist of 12:2-13:6. Nothing can be more final in an existential sense than a state of being in which Yahweh declares, "They are my people," and in which each individual responds, "Yahweh is my God" (13:9). This is in fact a direct reaffirmation of the eschatology of Hos 2:18-25 [Engl. 2:16-23], as well as a prolepsis of 1 Pet 2:10. Thus Zechariah 9-13 defines what is ultimate in a spiritual sense rather than final in chronological sequence. Zechariah 14 by itself reconstructs the entire cosmos, making future attacks on Israel impossible by bringing all the nations under allegiance to Yahweh as the universal King, drastically rearranging the land and the city, while removing any and all distinctions between what is holy and what is profane.

It should also be observed that Zechariah 14 goes beyond Ezekiel 38-39 in focusing futuristic expectation on Jerusalem and the temple, rather than on the land of Israel. Both in the sections belonging to its original core (Ezek 38:8, 39:2, 4, 17) and in the redactional additions (38:1-11, 16, 18-19, 39:9, 12-15, 28), the Gog apocalypse of Ezekiel is concerned with the imperilment of the *land* following Israel's return, while Jerusalem's peril remains unmentioned.

The Gog apocalypse remains thus within the patriarchal tradition of the promise of land and peoplehood. True, this changes drastically in Ezekiel 40-48, which proves to be the major source for the imagery of Zechariah 14. With reminiscences of the Isaianic tradition of an inviolable Zion, the menace to Jerusalem rather than to the land of Israel becomes thematic in this chapter, as it has been in Zechariah 12:1-13:6. Hope for the land as such has been given up and everything has been concentrated in Jerusalem, now viewed less as a political entity than as a single cultic center for the entire cosmos. The apocalypticists of Zechariah 12—14, but especially those of chapter 14, have relativized all that is secular and historical within Israel's futuristic expectations, substituting an image that is at the same time narrowly particularistic and ideologically transhistorical.

III. Summary Comparison Between the Two Groups of Minor Prophets

I shall conclude this presentation by citing the following paragraphs from my study *From Old Revelation to New*.[12] They summarize my main observations concerning the postexilic *versus* the preexilic use of futuristic transitions, and what they show in general about the connection between the rival eschatologies at work, together with the redactional processes behind the verbal expressions that reflect these eschatologies. For my detailed sup-

---

[12] De Vries, *From Old Revelation to New*, 236-7. Permission granted by Eerdmans to publish this lengthy quotation.

port of my analysis of individual passages under discussion, one should turn
to the relevant pages of this work.

    I see that the integral temporal transitions that appear frequently in the pre-exilic
minor prophets have become rare in the post-exilic minor prophets. Of the
passages that do contain them, two give strong expression to an imminentistic
expectation (Hag 2:20-23, Zech 8:9-13), while the one that remains (Zech 12:2a,
3b-4a) employs the temporal formula to introduce the climax of a divine act that is
scheduled for the present crisis to which it speaks.

    Occurrences that introduce redactional expansions, on the other hand, are even
more strongly in the ascendancy in the postexilic minor prophets than in the pre-
exilic passages, and the variants, ההוא ביום and ביום ההוא והיה ההוא, now hold
almost complete sway. The peculiar eschatological program of the late additions to
Joel   seems to have occasioned a choice of formulas of transition not found
elsewhere (אחרי־כן והיה, 3:1; ההמה ובעת ההיא כי הנה בימים, 4:1), while
בימים ההמה in Zech 8:23 relates the naively idealistic expectation of ten gentiles
seizing a Jew's robe to a whole series of sanguinary prognostications within the
preceding context.

    Within the book of Zechariah the formula ההוא ביום (והיה) has come to
special prominence. The influence of the additions to Isaiah and of the Gog
apocalypse in Ezekiel is evident; but, as we have seen, these are found only in the
proto-apocalyptic sections of Zechariah (12:1-13:6 and 14:1-21. The word והיה,
used in these pericopes also without a following ההוא ביום, seems especially
appropriate for introducing drastically different and permanent conditions or states
of being. This is to say that the eschatology of these sections is not concerned with
unitary events except when an event introduces a permanent change, as in 12:3.

    Initial levels of redaction in Zech 12:1ff. and 14:1ff. are marked by the styling
והיה ביום ההוא, while the formula without והיה usually introduces late levels
of redaction. It is especially remarkable that the epitome in 14:21b and several of
the expansions introduced by a temporal transition (13:1, 14:9b, 20; also 14:6, 13
with foregoing והיה) have a form of היה (be or become) as the main verb. Here
the expectation has already moved beyond what historical event might produce --
or even beyond what Yahweh's direct action in historical event might produce -- to
a transcendental state that has virtually independent existence.

    It is significant that among the postexilic prophets only Joel (3:1, 4:18) has a
temporal formula in anacrusis -- a construction prevalent among the pre-exilic
minor prophets. This was apparently the form best suited for attaching traditional
materials, but Zechariah does entirely without anything of the sort. The new
material in Zechariah that is introduced by a temporal transition occurs exclusively
in prose. As elsewhere in the prophetic collection, prose proves also to be the
form that is best suited to the communication of speculative concepts. Though
motifs from the past may be recalled in some of these prose expansions, they tend
to be bold and innovative in imaging the future. This is one among several items
of evidence that traditional prophecy was surely coming to an end as oracular
revelation was being supplanted by reflective interpretation and speculation.

    Finally, it is worth pointing out that the predominant theme of the postexilic
minor prophets is the punishment of the nations as a prerequisite to Israel's full
salvation (Joel 4:1, Zech 12:1ff., 14:1ff.; cf. Hag 2:20-23). In this too the influence

of Ezekiel 38-39 is evident -- that is, the original Gog apocalypse with its early expansions, apart from 39:23-29, the original redactional conclusion to an early collection. The assumption is that although the return had already occurred, restored Israel remained in peril. In the additions to Joel this problem is solved in terms of a final judgment upon the nations. In Zechariah 12-13 it is solved in terms of Yahweh's victory over enemies attacking Jerusalem, leading to stringent reforms in 12:1ff., and in 14:1ff. to Yahweh's universal kingship and comprehensive holiness throughout his land and among his people.

Haggai-Zechariah: Prophecy after the Manner of Ezekiel

Steven S. Tuell

The role of the book of Ezekiel in the formation of the canon seems ambiguous, to say the least. The important role of books such as Isaiah or Jeremiah, which were quoted from and alluded to with considerable frequency in the texts of developing Judaism and Christianity, is obvious. By contrast, Ezekiel was more usually seen as a problem in need of a solution. Rabbinical Judaism considered the study of this book dangerous for any but the mature scholar.[1] Three times (*b. Shabbat* 13b; *b. Ḥagigah* 13a; and *b. Menaḥot* 45a) Talmud records the story of Hananiah ben Hezekiah, leader of the school of Shammai, who burned three hundred jars of oil laboring over the texts until all the contradictions between Ezekiel and the Torah of Moses were resolved. Even so, *b. Menaḥot* 46a observes that only when Elijah comes will all the discrepancies be explained.

Difficult as the book may be, the rightful place of Ezekiel in the canon was unquestioned.[2] Indeed, Ezekiel is today sometimes identified as the key figure in the transition between the pre-exilic prophets and the post-exilic scribes, and hence between ancient Israelite religion and second-temple Judaism.[3] But the influence of Ezekiel is still most apparent in the literature of fringe communities: in apocalypses such as Daniel (especially chapters 7 and 10), the Book of the Watchers (1 Enoch 4:8-25), and Revelation (Rev 11:1; 21:10-21; 22:1-6), and in the life and liturgy of the Essenes.[4] Ezekie-

---

[1]   In a letter to Paulinus, bishop of Nola, Jerome reports a Jewish regulation of his day barring anyone under the age of thirty from reading either the beginning (chapters 1—3, the vision of the chariot throne), or the ending (chapters 40 — 48), of Ezekiel's book (cf. *St. Jerome,* W. H. Freemantle, A Select Library of Nicene and Post-Nicene Fathers of the Christian Church, 2/6 [New York: Christian Literature, 1893] 502).

[2]   Cf. *b. Baba Bathra* 14b, 15a, which claims the authority of the Great Synagogue for Ezekiel, as well as Daniel, Esther, and the Book of the Twelve.

[3]   For Ezekiel as a liminal figure between prophet and scribe, see Ellen Davis, *Swallowing the Scroll: Textuality and the Dynamics of Discourse in Ezekiel's Prophecy* (JSOT 78; Sheffield: Almond Press, 1989), 65-66.

[4]   For a general treatment of the apparent influence of Ezekiel on the Essene community, cf. Ben Zion Wacholder, "Ezekiel and Ezekielianism as Progenitors of Essenianism," in *The Dead Sea Scrolls: Forty Years of Research* (ed. Devorah Dimant and Uriel Rappaport; Leiden: Brill, 1992), 186-196. Allusions to Ezekiel appear in particular in the Shabbat Shirot from Qumran. The description of the throne chariot of YHWH in

lian influence on more mainstream texts within the canon is less apparent, and more subtle.[5]

This study will explore the influence the book of Ezekiel may have had upon Haggai-Zechariah[6] by investigating four possible points of connection: the centrality of temple and cult in Haggai-Zechariah; the dating formulae, precise to the day, which structure this composite work; Zechariah's vision reports; and the use of the first person in Zechariah. Once the likelihood of Ezekielian influence has been established, this study will raise questions concerning the nature of that influence, and its significance for the redaction of Haggai-Zechariah and the Book of the Twelve.

4Q404, 1,2:1-16 (Carol Newsom, *Songs of the Sabbath Sacrifice: A Critical Edition* [HSS 7; Atlanta: Scholars, 1985], 226) and 4Q405, 20-21-22 (Newsom, *Songs*, 303) obviously derives from Ezekiel 1, as Newsom has noted (*Songs*, 52 and 55-56). The interest of Ezek 40 — 42 in the temple gates also appears to find a parallel in the Songs. Note that the words used to describe the entrances and exits of the heavenly temple in 4Q405 (בוא, אצי, שער, פתח) appear together only in Ezekiel: the first two in 40:11, 38, 40 and 46:3; all together in 46:2-3 (as noted by Newsom in *Songs*, 42).

5   For example, compare Ezek 44:1-14 and Isa 56:1-8; on this parallel, cf. Michael Fishbane (*Biblical Interpretation in Ancient Israel* [Oxford: Clarendon, 1985] esp. 138 and 142) and Walther Zimmerli (*Ezekiel*, 2 vols.; trans. Ronald E. Clements; Hermeneia; Philadelphia: Fortress, 1979] 2.453-4).

6   This study will deal with Haggai and Zechariah 1—8. Scholarly consensus holds that Zechariah 9—14 represents a later, apocalyptic addition to Zechariah. Evidence indicates that Haggai and Zechariah 1—8 have been edited together; so Peter Ackroyd, "The Book of Haggai and Zechariah I-VIII," *JJS* 3 (1952) 155-56; W. A. M. Beuken, *Haggai-Sacharia 1-8: Studien zur Überlieferungsgeschichte der Frühnachexilischen Prophetie* (Assen: Van Gorcum, 1967), 331; Carol L. and Eric M. Meyers, *Haggai, Zechariah 1-8* (AB 25B; Garden City, N. Y.: Doubleday, 1987), xliv-xlviii and especially xlix, which demonstrates the redactional links particularly between Haggai and Zech 7-8; Paul L. Redditt, *Haggai, Zechariah, Malachi* (NCB; Grand Rapids: Eerdmans, 1995), 37; 42-3; Seth Sykes, *Time and Space in Haggai-Zechariah 1-8: A Bakhtinian Analysis of a Prophetic Chronicle* (Studies in Biblical Literature 24; New York: Peter Lang, 2002), 25-46. David Petersen (*Haggai and Zechariah 1-8*, OTL [Philadelphia: Westminster, 1984], 124), while insisting on the distinct composition and redaction of Haggai and Zechariah, nonetheless views Zechariah as a response to Haggai. The early proposal of A. Klostermann (*Geschichte des Volkes Israel bis zur Restauration unter Esra und Nehemia* [Munich: C. H. Beck, 1896], 212-13) that Haggai-Zechariah was a single original narrative secondarily divided into two books (cited by Beuken, *Haggai, Sacharja 1-8*, 11), while rendered impossible by the distinctiveness of Haggai and Zechariah, nonetheless affirms the unity achieved by their redaction. As James Nogalski (*Literary Precursors of the Book of the Twelve*, BZAW 217 [Berlin: de Gruyter, 1993], 278, and *Redactional Processes in the Book of the Twelve*, BZAW 218 [Berlin: de Gruyter, 1993], 274-79) has demonstrated, Haggai and Zechariah 1— 8 were combined prior to their incorporation into the Book of the Twelve, and Zechariah 9 —14 was added subsequent to this incorporation. As this study is concerned with the composition and redaction of Haggai-Zechariah and, secondarily, of the Book of the Twelve, consideration of Zechariah 9 —14 was not deemed relevant.

I. Possible Points of Influence

A. The Centrality of Temple and Cult

The editorial superscription to Ezekiel identifies this prophet as a priest (Ezek 1:3). The content of the book, however, would lead the reader to this conclusion, even without that explicit statement. The prophet's concern for right worship and ritual purity (i.e., Ezek 18:5-6; Ezek 8) and the parallels in style and content between Ezekiel and the Holiness Code (for example, in Lev 18:6-19//Ezek 22:8-12) make the relationship between the book of Ezekiel and Jerusalemite priestly circles evident.

As we might expect from a prophet-priest, concerns for the temple affect both the content and the structure of Ezekiel. The book is punctuated by three great visions (1—3, 8—11, 40—48). These complex vision reports are linked by the experience of the divine glory, the כבוד, which in priestly texts signifies the presence of YHWH in sacred space.[7] In Ezekiel, however, the כבוד is encountered in an unclean land, among the exiles. In the first vision (Ezek 1—3), the כבוד comes to be with Ezekiel and his fellow exiles in Babylon, beside the river Chebar. This gracious presence of YHWH with the exiles, however, implies the divine absence from the Jerusalem temple,

---

[7]   First at the mountain of God (Exod 24:16, 17; 29:43; 40:34, 35; Lev 9:6, 23), later at the tabernacle (Num 14:10, 21, 22; 16:19; 17:7 [16:42]; 20:6). The sole apparent exception to this rule, the appearance of the glory at the giving of the manna in Exodus 16:7, 10, proves on closer examination rather to confirm the rule. Not only is this incident set in the immediate vicinity of the mountain of God (cf. Exod 17:6), but the mention of a jar of manna being placed לפני העדת ("before the testimony") in v. 34 demonstrates that, in an earlier form of the tradition, this account belonged to the period after Sinai, in connection with the tabernacle and the Ark. Although in Num 14:21 the earth is said to be filled with the כבוד יהוה (cf. Isa 6:3), the particular manifestation of the כבוד remains tied to sacred space. Indeed, care must be taken to ensure that unauthorized contact with the כבוד does not occur (cf. the Korah rebellion, Num 16:1-11, 16-22, 35 — 17:15 [Eng. 16:50]), suggesting that the manner in which the כבוד fills the earth is very different from the manner in which it is present on Sinai and in the tabernacle. The language used of the כבוד in the Jerusalem temple (1 Kgs 8:11; Pss 24:7, 10; 26:8; 29:3; Isa 6:3) is, thus, in direct continuity with P: not surprising, as the writers and redactors responsible for P are of the same lineage as the Zadokite priests of the pre- and post-exilic temple establishments.

where the כבוד would normally be manifested.[8] In the second vision (Ezek 8—11), this implication is confirmed: the כבוד has abandoned the temple and the city, leaving both ripe for destruction.

In the third and final vision (Ezek 40 — 48), the כבוד appears for the last time, inhabiting a glorious visionary temple. Many scholars would agree, with Blenkinsopp[9], that this vision involves the rebuilding of the temple, in fulfillment of the promise in Ezek 37:26b-27: "I will bless and multiply them, and will set my sanctuary among them forevermore. My dwelling place shall be with them; and I will be their God, and they shall be my people."[10]   However, this researcher has argued elsewhere that the temple description in Ezekiel 40—42 does not fit the pattern of temple-building texts in the ancient Near East. Rather, the original text of Ezekiel 40—48 depicted a heavenly ascent; the temple the prophet describes is the original, archetypal dwelling of God.[11]   Ezekiel's description of this structure would have served in his community as a substitute for the Jerusalem temple and its iconography, which provided for worshipers a connection to divine reality (cf. Ps 48:13-15). In its final form, however, the function of the final nine chapters of Ezekiel has been redirected. By a thoroughgoing Zadokite redaction, probably dating to early in Darius' reign, Ezekiel's visionary experience of YHWH's presence has become a law, the Law of the Temple, describing the means by which the divine presence may legitimately be approached: through right cult (43:18-27; 44:13—46:15) and right priesthood (44:4-31).[12]

---

[8]   Little wonder, as Samuel Terrien observes, that Ezekiel's call begins with the heavens being torn open: "As the member of a priestly family, the young deportee had doubtless believed that Yahweh dwelt in Zion. He could not expect that Yahweh would manifest his presence in a remote and totally alien land except through some shattering of the cosmic order" (*The Elusive Presence: The Heart of Biblical Theology*, [Religious Perspectives 26; San Francisco: Harper and Row, 1978], 258).

[9]   Blenkinsopp further argues that the Temple vision originally followed Ezekiel 37 (*Ezekiel*, Interpretation [Louisville, Kentucky: John Knox, 1990], 177-178; 179-180; 194).

[10]   Unless otherwise stated, English Bible quotations will be from the NRSV.

[11]   Steven Tuell, "Ezekiel 40—42 as Verbal Icon," *CBQ* 58 (1996) 649-64.

[12]   For a detailed analysis of the redaction of Ezekiel 40—48, see Tuell, *The Law of the Temple in Ezekiel 40—48* (HSM 49; Atlanta: Scholars Press, 1992), Chapter Two. By means of this redactional expansion, the center of the text has been subtly shifted from the divine promise of presence (Ezek 43:7a) to the means by which the presence can be encountered. A liturgy is set forth, together with a cult calendar and a hierarchy of Temple personnel. The funding of the cult is arranged, and hence its continuance is guaranteed. Within this scheme are evidences of gritty reality. Political problems are revealed in the three prophetic critiques of the leader in the land, the נשיא (45:8; 45:9; and 46:18). Tensions in the Temple leadership are evidenced by the polemic against the Levites, especially in 44:6-14. The society depicted in the Temple Vision is no

These same concerns for temple, cult, and priesthood animate Haggai-Zechariah. Even outside the books that bear their names, the prophets Haggai and Zechariah are remembered in connection with the rebuilding of the temple (Ezra 5:1 and 6:15). Within the text of these prophets, these issues are primary, suggesting that Ezekielian influence may be found at this point.

Clearly, the rebuilding of the temple and the reestablishment of Judah as a nation are the principal themes of Haggai's prophecy.[13] Haggai 1:2-11 echoes the theme of material prosperity, linked to the divine presence enshrined and celebrated in the right temple with the right cult, which is communicated in Ezek 47:1-12[14]—though in a negative, rather than a positive sense. The failure to rebuild the temple, Haggai declares, has meant disaster not only for the human community, but also for the land itself. Without the temple, the land has suffered the curse of infertility and drought (Hag 1:11). Only when YHWH's house is rebuilt will the land be blessed once more.

In Zechariah as well, the rebuilding of the temple is a prominent concern. Zech 2:14-17 (10-13)[15] describes Jerusalem as the place of YHWH's dwelling, in language reminiscent of Ezek 37:24-28.[16] In particular, the rebuilding of the temple is the subject of the intertwined vision report and oracle found in Zech 4:1-14. In his vision, Zechariah sees a golden lampstand (Zech 4:1-5). As lampstands in the ancient world were customarily made of clay, it is likely that Zechariah's golden lampstand is

---

ideal projection, but an actual society, centered on a state-supported Temple in which the secular leadership played an important role. The evidence suggests that this society was Restoration Judea. Persian interventions in the religious institutions of other subject peoples tended to follow the pattern described here. The sixty-shekel mina from the table of weights and measures in 45:10-12 corresponds to the system of weights and measures instituted by Darius I. The title נשיא, given to the leader of the society portrayed in the Temple Vision, was also given to Sheshbazzar, first governor of the Persian province of Yehud. The restriction of priesthood to the Jerusalemite altar clergy can best be explained as a transitional stage between First and Second Temple periods, operative until the time of Ezra's Mosaic torah. Even the borders depicted in 47:15-20 roughly coincide with the borders of the Persian province Abar-Nahara, of which Judah was a part (so Tuell, "The Southern and Eastern Borders of Abar Nahara," *BASOR 284* [1991] 51-58). Particularly suggestive (see n. 59, below) is the Demotic Chronicle, which details the demand of Darius that the Egyptian clergy produce a law of the temples. As 43:12 explicitly states, in its final form, the Temple Vision is just such a code: it is תורת הבית, the Law of the Temple.

[13] So Peter R. Ackroyd, "Haggai," *HBD* , 1985), 367; Redditt, *Haggai, Zechariah, Malachi*, 13.
[14] Tuell, *Law*, 68-71; cf. also "The Rivers of Paradise: Ezek 47:1-12 and Gen 2:10-14," in *God Who Creates* (ed. S. Dean McBride, Jr. and William Brown; Eerdmans, 2000), 171-89, esp. 181-86.
[15] When the Hebrew and English chapter/verse enumeration differ, the Hebrew will be given first.
[16] Meyers and Meyers, *Haggai, Zechariah 1-8*, 168.

meant to suggest the golden lampstands of the tabernacle (Exod 25:31-40) and the temple of Solomon (1 Kgs 7:49). Between this vision (Zech 4:1-5) and its interpretation (4:10b-14), an oracle concerning Zerubbabel (Zech 4:6-10a) has been inserted, which confirms the temple connection.[17] The specific provisions of the Zerubbabel oracle relate to the rituals of temple rebuilding usually performed by the king. Before Zerubbabel, the Lord declares, the top of the temple mount shall become a smooth, level place, prepared for rebuilding.[18] Into this building site Zerubbabel will carry האבן הראשה ("the top stone"), while all the people cheer (Zech 4:7). The "top stone," or, perhaps better the "first" or "premier stone," could be the equivalent of the first brick in Babylonian temples, ceremonially placed by the king. Alternatively, Zerubbabel's "top stone" could be a stone from the first temple, ceremonially preserved from the ruins for inclusion in the new temple. This custom, too, was followed in Babylon.[19]

Also said to be in Zerubbabel's hand is האבן הבדיל (literally, "the tin stone;" Zech 4:10). If the Hebrew phrase refers to a plummet,[20] then the intention once more is to depict Zerubbabel in the act of rebuilding—here, checking that the temple walls are laid true. However, deposits of precious materials and of symbolic metal objects such as nails were often placed in temple foundations. Perhaps האבן הבדיל is such a foundation deposit.[21] In any case, seeing this object in the hands of Zerubbabel is convincing proof, even to the skeptics who "despised the day of small things," that the spirit of the Lord is at work in Zerubbabel. Having restored the foundations of the temple, he will also complete the rebuilding (Zech 4:9).

The priesthood as well figures prominently in Haggai-Zechariah. Two of Haggai's four oracles are addressed to Joshua the high priest, as well as to Zerubbabel the governor (Hag 1:1; 2:2, 4; note that Joshua also figures prominently in the narrative depicting the temple rebuilding in Hag 1:12-15).

---

[17] Many scholars (for example, Paul D. Hanson, "Zechariah, Book of," *IDBSup*, 982; Petersen, *Haggai and Zechariah 1-8*, 244; Redditt, *Haggai, Zechariah, Malachi*, 39) hold that this insertion was made by later editors. However, Meyers and Meyers (*Haggai, Zechariah 1-8*, 242) persuasively argue that the oracle and the vision belong together, and were likely arranged together by Zechariah himself.

[18] Meyers and Meyers, *Haggai, Zechariah*, 244-45.

[19] Meyers and Meyers, *Haggai, Zechariah 1-8*, 246-48; see also Petersen, *Haggai and Zechariah 1-8*, 240-41.

[20] As it has traditionally been rendered; so AV, NIV, NRSV. JPSV emends the text to read "stone of distinction."

[21] Meyers and Meyers, *Haggai, Zechariah*, 253-54; Petersen, *Haggai and Zechariah 1-8*, 243-44.

Another oracle involves the request for, and response to, a priestly torah (Hag 2:10-19).[22]

The importance of the priesthood in Zechariah is indicated in many ways. In Zechariah 3, the prophet sees the high priest Joshua on trial in the heavenly court, accused by הַשָּׂטָן. He is, however, vindicated. YHWH rebukes הַשָּׂטָן and declares, "Thus says the LORD of hosts: If you will walk in my ways and keep my requirements, then you shall rule my house and have charge of my courts, and I will give you the right of access among those who are standing here" (Zech 3:7). As Paul Hanson observes, "This passage both reflects the exalted position of the Zadokite high priest at this period and hints at the existence of intercommunity controversy over his appointment."[23]   Another, implicit affirmation of Joshua comes in the interpretation of Zechariah's vision in chapter 4. The two olive trees are identified as "the two anointed ones who stand by the Lord of the whole earth" (Zech 4:14)—referring, evidently to Zerubbabel the governor and Joshua the high priest. בְּנֵי הַיִּצְהָר, the Hebrew phrase translated "anointed ones" in the NRSV, means literally "sons of oil." The term יִצְהָר usually refers to fresh olive oil, and is never used elsewhere for anointing oil. The point does not appear to be that Joshua the high priest and Zerubbabel the governor are messiahs.[24] Rather, just as the two olive trees in Zechariah's vision provide oil for the lamps, the high priest and the governor together are expected to provide for the temple, where God's presence will be experienced and celebrated. Note, too, that in Zechariah as in Haggai, the priests are approached for an authoritative ruling (Zech 7:1-3), which again provides the occasion for a prophetic oracle.

To be sure, Ezekiel and Haggai-Zechariah manifest a common interest in temple, cult, and priesthood. However, the general ideas concerning the temple expressed in Haggai-Zechariah can be found elsewhere throughout the ancient Near East and in the Hebrew Bible, and do not indicate depend-

---

22   For a brief summary of the various approaches to this enigmatic text, see Brevard Childs, *Introduction to the Old Testament as Scripture* (Philadelphia: Fortress, 1979), 464-65.

23   Paul D. Hanson, "Zechariah," *HBD*, 1159. Note, for example, that while the Law of the Temple in Ezek 40 — 48 affirms an exclusively Zadokite priesthood, it makes no mention of a high priest (cf. Tuell, *Law*, 146-151).

24   Note, though, the mention of the crowns in Zech 6:9-15. Although only the crown for Joshua is mentioned in the final form of the text, the use of the plural in vv 11 and (possibly) 14, and the reference to "a priest by his throne" in v 13, show that the original form of the text envisioned crowns for both Joshua and Zerubbabel (so Hanson, "Zechariah," 983). The Essenes did expect two messiahs, one a priest and one a king. Cf. Geza Vermes, *The Dead Sea Scrolls in English* (4th ed.; London: Penguin, 1995), 60.

ency upon Ezekiel. Further, Ezekiel's characteristic terminology is not used. The term היכל, used in Ezek 41:1 and elsewhere for the long central chamber of the temple, is in Haggai (2:15, 18) and Zechariah (8:9) used interchangeably with בית יהוה, for the entire temple. Ezekiel's term for divine presence, כבוד, does appear in Hag 2:3, 7, and 9. However, it is used differently than in Ezekiel. In Haggai, כבוד simply means "splendor," and does not explicitly indicate divine presence.[25] In Zechariah, on the other hand, כבוד is definitely used with reference to the divine presence (Zech 2:9 [5]), and even as a circumlocution for the divine name (Zech 2:12 [8]). However, in both Haggai and Zechariah, the term כבוד appears together with the expression יהוה צבאות, which in texts expressive of the old Zion theology depicts YHWH enthroned above the cherubim in the most holy place. Indeed, as Meyers and Meyers observe יהוה צבאות is a characteristic expression of Haggai-Zechariah.[26] This term never appears in Ezekiel; indeed, Tryggve Mettinger proposes that it has been polemically excluded.[27] Also conspicuous by its absence from Haggai-Zechariah is any reference to the detailed legislation in the final form of Ezekiel 40 — 48, or to the temple plan in Ezekiel 40 — 42. Note, too, that while the role of Joshua as high priest is an important theme in Haggai-Zechariah, the cultic legislation in Ezekiel 40 — 48 makes no mention of a high priest. In short, while temple, cult, and priesthood are shared interests of Ezekiel and Haggai-Zechariah, the concrete expression of these ideas in Haggai-Zechariah does not derive from Ezekiel.[28]

B. The Dating Formulae

Sixteen different occurrences of the date formula can be found in Ezekiel, each time as the heading of a unit. Of these, eleven are precise to the year, month and day (Ezek 1:1; 8:1; 20:1; 24:1; 29:1; 29:17; 30:20; 31:1; 32:1; 33:21; and 40:1). Three others (1:2; 26:1; and 32:17) are precise to the year and day, while two date in reference to some fixed event (3:16 refers to the

---

[25] *Contra* Meyers and Meyers, *Haggai, Zechariah 1-8*, 54.

[26] Ibid., 18. While Haggai constitutes only .2% of the Hebrew Bible, it contains 14 occurrences of יהוה צבאות: 5% of the total references. Similarly Zechariah 1—8, at .6% of the Hebrew Bible, accounts for 14% of the total references (44 occurrences).

[27] Tryggve N. D. Mettinger, *The Dethronement of Sabaoth: Studies in the Shem and Kabod Theologies* (trans. Frederick H. Cryer; CBOTS 18; Lund: C. W. K. Gleerup, 1982), 11, 109-113.

[28] *Contra* Paul D. Hanson, who argues that Haggai and Zechariah were attempting to enact the program in Ezekiel 40 — 48 (*The Dawn of Apocalyptic* [Philadelphia: Fortress, 1975], 174).

date of the call vision, and sets its vision seven days later, while a second date in 40:1 specifies the year as the fourteenth after the fall of Jerusalem). Interestingly, both the first use of the date formula (Ezek 1:1- 2) and the last (Ezek 40:1) are doubled dates. The dates in Ezekiel are mainly sequential,[29] and are calculated by the years of Jehoiachin's exile, which also happen to be the years of exile for Ezekiel and his fellows. The sole exception, the enigmatic "thirtieth year" of Ezek 1:1, would appear to be a reference to Ezekiel's age at the time that his career as a prophet began.[30]

There are eight occurrences of the dating formula in Haggai-Zechariah (Hag 1:1, 15; 2:1, 10, 20; Zech 1:1, 7; 7:1). All but two are precise to the year, month and day: Hag 2:20, which gives only the day, but refers explicitly to the date in 2:10; and Zech 1:1, which gives only the year and month. Usually, as in Ezekiel, these date formulae introduce a unit. But the date formula in Hag 1:15 appears to be free-floating, suggesting that the text has been disarranged[31]; moreover, the "second year of King Darius" in Hag 1:15b seems to do double duty, defining both the date in 1:15 and the following date in 2:1. However, Meyers and Meyers note that 1:15 forms a neat envelope with 1:1 (while 1:1 gives year, month, and day, 1:15 presents the date as day, month, year), and so propose that it is intended to conclude the first unit.[32] Two of the date formulae (Hag 2:10 and 20) refer to the

---

[29] Only three dates are out of sequence: 26:1, which postdates 29:1 by about a year; 29:17, the latest date in Ezekiel, which introduces a later appendix to Ezekiel's original prophecy; and 32:1, which postdates 33:21 by about two months. Note that G of 32:17 specifies the first month, which likewise predates 32:1.

[30] Cf. the discussion in Margaret Odell, "You Are What You Eat: Ezekiel and the Scroll," *JBL* 117 (1998) 238-41. Rudolf Smend held that the thirtieth year was the year of the book's completion (*Der Prophet Ezechiel* [KEH; Leipzig: S. Hirzel, 1880], xxii). C. C. Torrey concluded from this date that the book had originally been written in the thirtieth year of Manasseh (*Pseudo-Ezekiel and the Original Prophecy* [New Haven: Yale University, 1930; reprint, Library of Biblical Studies {New York: Ktav, 1970}], 17-18; 64).

[31] Hans Walter Wolff believes that the "Haggai-chronicler," as he calls the final redactor of this text, moved the oracle now found in 2:15-19 from its original position following 1:15, so that the promised blessing was associated, not with rebuilding, but with the rejection of the unclean from participation. This left 1:15, which had introduced that oracle, as a free-floating fragment. Cf. Hans Walter Wolff, *Haggai: Eine Auslegung* (BSt 1; Neukirchen-Vluyn: Neukirchener Verlag, 1951), 20-21.

[32] Meyers and Meyers, *Haggai, Zechariah 1-8*, 36. They further propose that the year may have dropped out of 2:1, due to haplography (37). Petersen (*Haggai and Zechariah 1-8*), on the other hand, proposes that Hag 1:1-15a be divided into two units, one beginning with a date formula (1:1-11; pp. 41-54), the other ending with one (1:12-15a; pp. 55-60); while the year designation in 1:15b is combined with the month and day in 2:1 (p. 62). However, these verses appear to make best sense as a single unit (so Beuken, *Haggai, Sacharja 1-8*, 31-33, and Meyers and Meyers, *Haggai, Zechariah 1-8*, 36).

same day: "On the twenty-fourth day of the ninth month, in the second year of Darius." This date is also emphasized in Hag 2:18: "Consider from this day on, from the twenty-fourth day of the ninth month." Meyers and Meyers propose that this was the date of the refoundation ceremony for the temple, and note that it stands at the center of Haggai-Zechariah, with three dates before it and three after.[33] The dates are sequential, with the exception of Zech 1:1, which predates Hag 2:10 and 20. Sykes proposes that these overlapping dates "reinforce a thematic connection between the two prophetic texts"; in this way, the overlap contributes to the unity of Haggai-Zechariah as a "unified, whole utterance."[34] Note finally that the dates in Haggai-Zechariah are calculated by the regnal years of a foreign king, the Persian monarch Darius — a move without precedent in the prophetic corpus.[35]

We have no reason to doubt the accuracy of these dates, either in Ezekiel or in Haggai-Zechariah. However, the date formulae in Ezekiel are less significant for the structure of that book, and appear to be original to the prophet. In Haggai-Zechariah, on the other hand, the dates are a major redactional link between Haggai and Zechariah, and a key structural feature, dividing the text into seven sections.[36] Obviously, in both books, the system of dating precise to the day shows a keen awareness of, perhaps even an obsession with, the passage of time. In Ezekiel's case, it is the slow passage of the exile that is in view. In Haggai-Zechariah, Meyers and Meyers propose, the dates are a "countdown" to the end of the disruption brought by exile, thanks to the rebuilding of YHWH's temple.[37]

That Haggai-Zechariah marks time by the regnal years of the Persian Darius would appear to indicate at least an acknowledgement and acceptance of Persian domination, and perhaps even a pro-Persian bias, on behalf of the text's redactor.[38] However, Sykes proposes rather that the "chronistic" structure of Haggai-Zechariah involves a transformation of the old Babylonian chronicle genre. The Babylonian chronicles[39] functioned to preserve the social order; in particular to maintain royal support of the temple and cult at Esagil. By selectively chronicling the reigns and vicissitudes of

---

[33] Meyers and Meyers, *Haggai, Zechariah 1-8*, xlvii.

[34] Sykes, *Time and Space*, 27.

[35] As Meyers and Meyers, *Haggai, Zechariah 1-8*, observe (5).

[36] See especially Sykes, *Time and Space*, 28-9.

[37] Meyers and Meyers, *Haggai, Zechariah 1-8*, 6.

[38] Ibid., 5-6; Petersen, *Haggai and Zechariah 1-8*, 42-3; Hanson, *Dawn*, 244-45.

[39] Sykes accepts the classification of A. Kirk Grayson, who identifies twenty-four texts as chronicles; cf. *Assyrian and Babylonian Chronicles* (Texts from Cuneiform Sources; Locust Valley, N.Y.: Augustin, 1975). Fourteen of these texts, those composed prior to Haggai-Zechariah, are analyzed by Sykes using the tools of Bakhtinian literary criticism, in order to uncover their sociopolitical setting and function (Sykes, *Time and Space*, 47-91).

"good" and "bad" kings, the Babylonian chronicles generate a portrait of the ideal king, who preserves Babylon and its temples, and so is blessed by the gods. By dating in accordance with the reign of Darius, Haggai-Zechariah may appear to be following in that same vein. However, the focus of the text is not on the rule of the Persian monarch, but (as the preponderance of references to the old title יהוה צבאות indicates) on the kingship of YHWH. Haggai-Zechariah, Sykes states, "subverts the historical reality of Persian imperial rule by depicting the universal and eternal rule of Yahweh."[40]

The consistent use of dating formulae precise to the day is a feature unique to Ezekiel and Haggai-Zechariah, and so a likely sign of Ezekielian influence on the later composition. However, note that this influence belongs to the level of the redactional combination of Haggai-Zechariah, not to the level of their composition. Further, while the form of Ezekiel's date citations has been followed in Haggai-Zechariah, it has been put to quite a different use.

C. Vision Reports

We have already considered the importance of the three great כבוד visions in the structure of Ezekiel. All three are dated precise to the day (1:1; 8:1; 40:1), and all are designated מראות אלהים ("visions of God;" Ezek 1:1; 8:3; 40:2).[41] In all three, the prophet is lifted out of himself into heavenly reality as the vision begins. The formula for expressing prophetic ecstasy, "the hand of (Lord) YHWH was upon me," occurs seven times in Ezekiel: not only in the three great vision complexes (Ezek 1:3; 3:14, 22; 8:1; 40:1), but also in 33:22 (where the יד יהוה removes Ezekiel's dumbness; cf. 3:22-27) and 37:1 (at the beginning of the vision of the dry bones). Zimmerli rightly regards the phenomenon of prophetic ecstasy as characteristic of Ezekiel, a point of continuity between this prophet and the pre-classical prophets.[42] With Ezekiel as well comes the first instance of a feature that will become more and more common in later texts: the presence of an angelic figure, to illustrate and interpret the prophet's visions (Ezek 40:3-4).

While vision reports play no role at all in Haggai, Zechariah's prophecy is characterized by weird symbolic visions. The message of this prophet is communicated in eight vision reports (1:7-17; 2:1-4 [1:18-21]; 2:5-9 [1-5]; 3:1-10; 4:1-5, 10b-14; 5:1-4; 5:5-11; and 6:1-8), interspersed with prophetic

---

[40]   Ibid., 149-50.

[41]   מַאֲרָה is relatively rare, occurring only eleven times in the Hebrew Bible: Gen 46:2; Num 12:6 (both E); 1 Sam 3:15; and Dan 10:7 (2x), 8, 16; as well as Ezek 1:1; 8:3; 40:2; and 43:3.

[42]   Zimmerli, *Ezekiel*, 1:42.

oracles (1:1-6; 2:10-17 [6-13]; 4:6-10a; 6:9-15; 7:1-14; 8:1-17, 18-23). An angel whom the prophet calls "the angel who talked with me" serves as Zechariah's guide and interpreter in these visions (Zech 1:9, 2:2 [1:19]; 2:7-9 [3-5]; 4:10-14; 5:3, 6-8, 10-11; 6:5-6). Like Ezekiel's visions, Zechariah's abound in fantastic imagery and odd, supernatural beings. These visions may be understood as dreams or night visions (Zech 1:8; 4:1; compare Dan 7:1-2). However, it is also possible that Zechariah, like Ezekiel, speaks out of a prophetic ecstasy, in which he is transported to the heavenly world. So, in Zech 3:1, the prophet is standing in the heavenly throne room. In Zech 4:1, moreover, the prophet says that the angel "wakened me, as one is wakened from sleep." This could mean that the vision of the lamp stand that follows came in a dream. However, the language of the verse suggests that the prophet may have intended a comparison: being summoned by the angel at the beginning of the vision was *like* being awakened from sleep. For Zechariah, the world of God's revelation is not less, but more real than the waking world. Entry into the visionary state was not like falling asleep, but like waking up![43]

On the one hand, then, Zechariah's visions seem in character very like Ezekiel's. On the other hand, Ezekiel's characteristic vocabulary is once again absent. Zechariah's visions are not titled מראות אלהים; nor are they dated. Ezekiel's formulaic expression for prophetic ecstasy does not appear in Haggai-Zechariah. Further, the content of Zechariah's visions is, generally speaking, entirely distinctive and unlike Ezekiel. We should note, by the way, that the presence of one or two words or images in both Zechariah and Ezekiel is not sufficient to indicate dependency. So, for example, Zech 5:1-4 involves a scroll (like Ezek 2:8 — 3:3), and elements of measurement (like Ezekiel 40 — 42, or 48:1-35). However, these are very common ideas, and are used in quite distinctive ways: Ezekiel eats his scroll, while Zechariah's flies through the air. No influence of Ezekiel upon Zechariah can be deduced from such specious parallels.

The exception that proves the rule is Zech 2:5-9 (2:1-5). Here, Zechariah sees "a man with a measuring line in his hand." This is certainly an allusion to Ezek 40:3, where the prophet describes a man with a linen cord and a measuring reed in his hand. Although different terms are used for the cord (חבל מדה in Zech, פתיל־פשתים in Ezek), the correspondence is striking. The linen cord is not mentioned again in Ezekiel,[44] suggesting that Zechariah's vision deliberately responds to Ezekiel's, providing an explanation for the cord. Each figure appears to be engaged in measurement: of the vision-

---

[43] Meyers and Meyers, *Haggai, Zechariah 1-8*, 229.

[44] Although in 47:3, the man uses a קו ("line") in his hand to measure the river flowing out from the temple.

ary temple complex and the fabulous river that flows out of it in Ezekiel, and of Jerusalem in Zechariah. Little wonder that Meyers and Meyers see a virtual correspondence between these two visions.[45]

One should note, however, that in fact Zechariah's vision is not a parallel to Ezekiel's, but a response, indeed a parody. First, it is no accident that the man in Ezekiel's vision measures the temple and *not* the city. The "very high mountain" (Ezek 40:2) to which Ezekiel is taken as this final vision report opens is, of course, Zion, the Jerusalem acropolis. In Ezekiel, however, the mountain is not *called* Zion, a term that never appears in this book. Indeed, in Ezekiel's vision the city, described in Ezek 48:30-35, is not located on the mountain, and the temple is not located within the city.[46] In the original vision, it was not the earthly, political Zion, but the heavenly, mythical Zion that was the ground of hope. True, the final form of Ezekiel 40 — 48, with its detailed legislation regarding both priest and prince, does emphasize concrete, political reality. But the Jerusalem focus in Zechariah remains at odds with Ezekiel's vision. Second, note that detailed, careful measurement is the point of Ezekiel 40 — 42. The perfect dimensions of the sanctuary serve to demonstrate its holiness. But in Zechariah's vision, the man with the measuring line never actually gets to measure anything. As Petersen observes, "An angelic interpreter interrupts these proceedings and proclaims that the new Jerusalem will exist without boundaries."[47] Zechariah clearly alludes to Ezekiel here. But, his own vision moves in an entirely different direction.

In the prominence given to vision reports, and in the role played by the interpreting angel, Zechariah has certainly been influenced by Ezekiel. However, in content the visions of Zechariah are quite distinct. Once more, it is in matters of form, rather than matters of content, that Ezekiel's influence is felt.

---

[45] Meyers and Meyers, *Haggai and Zechariah 1-8*, 151.

[46] Zimmerli (*Ezekiel*, 2:547), observes that the "last sentence of the book of Ezekiel shows how the old tradition of the city of God has forcefully obtained justice for itself against the priestly reform project, which, through the separation of city and temple, has robbed the city of much of its dignity." He therefore classes Ezek 48:30-35 with the similar exaltations of the city in Deutero- or even Trito-Isaiah (2:545), and views it as a later addition to the text. Based on the parallel between the city in 48:30-35 and the "construction like a city" in 40:1-4, this researcher has proposed that 48:30-35 was a part of the prophet's original vision (Tuell, *Law*, 73-74). Only by explicitly describing the city as distinct from the mountain could Ezekiel adequately express his point: that the true dwelling of God has been cut loose from its associations with Jerusalem (Tuell, "Rivers," 186-89).

[47] David L. Petersen, "Zechariah," *HBC*, 748. He also understands Zechariah here as a repudiation of Ezek 40 — 48 (see Petersen, *Haggai and Zechariah 1—8*, 169).

D. The Use of the First Person

Both Ezekiel and Zechariah are written predominantly in the first person. Margaret Odell proposes that the use of the first person in Ezekiel reflects the transformation of the building inscription, an ancient Mesopotamian genre that also used the first person.[48] This genre functioned to exalt the king who had established the building's foundations. However, in Ezekiel's adaptation of the genre it is YHWH, not the prophet, who is king; Ezekiel is בֶּן אָדָם, the loyal subject. While certainly intriguing, Odell's proposal is not finally convincing. Apart from the use of the first person, the text of Ezekiel does not match the features of the building inscription. Further, it is unclear how public such inscriptions would have been, and so what access Ezekiel could have had to exemplars of this genre.

Another ancient "autobiographical" genre is the votive inscription. A fine example is the inscription upon the statue of Udjahoresne, an intriguing sixth-century figure who seems to have been for Egypt what Ezra was for Judah: a legal/religious authority, acting under Persian auspices.[49] In the inscription, Udjahoresne is called "the chief physician,"[50] probably owing to his high position, not only in the temple of Neith, but in the House of Life, an institution dedicated to medicine and the healing arts as well as to religious ritual.[51] However, he had also served as the commander of the Egyptian fleet before his defection to the Persians under Cambyses.[52] It was Udjahoresne who composed the titulary of Cambyses in Egypt: Mesutire, meaning Son of Re, the sun god.[53] Under this name, Cambyses ruled as king of Upper and Lower Egypt. In return, the Persian monarch gave Udjahoresne the authority to expel the "foreigners" from the temple of Neith, even to destroy their houses and property, and to restore the temple to its former glory.[54]

Clearly, Ezekiel could not have been influenced by the Udjahoresne inscription, although the political and religious situation it describes sounds much like that of the Law of the Temple[55] — or, for that matter, like that of Haggai-Zechariah. Still, Ezekiel could well have been familiar with

---

48   Margaret S. Odell, "Genre and Persona in Ezekiel 24:15-24," in *The Book of Ezekiel: Theological and Anthropological Perspectives* (ed. Margaret Odell and John Strong; SBLSymS 9 (Atlanta: Scholars Press, 2000), 195-219, esp. 210-17.
49   Joseph Blenkinsopp, "The Mission of Udjahoresnet and Those of Ezra and Nehemiah," *JBL* 106 (1987) 417.
50   Miriam Lichtheim, *Ancient Egyptian Literature*, Vol. 3: *The Late Period* (Berkeley: University of California Press, 1980) 39.
51   Lichtheim, *Ancient Egyptian Literature*, 36.
52   Ibid., 37.
53   Ibid., 38. The name is translated on p. 40.
54   Ibid., 38.
55   Tuell, *Law*, 84-85; 90-91.

Egyptian votive inscriptions. Blenkinsopp observes a formal parallel between the Udjahoresne inscription and the memoirs of Nehemiah, suggesting in particular that Nehemiah 13 "was modeled on the Egyptian autobiographical votive inscription."[56] Such borrowing could perhaps also be indicated by the first-person style of Ezekiel and Zechariah. However, neither Ezekiel nor Zechariah really read like autobiographies. Despite the fact that these books are written in first person, we learn surprisingly little from them about the prophets themselves. In the foreground is not the personality of Ezekiel or Zechariah, but the word of YHWH.[57]

The most likely explanation for the use of the first person in Ezekiel, and perhaps for the preponderance of dates as well, comes from the predominant role played by visions in his prophecy. Vision reports are typically in the first person, and are usually dated.[58] It is little wonder, then, that in the work of a visionary such as Ezekiel the first person style became generalized across the narrative. It is perhaps possible that Zechariah could have adopted the first person independently, for the same reasons. However, as we know that Zechariah made use of Ezekiel, and as Ezekiel is the only other predominately first-person text in the prophetic corpus, it is more likely that the first-person style in Zechariah is due to Ezekielian influence.

E. The Nature and Significance of Ezekielian Influence on Haggai-Zechariah

It is apparent that Ezekiel has influenced Haggai-Zechariah. However, this composite work never refers to Ezekiel the prophet or quotes from his book. Allusions to Ezekiel are few, and distant. The closest parallels between Ezekiel and Haggai-Zechariah are found in the text of Zechariah; the most probable sign of Ezekielian influence in Haggai, the use of the date formulae, comes from the redactional layer linking Haggai to Zechariah. This connection supports the proposal of Meyers and Meyers, that either Zechariah himself or a close disciple is responsible for the redaction of Haggai-Zechariah.[59]

Ezekielian influence upon Haggai-Zechariah relates most reliably to matters of form rather than content. Rather like a painter producing a still life in the style of Picasso, or a composer creating a fugue in the style of Bach, the author/redactor of Haggai-Zechariah has produced a book of prophecy after the manner of Ezekiel. We have in the New Testament gospel of Luke an intriguing parallel to this usage of an earlier text. As I. Howard Marshall observes, Luke's "use of a LXX style must raise the

---

[56] Blenkinsopp, "Udjahoresne," 417.

[57] Cf. Joel Rosenberg, "Jeremiah and Ezekiel," in *The Literary Guide to the Bible* (ed. Robert Alter and Frank Kermode; Cambridge: Belknap, 1987), 196.

[58] Adela Yarbro Collins, "Vision," *HBD*, 1115.

[59] Meyers and Meyers, *Haggai, Zechariah 1-8*, xliv-xlviii.

question whether he thought of himself as writing a work of the same kind and thus continuing the 'salvation history' which he found in it."[60] Analogously, it appears that Zechariah, in his prophetic activity and particularly in his composition and editing work, understood himself to be working in the tradition of Ezekiel.

II. Ezekiel and the Emergence of Scripture

The early Persian period, indeed the reign of Darius, marks the compilation of Haggai-Zechariah, the final redaction of Ezekiel, and quite possibly the beginnings of both the Chronicler's History[61] and the Mosaic torah. The probable impetus for this tremendous burst of literary creativity was a decree of Darius, described in the so-called Demotic Chronicle:

> As for Darius, it heeded him . . . the land (of Egypt) in its entirety because of the excellence of his character. He issued a decree concerning Egypt to his satrap in (his) third regnal year, as follows: "Let be brought unto me the learned men . . . from among the (military) officers, the priests, (and) the scribes of Egypt so that, being assembled together, they may in concert write the law of Egypt which had been (observed) formerly through the forty-fourth regnal year of Pharaoh Amasis, (that is) the fifth pharaonic law, (concerning) the temples (and) the people."[62]

Eric Meyers suggests that "Persian encouragement to codify laws in the provinces could well have been the impetus to combine Zechariah 1-8 with Haggai into a single composite piece that was probably intended for presentation at the rededication ceremony of the Second Temple."[63] But Haggai-Zechariah scarcely fills the bill as a "law ... (concerning) the temples (and) the people." Ezekiel 43:12, though, is a striking literary parallel to the Demotic Chronicle. While the Chronicle records Darius's demand for the "law (concerning) the temples" in Egypt, Ezek 43:12 (the superscription to

---

[60]   I. Howard Marshall, "An Assessment of Recent Developments," in *It Is Written: Scripture Citing Scripture* (ed. D. A. Carson and H. G. M. Williamson; Cambridge: Cambridge University, 1988), 9.

[61]   So David N. Freedman, "The Chronicler's Purpose," *CBQ* 23 (1961) 439-440; William M. Schniedewind, *The Word of God in Transition: From Prophet to Exegete in the Second Temple Period* (JSOT 197; Sheffield, 1995), 249; and Steven Tuell, *First and Second Chronicles*, (Interpretation; Louisville: John Knox, 2001), 10-12.

[62]   Wilhelm Spiegelberg, *Die sogenannte demotische Chronik des Pap. 215 der Bibliotheque Nationale zu Paris, nebst den auf der Rückseite des Papyrus stehenden Texten* (Demotische Studien 7; Leipzig, 1914) 30-31. Translated here from the Demotic by S. Dean McBride, Jr.

[63]   Eric M. Meyers, "The Persian Period and the Judean Restoration: From Zerubbabel to Nehemiah," in *Ancient Israelite Religion* (eds. Patrick Miller, Paul Hanson and S. Dean McBride, Jr.; Philadelphia: Fortress, 1987) 513. Cf. also Meyers and Meyers, *Haggai, Zechariah 1-8*, 380.

the juridical corpus that follows) declares "This is the law of the temple." In its final form, Ezekiel 40 — 48 is one Judean answer to Darius' command: this is the law of *our* temple, in Jerusalem.

Even if such an order as described in the Demotic Chronicle was not given directly to the Judean priestly establishment, Persian concern for an official codification of Egyptian temple laws would surely have galvanized the YHWHistic priestly communities, both in Babylon and in Palestine, to formulate their own authoritative canons. In Babylon, the process of compilation would eventually result in the Mosaic torah, our Pentateuch.[64] In Jerusalem, the first fruit of this labor was Ezekiel 40 — 48 in its final form: the Law of the Temple, founded upon Ezekiel's last vision report.

That the prophecy of Ezekiel should have become an authoritative text is not surprising. At least since Smend in 1880, scholars have stressed the explicitly literary character of the book of Ezekiel.[65] The unique function of Ezekiel as a written text has been a particular concern of Ellen Davis.[66] She finds great significance in the report of Ezekiel's call vision, where the prophet describes a scroll, covered front and back with writing, which he is told to eat (Ezek 2:8 — 3:3). Thus revelation "comes to Ezekiel already *as a text*."[67] The point may, of course, be overstated; certainly written prophecy did not originate with Ezekiel. However, while earlier prophetic "books" are clearly written collections of oral performances, Ezekiel's work has the consistency of style and theme characteristic of written composition. Unlike his prophetic forebears, Ezekiel has written a book.[68]

I propose that, in Haggai-Zechariah, Zechariah too has written a book, modeled after Ezekiel. Meyers and Meyers observe in the later prophets "an increasingly greater awareness of and dependence on sacred literature";

---

[64] Blenkinsopp ("Mission," 414) has also proposed a link between the codification of the legal material in the Pentateuch and the Demotic Chronicle.

[65] Smend, *Ezechiel*, xxi. He was so impressed by the tight structure and unity of vision in Ezekiel as to write "man könnte kein Stück herausnehmen, ohne die ganze Ensemble zu zerstören" (one could not remove any part without destroying the whole structure). Robert Wilson ("Ezekiel," *HBC*, 657) has argued forcefully that "Ezekiel was a written composition from the beginning." He gives three reasons for this claim. First, Ezekiel is rarely depicted delivering oracles, but is rather encountered sitting his home. Second, the complexity of the oracles suggests that they were not delivered orally, but were written compositions from the beginning. Third, written prophecy would have been most conducive to wide distribution among the broadly dispersed exilic community.

[66] Ellen Davis, *Swallowing the Scroll: Textuality and the Dynamics of Discourse in Ezekiel's Prophecy* (JSOT 78; Sheffield: Almond Press, 1989), 65-66.

[67] Davis, *Scroll*, 51 (emphasis hers). Contrast the emphasis on written text in the call of Ezekiel with the emphasis on orality in the call of Jeremiah (Jer 1:9).

[68] So Hermann Gunkel, "Die israelitische Literatur," in *Die orientalischen Literaturen* (ed. P. Hinnenberg; Die Kultur der Gegenwart 1/7; Berlin, Tuebner,1906), 82.

indeed, they suggest that "the availability of written, sacred tradition as revelation from God must have been one critical factor" in the eventual disappearance of prophecy.[69] The emerging notion of written text, rather than oral pronouncement, as word of God extends in a broad continuum from Ezekiel onward. The Chronicler, who like Ezekiel has often been cited in connection with Haggai-Zechariah,[70] stands in this same tradition. Here, the plan for the temple and its liturgy is revealed to David as a written text: "All this, in writing at the LORD's direction, he made clear to me—the plan of all the works" (1 Chr 28:19). The Chronicler is a student of Scripture, and understands the will of God to be expressed through the written word.[71] The portions of the Chronicler's History which deal with the post-exilic restoration of Judah (that is, Ezra-Nehemiah) continue this same theme.[72] With the exception of Haggai and Zechariah, prophets and prophecy no longer function as the means of God's revelation. So, Ezra is not a prophet, but rather "an inspired text interpreter."[73] The text of Scripture has become the means of divine revelation. The great Temple Scroll from Qumran marks a far point on this continuing trajectory. This text, a plan for a massive temple complex, presents itself as the תבנית ("plan") originally revealed to Moses (Exod

---

[69] Meyers and Meyers, *Haggai, Zechariah 1-8,* 201. Cf. also Benjamin D. Sommer ("Did Prophecy Cease? Evaluating a Reevaluation," *JBL* 115 [1996] 46-47), although he attributes the decline of prophecy to the end of kingship and the destruction of the temple.

[70] So Beuken, *Haggai, Sacharja 1-8,* 331-336; Ackroyd, *HBC,* 745.

[71] In the text of Chronicles, "the word of the Lord" refers always either to prophetic revelation (1 Chr 11:3, 10; 22:8; 2 Chr 11:2; 12:7; 18:4, 18; 36:21) or to the word of Scripture, specifically the torah of Moses (1 Chr 15:15; 2 Chr 30:12; 34:21; 35:6). Indeed, this may be an artificial distinction, since in the Chronicler's view prophets write books (so Samuel, Nathan and Gad in 1 Chr 29:29; Nathan, Ahijah, and Iddo in 2 Chr 9:29; Shemaiah and Iddo in 2 Chr 12:15; Iddo in 2 Chr 13:22; Jehu ben Hanani in 2 Chr 20:34; Isaiah in 2 Chr 26:22 and 32:32), and so may be seen as composers of Scripture. With Geza Vermes (Emil Schürer, *The History of the Jewish People in the Age of Jesus Christ [175 B.C.—A.D. 135]*, III.1, rev. and ed. by Geza Vermes, Fergus Millar, and Martin Goodman [Edinburgh: T&T Clark, 1986], 326) and Philip S. Alexander ("Retelling the Old Testament," in *It Is Written: Scripture Citing Scripture,* 100), this researcher views Chronicles as an exemplar of the "rewritten Bible" genre (cf. Tuell, *Chronicles,* 7-8, 12-14).

[72] With Frank Moore Cross, Jr., "A Reconstruction of the Judean Restoration," *Int* 29 (1975) 194-98; Joseph Blenkinsopp, *Ezra-Nehemiah* (OTL; Philadelphia: Westminster, 1988) 43-54; and Tuell, *Chronicles,* 8-10; *contra* H. G. M. Williamson, *Israel in the Books of Chronicles* (Cambridge: Cambridge University Press, 1977), 69; Sara Japhet, *I & II Chronicles,* OTL (Louisville: Westminster/John Knox, 1993), 4-5; Ralph Klein, "Chronicles, Book of 1-2" *ABD* 1:993.

[73] Schniedewind, *Word,* 250.

25:9, 40), then handed on to Solomon by David (1 Chr 28:19).[74] For the
Qumran community, not only were the revelations to Moses and David seen
as one and the same, but this unified revelation was contained not in a
vision, but in a book.

Along this trajectory, of course, falls the Book of the Twelve. That the
Book of the Twelve *is*, in fact, a book has been ably demonstrated by
Nogalski's careful documentation of redactional connections among its
members.[75] With Odil Steck, Nogalski identifies the tradents responsible for
the redaction of Isaiah as also being responsible for the redaction of the
Twelve.[76] However, the impetus for collecting these twelve disparate
prophetic collections and combining them as a book may well have
originated with Ezekiel: arguably, the first *author* in Israel. Further, the final
form of Ezekiel, culminating in the Law of the Temple, may mark the first
step toward the canon as we know it. Ezekiel may well be the inventor of
Scripture.

---

[74]   Yigael Yadin, *The Temple Scroll, Volume 1: Introduction*   (Jerusalem: Israel
      Exploration Society, 1983), 177 and 182.
[75]   See n. 6, above.
[76]   Nogalski, *Redactional Processes*, 280; Odil Steck, *Der Abschluß der Prophetie im
      Alten Testament: Ein Versuch zur Frage der Vorgeschichte des Kanons* (Biblisch-
      Theologische Studien 17; Neukirchen-Vluyn: Neukirchener Verlag, 1991).

The Perspective on the Nations in the Book of Micah as a "Systematization" of the Nations' Role in Joel, Jonah and Nahum? Reflections on a Context-Oriented Exegesis in the Book of the Twelve[1]

Burkard M. Zapff

I. Preliminary Hermeneutical Reflections on an Exegesis of the Dodekapropheton

Scholars engaged in research today on the Book of the Twelve as a whole or individual books within the Dodekapropheton cannot do so – in view of the present discussion in the discipline[2] – without elucidating their hermeneutical principles. If one reads one of the commentaries by Hans Walter Wolff on partial books[3] in the Twelve, one will notice that the exegesis is handled with nearly the same criteria as a book of the so-called great prophets – e.g. Ezekiel.[4] Normally, these commentaries emphasize questions concerning the person of the prophet, his historical background, the message of the book, its literary unity, and the history of its origin. In short until the beginning of the 1990s – apart from a few exceptions – the individual books

---

[1]   I thank James Nogalski for correcting the first English translation.

[2]   On the present discussion of the Dodekapropheton, cf. in particular: J. W. Watts and P. R. House, *Forming Prophetic Literature. Essays on Isaiah and the Twelve in Honor of J. D. W. Watts* (JSOTS 235; Sheffield: Sheffield Academic Press, 1996), especially the essays on pp. 86-302; James Nogalski, *Literary Precursors to the Book of the Twelve* (BZAW 217, Berlin/New York: de Gruyter, 1993); James Nogalski, *Redactional Processes in the Book of the Twelve* (BZAW 218; Berlin/New York: de Gruyter, 1993); Barry A. Jones, *The Formation of the Book of the Twelve. A Study in Text and Canon* (SBLDS 149; Atlanta: Society of Biblical Literature, 1995; Burkard M. Zapff, *Redaktionsgeschichtliche Studien zum Michabuch im Kontext des Dodekapropheton* (BZAW 256; Berlin, New York: de Gruyter, 1997), especially 241-47; Aaron Schart, *Die Entstehung des Zwölfprophetenbuchs* (BZAW 260: Berlin/New York: de Gruyter, 1998), with an extensive history of the research (pp. 6-21).

[3]   Cf., e.g., the 4th edition of the commentary to the book of Hosea: Hans Walter Wolfe, *Dodekapropheton 1, Hosea* (BKAT XIV[1]; 4th ed.; Neukirchen-Vluyn: Neukirchener Verlag, 1990).

[4]   Cf. Walter Zimmerli, *Ezechiel 1-24* (BKAT XIII[1]; 2d ed.; Neukirchen-Vluyn: Neukirchener Verlag, 1979).

of the Twelve were treated like other individual prophetic writings of the OT, without considering the possibility that each book perhaps should be read and understood in the context of the other books of the Dodekapropheton.[5]

Recently scholars have begun to pay attention to the opinion[6] of Pirke de Rabbi Eliezar concerning the sequence of Jonah and Nahum. His words show that a context-oriented reading of the Book of the Twelve is not just a modern desideratum. According to Eliezar's interpretation the repentance of the inhabitants of Nineveh based on the sermon of Jonah was only temporary, so that in the subsequent book of Nahum the judgment of Yahweh befell Nineveh justly.[7] Indeed in his commentary on Obadiah and Jonah, Wolff reflects upon their respective canonical positions, noting that Obadiah would make a suitable completion of Joel 4, while Jonah could well be understood as the messenger in Obad 1 that was sent among the nations.[8] However, Wolff's interpretation does not extend beyond the boundary of either individual book. One could possibly characterize this view as a blind spot in traditional research of the Book of the Twelve, if there were not some indications that the previous means of proceeding did have some justification. As Ehud Ben Zvi has recently emphasized,[9] a survey of the individual books of the Twelve shows that – apart from the book of Jonah – every book of the Dodekapropheton has a heading of its own similar to those of the books of Isaiah or Jeremiah. This fact seems to support the assumption that the books of the Dodekapropheton should be read and interpreted as isolated units. On the other hand, a few of the headings in the Book of the Twelve give evidence that some books of the Dodekapropheton were handed down as a chronologically arranged collection and should be understood in this way. The so-called D-Corpus (cf. Schart), composed of

---

5   Indeed attempts in this direction were undertaken early, but they found little acceptance. Cf. Karl Budde, "Eine folgenschwere Redaktion des Zwölfprophetenbuches," ZAW 39, 1921, 218-229; Roland E. Wolfe, "The Editing of the Book of the Twelve," ZAW 53 (1935) 90-123.

6   Zapff, *Studien*, 274, n. 124; Schart, *Entstehung*, 27.

7   Cf. Louis Ginzberg, *The Legends of the Jews* (7 vols.; Philadelphia: Jewish Publication Society, 1913) 4.252-53.

8   Hans Walter Wolff, *Dodekapropheton 3, Obadja, Jona* (BKAT XIV[3;] 2d ed.; Neukirchen-Vluyn: Neukirchener Verlag, 1991) 2.

9   Ehud Ben Zvi, "Twelve Prophetic Books or 'Twelve': A Few Preliminary Considerations," *Forming Prophetic Literature: Essays on Isaiah and the Twelve in Honor of John D. W. Watts* (ed. James W. Watts, Paul R. House; JSOTSup 235; Sheffield: Sheffield Academic Press, 1996) 125-156, here 137: "The most significant and unequivocal internal evidence, namely that of the titles (incipits) of the prophetic books, set them on the same level with Isaiah or Jeremiah or Ezekiel, namely as separate prophetic books."

the books Hosea, Amos, Micah, and Zephaniah,[10] is an example of this evidence. According to the well-founded conclusion of Schart, the common system of headings in Hos 1:1, Amos 1:1, Mic 1:1 and Zeph 1:1 was designed for this specific collection of prophetic writings.[11] This raises the presumption that one also has to reckon with context-oriented revisions within the mentioned books.

The different arrangement of the books in the Twelve presents a more serious impediment to a contextual reading of the Book of the Twelve. Specifically, one finds varying sequences of the individual books in the MT, the LXX and a Qumran fragment of the Book of the Twelve – 4QXII[a].[12] This fact seems to confirm the opinion that there was no established sequence of the books in the Dodekapropheton, so consequently the task of contextual exegesis is founded on uncertain ground. If one considers the evidence available on this issue more closely, however, one will get the following results: 4QXII[a] (circa 150 BC) presents Jonah in final position, whereas 4QXII[g] (circa 50 BC), the Twelve Prophets scroll from the Wadi Nurabba'at (circa 50 BC), and the Greek written manuscript of the Dodekapropheton from Nahal Hever 8Hev XII (circa 50 BC) attest the position of the book of Jonah in the sequence of the MT, i. e., before the book of Micah. In his dissertation Barry A. Jones has argued for the originality of the sequence of 4QXII[a] vis-à-vis the LXX and the MT. Space does not allow a discussion of his argument, but if Jones says that Jonah has a different position in each of the transmitted sequences, a careful examination shows that both the LXX and the MT list the book of Jonah in the position after Obadiah and before Nahum – though in the MT Jonah is separated from Nahum by the book of Micah. It is not, therefore, the book of Jonah but the book of Micah that appears in different places in the MT and the LXX. Hence, one may not simply say that the book of Jonah is more loosely integrated into the Dodekapropheton than the other books and draw the conclusion that its position in the Dodekapropheton was determined relatively late.[13] In my opinion one has to affirm the stronger literary and thematic relationship between Jonah and the books of Joel, Micah and Nahum instead of the literary relationship between Malachi and Jonah that Jones builds on (i. e., the mention of Elijah [Mal 3:23-24, Eng. 4:5-6] and the positive view of the nations in view of the accusation of Israel because of the profanation of Yahweh's name [Mal 1:11-14]). However, I will enter

---

[10]   Schart, *Entstehung*, 218ff.
[11]   Ibid., 45.
[12]   For detailed representation, cf. Jones, *Formation*, 2-42. The order in the MT is as follows: Hosea-Joel-Amos-Obadiah-Jonah-Micah-Nahum; in the LXX: Hosea-Amos-Micah-Joel-Obadiah-Jonah-Nahum; in 4QXII[a]: Malachi-Jonah.
[13]   Jones, *Formation*, 222.

into this issue later. To my mind there are better reasons for the view that the sequence of 4QXII[a] is an exception,[14] for which opinion Odil Hannes Steck has recently argued.[15]

If one examines the remaining sequences of the MT and the LXX, one will notice that it is possible to limit the problem to the different positions of the books of Joel and Micah. While it is difficult to derive the sequence of the MT from the sequence in the LXX, the reverse derivation is no problem. The sequence in the LXX oriented itself on the one hand on the criterion of the common headings of the D-Corpus (Hosea, Amos, Micah, and Zephaniah, the position of which is the same in the MT and the LXX), and on the other hand on thematic criteria. On the basis of its heading and its greater length (seven chapters, as opposed to four for Joel, one for Obadiah, and four for Jonah), Micah seems to have appeared to the editor(s) of the LXX to have belonged after the book of Amos rather than after Jonah. Nevertheless, the relative positions of Jonah and Nahum remained the same, though because of the relocation of Micah the book of Jonah comes to stand directly before the book of Nahum. Because of the theme of Nineveh, this arrangement actually seems to be an improvement on the sequence of the MT. Moreover, on the basis of the theme of Edom in Joel 4:19, a position of the book of Joel before the book of Obadiah also seems to be more appropriate. Therefore it seems that the sequence of the MT as the *lectio difficilior* is the original sequence, since it is more difficult to explain the subsequent transposition of the book of Micah from a former position between Amos and Joel in the LXX to a later position between Jonah and Nahum in the MT.[16]

Even if one concludes that the sequence of the MT was earlier than that of the LXX or 4QXII[a], one still has not determined whether one should understand the books of the Twelve solely as single and isolated units. It is, to be sure, quite conceivable that only chronological and thematic criteria were responsible for the sequence of the books. Wolff, for example, tries to explain the position of the book of Jonah before Micah on such grounds alone. He notes that 2 Kgs 14:23-25 speaks of a prophet named Jona ben Amittai, who flourished during the time of king Jeroboam II. This king also is mentioned in the heading of Hosea and Amos as a contemporary of king Uzziah of Judah. The superscription in Hos 1:1 mentions three kings of Judah, Jotham, Ahaz, and Hezekiah, as successors of Uzziah. Only the last two of

---

[14]   Cf. Schart, *Entstehung*, 2.

[15]   Cf. O. H. Steck,"Mitteilungen: Zur Abfolge Maleachi - Jona in 4 Q76 [4QXII[a]]," *ZAW* 108 (1996) 249-53.

[16]   So Jones (*Formation*, 232) is forced to admit: "The relationship between Jonah and its context in the MT Book of the Twelve is less easily explained than the contexts of the Book of Joel and Obadiah."

these kings are found in the heading of the book of Micah (1:1), so it would be logical for an editor to conclude that Micah prophesized *after* Jonah.[17] Jones tries to explain the secondary sequence – in his view – of Jonah and Micah in the MT with the similar career and message of both prophets: "(they) confronted a nation (Judah/Nineveh) with words of doom (Mic 3:12/Jon 3:4) that provoked the response of the king (Hezekiah/ king of Nineveh) and led to change of heart on the part of both the nation and the deity (Jer 26:19/ Jon 3:10)."[18]

If, then, one wishes to pursue a contextual reading of the Book of the Twelve, one needs to find criteria internal to the Twelve that point to a deliberate connection of the individual books. On principle there are two possibilities: an originally independent book was rewritten by a redactional process to be read as a part of a greater collection of prophetic books, or a book was specially written for this collection.

I do not deny the possibility of a circular logic on this issue, but I do not see it as inevitable as does Ehud Ben Zvi. He challenges the validity of Nogalski's view that the existence of catchwords between the closing chapters of the books of the Twelve and the beginnings of the next shows deliberate redactional activity tying together the various books. Ben Zvi argues that the assumption of the unity of the Twelve already underlies these observations and that Nogalski's argument is circular and, thus, flawed. Consequently, the "catchwords" do not prove the unity of the Book of the Twelve.[19] With regard to the sequence of the books chosen for this study, the charge of circularity could apply when on the one hand I find texts in the book of Micah which one could interpret with a view to the MT sequence Jonah-Micah-Nahum, and on the other hand when I attempt to prove with these texts a contextual reading of these same books.

The problem is not solved, however, if one simply does without contextual exegesis, for behind Ben Zvi's rejection of Nogalski's argument there is also a presupposition, namely that every book of the Dodekapropheton arose independently of its context and therefore has to be understood irrespective of its context. This emphasis on an a priori isolation of the books could result in a failure to understand some texts properly, since one would

---

[17]   Wolff, *Obadja, Jona*, 53.

[18]   Jones, *Formation*, 233.

[19]   Ben Zvi ("Twelve Prophetic Books," 142) says of the catchword phenomenon in the Book of the Twelve: "This discussion ... strongly suggests that, rather than providing the unity of the Twelve, these observations and especially any interpretation of them that points to a unified understanding of the Twelve are based on a pre-ordinate conception of the unity of the Twelve. As such, these considerations fall under the category of 'providing what was already assumed,' that is circular thinking."

not see the whole literary context for reading them. Therefore the return to a traditional, single-book-oriented exegesis is not a solution. As a way to avoid the two problems just outlined, the following proceeding seems appropriate. First a book-oriented exegesis will be carried out, employing the traditional methods of literary and redactional criticism. Based on the results of this exegesis, I will ask whether there are thematic or literary phenomena which could serve as evidence for a context-oriented redactional revision of this reading. From there, I must once again ask what role this book as a whole plays. Or, I must ask what role this book plays based on the character given to it by redactional revisions in the context of the Dodekapropheton. This task should always be undertaken from a diachronic perspective, i.e. in view of the hypothetical history of the rise of the Book of the Twelve.

Schart already has shown how effectively this method works. I tested this method in a more limited way in respect to the *Redaktionsgeschichte* of the book of Micah. In the following discussion I will refer to the results of both Schart's work and mine several times.

The first extensive study to deal with the origin of the Book of the Twelve, and that not only in the sense of a collection of former independent prophetical books, is the work of Nogalski in 1993. Proceeding from the striking phenomenon of the catchword-connections between the opening and closing chapters of the books of the Twelve, Nogalski develops a theory about the redactional processes in the Dodekapropheton. With regard to the MT sequence Jonah-Micah-Nahum, his work is important as far as he can make it sufficiently probable that the sequence of the LXX is secondary vis-à-vis that of the MT. To do so he shows that there are strong thematic and lingual connections on the one hand between Joel and Amos[20] and on the other hand between Amos 9 and Obad 1-9.[21] In view of those connections, one has indirect confirmation for the position of the book of Micah, not after the book of Amos as in the LXX, but corresponding to the MT between Nahum and Jonah.

---

[20] Nogalski, *Processes*, 42-48; Schart, *Entstehung*, 262-63.
[21] Nogalski, *Processes*, 61-74; Schart, *Entstehung*, 271-72.

II. The Book of Jonah in the Twelve;
Intertextuality Among Jonah, Joel and Nahum

Among the numerous problems in the book of Jonah discussed today,[22] the question of the relationship between it and the Dodekapropheton seems to be of particular importance. Based on the characterization of the book Jonah as a satire,[23] scholars normally conclude that it was inserted in the Book of the Twelve last.[24] There are, however, a few hints that suggest that the book implies its present context, a fact which needs to be explained.

There are no traces of a redactional revision of the book of Jonah – perhaps apart from the disputed psalm in Jon 2:3-10,[25] but this observation is not absolutely crucial for the question of whether or how the book of Jonah is connected with its context. It is conceivable that the book of Jonah was composed for its present context, and that context – especially the books of Micah and Nahum – was redactionally revised during this process. A striking piece of evidence for a contextual orientation is the fact that the book of Jonah, in contrast to the other books of the Twelve, has no superscript. It starts with the sentence: ויהי דבר יהוה אל יונה בן אמתי לאמר. Normally this fact is interpreted to mean that the book of Jonah was inserted after Obadiah, since Jonah was considered as a continuation of Obad 1, which announced that a messenger had been sent to the nations.26 Moreover after the destruction of Edom, it is suggested that the Twelve turns to the more powerful enemy Nineveh. As mentioned in connection with the position of the book of Jonah between Obadiah and Micah, the name Jonah ben Amittai is held especially responsible for the placement of the book. Few scholars, however, ever ask about this reason for this idea. The etymological interpretation of Wolff (Jonah = pigeon) as a characterization of the prophet in his inconstancy ("nach Ninive soll er, nach Tarschisch will

---

[22]   For the full discussion, cf. Erich Zenger, *Einleitung in das Alte Testament* (Stuttgart/Berlin/Köln: W. Kohlhammer, 1995) 399-405 with literature; for a survey, cf. Zapff, *Studien*, 252-255.

[23]   Cf. Wolff, *Obadja, Jona*, 62-64; F. W. Golka, *Jona* (Calwer Bibelkommentare; Stuttgart: Calwer, 1991; J. Magonet, *Form and Meaning. Studies in literary Techniques in the Book of Jonah* (2d ed.; Sheffield: Sheffield Academic Press, 1983).

[24]   This is, as far as I can see, the *consensus communis* in the discipline; cf. Schart, *Entstehung*, 289.

[25]   Recently Golka argued for the originality of the psalm; cf. *Jona*, 72; K. M. Craig, *A Poetic of Jonah* (New York: Columbia: University of South Carolina Press, 1993; and Theodor Lescow, "Die Komposition des Buches Jona," *BN* 65 (1992):29-34. Wolff (*Obadja, Jona*, 104ff) raised grave counter-arguments; cf. Nogalski, *Processes*, 254.

[26]   Cf. Schart, *Entstehung*, 290.

er"),[27] is ingenious, no doubt, but does not explain the identification with Jonah *ben Amittai*.[28] Is it not conceivable that this identification is a deliberate fiction? This suggestion is all the more attractive if the book of Jonah was actually composed for its position between Micah and the complex of Hosea-Joel-Amos-Obadiah. In that case, the name of the eighth-century prophet "Jonah ben Amittai" was chosen to make the book contemporary with the other eighth-century prophets.

However plausible, this is but a supposition. Much more important are the observations of Schart, who has pointed to specific connections between the books of Jonah and Joel.[29] For example, there is the correspondence between Jon 3:9 and Joel 2:14: מִי יוֹדֵעַ יָשׁוּב וְנִחָם: "who knows (if) he will turn back and repent?" In the book of Joel this sentence is found in the mouth of the prophet, who calls his people to repentance, whereas in the book of Jonah the king of Nineveh speaks these words. Likewise the correspondence between Joel 2:13 and Jon 4:3, based on the grace formula of Exod 34:6, is impressive.[30] On the one hand, it functions as a reason to motivate Israel to return to Yahweh; while on the other hand it functions as a reproach to Yahweh because of his patience with Nineveh, put in the mouth of Jonah with satirical intention. The fact that both equivalents stand close to each other in their respective books shows that their twofold appearance was no accident. The strong connection of these verses to their contexts precludes any assumption of a subsequent redactional revision of the book of Jonah with the book of Joel in view, or vice versa. The aim of the book of Jonah with respect to the book of Joel is – so Schart – to criticize satirically its position of a nationalistic-particularistic isolation.[31] Beside these verbal connections, other connections between the book of Jonah and the book of Nahum are remarkable.

In the case of the book of Nahum, I have to restrict myself to the question of possible intertextuality. I presume the consensus *communis* that the

---

27 Wolff, *Obadja, Jona*, 76.
28 Wolff (*Obadja, Jona*, 76) argues that the author intended to choose a prophet of salvation from the 8th century of whom little is known.
29 Schart, *Entstehung*, 287-88.
30 For the usage of this formula in the final form of the Twelve, cf. Raymond C. Van Leeuwen, "Scribal Wisdom and Theodicy in the Book of the Twelve," *In Search of Wisdom* (Louisville: Westminster, 1993) 33: "Exodus 34, 6-7, in the final form of the Twelve, is used as the redactors' crucial commentary on the bitter eight-century prophets, Hosea, Amos, and Micah, thus combining judgment with theodicy and hope for the future."
31 Cf. Schart, *Entstehung*, 289.

book of Nahum arose between 664 and 614 BC.[32] During its inclusion in the developing Book of the Twelve it was probably enlarged by the semi-acrostic psalm in Nah 1:2-8 to connect it with Hos 4:3, Amos 1:2, and Mic 1:3 by means of the theophany of Yahweh.[33] In any case one can reasonably assume that the book of Jonah already presupposes the book of Nahum. Besides the common theme "Nineveh" – in the book of Jonah with the perspective of repentance, in the book of Nahum with the perspective of total judgment – it is striking that both books end with a question.[34] In the book of Jonah, God asks: "Shouldn't I be in mourning for Nineveh?" By contrast, in the book of Nahum the prophet rhetorically asks Assyria: "Whom didn't your wickedness strike continually?" In Jon 4:11, the mercy of YHWH concerning Nineveh is contrasted with the wickedness of Nineveh that overtook everyone עַל נִינְוֵה. Particularly striking, however, is the redactional insertion in the semi-acrostic psalm Nah 1:2-3, which extends the א line vis-à-vis the following lines disproportionately. The redactional insertion is found in vv 2b.3a.[35] These verses further illustrate the characterization of Yahweh by the application of the catchword נקם. With reference to the grace formula in Exod 34:6 (אֶרֶךְ אַפַּיִם) and Exod 34:7 (לֹא יְנַקֶּה וְנַקֵּה), it is made clear that the opponents of Yahweh – the Ninevites – should not expect mercy, but total judgment. Vis-à-vis the use of Exod 34:6 in the books of Joel and Jonah, Nahum not only changes רַב חֶסֶד into כֹּחַ, which originates from the context of Exodus (cf. Exod 32:11; Deut 4:37; 9:29; 2 Kgs 17:36), but also includes in its argument Exod 34:7, which announces the certain punishment of evil until the third generation of the sinners.[36] If one accepts the rule, correctly stated by Schart, that the Book of the Twelve ought to be read sequentially,[37] then in the view of this redactional insertion the book of Nahum should be understood as a correction of the per-

---

[32] For the current results of discipline cf. Zenger, *Einleitung*, 411-414; Zapff, *Studien*, 256-259 with literature.

[33] So Nogalski, *Processes*, 115; Schart, *Entstehung*, 246.

[34] Cf. T. F. Glasson, "The Final Question – In Nahum and Jonah," *ExpTim* 81 (1969/70), 54-55.

[35] Nogalski, *Redactional Processes*, 106-7.

[36] Van Leeuwen, "Wisdom," 49: "By using the full, bipolar contrast of mercy and justice from Exod 34:6-7, the redactor affirms, on the one hand, that YHWH is free to exercise his forgiveness and mercy toward *any* who repent, and, on the other, that he will not be held forever hostage to the evil of the wicked."

[37] Schart, *Entstehung*, 26: "Ein Text muß sukzessive, von vorne nach hinten fortschreitend gelesen werden," and "Gilt diese Leserichtung 'von vorne sukzessiv nach hinten' für die einzelnen Prophetenschriften, so sollte das auch für das Zwölfprophetenbuch gelten, insbesondere deshalb, weil die Überschriften dem ganzen ein narratives Grundgerüst geben."

spective of the book of Jonah,[38] without, however, canceling its validity. The restriction of the judgment only to opponents and enemies of Yahweh by the redactional insertion of Exod 34:6-7 into Nah 1:2 shows that here a universal, undiscriminating judgment in the sense of Joel 4 is no longer in view.

If the book of Jonah is a correction of the perspective of the book of Joel (especially Joel 4:9-14), and also extends the mercy and pardon of Yahweh to the city of Nineveh (which functions as a symbol of the anti-Israel-nations), then the redactional revision of the semi-acrostic psalm in the book of Nahum responds to the view of the book of Jonah by restricting the judgment to the enemies of Yahweh, among whom in distinction to the book of Jonah, however, Nineveh is reckoned once again.

How should these observations be interpreted with regard to the "Redaktionsgeschichte"? This question is not easy to answer. The correspondences between the book of Jonah on the one hand and the books of Joel and Nahum on the other suggest that the book of Jonah was deliberately composed for its place the Book of the Twelve.[39] But can one imagine that the book of Jonah was intentionally composed against the background of the following book of Nahum, so that the message of the book of Jonah composed in satirical manner is immediately depreciated by the book of Nahum, and that the prophet Jonah, who announced the destruction of Nineveh, maintains his point ultimately? Probably not.

In my opinion, therefore, one has to distinguish between the origin of the book of Jonah and its insertion in the Book of the Twelve. I suppose that whoever did the latter is also responsible for the redactional insertion in Nah 1:2b.3a, in an effort to explain why the judgment came over Nineveh not in spite of, but because of Exod 34:6-7.

What function in this threefold connection Joel-Jonah-Nahum does the book of Micah now have, since Micah stands between Jonah and Nahum in the sequence of the MT?

III. The Position of the Book of Micah in the Dodekapropheton

A. The Structure and the Message of the Book of Micah

One of the great problems of the research in the book of Micah is the correct description of the structure of the book.[40] The proposed alternatives

---

[38] Cf. Duane L. Christensen, "The Book of Nahum: A History of Interpretation," *Forming Prophetic Literature: Essays on Isaiah and the Twelve in Honor of John D. W. Watts* (ed. James W. Watts and Paul R. House; JSOTSup 235. Sheffield: Sheffield Academic Press, 1996) 187-194, esp. 187-88.

[39] So, e.g., Van Leeuwen, "Wisdom," 44.

[40] For a detailed description of the alternatives cf. Zapff, *Studien*, 7-9.

orient themselves partly on criteria of content and partly on criteria of the form. In this debate the call to hear plays a key function (cf. Mic 1:2, 3:1, and 6:1), as does the *inclusio* between Mic 1:2 and 5:14: שמעו עמים/ שמעו את־הגוים אשר לא. The decision depends upon whether one emphasizes content or form. On the one hand, John T. Willis[41] advocates a threefold structure, but ignores the *inclusio* between Mic 1:2 and 5:14; on the other hand, James L. Mays[42] advocates a twofold structure, but neglects the call to hear (1:2; 3:1; 6:1) in favor of his model.

In my opinion one has to solve the problem diachronically. The structures in the book of Micah are superimposed upon another, with the twofold structure being newer than the threefold. The most important argument for this view is that throughout Micah 4/5 and 7 one finds the latest texts of the book,[43] whereas the texts in Micah 1-3 and Micah 6, which are arranged by the calls to hear in Mic 3:1 and 6:1 (perhaps in Mic 1:2), belong to the older core of a Deuteronomistic version of the book of Micah.[44] According to my research, the twofold structure is a product of a redactional rewriting, which revises an already existing book of Micah.[45] It expresses itself in Micah 4/5 as a redactional revision, rearranging a preexisting text with several insertions and supplements. Micah 7, on the contrary, may be seen as an extensive "Fortschreibung" (Mic 7:4b,7-20). The resulting first cycle in Mic 1:2-5:14 thereby presents a sequence of judgment and salvation, which has as subjects not only the reconstruction of Zion, but also the inclusion of the nations in the salvation of Yahweh. The latter theme is extensively unfolded in Micah 4/5, which is problematic for a diachronic analysis. Unlike Schart, I think that in Micah 4/5 the problem is not the question of a documentation of contradicting theological positions.[46] One should pay attention instead to the redactionally placed text markers: עתה(ו) "(and or but) now" (Mic 4:9,11,14) on the one hand, and והיה (Mic 5:6,9), followed by הימים באחרית והיה (Mic 4:1) or ההוא ביום (Mic 4:6) on the other hand. (Cf. the markers in Mic 7:4b,10 [עתה – marking the distress of Zion] and in 7:11, 12 [there יום and הוא יום respectively – marking the deliverance and re-

---

[41]   John T. Willis, "The Structure, Setting and Interrelationship of the Pericopes in the Book of Micah," *Dissertation Abstracts* 22, Vanderbilt Univ. 1966, 12.

[42]   James L. Mays, *Micah. A Commentary* (OTL; Westminster: Philadelphia 1976) 6; recently Gabriele Metzner, *Kompositionsgeschichte des Michabuches* (Frankfurt: Peter Lang, 1998) 58.

[43]   For Mic 7:8-20 cf. recently Metzner, *Kompositionsgeschichte*, 163: "hellenistische Zeit."

[44]   Cf. Schart (*Entstehung*, 191-204), who includes Mic 1-3*.6 in the dtr. book of Micah; so also Nogalski.

[45]   Cf. Zapff, *Studien*, 237-240.

[46]   Cf. Schart, *Entstehung*, 275-6.

construction of Zion.]) Such a reading will reveal a structure that reminds one of the sequence of Zechariah 14,[47] an observation which Bernard Renaud already made in the seventies regarding Micah 4/5.[48] Because of the sins of Israel the nations march against Zion, which is devastated and humiliated (cf. Mic 1-3; 4:10-11, 14; also Mic 6:1-16; 7:1-7, especially 4b). But with the punishment of Zion, Yahweh rises at the same time against the nations and destroys them (Mic 4:11-13; cf. Mic 7:10). The destruction has the consequence of the return home of the dispersed persons of Israel (Mic 4:6f.; Mic 7:11), which entails the pilgrimage of the nations to Mount Zion (Mic 4:1-3; cf. Mic 7:12.16f.). This brings about an acknowledgment of Yahweh by (some of) the nations. The nations, however, who still show themselves hostile to Yahweh will be destroyed ultimately (Mic 5:7-14; cf. Mic 7:13). These passages show that there are close thematic connections between Micah 4/5 and 7.[49] These connections argue for the assumption that the author of the "Fortschreibung" in Mic 7:4b.8-20 was the same as the redactor that shaped Micah 4/5.

In the resulting version of Micah, the two cycles do not merely narrate the same thing in diverse ways. Whereas in cycle A (Mic 1:2-5:14) the sequence of judgment and salvation is well to the fore (judgment over Israel – judgment over the nations, who march against Zion – peaceful pilgrimage of the nations to Zion – final judgment over the nations, who do not obey), in cycle B (Mic 6:1-7:20) the question to the fore is how the distressed Zion can experience the world-changing power of Yahweh by the reception of the divine word and thus receive revival and forgiveness of its sins. With that question, a connection is formed to Mic 1:1-7, where the theme of guilt is already mentioned as a reason for the judgment of Yahweh.[50]

B. The Relation of the Perspective of the Nations in the Book of Micah to the Books of Jonah, Joel and Nahum

If one considers this perspective of the nations in the book of Micah (oriented structurally as it is to Zechariah 14) in connection with the position of Micah between Jonah and Nahum, one will conclude that the similarity is no accident. Rather, one will see that the sequence of the different perspectives of the nations appears also in the books of Joel, Jonah, and Nahum. The judgment on the nations before Mount Zion described in the book of

---

[47]   Cf. Zapff, *Studien*, 124ff.
[48]   Bernard Renaud, "La formation du livre de Michée. Tradition et Actualisation," (*Ebib*; Paris: J. Gabalda, 1977) 26.
[49]   For details cf. Zapff, *Studien*, 231ff.
[50]   Cf. Zapff, *Studien*, 237ff.

Joel finds its equivalent in Mic 4:11-14; 7:10. The prospect of the possibility of the repentance of the nations and of the readiness of Yahweh for forgiveness offered in the book of Jonah has its equivalent in the pilgrimage of the nations to Mount Zion in Mic 4:1-3; 7:12. Likewise the final judgment on all the nations who "do not obey," i.e. who do not go on pilgrimage (Mic 5:14; 7:13) can be found in Nahum 1, where a distinction is made between the "enemies of Yahweh" (Nah 1:2b) and "those who take their refuge to Yahweh" (Nah 1:7).

The perspective of the nations in this view would be a kind of systematization of the different views of the nations in Joel, Jonah and Nahum. Since the three books have been dated differently, one has to reckon with a redactional "Fortschreibung," before which these three books already existed in the sequence of the MT. At the time of this extension, the book of Jonah was inserted in the emerging Book of the Twelve. The similarity with Zechariah 14 could point to a relatively late dating of this redactional layer, which would correspond well with the similar late dating of Joel, Jonah, and Nahum. So we would already have a logical draft of the different perspectives of the nations in the Dodekapropheton prior to the time of Zechariah 14,[51] located in the middle of the Book of the Twelve, where the question arises of how to bridge the almost unbridgeable contrast between Jonah and Nahum, and between Joel and Jonah too.

The crucial question for the verification of this hypothesis is whether one can find redactional connections between the layer of the "Fortschreibung" in the book of Micah and the other three books of Joel, Jonah, and Nahum.

C. The Connection between the Book of Nahum and the Book of Micah

Credit belongs to Nogalski for pointing out the striking connections between the semi-acrostic psalm in Nah 1:2-8 and Micah 7.[52] Hence – so Nogalski – with regard to Micah 7, Nahum 1 was revised and connected with this chapter through catchwords, whereby the semi-acrostic schema was partly destroyed[53] in lines ד, ז, and ע, and through the previously-mentioned insertion in vv. 2b.3a. Whereas Nogalski thinks that this revision was undertaken based on the already existing chapter 7 of the book of Mi-

---

[51]   Contra Schart, *Entstehung*, 275ff.

[52]   Nogalski, *Precursors*, 103ff.

[53]   Ibid., 104: "A notable phenomenon within these breaks in the acrostic must be born in mind, namely *all four* interruptions can be explained as deliberate alterations to an existing poem, and at least two of the remaining interruptions (possibly all three) can be tied directly to the redactional process of linkage to Micah 7."

cah,[54] in my opinion one has to consider this revision of the semi-acrostic psalm in connection with the insertion of Mic 7:4b.8-20 as a redactional "Fortschreibung" of the book of Micah. It is possible to show catchword connections between Micah 7 and the psalm of Nahum, which on the one hand are constitutive for the acrostic schema and on the other hand relate to verses of the semi-acrostic psalm, where one cannot observe a subsequent revision.[55] Moreover, Micah 7 anticipates the theme of Nineveh in Nahum 1 through the humiliation of "the (female) enemy" of Zion. This redactional connection between Micah 7 and Nahum 1 becomes particularly clear through the allusion to the grace formula of Exod 34:6-7,[56] which one can also observe in Mic 7:18-19. If the relatively free allusion to Exod 34:6-7 in Mic 7:18 serves to strengthen the confidence of Israel in the grace and readiness of Yahweh to remit sin, who does not cling to his wrath that he had already executed on Israel (!), then the reference to Exod 34:6-7 in Nah 1:2-3 expresses the certainty that in spite of the patience of Yahweh his judgment surely will be executed over his enemies.[57] With regard to Israel and perhaps to the nations that are ready to repent, Exod 34:6-7 is used as an argument for the readiness of Yahweh to forgive; whereas in Nah 1:2, Exod 34:6-7 supplies the reason for the judgment of Yahweh on his enemies. So Mic 7:18 binds together the interpretation of Exod 34:6 in the book of Joel with regard to Israel and in the book of Jonah with regard to Nineveh as a symbol for the nations, who are ready to repent. By contrast, the book of Nahum stresses the destruction of Nineveh by making the same scribal allusion to Exod 34:6-7, except that (based on the insertion in Nah 1:2) Nineveh now is a symbol of the enemies of Yahweh. This intention finds its confirmation through another analogy between Micah 7 and Nahum 1. The incomparability of Yahweh in his readiness to forgive in Mic 7:18 finds its equivalent in Nah 1:6, where nobody can stand the rage and the burning wrath of Yahweh.

---

[54]   Ibid., 110-11.

[55]   So, e.g., Mic 7:12/ Nah 1:4 יָם; Mic 7:12/ Nah 1:4 נהר and נהרות respectively; Mic 7:12/ Nah 1:4 הר, and הרים respectively; Mic 7:13/ Nah 1:5 אֶרֶץ; and above all Mic 7:18/ Nah 1:2 אל.

[56]   Cf. the catchwords in 18 (אל, נשא עון, פשע, אפו, חסד) and in 19 (רחם, התאה, חסד, אמת); nearby one can observe a very free usage of Exod 34:6-7, corresponding to the situation of Mic 7. As in Exod 34:6-7, so also here Yahweh carries the guilt, but he does not prolong his wrath (Exod 34:6b); rather he no longer holds on to his wrath against Israel, which he had already executed (Mic 7:18c). It is not simply that his grace is great (Exod 34:6b); rather it belongs to the essence of Yahweh to be gracious.

[57]   Zapff, Studien, 270.

D. The Connection of the Book of Jonah with the Book of Micah

If one searches for traces of a connection between the book of Jonah and the book of Micah, one finds it in the psalm of Jonah (Jon 2:3-10). Already Nogalski pointed to several catchwords, which connect this psalm with the first chapter of the book of Micah.[58] However apart from היכל קדש (Mic 1:2; Jonah 2:8), these catchwords are everyday words, so they cannot support the thesis of an intentional connection by catchwords between the book of Micah and the book of Jonah corresponding to the model of the catchword connections between Nahum 1 and Micah 7. Besides, there are several thematic connections between the book of Jonah and the book of Micah that one can explain as instances of a redactional "Fortschreibung" in the book of Micah to an already existing book of Jonah. Furthermore, it is important that one finds these references again especially in Micah 7, the chapter that plays such a crucial role in the connection between the book of Micah and the book of Nahum.

Nogalski has pointed to the phrase ותשליך במצלות in Mic 7:19b and ותשליכני מצולה in Jon 2:4a. However, he wants to understand the former as a gloss inserted in Micah 7 to create a connection between the two books.[59] For this suggestion, however, there is no evidence. One can find instead, however, several other connections between Micah 7 and the book of Jonah.[60] For example, the confidence of the prophet in Mic 7:7 that Yahweh will hear him has its equivalent in the confession of Jonah that Yahweh heard him (Jon 2:3). On the whole Jonah is characterized very positively in the psalm of Jonah (similar to Zion in Mic 7:8ff), to the extent that both confess their total dependence on Yahweh. One can also observe this similarity in the analogy between Mic 7:9 and Jon 2:7, insofar as the confidence of Zion that Yahweh will lead her to the light has its equivalent in the confession of Jonah that Yahweh has led him out of the grave. The designations of god in the psalm of Jonah – by the way, in contrast to the designations of god in the rest of the book of Jonah – find their equivalent in Mic 7:10.17, where the name Yahweh is connected with אלהים, which has a suffix. Thus Yahweh is emphasized as the god of Jonah, and likewise the god of Zion. Finally the confession of confidence made by Zion in Mic 7:8-9 has a similar function in its context as does the psalm in the book of Jonah. The confidence of Jonah in Yahweh and his subsequent deliverance is the precondition for the repentance and the subsequent sparing of Nineveh, caused by the prophetic message of judgment. Something similar

---

[58] Nogalski, *Processes*, 266.
[59] Ibid., 153.
[60] Cf. Zapff, *Studien*, 259-60.

is true for the confession of confidence of Zion in Mic 7:8-9 and her expected deliverance by Yahweh. Ultimately this is the precondition for the
confidence of the nations in Yahweh; indeed the deliverance of Zion is the
signal through which the nations turn to Yahweh (Mic 7:16).

Thematically there are other connections between Micah 7 and the book
of Jonah. First there is the theme of remission of sins, which is found both
in Jonah 3-4 and in Mic 7:18ff. In addition, I have already pointed to the
common use of Exod 34:6. Further, Jon 1:16 tells us that the sailors "feared
Yahweh with great fear" (וייראו האנשים יראה גדולה את יהוה), offered
sacrifice, and made many vows to him. This description finds its equivalent
in Mic 7:17, where with regard to Hos 3:5 (where the subject is "sons of
Israel") the prophet expects a return of the nations to Yahweh in the sense
of an acknowledgement of his divinity: "and they will be afraid of you"
(אויראו ממך). Finally regarding the Jonah's desire to see the destruction of
Nineveh, the book opposes the fulfillment of the expectation that Zion
would see not only the humiliation of her enemy but also the miraculous
deeds of Yahweh as in the days of the Exodus from Egypt. Thus, Micah 7
takes up different themes of the book of Jonah, and Zion even slips into the
role of Jonah.

In Micah, however, there is a distinction between the nations who are
ready to return and the enemy of Zion, who does not want to return, and
who – symbolized through Nineveh in the book of Nahum – is finally destroyed. Against this background one can also explain the call to hear addressed to the nations in Mic 1:2, which is reflected in Mic 5:14; namely,
that all the nations who do not obey are in danger of reaping Yahweh's
wrath. Thus the book of Jonah is understood as a paradigm for all nations.
As was true of Nineveh, the judgment of Yahweh menaces them; but there
is a possibility the nations can avert this judgment: if they will hear the
message of the book of Micah, take the judgment of Yahweh on Israel to
heart, turn back to Yahweh, and not close their minds to hearing the call.
However, if they persist in disobedience and become enemies of Zion and
Yahweh, the fate of Nineveh in Nahum 1 menaces them. In the view that
the book of Micah develops, Nineveh in the book of Jonah and Nineveh in
the book of Nahum become paradigms for the salvation or destruction of
the nations respectively. This bridging of the two books performs a redactional "Fortschreibung" in the book of Micah, which in analogy to
Zechariah 14 describes diverse, temporally differentiated behaviors of the
nations vis-à-vis Zion, and aims at a final alternative: either pilgrimage to
Zion or judgment by God. This perspective, however, leads beyond the
books of Nahum and Jonah, which describe only the fundamental alternative for the nations: sparing or judgment. With regard to the question of the

"Redaktionsgeschichte," one should interpret this observation as follows: the redactional "Fortschreibung" in the book of Micah already presupposes the book of Jonah, wherein it is perhaps responsible for the insertion of the psalm of Jonah[61] into the book together with the insertion of Jonah into the Book of the Twelve.

E. Connections between the Book of Micah and the Book of Joel

A connection between the book of Joel[62] and the book of Micah is established by the pilgrimage of the nations to Mount Zion, which Joel 4:1-21 changes into an assembly of the nations, initiated by Yahweh for judgment. Wolff writes: "Das große Wort von der Völkerwallfahrt, bei der die Völker in Jerusalem Heil und Frieden finden, ist in einen kriegerischen Aufmarsch umgedichtet, an dessen Ende der Untergang steht."[63] One can show this connection by means of Joel 4:10: לחרבות ומזמרתיכם לרמחים, which reverses the corresponding formulation in Isa 2:4/Mic 4:3: למזמרות וכתתו חרבתיהם לאתים וחניתתיהם. Isa 2:1-4/ Mic 4:1-4 usually is dated by scholars in the fifth century BC, i. e., in the middle of the Persian period,[64] whereas the book of Joel is dated in the fourth century BC,[65] i. e., in the late Persian or the early Hellenistic period. Moreover, the majority of exegetes think the text of Micah is not only the older version of the pilgrimage to Mount Zion (on which the version in the book of Isaiah depends),[66] but

---

[61] Cf. Nogalski (*Processes*, 256ff.), who reckons with a subsequent insertion of the psalm of Jonah in the book of Jonah. One also finds observations which speak for a literary separation of the psalm from its context in Wolff, *Obadja, Jona*, 104ff. and P. Weimar, "Jona 2,1-11, Jonapsalm und Jonaerzählung," *BZ* NF 28 (1984) 43-68.

[62] With respect to the literary unity of the book of Joel there is no consensus in the discipline; cf. Siegfried Bergler, *Joël als Schriftinterpret* (Frankfurt: Lang, 1988); Willem S. Prinsloo, "The Unity of the Book of Joel," *ZAW* 104 (1992) 66-81; Nogalski, *Processes*, 1-57; Erich Bosshard-Nepustil, *Rezeptionen von Jesaja 1-39 im Zwölfprophetenbuch* (OBO 154; Freiburg/Schweiz, Vandenhoeck & Ruprecht, 1997). Based on the relation between the book of Joel and Jonah on the one hand and the redactional relations between the book of Micah and the books of Jonah and Nahum on the other hand, I assume that before a redactional "Fortschreibung" in the book of Micah had been undertaken the book of Joel was already a part of the Book of the Twelve.

[63] H. W. Wolff, *Dodekapropheton 2, Joel-Amos* (3d ed.; BK XIV/2; Neukirchen-Vluyn: Neukirchener Verlag, 1969), 96.

[64] Recently again Bosshard-Nepustil, *Rezeptionen*, 253). Ulrich Berges (*Das Buch Jesaja* [HBS 16; Freiburg/Breisg,. 1998], 75) believes that Isa 2:2-4 was taken over from the book of Micah to the book of Isaiah after 482 BC.

[65] Nogalski (*Processes*, 57): "late Persian period."

[66] E.g. John T. Willis, "Thought on a Redactional Analysis on the Book of Micah," *SBL Seminar Papers, 1978* SBLSP 15; Chico, Calif.: Scholars Press, 1978) 99; O. Kaiser, *Das Buch des Propheten Jesaja, Kapitel 1-12* (ATD 17/5; rev. ed.; Göttingen: Van-

also the text to which Joel 4:10 refers, modifying the pilgrimage of the nations into an assembly of the nations which Yahweh will judge.[67] I opposed the first assumption in my study on Micah, and recently I received support from Bosshard-Nepustil with similar observations.[68] Furthermore, he points to the fact that everything "was in Mic 4,1-4 anders ist als in Jes 2,2-4 ..., seinen Anhalt zu einem großen Teil im Zwölfprophetenbuch (hat)."[69] In this context the equivalents with the book of Joel are striking: Mic 4:3a and Joel 1:6 use synonymously the terms גוי and עצום; Mic 4:4 and Joel 1:7 use the word pair גפן and תאנת. The impending assault of locusts, which in Joel 1:17 leads to the destruction of the *vine* and the *fig tree*, becomes the pilgrimage of the nations in Mic 4:1-3, in which God opposes the coming of the mighty to Mount Zion. The picture culminates (4:4) in a paradisiacal state, where people sit peacefully under the *vine* and the *fig-tree* – a picture taken over nearly verbatim from 1 Kgs 5:5.[70]

Based on these observations, the question concerning the relation of both texts arises once more. If one strictly Schart's principles to this problem, according to which (1) the Book of the Twelve is to be read from beginning to end as a reader might be expected to do, and (2) one may use in interpreting a passage only the information a reader had already gained to that point, it will not be possible to hold to the conclusion that the book of Joel wants to correct the pilgrimage of the nations found in the subsequent following book of Micah. These principles are not fatal to my view, however, because I presume that in this passage the book of Joel, which also shows relations to the book of Isaiah elsewhere, refers here also to the Isaianic version of the nations' pilgrimage and wants to correct the positive view of the nations there. The view that the judgment of Yahweh on the

---

denhoeck & Ruprecht, 1981) 63; L. Schwienhorst-Schönberger, "Zion – Ort der Tora. Überlegungen zu Mic 4,1-3," in *Zion – Ort der Begegnung, Festschrift für L. Klein zur Vollendung des 65. Lebensjahres* (BBB 90, Bodenheim: Athenäum Hain Hanstein, 1993), 109-125, here 110f.; recently again F. Sedlmeier, "Die Universalisierung der Heilshoffnung nach Micha 4,1-5," *TTZ* 107 (1998) 62- 81, here 66; Berges, *Jesaja*, 73.

[67] Erich Bosshard, "Beobachtungen zum Zwölfprophetenbuch," *BN* 40 (1987) 42; Schart, *Entstehung*, 268.

[68] For details cf. Zapff, *Studien*, 64-74; Bosshard-Nepustil, *Rezeptionen*, 416 n.1.

[69] Bosshard-Nepustil, *Rezeptionen*, 416 n. 1, e.g. Mic 4:3a/ Joel 1:6 גוי + עצם, Mic 4:3a/ Hab 1:8; Sach 6:15 רחוק (עד) ; Mic 4:4a/ Joel 1:7.

[70] One finds another connection to the book of Joel with a similar tendency in Mic 7:10, where the question of the enemy of Zion "Where is Yahweh your god?" (אין יהוה אלהיך) in the book of Joel is used in the context of the complaint of the priests, who quote the nations: "Where is their god?" (איה אלהים). Evidently Mic 7:10 looks back to Joel from the perspective of trouble already endured; cf. Metzner, *Komposition*, 163.

nations can follow their pilgrimage to Jerusalem as a means of correcting them is verified as a pattern for the book of Isaiah by the relation between Isa 2:1-3 and Isaiah 13.[71] In this connection it should be mentioned that Joel 4 is closely connected with a redactional layer in the book of Isaiah that O. H. Steck terms the "Jes I – Fortschreibung." According to Steck this "Fortschreibung" promises the revival and return home of Israel in Isaiah 35 after a total judgment on the nations in Isaiah 13.[72]

In the present arrangement of the Book of the Twelve, however, the version of the nations' pilgrimage in the book of Micah seems to answer to the judgment of the nations in the book of Joel. Irmtraud Fischer tries to describe the relation between these contradictory passages as follows: the nations, who make the pilgrimage to Mount Zion in Mic 4:1-3, are those people who did not march against Zion in Joel 4:10-11, but recast their weapons to ploughs.[73] I do not believe, however, that this assumption solves the tension between Joel 4:10ff. and Mic 4:1-3. Rather, the book of Micah itself gives us a hint. An assault of the nations against Mount Zion is also described in Mic 4:11-13, but Zion can prevent it with the help of god, and the nations will sustain a defeat.[74] Based on the word ועתה (and now), I argue that this event is placed in the present time or in the near future. By contrast, the pilgrimage of the nations will take place at the end of the days וְהָיָה יָם־ בְּאַחֲרִית הַיָּם (Mic 4:1), and as in Mic 4:11 there are "many nations" that will make a pilgrimage to Mount Zion.[75] They are the same nations who first march against Mount Zion with hostile intention and then want to profit from the benefits of the Torah.

Reading this way, Micah 4 bridges the tension between the nations' assault and the nations' pilgrimage, transferring the former to the near future, and the latter to the end of the time. The previously mentioned observations of Bosshard-Nepustil and my description of the integration of the redactional revision of Micah 4/5 offered above point to the fact that the pilgrimage of the nations was inserted as an answer to Joel 4, and not earlier than this redactional revision of the book of Micah.

---

[71] Cf. Zapff, "Schriftgelehrte Prophetie – Jes 13 und die Komposition des Jesajabuches," *FzB* 74 (1995) 56.

[72] O.H. Steck, *Der Abschluß der Prophetie im Alten Testament* (Neukirchener Verlag: Neukirchen-Vluyn 1991, 37.197; Zapff, *Schriftgelehrte Prophetie*, 302ff.

[73] Irmtraud Fischer, "Schwerter oder Pflugscharen? Versuch einer kanonischen Lektüre von Jes 2, Joël 4 und Micha 4," *BL* 69 (1996) 208-216.

[74] Already Wolff (*Obadja, Jona*, 97) pointed to this relation ship; Schart (*Entstehung*, 269) says that Mic 4:11-13 "konzeptionell auf der Seite von Joel 4 steht."

[75] In my opinion one cannot say that "der Beitrag Mic 4,11-13 als emphatisches Festhalten an der Konzeption von Joel 4,12-13 gelesen (wird)" as Schart does (*Entstehung*, 269).

At the level of this redactional revision, an interpretation arises that tries to understand the sequence of the books of Joel-Jonah-Nahum corresponding to the scheme of Zechariah 14. Joel 4:10ff. describes the assault of the nations against Mount Zion corresponding to Zech 14:1ff. (which itself corresponds to Mic 4:11-13). Yahweh, however, wards off this assault. The book of Jonah describes the possible conversion of the nations on the example of Nineveh, corresponding to Zech 14:16 (which corresponds to Mic 4:1-4) and finally Nahum depicts the final destruction of the nations on the example of Nineveh, corresponding to Zech 14:17 (which corresponds to Mic 5:6-14).

IV. Conclusions for the "Redaktionsgeschichte"

The conclusions one should draw from this study already have become apparent. First, the assumption that the book of Jonah presupposes the book of Joel is somewhat certain.[76] Moreover there is the question of whether the book of Jonah first existed as an independent scroll outside the developing Book of the Twelve albeit with knowledge of the book of Joel, or whether it was composed for its position in the Book of the Twelve. I do not believe that at present it is possible to answer this question definitively, because there is evidence for both possibilities.

Second, the redactional revision of the book of Micah (hereafter designated FSM for "Fortschreibung Micah"), which one encounters in the psalm of Jonah and the redactional revision of Nahum 1, bridges the opposing conceptions of the fate of Nineveh found in Jonah and Nahum, and integrates the book of Jonah more closely into the Dodekapropheton. Based on the thematic relationship to Zechariah 14, it is possible that this redactional revision communicates with the so-called "Mehrprophetenbuch Fortschreibung III" postulated by Steck for Zechariah 14 and the end of the

---

[76] E.g. P. L. Redditt, "Zechariah 9-14, Malachi and the Redaction of the Book of the Twelve," in *Forming Prophetic Literature: Essays on Isaiah and the twelve in Honor of John D. W. Watts* (ed. James W. Watts, Paul R. House; JSOTSup 235; Sheffield: Sheffield Academic Press, 1996), 245-268, here 257. Contra Bergler (*Schriftinterpret*, 230), who presupposes the reverse dependence, Schart (*Entstehung*, 289) writes: "Macht man die Gegenprobe und spielt den Gedanken durch, was denn Joel bewegt haben könnte, Jona zu zitieren, so kommt man mit Bergler wohl darauf, daß Joel die Heiden gegenüber Israel als Vorbild hinstellen will, etwa in dem Sinn, daß Israel erst recht und vielleicht sogar besser leisten müßte, was die Heiden bereits vorgemacht haben. Diese Vorbildfunktion Ninives vertrüge sich aber kaum mit der Einschätzung der Völker in Joel 4. Dort wird ihre Bosheit als so groß gezeichnet (Joel 4,13), dass Jahwe nur durch ihre Vernichtung dem Zion Ruhe vor seinen Bedrängern verschaffen kann."

Book of the Twelve.[77] Moreover, this redactional "Fortschreibung" shows close contacts to similar redactional processes in Trito-Isaiah. Even the existing contacts between FSM and the book of Isaiah – particularly based on the pilgrimage of the nations to Mount Zion – seem to support this thesis. In any case, however, it is an interesting attempt to integrate opposing conceptions of the OT into a system, though this attempt is connected with a leveling of the pointed message of the single books, especially of the book of Jonah.

---

[77]   Steck, *Abschluß*, 43-60.

Endings as New Beginnings: Returning to the Lord, the Day of the Lord, and Renewal in the Book of the Twelve

Paul R. House

When I began to write *The Unity of the Twelve*[1] in 1986, relatively few works on the Book of the Twelve existed. Of course, this situation has changed dramatically, as Paul Redditt, James Nogalski, Aaron Schart, Marvin Sweeney, and others have shown.[2] There are now several redaction-oriented studies of the Twelve that suggest how the corpus came to be in its present form.[3] There are also studies that stress the differences between the Masoretic Text and the Septuagint,[4] and some that discuss the appropriateness of reading the twelve separate books as a whole.[5] There are still others that analyze key themes that provide coherence or reveal possible redactional seams in the Twelve, or that debate the viability of synchronic versus

---

[1]   Paul R. House, *The Unity of the Twelve* (JSOTSup 97; BLS 27; Sheffield: Sheffield Academic Press, 1990).

[2]   Note the surveys of literature in Paul L. Redditt, "The Production and Reading of the Book of the Twelve," *Reading and Hearing the Book of the Twelve* (SBLSymS 15; ed. James D. Nogalski and Marvin A. Sweeney; Atlanta: Society of Biblical Literature, 2000) 11-33; idem, "Recent Research on the Book of the Twelve as One Book," *CurBS* 9 (2001) 47-80; James D. Nogalski, *Literary Precursors to the Book of the Twelve* (BZAW 217; Berlin and New York: de Gruyter, 1993); idem, *Redactional Processes in the Book of the Twelve* (BZAW 218; Berlin and New York: de Gruyter, 1993); Aaron Schart, *Die Enstehung des Zwolfprophetenbuchs* (BZAW 260; Berlin and New York: de Gruyter, 1998); and Marvin A. Sweeney, *The Twelve Prophets* (2 vols.; Berit Olam; Collegeville, MN: The Liturgical Press, 2000) 1.xv-xxxix.

[3]   Representative examples of redactional studies of the Twelve include Nogalski, *Literary Precursors* and *Redactional Processes*; Schart, *Die Enstehung*; and Byron Curtis, "The Zion-Daughter Oracles: Evidence on the Identity and Ideology of the Late Redactors of the Book of the Twelve," *Reading and Hearing the Book of the Twelve* (SBLSymS 15; ed. James D. Nogalski and Marvin A. Sweeney; Atlanta: Society of Biblical Literature, 2000) 166-184.

[4]   Barry Alan Jones, *The Formation of the Book of the Twelve: A Study of Text and Canon* (SBLDS 149; Atlanta: Scholars Press, 1995).

[5]   See especially Ehud ben Zvi's programmatic article "Twelve Prophetic Books or 'The Twelve': A Few Preliminary Considerations," *Forming Prophetic Literature: Essays on Isaiah and the Twelve in Honor of John D.W. Watts* (JSOTSup 235; ed. James W. Watts and Paul R. House; Sheffield: Sheffield Academic Press, 1996) 125-156.

diachronic readings.[6]   In other words, in many ways scholarship on the Book of the Twelve now reflects the unsettled state of Old Testament scholarship in general.

There have been fewer studies of the Twelve's theological emphases, but treatments of this topic have appeared in the past few years. Led by Rolf Rendtorff and James Nogalski, some of this material has focused on the day of the Lord and related judgment metaphors.[7]   Such interest is well founded, since this judgment motif spans the whole of the Twelve, and since other themes develop in relationship to it. After all, some form of the judgment motif appears in every separate book of the Twelve, whether as the "day of the Lord," "that day," or as sheer description of impending or accomplished divine punishment.

Quite significantly, as Rendtorff points out, in several of the individual books themes related to the concept of the need for changed behavior, whether in the form of "returning to the Lord," "seeking the Lord," or "taking refuge in the Lord," precede or stand alongside the judgment motif.[8] These connected ideas often emerge early in the books, develop as the text unfolds, then merge at the end of individual books to form a resolution to the problems that they have introduced. As they do so they produce a cumulative effect of stressing endings as new beginnings that marks the Book of the Twelve as a whole. This paper seeks to analyze these patterns in an introductory way. Particular attention will be paid to the relationship between calls for change and the people's response to them, coming judgment, and renewal.

I. Methodology

As was noted above, the Book of the Twelve has been examined from a variety of methodological angles in the past several years. My own contributions to the subject have utilized a synchronic approach in order to grasp certain elements of literary unity that divulge theological themes, and this article will try to do the same. Thus, this article will apply a methodology that is similar to, though not identical with, that used in recent works by Marvin Sweeney and Rolf Rendtorff.

---

[6]   For representative examples of these arguments, see Watts and House, *Forming Prophetic Literature*, 158-302.

[7]   Rolf Rendtorff, "How to Read the Book of the Twelve as a Theological Unity," *Reading and Hearing the Book of the Twelve* (SBLSymS 15; ed. James D. Nogalski and Marvin A. Sweeney; Atlanta: Society of Biblical Literature, 2000) 75-87; and James D. Nogalski, "The Day(s) of Yahweh in the Book of the Twelve," *SBL Seminar Papers, 1999* (SBLSP 38; Atlanta: Society of Biblical Literature, 1999) 617-642.

[8]   Rendtorff, "How to Read the Twelve as a Theological Unity," 86.

Sweeney's two-volume commentary on the Twelve utilizes at least five key methodological components. First, he "focuses on a synchronic literary analysis." Second, he "points to the Book of the Twelve as a collection of twelve individual prophetic books that were placed together to form at least two versions [Septuagint and Masoretic] of the Twelve." Third, he "treats the individual books as discrete units within the Twelve." Fourth, he "considers their interrelationships within the sequences of both the Masoretic and Septuagint forms of the book." Fifth, he "includes diachronic considerations in order for the synchronic analysis to make sense."[9] This article adopts the same principles except that it offers no observations on the Septuagint order, a decision that in no way attempts to argue that the Masoretic text reflects the Twelve's original sequence. Rather, the attempt here is simply to work with one of the major traditions of the Twelve's order.

In his "How to read the Book of the Twelve as a Theological Unity," Rendtorff offers a very straightforward approach. First, he reads the text as a unity without referencing its compositional development.[10] Second, he traces the "day of the Lord" theme through the Twelve, and notes the relationships between the various books' presentation of this motif.[11] Third, having done his analytical work, he concludes:

> Finally, I point out that in studying the Book of the Twelve as a whole there is no simple alternative between "diachronic" and "synchronic" reading. The diachronic features are not only obvious but are marked explicitly by the different datings of a number of writings. On the other hand, those who gave the writings their shape (whatever we call them) obviously wanted the reader to read the writings as a connected whole and to reflect on their different messages.[12]

Thus, like Sweeney, Rendtorff attempts to blend synchronic reading informed by diachronic textual markers to achieve thematic results.

Of course, the procedures outlined above are based on the belief that interpreting the Twelve *as a whole* is a viable methodology. Ben Zvi has argued that the redaction-critical studies of the Twelve have failed to yield the necessary data to conclude that the books *must* be read as a whole, though he grants that one *may* read the books this way if one wishes. Yet, he writes, "It certainly does not follow from this observation that the twelve prophetic books were intentionally written or edited so as to convey a sense of close unity among them that set them apart as a unit from the other prophetic books, that is, Isaiah, Jeremiah, and Ezekiel."[13]

---

9   Sweeney, *The Twelve Prophets*, 1.xxxix.
10 Rendtorff, "How to Read the Twelve as a Theological Unity," 76.
11 Ibid., 76-86.
12 Ibid., 87.
13 Ben Zvi, "Twelve Books or 'The Twelve,'" 130.

Further, he claims, even if one grants the historical evidence that the Twelve were read as a single scroll from the second-century BCE onward, "this evidence is not necessarily helpful for the study of composition, redaction, and above all, for reconstructing the way in which these prophetic books were read and (re) read within the communities within which and for which they were written."[14] After a thorough defense of his position,[15] ben Zvi concludes by noting that perhaps a different sort of unity exists in the Twelve. He suggests:

> Rather than assuming a unified book that is read and redacted as such, it is perhaps better to focus on the common repertoire of a relatively small social group consisting of educated writers and readers within which and for which prophetic—and other "biblical"—books were written, at the very least in their present form. Such a focus is likely to uncover a (largely) shared discourse, a common linguistic heritage, implied "intertextuality," and shared literary/ideological tendencies.[16]

In other words, the prophetic books share common literary motifs and common audiences that would have appreciated those motifs. Though the books share this sort of unity and may have come to be read together by communities as they read and reflected upon them over time, he concludes that there is no solid evidence to suggest that they were written or redacted for this purpose.

Writing about Obadiah in his commentary on Joel and Obadiah, John Barton basically agrees with ben Zvi's assessment. Noting ben Zvi in contrast to my work and to Nogalski's, he concludes, "At best, then, we should probably think of the positioning of Obadiah in the canon as a result of perceived similarities with the two books that precede it but not, with Nogalski, suppose the text has actually been reworked to make it fit better in its present position—still less that is was designed to function as merely one chapter in a larger work, 'the Twelve.'"[17] Perhaps one correction is in order. If Barton thinks that I have argued that Obadiah was written to be "chapter four" in "The Twelve Prophets," then I need to be clearer. I do not think that such was the case, nor do I argue for this position in *The Unity of the Twelve*. Rather, like Barton I believe that Obadiah was probably placed in its current position because of the similarity of its content to the books around it. Still, I continue to conclude that the skillful placement of Obadiah and the other books results in a Book that has historical, thematic, and plot-like unity.

---

[14]   Ibid., 131.
[15]   Ibid., 132-154.
[16]   Ibid., 155.
[17]   John Barton, *Joel and Obadiah* (OTL; Louisville: Westminster John Knox Press, 2001) 117.

Ben Zvi and Barton make some excellent observations that aid a thematic approach to the Book of the Twelve. Barton focuses on how Joel and Obadiah contain material that led the collectors of the twelve prophecies to place the books where they did. Both he and ben Zvi insist on treating the separate books as important in and of themselves before then asking questions about how they fit into a larger picture. Ben Zvi's emphasis on the original readers offers insight into how prophetic books were written, read, and understood as *prophecies*, not just as general religious literature. In other words, his emphasis on literary features understood by a unique audience aids an awareness of how the prophetic genre operates. All these elements of analysis are appropriate characteristics of a careful reading of the Twelve. This being said, it is also proper to note that ben Zvi and Barton remain skeptical of reading the Twelve as a whole, or at least of reading them primarily as a whole.

Given these preliminary considerations, this paper utilizes the following methodology. First, the texts will be read primarily synchronically, yet with primary diachronic markers in mind. For example, the superscriptions and clear historical references will be noted at times to aid the discussion of thematic progression.[18] Second, each book's contribution to themes related to the need for returning to the Lord, the threat of the day of the Lord, the people's return to the Lord, the day of the Lord, and renewal will be noted briefly. Though this article cannot analyze these books in the depth they deserve, perhaps this attempt may at least be a good faith effort to treat each book's contribution to these themes as a separate part of an emerging whole. Third, the books will be read as specific examples of the prophetic genre that together form a larger, unified corpus of prophetic literature. The prophetic writers produced the books' themes, literary skill, and passion. Their audiences eventually placed them in their current order. Fourth, the books will be read synthetically for theological purposes. As was just stated, specific themes that clearly exist in the Twelve will be charted.

It is also important to state what this article does not do. It does not attempt to get behind the text to determine redactional layers. Nogalski, Redditt, Schart, and others are the experts to read on that subject. Like Rendtorff, despite having opinions on the matter I assume the development of the books and try to read the books as a unity. At the same time, I try to keep the value of each individual book in mind. This article does not argue that a specific book was written to fit into the whole, but operates as if the community of faith placed the books strategically in their current location. It

---

[18] For a study on the significance of the superscriptions in the Twelve consult John D.W. Watts, "Superscriptions and Incipits in the Book of the Twelve," *Reading and Hearing the Book of the Twelve* (SBLSymS 15; ed. James D. Nogalski and Marvin A. Sweeney; Atlanta: Society of Biblical Literature, 2000) 110-124.

does not deal with the Septuagint order. Sweeney and Jones offer excellent readings of the Greek order and they should be consulted by those interested in the topic. This decision simply means that this article attempts to work with themes as they unfold in the Masoretic tradition. Perhaps separate labors in both orders of the book will yield helpful results, especially in the last six books, where the orders are the same.

II. Calls for Change, the Day of the Lord, and Renewal

Every book in the Twelve depicts the sins of Israel (either Israel or Judah or both), the nations, or Israel and the nations. There is no debate among scholars that sin is the problem the prophets address in the most detail. Where the scholarly debate starts is on the subject of calls for change and their relationship to the books' many threats of judgment. Some scholars argue that the threats are primary to the text, and that the calls for returning to the Lord may well be additions to the text. The thinking is that the threats of punishment are so absolute that by definition they eliminate the possibility for repentance and resultant forgiveness. Others conclude that the history of Israel proves that the possibility of repentance plays a minor role in the books. After all, Assyria and Babylon eventually defeated the people. How essential could the repentance theme be?

A synchronic reading of the Twelve yields a pattern found in other major segments of the Old Testament. This pattern includes threats brought about by covenant disobedience, calls for change, promises associated with change, larger threats for rejecting the opportunity to change, and promises of eventual renewal. In other words, this pattern is similar to that found in Deuteronomy 27—30, 2 Kings 17, and Isaiah 1—5, to name just a few texts. Due to the constraints of this paper these themes will be developed in more detail in the first six books of the Twelve, while later six will be discussed in a more cursory manner.

A. Hosea

Hosea features statements about change in the beginning, middle, and end of the book. These statements are necessitated by explicit sin committed by Israel and Judah. Set in pre-722 BCE Israel according to the book's superscription, Hosea 1—2 depicts Israel's sin as spiritual infidelity through the symbolic acts of Hosea in his marriage to Gomer. Because Israel has committed "great whoredom by forsaking the Lord" (1:2),[19] the Lord will "punish...will put to an end...the kingdom of the house of Israel" (1:4). Yet the text also promises that the Lord will make them his people on "the day

---

[19] Unless noted otherwise, all scriptural quotations are from the *English Standard Version*.

of Jezreel" (1:10-11), which is otherwise portrayed as a quite ominous day. Further, the Lord pledges to treat Israel in ways that will cause the people to "return to" him (2:7, 9-10). At a time simply called "that day" (2:16, 2:21) the Lord will give Israel hope, security, prosperity, mercy, and a fresh relationship with their God (2:14-23).

A second episode between Hosea and his wife underscores how this redemptive process will occur. Hosea buys back his wife and does not have sexual relations with her for a set amount of time (3:1-3). Similarly, Israel will live without a king or prince—in other words in exile—for a time. But "afterwards" Israel "shall return and seek the Lord their God, and David their king, and they shall come in fear to the Lord and to his goodness in the latter days" (3:5). This passage, like 1:2-11 and 2:1-23, follows a distinct, connected pattern. Israel's sins are declared, God takes action to bring them back, and on some distant difficult "day" the people "return and seek" their God. Coupled with God's work, this returning and seeking leads to a restoration of fortunes for the one formerly out of favor.

The renewal of Israel described in Hosea 1—3 clearly occurs in the future. But the book also indicates that return and seeking had immediate relevance to the lives of eighth-century Israelites. Before the exile there was the ministry of the prophets, the compassion of God, and the opportunity to forestall punishment. Lodged within an extended description of the people's sins in chapters 4—5 is the telling comment, "Their deeds do not permit them to return to their God. For the spirit of whoredom is within them, and they do not know the Lord" (5:4). Thus, the prophet, perhaps using words the priests commonly employ halfheartedly for this purpose, urges the people to "return" in 6:1-3. God has torn in order to heal. Returning to God, then, will stave off further pain and disaster. Sadly, Israel's and Judah's love for God has been "like the dew that goes early away" (6:4). Thus, prophets must announce judgment (6:5).

God would heal, but "they deal falsely" (7:1-7). Because of their corruption "days of punishment have come" (9:7-9), which means that Ephraim will be bereft of her children (9:11-14), her king shall perish (10:7), and nations will gather against her (10:10). The only remedy for these impending punishments is a "seeking" of the Lord that results in sowing righteousness (10:11-12). In the text "seeking" has the same results as "turning." After all, without such seeking their sowing of wickedness will reap the horrors of war (10:13-15). The possibilities are clear: seeking and returning or war and loss.

God's most heartrending appeal for change appears in 11:1-9. Here the Lord states, "When Israel was a child, I loved him and out of Egypt I called my son" (11:1). This reference to the exodus is similar to the one in 9:10, and will soon be joined by other references to the people's past. Tragically, the more God called his son the more the child rebelled, in this instance by running after Baal worship (11:2). Despite their rebellion, however, the Lord decides not to execute his "burning anger" because of his compassion for the "child" (11:8-9). Rather, the Lord will wait before acting. While waiting, God "roars like a lion," a phrase that announces judgment here, in Joel 3:16, and again in Amos 1:2, against Judah and Ephraim (11:10-12:1). He also presents an indictment of their activities (12:2-9). The Lord reminds the people that a prophet brought them out of Egypt and that they are hearing from prophets now (12:10-14). Unfortunately, just as they rejected the Lord in the past, so they now reject the Lord by dismissing the word of the Lord sent through the prophets (13:4-11). Given this grim historical situation, Samaria can expect to bear her guilt eventually (13:15-16).

Thus, Israel's hope remains a "return" to the Lord as the book ends (14:1-9). This return amounts to an acceptance of "what is good" (14:2), which requires looking to the Lord, not Assyria, for deliverance, rejecting idols, as well as a general movement away from iniquity (14:2-3). In response, God will "heal their apostasy" and "love them freely" (14:4; see 6:1-3). Renewal is not automatic; it requires a change of Israel's attitude and actions. Harvest and growth imagery adorns the pledge given, and the wise ones are counseled to accept this course of action (14:5-9). In other words, these promises fit with those made in 3:4-5 and 6:1-3, though they fit more closely with 6:1-3.

Read as a whole, the book of Hosea stresses the possibility of renewal based on returning/seeking. This possibility will become reality on "the day of Jezreel" (1:10-11) and "afterward" (3:5). In the interim, while the Lord's compassion compels waiting before releasing disaster (11:8-9), the people may and ought to return. Though both Judah and Israel are in danger, the chief danger is to Israel (Ephraim). Therefore hope remains, however slender it may appear. With each reference to return and the promises associated with them there resides the possibility of a new beginning for the people the Lord brought out of Egypt.[20] As the book ends, readers are reminded that there was always a new beginning available to their ancestors. Yet as they read they recall that no such turning came and Samaria was destroyed in 722. At the same time they read that even when that new beginning was rejected there remained the new beginning forced by the "day of Jezreel."

---

[20]   James D. Nogalski, "Joel as 'Literary Anchor' for the Book of the Twelve," *Reading and Hearing the Book of the Twelve* (SBLSymS 15; ed. James D. Nogalski and Marvin A. Sweeney; Atlanta: Society of Biblical Literature, 2000) 96.

B. Joel

As is well known and has been thoroughly discussed, it is virtually impossible to establish a certain date for Joel. The superscription offers the important notice that what follows is "the word of the Lord" (1:1), yet does not specify an era for the book. Rather, the text announces an unprecedented locust plague that deserves to be described to future generations (1:2-4). This plague transforms into a military invasion in chapter two, and thus becomes the impetus in the book for a lengthy call for returning to the Lord that runs alongside descriptions of the day of the Lord. Renewal emerges in the latter stages of the book as a result of human response and divine judgment. Thus, Hosea and Joel are joined thematically through these emphases.[21]

In 1:5-14, the prophet commands various segments of the population to realize what is occurring. The drunkards are told to "awake" (1:5-7), the farmers are counseled to "lament" (1:8-10), and the priests are admonished to "put on sackcloth and lament" (1:13-14). After all, because of the locusts' thoroughness the drunkards will have no wine, the farmers no crops, and the priests no offerings. Due to this coming "day of the Lord" their crops will be consumed (1:15-18). As all the pastures and trees suffer under this affliction, the prophet cries to the Lord (1:19-20). At this point in the book there is no overt admission of guilt expressed. At the very least, however, there exists an extreme need to receive help from the Lord. It is his "day" that is coming, and only he can help.

The use of locust imagery to describe the day of the Lord does not just occur in Joel. As James Nogalski has observed, "Locust imagery unites diverse material presupposing threats from locust, drought, and enemy attack. Later in the Twelve, several passages (Amos 4:9; Nah 3:16b, 17; Hab 1:9; Mal 3:10) use locust metaphors to refer to divinely-initiated threats to Yahweh's people."[22] Apparently locust swarms were a typical part of the prophetic stock phrases for the day of the Lord.

Next, Yahweh announces the nearness and terrible nature of the day of the Lord by commanding that a trumpet be blown in Zion (2:1). Like the Lion's roar the blowing of the trumpet signals disaster and the need to respond to it (see Hos 5:8; 8:1). The reference to Zion probably indicates that Judah is the nation under attack.[23] Whereas the first chapter warned of the danger to the countryside, the second chapter depicts the threat against Jeru-

---

[21] Ibid., 94-100.

[22] James D. Nogalski, "Intertextuality in the Twelve," *Forming Prophetic Literature: Essays on Isaiah and the Twelve in Honor of John D.W. Watts* (JSOTSup 235; ed. James W. Watts and Paul R. House; Sheffield: Sheffield Academic Press, 1996) 117.

[23] Sweeney, *The Twelve Prophets*, 1.161.

salem.[24] This danger is immediate, for "the day of the Lord is near" (2:1; see Obadiah 15). It is a day of darkness (2:2; see Amos 5:18 and Zeph 1:14-16), one in which a great and powerful army stands ready to invade (2:2). These invaders turn a place as verdant as the Garden of Eden into a wasteland (2:3). They are a consuming fire (2:3-5), everyone fears them (2:6), and they are fiercely and horribly efficient (2:7-9). Indeed, this is God's army and God's day (2:11). Who can endure it, and under what conditions?

As in Hos 6:1-3 and 14:1-9, the only hope for the people is in returning to the Lord, in this instance with their whole hearts, with "fasting, with weeping, and with mourning" (2:12). They must rend their hearts and not their garments (2:13). God is "gracious and merciful, slow to anger, and abounding in steadfast love; and he relents over disaster" (2:13). This conviction reminds readers of Exod 34:6-7, which follows the golden calf incident, and Jon 4:2, which offers God's reasons for forgiving Nineveh. Thus, the Lord may turn and have compassion as in the golden calf incident or the Nineveh repentance (2:14). In other words, their returning may well lead to God returning to a favorable view of them.

Once again the prophet commands that the trumpet be blown (2:15). The priests must lead the people in prayer and fasting (2:15-17). They should pray in a manner similar to Moses after the golden calf incident (Exod 32:11-14) in the sense that they should petition God based on Israel's status as the elect nation, yet more importantly based on the Lord's reputation among the nations (2:17). "Returning" therefore has a specific content here. It at least begins with humility, fasting, prayer, and intercessory lament. It is not simply a psychological crisis that does not result in changed behavior.[25]

When the people turn and seek in this manner the Lord will have pity (2:18). Yahweh will restore the produce (2:19), the invader will leave (2:20), the animals will revive (2:21-22), rains will fall (2:23), vats will be full (2:24), crops will be restored (2:25), and the people will be fed again (2:26). This positive agricultural imagery coincides with that found in Hos 14:4-9.[26] Most importantly, they will know that the Lord is their God and there is no other (2:27), a conviction shared with Deut 32:39 and Isaiah 40—48. Clearly, there is a direct connection between returning and renewal here. Either the proposed invasion does not occur or it is shortened. The threat was enough to move the people to appropriate action prescribed by

---

[24]   Barton, *Joel and Obadiah*, 70.
[25]   Ibid., 78-79.
[26]   On this imagery see Nogalski, "Joel as 'Literary Anchor' for the Book of the Twelve," 100-104.

the Lord, a pattern that occurs again in Jonah, Haggai, Zechariah, and Malachi (see below).

Now the text moves farther into the future. At some point in time, which is simply described as "afterward" (2:28), God will pour out his spirit on all flesh, resulting in prophesying by all groups of people in Israel (2:28-29). Signs will accompany this "great and awesome day of the Lord" (2:30), a designation that ties this day of the Lord to the one mentioned in Joel 2:11.[27] But this day is different in at least one particularly significant way. As James Crenshaw writes, "Now Joel implies that other nations will undergo that same frightening experience, while God's people will escape the divine fury this time."[28] Zion will be the place where those who call upon the Lord will come for refuge (2:32). In the rest of the book Zion stands as the holy place where God dwells (3:16-17, 21), as it does in Mic 4:2-13, Zeph 3:14-16, and Zech 9:9. As for the other nations, however, they will be judged "in those days" (3:1-8). Whatever army comes will fail (3:9-12), for the Lord roars (3:16; see Amos 1:2) against the wicked, which means that their day of punishment is "near" (3:14; see Obadiah 15).

The result of this "day" is at least threefold. First, the nations will join Israel in the knowledge that the Lord alone is God (3:17; see 2:27). Second, Jerusalem and Zion will be holy (3:17), and God will restore the land (3:18; see 2:18-27 and Hos 14:4-9). Third, God will make Egypt and Edom (see Obadiah) desolate (3:19), but Judah will be inhabited (3:20), for the Lord dwells in Zion (3:21). These renewal elements become staples in future texts such as Micah 4—5 and Zeph 3:6-20.

To summarize, in chapter one a terrible invasion is on the horizon. The prophet believes that a terrible locust swarm has prefaced this invasion. He seems to realize what the people in Amos 4:6-13 will not: such "natural" disasters constitute divine warnings. Thus, in chapter two he calls for and receives change based on the belief that the day of the Lord is near. This renewal, brought on by returning, is like the one described in 2:28-3:17, with the first day of the Lord threatening Judah and the second facing the nations. Thus, the renewal through returning spans the whole book, as it does in Hosea. In both books returning is the key to averting the day of the Lord; in both books agricultural imagery describes both punishment and blessing, and in both books renewal is the final word.[29] Either returning to the Lord or the onset of the day of the Lord can give Israel a new beginning, since either option produces the end of dominant sin and the beginning of divine favor.

---

[27]   James L. Crenshaw, *Joel* (AB 24C; New York: Doubleday, 1995) 169.
[28]   Ibid., 196.
[29]   See Nogalski, "Joel as 'Literary Anchor' for the Book of the Twelve," 97-98.

C. Amos

Hosea's and Amos' superscriptions place the books in the same era, the latter half of the eighth century. Though scholars have generally argued that Amos was written before Hosea, Jörg Jeremias has argued that the editors of Amos sought to read the book in light of Hosea's message.[30] According to Jeremias the disciples of both prophets "did not want the words of either Hosea or Amos to be read with historical interest for a distant past but with a current interest in their words as a help for present problems. They were asking about the one message of God by two messengers (but without creating something like Tatian's harmony of the gospel)."[31] If so, this audience was interested in the interaction of returning, renewal, and the future of God's people, since Amos continues the emphasis on these subjects begun in Hosea and Joel.

Amos starts with three connections to Hosea and Joel. First, the book opens with the Lord roaring from Zion (1:2; see Hos 3:16). Second, 1:2—2:3 describes the sins of the nations, a theme begun in Joel 3, and 2:4-16 continues with a description of Israel's and Judah's sins, a theme that originates in Hosea 1—3. Though this depiction of sin is more stylized than anything found in Hosea or Joel, historical summaries and similar themes such as rebellion against the law and covenant breaking are also prominent in Hosea (see Hos 11:1—12:14). Third, this rebellious behavior will bring punishment (2:4, 6) on "that day" (2:16). These connections may well be typical elements of prophetic literature, since they also appear in texts like Jeremiah 2—6, though each prophet puts his own particular stamp on the chosen element.

God is angry at the "whole family" that he "brought up out of the land of Egypt" (3:1). He has chosen them out of all the nations of the earth, so their sin is presented as all the more heinous because of their privileged position (3:2). As in Hosea and Joel, the lion has roared and the trumpet has blown, both of which indicate approaching judgment (3:3-8). Why does judgment come? Because the people had not listened to the prophets (3:7-8). Because they "do not know how to do right" (3:10). As in Hos 9:7—10:15, such behavior can only bring an invasion by an "adversary" that will purge the land (3:11-15). Idolatrous altars such as Bethel will be destroyed (3:14), a theme also found in Hos 4:15-19 and 10:5, 15.

---

[30]   Jörg Jeremias, "The Interrelationship between Amos and Hosea," *Forming Prophetic Literature: Essays on Isaiah and the Twelve in Honor of John D.W. Watts* (JSOTSup 235; ed. James W. Watts and Paul R. House; Sheffield: Sheffield Academic Press, 1996) 185-186.

[31]   Ibid., 185.

Amos 4:6-13 agrees with Hos 6:1-3, Hos 14:1-3, and Joel 2:1-17 that the key to avoiding terrifying judgment is to return to the Lord. Unlike the earlier books, however, Amos states the case negatively. That is, Amos 4:6-13 argues that no matter what the Lord did to awake them from their moral slumber they did not return to the Lord (4:7, 9, 10, 11). Thus, the text calls for a lament for fallen Israel (5:1-3). Despite this failure to return to the Lord, however, there remains time to "seek the Lord and live" (5:4, 5, 6, 14), a theme found earlier in Hos 3:5, 5:6, 5:15, and 10:12. In this passage "seeking" and "returning" amount to the same thing, since they require forsaking cultic centers such as Gilgal and Bethel (5:4-5) in favor of the Lord. Further, since they are to "seek good, and not evil" (5:14), to "hate evil, and love good, and establish justice in the gate" (5:15), and to "let justice roll down like the waters" (5:27), returning to a previous behavior is more than implied. Indeed, it is required if the day of the Lord is to be avoided (5:18-20).

Sadly, Amos 6:1—9:10 offers no indication akin to that found in Joel that returning/seeking occurs. Amos' prayers for mercy delay the judgment for a time (7:1-9), but the book's penultimate promise is that the sword, or military defeat, awaits the disobedient nation (9:10). God's willingness to forestall judgment because of the prophet's prayers indicates that returning/seeking would have had the same effect. Israel cannot escape. The nation will go into captivity (9:4), a threat that the original readers of the Twelve knew came true in 722.

Having experienced God's wrath, Israel will eventually enjoy God's blessing again. "In that day" Yahweh will restore David's tent and subsume Edom under that authority (9:11-12). "Days are coming" for the renewal of land (9:13), returning of fortunes (9:14), and restoration of security in the land (9:15). In other words, the text uses language quite similar to that found in Joel 3:18 to describe the people's future. Returning is not mentioned directly in this segment, but by this point in Amos one has to wonder if some form of returning should be assumed.

In Amos, as in Hosea and Joel, the threat of the day of the Lord brings with it the chance for new beginnings. Those who heed the threats may seek the Lord, return to him, and thus find forgiveness and renewal. The prophets who carry the threat may pray and preach in a manner that forges a new beginning for the people. If the prophets' efforts fail due to lack of returning, the day of the Lord itself will effect a new beginning. The day purges sin from the people and leaves persons like the prophets as representatives of the living God. Post-exilic readers of the Twelve could decide for themselves if their own situation called for new beginnings, and they could also decide by what means they wished that fresh start to come.

D. Obadiah

Obadiah's superscription reveals only the prophet's name. The book probably references the fall of Jerusalem in 587, but the text is not explicit about that fact.[32] Ben Zvi suggests that in this book Edom is a symbol for all nations that oppose God's people.[33] Edom opposed Judah at a number of junctures, so it is a historically based symbol at the very least.

Obadiah certainly mentions the day of the Lord, but lacks calls for returning/seeking. As in Joel and Amos, this foreign nation faces God's wrath, not God's forgiveness. At this point in time "the day of the Lord is near upon all the nations" (15), a phrase found in Joel 3:1-21, Amos 1—2, Nahum, and Zeph 2:4-15. Edom will suffer for all it has done against God's holy mountain, Zion (15-16). The nations that have drunk Jerusalem's destruction will soon drink their own (16).

In Zion, though, some people will escape, and Jacob will be fire to Edom/Esau's stubble (18). Jerusalem's exiles will possess Canaan again, and the northern tribes will go back to their places, so a new conquest will occur at that time (19-21). These escapees are not defined by any action of their own, for they need deliverers (21). This new beginning requires the judgment of Israel's foes, as is true in Joel and Amos. It also requires the repatriation of exiles. In Obadiah the day of the Lord falls on the nations for their joy at the day of the Lord falling on Israel. In this setting the lack of repentance on either side leaves the day of the Lord as the only possible new beginning.

E. Jonah

Jonah's superscription merely reveals the prophet's name and father, but a reference to a prophet by the same name having the same father in 2 Kgs 14:25 almost certainly indicates that the same person is intended in both passages. If so, then the eighth century is the setting for the book, as it is for Hosea, Amos, and Micah. The issue here is whether a nation as corrupt as Assyria could repent and find God relenting from the promised punishment. In other words, was it inevitable that Assyria become an instrument (see Isa 10:5-11) and recipient (see Isa 10:12-34; Nahum 1—3) of wrath, or could this most vicious of nations have turned and sought the Lord?

Though Amos may be the book in the Twelve most discussed by scholars, it is likely that Jonah is the best known of the so-called Minor Prophets. As the familiar account goes, Jonah does not wish to preach to Nineveh,

---

[32] Barton, *Joel and Obadiah*, 120-123.
[33] See Ehud ben Zvi, *A Historical-Critical Study of the Book of Obadiah* (BZAW 242; Berlin and New York: de Gruyter, 1996).

though when under divine punishment himself he truly wishes to be released from the belly of the fish (2:1-10). He seeks God and finds a new beginning, but does he now wish the same for the Assyrians? When he does preach in Nineveh he speaks only of judgment, and not in specific day of the Lord terminology (3:1-4). Certainly he offers no call for change and no hope for renewal.

Despite the lack of returning/seeking terminology the hearers respond, as they ought. They "believed God. They called for a fast and put on sackcloth, from the greatest of them to the least of them" (3:5). In other words, they acted just as the Lord asked Israel to act in Joel 2:12-13. The king calls for changes that include turning away from violence and evil, which in effect is what the Lord commands Israel to do in Amos 2:6-7, 3:9-10, and 5:24-27. The monarch's hope is that the Lord will "turn and relent and turn from his fierce anger" (3:9), language nearly identical to that found in Joel 2:12-14 and Amos 7:1-9, as well as in Jer 18:1-12. Indeed the Lord does exactly what the king hoped. God does relent based on their turning from their wicked ways (3:10), an action that angers the prophet, even as he confesses that the Lord is gracious and kind (see Exod 34:6-7 and Joel 2:12-14). God's response is that it was right for him to take pity on such an evil place when they turn from that evil (4:11).

Jonah deals with several issues vital to the Twelve's approach to returning and renewal. First, as Marvin Sweeney concludes, the book "takes up the question posed in Joel 2:12-14 as to whether YHWH will respond to repentance by relenting from an earlier decision to punish."[34] On the one hand, where God's willingness to forgive is concerned, the answer to the question is a resounding "Yes." At the same time, it may be important to question the question. In the book of the Twelve, and in the Old Testament as a whole, the Lord's "decision to punish" is not necessarily a punctiliar mental decision, nor is the Lord's "decision not to punish" a second, corrective decision. Rather, the Lord always and at all times threatens punishment for sin when a person or some persons do not repent. Such is the nature of the Lord's will. Disaster inevitably awaits those who do not return and/or seek the Lord. At the same time, forgiveness awaits those who return/seek.

Second, Jonah indicates that the offer of return and renewal applies to gentiles. Though other passages appeal to this same principle, this text is the only example of a large group of gentiles changing on account of a prophetic word. H.W. Wolff writes, "Jer 18:7f. proclaims the doctrine that the message of judgment will be withdrawn from the Gentiles too, if it brings about repentance. The passage is unique in the Old Testament; and it is in our present scene alone that this message is shown as reaching fulfill-

---

[34] Sweeney, *The Twelve Prophets*, 1.303.

ment."[35] This message should have an effect on Israel. Wolff continues, "In presenting this the narrator does not merely take over Jeremian-Deuteronomistic doctrinal tenets; by doing so he also offers a challenge to life in Jerusalem as it was really lived. In this way the narrator introduces into his story an unheard-of hope for the Gentile world."[36] Though not as explicitly as in Jonah, the same theme will occur again in renewal passages like Zeph 3:9-20.

Third, the book's canonical placement asserts that God's mercy and God's justice work cooperatively. Sweeney notes that Jonah shows God's forgiveness of Nineveh, yet the book is followed later by Nahum, which relates God's punishment of Nineveh. Thus, the book of Jonah "points to the necessary interrelationship of YHWH's justice together with YHWH's mercy. YHWH can show mercy to Nineveh when it repents, but YHWH will punish Nineveh when it sins."[37] This interrelationship means that repentance is not a one-time event that precludes judgment for centuries. Sin must cease or be repented of for mercy to continue.

Fourth, Jonah 3—4 follows the announcement of sin—seeking/returning—forgiveness/renewal pattern found in the earlier books of the Twelve. These chapters appear to stress that this pattern is ingrained in the text because it is ingrained in the character of God. New beginnings are possible for any nation or person that changes in the ways God desires.

F. Micah

Micah concludes the Twelve's emphasis on the eighth century. The superscription places the book in the last decades of that century, a time in which Samaria fell to Assyria and in which Assyria invaded and devastated Judah. Though the Sennacherib crisis (c. 701) was the most extreme case of that harassment, it was by no means the only instance of it. Without question, Micah reads these events as divine judgment that should inspire change. Only at the end of the book, however, is there any indication that the message has been heard. In Micah the Lord forges a new beginning primarily through the means of punishment, so in this way the book mirrors Amos more than it does Hosea, Joel, or Jonah. Yet it also stresses the importance of confession, which is a new emphasis in the Twelve.

Micah 1—3 details the people's sins and the consequences of those sins in what are familiar terms by this point in the Twelve. In 1:2, 3:1, and 3:9 the prophet warns the people to "hear" the message. Due to their "prostitu-

---

[35]   Hans Walter Wolff, *Obadiah and Jonah: A Commentary* (trans. Margaret Kohl; Minneapolis: Augsburg, 1986) 146.
[36]   Ibid.
[37]   Sweeney, *The Twelve Prophets,* 1.303.

tion" (see Hosea 1—3) with idols the Lord is coming with great wrath to judge (1:2-7). Now Judah, not just Israel, will be punished (1:8-9). Lamenting and mourning are appropriate at this time (1:10-16).

"Woe" awaits wicked oppressors on "that day" (2:1-5). They have wanted the prophets to preach about wine and strong drink (2:6-11), so the Lord will gather them for punishment (2:12). In fact, the Lord will marshal an army against them (2:13), a theme previously expressed in Joel 2:11. Corrupt prophets, priests, and officials will lead the nation into disaster (3:1-12; see Hosea 4—5). Zion will be plowed like a field, and Jerusalem will become a heap of ruins (3:12). The people want God's favor, but they do not return or seek in the manner prescribed earlier in the Twelve, nor in the manner set forth in Mic 6:1-8.

Micah 4—5 offers the same solution to these problems as Amos 9:1-15: defeat. Renewal flows from the day of the Lord only, not through any returning/seeking on the people's part. Unlike Amos, though, Micah begins with a description of renewal, then concludes with the effects of judgment. Renewal will be evident when "in the latter days" (4:1) the people of "many nations" (4:2) shall come to the "mountain of the Lord" (4:2) to learn "the law" and hear "the word of the Lord" (4:2). God will judge them and lead them into a peaceful and secure way of life (4:3-4) based on worshiping the Lord alone (4:5). God's word and will for Israel will at that time become his word and will for the nations. In the meantime, Zion will mourn for lack of a king (4:9), shall go to Babylon (4:10), and will eventually be rescued (4:10). Current defeat will become certain victory in due time (4:11-13).

Such victory will only come after Judah has been struck on the cheek (5:1), a reference to the same exile noted in 4:8-10. In the future, a Davidic ruler "whose origin is from of old, from ancient days" will arise from Bethlehem and bring peace (5:2) and make the people secure (5:3-5a). In the short run, shepherds will deliver them from the Assyrians (5:5b-6). A remnant of God's people will live among the nations, yet will not be at the mercy of the nations (5:7-9). They will not perish in exile. Rather, the Lord will use their defeat to remove idolatry from them (5:10-15). Thus, defeat can serve the same purpose as returning/seeking.

Micah 6—7 offers a new twist on return and renewal by using first-person confession as a means of expressing change. Before offering this new option, the passage concludes God's case against his people (6:1-5), explains what God requires of the straying people (6:6-8), and notes that walking in Ahab's and Omri's ways has led to their punishment by the Lord (6:9-16). Then a first-person speaker declares, "Woe is me!" (7:1). Why? Because the punishment described in 6:9-16 has occurred (7:1-6). Though other options are possible,[38] it is probable that the prophet speaks here, either on behalf of the people or for himself only.[39] He states that he will "look to the Lord" and "wait for the God of my salvation," and confesses that "my God will hear me" (7:7). This confession of faith in God's willingness to hear those who wait for him leads to the confident assertion that "when I fall, I shall rise; when I sit in darkness, the Lord will be a light to me" (7:8). The prophet is willing to bear God's indignation because he has sinned and because the Lord "executes judgment" on his behalf (7:9). Such confidence leads both to a declaration of future victory over enemies (7:10-17) and to a confession of faith in God's willingness to pardon sin and have compassion (7:18-20). God's covenant with Abraham and Jacob is the foundation for belief in these future blessings (7:20).

Mic 7:9 lies at the heart of the prophet's hopes for renewal. He looks to the Lord even as he confesses his sin. It is this turning from his sin, coupled with the Lord's forgiving nature, that evokes confidence in the speaker. In Joel and Jonah, fasting and mourning lead to returning and renewal, while here confession and waiting produce the same result. In Micah the Lord's punishment awakens the one confessing, while preaching effects that outcome in earlier books, as well as in later books such as Haggai and Malachi. Thus, by now the Book of the Twelve has announced several nearly identical avenues to renewal. One may return, seek, wait, or confess. Each term allows the people to receive a new beginning with the Lord. Throughout the books if these means of forging new beginnings fail, the day of the Lord will do what preaching alone did not effect.

G. Nahum

Nahum's superscription provides no specific date, yet most scholars think it prefigures or depicts the fall of Nineveh in 612. If so, the Twelve has finally moved out of the eighth century for good, and now proceeds to focus on messages that revolve around the momentous days when Babylon supplanted Assyria as the chief world power and threatened Judah while doing so. Samaria is no longer a political factor, which means that threats expressed in the first six books have come to fruition. Since Nineveh is the chief city both here and in Jonah it is apparent that returning and relenting are not actions that one generation can do and gain from God on behalf of their descendants. Each new generation must seek the Lord themselves.

---

[38]   See James Luther Mays, *Micah* (OTL; Philadelphia: Westminster Press, 1976) 150-151.

[39]   See Francis I. Andersen and David Noel Freedman, *Micah* (AB 24E; New York: Doubleday, 2000) 564-578.

The fact that Nineveh, Judah and the whole of creation have failed to grasp this truth dominates Nahum, Habakkuk, and Zephaniah.

It is important to note that Nahum begins this three-book emphasis on judgment by asserting the Lord's patience. Though he is jealous and avenging (1:2), the Lord is at the same time "slow to anger" (see Exod 34:6; Joel 2:13; Jon 4:2), yet unwilling to clear the guilty (1:3). Because he can make Carmel wither (1:4; see Joel 3:16 and Amos 1:2) when he judges, no one can stand before his indignation (1:6). As Nineveh discovered in earlier days, the Lord is a refuge for those who seek him (1:7), but as they will now discover he can also be a terrifying judge. Nineveh may plot against the Lord, but will perish even if its armies are at full military strength (1:9-15).

Time has run out for change. Nineveh will be destroyed (2:1-13). But the Lord will restore "the majesty of Jacob" (2:2) at some future time. Nineveh has been a prostitute, and now she will be uncovered, stripped bare (3:1-7). Once Nineveh multiplied like grasshoppers (see Joel 1:4, 6), yet now will be devoured by fire (3:15; see Joel 2:3 and Amos 1:2-2:3). They will be scattered with no one to gather them (3:18). No message of returning/seeking is offered.

The only new beginning mentioned here is for those Nineveh has oppressed. God promises to break the Assyrian yoke (1:12-13), which will lead to Jacob's renewal (2:2). In other words, the day of the Lord may lead to a new beginning for Israel either because it leads Israel to a returning to the Lord or because it frees Israel from oppression. As the exile unfolded and continued both possibilities probably occupied the minds of the Twelve's readers.

H. Habakkuk

Habakkuk's date is impossible to fix with certainty, though its general time frame is possible to determine. The book announces the rise of the Babylonians, so the date may be in the last quarter of the seventh century or later, and may well revolve around one of the Babylonian incursions into Judah.[40] Regardless of the specific date, the fact is that Judah has little time before facing the same fate as Nineveh. Time is running out for real returning and seeking.

Like Mic 7:1-20, Habakkuk is dominated by first-person speech. Here the prophet asks questions of and receives answers from the Lord. When he asks if the wicked in Judah will remain free from judgment (1:2-4), he is told that Babylon will punish Judah's wicked (1:5-11). When he asks if wicked Babylon will go unpunished (1:12-2:1), he is told to live by faith (2:2-5), for the Babylonians will also be punished (2:6-20). Some day the

---

[40]   See Sweeney, *The Twelve Prophets*, 2.454-5.

plunderer will be plundered (2:9), so they will share the same fate as the old plunderer, Nineveh (see Nah 2:2).

In the concluding section, Habakkuk rejoices in the Lord. He uses creation imagery to express God's power to save and to judge. Indeed, the prophet will rejoice no matter how difficult the times may become (3:17-19). In this way Habakkuk demonstrates the same faith as that expressed by Micah. Both prophets return and seek through confessions of faith, though Habakkuk includes no confession of sin. These prophets may speak only for themselves, yet even so they point the way to how others may likewise find renewal. The readers of the Twelve learned that this method is as old as Hos 6:1-3 and 14:1-9, and is available to individuals, to cities, and to nations. In Nahum and Habakkuk, the fact is that only individuals avail themselves of this opportunity. The larger groups opt to gain the opportunity for renewal the hard way—through the day of the Lord.

I. Zephaniah

Set sometime during the reign of Josiah (640-609), the prophet Zephaniah concludes the Twelve's emphasis on the seventh century by stressing the coming of divine judgment on all creation. Human beings, animals, and idols will all be "swept away" in the wake of God's wrath (1:2-3). Despite the universal scope of this destruction, Judah remains the focal point of the prophet's message (1:4-6). Thus, Zephaniah continues the strong judgment themes found in Nahum and Habakkuk. At the same time, unlike Nahum and Habakkuk this book includes calls for change in Judah and includes the possibility of renewal for both Judah and the nations.

Zephaniah's portrait of the day of the Lord emphasizes the event's totality. All persons (1:3, 17, 18), all the earth (1:18), every idolater (1:9), every violent person (1:9), and every fortified city (1:16) will experience this dark and terrifying day (1:14-16; see Amos 5:18-20). The reason for this judgment is that "they have sinned against the Lord" (1:17). As in Amos 1:2—2:6, this punishment will be shared by Judah and her enemies (2:4-15). Time seems to have run out for everyone concerned. All the gods of the earth and all the lands of the earth will bow down to the Lord (2:11).

Despite the fact that "the day of the Lord is near" (1:7; see Joel 1:15, 2:1, 11, 15, 31; Amos 5:18; and Obadiah 15), the prophet calls on the people to "seek the Lord" (2:3). Here seeking the Lord means "seek righteousness; seek humility" (2:3). Such seeking may lead to their being "hidden on the day of the anger of the Lord" (2:3). Interestingly enough, this seeking will not forestall the day of the Lord, as was true earlier in the Twelve. Now such seeking will merely hide the persons who seek the Lord in the midst of the inevitable day of the Lord. The "humble of the land" (2:3) should take refuge in the Lord, but this refuge pertains only to them. They will be preserved, but the nation will not. A text like this one may have helped early readers of the Twelve understand why the "humble of the land," people like Habakkuk and Jeremiah, for instance, suffered when the land was destroyed. The time has passed for a more general seeking and finding of the Lord.

Now the book begins its final movement towards the punishment that will bring renewal. The prophet declares "woe" (3:1) on the nation. This woe could have been avoided, as 2:1-3 has already indicated, had the people been willing to accept the Lord's correction (3:7). Given their evident eagerness to act corruptly (3:7), the Lord decides to pour out his indignation, with the result that "all the earth shall be consumed" (3:8). Never to this point has the Book of the Twelve offered such a picture or worldwide judgment.

Through this judgment the Lord will renew both the nations and Judah. The Lord "will change the speech of the peoples to a pure speech, that all of them may call upon the name of the Lord and serve him with one accord" (3:9). Adele Berlin notes that "the idea seems to be universal worship of the Lord, reminiscent of, or actually going beyond, the idea in 2:11."[41] Further, exiles shall come from a distance to worship the Lord (3:10), and the Lord will leave in land "a people humble and lowly. They shall seek refuge in the name of the Lord" (3:12). For these renewed people the Lord will do great things. He will gather them (3:18), deal with their oppressors (3:19), heal their lame (3:19), remove their shame (3:19), and renew them fully (3:20). Truly the renewal has been as thorough as the punishment. A truly new beginning has been forged out of the punishment inflicted on the nations and on Judah.

Both means of renewal unfold in Zephaniah. The people may either seek the Lord or experience the day of the Lord. The "humble of the land" are likely those who did seek God, and they will be joined by a purified group of people after the full force of the day of the Lord has been felt. In this way Zephaniah acts as a summary of how judgment comes to Israel and the nations without that judgment being the final word. Renewal is the final word, and that word may well have encouraged the Twelve's first audience.

J. Haggai

Haggai's superscription (1:1) places it in the Persian period. More specifically, it sets the book in the years 520-515, the period in which the temple was rebuilt. Thus, this book marks the Twelve's movement out of the seventh century and into the sixth, and thereby reminds readers that the people

---

[41]   Adele Berlin, *Zephaniah* (AB 25A; New York: Doubleday, 1994) 133.

have begun to come back to the land. God has not left them in exile, just as the previous books promised (see Zeph 3:12-13). The book testifies to the Lord's ability to give Israel a new beginning. At the same time, this era was not kind to those who came to Jerusalem. The land was poor and the people felt keen disappointment at their circumstances. In this setting the prophet Haggai offers a familiar message of returning and renewal.

Probably due to their circumstances, the people have not felt able to re-build the temple, though they have felt able to build their own houses. Haggai indicts them for this hypocrisy, and states that their hard times are due to their unwillingness to attend to God's house (1:2-6). He urges them to "consider" their ways and their situation and act (1:7-11). In this passage the word "consider" has much the same force as returning and seeking do in earlier books.

Though the word "return" does not appear, the people's consideration leads to fear of the Lord and to work on the Lord's house (1:12-15). A finer response to a message could hardly be conceived. Based on their response, the Lord promises to renew the covenant promises made when Israel came out of Egypt (2:5; see Hos 11:1-9; Amos 3:1-8; and Mic 7:18-20). Cove-nant blessings will likewise emerge (2:6). In fact, the Lord will "shake all nations" so that the temple will be filled with wealth and glory. In the past the people did not respond to the Lord's message. In language clearly reminiscent of Amos 4:6-13, God claims, "I struck you and all the products of your toil with blight and with mildew and with hail, yet you did not re-turn to me" (2:17). But now the people have indeed turned to the Lord, so they will indeed be blessed (2:18-19). The book concludes with a special blessing for the people's leader (2:20-23).

As in Joel and Jonah, turning to the Lord, not the day of the Lord, has led to renewal. In previous books returning/seeking meant fasting, con-fessing, changing behavior, and acting justly and faithfully. In Haggai the meaning of returning/seeking is "consider and build." In every context obeying God's specific commands is the chief way of knowing how to de-fine the key terms. The people have a fresh start with the Lord, but it re-mains to be seen how well they will build on that new beginning.

K. Zechariah

Zechariah's superscription places its opening message at the same time as Haggai, the second year of Darius (1:1). Therefore, this book shares its immediate predecessor's historical context, and it also shares its interest in the restoration of Jerusalem and the rebuilding of the temple. In expressing these interests, the book includes passages that stress returning to the Lord, God's mercy, the day of the Lord, and ultimate renewal.

The book begins with a strong statement about the people's past and their current opportunity. In the past the Lord was angry with their ancestors, and told them to "return to me and I will return to you" (1:2-3), a plea that was generally rejected (1:4-5). Thus, the prophets' threats overcame these ancestors (1:6). Judgment fell. But now the people repent and testify to God's just actions (1:6). Their attitude leads to prayer and to God's promise to return to them because they have returned to him (1:16).

In Zech 1:17—6:15, God's merciful turning to the people leads to renewal. Blessing will come in the future as surely as judgment came in the past (1:17). When those days of blessing arrive, the Lord will plunder those who plundered Israel (2:8; see Nah 2:2), and many nations will "join themselves to the Lord" and become the Lord's people (2:11). Israel's repentance will inspire other countries to do the same. The high priest's sins will be forgiven and the temple ministry purified (3:1-10). Israel's civil leader will be empowered (4:1-14; see Hag 2:20-23). The wicked will be removed from the land (5:1-3), and the crown and the temple shall be restored (6:9-15).

Zechariah 7—8 reminds readers that these blessings result from a change in attitude and action that marks a clear break with earlier generations. In those days the people "made their hearts diamond-hard lest they should hear the law and the words that the Lord of hosts had sent by his Spirit through the former prophets" (7:12). Thus, they experienced God's anger (7:12). Now the people have responded positively to the Lord's word, so God has returned to Zion, and the results will be astoundingly positive (8:1-13). Just as God had once sent disaster, so he will now send good things (8:14-17). The past days of the Lord have been the evidence the people needed to accept God's demand for change. Judgment has led to repentance, which has in turn led to renewal. Once more the text states that Israel's seeking of the Lord will lead other peoples to do the same (8:20-23; see Mic 4:1-5; Zeph 3:9).

After focusing on the coming of the king and subsequent days of salvation in chapters 9 – 11, the book concludes with descriptions of the coming day of the Lord and its results in chapters 12 – 14. In the past the day of the Lord only benefited Israel in a secondary way. That is, they benefited from the fall of Assyria because it gave them relief, but they were not protected by a day of the Lord. All this changes in this last section. Here the creator of the heavens and earth (12:1) will bring the day of the Lord to devour those who oppose Jerusalem (12:2-9). That day will cleanse Israel from idolatry and other types of sins (13:1-6). On that day the Lord will defeat all Jerusalem's enemies (14:1-5), be king over the whole earth (14:9), welcome worshipers from all lands to the Feast of Booths (14:16-19), and make

Jerusalem "holy to the Lord" (14:20-21). This futuristic picture is forged by judgment on behalf of people who turn to the Lord.

In Zechariah, then, there is a virtually perfect blending of repentance, renewal, and the effects of the day of the Lord. Each one contributes to the remaking of Jerusalem into a holy city and to the restoration of creation. In many ways Zechariah is the high point of the Twelve's theological message. After all, the people are changed, Jerusalem is holy, and the Lord has returned to the people who have returned to him. The Book of the Twelve does not end here, however. It ends with a book that calls the nation once more to return to their God.

L. Malachi

Malachi's superscription offers no information on the prophet's date or family. He is certainly a post-exilic prophet like Haggai and Zechariah, but even this conclusion must be drawn from an analysis of the book's contents. These contents portray the people as questioning God's love (1:2-5), offering polluted offerings (1:6-14), countenancing priests who do not instruct them properly (2:1-9), profaning the covenant with God and the covenant made with their spouses (2:10-16), and robbing God in their offerings (3:6-14). Clearly, the glorious renewal described in Zechariah does not apply to Malachi's era.

Scholars have often associated this rather dismal picture with Ezra and Nehemiah's time,[42] though Paul Redditt rightly concludes that the Malachi's contents only fit a time span of 515-445 as the possible range for the book's composition.[43] Andrew Hill suggests that the book's linguistic data indicate that it was probably written c. 500, so Malachi addresses a situation nearer to the time of Haggai and Malachi.[44] If Hill is correct, then Malachi deals with the people's early attempts at worship and general disappointment with its failure to usher in the sort of glory promised in Haggai and Zechariah. He does so in part by utilizing calls for change and promises of renewal.

After the messages concerning the people's lack of confidence in the Lord's love for them (1:2-5) and their polluted offerings (1:6-14), the prophet uses new phrases to call for change. He tells them "take it to heart" (2:2), which seems to be a near parallel to Haggai's demand that they consider their ways (Hag 1:7). He follows this command with admonitions to "guard their spirits" and change their behavior (2:15, 16). This sort of ac-

---

[42] Marvin A. Sweeney expresses this point of view in *The Twelve Prophets*, 2.715-716.

[43] See Paul L. Redditt, *Haggai, Zechariah, Malachi* (NCB; Grand Rapids: Eerdmans, 1995) 150.

[44] See Andrew E. Hill, *Malachi* (AB 25D; New York: Doubleday, 1998) 80-84.

tion must replace false weeping and groaning (2:13). Though not identical with earlier *terms* for change, the *effects* are the same.

As in Joel, Jonah, Haggai, and Zechariah, some hearers do respond to the message. As in Hag 1:12, some persons fear the Lord, take stock of their situation, and receive God's forgiveness (3:16-18). These people will be God's special possession (3:17; see Exod 19:5), and God will spare them "as a man spares his son who serves him" (3:17; see Hos 11:1-9). As always, those who obey God's call to turn to him find that judgment is no longer necessary.

Malachi concludes the Book of the Twelve with one final reference to the day of the Lord. Wicked persons should fear the day (4:1; see Amos 5:18-27), but those who fear the Lord, another way of expressing the fact that they turn to God, will be blessed at that time (4:2-3). One last time the people are told to adhere to the covenant standards (4:4), and they are warned to avoid a future "utter destruction" prefigured by the appearance of a new Elijah (4:6). As before, what returning, seeking, fearing, considering, and guarding does not do will be accomplished by the day of the Lord. Regardless of the people's choice, the Lord will remove sin and restore the humble of the land to their rightful place in Zion. Thus, the one who is Israel's father (1:6; 2:10), king (1:14), and judge (3:2-3) has an unshakeable love for those who respond to his covenant love (1:2-5).[45]

III. Conclusion

This article has sought to chart some of the ways themes such as returning to the Lord, seeking the Lord, considering one's ways, and fearing the Lord relate to the day of the Lord and promises of renewal. What seems clear is that Rendtorff's conclusion that these themes are tightly interrelated is correct.[46] These ideas intersect so often that it seems reasonable to conclude that they provide several unifying elements to the Twelve. They also indicate certain things about the Twelve's theology and about its audience.

To be sure, the Twelve stresses a God who defines and denounces sin, and who announces judgment for that sin. At the same time, it also claims that this same God is the creator, the king of the universe, and the one who forgives. The messages of condemnation are given through the prophets to effect returning to the Lord and his standards. Even judgment itself occurs so that renewal may be forged out of its fiery embers. In short, the Twelve presents a God whose pursuit of new beginnings will not be denied. This God loves Israel, and will not let them go (see Hos 11:1-9). Likewise, he loves the nations, and is concerned when they do not know their left hand

---

45   Redditt, *Haggai, Zechariah, Malachi,* 187.
46   Rendtorff, "How to Read the Book of the Twelve as a Theological Unity," 86.

from their right because of their sins (see Jon 4:1-11). Thus, the Lord will bring Israel and the nations to his holy mountain, where sin is no longer relevant (Mic 4:1-5; Zech 14:20-21).

As for its audience, the Twelve offers a post-exilic readership a clear choice based on their spiritual heritage. Those who first held the whole corpus in their hands lived between the day of the Lord that brought exile and the day of the Lord that would bring them final security. They were people in the middle of times, people who had neither participated in the cataclysms of the past nor the glorious victories set for the future. Thus, they awaited a new beginning. As they waited, they had the chance to turn to the Lord and avoid the judgments of their day. In other words, they could read these prophets, consider their ways, and seek the Lord's favor, thereby gaining membership among the humble of the land.

Works Cited

Ackroyd, Peter. "The Book of Haggai and Zechariah I-VIII." *Journal of Jewish Studies* 3 (1952): 151-56.

Ådna, Josten. "James' Position at the Summit Meeting of the Apostles and the Elders in Jerusalem (Acts 15)." Pages 125-61 in *The Mission of the Early Church to Jews and Gentiles.* Edited by Jostein Ådna and Hans Kvalbein; Wissenschaftliche Untersuchungen zum Neuen Testament 127; Tübingen: Mohr-Siebeck, 2000.

Aichele, George, and Gary A. Philips, (eds). *Intertextuality and the Bible.* Semeia 69-70. Atlanta: Society of Biblical Literature, 1995.

Alexander, Philip S. "Retelling the Old Testament." Pages 99-121 in *It Is Written: Scripture Citing Scripture.* Edited by D. A. Carson and H. G. M. Williamson. Cambridge: Cambridge University, 1988.

Anderson, Francis. I. and David Noel. Freedman. *Hosea.* Anchor Bible 24A; Garden City: Doubleday, 1980.

Andersen, Francis I. and David Noel Freedman. *Micah.* Anchor Bible 24E. New York: Doubleday, 2000.

Albertz, Rainer. "Jer 2-6 und die Frühzeitverkündigung Jeremias." *Zeitschrift für die alttestamentliche Wissenschaft* 94 (1982): 20–47.

Albertz, Rainer. *A History of Israelite Religion in the Old Testament Period.* 2 vols. Old Testament Library. Louisville: Westminster, 1992.

Albertz, Rainer. "In Search of the Deuteronomists: A First Solution to a Historical Riddle." Pages 1-17 in *The Future of the Deuteronomistic History.* Edited by T. Römer. Bibliotheca Ephemeridum theologicarum Lovaniensium 147. Leuven: Leuven University Press & Peeters, 2000.

Albertz, Rainer. *Die Exilszeit: Das 6. Jahrhundert.* Biblische Enzyklopädie 7. Stuttgart: Kohlhammer, 2001.

Babylonian Talmud. Translated into English with notes, glossary and indices. Edited by Isidore Epstein. 35 vols. London: Soncino Press, 1935-1952.

Baldwin, Joyce G. *Haggai, Zechariah, Malachi: An Introduction and Commentary.* Tyndale Old Testament Commentaries. Downers Grove: Inter-Varsity Press, 1972.

Barton, John. *Joel and Obadiah.* Old Testament Library. Louisville: Westminster John Knox, 2001.

Barton, John. *Reading the Old Testament: Method in Biblical Study.* London: Darton, Longman and Todd, 1984.

Batto, Bernhard F. "The Covenant of Peace: A Neglected Ancient Near Eastern Motif" *Catholic Biblical Quarterly* 49 (1987): 187-211.

Baumann, Gerlinde. "Connected by Marriage, Adultery and Violence: The Prophetic Marriage Metaphor in the Book of the Twelve and in the Major Prophets." Pages 552-69 in *SBL Seminar Papers 1999*. Society of Biblical Literature Seminar Papers 38. Atlanta: Society of Biblical Literature, 1999.

Baumann, Gerlinde. *Liebe und Gewalt. Die Ehe als Metapher für das Verhältnis JHWH – Israel in den Prophetenbüchern.* Stuttgarter Bibelstudien 185. Stuttgart: Katholisches Bibelwerk, 2000.

Baumann, Gerlinde. "Prophetic Objections to YHWH as the Violent Husband of Israel: Reinterpretations of the Prophetic Marriage Metaphor in Second Isaiah (Isaiah 40-55)." Pages 88-120 in *Prophets and Daniel. A Feminist Companion to the Bible.* Second Series 8. Edited by Athalya Brenner; Sheffield: Sheffield Academic Press, 2001.

Becker, Uwe. *Jesaja – von der Botschaft zum Buch.* Forschungen zur Religion und Literatur des Alten und Neuen Testaments 178. Göttingen: Vandenhoeck & Ruprecht, 1997.

Becker, Uwe. "Der Prophet als Fürbitter: Zum literarhistorischen Ort der Amos-Visionen. *Vetus Testamentum* 51 (2001): 141-165.

Bellefontaine, Elizabeth. "Reviewing the Case of the Rebellious Son" *Journal for the Study of the Old Testament* 13 (1979): 13-31.

Bellinger, Willam H. *Psalmody and Prophecy.* Journal for the Study of the Old Testament Supplement Series 27. Sheffield: JSOT Press, 1984.

Benjamin, Don C. "Israel's God: Mother and Midwife." *Biblical Theology Bulletin* 19 (1989): 115-20.

Ben Zvi, Ehud. *A Historical-Critical Study of the Book of Obadiah.* Beiheft zur Zeitschrift für die alttestamentliche Wissenschaft 242. Berlin and New York: de Gruyter, 1996.

Ben Zvi, Ehud. *Micah.* Forms of the Old Testament Literature XXIB. Grand Rapids: Eerdmans 2000.

Ben Zvi, Ehud."Twelve Prophetic Books or 'The Twelve': A Few Preliminary Considerations." Pages 125-56 in *Forming Prophetic Literature: Essays on Isaiah and the Twelve in Honor of John D. W. Watts.* Edited by James W. Watts and Paul R. House. Journal for the Old Testament Supplement Series 235. Sheffield: Sheffield Academic Press, 1996.

Berger, Peter L. *The Sacred Canopy: Elements of a Sociological Theory of Religion.* Garden City: Doubleday, 1969.

Berges, Ulrich. *Das Buch Jesaja.* HBS 16; Freiburg/Breisg, 1998.

Bergler, Siegfried. "'Auf Der Mauer - Auf Dem Altar': Noch einmal die Visionen des Amos." *Vetus Testamentum* 50 (2000): 445-471.

Bergler, Siegfried. *Joel als Schriftinterpret*. Beiträge zur Erforschung des Alten Testaments und des antiken Judentum 6. Frankfurt/Main: Lang, 1988.

Berlin, Adele. *Zephaniah*. Anchor Bible 25A. New York: Doubleday, 1994.

Berry, Donald K. "Malachi's Dual Design: The Close of the Canon and What Comes Afterward." Pages 269-302 in *Forming Prophetic Literature: Essays on Isaiah and the Twelve in Honor of John D. W. Watts*. Edited by James W. Watts and Paul R. House. Journal for the Old Testament Supplement Series 235. Sheffield: Sheffield Academic Press, 1996.

Beuken, W. A. M. *Haggai-Sacharia 1-8: Studien zur Überlieferungsgeschichte der Frühnachexilischen Prophetie*. Assen: Van Gorcum, 1967.

Bickerman, Elias. "Les deux erreurs du prophète Jonas." *Revue d'histoire et de philosophie religieuses* 45 (1965): 232-264.

Bickerman, Elias. *Four Strange Books of the Bible. Jonah / Daniel / Kohelet / Esther*. Schocken Books: New York, 1967.

Biddle, Mark E. "The Figure of Lady Jerusalem: Identification, Deification and Personification of Cities in the Ancient Near East." Pages 173-94 in *The Biblical Canon in Comparative Perspective*. Edited by B. Batto et al. Scripture in Context 4. Lewiston, NY: Mellen, 1991.

Bird, Phyllis. "'To Play the Harlot': An Inquiry into an Old Testament Metaphor." Pages 75-94 in *Gender and Difference in Ancient Israel*. Edited by P. L. Day. Minneapolis: Fortress Press, 1989.

Biser, Eugene. "Zum frühchristlichen Verständnis des Buches Jonas." Bibel und Kirche 17 (1962): 19-21.

Blenkinsopp, Joseph. *Ezra-Nehemiah*. Old Testament Library. Philadelphia: Westminster, 1988.

Blenkinsopp, Joseph. *Ezekiel*. Interpretation. Louisville: John Knox, 1990.

Blenkinsopp, Joseph. *A History of Prophecy in Israel*. 2d ed. Louisville: Westminster John Knox, 1996.

Blenkinsopp, Joseph. "The Mission of Udjahoresnet and Those of Ezra and Nehemiah." *Journal of Biblical Literature* 106 (1987): 409-21.

Bosshard, Erich. "Beobachtungen zum Zwölfprophetenbuch." *Biblische Notizen* 40 (1987): 30-62.

Bosshard-Nepustil, Erich. *Rezeptionen von Jesaia im Zwölfprophetenbuch. Untersuchungen zur literarischen Verbindung von Prophetenbüchern in Babylonischer und Persischer Zeit*. Orbis biblicus et orientalis 154. Freiburg, Göttingen: Vandenhoeck & Ruprecht, 1997.

Bosshard, Erich and Reinhard G. Kratz, "Maleachi im Zwölfprophetenbuch," *Biblische Notizen* 52 (1990): 27-46.

Botterweck, G. Johannes, Helmer Ringgren, and Heinz-Josef Fabry, eds. *Theological Dictionary of the Old Testament.* 11+ vols. Grand Rapids: Eerdmans, 1974ff.

Braaten, Laurie J. "Earth Community in Hosea 2." Pages 4.185-203 in *The Earth Bible: Earth Story in the Prophets.* Edited by Norman C. Habel. 4 vols. Sheffield: Sheffield Academic Press, 2001.

Braaten, Laurie J. "God Sows the Land: Hosea's Place in the Book of the Twelve." Pages 218-42 in *SBL Seminar Papers, 2000.* Society of Biblical Literature Seminar Papers 39. Atlanta: Society of Biblical Literature, 2000.

Braaten, Laurie J. "Parent-Child Imagery in Hosea." Ph.D. dissertation, Boston University, 1987.

Braaten, Laurie J. "That God May Heal the Land: A Liturgical Setting for the Book of the Twelve." Paper presented at the New England Society of Biblical Literature, Boston, Mass., April 27, 2001.

Bright, John. *A History of Israel.* Philadelphia: Westminster, 1975.

Brown, Robert McAfee. Introduction E. Wiesel's play, *The Trial of God.* New York: Schocken, 1995.

Brueggemann, Walter. *1 and 2 Kings.* Macon, Ga: Smyth & Helwys, 2000.

Brueggemann, Walter. *The Land: Place as Gift, Promise and Challenge in Biblical Faith.* Overtures to Biblical Theology. Philadelphia: Fortress, 1977.

Brueggemann, Walter. "Theodicy in a Social Dimension." *Journal for the Study of the Old Testament* 33 (1985): 3-24.

Budde, Karl. "Eine folgenschwere Redaktion des Zwölfprohetenbuchs." *Zeitschrift für die alttestamentliche Wissenschaft* 39 (1921): 218-229.

Carroll, Robert P. "Night without Vision: Micah and the Prophets." Pages 74-84 in *The Scriptures and the Scrolls: Studies in Honour of A.S. van der Woude's 65th Birthday.* Edited by G. Martínez, A. Hilhurst, and C. J. Labuschagne. Leiden: Brill, 1992.

Cathcart, K. J. and R.P. Gordon. *The Targum of the Minor Prophets.* The Aramaic Bible 14. Edinburgh: T&T Clark Ltd, 1989.

Chapman, Stephen B. *The Law and the Prophets.* Forschungen zum Alten Testament 27. Tübingen: Mohr Siebeck, 2000.

Cheyne, T. K. *Hosea, with Notes and Introduction.* Cambridge Bible. Cambridge: University Press, 1884.

Childs, Brevard Springs. "The Canonical Shape of the Prophetic Literature," *Interpretation* 32 (1978): 46-55.

Childs, Brevard S. *Introduction to the Old Testament as Scripture.* Philadelphia: Fortress, 1979.

Childs, Brevard Springs. "Retrospective Reading of the Old Testament Prophets." *Zeitschrift für die alttestamentliche Wissenschaft* 108 (1996): 362-377.

Christensen, Duane A. "The Book of Nahum: A History of Interpretation." Pages 187-94 in *Forming Prophetic Literature: Essays on Isaiah and the Twelve in Honor of John D. W. Watts.* Edited by James W. Watts and Paul R. House. Journal for the Old Testament Supplement Series 235. Sheffield: Sheffield Academic Press, 1996.

Coggins, R. J. "The Minor Prophets--One Book or Twelve?" *Crossing the Boundaries.* Biblical Interpretation 8. Fest. M. D. Goulder Edited by John Barton and D. J. Reimer. Macon, GA: Mercer University Press, 1996.

Cohen, N. G. "From *Nabi* to *Mal'ak* to 'Ancient Figure.'" *Journal of Jewish Studies* 36 [1985]: 12-24.

Collins, Terence. *The Mantle of Elijah: The Redaction Criticism of the Prophetical Books.* The Biblical Seminar 20. Sheffield: Sheffield Academic Press, 1993.

Conrad, E. W. "The End of Prophecy and the Appearance of Angels/Messengers in the Book of the Twelve." *Journal for the Study of the Old Testament* 73 (1997): 65-79.

Conrad, Edgar W. "Prophet, Redactor and Audience: Reforming the Notion of Isaiah's Formation." In *New Visions of the Book of Isaiah* (ed. R. Melugin and M. Sweeney. Journal for the Study of the Old Testament Supplement Series 214; Sheffield: Sheffield Academic Press, 1996.

Conrad, Edgar W. *Reading Isaiah.* Overtures to Biblical Theology. Minneapolis: Fortress Press, 1991.

Conrad, Edgar W. "Reading Isaiah and the Twelve as Prophetic Books." Pages 3-17 in *Writing and Reading the Scroll of Isaiah: Studies of an Interpretive Tradition.* Supplements to Vetus Testamentum 70/1. Edited by Craig C. Broyles and Craig A. Evans. New York: Brill, 1997.

Conrad, Edgar W. *Zechariah.* Readings: A New Biblical Commentary. Sheffield: Sheffield Press, 1999.

Cook, Stephen L. Pages 167-209 in *Prophecy and Apocalypticism: The Post-Exilic Social Setting.* Minneapolis: Fortress, 1995.

Cooper, Alan. "In Praise of Divine Caprice: The Significance of the Book of Jonah." Pages 159-63 in *Among the Prophets: Language, Image and Structure in the Prophetic Writings.* Edited by P. R. Davies and D. J. A. Clines. Journal for the Study of the Old Testament Supplement Series144; Sheffield: JSOT, 1993), 159-63.

Coggins, R. J. "The Minor Prophets—One Book or Twelve?" Pages 57-68 in *Crossing the Boundaries.* Edited by S. E. Porter, P. Joyce, and D. E. Orton. Leiden: Brill, 1994.

Collins, Terrence. *The Mantle of Elijah: The Redaction Criticism of Prophetical Books.* Biblical Seminar 20; Sheffield: Sheffield Academic Press, 1993.

Cooper, Alan. "In Praise of Divine Caprice." Pages 144-163 in *Among the Prophets; Language, Image and Structure in the Prophetic Writings.* Edited by Philip R. Davies and David J. A. Clines. Sheffield: JSOT Press, 1993.

Craig, Kenneth M., Jr. "Interrogatives in Haggai and Zechariah: A Literary Thread?" Pages 224-44 in *Forming Prophetic Literature: Essays on Isaiah and the Twelve in Honor of John D. W. Watts.* Edited by James W. Watts and Paul R. House. Journal for the Old Testament Supplement Series 235. Sheffield: Sheffield Academic Press, 1996.

Craig, Kenneth M., Jr. *A Poetic of Jonah.* New York: Columbia: University of South Carolina Press, 1993.

Crenshaw, James L. "The Concept of God in Old Testament Wisdom." Pages 1-18 in *In Search of Wisdom: Essays in Memory of John G. Gammie.* Edited by Leo G. Perdue, Bernard Scott, and William Wiseman. Louisville: John Knox, 1993.

Crenshaw, James L. *Education in Ancient Israel: Across the Deadening Silence.* New York: Doubleday, 1998.

Crenshaw, James L. *Hymnic Affirmation of Divine Justice.* Society of Biblical Literature Dissertation Series 24; Missoula, Mon.: Scholars Press, 1975.

Crenshaw, James L. *Joel.* Anchor Bible 24C. New York: Doubleday, 1995.

Crenshaw, James L. "Joel's Silence and Interpreter's Readiness to Indict the Innocent." In *"Lässet uns Brücken bauen..." Collected Communications to the XVth Congress of the International Organization for the Study of the Old Testament Cambridge, 1995.* Beiträge zur Erforschung des Alten Testaments und des antiken Judentum 42; Frankfurt: Lang, 1998.

Crenshaw, James L. "A Liturgy of Wasted Opportunity: Am. 4:6-12; Isa. 9:7-10:4." *Semitics* 1 [1971]: 27-37.

Crenshaw, James L. "Popular Questioning of the Justice of God in Ancient Israel." *Zeitschrift für die alttestamentliche Wissenschaft* 82 (1970): 380-95.

Crenshaw, James L. *Prophetic Conflict: Its Effect Upon Israelite Religion.* Beiheft zur Zeitschrift für die alttestamentliche Wissenschaft 124. Berlin and New York: de Gruyter, 1971.

Crenshaw, James L. *The Psalms: an Introduction.* Grand Rapids: Eerdmans, 2001.

Crenshaw, James L. "The Sojourner Has Come to Play the Judge: Theodicy on Trial." Pages 83-92 in *God in the Fray: A Tribute to Walter Brueg-*

gemann. Edited by Tod Linafelt and Timothy K. Beal. Minneapolis: Fortress, 1998.

Crenshaw, James L. *Theodicy in the Old Testament.* Philadelphia: Fortress, 1983.

Crenshaw, James L. "Theodicy, Theology, and Philosophy: Early Israel and Judaism." In *Religions of the Ancient World: A Guide.* Cambridge, Mass.: Harvard University Press, forthcoming.

Crenshaw, James L. *Urgent Advice and Probing Questions: Collected Writings on Old Testament Wisdom.* Macon: Mercer University, 1995.

Crenshaw, James L. "Who Knows What Yahweh Will Do? The Character of God in the Book of Joel." Pages 185-96 in *Fortunate the Eyes That See: Essays in Honor of David Noel Freedman* Edited by Astrid Beck et. al. Grand Rapids: Eerdmans, 1995.

Cross, Frank Moore, Jr. "A Reconstruction of the Judean Restoration." *Interpretation* 29 (1975): 187-203.

Cuffey, Kenneth H. "Remnant, Redactor, and Biblical Theologian: A Comparative Study of Coherence in Micah and the Twelve." Pages 185-208 in *Reading and Hearing the Book of the Twelve.* Edited by James D. Nogalski and Marvin A. Sweeney. Society of Biblical Literature Symposium Series 15. Atlanta: Society of Biblical Literature, 2000.

Curtis, Byron G. "The Zion-Daughter Oracles: Evidence on the Identity and Ideology of the Late Redactors of the Book of the Twelve." Pages 166-84 in *Reading and Hearing the Book of the Twelve.* Edited by James D. Nogalski and Marvin A. Sweeney. Society of Biblical Literature Symposium Series 15. Atlanta: Society of Biblical Literature, 2000.

Dassmann, Ernst. "Umfang, Kriterien und Methoden frühchristlicher Prophetenexegese." *Jahrbuch für biblische Theologie* 14 (1999): 117-143.

Davies, Philip. *Scribes and Schools: The Canonization of the Hebrew Scriptures.* Louisville: Westminster/John Knox, 1998.

Davis, Ellen. *Swallowing the Scroll: Textuality and the Dynamics of Discourse in Ezekiel's Prophecy.* Journal for the Study of the Old Testament Supplement Series 78. Sheffield: Almond Press, 1989.

Delkurt, Holger. *Sacharjas Nachtgesichte. Zur Aufnahme und Abwandlung prophetischer Traditionen.* Beiheft zur Zeitschrift für die alttestamentliche Wissenschaft 302; Berlin, New York: de Gruyter, 2000.

Dentan, Robert C. "The Literary Affinities of Exodus XXXIV6f." *Vetus Testamentum* 13 (1963): 34-51.

De Roche, Michael. "The Reversal of Creation in Hosea." *Vetus Testamentum* 31 (1981): 400-409.

De Vries, Simon J. *From Old Revelation to New: A Tradition-History and Redaction-Critical Study of Temporal Transitions in Prophetic Prediction.* Grand Rapids: Eerdmans, 1995.

De Vries, Simon J. *Yesterday, Today and Tomorrow.* Grand Rapids: Eerdmans, 1975.

Dozeman, Thomas B. "Inner-Biblical Interpretation of Yahweh's Gracious and Compassionate Character." *Journal of Biblical Literature* 108 (1989): 207-23.

Draisma, Sipke, ed. *Intertextuality in Biblical Writings: Essays in Honor of Bas van Iersel.* Kampen: J. H. Kok, 1989.

Duhm, Bernhard. "Anmerkungen zu den Zwölf Propheten." *Zeitschrift für die alttestamentliche Wissenschaft* 31 (1911): 1-43, 81-110, 161-204.

Duhm, Bernhard. *Die Theologie der Propheten als Grundlage für die innere Entwicklungsgeschichte der israelitischen Religion.* Bonn: Marcus 1875.

Duval, Yves-Marie. *Le livre de Jonas dans la littérature chrétienne grecque et latine. Sources et influence du Commentaire sur Jonas de saint Jérôme.* Vol. I. *Sources Augustiennes;* Vol. II. *Index *Metanoia; *Pénitence nécessaire des païens.* Paris: Études Augus-tiennes, 1973.

Eaton, John H. *Vision in Worship.* London: SCM Press 1981.

Eco, Umberto. *Interpretation and Overinterpretation.* Ed. S. Collini; Cambridge: Cambridge University Press, 1992.

Eco, Umberto. *The Limits of Interpretation.* Bloomington: Indiana University Press, 1990.

Eco, Umberto. *The Role of the Reader: Explorations in the Semiotics of Texts.* London: Hutchinson, 1981.

Ego, Beate. *Buch Tobit.* Jüdische Schriften aus hellenistisch-römischer Zeit. Vol. II: *Unterweisung in erzählender Form.* Gütersloh: Gütersloher Verlagshaus, 1999.

Ego, Beate. "Denn die Heiden sind der Umkehr nahe. Rabbinische Interpretationen zur Buße der Leute von Ninive." Pages 158-76 in *Die Heiden. Juden, Christen und das Problem des Fremden.* Edited by R. Feldmeier, U. Heckel. Wissenschaftliche Untersuchungen zum Neuen Testament 70 Tübingen: J.C. B. Mohr [Paul Siebeck], 1994.

Ego, Beate. "The Repentence of Nineveh in the Story of Jonah and Nahum's Prophecy of the City's Destruction: Aggadic Solutions for an Exegetical Problem in the Book of the Twelve." Pages 243-53 in *SBL Seminar Papers, 2000.* Society of Biblical Literature Seminar Papers 39. Atlanta: Society of Biblical Literature, 2000.

Elliger, Karl. *Deuterojesaja in seinem Verhältnis zu Tritojesaja.* Beiträge zur Wissenschaft vom Alten (und Neuen) Testament. Stuttgart: Kohlhammer, 1933.

Everson, A. Joseph. "The Days of Yahweh." *Journal of Biblical Literature* 93 (1974): 329-337.

Everson, A Joseph. "Serving Notice on Babylon: The Canonical Function of Isaiah 13-14." *Word and World* 19 (1999): 133-40.

Ewald, Heinrich. *Die Propheten des Alten Bundes erklärt.* 2d ed. Göttingen: Vandenhoeck & Ruprecht, 1868.

Fensham, F. Charles. "Widow, Orphan, and the Poor in Ancient Near Eastern Legal and Wisdom Literature." *Journal of Near Eastern Studies* 21 (1962): 129-39.

Fewell, Dana N., ed. *Reading Between Texts: Intertextuality and the Hebrew Bible.* Louisville: Westminster / John Knox, 1992.

Fischer, Irmtraud. "Schwerter oder Pflugscharen? Versuch einer kanonischen Lektüre von Jes 2, Joël 4 und Micha 4." *Bibel und Liturgie* 69 (1996): 208-216.

Fish, Stanley. *Is There a Text in This Class? The Authority of Interpretive Communities.* Cambridge: Harvard University Press, 1980.

Fishbane, Michael. *Biblical Interpretation in Ancient Israel.* Oxford: Clarendon Press, 1985. Corrected ed. 1986.

Fitzgerald, Aloysius. "The Mythological Background for the Presentation of Jerusalem as a Queen and False Worship as Adultery in the OT." *Catholic Biblical Quarterly* 34 (1972): 403-416.

Freedman, David N. *The Anchor Bible Dictionary.* 6 vols. New York et al.: Doubleday, 1992.

Freedman, D. N. "The Chronicler's Purpose." *Catholic Biblical Quarterly* 23 (1961): 463-42.

Freedman, David N. "Headings in the Books of the Eighth Century Prophets." *Andrews University Seminary Studies* 25,1 (1987): 9-26.

Fretheim, Terence E. "Jonah and Theodicy." *Zeitschrift für die alttestamentliche Wissenschaft* 90 (1978): 227-37.

Frymer-Kensky, Tivka. "Pollution, Purification, and Purgation in Biblical Israel." Pages 399-414 in *The Word of the Lord Shall Go Forth; Essays in honor of David Noel Freedman in Celebration of His Sixtieth Birthday.* Edited by Carol L. Meyers and M. O'Connor. Eisenbrauns: Winona Lake, Ind, 1983.

Fuller, Russell. "The Form and Formation of the Book of the Twelve: The Evidence from the Judean Desert." Pages 86-101 in *Forming Prophetic Literature: Essays on Isaiah and the Twelve in Honor of John D. W. Watts.* Edited by James W. Watts and Paul R. House. Journal for the Old Testament Supplement Series 235. Sheffield: Sheffield Academic Press, 1996.

Galambush, Julie. *Jerusalem in the Book of Ezekiel: The City as Yahweh's Wife*. Society of Biblical Literature Dissertation Series 130. Atlanta: Scholars Press, 1992.

Galling, Kurt. "Die Exilswende in der Sicht des Propheten Sacharja." In *Studien zur Geschichte Israels im persischen Zeitalter*. Tübingen: Mohr, 1964.

Gerstenberger, Erhard S. "Gemeindebildung in Prophetenbüchern?" Pages 82-97 in Volkmar Fritz (ed.), *Prophet und Prophetenbuch*. Beihefte zur Zeitschrift für die Alttestamentliche Wissenschaft 185. Berlin: de Gruyter, 1989.

Gerstenberger, Erhard S. "Psalms in the Book of the Twelve: How Misplaced Are They?" Pages 254-62 in *SBL Seminar Papers, 2000*. Society of Biblical Literature Seminar Papers 38. Atlanta: Society of Biblical Literature, 2000.

Gerstenberger, Erhard S. *Psalms Part I*. Forms of the Old Testament Literature X. Grand Rapids: Eerdmans 1988; *Psalms, Part II*. Forms of the Old Testament Literature XV. Grand Rapids: Eerdmans, 2001.

Gese, Hartmut. "Jona ben Amittai und das Jonabuch." Pages 122-38 in *Alttestamentliche Studien*. Tübingen: J.C.B. Mohr [Paul Siebeck], 1991.

Ginzberg, Louis. *The Legends of the Jews*. 7 vols. Philadelphia: The Jewish Society of America, 1946-1955.

Gitay, Jeoshua. "Prophetic Criticism—'What are they Doing?' The Case of Isaiah—A Methodological Assessment." *Journal for the Study of the Old Testament* 96 (2001): 101-27.

Glasson, T. F. "The Final Question – In Nahum and Jonah." *Expository Times* 81 (1969/70): 54-55.

Glazier-McDonald, Beth. *Malachi: Divine Messenger*. Society of Biblical Literature Dissertation Series 98. Atlanta: Scholars Press, 1987.

Golka, F. W. *Jona*. Calwer Bibelkommentare. Stuttgart: Calwer, 1991.

Gowan, Donald E. *The Triumph of Faith in Habakkuk*. Atlanta: John Knox, 1976.

Grayson, A. Kirk. *Assyrian and Babylonian Chronicles*. Texts from Cuneiform Sources. Locust Valley, N.Y.: Augustin, 1975.

Green, William Scott. "Facing the One God Together." *Perspectives in Religious Studies* 26 (1999): 303-316.

Greenberg, Moshe. *Biblical Prose Prayer as a Window to the Popular Religion of Ancient Israel*. Berkeley: University of California, 1983.

Grossfeld, Bernard. *The Two Targums of Esther, translated with Apparatus and Notes*. The Aramaic Bible 18. Edinburgh: T&T Clark, 1991.

Gunkel, Hermann and Joachim Begrich. *Einleitung in die Psalmen*. Göttingen: Vandenhoeck & Ruprecht, 1933.

Gunkel, Hermann. "Die israelitische Literatur." Pages 53-112 in *Die orientalischen Literaturen.* Edited by P. Hinnenberg. Die Kultur der Gegenwart 1/7. Berlin: Tuebner, 1906.

Gunkel, Hermann. "The Prophets as Writers and Poets." In *Prophecy in Israel: Search for Identity.* Translated by J. L. Schaaf. Edited by D. L. Petersen. Issues in Religion and Theology 10. Philadelphia: Fortress, and London: SPCK, 1987.

Haak, Robert D. *Habakkuk.* Supplements to Vetus Testamentum 44. Leiden: Brill, 1991.

Hanson, Paul D. *The Dawn of Apocalyptic.* Philadelphia: Fortress, 1979.

Hare, D. R. A. (trans.) "The Lives of the Prophets." Pages 397-400 in *The Old Testament Pseudepigrapha. Volume 2.* Edited by J. H. Charlesworth. Garden City, New York: Doubleday, 1985.

Hartenstein, Friedhelm. *Die Unzugänglichkeit Gottes im Heiligtum. Jesaja 6 und der Wohnort JHWHs in der Jerusalemer Kulttradition.* Wissenschaftliche Monographien zum Alten (und Neuen) Testament 75. Neukirchen-Vluyn: Neukirchener Verlag, 1997.

Hartenstein, Friedhelm. "Wolkendunkel und Himmelsfeste: Zur Genese und Kosmologie der Vorstellung des himmlischen Heiligtums JHWHs." Pages 125-79 in *Das biblische Weltbild und seine altorientalischen Kontexte.* Edited by Bernd Janowski and Beate Ego; Forschungen zum Alten Testament 32. Tübingen: Mohr Siebeck, 2001.

Hayes, Katherine M. "'The Earth Mourns': Earth as Actor in a Prophetic Metaphor." Ph.D. dissertation, Catholic University of America, 1997.

Heinemann, Joseph. *Aggadot we-toledotehen.* Sifriyat Keter. Jerusalem: Keter Publishing House, 1974.

Heinemann, Joseph. *Prayer in the Talmud. Forms and Patterns.* Studia judaica 9. Berlin/New York: de Gruyter, 1977.

Heyns, Darlene. "Theology in Pictures: the Visions of Amos." Pages 132-72 in *"Feet on Level Ground": A South African Tribute of Old Testament Essays in Honor of Gerhard Hasel.* Edited by Koot van Wyk. Berrien Springs, Mich.: Hester, 1996.

Hiebert, Theodore. "The Book of Habakkuk." Pages 623-55 in *The New Interpreter's Bible.* Vol. 7; Nashville: Abingdon, 1996.

Hill, Andrew E. *Malachi.* Anchor Bible 25D. New York: Doubleday, 1998.

Hillers, Delbert R. "'The Roads to Zion Mourn' (Lam 1:4)." *Perspective* 12 (1971): 121-34.

Hoffmann, Yair. "The Day of the Lord as a Concept and a Term in the Prophetic Literature." *Zeitschrift für die alttestamentliche Wissenschaft* 93 (1981): 37-50.

House, Paul R. "Dramatic Coherence in Nahum, Habakkuk, and Zephaniah." Pages 195-208 in *Forming Prophetic Literature: Essays on*

Isaiah and the Twelve in Honor of John D. W. Watts. Edited by James W. Watts and Paul R. House. Journal for the Study of the Old Testament Supplement Series 235. Sheffield: Sheffield Academic Press, 1996.

House, Paul R. "The Character of God in the Book of the Twelve." Pages 125-145 in *Reading and Hearing the Book of the Twelve.* Edited by James D. Nogalski and Marvin A Sweeney. Society of Biblical Literature Symposium Series 15. Atlanta: Society of Biblical Literature, 2000.

House, Paul R. *The Unity of the Twelve.* Journal for the Study of the Old Testament Supplement Series 97. Sheffield: Sheffield Academic Press, 1990.

Hurtado, Larry W. "The Origin of the Nomina Sacra: A Proposal." *Journal of Biblical Literature* 117 (1998): 655-673.

Irvine, Stuart A. "Enmity in the House of God." *Journal of Biblical Literature* 117 (1998): 645-53.

Irvine, Stuart A. "Politics and Prophetic Commentary in Hosea 8:8-10." *Journal of Biblical Literature* 114 (1995): 292-94.

Japhet, Sara. *I & II Chronicles.* Old Testament Library. Louisville: Westminster/John Knox, 1993.

Jepsen, Alfred. "Kleine Beiträge zum Zwölfprophetenbuch." *Zeitschrift für die alttestamentliche Wissenschaft* 56 (1938): 85-100; 242-51.

Jeremias, Jörg. "Die Anfänge des Dodekapropheton: Hosea und Amos." Pages 34-54 in Jörg Jeremias. *Hosea und Amos: Studien zu den Anfängen des Dodekapropheton.* Forschungen zum Alten Testament 13. Tübingen: Mohr, 1996.

Jeremias, Jörg. "Die Deutung der Gerichtsworte Michas in der Exilszeit." *Zeitschrift für die alttestamentliche Wissenschaft* 83 (1971): 330–354.

Jeremias, Jörg. "The Interrelationship Between Amos and Hosea." Pages 171-86 in *Forming Prophetic Literature: Essays on Isaiah and the Twelve in Honor of John D. W. Watts.* Edited by James W. Watts and Paul R. House. Journal for the Old Testament Supplement Series 235. Sheffield: Sheffield Academic Press, 1996.

Jeremias, Jörg. *Der Prophet Hosea.* Das Alte Testament Deutsch 24,1. Göttingen: Vandenhoek & Ruprecht, 1983.

Jeremias, Jörg. *Der Prophet Amos.* Das Alte Testament Deutsch 24,2. Göttingen: Vandenhoeck & Ruprecht, 1995. Eng. trans. *The Book of Amos.* Old Testament Library. Louisville: Westminster John Knox, 1998.

Jeremias, Jörg. "Rezeptionsprozesse in der prophetischen Überlieferung - am Beispiel der Visionsberichte des Amos." Pages 29-44 in *Rezeption und Auslegung im Alten Testament und in seinem Umfeld.* Edited by Reinhard Gregor Kratz and Thomas Krüger. Orbis Biblicus et Orientalis

153. Freiburg, Schweiz / Göttingen: Universitätsverlag / Vandenhoeck & Ruprecht, 1997.

Jeremias, Jörg. "Das unzugängliche Heiligtum. Zur letzten Vision des Amos (Am 9,1-4)." Pages 244-56 in *Hosea und Amos: Studien zu den Anfängen des Dodekapropheton*. Forschungen zum Alten Testament 13; Tübingen: Mohr Siebeck, 1996.

Jones, Barry A. "The Book of the Twelve as a Witness to Ancient Biblical Interpretation." Pages 65-74 in *Reading and Hearing the Book of the Twelve*. Edited by James D. Nogalski and Marvin A. Sweeney. Society of Biblical Literature Symposium Series 15. Atlanta: Society of Biblical Literature, 2000.

Jones, Barry A. *The Formation of the Book of the Twelve: A Study in Text and Canon*. Society of Biblical Literature Dissertation Series 149. Atlanta: Scholars Press, 1995.

Jerome. Edited by W. H. Freemantle. *A Select Library of Nicene and Post-Nicene Fathers of the Christian Church*, 2/6. New York: Christian Literature, 1893.

Josephus. Translated by Ralph Marcus. Loeb Classical Library. London: Heinemann; Cambridge, Mass.: Harvard University Press, 1958.

Kaiser, Otto. *Das Buch des Propheten Jesaja, Kapitel 1 – 12*. Das Alte Testament Deutsch 17. 5th ed. Göttingen: Vandenhoeck & Ruprecht, 1981.

Kapelrud, Arvid S. *Joel Studies*. Uppsala Universitetsårkrift 4; Uppsala: A.-B. Lundequist; Leipzig: Otto Harrassowitz, 1948.

Katz, Steven T. "Holocaust: Judaic Theology and the." Pages 406-420 in *The Encyclopedia of Judaism*. Edited Jacob Neusner, Alan Avery-Peck, and William Scott Green. Leiden: E. J. Brill, 1999.

Keil, C. F. *Biblical Commentary on the Twelve Minor Prophets*. 2 vols. Edinburgh: T & T Clark, 1869.

Kessler, Rainer. *Micha*. Herders Theologischer Kommentar zum Alten Testament. Freiburg: Herder, 1999.

Kessler, Rainer. "Mirjam und die Prophetie der Perserzeit." Pages 64-72 in *Gott an den Rändern. Sozialgeschichtliche Perspektiven auf die Bibel. Für Willy Schottroff zum 65. Geburtstag*. Edited by U. Bail and R. Jost. Gütersloh: Chr. Kaiser/Gütersloher Verlagshaus, 1996.

Kessler, Rainer. "Zwischen Tempel und Tora. Das Michabuch im Diskurs der Perserzeit." *Biblische Notizen* 44 (2000): 21-36.

Klostermann, August. *Geschichte des Volkes Israel bis zur Restauration unter Esra und Nehemia*. Munich: C. H. Beck, 1896.

Knierim, Rolf. "Criticism of Literary Features, Form, Tradition, and Redaction." Pages 123-65 in *The Hebrew Bible and its Modern Interpre-*

ters. Edited by Douglas Knight and G. M. Tucker. Chico: Scholars Press, 1985.

Knierim, Rolf. Old Testament Form Criticism Reconsidered." *Interpretation* 27 (1973): 435-448.

Koch, Klaus. "Some Considerations on the Translation of *kapporet* in the Septuagint." Pages 65-75 in *Pomegranates and Golden Bells.* Edited by David P. Wright, David Noel Freedman, and Avi Hurvitz. Winona Lake, Ind.: Eisenbrauns, 1995.

Krause, Gerhard and Gerhard Müller, eds. *Theologische Realenzyklopädie.* Berlin: de Gruyter, 1977ff.

Kristeva, Julia. *Desire in Language: A Semiotic Approach to Literature and Art.* Edited by L. S. Roudiez. Translated by T. Gora, A. Jardine, and L. S. Roudiez. New York: Columbia University Press, 1980; French editon 1969.

Kutsko, John F. *Between Heaven and Earth: Divine Presence and Absence in the Book of Ezekiel.* Biblical and Judaic Studies 7; Winona Lake, Ind.: Eisenbrauns, 2000.

Landy, Francis. *Hosea.* Readings: A New Biblical Commentary. Sheffield: Sheffield Academic Press, 1995.

Lang, Bernhard. *Ezechiel. Der Prophet und das Buch.* Erträge der Forschung 153. Darmstadt: Wissenschaftliche Buchgesellschaft 1981.

Langevin, Paul Emile. "Sur l'origine du 'Jour de Yahvé.'" *Sciences Ecclésiastiques* 18 (1966): 359-370.

Lee, Andrew Y. "The Canonical Unity of the Scroll of the Minor Prophets." Ph. D. diss., Baylor University, 1985.

Lemaire, André and Magne Saebø (eds.) *Congress Volume: Oslo 1998.* Supplements to Vetus Testamentum 80. Leiden: Brill, 2000.

Lescow, Theodor. *Das Buch Maleachi: Texttheorie—Auslegung—Kanontheorie.* Arbeiten zur Theologie 75. Stuttgart: Calwer, 1993.

Lescow, Theodor. "Die Komposition des Buches Jona," *Biblische Notizen* 65 (1992): 29-34.

Levin, Christoph. "Amos und Jerobeam I," *Vetus Testamentum* 45 (1995): 307-317.

Lewis, C. S. *Reflections on the Psalms.* New York: Harcourt, Brace, 1958.

Lichtheim, Miriam. *Ancient Egyptian Literature*, Vol. 3: *The Late Period.* Berkeley: University of California, 1980.

Linville, James R. "Visions and Voices: Amos 7-9." *Biblica* 80 (1999): 22-42.

Lohfink, Norbert. "Gab es eine deuteronomistische Bewegung?" Pages 65-142 in *Studien zum Deuteronomium und zur deuteronomistischen Literatur III* Stuttgarter Biblische Aufsatzbände 20. Stuttgart: Katholisches Bibelwerk, 1995.

Marshall, I. Howard. "An Assessment of Recent Developments." Pages 1-21 in *It Is Written: Scripture Citing Scripture*. Edited by D. A. Carson and H. G. M. Williamson. Cambridge: Cambridge University Press, 1988.

Mason, Rex A. "The Relation of Zech 9-14 to Proto-Zechariah." *Zeitschrift für die alttestamentliche Wissenschaft* 88 (1976): 227-39.

Mason, Rex. *Zephaniah, Habakkuk, Joel*. Old Testament Guides. Sheffield: JSOT Press, 1994.

Mathias, Dietmar. "Beobachtungen zur fünften Vision des Amos (9,1-4)." Pages 150-74 in *Gedenkt an das Wort*. Edited by Christoph Kähler and Werner Vogler. Leipzig: Evangelische Verlagsanstalt, 1999.

Mays, James L. *Micah: A Commentary*. Old Testament Library. London: SCM, 1976.

Macintosh, A. A. *Hosea*. International Critical Commentary. Edinburgh: T & T Clark, 1997.

Magonet, J. *Form and Meaning. Studies in Literary Techniques in the Book of Jonah*. 2d ed. Sheffield: Sheffield Academic Press, 1983.

Mettinger, Tryggve N. D. *The Dethronement of Sabaoth: Studies in the Shem and Kabod Theologies*. Translated by Frederick H. Cryer. Coniectanea Biblica Old Testament Series 18. Lund: C. W. K. Gleerup, 1982.

Metzner, Gabriele. *Kompositionsgeschichte des Michabuches*. Frankfurt: Lang, 1998.

Meyers, Carol L. and Eric M. Meyers. *Haggai, Zechariah 1-8*. Anchor Bible 25 B. Garden City: Doubleday, 1987.

Meyers, Carol L. and Meyers, Eric M. *Zechariah 9-14*. Anchor Bible 25C; New York: Doubleday, 1993.

Meyers, Eric."The Persian Period and the Judean Restoration: From Zerubbabel to Nehemiah." Pages 509-21 in *Ancient Israelite Religion*. Edited by Patrick Miller, Paul Hanson and S. Dean McBride, Jr. Philadelphia: Fortress, 1987.

Miller, Patrick D. "Divine Council and the Prophetic Call to War." *Vetus Testamentum* 18 (1968): 100-107.

Mowinckel, Sigmund. *Psalmenstudien III* (1923). Repr. Amsterdam: Schippers 1961.

Miscall, Peter D. *Isaiah*. Readings. Sheffield: JSOT Press, 1993.

Nägele, Sabine. *Laubhütte Davids und Wolkensohn: Eine auslegungsgeschichtliche Studie zu Amos 9:11 in der jüdischen und christlichen Exegese*. Arbeiten zur Geschichte des antiken Judentums und des Urchristentums 24; Leiden, et al.: Brill, 1995.

Neusner, Jacob. *The Talmud of the Land of Israel. A Preliminary Translation and Explanation*. Vol. 18; *Besah and Taanit*. Chicago Studies in the History of Judaism. Chicago: The University of Chicago, 1987.

Newsom, Carol. *Songs of the Sabbath Sacrifice: A Critical Edition.* Harvard Semitic Studies 7. Atlanta: Scholars, 1985.

Nicholson, Ernest W. *Preaching to the Exiles.* Oxford: Blackwells, 1960.

Nissinen, Martti. *References to Prophecy in Neo-Assyrian Sources.* State Archives of Assyrian Studies 7. Helsinki: The Neo-Assyrian Text Corpus Project, 1998.

Nissinen, Martti. "Spoken, Written, Quoted, and Invented: Orality and Writtenness in Ancient Near Eastern Prophecy." Pages 235-71 in *Writings and Speech in Israelite and Ancient Near Eastern Prophecy.* Edited by Ehud Ben Zvi and Michael H. Floyd. Atlanta: Society of Biblical Literature, 2000.

Noble, Paul R. "Amos and Amaziah in Context: Synchronic and Diachronic Approaches to Amos 7-8." *Catholic Biblical Quarterly* 60 (1998): 423-439.

Nogalski, James D. "The Day(s) of Yahweh in the Book of the Twelve." Pages 617-41 in *SBL Seminar Papers, 1999.* Society of Biblical Literature Seminar Papers 38. Atlanta: Society of Biblical Literature, 1999.

Nogalski, James D. "Intertextuality in the Twelve." Pages 102-124 in *Forming Prophetic Literature: Essays on Isaiah and the Twelve in Honor of John D. W. Watts.* Edited by James W. Watts and Paul R. House. Journal for the Old Testament Supplement Series 235. Sheffield: Sheffield Academic Press, 1996.

Nogalski, James D. "Jeremiah and the Twelve: Intertextual Observations and Postulations." Paper presented at the annual meeting of the Society of Biblical Literature. Orlando, Fla., November 22, 1998.

Nogalski, James D. "Joel as 'Literary Anchor' for the Book of the Twelve." Pages 91-109 in *Reading and Hearing the Book of the Twelve.* Society of Biblical Literature Symposium Series 15. Atlanta: Society of Biblical Literature, 2000.

Nogalski, James D. *Literary Precursors to the Book of the Twelve.* Beihefte zur Zeitschrift für die alttestamentliche Wissenschaft 217. Berlin, New York: de Gruyter, 1993.

Nogalski, James D. "The Problematic Suffixes of Amos 9:11." *Vetus Testamentum* 43 (1993): 411-418.

Nogalski, James D. *Redactional Processes in the Book of the Twelve.* Beihefte zur Zeitschrift für die alttestamentliche Wissenschaft 218. Berlin, New York: de Gruyter, 1993.

Nogalski, James D. "The Redactional Shaping of Nahum 1 for the Book of the Twelve." Pages 193-202 in *Among the Prophets; Language, Image and Structure in the Prophetic Writings.* Edited by Philip R. Davies and David J. A. Clines. Sheffield: Sheffield Academic Press, 1993.

Nogalski, James D. "The Use of Stichwörter as a Redactional Unification Technique in the Book of the Twelve." Th. M. thesis, Baptist Theologoical Seminary, Ruschlikon, Switzerland.

Nogalski, James D. "Zephanaiah 3: A Redactional Text for a Developing Corpus." Pages 207-18 in *Schriftauslegung in der Schrift, FS für O.H. Steck.* Edited by R.G. Kratz, Th. Krüger and K. Schmid. Beiheft zur Zeitschrift für die alttestamentliche Wissenschaft 300; Berlin and New York: de Gruyter, 2000.

O'Brien, Julia M. "Judah as Wife and Husband: Deconstructing Gender in Malachi." *Journal of Biblical Literature* 115 (1996): 241-250.

O'Brien, Julia. *Priest and Levite in Malachi.* Society of Biblical Literature Dissertation Series 121. Atlanta: Scholars Press, 1990.

O'Day, Gail. "Jeremiah 9:22-23 and 1 Corinthians 1:26-31. A Study in Intertextuality." *Journal of Biblical Literature* 109 (1990): 259-67.

Odell, Margaret S. "Genre and Persona in Ezekiel 24:15-24." Pages 195-220 in *The Book of Ezekiel: Theological and Anthropological Perspectives.* Edited by Margaret Odell and John Strong; Society of Biblical Literature Symposium Series 9. Atlanta: Scholars Press, 2000.

Odell, Margaret S. "The Prophets and the End of Hosea." Pages 158-70 in *Forming Prophetic Literature: Essays on Isaiah and the Twelve in Honor of John D. W. Watts.* Edited by James W. Watts and Paul R. House. Journal for the Old Testament Supplement Series 235. Sheffield: Sheffield Academic Press, 1996.

Odell, Margaret S. "Who were the Prophets in Hosea?" *Horizons in Biblical Theology* 18 (1996): 78-95.

Odell, Margaret S. "You Are What You Eat: Ezekiel and the Scroll." *Journal of Biblical Literature* 117 (1998): 229-48.

Ogden, Graham S. "Joel 4 and Prophetic Responses to National Laments." *Journal for the Study of the Old Testament* 26 (1983): 97-106.

Overholt, Thomas W. "The End of Prophecy: No Players without a Program." *Journal for the Study of the Old Testament* 42 (1988): 103-115.

Owen, Henry. *Critica Sacra; or, a Short Introduction to Hebrew Criticism.* London: W. Bowyer and J. Nichols, 1774.

Paas, Stefan."Seeing and Singing: Visions and Hymns in the Book of Amos." *Vetus Testamentum* 52 (2002): 253-274.

Parker, Simon B. *The Pre-Biblical Narrative Tradition. Essays on the Ugaritic Poems* Keret *and* Aqhat. Society of Biblical Literature Sources for Biblical Study 24. Atlanta: Scholars Press, 1989.

Parpola, Simo. *Assyrian Prophecies.* State Archives of Assyria 9. Helsinki: Helsinki University Press, 1997.

Paul, Shalom M. *Amos.* Hermeneia; Minneapolis: Fortress, 1991.

Paul, Shalom M. "Heavenly Tablets and the Book of Life." *Journal of the Near Eastern Society of Columbia University* 5 (1973): 345-53.

Penchansky, David and Paul L. Redditt, eds. *Shall Not the Judge of all the Earth Do What Is Right: Studies on the Nature of God in Tribute to James L. Crenshaw.* Winona Lake: Eisenbrauns, 2000.

Penchansky, David. *What Rough Beast? Images of God in the Hebrew Bible.* Louisville: Westminster John Knox, 1999.

Perlitt, Lothar. *Bundestheologie im Alten Testament.* Wissenschaftliche Monographien zum Alten und Neuen Testament 36. Neukirchen-Vluyn: Neukirchener Verlag, 1969.

Person, Raymond F. *Second Zechariah and the Deuteronomistic School.* Journal for the Study of the Old Testament Supplement Series 167. Sheffield: JSOT Press, 1993.

Petersen, David L. "A Book of the Twelve?" Pages 1-10 in *Reading and Hearing the Book of the Twelve.* Edited by James D. Nogalski and Marvin A. Sweeney. Society of Biblical Literature Symposium Series 15. Atlanta; Society of Biblical Literature, 2000.

Peterson, David L. *Haggai and Zechariah 1-8.* Old Testament Library. Philadelphia: Westminster, 1984.

Petersen, David L. *Zechariah 9-14 and Malachi.* Old Testament Library. Louisville: Westminster / John Knox, 1995.

Phillips, Elaine A. "Serpent Intertexts: Tantalizing Twists in the Tales." *Bulletin for Biblical Research* 10 (2000): 233-45.

Polanski, Donald C. "Reflections on a Mosaic Covenant: The Eternal Covenant (Isaiah 24.5) and Intertextuality." *Journal for the Study of the Old Testament* 77 (1998): 55-73.

Prinsloo, Willem S. "The Unity of the Book of Joel." *Zeitschrift für die alttestamentliche Wissenschaft* 104 (1992): 66-81.

Rad, Gerhard von. "Origin of the Concept of the Day of Yahweh." *Journal of Semitic Studies* 4 (1959): 97-108.

Raven, John H. *Old Testament Introduction: General and Special.* New York: Revell, 1906.

Roberts, Colin Henderson. "Nomina Sacra: Origins and Significance." Pages 26-48 in *Manuscript, Society and Belief in Early Christian Egypt.* London: Oxford University Press, 1979.

Roberts, J. J. M. *Nahum, Habakkuk, and Zephaniah.* Old Testament Library. Louisville: Westminster/John Knox, 1991.

Redditt, Paul L. "The Book of Joel and Peripheral Prophecy." *Catholic Biblical Quarterly* 48 (1986): 225-40.

Redditt, Paul L. *Haggai, Zechariah, Malachi.* New Century Bible. London: HarperCollins, and Grand Rapids: Eerdmans, 1995.

Redditt, Paul L. "The Production and Reading of the Book of the Twelve." Pages 11-33 in *Reading and Hearing the Book of the Twelve*. Edited by James D. Nogalski and Marvin A Sweeney. Society of Biblical Literature Symposium Series 15. Atlanta: Society of Biblical Literature, 2000.

Redditt, Paul L. "Recent Research on the Book of the Twelve as One Book." *Currents in Research: Biblical Studies* 9 (2001): 47-80.

Redditt, Paul L. "Zechariah 9-14, Malachi, and the Redaction of the Book of the Twelve." Pages 245-68 in *Forming Prophetic Literature: Essays on Isaiah and the Twelve in Honor of John D. W. Watts*. Edited by James W. Watts and Paul R. House. Journal for the Old Testament Supplement Series 235. Sheffield: Sheffield Academic Press, 1996.

Rendtorff, Rolf. "Alas for the Day! The 'Day of the LORD' in the Book of the Twelve." Pages 186-97 in *God in the Fray: A Tribute to Walter Brueggemann*. Edited by T. Linafelt and T. K. Beal. Minneapolis: Fortress Press, 1998.

Rendtorff, Rolf. "How to Read the Book of the Twelve." Pages 75-87 in *Reading and Hearing the Book of the Twelve*. Edited by James D. Nogalski and Marvin A Sweeney. Society of Biblical Literature Symposium Series 15. Atlanta: Society of Biblical Literature, 2000.

Reventlow, Henning Graf. *Liturgie und prophetisches Ich bei Jeremia*. Gütersloh: Mohn, 1963.

Rosenberg, Joel. "Jeremiah and Ezekiel." Pages 184-206 in *The Literary Guide to the Bible*. Edited by Robert Alter and Frank Kermode. Cambridge: Belknap, 1987.

Rudolph, Wilhelm. *Joel, Amos, Obadja, Jona*. Kommentar zum Alten Testament 13,2. Gütersloh: Mohn, 1971.

Rudolph, Wilhelm. *Haggai—Sacharja 1—8—Sacharja 9—14—Maleachi*. Kommentar zum Alten Testament 13,4. Gütersloh: Mohn, 1976.

Rudolph, Wilhelm. *Hosea*. Kommentar zum Alten Testament XIII,1. Gütersloh: Mohn, 1966.

Saebø, Magne. *Sacharja 9-14, Untersuchungen von Text und Form*. Neukirchen-Vluyn: Neukirchener Verlag, 1969.

Sailhamer, John H. *Introduction to Old Testament Theology: A Canonical Approach*. Grand Rapids: Zondervan, 1995.

Sasson, Jack M. *Jonah*. Anchor Bible 24B. New York: Doubleday, 1990.

Scharbert, Josef. "Formgeschichte und Exegese von Ex 34,6f und seine Parallelen." *Biblica* 34 (1957): 130-50.

Schart, Aaron. "Combining Prophetic Oracles in Mari Letters and Jeremiah 36." *Journal of the Ancient Near Eastern Society* 23 (1995): 75-93.

Schart, Aaron. *Die Entstehung des Zwölfprophetenbuchs*. Beihefte zur Zeitschrift für die alttestamentliche Wissenschaft 260. Berlin, New York: de Gruyter, 1998.

Schart, Aaron. "Zur Redaktionsgeschichte des Zwölfprophetenbuches." *Verkündigung und Forschung* 43 (1998): 13-33.

Schmidt, Werner H. "Die deuteronomistische Redaktion des Amosbuches. Zu den theologischen Unterschieden zwischen dem Propheten und seinem Sammler." *Zeitschrift für die alttestamentliche Wissenschaft* 77 (1965): 168–193.

Schmitt, John J. "The Gender of Ancient Israel" *Journal for the Study of the Old Testament* 26 (1983): 115-25.

Schmitt, John J. "The Motherhood of God and Zion as Mother." *Revue biblique* 92 (1985): 557-569.

Schmitt, John J. "The Wife of God in Hos 2" *Biblical Research* 39 (1989) 5-18.

Schneider, Dale. "The Unity of the Book of the Twelve." Ph. D. diss., Yale University, 1979.

Schniedewind, William M. *The Word of God in Transition: From Prophet to Exegete in the Second Temple Period*. Journal for the Study of the Old Testament Supplement Series 197. Sheffield: Sheffield Academic Press, 1995.

Schultz, Richard L. *The Search for Quotation: Verbal Parallels in the Prophets*. Journal for the Study of the Old Testament: Supplement Series 180. Sheffield: Sheffield Academic Press, 1999.

Schulz-Rauch, M. *Hosea und Jeremia. Zur Wirkungsgeschichte des Hoseabuches*. Calwer Theologische Monographien 16. Stuttgart: Calwer Verlag, 1996.

Schunck, Klaus Dietrich. "Die Eschatologie der Propheten des Alten Testaments und ihre Wandlung in exilisch-nach-exilischer Zeit." Pages 116-32 in *Studies on Prophecy*. Supplements to Vetus Testamentum 26. Leiden: Brill, 1974.

Schunck, Klaus Dietrich. "Strukturlinien in der Entwicklung der Vorstellung vom Tag Jahwes." *Vetus Testamentum* 14 (1964): 319-330.

Schürer, Emil. *The History of the Jewish People in the Age of Jesus Christ (175 B.C.—A.D. 135)*. Revised and edited by G. Vermes, F. Millar, and M. Goodman. 3 vols. Edinburgh: T&T Clark, 1973-1987.

Schwienhorst-Schönberger, L. "Zion – Ort der Tora. Überlegungen zu Mic 4,1-3." Pages 109-125 in *Zion – Ort der Begegnung, Festschrift für L. Klein zur Vollendung des 65. Lebensjahres*. Bonner biblische Beiträger 90. Bodenheim: Athenäum Hain Hanstein, 1993.

Schwemmer, Anna Maria. *Die Viten der kleinen Propheten und der Propheten aus den Geschichtsbüchern. Übersetzung und Kommentar. Vol. 2* of *Studien zu den frühjüdischen Prophetenlegenden Vitae Prophetarum. Texte und Studien zur antiken Judentum* 50. Tübingen: Mohr Siebeck, 1996.

Scoralick, Ruth. *Gottes Güte und Gottes Zorn: Die Gottesprädikationen in Ex 34,6f. und ihre intertextuellen Beziehungen zum Zwölfprophetenbuch.* Herders Biblische Studien 33. Freiburg: Herder, 2002.

Seifert, E *Tochter und Vater im Alten Testament. Eine ideologiegeschichtliche Untersuchung zur Verfügungsgewalt von Vätern über ihre Töchter.* Neukirchener Theologische Dissertationen und Habilitationen 9. Neukirchen-Vluyn: Neukirchener Verlag, 1997.

Sedlmeier, F. "Die Universalisierung der Heilshoffnung nach Micha 4,1-5." *Trierer theologische Studien* 107 (1998): 62- 81.

Setel, T. D. "Prophets and Pornography." Pages 86-95 in *Feminist Interpretation of the Bible.* Edited by L.M. Russell. Oxford: Basil Blackwell, 1985.

Seybold, Klaus. *Satirische Prophetie: Studien zum Buch Zephanja.* Stuttgarter Bibelstudien 120. Stuttgart: Katholisches Bibelwerk, 1985.

Sherwood, Yvonne. "Of Fruit and Corpses and Wordplay Visions: Picturing Amos 8.1-3." *Journal for the Study of the Old Testament* 92 (2001): 5-27.

Siegert, Folker. *Drei hellenistisch-jüdische Predigten. Ps.-Philon, "Über Jona," "Über Simson" und "Über die Gottesbezeichnung 'wohltätig verzehrendes Feuer.'"* Vol. I *Übersetzung aus dem Armenischen und sprachliche Erläuterungen.* Wissenschaftliche Untersuchungen zum Neuen Testament 20; Tübingen: J.C.B. Mohr [Paul Siebeck], 1980. Vol. II: *Kommentar nebst Beobachtungen zur hellenistischen Vorgeschichte der Bibelhermeneutik.* Wissenschaftliche Untersuchungen zum Neuen Testament 61. Tübingen: J.C.B. Siebeck [Paul Mohr], 1992.

Smend, Rudolf *Der Prophet Ezechiel.* Kurtzgefasstes exegetisches Handbuch. Leipzig: S. Hirzel, 1880.

Smith, Ralph L. *Micah-Malachi.* Word Biblical Commentary; Waco: Word, 1984.

Snyman, S. D. "Yom (YHWH) in the Book of Obadiah." In Goldene Äpfel in silbernen Schalen. Beiträge zur Erforschung des Alten Testaments und des antiken Judentums 20. Frankfurt: Lang, 1992.

Sommer, Benjamin D. "Did Prophecy Cease? Evaluating a Reevaluation." *Journal of Biblical Literature* 115 (1996): 31-47.

Sommer, Benjamin D. "Exegesis, Allusion and Intertextuality in the Hebrew Bible: A Response to Lyle Eslinger." *Vetus Testament* 46 (1996): 479-89.

Spieckermann, Hermann. "Dies irae: der alttestamentliche Befund und seine Vorgeschichte." *Vetus Testamentum* 39 (1989): 194-208.

Spiegelberg, Wilhelm *Die sogenannte demotische Chronik des Pap. 215 der Bibliotheque Nationale zu Paris, nebst den auf der Ruckseite des Papyrus stehenden Texten.* Demotische Studien 7. Leipzig, 1914.

Steck, Odil Hannes. *Der Abschluss der Propheite im Alten Testament: Ein Versuch zur Frage des Vorgeschichte des Kanons.* Biblisch-Theologische Studien 17. Neukirchen: Neukirchener Verlag, 1991.

Steck, Odil Hannes. *Die Prophetenbücher und ihr theologisches Zeugnis: Wege der Nachfolge und Fährten zur Antwort.* Tübingen: Mohr, 1996. (English translation: *The Prophetic Books and their Theological Witness.* St. Louis: Chalice, 2000).

Stemberger, Günter. *Einleitung in Talmud und Midrasch.* 8th ed. Munich: C.H. Beck, 1992.

Steuernagel, Carl. *Lehrbuch der Einleitung in das Alten Testament* Tübingen: Mohr, 1912.

Stowasser, Martin. "Am 5,25-27; 9,11f. in der Qumranüberlieferung und in der Apostelgeschichte: Text- und traditionsgeschichtliche Überlegungen zu 4Q174 (Florilegium) III 12/CD VII 16/Apg 7,42b-43; 15,16-18." *Zeitschrift für die Neutestamentliche Wissenschaft und die Kunde der älteren Kirche* 92 (2001): 47-63.

Striek, Marco. *Das vordeuteronomistische Zephanjabuch.* Beiträge zur biblischen Exegese und Theologie 29. Frankfurt am Main: Lang, 1999.

Stuart, Douglas. *Hosea-Jonah.* Word Biblical Commentary 31; Waco: Word, 1987.

Stuart, Douglas. "The Sovereign's Day of Conquest." *Bulletin of the American Schools of Oriental Research* 221 (1976): 159-164.

Sweeney, Marvin A. "Form Criticism." Pages 58-89 in *To Each Its Own Meaning: Biblical Criticisms and their Application.* Edited by S. L. McKenzie and S. R. Haynes. Revised and expanded edition. Louisville: Westminster John Knox, 1999.

Sweeney, Marvin A. "Formation and Form in Prophetic Literature." Pages 113-26 in *Old Testament Interpretation: Past, Present and Future.* Edited by J. L. Mays, D. L. Petersen, and K. H. Richards. Nashville: Abingdon, 1995.

Sweeney, Marvin A. *Isaiah 1-39, with an Introduction to Prophetic Literature.* Forms of the Old Testament Literature 16. Grand Rapids and Cambridge: Eerdmans, 1996.

Sweeney, Marvin A. *King Josiah of Judah: The Lost Messiah of Israel.* New York: Oxford, 2001.

Sweeney, Marvin A. "Micah's Debate with Isaiah." *Journal for the Study of the Old Testament* 93 (2001): 111-24.

Sweeney, Marvin A. "The Place and Function of Joel in the Book of the Twelve." Pages 570-95 in *SBL Seminar Papers, 1999.* Society of Biblical Literature Seminar Papers 38. Atlanta: Society of Biblical Literature, 1999.

Sweeney, Marvin A. "Sequence and Interpretation in the Book of the Twelve." Pages 49-64 in *Reading and Hearing the Book of the Twelve.* Edited by James D. Nogalski and Marvin A Sweeney. Society of Biblical Literature Symposium Series 15. Atlanta: Society of Biblical Literature, 2000.

Sweeney, Marvin A. "Three Recent European Studies on the Composition of the Book of the Twelve." *Review of Biblical Literature* 1 (1991): 22-37.

Sweeney, Marvin A. *The Twelve Prophets.* 2 vols. Berit Olam. Collegeville: Liturgical Press, 2000.

Sykes, Seth. *Time and Space in Haggai-Zechariah 1-8: A Bakhtinian Analysis of a Prophetic Chronicle.* Studies in Biblical Literature 24. New York: Lang, 2002.

Terrien, Samuel. *The Elusive Presence: The Heart of Biblical Theology.* Religious Perspectives 26. San Francisco: Harper and Row, 1978.

Tilley, Terrence W. *The Evils of Theodicy.* Eugene, Oregon: Wipf and Stock, 2000.

Toorn, Karel van der. "From the Oral to the Written: The Case of Old Babylonian Prophecy." Pages 219-34 in *Writings and Speech in Israelite and Ancient Near Eastern Prophecy.* Edited by Ehud Ben Zvi and Michael H. Floyd: Atlanta: Society of Biblical Literature, 2000.

Toorn, Karel van der. "Mesopotamian prophecy between immanence and transcendence: a comparison of Old Babylonian and Neo-Assyrian Prophecy." Pages 1-87 in *Prophecy in its Ancient Near Eastern Context.* Edited by Martti Nissinen. Society of Biblical Literature Symposium Series 13. Atlanta: Society of Biblical Literature, 2000.

Torrey, C. C. *Pseudo-Ezekiel and the Original Prophecy.* New Haven: Yale University, 1930. Repr. Library of Biblical Studies. New York: Ktav, 1970.

Tov, Emanuel. *The Text-critical Use of the Septuagint in Biblical Research.* Jerusalem Biblical Studies 8. 2d revised and enlarged ed. Jerusalem: Simor, 1997.

Trobisch, David. *Die Endredaktion des Neuen Testaments: Eine Untersuchung zur Entstehung der christlichen Bibel.* Novum Testamentum et Orbis Antiquus 31; Freiburg (Schweiz) / Göttingen: Universitätsverlag / Vandenhoeck & Ruprecht, 1996.

Tucker, Gene M. "Prophetic Superscriptions and the Growth of a Canon." Pages 56-70 in *Canon and Authority: Essays in Old Testament Religion and Theology.* Edited by George W. Coats and Burke O. Long. Philadelphia: Fortress, 1977.

Tuell, Steven S. "Ezekiel 40—42 as Verbal Icon." *Catholic Biblical Quarterly* 58 (1996): 649-64.

Tuell, Steven S. *First and Second Chronicles.* Interpretation. Louisville: John Knox, 2001.

Tuell, Steven S. "Haggai-Zechariah: Prophecy After the Manner of Ezekiel." Pages 263-86 in *SBL Seminar Papers, 2000.* Society of Biblical Literature Seminar Papers 38. Atlanta: Society of Biblical Literature, 2000.

Tuell, Steven S. "The Rivers of Paradise: Ezek 47:1-12 and Gen 2:10-14." Pages 171-89 in *God Who Creates.* Edited by S. Dean McBride, Jr. and William Brown. Grand Rapids: Eerdmans, 2000.

Urbach, Ephraim. "Teshuvat anshe ninive wehaviquah hayehudy nosry." *Tarbiz* 20 (1949/50) 118-122.

Utzschneider, Helmut. *Künder oder Schreiber? Eine These zum Problem der "Schriftprophetie" auf Grund von Maleachi 1,6 – 2,9.* Beiträge zur Erforschung des Alten Testaments und des antiken Judentum19. Frankfurt: Lang 1989.

Van Leeuwen, Raymond C. "Scribal Wisdom and Theodicy in the Book of the Twelve." Pages 31-49 in *In Search of Wisdom: Essays in Memory of John G. Gammie.* Edited by Leo G. Perdue, Bernard Scott, and William Wiseman. Louisville: John Knox, 1993.

Van Leeuwen, Raymond C. "The Prophecy of the Yom YHWH in Amos v 18-20." Pages 113-34 in *Language and Meaning.* Oudtestamentische Studien 19. Leiden: Brill, 1974.

Vermes, Geza. *The Dead Sea Scrolls in English.* 4th ed. London: Penguin, 1995.

Vieweger, Dieter. *Die literarischen Bezüge zwischen den Büchern Jeremia und Ezechiel.* Beiträge zur Erforschung des Alten Testaments und des antiken Judentums 26; Frankfurt: Peter Lang, 1993.

Wacholder, Ben Zion. "Ezekiel and Ezekielianism as Progenitors of Essenianism." Pages 186-96 in *The Dead Sea Scrolls: Forty Years of Research.* Edited by Devorah Dimant and Uriel Rappaport. Leiden: Brill, 1992.

Watts, James W. "Psalmody in Prophecy: Habakkuk 3 in Context." Pages 209-223 in *Forming Prophetic Literature: Essays on Isaiah and the Twelve in Honor of John D. W. Watts.* Edited by James W. Watts and Paul R. House. Journal for the Old Testament Supplement Series 235. Sheffield: Sheffield Academic Press, 1996.

Watts, John D. W. "A Frame for the Book of the Twelve." Pages 209-217 in *Reading and Hearing the Book of the Twelve.* Edited by James D. Nogalski and Marvin A Sweeney. Society of Biblical Literature Symposium Series 15. Atlanta: Society of Biblical Literature, 2000.

Watts, John D. W. "Superscriptions and Incipits in the Book of the Twelve." Pages 110-24 in *Reading and Hearing the Book of the Twelve*. Edited by James D. Nogalski and Marvin A. Sweeney. Society of Biblical Literature Symposium Series 15. Atlanta: Society of Biblical Literature, 2000.

Weimar, P. "Obadja. Eine Redaktionskritische Analyse." *Biblische Notizen* 27 (1985): 18-99.

Weiser, Artur. *Das Buch der zwölf kleinen Propheten.* Das Alte Testament Deutsch 24,1. 2nd ed. Göttingen: Vandenhoeck & Ruprecht, 1956.

Wellhausen, Julius. *Die kleinen Propheten.* 3rd ed. Berlin: Georg Reimer, 1898.

Williamson, H. G. M. *Israel in the Books of Chronicles.* Cambridge: Cambridge University Press, 1977.

Willey, P. T. *Remember the Former Things. The Recollection of Previous Texts in Second Isaiah.* Society of Biblical Literature Dissertation Series 161. Atlanta: Scholars Press, 1997.

Willi-Plein, Ina. *Vorformen der Schriftexegese innerhalb des Alten Testaments.* Beiheft zur Zeitschrift für die alttestamentliche Wissenschaft 123. Berlin: de Gruyter 1971.

Williamson, Clark M. *Way of Blessing Way of Life: A Christian Theology.* St. Louis: Chalice, 1999.

Willis, John T. "The Structure, Setting and Interrelationship of the Pericopes in the Book of Micah." *Dissertation Abstracts* 22, Vanderbilt University, 1966.

Willis, John T. "Thought on a Redactional Analysis on the Book of Micah." *SBL Seminar Papers, 1978.* Society of Biblical Literature Seminar Papers 15. Chico, Calif.: Scholars Press, 1978.

Wolfe, Rolland E. "The Editing of the Book of the Twelve." Ph. D. diss., Harvard University, 1933.

Wolfe, Rolland E. "The Editing of the Book of the Twelve." *Zeitschrift für die alttestamentliche Wissenschaft* 53 (1935): 90-129.

Wolff, Hans Walter. *Dodekapropheton 2: Joel und Amos.* Biblischer Kommentar Altes Testament XIV,2. Neukirchen-Vluyn: Neukirchener Verlag, 1969. Eng. trans. *Joel and Amos.* Hermeneia; Philadelphia: Fortress, 1977.

Wolff, Hans Walter. *Dodekaproheton: Micha.* Biblischer Kommentar Altes Testament XIV,4. Neukirchen-Vluyn: Neukirchener Verlag, 1982.

Wolff, Hans Walter. *Haggai: Eine Auslegung.* Biblische Studien 1. Neukirchen-Vluyn: Neukirchener Verlag, 1951.

Wolff, Hans W. Hosea. Biblisher Kommentar, Altes Testament XIV/1. 2d ed. Neukirchen-Vluyn: Neukirchener Verlag, 1965; Eng. Translation. *Hosea.* Hermeneia. Philadelphia: Fortress, 1974.

Wolff, Hans Walter. *Obadiah and Jonah: A Commentary.* Minneapolis: Augsburg, 1986.

Wright, Christopher J. H. *God's People in God's Land: Family, Land, and Property in the Old Testament.* Grand Rapids: Eerdmans, 1990.

Yadin, Yigael. *The Temple Scroll. Volume 1: Introduction.* Jerusalem: Israel Exploration Society, 1983.

Yee, Gale A. *Composition and Tradition in the Book of Hosea: A Redaction Critical Investigation.* Society of Biblical Literature Dissertation Series 102. Atlanta: Scholars Press, 1987.

Zapff, Burkard M. "The Perspective of the Nations in the Book of Micah as a 'Systematization' of the of the Nations' Role in Joel, Jonah, and Nahum? Reflections on a Context-Oriented Exegesis in the Book of the Twelve." Pages 596-616 in *SBL Seminar Papers, 1999.* Society of Biblical Literature Seminar Papers 1999. Atlanta: Society of Biblical Literature, 1999.

Zapff, Burkard M. *Redaktionsgeschichtliche Studien zum Michabuch im Kontext des Dodekapropheton.* Beihefte zur Zeitschrift für die alttestamentliche Wissneschaft 256. Berlin, New York: de Gruyter, 1997.

Zapff, Burkhard M. "Schriftgelehrte Prophetie – Jes 13 und die Komposition des Jesajabuches." *Forschungen zur Bibel* 74 (1995): 56.

Zenger, Erich. "'Durch Menschen zog ich sie …' (Hos 11,4). Beobachtungen zum Verständnis des prophetischen Amtes im Hoseabuch." Pages 183-201 in *Künder des Wortes. Beiträge zur Theologie der Propheten. Josef Schreiner zum 60. Geb.* Edited by Lothar Ruppert, Peter Weimar and Erich Zenger. Würzburg: Echter, 1982.

Zenger, Erich. *Einleitung in das Alte Testament.* Stuttgart/Berlin/Köln: W. Kohlhammer, 1995.

Zenger, Erich. "Das Zwölfprophetenbuch." Pages 467-533 in *Einleitung ins Alte Testament.* 3d ed. Edited by E. Zenger et al. Stuttgart: Kohlhammer, 1998.

Zimmerli, Walther. *Ezechiel 1-24.* Biblischer Kommentar, Altes Testament XIII/1. 2d ed. Neukirchen-Vluyn: Neukirchener Verlag, 1979. Eng. trans. *Ezekiel.* Hermeneia. Philadelphia: Fortress, 1979.

Scripture Index

Old Testament

Genesis

12:28	57 n. 40
49:10-11	36

Exodus

10:1-2	144
10:1-20	143
10:4, 5, 12, 15	144
10:6, 14	144
10:17, 19	144
10:21-29	143, 145
14-15	145
19:5	337
23:20	30
24:7	86
25:9, 40	290-91
32:12, 14	39
34	14
34:6	39, 299, 307, 331
34:6-7	5, 10, 23, 37, 38, 40, 181 n. 14, 188, 189, 190, 215, 300-01, 305, 305 n. 56, 327
34:6-11	322

Leviticus

18:6-19	275
19:29	109 n. 18

Numbers

6:25	30
35:33	109 n. 18

Deuteronomy

5:16a	131
5:16b	132
18:15-22	226
28:30b	40
28:38-40	40
31:10-11	86
32:6	30
32:39	11, 191
32:44-47	131
32:47	132
34	20

Joshua

1	131
8:34	86

Judges

20:18-28	199

I Samuel

9:9	87

I Kings

4:25	266
13:34	55

II Kings

14:23-25	295
14:25	326
22:8, 10	86
23:25	172

Isaiah

1	107, 154
1:1-2	100
1:21	219
1-11	21
2:1-3	310
2:1-4	45, 43
2:2-4	148-49, 308-09
2:3	38
2:4	13, 36
2:6-21	146